Years of Recovery

Alec Cairncross

# YEARS

# OF
British economic
policy 1945–51

# RECOVERY

METHUEN

First published in 1985 by
Methuen & Co. Ltd
11 New Fetter Lane
London EC4P 4EE

First published as a University Paperback
in 1987

Typeset in Great Britain by
Scarborough Typesetting Services
and printed at the
University Press, Cambridge

*British Library Cataloguing in
Publication Data*

Cairncross, *Sir*, Alec
Years of recovery: British economic
policy 1945–51.
1. Great Britain – Economic policy –
1945–
I. Title
330.941′ 0854     HC256.6

ISBN 0-416-04042 X

# CONTENTS

| | | |
|---|---|---:|
| | *List of figures* | vii |
| | *List of tables* | viii |
| | *Preface* | xi |

**PART ONE**

| | | |
|---|---|---:|
| one | The post-war situation | 3 |
| two | The years of recovery: an overview | 17 |
| three | The machinery of government | 47 |

**PART TWO**

| | | |
|---|---|---:|
| four | External economic policy: the background | 61 |
| five | The American loan | 88 |
| six | The convertibility crisis of 1947 | 121 |
| seven | Devaluation, 1949 | 165 |
| eight | Rearmament, 1950–1 | 212 |
| nine | Robot, 1952 | 234 |
| ten | Britain and Europe | 272 |

**PART THREE**

| | | |
|---|---|---:|
| eleven | The planned economy | 299 |
| twelve | Direct controls | 333 |
| thirteen | The coal crisis | 354 |

fourteen  Manpower and the labour market  385
fifteen  Fiscal policy, demand management and inflation  409
sixteen  Monetary policy  427
seventeen  Capital investment  446
eighteen  Nationalization  463


PART FOUR

nineteen  Conclusions  499

*Select bibliography*  510
*Index*  519

# LIST OF FIGURES

| | | |
|---|---|---|
| 2.1 | Excess demand, unemployment and vacancies 1946–52 | 23 |
| 2.2 | Volume of exports and retained imports 1945–53 | 36 |
| 2.3 | Fluctuations in wages and prices 1945–52 | 40 |
| 2.4 | United Kingdom trade with the dollar area 1946–53 | 44 |
| 4.1 | United Kingdom import and export prices and the terms of trade 1945–52 | 64 |
| 4.2 | Volume of exports and imports by quarter 1945–52 | 85 |
| 6.1 | Imports from dollar and non-dollar sources 1946–54 | 146 |
| 6.2 | Quarterly gold and dollar balance of the United Kingdom 1946–8 | 161 |
| 7.1 | Gold and dollar balance of the United Kingdom 1948–50 | 203 |
| 7.2 | British trade with dollar and sterling areas 1948–54 | 208 |
| 9.1 | Gold and dollar balance of the United Kingdom and balance on current account 1950–3 | 239 |
| 16.1 | Interest rates 1946–52 | 439 |
| 17.1 | Gross domestic fixed capital formation 1945–54 | 453 |

# LIST OF TABLES

2.1 Change in allocation of resources 1945–52     24
2.2 The pattern of consumer spending 1938–56     29
2.3 Consumers' expenditure 1945–51     31
2.4 Changes in consumers' expenditure 1938–46 and 1946–50     32
2.5 Public expenditure 1935–52     33
2.6 The finance of investment 1945–52     35
2.7 Changes in the price structure 1939–52     42

4.1 Pattern of British trade 1938–50     66
4.2 The dollar shortage 1925–51     70
4.3 Reconciliation of gold and dollar deficit and current account 1946–52     79
4.4 Balance-of-payments forecasts 1945–52     84

5.1 Forecasts of balance of payments of the United Kingdom 1946–8     112
5.2 Sources of dollar finance 1945–52     116
5.3 Analysis of the dollar drain 1945–52     117
5.4 Sectoral balance-of-payments surpluses and deficits 1945–52     118
5.5 Transactions with the sterling area 1945–52     118

6.1 UK trade with non-dollar, non-sterling countries 1946–51     148

6.2 Flunctuations in gold and dollar payments 1946–7 and
    1947–8                                                     150
6.3 Current account, gold and dollar deficit and net capital
    exports 1946–52                                            154
6.4 Successive official estimates of UK balance of payments
    for 1947                                                   155
6.5 Balance of payments on current account of sterling area
    countries 1946–51                                          158
6.6 Balance of payments of rest of sterling area (RSA) 1947    159

7.1 British trade and payments 1946–52                         201
7.2 British trade with the dollar area 1946–52                 201
7.3 UK gold and dollar accounts 1946–54                        202
7.4 Sterling area trade with the United States 1948–50         204
7.5 US trade and national income 1948–54                       210

8.1 Defence expenditure 1950–3                                 215
8.2 Planned expenditure on defence production 1950–4           223
8.3 Distribution of supplies of metal goods 1950–2             229

9.1 Imports into the sterling area from the dollar area and
    OEEC countries 1950–2                                      266

12.1 Analysis of 1950 import programme according to degree
     of control exercised                                      340
12.2 Extent of import control 1945–58                          341

13.1 Output, consumption and stocks of coal 1938–52           355
13.2 Employment, recruitment, wastage and absenteeism in
     coal-mining 1938–52                                       357
13.3 Stocks of coal at power stations and gasworks 1946–7     371
13.4 The summer coal budget May–November 1947               372
13.5 Recruitment to coal-mining 1946–7                        379

14.1 The progress of demobilization 1945–8                   388
14.2 Employment in the 'undermanned' and other industries
     1939–53                                                   394
15.1 National income and expenditure 1946                     412
15.2 Budget surplus or deficit and public sector savings
     1946–52                                                   421
15.3 Analysis of Budget tax changes 1945–52                  423

16.1 Exchequer financing 1945–51                              434

16.2   Exchequer financing and the money supply 1945–52          437

17.1   Domestic capital investment in the United Kingdom
       1938 and 1945–7                                           449
17.2   Gross fixed capital formation in the United Kingdom
       1946–53                                                   456
17.3   Changes in the pattern of gross domestic fixed capital
       formation 1938–58                                        459

18.1   Nationalization measures                                 466

# PREFACE

This book started out as a study of successive crises or turning-points in the period of transition after World War II. Episodes such as the coal and convertibility crises of 1947, devaluation in 1949 and rearmament in 1951, had not only a dramatic interest of their own but lit up the dilemmas of policy, the underlying economic trends and pressures and the problems these posed for economic management in a country unaware that it was virtually bankrupt.

A treatment of the period exclusively in terms of crises, however, would have given a false as well as an incomplete picture of developments. Even the crises themselves had to be put in context. Inevitably, therefore, the book grew into a study of the whole period, from the end of the war to the downfall of the Labour government in 1951. I was the more ready to embark on this because no detailed study has appeared since Christopher Dow's *The Management of the British Economy 1945–60* in 1964 and the Oxford symposium on *The British Economy 1945–1950* edited by Worswick and Ady in 1952. I have not attempted to provide a continuous narrative of events but have combined with an account of the various crises with which the book began, a treatment of some of the more important aspects of policy as they developed over the period. To keep within reasonable length I have been obliged to deal very lightly with many topics and to omit any extended discussion of regional, commercial and industrial policy, concentrating largely on policy as seen from the Treasury.

The emphasis throughout is on policy rather than performance although inevitably the one has to be seen in the context of the other. It is the government that is in the forefront – not just the Cabinet but the whole policy-making machine. The angle from which the events of the period are examined is not that of economic theory and the verification of doctrine; nor is it that of the quantitative economic historian seeking to establish after the event how the economy actually functioned. It is essentially that of economic management. How did events present themselves to a government which had to appraise them and decide how to respond to them? How were major decisions of economic strategy taken (if taken at all) and by what factors were they influenced and constrained? Did the government have an accurate picture of what was going on and could it form a reliable view of the dangers it was running? What was the state of the art of diagnosis and prognosis? How well was the government advised and how much did it profit from the advice? These are not questions specifically addressed one by one in what follows. But they are the kind of questions that have coloured my choice of topic and of treatment.

A particular difficulty has been the weaving together of domestic and external aspects of policy. The connection between the two was not always apparent to ministers (and indeed was vigorously denied by the Prime Minister). While I hope that the connection will be apparent to the reader, I have nevertheless opted for a systematic exposition of the problems of external economic policy before expounding the different aspects of domestic policy. This has not prevented me from sandwiching the chapter on rearmament (apparently a domestic matter) between those on devaluation in 1949 and the Robot scheme for a floating rate of exchange in 1952 because the fluctuations in the balance of payments in 1951–2 were so intimately bound up with domestic expenditure on defence.

A second difficulty has lain in the shifting sands of statistical revision. Our knowledge of the past is necessarily incomplete and tentative; but we are often inclined to put a trust in official statistics of past events that we rightly deny to other, non-quantitative information. When the Central Statistical Office revises its estimates, even after thirty years or more, it is a little more difficult to accord to the latest figures the simple trust that we gave to their predecessors. I have drawn attention to some of the major revisions and accepted them; but I am conscious that this gives rise to occasional inconsistencies between the figures that have been revised and those that have not. The frequency and magnitude of the revisions not only introduce a special element of arbitrariness into any assessment of economic performance but are liable also to warp one's judgement of policies shaped by the same statistics in an earlier incarnation. I have therefore tried to draw attention to some of the more conspicuous gaps between what statisticians say now and what they said at the time about economic data.

Although I played some part in the events described, first as Economic Adviser to the Board of Trade from October 1946 to December 1949 and then as head of the Economic Division of OEEC in Paris for the ensuing year, my recollection of events was of much less value than I had hoped, especially as I have recoiled from giving to micro-economic policy (which was my main concern) the extended treatment that I have given to macro-economic policy. The period covered was the most recent period for which it was possible to have access to official documents and this was obviously of advantage in analysing and assessing policy decisions. The story told in the following pages does not, it is true, depart much from what was already known. The papers in the Public Record Office supply some piquant details on the lines of argument ministers were prepared to entertain but they do not add a great deal to our knowledge of what they decided. What the papers do reveal more adequately is what went on at the official level, the techniques of analysis that were being developed, the possibilities of action that were canvassed, the thinking and differences of opinion that underlay the ministerial pronouncements. I am grateful to the Controller of Her Majesty's Stationery Office for permission to include references to the Crown Copyright material in the Public Record Office.

I have made free use in some chapters of published work, especially that of Christopher Dow and (in chapter 18) of Norman Chester. Where research has been undertaken with the thoroughness and skill of these writers I have seen no point in duplicating it.

Russell Jones has kindly allowed me to draw on his unpublished MA thesis on 'The wages problem in employment policy 1936–48'. I am also greatly indebted to George Peden, Peter Mathias, Kenneth Morgan and Lord Roberthall for much useful advice and information and to all of them for reading through the entire work in manuscript and making extensive comments. Others who have helped me with particular chapters are William Ashworth (chapter 13), Philip Cottrell (chapter 6), Leslie Pressnell (chapters 5 and 7) and Brian Tew (chapter 16). To them and to those from whose contributions to the Post-war History Seminar at All Souls College I have profited I am very grateful. My task has also been much simplified by Anne Robinson's impeccable translation of my scribbles into typescript and by Jane Morgan's help with my untidy footnotes.

The completion of the book was assisted and encouraged by the grant of an Emeritus Fellowship by the Leverhulme Trust to whom I take this opportunity of expressing my gratitude.

In this paperback edition I have corrected some obscurities and errors of fact to which Douglas Jay and David Worswick have kindly drawn my attention.

Throughout this volume 'billion' is used to mean 'thousand million'.

ALEC CAIRNCROSS

# PART ONE

# Chapter one

# THE POST-WAR SITUATION

World War II ended unexpectedly early. Not the war with Germany which the British Chiefs of Staff in 1944 had forecast would end four months before the actual surrender on 9 May 1945. It was the collapse of Japan soon afterwards in mid-August that had not been foreseen: no one knew for sure how the first atomic bombs would work.[1] An interval of eighteen months between the two surrenders – christened Stage II – had been envisaged in Anglo-American planning before the death of Roosevelt in April. The new President and the new administration that succeeded him had had too little time to adapt those plans to the very different prospects opened up by the atomic bomb. In Britain, welcome as the earlier conclusion of hostilities was bound to be, it did away with the period of transition in which a more gradual adjustment might have been made from an economy tightly organized on a wartime footing to one that could sustain itself in the changed conditions of peace. As in the United States, a new government faced a sudden change of circumstances without adequate preparation. Taking office on 26 July, in the middle of the Potsdam Conference with Russia and the United States and only eleven days before the dropping of the first atomic bomb on Hiroshima, Mr Attlee and his colleagues were deprived of the breathing-space between all-out war and the final cessation of the armed struggle that a continuation of the war with Japan would have provided. Three weeks after the July General Election, the war was over.

1  Clarke (1982), p. 23.

The first consequence of its sudden end was the equally abrupt termination of Lend-Lease. The new American President stuck to the letter of the law and the categorical assurances given by the administration to Congress and decided two days after the Japanese surrender to stop all Lend-Lease shipments forthwith. Not only were there to be no new contracts but supplies in the pipeline would have to be paid for and an inventory was to be prepared of all items still under United Kingdom control. Thus what had provided the United Kingdom with roughly two-thirds of the funds needed to finance a total external deficit of £10,000 million over six years of war was withdrawn unilaterally and without prior negotiation.[2]

No doubt there should have been no occasion for surprise. As far back as March, Congress had insisted that Lend-Lease should terminate with the war and that it should not be used for post-war relief, rehabilitation and reconstruction. Later, President Truman, responding to the 'wave of economy' that followed VE Day, directed that military supplies under Lend-Lease should be confined to those required for operations against Japan, without regard to earlier agreements with the United Kingdom. The Lend-Lease Continuation Act passed by Congress in June had introduced this restriction and the Administration, new to its responsibilities and unprepared for the end of the war, made no attempt to obtain fresh legislation in place of the Lend-Lease Act.[3]

A second consequence was a change of attitude in the United States: a natural sense of release from the obligations that war imposes, an anxiety to proceed as fast as possible with reconversion, and a disposition to leave other countries to work out their own economic salvation. America was prepared to offer help in the form of loans on commercial terms but saw no reason to make outright grants except through UNRRA or to temper the interest charge on loans in consideration of past services. There was no wish to reconsider the distribution between the Allies of the financial burdens inherited from the war: the United States, having shown unprecedented generosity in meeting the whole cost of Lend-Lease, thought that it must now look to its own interests including, of course,

2  Sayers (1956), pp. 480, 500. Lend-lease aid from the US totalled £6700 million but against this total should be set about £1300 million in reciprocal aid to the United States.
3  ibid., p. 477.

its commercial interests.[4] It was the future, not the past, that should govern financial arrangements for the peace.

The cutting off of Lend-Lease was no more than a symptom of this change of attitude and there was to be fresh evidence of the change before the winter was over. The pooling of resources that had formed the basis of the war effort was at an end.[5] On the other hand, the collaboration envisaged at Bretton Woods in 1944 and eventually embodied in the IMF and the World Bank had still to take concrete shape and in any event was not designed to cope with the stresses of a world completely out of balance.

What shocked British opinion was the unilateral manner in which the United States had acted over Lend-Lease and the ominous absence of regard for the situation so created. Since February 1942 aid had been on a reciprocal basis and although the UK was a very large net recipient, she put a great deal into the pool from a much smaller economy and one already strained to the limit. 'Relative to her resources', as Sir Roy Allen has pointed out, 'the UK contribution in the form of reciprocal aid to the United States may have been rather less, but certainly not much less, than the US contribution in the form of lend-lease aid to the British Empire.'[6] Moreover, aid received under Lend-Lease by the UK was not unconditional – as aid to the USSR and reciprocal aid supplied by Britain was; and the extreme to which it allowed Britain to push her military effort enhanced the risk of economic collapse when peace returned.

The situation was indeed alarming. As Mr Attlee explained in the House of Commons on 24 August:

> We can, of course, only demobilise and reconvert gradually, and the sudden cessation of a support on which our war organisation has so largely depended puts us in a very serious financial position. . . . Our overseas outgoings on the eve of the defeat of Japan were equivalent to expenditure at the rate of about £2000 million a year, including the essential food and other non-essential supplies which we have received hitherto under lend-lease but must now pay for. Towards this total in the present year, 1945, our exports are contributing £350 million and certain sources of income, mainly temporary, such as receipts from the

4  The Lend-Lease Act 'was alleged by interested parties to threaten a handicap in the post-war race for markets' (Sayers (1956), p. 476).
5  Clarke (1982), pp. 23–6.
6  Allen (1946) reprinted in Sayers (1956), pp. 544–5; Clarke (1982), pp. 26–7.

United States Forces in this country and reimbursements from the Dominions of war expenditure which we have incurred on their behalf, £450 million. Thus the initial deficit with which we start the task of re-establishing our economy and of contracting our overseas commitments is immense.[7]

Britain's ability to pay for the imports which were indispensable to her livelihood had been seriously compromised in her wholehearted mobiliz-ation for war. First of all, exports had been allowed to fall away to 30 per cent of their pre-war level. One reason for this lay in the limitations imposed on the use of raw materials in order to allay any suspicion that materials supplied under Lend-Lease were finding their way into exports competing with American goods. No concessions had been sought from the Americans until November 1944 when it was accepted somewhat grudgingly that the United Kingdom should enjoy, in Keynes's words, 'the certainty of complete export freedom after VE day and by adminis-trative action, the substance of it from 1 January 1945'.[8] But restrictions deriving from Lend-Lease obligations were a secondary matter. Exports had been run down deliberately as part of a general strategy of freeing as much British manpower as possible for the prosecution of the war. To quote Attlee again:

> It has been made possible for us . . . to mobilise our domestic man-power for war with an intensity unsurpassed elsewhere . . . without having to pay for our imports of food and raw materials or to provide the cash we were spending abroad. The very fact that this was the right division of effort between ourselves and our allies leaves us, however, far worse off, when the sources of assistance dry up, than it leaves those who have been affording us the assistance.[9]

From the British point of view it was not possible to disentangle the future from the past. The difficulties Britain was now to experience in paying her way were the direct consequence of a distribution of responsi-bilities in wartime to which her allies were party. Having taken risks with her economy which they had not had to face and which worked to their advantage, she felt entitled in fairness to sympathy and support when the penalties of neglecting exports eventually came home. No one could tell

7  *H. C. Deb.*, 5th ser., vol. 413, col. 956.
8  Clarke (1982), p. xvii.
9  *H. C. Deb.*, 5th ser., vol. 413, col. 955, 24 August 1945.

how long it might be before exports could be boosted to the necessary volume.

In calculating how large that volume would have to be, British officials had formed the conclusion long before the end of the war that a very substantial excess over the pre-war volume of exports was indispensable[10] and that it was likely to take three to five years to reach the target. The war had reduced income from invisible as well as visible trade. There had been heavy shipping losses. The gross tonnage lost (before adding back replacements) amounted to not much less than the total on the British Register at the outbreak of war: the net loss of tonnage at the end of the war was 28 per cent. To the loss in freights had to be added the reduction in income from foreign assets which in 1938 had paid for one quarter of retained imports. A large part of private portfolio holdings had been disposed of either after requisitioning or voluntarily: sales of investments during the war were in excess of £1000 million. Other foreign assets – in Malaysia, for example – would take time to yield an income or yield an income that fell short of pre-war earnings, especially if allowance was made for the large and continuing fall in the value of money.[11] The change on the assets side of the account was dwarfed, however, by the debts that had been run up all over the world, mostly in countries like India and Egypt where the occupying power had incurred heavy military and other expenditure for which payment was made in sterling. The sterling and dollar liabilities accumulated during the war reached a total at the end of 1945 of £3500 million. When sales of foreign investments and of a small amount of gold and dollars are added in, the net change on capital account between the outbreak of war and the end of 1945 amounted to no less than £4700 million.[12] The United Kingdom ended the war with the largest external debt in history.[13]

There had been a time, before the First World War, when the United Kingdom was by far the world's largest creditor. In 1913 her net overseas assets were comparable in magnitude with the net value of her domestic stock of fixed assets other than dwellings. By 1945 net overseas assets were a minus quantity.[14] In the First World War 15 per cent of the country's

10  Estimates varied between 50 and 75 per cent.
11  Income from foreign investments in 1946 is now estimated to have been not much lower in money terms than in 1938; but in command over imports, less than half.
12  Sayers (1956), p. 498.
13  ibid., p. 486.
14  Matthews et al. (1982), p. 129.

wealth had been wiped out by disinvestment in foreign assets and increased foreign indebtedness; in the Second World War the loss was 28 per cent – nearly twice as great proportionately.[15] Over nearly forty years, between 1913 and 1951 there was no net increase in the total real wealth of the country: an increase by half in the stock of domestic assets was offset by disinvestment and higher external indebtedness in the two World Wars.[16] No other major country suffered such a setback.

This change in Britain's external position meant more than a loss of wealth. For many years to come, an enormous weight of liquid liabilities overhung the balance of payments, threatening a flight from the pound, limiting the freedom of action of the government and contributing to the jerkiness of post-war growth which was later to be christened 'Stop-go'. Britain's position as an international banker suffered since the excess of liabilities over assets reflected on the strength of sterling and the confidence with which further commitments abroad could be entered into. The balance of payments had moved so far into deficit that further borrowing was inevitable. Over the war years the deficits had amounted in the aggregate to £10 billion of which nearly half had been met out of capital through disinvestment in overseas securities or by incurring fresh liabilities while the other half represented the balance of Lend-Lease from the United States over reciprocal aid supplied by the United Kingdom. In 1944 the deficit on current account was running at £2500 million. Such a deficit would not disappear quickly. It might even be doubted whether, without a catastrophic reduction in imports and in living standards, it would disappear at all.

The immediate danger was to imports. These had fallen during the war to a little over 60 per cent of the 1938 level, partly in order to save foreign exchange and partly for lack of shipping space. The demand for imports might be expected, however, to recover to its pre-war level once peace-time conditions were restored; and indeed, more imports would be required with a larger and more fully employed working population, especially if productivity continued to improve. How was such an enlarged volume of imports to be paid for? Since shipping earnings, income from foreign investments and other invisibles were all well below the pre-war level and were unlikely to recover quickly, the only hope lay in exports. With no German or Japanese competition to be reckoned with, foreign markets, initially at least, could absorb all that the United

15 ibid.
16 ibid.

Kingdom could supply. But the scale of expansion required was very large, even without providing against the kind of sharp unfavourable movement in the terms of trade that was about to occur. Exports could certainly not grow to the necessary volume instantaneously; the longer they took, the greater the competition they would have to face as other countries recovered. The struggle to export manufactures would be the more acute the more the primary producing countries sought to industrialize themselves and edged out of their traditional pursuits.

On the best estimates the government's advisers could make, there was likely to be a deficit in the United Kingdom's balance of payments stretching out over the next three to five years and amounting to no less than £750 million (half as much again as the entire reserves of gold and dollars) in 1946 alone. Over the succeeding years a further deficit of some £500 million was expected to bring the total to £1250 million. This formidable total, although no more than a very precarious estimate, was 'fully as optimistic as any prudent person would adopt as a basis of a decision', since it took credit for a rapid recovery in exports to their pre-war level by the end of 1946 and a volume of imports no higher than before the war in spite of the intervening increase in employment and productivity.[17] There seemed no escape from heavy further borrowing; and since the pre-war level of exports was insufficient to prevent a large deficit, it would be necessary, in order to bring the balance of payments back into equilibrium, to aim at a much larger volume of exports – at least 50 per cent and more probably 75 per cent above the pre-war level. Imports would be the residual: at the mercy of failure to reach export targets, less favourable terms of trade, and any limits that had to be set to foreign borrowing. So, far from exceeding the pre-war volume, it was conceivable that they might have to be kept to the wartime level or even reduced below it.

There was another reason why, immediately after the war, imports might remain low. All over the world economic life had been disrupted by the war. Some countries had been fought over or extensively bombed. Others had organized their economies on a war footing or to supply the

---

17 *Statistical Material presented during the Washington Negotiations*, Cmd 6707, HMSO, December 1945. The current account deficit in 1944 had reached £2500 million of which £1800 million was provided through Lend-Lease (Sayers (1956), p. 499). The latest estimates of the CSO in 1983 put the current account deficit in 1946 at £230 million and in 1947 at £381 million. By 1948 the deficit had been virtually extinguished. On the other hand, the gold and dollar deficit, which was what mattered from the point of view of drawings on reserves, reached a cumulative total of £1250 million by the end of 1947 and £2000 million by the end of 1949.

special requirements of war. All had pressing requirements which they hoped to meet as soon as peace was established. But few could meet these requirements from their own resources. Only the countries of the Western Hemisphere had any margin to spare and only North America was in a position to offer financial help. Thus post-war import demands were likely to be concentrated on one particular group of suppliers, whose prices would determine world prices and were not likely, in the circumstances, to fall. Some of those suppliers might find it possible to make matching increases in their purchases from abroad. But, particularly in North America, the prospect was one of acute imbalance with the rest of the world unable to make payment in goods and services and obliged either to go short of the imports it needed or to borrow from the one country in a position to lend, viz. the United States. In the scramble for supplies and for the borrowed dollars with which to buy them, the United Kingdom might have to content itself with less than it would have liked.

There was another joker in the pack. Government expenditure overseas, most of it military expenditure although munitions were excluded, had been running at £700 million a year in 1943–4 and was somewhat higher in 1945. At that level it could be held to account for the whole of the 1945 financial deficit of £800 million and was almost as large as total imports of food, raw materials and semi-manufactures. If this expenditure was not run down fast, the estimates of the experts would err on the side of optimism while if it was cut drastically, the prospect would not be so dark. Unfortunately, with the need for garrisons in Germany and elsewhere and the large number of trouble spots throughout the world, it could not be taken for granted that military expenditure overseas would dwindle rapidly to a normal peacetime level.

The gravity of the situation was enhanced by the public mood. It was difficult for a country rejoicing in victory after six long years of war to grasp the dangers ahead and entertain the possibility that things might get worse, not better, and recovery take years, not months. As Lord Keynes pointed out 'the financial problems of the war have been surmounted so easily and so silently that the average man sees no reason to suppose that the financial problems of the peace will be any more difficult.' But the reality could best be described, 'without exaggeration and without implying that we should not eventually recover from it, [as] a financial Dunkirk'.[18]

18  Keynes (1979), vol. XXIV, pp. 64, 410, quoted by Hancock and Gowing (1949), pp. 546, 553.

While officials might map out with some accuracy the dimensions of the adjustments required it was difficult to foresee how readily the public would acquiesce in these adjustments. Peace always raises expectations; and it was natural that the public should feel, after six years of wartime austerity, that there should be some reward in higher levels of consumption and greater freedom from control. The damage and destruction within the country were visible and their consequences comprehensible; but debts, disinvestment in paper assets and balance-of-payments constraints were quite another matter. How was the public mood to be attuned to the hardships that lay ahead? How was the government itself to be brought to a true appreciation of what Adam Smith called 'the real mediocrity of [the country's] circumstances'?

The very fact that Britain had been successful in war made the task all the more difficult. Since the conflict was worldwide, Britain was obliged to man a worldwide front and take on ever-wider international responsibilities. A war of liberation in Europe stirred parallel ambitions throughout the colonial empires of Asia: the overthrow of Japanese rule from Burma to Indonesia left a temporary vacuum in which national aspirations were free to expand, and fuel a long struggle for self-government. In the turmoil that followed the war, British forces were maintained all over the world on a scale that an impoverished country could no longer afford.

The solitary struggle against a triumphant Germany and the subsequent partnership with the United States had raised British influence in the world to a pitch that could not be sustained. The underlying weakness of the British economy was concealed in the euphoria of victory. It was accepted without question that Britain was still a world power and should have a world presence. Hardly anyone appreciated how complete was the ascendancy of the United States in world affairs, how far out of balance the dollar and sterling worlds had become, and how much more akin were Britain's economic prospects to those of the liberated countries of Europe than to those of the affluent North American continent. It was a shock to British pride to have to borrow so heavily when the war had just been won and to find that borrowing was possible only on the lender's terms.

The skill with which the country had been organized for war encouraged complacency at a different level. Although consumption per head had been reduced by about 16 per cent at the height of the war, the level of wages had more or less kept pace with prices. The financial resources necessary for the conduct of the war had not come from any reduction in the real level of remuneration of the average wage-earner. Real wage rates may have been slightly lower at the end of the war but real earnings were much higher even if, after paying taxes and saving more, many wage-earners may have consumed less.[19] The average worker, unaware of how the war was being financed, could be excused for thinking that if he could earn more in wartime he should be still better off now that peace had returned.

But how had the war been financed? In part, as we have seen, by realizing foreign assets requisitioned from their owners and by running up debts to other countries on an unprecedented scale; in part also out of Lend-Lease. Taking these together and deducting the reciprocal aid given by Britain to her Allies, the total amount made available from capital for war purposes between 1939 and 1945 was £10,000 million – more than two years' output of the entire labour force. Not all of that had gone on direct war expenditure and not all the 'war expenditure' would cease forthwith. It would be necessary to find resources within the United Kingdom to make up the difference. Another contribution had come from additional production through the absorption into employment or the armed forces of previously unemployed workers; the entry into the labour force of over 2 million more women and the re-entry of workers who had retired; and the extra hours of overtime throughout the entire economy. Part of these gains might continue in peacetime but part represented abnormal exertions that would cease. Then there was the contribution made by diminished consumption: consumers are estimated to have absorbed only 57 per cent of the national income in 1944 compared with 87 per cent in 1938.[20] This reflects both higher taxation and higher saving, the first augmented by a shift in spending towards higher-taxed items such as tobacco, the latter through the obstacles to spending presented by rationing and other restrictions. While taxation lay within the government's control, it was not easy to visualize the maintenance of income tax at 50 pence in the pound in peacetime or a level of indirect taxation levied on personal consumption that would continue to bring in more than double the pre-war revenue (at unchanged prices). As for savings, there was no

19 Consumer prices were about 55 per cent higher in 1945 than in 1938 while weekly wage rates were about 50 per cent higher and manual workers' earnings about 75 per cent higher (calculated from Feinstein (1972), tables 24 and 25 and from *British Labour Statistics: Historical Abstract*, tables 13 and 40). However, the rise in the only index of prices available at the time (the official working-class cost-of-living index) was only 30 per cent, giving a misleading impression of a big increase in real wages (see pp. 39–40).

20 *Statistical Material presented during the Washington Negotiations*, Cmd 6707, 1945, p. 15.

chance of a level of savings reaching, as in wartime, over 15 per cent of personal disposable income; it was much more likely that personal savings would fall to zero or less once goods came on the market in quantities and descriptions to tempt peacetime buyers.

One further item that contributed to meeting the cost of the war was the failure to maintain the stock of capital by postponing replacements, renewals and maintenance. The nation had lived less on domestic capital than foreign capital: but it had drawn on the stock of domestic assets none the less. Half a million houses had been destroyed or made uninhabitable by enemy action and four million more had been damaged. Very few houses had been built since the war began. Offices, warehouses, shops and factories had all suffered similar damage; and although some repairs had been carried out and a good deal of construction of factories and works had gone on during the war, there were still large arrears to be made good even to get back to pre-war equipment levels.[21] Fortunately it is easier to replenish domestic assets than overseas investments and the task seems to have been accomplished earlier than most people supposed.[22] But capital requirements had themselves expanded as incomes increased over the post-war years so that it was necessary to expand capacity well beyond the pre-war level. This necessity put yet a further strain on the resources of the country.

Thus the situation was one in which the cessation of war expenditures on an enormous scale would be offset to a considerable extent by the cessation of exceptional wartime expedients. The external deficit could not be allowed to continue indefinitely; nor could the capital stock be allowed to go on running down through failure to maintain and renew existing assets; factories, warehouses and shops would have to rebuild stocks of all kinds; new industrial capacity would have to be created and new dwelling-houses built; the work force would shrink and work shorter hours; above all, the level of consumption could not easily be held

21 Sayers (1956) shows a total for gross domestic capital formation of £1300 million over the war years and a provision for depreciation totalling over £3000 million (p. 491). The first of these figures is a residual, not a direct estimate and the second is based on historic cost and takes no account of bomb damage. Feinstein (1972) puts gross domestic capital formation in the six years 1940–5 at £2460 million.

22 According to Matthews et al. (1982), the stock of reproducible fixed assets was one-sixth larger in 1951 than in 1937 and inventories were nearly half as large again (p. 129). Domestic assets in the aggregate were higher by £3500 million at 1938 prices. Feinstein (1972) shows an increase of 6 per cent in the reproducible capital stock between 1938 and 1948 (table 44).

down to 57 per cent of the national income when income-earners had ample funds to spend. In these circumstances, resources in the post-war economy would be severely strained by excess demand and there was little immediate danger of unemployment.

The Coalition government's assessment of the situation, in its White Paper on *Employment Policy* issued in May 1944, was on similar lines. There would be 'no problem of general unemployment in the years immediately after the end of the war in Europe'.[23] On the contrary, the period would be one of shortages, including manpower shortages. Unemployment had fallen to 75,000 in 1944 and no doubt this would be swollen as reconversion proceeded because of the very large shifts in employment that would have to be accomplished in a short time. With 42 per cent of the nation's manpower in the armed forces at the end of the war and only 2 per cent producing exports,[24] there were bound to be bottlenecks holding up the process of reallocation. But the resulting patches of unemployment would not be widespread or persistent. It was only later that it would be necessary to experiment with the measures outlined in the White Paper for averting mass unemployment.

What was seen as the more immediate danger was that excess demand would bring on an inflationary boom such as had occurred in 1919–20 and that it in turn would produce the kind of slump that had raised unemployment within a few months in the second half of 1920 from 4 to over 20 per cent. There was no lack of money: the economy was awash with liquid funds. There was also a vast amount of suppressed demand which would become effective as soon as supplies became available. Throughout the war inflation had been held at bay in spite of excess demand by the battery of controls that limited access to goods, by shop shortages and the extra effort shopping involved, and by the sheer absence from the market of the things that people would have been willing to buy. Since consumers could not buy what they wanted, they saved for the day when they could. Demand was deflected to goods with a low labour or import content (and often with a high tax content like tobacco). The inflationary pressure was also partially concealed by subsidies to rationed items, which continued to be given the weight in the cost of living index appropriate to peacetime consumption. Not that there was no inflation. On the contrary, prices rose in wartime by at least 50 per cent.

Foreseeing the continuation of inflationary pressure, the White Paper

23 *Employment Policy*, Cmd 6527, 1944, foreword.
24 *Economic Survey for 1947*, Cmd 7046, para. 30.

called for the retention of wartime controls, including rationing and price control. Changes in the supply of rationed goods could then take effect through variations in the rations rather than in their price. The pressure of demand could also be contained by saving: the more people saved and refrained from 'a scramble to buy', the better. The government would regulate the flow and direction of investment in an effort to keep down interest rates and avoid a 'scramble to borrow'. These contributions to the stabilization of demand would require to be supplemented by co-operation in keeping down the level of domestic costs (principally wages). Price control was only effective if accompanied by stability in the general level of costs; and this the government could not guarantee, both because import costs were settled on world markets and subject to fluctuations that could not be foreseen and because wage and other costs were also outside the government's control. The most the government could promise was to continue its policy of providing subsidies 'to prevent temporary and considerable rises in the cost of living'.[25]

What seized public attention, however, were not the passages in the White Paper on the danger of inflation but the Coalition government's public commitment to 'a high and stable level of employment' as one of its 'primary aims and responsibilities'. This was a revolution in economic policy and the commitment by itself was likely to make the policy more workable. But not everyone put their trust in the commitment. The average man continued to regard unemployment as a serious danger. The more sophisticated doubted the government's power to make good its promise. The TUC would settle for nothing less than 'full' employment.[26] The government itself had many reservations. It emphasized that the level of employment did not depend only upon conditions in Britain and required effective collaboration with other countries. Workers would have to move to places and occupations where they were needed or an increase in spending would merely create a dangerous rise in prices rather than in employment. The same would happen in the absence of 'moderation in wage matters': unless wages and prices were kept 'reasonably stable', action by the government to maintain the flow of expenditure so as to preserve full employment would be 'fruitless'.[27]

25 *Employment Policy*, para. 15.
26 TUC (1944).
27 *Employment Policy*, para. 49. Insistence on the need for this condition to be attached to the government's commitment is said to have been due to Hubert Henderson (Russell Jones (1983), unpublished MA thesis, p. 49).

But would there be 'moderation in wage matters'? The few phrases in the White Paper conceal long debates within the government throughout the later years of the war on the compatibility between high levels of employment and stability in prices and wages. Different hypotheses were advanced as to trade-union behaviour in claiming wage increases and the likely influence on wage settlements of a higher pressure of demand.[28] The trade unions themselves were non-committal:

> the TUC would have at all times to consider whether it was, on balance, better that the objective [of full employment] should be modified rather than that methods incompatible with the rights of work people and the objectives of Trade Unionism should be used to achieve it.[29]

No one really knew what would happen. As Keynes confessed in June 1945: 'One is also, simply because one knows no solution, inclined to turn a blind eye to the wages problem in a full employment economy.'[30]

So, as the war drew to an end, the government faced many grave economic problems, some arising from the all-out effort of war, some of the government's own making in nourishing hopes of a better future. A balance-of-payments constraint of unparalleled severity conditioned the pursuit of full employment without inflation.

28  For the pre-war and wartime discussions see Russell Jones (1983), pp. 1–75.
29  TUC, *Interim Report on Post-War Reconstruction*, quoted in Russell Jones (1983), p. 53.
30  Kahn (1974), p. 387.

# Chapter two

# THE YEARS OF RECOVERY: AN OVERVIEW

The six years of Labour government from 1945–51 have a unity in retrospect that they did not possess at the time. By 1951 a mass of legislation had given effect to one after another of the proposals on which the party came into office. The Bank of England (and Cable and Wireless) had been brought into public ownership; coal, gas and electricity had all been nationalized; so had the railways, the airlines and a large part of road transport; so, too, after a long struggle, had the steel industry. A score of light industries from cotton to pottery had been reported on by the Working Parties set up by Sir Stafford Cripps and in four of them tripartite Development Councils or their equivalent had been set up. A series of productivity teams had been dispatched to the United States to see for themselves the ways in which productive methods and techniques might be improved.

What did more to catch the popular imagination was the establishment of what came to be known as the Welfare State. It is, of course, an illusion to suppose that this sprang into being in the first six post-war years. The Labour government built on foundations laid many years previously. Pensions legislation, for example, went back before the First World War. Other social services also existed in one form or another. The National Health Service, although a major innovation of the post-war period, had been accepted in principle by the Coalition government in its White Paper of February 1944. The Education Act which laid the basis of modern secondary education was passed in 1944 under the Coalition government even if it was the Labour government three years later that raised the school-leaving age to fifteen. The food subsidies were another inheritance from the war although they did not endure as a social service. The housing subsidies which, unlike the food subsidies, did endure have come nearer to being regarded as another social service.

What the Labour government did was to give substance to the scheme for a National Health Service and to bring together under the National Insurance Act of 1946 a wide range of social services that were previously unconnected with one another, uniting them in a comprehensive national system of benefits as Sir William Beveridge had proposed in his wartime report on *Social Insurance and Allied Services*. There was to be public protection for all, as Beveridge put it, 'from the cradle to the grave', covering maternity, sickness, retirement, death and other contingencies.

Although all these forms of social expenditure were brought under a single label, what gave unity to the idea of the Welfare State was just as much how it was financed as the comprehensiveness of the provision made for social welfare. The Labour government did not put the whole cost on the taxpayer, for social security contributions met a substantial proportion, but it did require the taxpayer to shoulder a far larger burden than before the war. Moreover the rates of tax and death duty were such as to absorb very high proportions of the income or wealth of the rich. The effort to guarantee a minimum standard of living was coupled with the effort to make the rich pay: inequality was to be attacked at both ends of the social scale.

The government's achievements were accompanied by economic recovery and rested heavily on it. Full employment of a kind never before experienced in peacetime was maintained almost throughout. Industrial production in the five years between 1946 and 1951 increased by one-third and gross domestic product, after a small reduction over the first two postwar years as the labour force fell back to peacetime strength, grew at 3 per cent per annum over the next four years – perhaps the largest post-war advance in a four-year period. New capital assets were created to make good the damage and arrears of war. Consumption levels improved, slowly at first but more rapidly in later years, although it was not until 1954 that all traces of consumer rationing disappeared. Real wages, which had been fairly well maintained in wartime, were little changed over the six years after 1945 but real earnings, which are perhaps a better measure of labour remuneration (especially as hours of work *fell*) seem to have increased by about 10 per cent.

This was roughly the same as the improvement in labour productivity as measured by the change in GDP per head, which averaged about 1.6 per cent per annum over the six years 1945–51 but improved to 2.5 per cent per annum in the last three years 1948–51. In manufacturing, the growth in labour productivity was about 1 per cent per annum faster, i.e. about 3.5 per cent per annum between 1948 and 1951.[1]

Economic recovery was coupled with far-reaching changes in the management of the economy. Macro-economic policy was born in the years after the war and survived more or less unchanged for at least two more decades. It is this, perhaps more even than the development of the welfare state, that gives these years a special coherence and significance, as if all that followed until well into the seventies was a comparatively uneventful extrapolation of post-war recovery. The very concept of managing the economy was new and little understood. While debate raged on abstract theories of planning, the practice of regulating economic activity through demand management was in course of development and improvement. Employment policy had been set forth in the White Paper of 1944. At that stage it was little more than an objective and the methods described gave only a rough sketch of how the policy might work. The White Paper had studiously avoided approval of unbalancing the Budget as a weapon of demand management and the use of monetary policy was viewed with no greater enthusiasm than fiscal policy. What was envisaged was an effort to stabilize investment through a mixture of public works and jockeying larger enterprises into parallel action, together with some miscellaneous expedients such as hire-purchase restrictions. By 1951 the techniques were much further advanced, the government machine was more willing to accept that the job could be done and the public had come to take for granted a degree of success which far surpassed what had been contemplated earlier.

1   These estimates are based on data in Feinstein (1972) which show a fall in GDP at factor cost of 2.5 per cent between 1945 and 1948 and a rise of a little over 10 per cent between 1948 and 1951, the corresponding changes in employment (including the Armed Forces) being a fall of 4.8 per cent in the first three years and an increase of 2.3 per cent in the next three (Feinstein, 'Statistical Tables of National Income, Expenditure and Output of the U.K. 1855–1965', table 20). Feinstein's figures also indicate an increase of 6.8 per cent in manufacturing employment between 1948 and 1951 while manufacturing output expanded by about 18.5 per cent (ibid., tables 51 and 59). Unfortunately he gives no estimate of manufacturing employment in 1946; but the figures in British Labour Statistics: Historical Abstract (table 116), taken in conjunction with Feinstein's index of manufacturing output, suggest an increase in productivity in manufacturing of about 5 per cent between 1946 and 1948 and a small increase of about 1 per cent between 1938 and 1946. If, however, Feinstein's employment figures for 1938 and 1949 are used, it was not until 1948 that manufacturing productivity recovered to the pre-war level.

Yet if one looks forward from 1945 rather than backwards from the 1980s the Labour government was ill-prepared for the hectic years ahead. It was committed to programmes of nationalization without having given much thought to the way in which nationalized industries should operate. It wished to embark on highly expensive schemes of social welfare which it had never costed. It had little idea what to do about inflation. It could not even count on the wholehearted support of key groups of manual workers such as the miners. Above all, it had not taken on board the limitations imposed on all aspects of policy by the sheer lack of importing power. It was not conscious of succeeding to the management of an almost bankrupt economy, critically dependent on what it could buy and borrow from other countries. It took a long time to learn, if it ever did, that the 'commanding heights' of the British economy lay, not in the steel industry, but in the balance of payments and energy supply.

Thus the economic problems encountered by the government were not, as a rule, those which it had expected. Equally, the solutions to the problems were rarely of the government's devising. There were exceptions, as when Bevin grasped at what became the Marshall Plan. But more commonly ministers were the reluctant pupils of their officials. On one economic issue after another – the American Loan, the coal crisis, the dollar problem, devaluation, the European Payments Union – they were slow to grasp the true options of policy and had great difficulty in reaching sensible conclusions.

When one looks more closely at the year-to-year changes in the economy, the sense of steady fulfilment of a prearranged programme rapidly evaporates. Instead of a smooth and continuous recovery to ever higher levels of activity, one finds a succession of major crises at two-yearly intervals and the years between are never free from anxiety.

At the very start in 1945 came what amounted to a crisis over the negotiations for a loan from America. The financial terms on which the loan was offered, although generous by commercial standards, took the Cabinet aback since they had hoped for a grant-in-aid; the conditions attached were the subject of acute controversy and proved impossible to fulfil; even the amount was of doubtful adequacy. Two years later, as the loan ran out, a fresh crisis broke out with the suspension, after a brief spell of five weeks, of the currency convertibility promised in the Loan Agreement.

Earlier in 1947, a breakdown in coal deliveries near the end of a particularly severe winter had brought a similar moment of truth to *domestic* economic policy. A large part of manufacturing industry had to shut down for lack of coal and electric power, leaving over two million workers in temporary unemployment. The loss of industrial production threw the export drive out of gear, intensified the shortage of steel and other materials and set back the whole process of recovery.

While 1947 was the major turning-point – for Europe as well as for Britain, since it was the year of the Marshall Plan – the next crisis, in 1949, marked the end of the post-war adjustment process. The devaluation of the pound set off a series of changes in parity against the dollar that laid the basis for the gradual disappearance of the dollar shortage and ushered in nearly twenty years of comparative tranquillity in exchange markets.

The last crisis, in 1951, was again in the balance of payments. It was partly the product of rearmament in Britain in the wake of the Korean War and partly the outcome of the steep rise in import prices that accompanied the war and was due mainly to American rearmament. The previous year, stocks of imported food and materials had been allowed to run down and restocking was delayed into 1951 when the import bill rose alarmingly and the reserves melted away.

If the odd years were all years of crisis, the even years were not entirely free of trouble. In 1946, half the year had gone before Congress voted the loan: so that those who thought in April, like Douglas Jay in No. 10, that things were going swimmingly and that equilibrium in the balance of payments might be only a year away, were liable to reflect with horror a week later that there might yet be no loan at all to protect the limited reserves of gold and dollars.[2] None the less, the process of reconversion from war to peace did go remarkably well in 1946 – much better than anyone had expected. The labour released from the armed forces was absorbed into civil employment without any appreciable rise in unemployment. In the eighteen months from the middle of 1945 to the end of 1946 the numbers of those who were either in the armed forces or engaged in making supplies for them dropped by over seven million while the numbers in civilian employment increased by five million or over 40 per cent. There was no inflationary splurge such as followed the First World War: consumer prices in 1946 were up by a modest 3 per cent. The balance of payments, which had been expected to show a deficit on current

---

2 Douglas Jay to Attlee, 27 April 1946: 'by [July 1947] on present prospects our exports should be paying for all our foreign commitments.' On 7 May in another minute he expresses concern that Congress may reject the loan (PRO PREM 8/195).

account of £750 million in 1946, was estimated at the time at half that amount and has since been revised downwards to £230 million. Exports had grown with reassuring speed, more than doubling in comparison with 1945 and reaching a level well above that of 1938 by the end of the year. The economy seemed well on the way to full recovery.

1948 offered a similarly hopeful intermission. After the trauma of 1947, when exports marked time and the problem of paying for imports seemed more and more insoluble, industry got its second wind, exports resumed their rapid climb and expanded by 25 per cent in volume while imports were held firmly down. The balance-of-payments deficit vanished; but like the Cheshire cat it left its grin behind, in the form of an intractable dollar deficit. A large surplus in 'soft', inconvertible currencies was offset by a continuing deficit in 'hard' currencies, bridged for the time being by Marshall Aid. It was this imbalance that provided the rationale for devaluation in 1949 although it was not what led up to it; a short-lived depression in the United States and a consequent sharp drop in the reserves were the proximate causes.

Two years later, in 1950, came another year relatively free from economic crisis. Production continued to expand, the balance of payments swung into substantial surplus for the first time since the war, while the reserves doubled in a year and continued to climb until well into 1951. But by the time the Labour Party left office in October 1951 the reserves were plunging downwards again and yet another balance-of-payments crisis had broken out.

Throughout the period, the economy suffered from chronic excess demand which the various controls could check but not entirely stifle. It expressed itself in acute shortages of all kinds, in an upward drift in prices and in an undertow that deflected potential exports to the home market. The excess diminished over time and was relatively mild between 1948 and 1950: so much so that ministers, from early 1948 onwards, were in constant expectation of deflationary symptoms. While they found evidence of a marked easing of pressure and the number of unfilled vacancies fell steadily until 1950, unemployment remained below 2 per cent and the trend was, if anything, downwards up to the middle of 1951 (see figure 2.1). Prices, on the other hand, kept rising. In the six years of war they had risen by about 50 per cent and in the first six years of peace they rose by 35 per cent: in twelve years they had more than doubled.

The steady recovery of production, especially after the balance of payments had been restored to equilibrium in 1948, helped to remove some of the shortages while the parallel recovery taking place in other

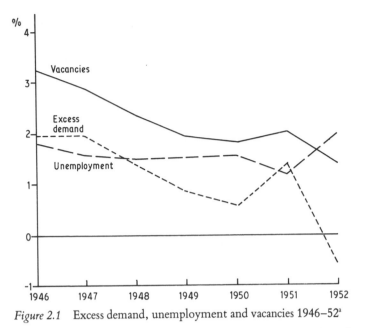

*Figure 2.1*   Excess demand, unemployment and vacancies 1946–52[a]

a Excess demand is roughly twice the difference between vacancies (%) and unemployment (%).

Source: J. C. R. Dow and L. Dicks-Mireaux, 'The excess demand for labour', *Oxford Economic Papers*, New Series, vol. 10, pp. 1–33.

countries increased supplies from abroad. This paved the way for a 'bonfire of controls' from 1948 onwards. Whereas in 1947 and 1948 30 per cent of consumer expenditure was on rationed goods, by 1950 the percentage had fallen to 11.[3] For raw materials the corresponding proportions of industrial input covered by allocation schemes were 83 per cent in 1947 and 47 per cent in 1950.[4]

The increase in production and the relaxation of controls did not imply a corresponding improvement in consumption. For reasons discussed below, any statistical measure of changes in living standards over the war and post-war years is necessarily suspect. But so far as one can trust the figures, consumer spending in total was about 7 per cent higher in real terms in 1951 than in 1946. With demobilization, however, the civilian population had increased – by about 1 million since the middle of 1946 – and the total population was also somewhat higher. It is unlikely, therefore, that consumption per head over those five years improved by more than about 1 per cent per annum.

3  Dow (1964), p. 173.
4  ibid., p. 175.

*Table 2.1*  Change in allocation of resources 1945–52 (increase from year to year in £m. at constant 1948 market prices)

| | 1946[a] | 1947 | 1948 | 1949 | 1950 | 1951 | 1952 | Change between 1946 and 1952 | |
|---|---|---|---|---|---|---|---|---|---|
| | | | | | | | | £m. | % |
| Consumers' expenditure | (750) | 274 | −48 | 145 | 209 | −45 | −49 | 486 | 5.9 |
| Public authorities' current expenditure | (−2,450) | −816 | −12 | 154 | −16 | 149 | 219 | −322 | −12.4 |
| Gross domestic fixed capital formation | (650) | 246 | 126 | 133 | 78 | 6 | 24 | 613 | 57.9 |
| Value of physical increase in stocks and work in progress | (325) | 414 | −181 | −112 | −251 | 588 | −395 | 63 | |
| Exports of goods and services | (650) | 93 | 416 | 238 | 324 | 129 | −55 | 1,145 | 77.3 |
| Total final expenditure | (−75) | 211 | 301 | 558 | 344 | 827 | −256 | 1,985 | 14.9 |
| Imports of goods and services | — | −144 | 28 | −172 | −37 | −384 | 292 | 417 | 14.5 |
| Gross domestic product | (−75) | 67 | 329 | 386 | 307 | 443 | 36 | 1,568 | 15.0 |
| Net property income from abroad | — | 35 | 50 | −20 | 115 | −105 | −50 | 25 | 24.5 |
| Gross national product | (−75) | 102 | 379 | 366 | 422 | 338 | −14 | 1,593 | 15.3 |

*Sources: National Income and Expenditure 1957*, table 12; Feinstein (1972), table 5, for 1946.

a The figures for 1946 are based on the data in Feinstein (table 5) and are not intended as more than a rough guide to the change in the allocation of resources in that year. The increments at 1938 prices have been recalculated at 1948 prices and adjusted to yield a fall in GDP of the same magnitude as in Feinstein.

Why did consumption grow so slowly when production was increasing much faster? The answer is to be found in the way in which the increment in resources was allocated from year to year. This is illustrated in table 2.1 which shows the annual changes taking place in the main claims on resources: first the claims exercised through consumers' expenditure; then the similar claims of public authorities through expenditure on goods and services; and then the claims represented by expenditure on fixed capital investment, on additions to stock, and on goods and services sold as exports. These items add up to the total demand for goods and services produced in the United Kingdom ('final demand'). When imports of goods and services are deducted, we are left with a measure of gross domestic product or GDP and if net property income from abroad is then added, we arrive at gross national product or GNP.

The figures in table 2.1 are neither the figures available at the time to the authorities nor the latest estimates prepared by the Central Statistical Office. History is rewritten over and over again as the statisticians arrive at fresh estimates of economic variables and this goes on many years after the events to which the figures relate. No set of figures is ever the last word. What appears in table 2.1 is based on the estimates published in 1957 by the CSO in *National Income and Expenditure 1957* and is intended to indicate the broad orders of magnitude of the changes taking place. Other official figures which are used later may tell a slightly different story but the picture they convey does not differ materially. The picture that ministers and officials had at the time, however, was a very different one. We shall have occasion in other chapters to draw attention to some of the more important revisions in official statistics that have taken place well after the event.

The main limitation of the figures in table 2.1 is of a different kind. We have fairly reliable measures of the various expenditure flows at current market prices; at least there is no major conceptual ambiguity and there are a number of cross-checks since GDP, for example, can be measured from the expenditure, income or output side from quite different data. But when we try to deflate current expenditure by price indices in order to eliminate the influence of inflation and express the estimates for successive years at constant prices, we find that there is no single set of price deflators that is unmistakably right. On the contrary, since the items making up expenditure vary from year to year, the weights appropriate to a price index are not themselves constant. The more they vary, the wider is the difference between a price index using the weights of year I and working forwards and a price index using the weights of year II and working backwards. This is particularly important in comparisons between pre-war years like 1938 and post-war years like 1948 when the pattern of expenditure had greatly changed.[5]

If we start by looking at the final column of table 2.1 we can see how the use of resources changed over the six years 1946–52 (leaving out 1945–6 but including 1951–2 as the aftermath of Labour policy decisions). The picture that emerges is dominated by the growth of exports, which

5  For example, if one tries to obtain a GNP deflator with a view to measuring the change in GNP between 1938 and 1948 one can either use 1948 weights, when the price increase works out at 93.8 per cent on Feinstein's figures, or use 1938 weights, when the rise is reduced to 83.4 per cent and the increase in real GNP is correspondingly greater. For a similar contrast in consumer price deflators see p. 30.

absorbed nearly three-quarters of the increment in GDP. Most of this went into improving the balance of payments and not much more than one-third was offset by additional imports. Investment made the next largest call on resources – about half as large as exports in the form of additions to fixed assets and a small further amount for the rebuilding of stocks. The net release of resources by the government, at first on an enormous scale, dwindled as increased claims emerged from 1949 onwards, particularly with rearmament in 1951–2. Consumers had to content themselves with a small net gain, equal to about one-third of the expansion in output.

When we turn to year-to-year changes the picture is much the same. At first, production fell slightly, as wartime pressures relaxed. Expansion for civil purposes was governed by the release of labour and other resources from military uses, either through demobilization or a rundown in the production of munitions. The call on resources by the authorities for military and other current purposes was reduced in 1946 by the equivalent of nearly 20 per cent of GDP and in the following year by a further 7 per cent. There was a small further reduction in 1948 and thereafter the long climb began in government spending for civil purposes.

How was this bonus in 1945–7 split between the three main contenders: consumption, investment and exports? The largest single beneficiary was investment which took about half of the resources freed from government use. Personal consumption took another third and what was left was absorbed by exports of goods and services. Proportionately, fixed capital investment increased fastest: by 1947 it had nearly trebled and was still increasing. Stock-building also rose over those two years and took over 40 per cent of the additional resources moving into investment. The increase in personal consumption was much more modest. Although it is not easy to measure unambiguously the change in consumption since before the war, it would seem that total expenditure by consumers had been restored within the first year of peace to its pre-war level and that in 1947 it was 14 per cent above the level in 1945. The share of personal consumption and fixed investment in the increment in resources available remained roughly equal in each of the two years, whereas personal consumption in the 1930s had normally absorbed about eight times the resources used in investment.

Exports of goods and services, on the other hand, moved erratically. In 1946, taking exports alone, there was a 70 per cent increase in volume over 1945 and by the end of the year the level of exports was higher than before the war. The following year there was a setback, occasioned by the fuel crisis among other things, and for the year as a whole there was little advance over the level of 1946. It is difficult to resist the impression that to some extent exports in 1947 were crowded out by other claims on resources and were not just victims of the fuel crisis.

Imports of goods and services were flat in both years and even in 1948 were lower in volume than they had been in 1945. This might seem to indicate a very firm grip on imports since GNP was running 10–12 per cent higher than before the war while imports of goods and services were down by some 14 per cent. But while imports of services were falling steeply with the reduction in wartime expenditure overseas there was an offsetting rise in imports of goods for civil use. Between 1945 and 1947 the increase in imports of goods was about 25 per cent and the level of imports had been raised to nearly 80 per cent of the 1938 level.

After the crises of 1947 the allocation of resources followed a different pattern, conditioned not by a further release from government employment, for of that there was very little, but by the steady expansion in output and the need to give priority to exports. In 1948 the whole of the increment in output and more went into exports. This transformed the balance of payments, wiping out the deficit on current account although not the deficit in hard currencies. The growth in personal consumption ceased while the further growth in fixed capital investment was more than offset by a lower rate of stock-building. In 1949, although exports suffered a check in the months before devaluation, the total for the year showed a further substantial increase that absorbed about two-thirds of the increase in output.

In 1950 exports continued to take the lion's share of the increment in output. Indeed, virtually the whole of the increase in output over the three years 1948–50 went into exports. For the third year running, more additional resources were absorbed by exports than went into consumption although consumption was several times larger than exports. As in 1948 this spurt in exports was partly at the expense of investment. Fixed capital investment continued to rise but the expansion was more than offset by a further reduction in stock-building involving quite heavy de-stocking. There was also, during 1950, quite a large increase in property income from abroad, partly because of the recovery in commodity prices as the brief American depression of 1949 came to an end and partly, no doubt, because of the transmission of larger funds from foreign branches and subsidiary companies after the devaluation of sterling.

The de-stocking in 1950 was violently reversed the following year; and since it took place after prices had been driven up steeply by the Korean

War the impact on the balance of payments was correspondingly severe. This is not brought out in a table showing volumes only. But even in volume terms the year is dominated by stock-building. This was coupled with a big increase in imports – greater than in any of the post-war years – and a marked check to the growth of exports. These changes in turn were associated with the pressure on resources as government spending on rearmament began to expand, squeezing out other claimants and making heavier demands on imports. Consumer spending fell for almost the first time since the war and fixed capital investment came near to falling, also for the first time. The economy was clearly out of balance.

The last year shown in table 2.1, 1952, was also one of disequilibrium. Government spending again made the running but the decline in stock-building was almost as violent as the upswing had been in 1951 so that final demand was extremely weak, in contrast to the previous year. Total production marked time and the changes in exports, investment and consumption were all relatively small.

By the end of the year the balance-of-payments crisis was over and the economy was set for a strong expansion, which raised GDP in three years by nearly as much as it had risen in the previous six. It was a very different expansion from that which came to an end in 1952. Now it was the consumer who was indulged while exports and investment lagged. In the three years after 1952 the increase in consumers' expenditure at 1948 prices was more than twice as great as in the previous six years and averaged 4 per cent per annum. It absorbed substantially more resources than did the simultaneous expansion in exports and fixed capital investment instead of less than one-third as in the years of Labour government. The great consumer boom was at last in full swing.

## Consumption

We can now look a little more closely at the changes in the main claims on resources, beginning with consumption.

There are obvious difficulties in measuring changes in living standards under wartime conditions. The subsequent changes when peace returns but rationing continues are equally hard to measure. Allowance has to be made for shop shortages, changes in rations and the absence of many kinds of commodity from the market. In wartime there were the added hardships of long queues, long hours of work with little time to shop, lack of settled housing accommodation, frequent air raids, lack of recreation and all the disruption of the ordinary routine of life. While peace put an end to

*Table 2.2*   The pattern of consumer spending 1938–56

| | Percentage of total expenditure | | | |
|---|---|---|---|---|
| | 1938 | 1946 | 1951 | 1956 |
| Food (household expenditure only) | 29.2[a] | 22.6 | 26.3 | 29.2 |
| Alcoholic drink | 6.5 | 10.1 | 7.9 | 6.7 |
| Tobacco | 4.0 | 8.4 | 8.0 | 7.0 |
| Housing | 11.8 | 9.2 | 8.4 | 8.3 |
| Durable household goods and private motoring | 8.5 | 6.6 | 9.2 | 10.7 |
| Clothing | 10.2 | 8.9 | 11.0 | 10.0 |
| All other | 29.8 | 34.2 | 29.2 | 28.1 |
| | 100.0 | 100.0 | 100.0 | 100.0 |

Source: National Income and Expenditure 1957.

a Including meals in restaurants, etc. (equal to 3.4 per cent of expenditure in 1956).

some of these hardships, others continued. Rationing was thought to be, if anything, more severe than before, especially when first bread was put on ration in July 1946 and then potatoes in November 1947; neither had been rationed in wartime. The way in which the government harped on austerity made it seem to exceed in rigour any wartime deprivations.

Nevertheless, if one examines the statistics, what is chiefly remarkable is how little, *on the average*, the goods and services purchased by consumers shrank in volume during the war and how quickly the level of consumption in 1938 was re-established. Taking 1944 as the year of fullest mobilization for war and comparing it with 1938, consumer spending by the civilian population is estimated to have fallen in volume by about 16 per cent.[6] The biggest falls were in motor cars (95 per cent), metal and electrical household goods (82 per cent), other household goods (51 per cent), personal effects (37 per cent), clothing and footwear (34 per cent) and miscellaneous services (33 per cent), the latter item reflecting the drop of about one million in the number of domestic servants. Spending on food, much the largest item, was down by 11 per cent per head. On the other hand, many items had increased: notably alcohol, tobacco, amusements, public transport, and postal and telephone services.

The shift in spending patterns (see table 2.2) was towards goods and services with a low resource content. Either there was a high tax element

6  *The Impact of the War on Civilian Consumption in the United Kingdom, the United States and Canada*, 1945, p. 23; Hancock and Gowing (1949), p. 500.

in the price or there was spare capacity that could be utilized at very little cost in additional employment. A return to pre-war spending patterns was liable, therefore, to involve a shift bearing more heavily on resources and appearing to reduce labour productivity. The measurement of shifts in spending of this kind depends critically on the weights assigned to the different elements in the consumer's budget. Prices tended to rise least for the items that were rationed, and on which therefore a lower proportion of income was spent. They rose most for unrationed items, consumption of which increased, *faute de mieux*. For example, consumers spent 18.8 per cent of their total outlay on drink and tobacco in 1948 compared with only 10.5 per cent in 1938, and the price of drink and tobacco rose by 238 per cent while consumer prices generally rose by only 95 per cent, using 1938 weights. If one jogs back from 1948, therefore, taking as a base the spending pattern in that year, the rise in consumer prices is exaggerated in comparison with the rise weighted in accordance with pre-war expenditure patterns. If 1948 weights are used the price increase is 95 per cent and if 1938 weights are used only 82 per cent.

So large a difference makes any judgement as to the change in consumer prices, and by implication, the change in the volume of consumption, over those ten years rather arbitrary. On the one basis the increase in consumption was almost negligible – there may even have been a slight fall.[7] On the other, there was an increase of 7.5 per cent.[8]

It is a little easier to trace the improvement in consumption from 1945 onwards. For this purpose it seems best to use 1948 as a base.

As table 2.3 brings out, there was a sharp rise in consumption in the first two post-war years and a particularly large increase in food consumption. Perhaps half of the increase in total consumers' expenditure can be accounted for by demobilization and the consequent increase in the number of consumers. This would not, however, apply to food consumption where an increase of 30 per cent in two years far exceeds what could be accounted for in this way.

The increase in consumption after the first two years was much more gradual and was concentrated in the period 1948–50. If one can trust the figures in table 2.3, three-fifths of the net increase in consumption between 1945 and 1947 was in food and between 1947 and 1951 two-thirds was in food. If we take 1948 as a base – which biases the calculation

7  The figures given in *National Income and Expenditure 1955* show a fall of 1 per cent at 1948 market prices.
8  Based on Feinstein (1972), table 5.

*Table 2.3* Consumers' expenditure 1945–51 (at 1948 prices)

| | Total consumers' expenditure (£m.) | Consumers' expenditure on food[a] (£m.) | Total consumers' expenditure (1945 = 100) | Consumers' expenditure on food[a] (1945 = 100) |
|---|---|---|---|---|
| 1945 | (7,472) | (1,533) | 100.0 | 100.0 |
| 1946 | 8,245 | 1,864 | 110.4 | 121.6 |
| 1947 | 8,519 | 1,994 | 114.0 | 130.1 |
| 1948 | 8,471 | 2,005 | 113.4 | 130.6 |
| 1949 | 8,616 | 2,099 | 115.1 | 136.9 |
| 1950 | 8,825 | 2,175 | 118.1 | 141.9 |
| 1951 | 8,780 | 2,168 | 117.5 | 141.4 |

*Sources: National Income and Expenditure 1957* for 1946–51; Feinstein (1972) for 1945.

a Excluding food consumed in hotels and restaurants.

towards a low increase in comparison with 1938 – food consumption had regained the pre-war level (but probably not the pre-war level *per head*) by 1947 and had more than recovered to the pre-war level per head by 1950. These estimates may seem difficult to reconcile with the introduction of bread rationing in 1946 and with the continued use of rationing well into the 1950s. But they seem on the whole to be cautious and some estimates imply an even more favourable comparison between 1950 and 1938.[9]

More detailed indications of food consumption are provided in the annual *Economic Surveys* that appeared from 1947 onwards. These show that although calorie intake was a little lower per head than before the war in 1947 and 1948 (and presumably also in 1945 and 1946), the intake of vegetable protein was consistently higher. The intake of animal protein had regained the pre-war level by 1947 and did not fall appreciably below it thereafter except in the first half of 1949. The biggest drop was in fat where the average intake in 1947 and 1948 was nearly 20 per cent below the pre-war figure. By 1950 all of these had recovered to at least the pre-war level. Then in 1950–1 there was a slight setback which brought the calorie intake temporarily below the pre-war average, fat intake more perceptibly below it and animal intake down to the pre-war average.

Even if we take meat consumption, where rationing was particularly severe, the lowest level reached – in 1948 – was two-thirds of the pre-war

9 It would seem, however, that the wartime estimate quoted above that civilian food consumption in 1944 had fallen by only 16 per cent is almost certainly an underestimate.

average and some part of the fall in meat consumption was balanced by a substantial increase in fish and poultry as well as by a much higher consumption of milk.

It must be admitted that consumers subject to rationing were not enjoying the same access to the items of their choice as they had before the war: they got a less satisfactory combination of goods for their money. There may in addition have been a greater falling-off in quality than is reflected in the allowances made for this in official price indices. On the other hand, there is nothing in the movement of the figures for food consumption after the removal of rationing to suggest that by 1950 any serious distortion of spending patterns remained. Much the fastest growth between 1950 and 1955, when all food rationing had ceased, was in sugar and confectionery.

By and large, therefore, the statistical indications are that over the first five post-war years, consumers' expenditure, both in total and in food, recovered to the pre-war standard with a little to spare.

*Table 2.4* Changes in consumers' expenditure 1938–46 and 1946–50 (at constant 1948 market prices)

| | Percentage change 1938–46 (%) | Percentage change 1946–50 (%) | Change in expenditure, 1946–50 at 1948 prices (£m.) |
|---|---|---|---|
| Food | −4.8 | +17.1 | +358 |
| Clothing | −22.7 | +38.3 | +278 |
| Durable household goods | −32.8 | +58.1 | +218 |
| Alcohol and tobacco | +13.2 | −11.9 | −210 |
| All other | −0.7 | −2.0 | −64 |
| | −3.7 | +7.0 | +580 |

*Source: National Income and Expenditure 1957.*

A broader picture of the changes in consumption is given in table 2.4. As one might expect, the biggest improvement over the post-war period was in the items that had been cut most in wartime. The biggest proportionate increase was in durable household goods, with clothing ranking second. Each of these had more than recovered its pre-war volume by 1950. Private motoring, later to become the main force behind the

*Table 2.5*  Public expenditure 1935–52 (£m. at current prices)

|  | Public expenditure on goods and services | Subsidies, welfare payments, etc. | Debt interest | Total |
|---|---|---|---|---|
| 1935 | 483 | 315 | 277 | 1,075 |
| 1939 | 1,179 | 329 | 288 | 1,796 |
| 1945 | 4,190 | 775 | 498 | 5,463 |
| 1947 | 1,735 | 1,206 | 565 | 3,506 |
| 1950 | 2,062 | 1,281 | 551 | 3,894 |
| 1952 | 2,883 | 1,397 | 655 | 4,935 |

*Source:* Feinstein (1972), table 14.

consumer boom, was held down by petrol rationing and the diversion of newly produced motor cars to export markets. Sales of new cars on the domestic market actually fell between 1946 and 1951 but doubled in the next two years and came near to doubling again in the two years following.

## Other claims on resources

We may deal briefly with other claims on resources since most of them are discussed in later chapters. Public expenditure on goods and services is discussed in chapters 13 and 15, investment in chapter 17 and exports in chapter 4.

### Public expenditure

The first of these, public expenditure on goods and services, contracted rapidly with demobilization after the war. From a peak of £5000 million in 1943–4 it fell to £1750 million in 1947–8 before rising again, mainly under the influence of rearmament, to £2400 million in 1951. These totals, even allowing for the fall in the value of money, were well above pre-war levels which remained below £500 million until after 1935. In 1950, before the rearmament programme had made much of a start, public expenditure on goods and services had roughly quadrupled in money terms and doubled in real terms since 1935. Debt interest over the same period had doubled in money terms but was no higher in real terms. Other public expenditure, in the form of subsidies, welfare payments and other transfer expenditure, changed little in the 1930s, but more than doubled during the war and continued to grow relatively fast in the first three years after the war before flattening out completely over the next three years to 1951. Taking the same span of time as for the other components, from 1935 to 1950, the increase was much the same as in expenditure on goods and services i.e. fourfold in money terms and doubling in real terms.

Thus in comparison with 1935 the main features of the changes in public expenditure, after the rundown in military expenditure in the first two years were the doubling in real terms of the two principal elements in the total and the success of the government in preventing any increase whatever during the early post-war years in the real burden of debt.

### Investment

Fixed investment shot up as soon as the war was over and had regained the pre-war level by 1947 or 1948 (depending on the basis of comparison). It continued to grow, but much more slowly, from 1947 until 1950 and then marked time for the next two years. The initial burst of investment was heavily concentrated on council housing but the expansion became quite general and continued long after the period covered here. Indeed, one of the major surprises of the post-war period was that after increasing by 1950 to 75 per cent above the highest inter-war year, 1938, fixed investment should then more than double in the next fifteen years.

The strength of the thrust behind investment is apparent from table 2.6, although, since the figures are expressed at current market prices and not adjusted for inflation, they exaggerate the rise. The volatility of stock-building stands out. The rapid expansion in total investment, intensified by the resumption of stock-building in 1947, put a considerable strain on domestic savings. Personal savings did little to meet this strain and were more or less negligible once supplies had improved and there was something worthwhile to buy. Company savings, at least when measured before deduction for depreciation and stock appreciation, were the largest single element in the finance of investment. But the biggest turnround was in the savings of public authorities which had been heavy borrowers in wartime and emerged in 1947–8 as large net contributors to the savings required to sustain the investment programme.

In the struggle to match savings and investment without having to borrow abroad as excess demand overflowed on to the balance of payments, it proved just as important to add to savings through the budget as to keep investment under control; and on the whole, savings were more

*Table 2.6* The finance of investment 1945–52[a] (£m.)

| | Investment[b] | | | Savings[c] | | | |
|------|-------|----------|-------|-------|----------|-----------|-----------|
| | Fixed | Stock-building | Total | Total | Personal sector | Companies | Public authorities |
| 1945 | 350 | −200 | 150 | .. | .. | .. | .. |
| 1946 | 929 | −102 | 827 | 542 | 315 | 575 | −348 |
| 1947 | 1,203 | 292 | 1,495 | 1,419 | 147 | 1,023 | 249 |
| 1948 | 1,426 | 175 | 1,601 | 1,783 | −25 | 1,146 | 662 |
| 1949 | 1,581 | 65 | 1,646 | 1,853 | 49 | 1,047 | 757 |
| 1950 | 1,712 | −210 | 1,502 | 2,419 | 92 | 1,458 | 869 |
| 1951 | 1,909 | 575 | 2,484 | 2,764 | 112 | 1,822 | 830 |
| 1952 | 2,134 | 50 | 2,184 | 2,184 | 332 | 1,246 | 606 |

*Sources: Economic Trends Annual Supplement 1981*, tables 9 and 156–7; for 1945, Feinstein (1972), table 2.

a The two sides of the table do not balance because (i) no account is taken of overseas transactions involving net investment abroad; (ii) the figures of savings are inflated by the inclusion of stock appreciation; and (iii) the figures of savings are incomplete because of the omission of additions to tax and dividend reserves (see Feinstein (1972), table 16).
b Fixed investment is gross of depreciation.
c Saving is estimated gross of depreciation and stock appreciation and does not include additions to tax and dividend reserves.

amenable than investment to short-term adjustments in the balance between the two.

## Exports

Of all the claimants to resources exports were regarded as taking pride of place: no other element in output enjoyed such encouragement. As with investment, the initial rise was steep but again, as with investment, the rise slowed down in 1947 and petered out in 1950. Figure 2.2 shows the year-to-year variations by volume from 1945 to 1953 and the simultaneous fluctuations in retained imports. While exports easily outstripped imports up to 1950 that was no longer true thereafter; and in 1947 and 1949, the years of crisis, imports either grew faster than exports or just as fast.

The expansion in British exports in post-war years has to be seen against the background of world markets. Neither Germany nor Japan had travelled very far along the road to recovery by 1950, their exports of manufactures in that year amounting to only 57 and 33 per cent respectively of the level reached in 1937. World trade in manufactures, however,

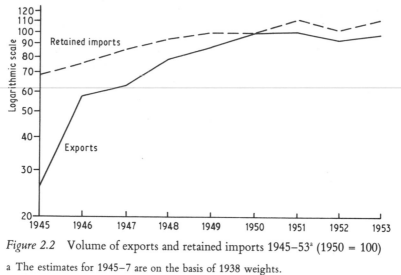

*Figure 2.2*   Volume of exports and retained imports 1945–53[a] (1950 = 100)

a The estimates for 1945–7 are on the basis of 1938 weights.

*Source: Annual Abstract of Statistics for 1953.*

was already above the pre-war level by some 21 per cent and the success of the British export drive owed more to this increase in the total than to the improvement in Britain's share in it from 17.5 per cent to 20.7 per cent. Seven years later, in 1957, when Britain's share had dipped well below the pre-war proportion to 14.7 per cent, and Japan had still not recovered her pre-war level of exports, the dominant factor in the continued growth of British trade was still more obviously the expansion in world markets, not some enhancement of Britain's competitive power.[10]

We may conclude this brief review of economic performance over the post-war years by examining the behaviour of employment, prices and the balance of payments.

## Employment and unemployment

We have already seen that throughout the first six post-war years unemployment was extremely low: so much so that except in the fuel crisis of 1947 it never approached the 3 per cent level which had been received with general scepticism when put forward as a target by Beveridge in 1944. Civil employment was correspondingly high and

10 The figures in this paragraph are based on Maizels (1963/1969), table A2 (revised).

expanding: there were three and a half million more workers in jobs outside the armed forces in June 1951 than six years previously. Such an outcome was gratifying to the government which was anxious above all to avoid any action that would add to the numbers unemployed. But it was also unexpected and unexplained. Why had things turned out so differently after the Second World War from the disastrous experience that followed the First?

So far as the answer is to be found within the territorial limits of the United Kingdom it can be readily deduced from table 2.1 (p. 24). In the first two post-war years, what drove the economy forward was a combination of the pressure from stock-building and consumer spending, which petered out thereafter as it had done after the First World War, and the more enduring pressure from fixed capital investment and exports, which did not falter until 1951–2. There is no need to spend time on the boom in stock-building and consumer spending since these are precisely the elements in common between the two post-war conjunctures and could be taken for granted in an economy drained of stocks and starved of consumer goods but amply supplied with cash. What has to be explained is why fixed investment and exports behaved so differently.

Since British experience was in no way unique, the explanation has to fit the situation in other countries as well. The secular boom that began after the war was worldwide and not confined to the United Kingdom. So far as it was the work of any one country, that country was the United States, not only because of its dominant position in the world economy, with an industrial production as large as that of the whole of the rest of the world, but because the United States financed much of the investment that took place in Europe and elsewhere and took care of the threats of imbalance that high investment generated in the balance of payments of the leading industrial countries.

The heart of the matter is the continuing high level of investment and low level of personal savings in the post-war years and the persistence of high investment even when savings began to recover. For this four factors were primarily responsible.

First, there was the obvious need to make good war damage and the accumulated arrears of maintenance and renewal after a war that was longer, more destructive, more all-embracing and more ruthless in its disregard of long-term civilian needs than the war of 1914–18. The accumulation of capital for civil purposes had been arrested with particular severity, leaving behind acute shortages of housing, electric generating capacity, transport equipment and other capital-intensive assets. Since the capital stock increases comparatively slowly, each year's savings adding no more than perhaps 2–3 per cent, it was likely to be many years before the damage and arrears could be made good.

On top of this, the move to full employment enormously enlarged the stock of capital required. The First World War had followed a long period of boom, including heavy investment in developing new sources of primary produce such as Canada. There was therefore little carry-over of capital requirements from before the war and more than enough primary production – a very capital-hungry form of activity – to match the industrial capacity then in use. The Second World War by contrast had put an end to an international depression of unprecedented length and severity in which much capital had fallen out of use or become obsolescent. No country wished to return to that state of affairs. One and all they were struggling not only to restore peace but to absorb in fruitful activities the resources that were formerly idle. This meant more than increasing employment, for if employment did increase so also would output, income and the standard of living: commitment to full employment meant commitment to prosperity. But if production had to be enlarged so had the infrastructure of capacity on which it rested. All over the world, investment had to be expanded to keep pace with the higher level of demand and output.

Once output began to expand to higher levels a third factor entered: the rate of innovation, technical, commercial and organizational. Expanding markets encouraged a speeding-up of innovation and this brought down costs and permitted a further expansion of markets. Wider markets also made for greater efficiency by a different route: the economies of large-scale production. To some extent, therefore, the expansion fed on itself; every expansion in demand and output enlarged the need for capital to keep pace with output and so sustained the high level of investment.

With these three factors went a fourth: the low cost of capital. In nearly all industrial countries nominal rates of interest were low, even by pre-war standards, and real rates of interest, if one could discount for the expected fall in the value of money, were much lower. Whereas in the 1920s prices had been falling and showed little sign of rising, in the 1940s and 1950s prices were rising and looked like continuing to rise. Debts contracted in money at low rates of interest were not burdensome while assets bought out of borrowings showed every sign of appreciating in value and could be fruitfully employed so long as the capital stock fell short of long-term requirements.

Even the four factors just listed would not have sufficed if inappropriate policies had been espoused by governments or if countries had experienced an acute shortage of liquidity for which they could devise no remedy or were unable to make the adjustments – in exchange rates or in costs and prices – that continued expansion required. Fortunately governments were in an expansionist mood and were, if anything, too ready to sustain demand while the public and financial markets had not yet learnt those self-fulfilling truths that made them treat increases in the money supply as the inevitable harbinger of inflation. At the same time, most important of all, a single country, the United States, had it in its power to prolong expansion by priming the European pump with Marshall Aid and manage the world economy in a way that prevented balance-of-payments deficits from interrupting the worldwide boom.

The United Kingdom, as we have seen, did not escape violent fluctuations in its balance of payments. But the fluctuations were largely confined to imports. Between 1945 and 1950 exports grews fourfold, giving a strong expansionary thrust to the economy. So far as the United Kingdom was concerned it was exports rather than fixed investment that sustained the pressure of demand until 1950 and helped to maintain it even in 1951. Growth in the post-war years was largely export-led. But it was export-led because of the lack of competition in the expanding markets of the sterling area rather than because of an exceptionally competitive edge possessed by British exporters. The origins of export growth lay predominantly outside the United Kingdom. It was the expansion in world markets for the reasons already discussed that generated this source of pressure on the economy; and to the extent that this was so, full employment was not home-made but reflected world forces that were at work in all the major countries, including Britain, to sustain demand and create ample job opportunities.

## Prices and inflation

The danger of inflation during and immediately after the war was well recognized. It had been held at bay in wartime with the help of food subsidies which were introduced in 1941 and had grown to £250 million a year by June 1945. These appeared to have been extremely successful in holding down the cost of living since the official index (which was based on working-class patterns of expenditure before the First World War) remained almost constant after 1941, the rise in the index up to June 1947 being no more than 2 per cent. The official index, however, was far from being a true measure of the change in the value of money. If instead one

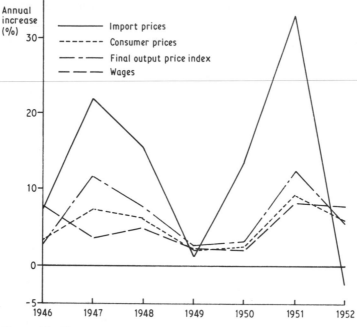

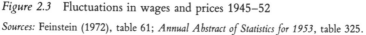

*Figure 2.3* Fluctuations in wages and prices 1945–52

*Sources:* Feinstein (1972), table 61; *Annual Abstract of Statistics for 1953*, table 325.

takes Feinstein's index of the price of final output the rise between 1941 and 1947 was 39 per cent and even his index of consumer prices shows a rise of 29 per cent. These figures express eloquently the divergence between the official index and the true rise in prices.[11]

If we turn to the period after 1945 the rise in the price of final output over the six years 1945–51 was 47 per cent, i.e. somewhat faster than in the six years following 1941. The fluctuations over the period are shown in figure 2.3. There were two peaks, one in 1947 when prices rose by 11.6 per cent and a second in 1951 when the rise was 12.5 per cent. In other years prices rose at around 3 per cent in 1946, 1949 and 1950 but at a faster rate in 1948 and 1952 when the rate of inflation was subsiding from the peak in the previous year. The rise in consumer prices was slower than in final output in almost every year – and especially in the two peak years

11 The pre-1947 cost-of-living index number used weights based on working-class budgets in 1904 and related to changes in price since 1914. It included items like flannelette and candles but not rayon goods or electric light and gave food a weight of 60 per cent when 40 per cent would have been enough in 1938 and 1948.

when it was 7.1 and 9.4 per cent respectively; exports and, to a lesser extent, capital goods on the other hand were increasing in price relatively fast. Whereas consumer prices increased by 35 per cent between 1945 and 1951, exports rose by 65 per cent and capital goods by 47 per cent.

The influences behind the inflation were in part external and in part domestic. The biggest single influence was the rise in import prices by 123 per cent. In face of this, a rise in consumer prices of 35 per cent was extremely modest and is some indication of the effectiveness of feeding in subsidies at key points in the economy in order to keep down prices. Import prices in the first peak year, 1947, rose by 22 per cent – three times as fast as consumer prices. In the second peak year, 1951, they rose by over 33 per cent – nearly as much as consumer prices in the whole period of six years. The volatility of import prices in comparison with consumer prices is clear from figure 2.3.

The second, domestic, element in inflation was wages. Average weekly wage rates increased over the six years by 33 per cent i.e. rather less than consumer prices. When real wages are falling it is difficult to regard wage settlements as a powerful initiating influence in inflation, however reasonable the fear of wage inflation in a fully employed economy may be. In 1947 when other prices were roaring up and excess demand was at its maximum, wage rates increased by no more than 3.6 per cent. The highest increase in the four years 1947–50 was 5 per cent in 1948. It was only after the breakdown of incomes policy with rearmament in 1951 that the rate of increase was plainly inconsistent with any conceivable rate of improvement in productivity. Earnings, it is true, outdistanced wage rates by 10 per cent or so but that still left not much more than a 1 per cent per annum improvement in real earnings.

The rate of increase in money wages up to 1951 was by current standards remarkably low. In the five post-war years it was exactly double the rate in the five pre-war years (4.4. per cent in 1945–50 compared with 2.2 per cent in 1934–9) although unemployment in the first period was over two million for most of the time and in the second period fluctuated around 300,000.

Nevertheless, although the rise in money wages may be regarded as induced rather than exogenous and moderate in relation to labour's bargaining power, the fact that money wages did increase contributed in its turn to the rise in prices. The rise in wages exceeded the rise in productivity and added to labour costs in each of the post-war years. Earnings, which were a more reliable guide to remuneration, rose at an average of 5.9 per cent, not 4.4 per cent, and both these figures exclude the explosive rise in 1951 and again in 1952. In those two years alone earnings leapt up by nearly 19 per cent.

The significant fact in the experience of those years was that money wages were not impervious to the fluctuations in import prices but rose with them in an effort to shuffle off the impact on wage-earners of an adverse shift in the terms of trade. Once set in motion, money wages contributed to the inflation and prepared the ground for fresh wage claims.

Other elements in the inflationary process responded in much the same way. Indirect taxes and employers' insurance contributions moved upwards from time to time as prices rose and this reinforced the rise. Profit margins appear also to have maintained a fairly steady proportionate relationship to prices. But all of these tended to echo inflation rather than set it going. Import prices were the most erratic and the most powerful influence in the inflationary process.

*Table 2.7*  Changes in the price structure 1939–52

| Price index for | 1939 | 1945 | 1952 |
|---|---|---|---|
| Final output | 100 | 153 | 239 |
| Consumer goods | 100 | 151 | 216 |
| Capital goods | 100 | 181 | 295 |
| Public authorities' goods and services | 100 | 147 | 217 |
| Exports of goods and services | 100 | 190 | 352 |
| Imports of goods and services | 100 | 196 | 428 |
| Gross domestic product at factor cost | 100 | 145 | 210 |

*Source:* Feinstein (1972), table 61.

What was perhaps just as important as the change in the price level was the change in the price structure. Table 2.7 shows how the structure changed between 1939 and 1945 and over the longer period between 1939 and 1952. During the war the main divergences were two: capital goods rose more steeply in price than other goods and services; and traded goods – both imports and exports – rose more than non-traded goods and services. Much the same is true over the longer period. But by 1952 import prices had shot ahead of export prices (in spite of a marked shift in the other direction between 1951 and 1952); and the price of capital goods had moved further out of line with consumer prices.

## The balance of payments

The balance-of-payments deficit bequeathed by the war gradually disappeared. Since export markets were buoyant and domestic inflation was held in check, all that was necessary was that output should grow and consumption (or rather, absorption) should be held in check. Exports made most of the running, growing fourfold in six years, and the government was in a position to limit imports directly. It was not long therefore before exports and imports were in balance although the balance was delayed in the first few years after the war by a sharp rise in import prices and a corresponding swing in the terms of trade. It was not until 1948, by which time the terms of trade were 17 per cent less favourable than in 1938, that the current account was restored to balance, with imports still one-fifth below the level of 1938 and exports over one-third above. Even so, the balance was precarious. In 1951 it was disturbed by a further sharp swing in the terms of trade to a position nearly 30 per cent less favourable than in 1938. Broadly speaking, however, we can date the restoration of balance in the current account to 1948 and regard the fluctuations over the next few years as transitory movements around an improving trend.

A more important question concerns the balance with the dollar area. This was in deficit throughout; the dollar drain ranked with the threat of unemployment as one of the two principal economic anxieties of the government in the post-war years. The dollar deficit too was brought under control, not perhaps by the time Labour left office in 1951 – for there was a major crisis immediately afterwards – but within a year or two after that. How was the gap eventually closed without the deflation that from time to time seemed about to be forced on the government as the reserves ran out?

There were three ways by which it might have been closed: by a direct assault on the American market designed to increase British exports; by cuts in imports, whether effected through deflation or devaluation or by discriminatory import restrictions or by turning to other sources of supply; or, finally, by earning dollars from other countries through multilateral trade.

As figure 2.4 illustrates, there was a steady upward trend in the value of British exports to the dollar area from 1946 onwards, with a slight dip in 1949, while imports moved rather unsteadily, with peaks in 1947 and 1951, and sharp drops in 1948, 1950 and 1952 as import cuts took effect. The deficit on trade account with the dollar area, which had reached $1760

*Figure 2.4* United Kingdom trade with the dollar area 1946–53

Sources: *United Kingdom Balance of Payments 1946 to 1953* (Cmd 8976) and *1946 to 1954* (Cmd 9291).

million in 1947, had fallen to $217 million by 1953. Exports, which before the war had covered about one-quarter of imports and in 1948–9 covered about one-half, had by 1953 risen to 85 per cent of imports from the dollar area. By that time, although the dollar gap had not been closed – for imports were limited by discriminatory restrictions – and the reserves were still far too low, a viable balance of payments had been achieved and the dollar shortage no longer dominated economic policy.

In the light of these trends in exports and imports we can form some judgement of the relative contribution made by each to reducing the dollar deficit. For this purpose we may compare 1948, the first year in which Marshall Aid was received and external balance achieved, and 1953, when Marshall Aid was at an end and trade had resumed a fairly normal pattern free from the disturbances associated with rearmament in 1951–2. Between 1948 and 1953 the trade deficit fell from $842 million to $217 million and of this narrowing of the gap by $625 million some 70 per cent came from higher exports and less than 30 per cent from lower imports. If we look at the changes in volume over those five years exports again appear to have undergone the bigger change: the reduction in the volume of imports was only 4 per cent while the increase in exports was 66 per cent. These changes ought, however, to be compared with the simultaneous changes in total imports and exports if we are to measure the deflection from the general trend on each side of the balance. On this test the increase in exports to the dollar area was not much in excess of the general increase (66 per cent compared with 53 per cent) while the fall in imports took place alongside an *increase* of 28 per cent in total imports.

It would be a mistake to lay too much emphasis on these rough calculations. But they suggest that, as one might expect, it was the pattern of imports that changed most in response to the dollar shortage. Nevertheless, given the difficulties of competing in the American market and the easier access enjoyed by British exporters to sterling area markets, it was a creditable result to have increased the proportion of British exports sold in dollar markets.

But what of the third possibility – the earning of dollars from third parties? There never seemed much likelihood of a substantial contribution of this kind to the dollar pool in the early post-war years in the absence of convertibility. The United Kingdom might run a surplus in some directions or even be in surplus on current transactions as a whole. But the surplus was unlikely to be paid off with gold and dollars and more likely to require additional credit or reflect the transfer of capital. The main exception was trade with the colonies which were able to pay in dollars (and a small amount of gold) from 1946 onwards, thanks to their earnings in dollar markets from the sale of primary produce. The rest of the sterling area, after allowing for sales of South African gold for sterling, drew heavily from the pool in 1947 but in most other years was close to balance or a small net contributor: from 1950 onwards a consistent and growing contributor except for a net withdrawal of £30 million in 1952. With the European members of the OEEC the United Kingdom had expected to be in surplus and at least to have little or no need to pay out dollars. But things fell out otherwise. A small surplus on current account there may have been except in 1951–2. It did not, however, prevent a substantial dollar drain to Europe from 1947 onwards. Belgium was the largest and most persistent creditor, with Switzerland, Sweden, and Portugal also drawing in dollars from time to time. France on the other hand was obliged to make substantial gold payments to the United Kingdom in the early post-war years.

Thus over the six years of Labour government there was little revival of the multilateral settlements that would have allowed the United Kingdom to earn the dollars it needed in its traditional markets. It was able now and then to put pressure on the members of the sterling area to cut their dollar commitments when they contributed heavily to the dollar drain. It sought to limit dollar payments to other countries through a series of monetary agreements. But it was never able to achieve complete inconvertibility and carry on trade outside the dollar area without any settlement of surpluses or deficits in dollars. Even in the European Payments Union formed in 1950 it had no hope of persuading the other members to eliminate gold and dollar settlements. Indeed, as the 1950s progressed it was to be to the countries of OEEC rather than to those in the dollar area that gold and dollar payments would have to be made.

# Chapter three

# THE MACHINERY OF GOVERNMENT

Until 1945 Labour had never been able to form a government with a majority over other parties in Parliament. There was corresponding jubilation that at last it could pursue its own programme to work a revolution in society untrammelled by compromise with the Liberals. Some felt like Hartley Shawcross, 'We are the masters now'; others were happy to find a broad consensus in all quarters in favour of ideas and measures that Labour claimed to have been preaching for a generation. 'High and stable', if not 'full', employment, greater social equality, a more active role for the state were all common ground.

The dominant figures in the new government had all held office during the war and were in no way new to the responsibilities of government. Attlee, a relatively obscure figure in 1931, had come to be leader of the Labour Party. After the débâcle of the 1931 general election he, unlike more prominent members of the Party, had retained his seat in the House of Commons. From 1940 to 1945 he had been Deputy Prime Minister under Churchill and, in turn, Lord Privy Seal, Dominions Secretary and Lord President of the Council. The new Foreign Minister, Bevin, never a member of the House of Commons before 1940, had been a highly successful Minister of Labour and National Service. Cripps, initially President of the Board of Trade, had been Ambassador to the USSR, Lord Privy Seal and Leader of the House of Commons, and then Minister of Aircraft Production. Dalton, Chancellor of the Exchequer, had been Minister of Economic Warfare and subsequently President of the Board of Trade. Morrison, Lord President of the Council, had a longer record of administration than any of them, first in local government and then as Minister of Supply and Home Secretary in the war.

Yet this experience was of limited value. Five years continuously in office, followed by six more equally strenuous years when the war was over, were a severe test of physical endurance. As the years went by, one after another of the ministers went down with illnesses that became progressively more severe. By October 1950 Cripps had had to resign office on grounds of health: he survived only two years more. Bevin, already showing signs of exhaustion in 1947 and frequently ill, died in 1951 soon after relinquishing office as Foreign Secretary. Morrison had a bad bout of illness in the first half of 1947 and was out of action for four critical months. The Prime Minister was in hospital throughout the dispute in Cabinet between Bevan and Gaitskell that ended with the resignation of Bevan, Wilson and Freeman in April 1951. Dalton exulted in his excellent health, dwelling in his diary on the illnesses of his colleagues and their failure to take a holiday or go on country walks: but even he was glad to have recourse to benzedrine.

While the war had provided a valuable education in management, it was management of a war economy with little foretaste of the problems of peace. The slogans of an earlier and very different decade continued to reverberate in ministers' speeches and, more damagingly, in their thinking. Although all of them had had some experience of economic issues, none – not even Dalton – was thoroughly versed in the kind of analysis necessary in the new situation.

In other respects, too, those long years in office in wartime were unhelpful. They had afforded little leisure for reconsideration of received opinion on economic policy. The Labour government of 1945 was almost as ill-prepared intellectually for handling the post-war situation as its predecessor in 1929 was for handling the Great Depression.

The bright young men in the party were not only not in the Cabinet. At the start many of them – Gaitskell and Callaghan, for example – were left on the back benches or, like Evan Durbin, were appointed to PPS posts of no great consequence. Harold Wilson, exceptionally, was made Parliamentary Secretary to the Ministry of Works while still in his twenties. Douglas Jay, not yet in Parliament, was brought in to help at No. 10 in 1945 and promoted in 1947 to be Economic Secretary to the Treasury while Gaitskell in May 1946 was appointed Parliamentary Secretary to the Ministry of Fuel and Power under Shinwell. Nye Bevan was the youngest member of the Cabinet at forty-seven when first appointed Minister of Health but, great as were his talents, Nye's interventions in matters of economic policy were rarely well-conceived.

More serious than any of these things was the lack of cohesion between the Big Five. Bevin was no admirer of Dalton and his relations with Morrison were never cordial. Cripps was trusted by none of them. Dalton, Cripps and Morrison were unanimous in deploring Attlee's indecisiveness. Things were at their worst in the episode in September 1947 when Cripps tried to arrange for Bevin to take over from Attlee without first consulting Bevin, and was repulsed by Morrison, who felt that if anyone took Attlee's place it should be he.[1] History has dealt kindly with Attlee and unkindly with Dalton. But if Dalton was the more controversial figure it was Morrison and Attlee who were more to blame for the failures in economic policy over the first two years. In the recovery that followed, Cripps played the leading part; but the worst was already over by 1948 and moreover he could count on support in Cabinet that was not offered to Dalton – support that might never have been forthcoming but for the coal and convertibility crises.

The air was full of threats of resignation. In 1947 Dalton, Cripps, Bevan, and no doubt others as well, contemplated resignation at least once or actually threatened it. Both Cripps and Bevan came near to it in October 1949 and in April 1951 both Bevan and Wilson did actually resign.

On most matters Attlee regarded himself as no more than chairman of the Cabinet, keeping the peace, summing up, and letting ministers get on with the job to which they were appointed. His might be the deciding voice on India, defence policy (including the bomb) and, to a lesser extent, social policy. But he made no attempt to whip ministers on or impose on them his own conception of economic strategy. His interests did not lie in the direction of economic policy, even if it was crucial to the success of his government. He did not even take a firm line with ministers whose incompetence was obvious, resisting repeated attempts by Dalton to get Shinwell sacked from Fuel and Power (perhaps because of his high nuisance value out of office), and protecting Alexander ('King Arthur') at Defence, often without much regard to the economic cost of the defence programme.

The Cabinet of 20 was much larger than wartime Cabinets of 5–9. This reflected the normal peacetime dispersion of authority, not just Attlee's preference for a more collegiate style of government. Even so, quite a number of ministers were excluded: for example, Food, Supply and Transport. The key economic departments were the Treasury and the Board of Trade, the latter swollen in size by most of the raw material

1  Dalton (1962), chapter XXIX.

controls and some residual functions bequeathed by the Ministry of Production.[2] The Treasury had fallen from its pre-eminence of pre-war days and become in wartime a department like other departments, a Ministry of Finance when finance was no longer the key to economic policy. Co-ordination had been the job of the Lord President with a kind of parallel Cabinet for civil affairs in the Lord President's Committee. But the Treasury had retained responsibility for overseas finance as well as for the Budget and both of these responsibilities were intimately bound up with macro-economic policy as it was coming to be understood: demand management, the import programme, the balance of payments, etc. It could be only a matter of time before the Treasury became the dominant economic ministry to an extent hardly imagined before the war. Unless the Lord President and the Chancellor were very like-minded and anxious to agree, the division of duties between them was likely to produce friction and became increasingly unworkable.

Morrison was not in fact a forceful co-ordinator and economic affairs were not in fact kept away from the Cabinet and settled by the Lord President's Committee. Dalton had cause to complain, not that he was overridden by Morrison, but that when he needed support in Cabinet he could not count on Morrison's backing nor, more important, on that of the Prime Minister. On the other hand, he did usually see eye to eye with Cripps at the Board of Trade.

At first, little change was made in the machinery of economic co-ordination inherited from wartime. The Ministry of Production was abolished when it might conceivably have been built up into a major co-ordinating department or even a Ministry of Economic Planning. No specific change was made in the functions of the Lord President's Committee which was reconstituted and continued to deal with a wide assortment of problems of domestic policy. Morrison, as Lord President, was quite explicitly put in charge of economic planning (although not of overseas economic policy, which was dealt with in a separate committee under the Prime Minister).[3]

2  Controls over the raw materials (mainly steel and other metals) used by the engineering and allied industries remained with the Ministry of Supply, now merged with the Ministry of Aircraft Production.

3  This committee was not set up until October 1946. Morrison asked that Stafford Cripps should not be made Deputy Chairman and no Deputy Chairman was appointed (PRO PREM 8/195).

The major issues of economic policy, however, came before, not the Lord President's Committee, but a small group of ministers consisting of Morrison as Chairman, Dalton (Chancellor of the Exchequer), Cripps (President of the Board of Trade) and Isaacs (Minister of Labour). This group was formally constituted as the Ministerial Committee on Economic Planning at the end of January 1946 but had already held several meetings from September 1945 onwards.[4] It was directed by the Prime Minister 'to exercise constant supervision over central economic planning' and advised at the official level by an inter-departmental committee of permanent secretaries, the Steering Committee on Economic Development, presided over by Sir Edward Bridges, who was both head of the Treasury and until 1946 Secretary of the Cabinet. This in turn drew on the work of a number of subordinate committees or working parties dealing with manpower, the balance of payments, capital investment, statistics and economic development. The Steering Committee sought to present to ministers a comprehensive and consistent picture of the economic situation in an *Economic Survey* prepared by the Economic Section of the Cabinet Office, submitting it with a lengthy covering note indicating the issues calling for decision together with its own suggestions and recommendations.[5]

The chief defect of this machinery was that Morrison had neither the authority nor the time to make it work. Planning decisions involving, say, the size of the armed forces concerned the entire Cabinet and could not be left to a handful of ministers in the civil departments. But even in less contentious issues, such as how to expand coal production, the machinery failed to grip. Financial policy was split off from economic policy when it lay increasingly at the heart of economic planning; and overseas economic policy was separated from domestic when it was beginning to dominate domestic economic management. The Treasury continued to be relegated to a subordinate role that was now quite inappropriate while the Ministry of Labour was given a front seat that was just as out of place, partly no doubt in deference to Isaacs's predecessor in office, Ernest Bevin, but partly

4  Initially the group was treated as 'the permanent nucleus of the Industry Sub-committee of the Lord President's Committee' (ED(45)2, in PRO CAB 124/891). The Socialization of Industries Committee, over which Morrison also presided, was formally appointed in the same month but had been meeting informally for some time.

5  For a full list of the 466 committees, 'standing, *ad hoc*, ministerial, official or a mixture of both breeds' in the Attlee governments – apart from twelve of which details have not been disclosed – see Hennessy and Arends (1983).

also because of the mistaken importance attached to the Ministry's contribution to manpower planning. Neither fiscal nor monetary policy was regarded as an important ingredient in economic planning.

No special steps were taken to build up a planning staff. Morrison had his own staff of civil servants headed by Alexander Johnston (later Chairman of the Board of Inland Revenue) and Max Nicholson (a temporary civil servant who before the war had been director of Political and Economic Planning, an influential research group) but none of them was a professional economist. Morrison was able to make use of the Economic Section which remained part of the Cabinet Secretariat but his relationship to it was very different from the wartime relationship with Anderson. Morrison's responsibilities were much too wide for him to give the necessary time to economic planning. He was deeply involved in the nationalization programme, with which he felt much more at home and in which he had far more interest. He was also in charge of the heavy legislative programme which the government intended to carry through within a comparatively short period. Apart from this, his authority over domestic economic policy was more open to challenge by other ministers, including such powerful figures as Dalton and Cripps, and could not be hived off, as in wartime, from a Cabinet preoccupied with more important matters. His contact with the Economic Section was more limited and less effective. Their ideas often remained obscure to him or failed to convince him and he in turn was either not sufficiently forceful in applying them when persuaded or found his colleagues unsympathetic or resistant. James Meade, who took over from Lionel Robbins as Director of the Economic Section in the autumn of 1945, had clear and consistent views about economic planning, as is evident from his diary,[6] but these were not views ever expounded by Morrison. The Economic Section were less on an inside track with the Lord President than they had been in wartime and had more difficulty in communicating effectively with him. On the other hand, by arrangement with the head of the Treasury, Sir Edward Bridges (who was also in 1945–6 Cabinet Secretary), James Meade was able to take a full part in the main economic and financial discussions in the Treasury. He was a member of the Budget and other Treasury committees, was in easy and frequent contact with Bridges and senior Treasury officials and joined them on appropriate occasions when they called on the Chancellor to offer advice. But he was in no sense Dalton's personal adviser.

In 1947 the machinery of policy-making underwent a series of changes.

6  A copy of the MS is in the Library of the London School of Economics.

Initially these took the form of strengthening the planning staff. Sir Edwin Plowden was appointed Chief Planning Officer in March with a small staff – the Central Economic Planning Staff – located initially along-side the Economic Section in the Cabinet Office and taking up its duties over the summer. An Economic Planning Board composed partly of civil servants and partly of representatives of both sides of industry was announced in March but not appointed until July. In March also, Hilary Marquand was promoted from the Department of Overseas Trade (where Harold Wilson took his place) to become Paymaster-General with rather vague duties to assist ministers in the co-ordination of economic policy.

These changes took place while Morrison was ill. In his absence between January and May Dalton deputized and Cripps began to take a more active part. At the end of September Morrison's role as economic co-ordinator virtually came to an end with Cripps's appointment as Minister of Economic Affairs. Six weeks later Dalton resigned after an error of judgement in disclosing the contents of his fourth Budget to a journalist on the way to delivering his Budget speech in the House of Commons. Cripps was appointed to succeed him and the Ministry of Economic Affairs amalgamated with the Treasury.

The situation was completely transformed. Cripps was in a far more powerful position than Morrison had been, with full responsibility for economic and financial policy, a strong department behind him and political protégés in several key departments (Harold Wilson, now President of the Board of Trade, Nye Bevan in the Ministry of Health, and Gaitskell at Fuel and Power). He could weld together economics and finance and at the same time keep an eye, as a former President of the Board of Trade, on industrial and commercial policy. He could also draw on the services of the new planning staff (now absorbed into the Treasury) and of the Economic Section.

After 1947 few changes were made in the machinery of policy-making. At the ministerial level a new Economic Policy Committee, chaired by the Prime Minister, became the main focus of co-ordination while the Steering Committee and the Economic Planning Board reviewed the main issues of policy before submission to ministers. Cripps resigned as Chancellor in October 1950 after nearly three years in office, remarking as he did so that 'we must not go back to having the Chancellor of the Exchequer separated from over-riding control in the economic field'.[7] Gaitskell took over as

7  Information from Lord Roberthall.

Chancellor, having already spent eight months in the Treasury as Minister of State for Economic Affairs and played a major role in the devaluation crisis of 1949.

Economic policy was thus increasingly dominated by the Treasury. This was true both of domestic and external policy. At the official level it took the lead, in conjunction with the Planning Staff, in the control of investment, with a small, reconstituted Investment Programmes Committee reporting to ministers annually on departmental programmes with appropriate recommendations. It also took a hand in the preparation of the *Economic Survey*, preparing an entirely new draft for publication in 1947 and editing the draft in later years with a vigour that ruffled the Economic Section. The Treasury also provided the chairman of the Import Programmes Committee, the Overseas Negotiations Committee and the London Committee dealing with the Marshall Plan and proposals for the economic integration of Western Europe. Although the Foreign Office continued to represent the government in negotiations abroad it was not equipped to deal with technical economic issues such as were involved in the setting-up of the European Payments Union or drawings on the IMF or payments agreements with foreign countries. Foreign economic policy was increasingly made by the Treasury.

The co-ordination of economic policy inevitably rested heavily on the calibre of the officials advising ministers, especially when, as in 1945–7, no minister (except Dalton) had any training in economics. Economic planning is by no means always undertaken by economists; but without *some* economists it is exposed to unnecessary hazards. At the end of the war, however, nearly all the economists in government service had left Whitehall and showed no inclination to return. Apart from the small group in the Economic Section of the Cabinet Office, few of whom were of much seniority, only one or two remained. Lord Keynes, the dominant figure in the Treasury, survived only until April 1946. Of those who had exercised a major influence on wartime planning, James Meade, Director of the Economic Section, and Austin Robinson, Economic Adviser to the Board of Trade, were the only two still available in 1945. Two years later Meade had gone and Austin Robinson, who had left in 1946, was back in Whitehall. One or two others, such as Robert Hall and Russell Bretherton, who had served in the Raw Materials Department of the Ministry of Supply, had remained in post when their department was absorbed by the Board of Trade. Eric Roll continued to serve in the Ministry of Food. But the Treasury in particular, and the Board of Trade in its main policy departments, relied almost exclusively on career civil servants with little or no training in economics. In the Treasury only 'Otto' (R.W.B.) Clarke had any real flair for general economic policy.

This did not appear to occasion any disquiet among ministers. Morrison was content to rely on the Economic Section and opposed to any effort to recruit a special staff of planners. Dalton felt that, as an economist, he was not in need of professional advice. Cripps, having failed in a take-over bid for the Economic Section, made use of Austin Robinson at the Board of Trade in 1945–6, but made no attempt to recruit other economists.

It was not until the succession of crises in 1947 that things changed. Even then, when Robert Hall took over in 1947 from James Meade (whose duties had given him stomach ulcers) and was urged by Morrison to recruit more staff, he had to point out that economists were not particularly eager to rally round the government and had university duties which they found very satisfying.

The main responsibility for economic advice rested with the Economic Section first under James Meade and then, from 1 September 1947, under Robert Hall. This was a small group of economists that had started life in the Cabinet Office at the beginning of 1940 as the staff of the Stamp Survey of Economic and Financial Plans and remained in the Cabinet Office until 1953 when it moved to the Treasury. In wartime it had served as the staff of the Lord President and when the war was over it continued to serve in that capacity. The Section never exceeded 12–15 in number but included economists of distinction both in wartime and afterwards. The older members of the Section, such as Lionel Robbins, returned to academic life either shortly after the war or over the next two years and it was difficult to find new staff. But the Economic Section's influence was conspicuous throughout the post-war period.

One reason for this was the absence of any other concentration of economists in Whitehall. With the death of Keynes the Treasury were left without any professional economist to advise them and felt the loss very severely. The Board of Trade had an economic adviser up to 1950 and there were one or two professional economists in administrative or statistical posts. Other departments, with the exception of Agriculture, Food and the Joint Intelligence Committee, had none or, at most, one.

When the Planning Staff was appointed in 1947 the position changed slightly. But the small group under Plowden did not include any professional economists apart from Austin Robinson (who left again in 1948) although most of them either had some training in economics or experience of economic planning. In general, Plowden looked to Robert

Hall for guidance on economic issues while Cripps was largely guided by Plowden. In the years when Cripps was Chancellor the influence of the Economic Section was at its zenith, as it had been under Sir John Anderson. When Gaitskell took over, the relationship was less close. Gaitskell had spent longer as a civil servant than as a minister and found it difficult to shake off the habits of a civil servant. He also counted himself an economist and was less willing on that account, too, to take on trust what his advisers suggested. Nevertheless the Economic Section, although not formally part of the Treasury, acted as the Treasury's think-tank and was regarded in that light by the Chancellor.

The influence of the Economic Section is very evident in at least three different directions: the budget; the exchange rate; and defence. James Meade was agitating for a budget surplus in 1946 and Robert Hall maintained the pressure successfully when Cripps became Chancellor. It was Dalton who, although no Keynesian, first budgeted for a surplus, but in doing so he was following a policy already accepted at the official level under the influence of the economists. The devaluation of 1949 was due more to Robert Hall than to any other individual. Similarly, the defence programme of 1950–1 owed more to him than to anyone else in the economic departments.

If economists played a smaller part than they had in wartime it was still a revolution to have professional economists brigaded alongside career administrators in Whitehall. Equally, the creation of the Central Statistical Office had revolutionized government statistics. In pre-war days, apart from the monthly trade returns, the unemployment figures, the cost-of-living index number and a few other series, statistics tended to be included in annual publications or at even longer intervals in censuses of population and production. Current statistics tended to be kept as scraps of information on file, not in the form of time series. The Bank of England's *Statistical Summary* and *The Economist* were among the few available sources of continuous statistical series. Although data on trade appeared in the *Board of Trade Journal* and on labour in the *Ministry of Labour Gazette*, there was no official publication like the *Monthly Digest* or *Economic Trends* devoted *exclusively* to their regular publication. Figures on any subject were harder to find and, when found, harder on the eye than nowadays. As for macro-economic data – GNP, the balance of payments, indices of production or of productivity, estimates of the components of final demand, and so on – they hardly existed. The quantitative treatment of economics was still in its infancy because of a shortage of raw material.

In the first half of 1940 much of this had changed – thanks largely to the efforts of Ely Devons in preparing a succession of secret monthly statistical bulletins on different aspects of the war economy. Of these what started as Series B began to appear in 1946 after Ministers agreed in January to its publication. The work of James Meade and Dick Stone in 1940–1 on macro-economic data had already borne fruit in the publication in 1941 of the first White Paper on national income[8] and the Coalition government had proposed, in the 1944 White Paper on *Employment Policy*, to develop this

> by providing a much more complete analysis than has hitherto been possible of the constituent parts of the country's total expenditure. In particular, direct estimates will be made of the various types of capital expenditure and the various sources of savings.[9]

Annual White Papers, both on national income and expenditure and on the balance of payments, appeared from 1946 onwards. The *Economic Survey*, which began to appear in 1947, supplemented these with an analysis of current trends and an outline of the targets for the coming year that the government had set.

All this meant a great advance, not just in public understanding of the workings of the economy, but in the approach of officials to economic problems. They became accustomed to a more quantitative treatment of these problems and to bringing to bear on them statistical information that was now readily available and more easily digested. They also acquired at least a nodding acquaintance with economic concepts to which at last definite magnitudes could be assigned.

Thus however formidable the problems that had to be faced, the government was much better informed and better advised than in pre-war days. The machinery of government might be under continuous strain; but it was not ill-adapted, by earlier standards, to post-war requirements.

8 *An Analysis of the Sources of War Finance and an Estimate of the National Income and Expenditure in 1938 and 1940*, Cmd 6261, 1941.
9 *Employment Policy*, Cmd 6527, 1944, para. 84.

# PART TWO

# Chapter four

# EXTERNAL ECONOMIC POLICY: THE BACKGROUND

We can now look at developments over the period in more detail with an eye to the influence of policy on these developments. Needless to say, most of what happened was not the direct outcome of deliberate policy and the impact of events on policy is easier to trace than that of policy on events.

The recurrence of balance-of-payments crises makes it natural to start from external events and pressures. It was obvious from the start that in a country so dependent on imports, so heavily in debt and so near to bankruptcy in its external accounts, the balance of payments was likely to prove the weakest link on the way to recovery. But it is never possible to dissociate external events and pressures from domestic policy, as some ministers, including the Prime Minister, tended to do.[1] Inflation, to take one example, and budget deficits to take another, do not exhaust their effects within the limits of the domestic economy but have an observable impact on the foreign exchanges. Even policies with no such direct effects, such as nationalization of the steel industry or the launching of a National Health Service, may influence market opinion and affect the strength of sterling or the government's power to borrow abroad. It is not possible to cut the economy in two and separate the external from the internal.

1 'During the years of Labour Government after 1945, it was a regular Opposition theme that Labour Chancellors thought too little about the relationship between the balance of the domestic economy and the external balance of payments' (Sir Edward Boyle, in J. K. Bowers (1979), p. 6). Attlee was still reluctant to link public expenditure and the balance of payments in November 1952 (ibid., p. 7). Cripps, however, became increasingly alive to the need to link internal and external financial policy (see, for example, EPC(50)44, para. 2, 27 April 1950, in PRO CAB 134/225).

From the point of view of exposition, however, it is convenient to deal separately with developments on the domestic front and on the external front. The four chapters that follow deal with events in each of the odd years between 1945 and 1951 when a balance-of-payments crisis threatened or occurred: the American Loan negotiations in 1945; the convertibility crisis of 1947; the devaluation crisis of 1949; the rearmament crisis of 1951. A later chapter looks at the renewed pressure for convertibility and the Robot scheme for combining this with a floating pound. The discussion of external economic policy then concludes with a chapter on relations with Europe, first in the early post-war years, then in OEEC in the days of Marshall Aid, over the Schuman Plan in 1950 and in the formation and operation of the European Payments Union. Thereafter we turn back to consider the problems of domestic economic management.

The present chapter is intended to provide the necessary background to external economic policy and to supplement the detailed account in later chapters of policy changes in the episodes of crisis by a more continuous outline of the evolution of policy. We begin by considering the outlook for the balance of payments in 1945, the structural and other changes that this appeared to require, and the instruments at the government's disposal for effecting these changes.

## The outlook in 1945

Britain's economic recovery was obviously bound up with world economic recovery since her economy was more closely integrated into the world economy than that of any other country. The dislocation of the world economy was so severe, especially in Europe and Asia, that reconstruction was likely to prove slow and painful, delaying recovery in Britain too: all the more if it was interrupted by the kind of worldwide depression that had followed the First World War. Added to this was the heavy cost of the international role that the United Kingdom was being asked to play. There were British troops in many different countries and the outlay involved weighed on the balance of payments. Large sums were required for UNRRA (i.e. for the rehabilitation of occupied countries), for feeding the Germans, for contributions to the IMF and IBRD, for credits to other countries and for other government expenditures abroad that brought no imports in return. Enormous debts had been accumulated and there seemed little chance of writing any of them off. The government felt obliged to offer support to the United States in her efforts to restore convertibility of currencies and non-discrimination in trade when these policies, however desirable once the world was in better balance, were calculated to reduce Britain's freedom of manoeuvre in a desperate situation.

Official forecasts, nevertheless, took a fairly robust view of the prospects: it was thought likely that world trade would reach or exceed the pre-war level by 1950 and might be 50 per cent higher than in 1937 by 1955.[2] This may have seemed optimistic at the time but it proved to be too cautious. World trade in manufactures, a more relevant measure, was 25 per cent higher by 1950 and over 70 per cent higher by 1955.

Officials were less successful in judging the outlook for world prices. In the first post-war calculations it was assumed that export and import prices would both double in comparison with pre-war prices, i.e. that the terms of trade would be unchanged.[3] It was on this basis that a deficit of £750 million in 1946 and a cumulative deficit of £1250 million to the end of 1948 were estimated; and it was on the same basis that the need was established for an increase in the volume of exports by 50–75 per cent above the pre-war level. But the course of prices was very different. In 1946 there was a worldwide food shortage prolonged into 1947 by bad harvests in Europe. Raw materials were also difficult to procure. The result was an abnormal dependence on supplies from the Western Hemisphere, which had escaped the devastation of war, and especially from the United States which acted as the world's marginal supplier. With the removal of price control, prices rose steeply in the United States, diminishing the real value of the dollar loan and raising import prices alarmingly. Between 1945 and 1949 import prices increased by 50 per cent and between 1949 and 1951 they increased again in the same proportion. Apart from the inflationary push that this gave to the British economy, it produced a sharp adverse change in the terms of trade. Already in 1945 they were slightly worse than before the war. By 1951 they were nearly 30

2 R. W. B. Clarke estimated in June 1945 that world trade would be up to 15 per cent more by volume in 1950 than in 1937 (Clarke (1982), p. 101). Austin Robinson in 1946 put the increase in world trade in manufactures by 1951 (over 1937) at 34 per cent on an optimistic view but 9 per cent less on a pessimistic view. British exports of manufactures would be 50 per cent higher on the first basis and 3 per cent higher on the second (Board of Trade memorandum on 'The Long-term Demand for British Exports of Manufactures', July 1946). The 'optimistic' picture proved in fact to err a little on the side of caution.

3 *Statistical Material presented during the Washington Negotiations*, Cmd 6707, December 1945 (referred to in what follows as '*Statistical Material*').

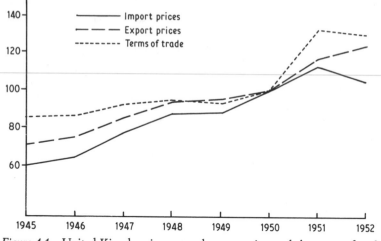

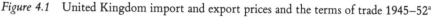

*Figure 4.1* United Kingdom import and export prices and the terms of trade 1945–52[a]

a Chain indices of unit value with 1938, 1947 and 1950 bases converted to uniform 1950 base. Figures for 1945 and 1946 are from Feinstein (1972), table 64.

*Source: Annual Abstract of Statistics for 1953, table 325.*

per cent worse (see figure 4.1). If a 50 per cent expansion in exports was a correct judgement of what was needed with unchanged terms of trade, an extra 30 per cent had become necessary by 1951.[4]

The estimates submitted by officials had two important implications. The first was the need for massive additional finance from the only available source – North America. The second was the need for a structural transformation of the British economy to make possible a 50–75 per cent increase in exports without any parallel expansion in imports above the pre-war level.

There were those who were not altogether convinced of the need for a large American loan and thought that it might be possible to get by with a limited amount of borrowing on commercial terms. But this postulated a swift withdrawal from military and political obligations to other countries and an acceptance of a much humbler role in international affairs; a posture in commercial policy that would have run counter to American ideas and might have produced a breach with other members of the Commonwealth; and a degree of austerity exceeding anything experienced in wartime.

4 The misjudgement was not confined to officials. Ministers kept on preparing for an American slump that never came and expected prices to be lower at some future date.

The Cabinet accepted the need for an immediate approach to the United
States for a grant (they did not at first contemplate a loan) on 23 August
1945. They also accepted in December the suggested target for exports but
without specifying a date.[5] To this end they would undertake 'with the
same energy as in time of war, whatever measure of industrial and marketing reorganisation and reconstruction may be necessary'.[6]

We discuss the subsequent negotiations with the Americans in chapter
5 and the means by which the government sought to influence the balance
of trade at pp. 74–5 below.

## The dollar problem

In 1945 the balance of payments was identified with the balance on current
account. It was taken for granted that a deficit with one country could be
set against an equal surplus with another and that all currencies were
equally 'hard'. But it was not long before it was recognized that this was
an oversimplification and that surpluses might be in soft currencies not
acceptable in settlement of deficits with hard currency countries.

What was not sufficiently emphasized at the start was the unique
position of the United States. Every country in the world seemed to be
queuing up to buy from the United States and they continued to queue
when the dollars they had to spend were running out fast. The United
States fed in enough dollars in 1946 to prevent any general scarcity but in
1947, with a virtual cessation of dollar lending and poor harvests in
Europe, the situation changed abruptly and only the launching of the
Marshall Plan allowed expansion to continue.[7] The United States was the
world's marginal supplier but at prices that rose steeply as controls were
removed. The United Kingdom, facing in one direction for her export
markets and in another for essential imports ended the year with a dollar
deficit more than twice as great as her current account deficit and very

---

5  *Statistical Material*, para. 13. It was not until November 1946 that the Cabinet set a
   target for the second half of 1947 of a volume of exports 50 per cent above the level of
   1938 – a target hastily reduced to 40 per cent in February 1947 in the middle of the
   fuel crisis (CM(46) 94 in PRO CAB 128/6).
6  ibid.
7  'For nearly a year to the spring of 1947 there had been practically no new cash lending
   by the United States.' (Bank for International Settlements, 17th *Annual Report*,
   1947, pp. 138–9.) Other countries drew down their reserves of gold and dollars in
   1947 by $4.5 billion.

*1. This implies that U.S. spending in WW II did not build up world dollar reserves.*

*Table 4.1*  Pattern of British trade 1938–50

| Source or market | Percentage of total imports | | | Percentage of total exports | | |
|---|---|---|---|---|---|---|
| | *1938* | *1946* | *1950* | *1938* | *1946* | *1950* |
| Western Hemisphere | 30.1 | 44.8 | 25.0 | 17.2 | 13.5 | 18.2 |
| Sterling area | 31.2 | 32.8 | 38.0 | 44.9 | 45.2 | 47.8 |
| OEEC countries (excluding Eire and Ireland) | 24.0 | 14.9 | 25.1 | 25.1 | 28.3 | 25.1 |
| Rest of the world | 14.8 | 7.5 | 11.9 | 12.8 | 13.0 | 9.0 |
| | 100.0 | 100.0 | 100.0 | 100.0 | 100.0 | 100.0 |

*Source: Annual Abstract of Statistics for 1953, tables 211 and 212.*

nearly ran out of dollars while in substantial surplus with non-dollar countries.

The world economy had become lopsided: there was an imbalance that might prove to be chronic between countries whose economies had flourished and expanded in wartime and those that had been devastated or turned upside down. Britain was having more success in finding markets in the latter group, which could not pay in convertible currency, while she relied heavily for supplies on the former group requiring payment in gold or dollars.

The change in the pattern of British trade is shown in table 4.1. Imports from the Western Hemisphere rose from 30 per cent before the war to 45 per cent in 1946 and then gradually fell to 25 per cent in 1950. On the other hand, exports to the Western Hemisphere fell from 17 per cent before the war to 13.5 per cent in 1946 before recovering to over 18 per cent in 1950. Trade with Europe and with the rest of the world followed the opposite pattern. Each shrank in importance as a source of supply immediately after the war and then recovered in the post-war years while the opposite was true of both areas as markets for British exports. These changes were accompanied by corresponding swings in the balance of trade: the trade deficit with the Western Hemisphere was inflated after the war and then shrank to more normal proportions by 1950 while an unusually favourable balance with Europe and the rest of the world in 1946 vanished between then and 1950.

Trade with the sterling area preserved a more stable relationship to total imports and exports, the proportion in 1946 being a little higher, and by 1950 perceptibly higher, on both sides of the account. One-third of

Britain's imports came from the sterling area and nearly half her exports were marketed there. Since this trade was all in sterling there were none of the payments difficulties associated with the use of hard currencies and it tended for that reason to be encouraged. But it did not escape the opposite danger, to which trade in soft currencies was subject, of absorbing British exports to excess without yielding in return the means of payment for imports from the dollar area i.e. the area requiring settlement in gold or dollars. Where at one time Britain had been able to run a deficit with the dollar area with impunity because other members of the sterling area were in surplus, it now looked in 1946–7 as if the rest of the sterling area would be taking from the dollar pool held centrally in London and putting very little back. The United Kingdom, instead of squaring its accounts multi-laterally, would have to resort to more desperate remedies for an impending dollar shortage.

What remedies would be appropriate depended on the view taken of the dollar shortage. On one view it was no more than an expression of the division of the world into hard and soft currencies and this in turn merely registered the lag in recovery in those parts of the world most devastated or dislocated by war. So long as Germany and Japan were in ruins, other countries were bound to turn to the United States for the manufactures they needed, especially if the United Kingdom was slow to deliver. As they recovered, the balance would change and there would be less need of dollars. Supplies from South-East Asia had also been disrupted by war and had been further reduced because rates of exchange were utterly un-realistic. These countries included some that might yet prove to be large dollar earners and offer the United Kingdom an easier route to converti-bility, by sharing in these dollars, than by making a direct attack on American markets. It would be well to guard against trying to effect a major structural adjustment in the world economy only to be left with a structural maladjustment within the British economy itself as a result of developing the wrong markets and the wrong industries. There was bound to be much waste and misdirected investment in any hastily implemented policy of dollar import substitution. This was as true of investment abroad as of investment at home. Attempts to produce groundnuts in East Africa, chickens in West Africa, and sorghum in Queensland, for example, demonstrated just how disastrous large and ambitious schemes of agricultural development in tropical or semi-tropical countries might prove.[8]

8  Morgan (1980).

1. If when Ger & Japan recovered they joined sterling currency Trading blocs they would be tied to the UK & Europe and be independent of US economic & political control. This very nearly happened.

On this view the dollar problem was a passing phase that recovery would cure. Some adjustment of exchange rates might also be necessary where currencies were clearly out of line. In the post-war years many exchange rates operated strongly against a recovery in exports and a closing of the trade gap. But there might also be a need for a more general alignment that made hard currencies dearer and soft currencies cheaper so that market forces could operate more powerfully to remedy the shortage of the one and the over-abundance of the other.

A widespread contrary view was that the dollar shortage would prove obstinate and enduring, if not irremediable. First of all the iron curtain that separated East and West had cut off traditional sources of grains and timber that might never again become available. Then, many of the less developed countries were turning away deliberately from primary products to manufactures in an effort of industrialization which they took to be the recipe for prosperity. This did not augur well for an early improvement in the supply of foodstuffs and materials. The United States, on the other hand, although a ready source of supply for primary products, which made up half her total exports, showed no great appetite for imports of manufactures and could not be depended upon to balance increased sales abroad with increased purchases of imports. In the years immediately before the war she had made dollars available to other countries through imports, remittances, grants, capital exports, etc., that represented no more than 4 per cent of her GNP; and even the large flow of aid in post-war years did not raise the proportion above 6.5 per cent – a lower proportion indeed than in the late 1920s.[9]

To break into the American market on any scale seemed beyond the powers of European manufacturers. America's superior industrial productivity was seen as self-reinforcing so that she could never be overtaken. Her competitive advantage would increase continuously, reinforced by success in foreign markets and in turn breeding fresh success. On this showing, the dollar problem was chronic and it was hopeless to expect market forces to eliminate it, whether through currency devaluation or a greater competitive effort. Equilibrium with America could only be restored by conscious planning, using state support to build up new industries and reconstruct old ones behind tariff walls or by the use of quota restrictions discriminating against imports from America. The argument has since become familiar in the literature of underdevelopment. The

9 Memorandum on 'World Supply and Use of Dollars', 25 June 1952, in PRO T 230/177.

advanced countries are alleged to have an unfair advantage because they dictate the rhythm of development to the latecomers who remain dependent on them and lag further and further behind. It is not a view of development that has much plausibility within the circle of advanced countries whatever may be thought of its applicability elsewhere. Later experience was soon to show that the dollar problem was anything but chronic.

There was also a common view, especially at the political level, that the dollar problem was somehow of America's own making and that it was up to the United States to take action to eliminate it. This had been true in the 1930s when the American slump, the Hawley-Smoot tariff and the suspension (indeed, reversal) of the flow of capital to other countries threw the American balance of payments into surplus, forced deflation on the rest of the world, drained away the reserves of countries that were slow in adjusting, and created a worldwide shortage of foreign exchange. In the late 1940s the situation was very different. It could be claimed that there was still a dollar shortage that would be relieved if only the United States made access to her domestic market easier or if she made larger grants and loans to her trading partners. But the dollar shortage no longer reflected deflation or protectionism in America. It was simply the American trading surplus seen from the other side when America alone could meet the urgent need for imports in countries trying to rebuild their economies and lacking the necessary capital. These countries could go on spending dollars only so long as America supplied them in grants or loans or so long as they had reserves to draw upon. No doubt it was also difficult for them to *earn* dollars by supplying the American market. But this difficulty arose as much from the rest of the world's hunger for goods that it could not spare and for capital that it could not save as from any obstacles to penetrating the American domestic market. Nearly every other country was in deficit with the United States and the total deficit to be financed (i.e. the American surplus) was becoming steadily larger up to the middle of 1947.

The balance between the demand for dollars and their supply over the post-war years is shown in table 4.2 which also shows how the two were brought into balance in pre-war years. The first line of the table shows the extraordinary bulge in exports in 1946–7 while imports were rising more gently so that the surplus in the current account of the balance of payments reached a peak of over $12 billion in 1947 before falling back to only $2.5 billion in 1950. While government grants and loans met most of this, America's trading partners had to supply $2 billion from their reserves in

Table 4.2  The dollar shortage 1925–51 ($m.)

| | 1925–9 (average) | 1935–9 (average) | 1946 | 1947 | 1948 | 1949 | 1950 | 1951 (provisional) |
|---|---|---|---|---|---|---|---|---|
| US exports of goods and services | 6,617 | 4,025 | 14,966 | 19,741 | 16,967 | 15,974 | 14,425 | 20,214 |
| US imports of goods and services | −5,525 | −3,462 | −7,167 | −8,463 | −10,268 | −9,603 | −12,128 | −15,163 |
| Errors and omissions | −224 | 397 | 155 | 1,004 | 1,037 | 785 | 156 | 648 |
| Excess of dollar payments | 868 | 960 | 7,954 | 12,282 | 7,736 | 7,156 | 2,453 | 5,699 |
| Met from: | | | | | | | | |
| Private financial resources (remittances, capital flows) | 1,453 | −133 | 933 | 1,295 | 1,534 | 1,111 | 1,797 | 1,162 |
| Public financial resources | | | | | | | | |
| Grants, unilateral transfers | 11 | 16 | 2,279 | 1,812 | 4,157 | 5,321 | 4,120 | 4,508 |
| Capital flows | −38 | — | 2,774 | 3,901 | 886 | 647 | 164 | 151 |
| Liquidation of gold and dollar assets of other countries | −558 | 1,077 | 1,968 | 4,513 | 780 | −60 | −3,645 | −122 |
| Dollars distributed by IMF/IBRD | | | | 761 | 379 | 137 | 17 | |
| Dollars made available | 868 | 960 | 7,954 | 12,282 | 7,736 | 7,156 | 2,453 | 5,699 |

Source: 'World Supply and Use of Dollars', 25 June 1952, in PRO T 230/177.

1946 and another $4.5 billion in 1947. In the crisis this produced, Marshall Aid came to the rescue and the drain on reserves fell away until by 1950, with American imports more closely aligned with her exports, the reserves of Britain and other countries began at last to be replenished.

From the point of view of policy what chiefly mattered was how long the dollar shortage would last. If it was a short-term affair it might be enough to prune current spending and defer investment outlays wherever possible. But if it had to be regarded as durable, all kinds of schemes would have to be devised to develop alternative sources of supply and lay on a more wholehearted effort to establish markets for British exports in North America.

The same applied, of course, to the deficit on current account. Here it had been accepted that the deficit was unlikely to last very long. That acceptance had not prevented efforts to increase self-sufficiency on a long-term footing: the agricultural expansion programme, for example, was not put in hand with any intention to reverse it three or five years later when exports and imports were in balance. The decision could be defended on the grounds that to leave the whole of the adjustment to market forces without some deliberate attempt to save imports by administrative action would have risked too large a shift in the terms of trade. Even a subsidy to agriculture might be cheaper than the losses inflicted by such a shift. In the same way it could be argued that balancing accounts with the United States posed a transfer problem that was better mitigated by a conscious effort to accelerate the development of dollar-saving sources of supply. Such an effort could be worthwhile even if the transfer problem were to fade away in a few years once relative prices made possible an adjustment on the scale necessary.

## Inconvertibility

The dollar shortage implied deficits and the deficits in turn meant a drain on the reserves and a growing reluctance to part with them. If the deficits were obstinate, and would not yield readily to the classical remedies of deflation or devaluation, the only thing to do was to seek agreements with other countries that whittled down the use of gold and dollars in settlements with them i.e. that limited convertibility. This might be done by receiving credit against deficits up to some agreed level or requiring the creditor to accept payment in the currency of the debtor. The next stage was likely to be a move to bilateral trade agreements designed to minimize imbalances between countries at the cost of distorting the flow of trade, reducing purchases from countries in bilateral surplus and forcing these countries to accept goods they would not otherwise take. Under such a system the pressure of a dollar shortage originating in the imbalance between the United States and the rest of the world would make itself felt in the trade of any country such as Canada or Belgium that had a particular need of dollars and earned them from third countries. It would also restrict the growth of world trade and injure countries like the United Kingdom that were highly dependent on that growth. It could in the long run be largely self-defeating if by confining trade within bilateral channels it divided the world economy and raised costs in the non-dollar world in relation to costs in the dollar world, so perpetuating the imbalance between the two.

Inconvertibility was never complete. Bilateral surpluses and deficits were not extinguished and had to be settled beyond agreed limits in gold and dollars. Sterling in non-resident hands was allowed a limited convertibility by 'administrative' and 'transferable' arrangements. So long as the bulk of Britain's trade was in government hands and exchange control was reinforced by monetary agreements with other countries, these arrangements were effective. It was only later, as these conditions changed, and markets in foreign-owned sterling grew up outside the limits of control by the monetary authorities, that doubts arose whether inconvertibility would not crumble as a parallel market in 'cheap sterling' developed.[10]

The threat of 'two worlds' on the one hand and of expanding markets in 'cheap sterling' on the other did not emerge in the first few years after the war. The dollar problem itself did not come to the front until 1947 although officials could see it coming in the middle of 1946.[11] By the spring of 1947 it was recognized that the recovery in Europe was in danger of being halted (or even reversed) if the flow of imports were not sustained, and that it could not be sustained out of Europe's dwindling reserves of foreign exchange. The Marshall Plan allowed recovery to continue. But it brought to a head the question: how long would the dollar shortage last? The picture put together in OEEC at the end of 1948 from forecasts provided by member countries showed a deficit not much less in 1952 than it had been in 1947 and strengthened opinion in London on the need for long-term measures. Yet two years later at the end of

---

10  Appendix on 'Inconvertible Sterling' to 'Plan for Overseas Sterling', 16 February 1952, in PRO T 236/3245.
11  Clarke (1982), p. 67.

1950, Marshall Aid to Britain was discontinued and a few years later still the United States became a deficit country. The dollar shortage was less prolonged than seemed likely; but it was the perception of it as enduring that governed policy.

There were thus two strands to the policy eventually adopted and the two came together in the middle of 1947. On the one hand was the need to effect a major transformation of the export–import balance and put an end to the external deficit; on the other, was the need to cope with the dollar problem and co-operate in restoring balance in the world economy.

## Control and adjustment

The first of these structural adjustments was never solely a matter of exports and imports. The balance of payments was largely shaped by major items lying outside the trade field altogether: military expenditure overseas; the release of sterling balances; the outflow of capital to Commonwealth countries; the investment of capital, much of it involving an outlay in dollars, by the oil companies.[12] In the early post-war period it was the rate of demobilization and the termination of military and political obligations abroad that was the main battleground of policy. While the struggle, as explained in chapter 14, was conceived in terms of manpower, it was also over government expenditure overseas and hence over a main source of the deficit in the balance of payments.

The change required in the trade balance seemed to imply that Britain would have to win a larger place in world export markets and supply a higher share of world trade in manufactures, not just while Germany and Japan were unable to compete but after their return as major competitors. Only if world trade was unexpectedly buoyant (as in fact it was) so that there was ample room for all, would it be possible to attain the necessary volume of exports with a falling share in total trade. New markets would have to be created and new industries developed. Since coal and cotton could play only a minor role, other industries would have to expand and establish themselves more strongly in world markets. The transformation required was thus not confined to trade but would affect the whole structure of British industry.

What role the government could play in the process of adjustment was

---

12  Clarke (1982), p. 70.

never very clear. Industrial policy was in its infancy. Stafford Cripps hoped for an improvement in industrial efficiency from the various working parties that he set up but it would be difficult to point to any such effect. Nationalization did nothing to enhance export prospects. The government relied mainly on its control over the allocation of materials to put pressure on firms to export more. It could either limit home market sales or tie the allocation of materials to an agreed export target. It could also speak soft words to the larger firms to enlist their support. When Cripps issued a set of export targets in 1947 they received much publicity and may have given a fillip to the export drive: but they had been prepared by the Board of Trade as a cock-shy, without consultation with the industries concerned, much less individual exporters, and were originally designed to show how an agreed target for total exports might plausibly be decomposed between the main exporting industries. Over the distribution of exports between markets the government had little or no influence except what could be exercised by the Dollar Exports Board – a circumstance creating some tension between the Treasury, with its list of desirable and undesirable markets, and the Board of Trade, more concerned to keep up the momentum behind exports, irrespective of destination. The plain fact was that there was no great need for the encouragement of exports in what remained a seller's market almost throughout the period of Labour government. Exports depended largely on what could be supplied and on the competitive attraction that the domestic market was allowed to exert.

The government had a firmer grip on imports since they were largely purchased on government account and rationed or allocated by government agencies after arrival. The import programme was the main instrument of control over the balance of payments and the leading example of successful economic planning. The government depended heavily on its power to restrict imports through a limitation of its own purchases or through import quotas, machinery licensing, and other devices. The pace of expansion in imports after 1945 was kept within the limits of a programme agreed to by the Cabinet, accelerating if things seemed to be going well and slowing down or giving way to cuts in a crisis. Decisions were taken as a rule on the basis of forecasts from the Balance of Payments Working Party in 1945–7 and by the Dollar Drain Committee or some other official body thereafter.

The government's control over imports was reduced as trade returned to private hands and rationing was abandoned. But as was shown in 1951, it was always in a position to make substantial cuts. It could put pressure on other Commonwealth countries as in 1949 and 1951–2 to take supporting action; and the trade agreements that were constantly being negotiated with other countries provided some additional leverage, on exports as well as imports.

There was a limit to the government's power to compress the volume of imports. In 1946 imports were not much above the wartime level and nearly one-third lower than in 1938. It was partly the easing up on this austere import programme that brought on the crisis in the autumn of 1947: the volume of imports in the middle quarters of 1947 was running over 20 per cent higher than in 1946. It was not surprising, therefore, that import cuts formed a major part of the subsequent retrenchment. In the later crises of 1949 and 1951 import cuts were again imposed, on both of those occasions in association with other sterling area countries after a conference of Commonwealth finance ministers.

There was always a tendency, when such cuts were made, to look for 'luxury' elements in the programme that could be cut with less hardship. Films and tobacco were favourite candidates. It was possible to do a deal with the American film companies and get them to accept partial payment in sterling. But any substantial cut in imports of American films would have meant closing down cinemas all over Britain. As for tobacco, nothing was half as successful in getting people to pay taxes and drain away excess demand. In any event, what the government took to be luxuries were not necessarily so regarded by consumers whose priorities, as expressed in their spending habits, might be rather different. It was inevitable that import cuts should in practice extend beyond what might be singled out as luxuries and embrace all the main categories of imports including food and raw materials.

Direct controls over the trade balance were supplemented by exchange control, which limited the outflow of capital to non-sterling countries, and control over invisibles such as tourist expenditure abroad. There was also a rather grudging acceptance, by Cripps at least, of the need to keep the pressure of demand under control through fiscal measures.

While the gradual restoration of balance was assisted by a progressive tightening of fiscal policy followed by devaluation, monetary policy played little or no part; and in the various crises that punctuated recovery, the action taken by the government made no use of any of these instruments of policy except in 1949 when devaluation was reluctantly and almost accidentally employed. Instead the government depended almost entirely on cuts in imports, sometimes alone as in 1947, sometimes, as in 1949 and 1951, in association with other sterling area countries.

## Foreign economic relations

The main aim of policy was thus to restore external equilibrium at a high level of activity and to put an end to the dollar drain. This had implications for relations with other countries that are not pursued very far in this book. It also required the adoption of policies that had sufficient impact on the balance of payments to keep it under control.

Britain's balance-of-payments problems chiefly affected her relations with the United States, the Commonwealth, and Western Europe. She was heavily dependent on the United States with whom she had hoped to be a full partner; and she experienced repeated disappointments in seeking American support when the role and responsibilities she was invited to assume proved beyond her strength. This was true, for example, of convertibility, then of European integration and finally of rearmament. The issue of convertibility in particular, continued to bedevil Anglo-American relations throughout the period, as the United States first insisted on it, accepted the need for patience in 1947, then began to exert fresh pressure in 1949 and at intervals thereafter. There were deep misunderstandings on both sides as to what the other could or would do: none perhaps so great as the British disposition to treat what American officials proposed as a commitment by Congress itself without regard to the very different relationship in Washington between the executive and the legislature. But however much at loggerheads, and whatever misunderstandings arose, the American connection was accepted as the basis of recovery and, even more, of military security.

With the Commonwealth, relations were on a very different footing. The consultations that took place were rarer, between ministers rather than officials, and intended to lead to resolutions, not take the form of negotiations. Here, too, the economic forces at work tended to weaken the British position. The United Kingdom was heavily in debt to some members and investing heavily in others. Both the debt and the investment were unwelcome but there was no possibility of repaying the debt or arresting the investment. The bonds that linked Commonwealth countries were gradually loosening just when Britain's dependence on Commonwealth trade was increasing. Membership of the sterling area (which by no means coincided with the Commonwealth) provided some community of interest in the strength of sterling; and there were at least two occasions – in 1949 and 1951 – when meetings of Commonwealth finance ministers agreed on effective action to bring world payments into better balance. But neither the sterling area nor the Commonwealth had the adminis-

trative machinery to make a prompt and co-ordinated response to dis-
equilibrating pressures.

Relations with Western Europe were changing rapidly throughout the
period. At first much weaker and in chronic deficit, the countries of
Western Europe were by 1951 rapidly overtaking the United Kingdom
and had all but given up counting on British leadership. The United
Kingdom, having begun by looking on Western Europe as a burden it
must not be asked to bear, debated two years later whether it could join
forces with continental countries in mounting a collaborative attack on
the dollar problem, helped to launch OEEC, but remained conscious that
her main interests lay outside Europe and dragged her feet at any
suggestion of economic integration. The most successful instrument of
European co-operation, the EPU, was born almost in spite of Britain and
there were times when British officials contemplated winding up OEEC
itself.

All these relationships were dominated by the dollar problem. So far as
any co-ordinated attack was made on the problem it was through the
OEEC, not, as might conceivably have happened, through the IMF. The
IMF in those years was one of the great disappointments to the United
Kingdom which had been led to believe that in conditions of dollar
shortage, the scarce currency clause could be invoked. Unfortunately, this
expectation overlooked the technicalities. A scarce currency had to be
scarce in the Fund and the United States took care to ensure that the Fund
was never short of dollars. One way in which this result was achieved was
by making access to the resources of the Fund subject to very stiff
conditions not envisaged by the signatories to the Bretton Woods Agreement. While the United Kingdom did succeed in 1947 in borrowing from
the Fund, the drawing it was able to make was roughly equal to what it
had already contributed in gold and dollars. So far as the early post-war
years were concerned, the Fund might as well never have been created.

### Forecasts, targets and performance

Government economic policy was dependent throughout on forecasts of
the balance of payments. There are few better indications of how the
government saw the situation. To begin with, it was necessary in 1945 to
judge how long it would be before equilibrium was restored and how
much it would be necessary to borrow abroad to cover the deficit before
that point was reached. It was necessary also to single out the strategic
elements in the balance of payments: not merely to be aware of the relative

magnitudes of its component parts, but to have a view also as to their sensitiveness to the instruments of policy at the government's disposal. Equilibrium would not come of itself without supporting policies; and any forecast stretching several years ahead to the point at which the deficit was eliminated implied a set of policies consistent with that elimination and a judgement as to their effectiveness.

The deficit in 1945, after all, was largely of the government's own making: its military expenditure overseas, the scale of its purchases of imports from abroad, the size of the rations it allowed to domestic consumers, and the materials it made available to exporters, were among the more obvious of the factors affecting the balance of payments. In collaboration with other governments, the government could help to promote an international order favourable to the expansion of international trade or it might actively obstruct all such efforts. A forecast of the post-war balance of payments was also, therefore, a forecast of trade policies, of the line that governments would take and the success they would enjoy.

Once equilibrium was restored, however precariously, the government's interest tended to have a more limited horizon, and the forecasts submitted to it usually looked only one year ahead. They came to be related to the import programme and were made the basis for a tightening or loosening of import restrictions, depending on the immediate prospect. Annual programmes were also required by the ECA for purposes of allocating Marshall Aid and were treated by them as a bid for aid. Since the purpose of Marshall Aid was to make Europe self-supporting, however, it was necessary once again to take a long view of the balance of payments, this time over the four years 1948–52, and forecast how and when Europe would no longer be in deficit on dollar account. As in 1945 this meant forecasting trade policies as well as trade patterns: only, on this occasion, the operation was not one for Britain alone but for collaborative action within OEEC.

Attempts had been made by the Economic Section to forecast the post-war balance of payments as far back as 1942 and there were several attempts in 1945 in preparation for the Loan Negotiations. The first post-war estimate was contained in Keynes's memorandum on 'Our Overseas Financial Prospects' circulated to ministers on 13 August 1945 just before VJ Day and the ending of Lend-Lease.[13] This suggested that the deficit in

13 It forms part of the longer memorandum on 'The Present Overseas Financial Position of the U.K.' reprinted in Keynes (1979), vol. XXIV, pp. 377 *et seq.*

*Table 4.3*  Reconciliation of gold and dollar deficit and current account 1946–52 (£m.)

|  | 1946 | 1947 | 1948 | 1949 | 1950 | 1951 | 1952 | Total 1945–52 |
|---|---|---|---|---|---|---|---|---|
| Net gold and dollar deficit | −225 | −1,024 | −406 | −348 | +308 | −407 | −174 | −2,276 |
| Reduction in sterling liabilities[a] | −2 | +122 | +184 | −12 | −220 | −349 | +347 | +70 |
| Other capital outflows (net) | −3 | +521 | +248 | +359 | +219 | +387 | −10 | +1,721 |
| Current account deficit | −230 | −381 | +26 | −1 | +307 | −369 | +163 | −485 |
| *Memorandum item* Change in sterling balances of sterling area | −34 | −131 | +68 | −12 | +381 | +59 | −113 | +218 |

Sources: *Economic Trends Annual Supplement 1981; United Kingdom Balance of Payments 1946 to 1953*, Cmd 8976.

a  Including change in official holdings of non-dollar currencies and credit balance in EPU.

1946 might be as high as £950 million even if determined efforts were made to expand exports and if the volume of imports was limited to 77 per cent of the pre-war level. Military expenditure overseas was expected to reach £450 million in 1946. On the assumption that exports reached the target level of 150 per cent of 1938 by 1949 and that equilibrium was restored by the end of 1948, Keynes put the cumulative deficit over the post-war transition period at £1700 million. Later, he revised his estimates by adding £50 million to exports and £100 million to invisibles so that the deficit in 1946 came down to £800 million. When the Washington negotiations opened this had been further reduced to £750 million and the cumulative deficit before the restoration of equilibrium to £1250 million.[14]

For the cumulative deficit this was not a bad guess, even if the latest estimates show a total for the three years 1946–8 of only £600 million. If one aggregates the first published estimates, the total is £1245 million, or, if one takes the total as it stood at the end of the three years in March 1949, it amounts to £1130 million. At the time it seemed as if the balance-of-payments forecasts accepted as the basis of policy in 1945 had proved remarkably accurate. What had not been foreseen, however, was that the balance of payments on current account and the change in the gold and dollar reserves would bear little relationship to one another (see table 4.3).

14  *Statistical Material*, para. 16. The total was made up of £750 million, £350 million and £150 million in 1946, 1947 and 1948 respectively. (Clarke (1982), p. 153.)

The drain from the reserves, which was not subject to later revision, amounted to £1250 million in the two years 1946–7, and there was a further drain of £750 million still to come in 1948–9. So far from being an overestimate of what it would be necessary to borrow, the forecasts made at the end of the war were a good deal too low.

The margin between the current account deficit and the gold and dollar deficit implied an outflow of capital to that amount from the United Kingdom. Some of this, in 1947–8 at least, represented a withdrawal of sterling balances; from year to year there was an agreed release from the wartime balances which the government had blocked. But since fresh accumulations of sterling took place over the period the *net* rundown in balances was very small: over the seven years 1945–52 it came to only £70 million. Most of the capital outflow took a different form: either credits in favour of countries with which the United Kingdom was in surplus, or longer-term investments, mainly in the Commonwealth but including also substantial amounts by the oil companies in the Middle East and elsewhere. The figures in table 4.3 imply a net capital outflow totalling over £1700 million over the seven years – a good deal more than the American and Canadian loans but less than the aggregate of foreign aid received over the post-war years.

In the succession of forecasts of the balance of payments for post-war years the estimate of £750 million for the deficit of 1946 is the one best remembered. It was spelt out in the draft 'Economic Survey for 1946' at the beginning of December 1945 and although the next two forecasts in February and April 1946 differed a good deal in detail they came fairly close in total to the December estimate. By October it was clear that the forecasts had been too pessimistic. The deficit was then put at £475 million and this was the figure published in February in the *Economic Survey for 1947*. The latest estimate of £230 million is much lower and would have been thought very surprising indeed in 1947. All the main items in the balance of payments turned out more favourably than expected. Exports, visible and invisible, were higher and imports and government expenditure overseas lower than seemed likely a year before.[15]

15  It is not altogether clear what the forecasting errors were. Exports in 1946 were expected to reach 75 per cent of the 1938 level instead of nearly 100 per cent and a deduction of £150 million was made from the recorded value for lags in payment. Thus although the forecast allowed for the 1938 level of exports to be regained before the end of 1946 it came to only £550 million compared with a recorded total of £960 million (including re-exports). Retained imports were put at only 3 per cent above 1944 so the error here cannot have been very serious. Government expenditure

As evidence of the rapid increase in exports became available and the outlook for the balance of payments improved, the Cabinet became increasingly optimistic. By the end of April they were accepting balance on current account in the first half of 1947 as a target[16] at a time when the Balance of Payments Working Party was forecasting a deficit of £125 million for the half year.

There had already been a struggle in Cabinet over the import programme for 1946.[17] The £1000 million shown for retained imports in the draft 'Economic Survey for 1946' in December had been raised to £1126 million in February and Dalton wanted a cut to £1075 million while Strachey, the Minister for Food, asked for authority to add £20 million to the import programme for food so as to allow him to place more long-term contracts. Cripps, for all his leanings towards austerity, was one of those who favoured higher food imports because without them the work effort would suffer and so would output and exports. Strachey got his extra imports but only by forfeiting an equivalent amount in the second half of the year. What was not commented on at the time but had been on the horizon for many months past was a sharp rise in procurement prices once the war ended and de-control set in in the United States.[18]

When the draft 'Economic Survey for 1946–47' came before ministers in July, they heralded approval of the American Loan by Congress with increases in the import programme for 1947 totalling $80 million including a 50 per cent increase in the petrol ration.[19] On the other hand, bread rationing was introduced almost simultaneously, on 21 July.

If ministers felt reassured, the Treasury was increasingly disquieted. They had never fully accepted the doctrine that there would be no dollar shortage and from the spring of 1946 they could point to a menacing change in the pattern of trade.[20] Imports from North America were running at over 38 per cent of total UK imports compared with 23 per

overseas, net of receipts, came to £300 million which may correspond to the draft 'Economic Survey' figure for 'overseas war expenditure' but is certainly below what Keynes feared in early 1946. Net receipts from invisibles, now estimated at £200 million, compare with an estimate of only £65 million for interest, profits and dividends from abroad (CP(46)32 in PRO CAB 129/6).

16  CM(46)38, 29 April 1946, in PRO CAB 128/5.
17  CM(46)13, 7 February 1946, in PRO CAB 128/5.
18  Sir Herbert Broadley in the Ministry of Food had drawn attention to this danger in July 1945 (PRO T 236/437).
19  MEP(46) 4th Meeting, 12 July 1946, in PRO CAB 134/503.
20  Clarke (1982), p. 72.

cent in 1938 while the proportion of UK exports marketed in North America had fallen from 11 to 8.5 per cent. The current account deficit in 1947 looked like working out between £200 and £250 million in all the forecasts from April onwards, but the more important dollar deficit (which the draft 'Economic Surveys' did not mention) was put, first at £450 million in June and then at £500 million in October. Dalton made the October forecast the basis of a paper warning his colleagues that the country was running through the American credits too fast.[21] Even before they were voted by Congress in July, the Treasury had concluded that there was every chance that the wiping-out of the external deficit would not put an end to a continuing outflow of gold and dollars: and that, if so, 'the burden of the world's transfer problem with North America becomes concentrated upon our reserves'.[22]

Whatever the Treasury's fears in 1946 they were much intensified in 1947 when the rest of the world was sucking in American imports at a great rate as recovery accelerated, drawing on their accumulated reserves and what dollars could be picked up from countries like the United Kingdom to whom America had lent or made grants since the war. The whole process of European recovery was in danger of slowing down drastically in 1947 as the supply of dollars dried up. But it was well into 1947 before this danger was fully appreciated.

Not much notice was taken of the Treasury's warnings before the convertibility crisis broke in the middle of 1947. This was partly because in other respects things seemed to be going well. The balance of payments continued to improve until the fuel crisis in February 1947. But it was partly also because Dalton's proposals for remedying matters were either not very specific or very modest and much of what needed to be done lay in his own hands. This was true not only of the financial measures that would have put the economy under greater pressure to seek markets abroad and limit the demands on manpower at home. It was true also of many of the more strategic changes of direction that were gradually put in hand: the need to expand British food production and to develop non-dollar sources of supply of food and raw materials in the sterling area and Western Europe; the need also to find ways of adding to energy supplies,

---

21 'The Import Programme 1947. Memorandum by the Lord President of the Council', covering a memorandum by the Chancellor of the Exchequer with the same title and a report by the Balance of Payments Working Party, 23 October 1946, in PRO CAB 129/14.

22 ibid.

whether of British coal or Middle Eastern oil, that would allow the non-dollar world to cover its requirements without a heavy expenditure of dollars; and the need to steer a higher proportion of British exports to dollar markets.

In any all-out effort of this kind, however, the United Kingdom was handicapped in 1946–7 by its obligation to refrain from discrimination against dollar sources of supply: an obligation which it was bound also to respect in any pressure it put on other members of the sterling area. It is true that this did not apply to efforts to produce more food or coal within the United Kingdom. But so far as these entailed subsidies or protection they too ran counter to the free-trade doctrines that were part of the current American philosophy. It was only when Marshall Aid made discrimination against dollar imports respectable that the Treasury was able to proceed wholeheartedly with a programme to restructure international trade.

The forecasts for 1946 had been too cautious: the deficit was reassuringly small, mainly because it was impossible to obtain the imports planned for. The forecasts for 1947, on the contrary, were too optimistic: the deficit proved to be alarmingly high. A forecast of £220 million in the draft 'Economic Survey for 1947' in December 1946 was hastily revised upwards to £350 million in the middle of the coal crisis: or at least this was stated by the government to be the limit within which they would finance a deficit although in the end they had to put up with much more. Exports fell away by 6 per cent in the first half of the year and recovered to show an improvement of 8 per cent in the second half (both figures in comparison with the second half of 1946). There was a comparable upset in imports which increased in value by 45 per cent instead of the 35 per cent approved in the October 1946 programme. Much of the increase reflected sharply higher prices, the increase by volume being no more than 14 per cent. The trade deficit which had been put as low as £128 million at the end of 1946 was instead £361 million whilst the dollar deficit which had been put at £500 million turned out to be over £1000 million, absorbing in a single year more than the whole of the American line of credit so painfully negotiated in 1945.

These figures were not available till months (or, in some cases, years) afterwards. But the trend was only too obvious. The convertibility crisis in August forced the government to act. The measures taken and the reasons why Dalton's repeated warnings had little effect earlier are discussed in chapter 5.

While the favourable experience of 1946 made the forecasts for 1947 too

*Table 4.4*   Balance-of-payments forecasts 1945–52 (£m.)

| | Current account as forecast at beginning of year | First published estimate of current account | Latest estimate of current account | Drain on reserves as forecast at beginning of year | Drain on reserves (actual) |
|---|---|---|---|---|---|
| 1946 | −750 | −450 | −230 | (750) | −225 |
| 1947 | −220 | −675 | −381 | (500) | −1,024 |
| 1948 | −(270)[b] | −120 | +26 | (450)[b] | −406 |
| 1949 | −(30)[b] | −70 | −1 | (400)[b] | −348 |
| 1950 | +50 | +229 | +307 | 280[c] | +308 |
| 1951 | −100 | −521 | −369 | | −407 |
| 1952 | — | +291[a] | +163 | | −175 |

*Sources: Economic Survey* for successive years; *Economic Trends Annual Supplement 1981.*

a  Including Defence Aid of £121 million.
b  Twice the forecast for the first half-year. For 1949–50 a deficit of £200 million was forecast in September 1948 and published in December 1948.
c  1950/51.

optimistic, the disastrous experience of 1947 had the opposite effect in 1948. The *Economic Survey for 1948* confined itself cautiously to a forecast for the first half of the year, estimating the current account deficit at £136 million and the drain on the reserves at £222 million. For the year as a whole, the current account was in fact marginally in surplus. The drain on the reserves, however, was close to the forecast: it amounted to £243 million in the first half of the year. In the second half it fell to £163 million, with Marshall Aid only a little less but enough to bring to an end the long fall in the reserves from the beginning of 1947 onwards.

The sharp change of policy precipitated by the crisis of 1947 halted the growth of imports and allowed exports to resume their expansion. The see-saw in the balance of trade is illustrated in figure 4.2 which shows how a flat year for exports in 1947 was followed by a flat year for imports in 1948. Exports in 1948 were 25 per cent larger by volume than in the previous year while imports were up by only 4 per cent. This brought exports at the end of 1948 close to the target of 50 per cent above the level of 1938 which the Cabinet had set, before the fuel crisis, for the end of 1947. Imports, on the other hand, were only 80 per cent of the pre-war level. The external deficit had gone but the dollar drain continued at £400 million a year.

The caution acquired in 1947 continued into 1949. Halfway through 1948 the official forecast for July 1948 to July 1949 was still showing a deficit on current account of £362 million; and in September 1948 the

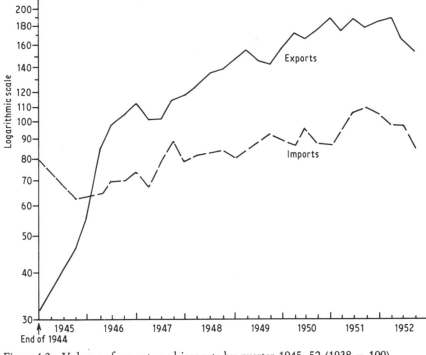

*Figure 4.2* Volume of exports and imports by quarter 1945–52 (1938 = 100)

Source: Monthly Digest of Statistics, various issues.

deficit for 1949–50 was put at £200 million.[23] But by March 1949 it was estimated that the current account had been in slight surplus since July 1948 and would remain approximately in balance in the first half of 1949. At that point, however, the growth of exports was arrested and reversed between spring and autumn by a temporary depression in export markets while imports resumed their climb. The gold and dollar deficit accelerated for long enough to produce an exchange crisis and in September the pound was devalued. But, taking the year as a whole, the dollar drain was less than in the previous year and the balance of payments on current account much the same.

The most that the *Economic Survey for 1950* would venture to predict was that the balance of payments 'might go back to a position of approximate balance or even show a surplus on current account'. A token surplus of £50 million was assumed. The only detailed forecasts published related

23 These were the figures submitted to ECA in December 1948 but prepared earlier (see *Economic Survey for 1949*, Cmd 7647, paras 59–60).

to the gold and dollar deficit for the year 1950–1. Once again the forecasts erred on the side of pessimism. The current account for 1950 showed a surplus of £307 million and for the first time the dollar drain was replaced by a net surplus in gold and dollars almost exactly equal to the large current account surplus.

Between 1950 and 1952 the balance of payments see-sawed between a large surplus in 1950, a still larger deficit in 1951 and a fresh surplus in 1952. Marshall Aid, which had sustained the dollar outflow in the three previous years, came to an end in 1951 and only a negligible amount of Defence Aid was received from the United States in that year. The swing in the balance of payments produced an even larger swing in the gold and dollar reserves which doubled in 1950, fell by half in the next fifteen months and held almost level in 1952, no higher than they had been at the end of 1948 and far too low to meet the strains to which they were exposed.

Rearmament in 1951–2 put an end to the export drive. The level of exports reached in 1950 – 80 per cent higher than in 1938 – was not regained until 1954. In the four years 1946–50 exports had more than doubled; in the next four years the increase was barely perceptible. Imports, too, lost a good deal of their momentum. In 1954 they were no more than 14 per cent above the level of 1950 whereas in 1950 they had grown by 28 per cent in the previous four years. They had barely recovered to their pre-war volume while exports were some 80 per cent higher and GDP was 35 per cent higher.

Meanwhile the practice of publishing a forecast of the balance of payments had virtually ceased. A token deficit of £100 million was shown in one of the tables in the *Economic Survey for 1951* but the Board of Trade thought that the deficit might amount to as much as £300 million.[24] A year later Butler was being warned that it might reach £750 million in 1952 and that the drain on the reserves might reach $1250 million, returning from the freak surplus of $862 million in 1950 to a little below the high level of 1948–9, without Marshall Aid to provide a compensating inflow.[25] Once again a crisis developed, less unexpectedly perhaps than in

---

24  A minute from David Butt, a member of the Economic Section, in PRO T 229/270 records that the Board of Trade expected a deficit of £250 million excluding stockpiling but suggested the use in the *Economic Survey for 1951* of a figure of £100 million. This figure appears in table 24.

25  'Notes for and record of conversation on financial and economic problems between J. W. Snyder and R. A. Butler', in PRO T 236/2989. The current account deficit is now put at £369 million and the dollar deficit was $1140 million.

1947 and 1949 but on a scale that took the government by surprise. And once again the forecasts for the following year erred on the side of caution. The most the Conservative administration would commit itself to was that the account would be in balance.

Thus, broadly speaking, there was a fresh balance-of-payments crisis every odd year but a fairly steep underlying trend towards equilibrium, first in the overall balance, which was reached in 1948, and then in the dollar balance, which can be said to have been reached in 1952.

# Chapter five

# THE AMERICAN LOAN

The most urgent problem facing the new government was the financing of a large and unavoidable external deficit over the next few years. When Lend-Lease ended the deficit was running at about £1200 million a year (excluding munitions)[1] and in 1946 it seemed unlikely to be less than £750 million.

The problem was coupled with two others. One related to the financial obligations arising out of Lend-Lease: these would involve negotiations at an early date with the United States and Canada. A second and larger issue, linked with the first, concerned the whole framework of international trade and payments in the post-war years. The Bretton Woods Agreements, providing for the creation of an International Monetary Fund and an International Bank for Reconstruction and Development, were currently under debate in Congress and would be presented to Parliament for ratification before the end of the year. Both of these institutions were as much British as American in conception although it had been American rather than British ideas that had prevailed at Bretton Woods. It was the United Kingdom, too, which had originated a proposal to establish alongside the IMF and IBRD a third international institution, the International Trade Organization (ITO), which would promote free, multilateral trade, banish discrimination and reduce trade barriers of all

---

1 This was the figure implied by Attlee when addressing the House of Commons (*H. C. Deb.*, 5th ser., vol. 413, col. 956, 24 August 1945). Keynes used an estimate of £1250 million (1979, vol. XXIV, p. 428). The draft 'Economic Survey for 1946' (CP(46)32 in PRO CAB 129/6) gives a figure of £1000 million for 1944.

kinds. The proposal went back to the Mutual Aid Agreement which had been signed by the United Kingdom in February 1942 after the introduction of Lend-Lease. This made provision in Article 7 for: 'agreed action . . . directed to . . . the elimination of all forms of discriminatory treatment in international commerce and to the reduction of tariffs and other trade barriers'. This much-disputed clause represented the 'consideration' which Congress had insisted should form part of the Lend-Lease settlement when agreeing to leave it to the President to decide what 'benefit to the United States' should be accepted in settlement. It was partly the need to give substance to the 'consideration' that had led to James Meade's proposal for a 'Commercial Union' in 1942 and to extensive discussion of the proposal (which blossomed into one for an International Trade Organization) in the Washington talks of September–October 1943. But in 1945 it remained unresolved how the United Kingdom was to give effect to Article 7. Moreover, even when the Bretton Woods Agreements were ratified there would still be an indefinite period of transition before undertakings such as the obligation to make sterling convertible at a fixed parity came into operation.

There was thus a good deal of unfinished business to be negotiated over Lend-Lease and over the commercial policy implications of Article 7. The Americans were likely to ask Britain to abbreviate the transition provided for in Article 14 of the Bretton Woods Agreement and to co-operate in accelerating the introduction of convertibility and non-discrimination in international trade. They took too little account of the impoverishment the world had suffered and the consequent imbalance between the dollar and non-dollar worlds.

These problems had exercised officials in Whitehall for several years. Keynes in particular had been brooding on how to meet the prospective deficit in Britain's balance of payments since his participation in the Stage II negotiations in Washington towards the end of 1944. Since it was he who was the dominant figure in the loan negotiations, first in shaping the proposals put to ministers and then in conducting negotiations in Washington on the basis of those proposals, we begin by outlining the way in which his thinking evolved and the considerations governing it. Until the negotiations were well under way, ministers played a very limited role and were content to leave things to Keynes *ad referendum*, i.e. reporting back to ministers whenever necessary for fresh instructions. Unfortunately there was a wide gulf between Keynes's presuppositions and those of ministers, most of whom had had little time to acquaint themselves with the complexities of the issues; and an equally wide gulf between Keynes's opening bid and the offers that the Americans were prepared to contemplate. The amount, the financial terms and the conditions attached to the eventual loan were all far removed from what Keynes had hoped for and led ministers to expect.

Keynes had foreseen from the start an overriding need to look to the United States for the finance necessary to cover Britain's post-war deficits but feared that an application for assistance would be treated on much the same footing as applications from other Allied countries. Any loans made were likely to be on commercial or near-commercial terms. Such terms might be appropriate to a country like France which had substantial reserves and no large external indebtedness. But a different approach was necessary in the British case, particularly if the United States wanted a Britain strong enough to engage in partnership in the construction of an open international economic system, free from discrimination and currency blocs. Britain was virtually bankrupt and could not afford to borrow on commercial terms. Her enormous external debts, which no other country had incurred, were the direct outcome of her war effort. Her overseas military expenditure had exceeded America's, and her mobilization for war had been deliberately allowed to absorb resources needed to pay for necessary imports. She was now, Keynes argued, entitled to ask for a reconsideration of the sharing of the costs of the war. While some prompting might be necessary, it would be best if the initiative in such a reconsideration was taken by the American side and some new idea, comparable in boldness with Lend-Lease, came as a stroke of policy from the President himself, taking everyone concerned by surprise.[2]

This approach, which struck others as too optimistic, he did not wish to be put to the Americans until a month or two after VE Day. Keynes did not want his ideas prematurely 'hawked round Washington'.[3] He set them out at length in a paper on 'Overseas Financial Policy in Stage III' drafted early in March 1945 and circulated to the War Cabinet after revision on 15 May.[4] In this he considered what freedom of action remained to the United Kingdom in financial arrangements with the United States and what options were open to the Cabinet in planning for the post-war years.

Keynes began by pointing out that at least Britain's war debts, with

2 Keynes to R. H. Brand, 15 February 1945, in Keynes (1979), vol. XXIV, pp. 248–9.
3 Keynes to F. G. Lee, 23 January 1945 in Keynes (1979), vol. XXIV, p. 251.
4 Reprinted in ibid., pp. 256–95.

minor exceptions, had been contracted entirely in sterling 'and it is pretty well understood by those concerned that they are in our hands'.[5] At the same time the gold and dollar reserves, which had fallen from £600 million at the beginning of the war to virtually nil in April 1941, had been built up again, mainly from American troop expenditures in Britain, to a total likely to reach £500 million. Payments agreements that had been concluded with some of the European countries, and were likely to be reached with others in Europe and elsewhere (when taken in conjunction with the sterling area and the special accounts system), established a *modus vivendi* for carrying on trade with nearly all countries outside the United States without immediate financial embarrassment. The currency was relatively stable in value and the exchange rate indicated a strong competitive position. On the other hand, overseas military expenditure outside Europe and the Western Hemisphere was largely out of control, and although practically none of it arose out of the war with Germany, was reckoned to be running at over £700 million a year – more than the rate of net dis-investment abroad. A sustained increase in exports to a level 50 per cent above pre-war was required but was unlikely to be achieved without major changes, especially if coal and cotton could no longer play a large part as in pre-war years. Finally, the sterling Dominions were leaving Britain to carry an excessive burden of imperial defence when they were all doing very well financially out of the war.

At that stage Keynes expected an external deficit in the first post-war year that would be not much under £1000 million. Three to five years would be necessary in order to restore equilibrium; and in that time the cumulative deficit was unlikely to be less than £2000 million. Nearly all of this, or perhaps more, would have to be borrowed outside the sterling area. At the very least, a cumulative deficit of £1000 million over the period of transition seemed a certainty; and the additional financial aid from the United States and Canada that would then be required ruled out any declaration of financial independence of North America. In any event, such a declaration, which would have to be accompanied by more stringent controls and rationing than any adopted in wartime and by national planning and direction of foreign trade, somewhat after the Russian model, would require the United Kingdom to practise, and indeed advocate, a policy of economic isolationism that would invite the strongest opposition from the United States, would be unlikely to commend itself to many other members of the sterling area, and would

5  ibid., p. 258.

receive little support from other countries that recognized their financial dependence on the United States.

There could be no guarantee, Keynes went on, that the Americans would make a fair offer allowing the United Kingdom to regain her strength in support of an open world economy in keeping with American ideas. But if they did, such a world was very much in Britain's interests as well, while the alternative of planned bilateralism would stifle enterprise, and disrupt the sterling area. The United Kingdom could not retain its position as the financial centre of the Commonwealth (Canada apart) unless sterling was freely convertible and available for the purchase of goods from any country. No doubt the system might break down and equilibrium might prove unattainable without a state monopoly of foreign trade. That could not be denied. But the only wise statesmanship was to start off from the other hypothesis.

While it would be right to reject what Keynes christened 'Starvation Corner' without representing it as utterly impracticable, it would also be right to avoid the opposite extreme which he called 'Temptation'. Keynes thought that it would be easy to negotiate a loan of $5 billion (which he regarded as probably the minimum required to permit of full multilateralism of trade and payments from the start), or even the $8 billion which might well be required, provided the conditions attached to such a loan were met. These conditions would be likely to involve a rate of interest of $2-2\frac{1}{2}$ per cent, with repayment spread over, say, thirty years but not beginning until after ten, and provisions for postponement in case of difficulty. There would be insistence on 'the unfettered conversion into dollars of the current earnings of the sterling area countries even during the provisional period' (i.e. in the period of transition immediately after the war) and perhaps even on a similar provision in relation to 'pre-zero hour' sterling balances. The Americans would also want the United Kingdom to subscribe to their views about the organization of international trade (e.g. their dislike of imperial preference, discrimination, cartels, state trading, etc.) which had already been pressed on the British and were to be pressed again in the abortive efforts to set up an International Trade Organization.

Since these terms are not so very different from those eventually accepted in December, although Keynes proved too optimistic about the amount of the loan, it is natural to ask what objections he urged in May. First of all, he argued that the immediate introduction of sterling convertibility, as opposed to its deferment until the end of the transition period as was envisaged under Bretton Woods, might result in the transfer of perhaps $2 billion, which the United Kingdom would otherwise owe to sterling area and other countries, into a debt to the United States. That is, countries that otherwise would be obliged to hold sterling, or already held sterling, would take the opportunity afforded by convertibility to transfer their sterling into dollars on a large scale, and the United Kingdom would be under an obligation to allow the transfer to proceed freely, if pre-zero hour sterling balances had been made convertible.

Secondly, debt service on a loan of $8 billion at a rate of $2\frac{1}{2}$ per cent would eventually absorb $500 million a year; and on top of this there would remain the sterling debts of $12,000 million. Such a burden might place the United Kingdom 'in a chronic condition of having to make humiliating and embarrassing pleas for mercy and postponement'. The total burden of debt, amounting to $20,000 million, would be exactly the sum which the Russians were proposing, but were unlikely ever to receive, as reparations from Germany. Was it not outrageous that Britain should be placed in relation to the United States in a position so similar to that of Germany in relation to the USSR? The war 'would end in Germany being forced into conformity with an economic policy designed from without: and the same here. She would plead to Russia from time to time for mercy and deferment: and so should we to the United States'.[6] Even if the terms were less stiff – if interest were charged at 1 per cent, if there was no obligation to release pre-zero hour sterling balances, and if no financial pressure was applied in negotiations on commercial policy – the injustice of such a settlement would remain.

What then was 'Justice', the third of the options to be discussed? Unless the balance was redressed, Britain, and only Britain, would end up 'owing vast sums, not to neutrals and bystanders, but to our own Allies, Dominions and Associates'.[7] Although this did not apply particularly to the United States, but applied all round, only action by the United States could make possible an agreed and just redistribution of the proper burden of the costs of the war. Such action might take the form of inviting her to refund to the United Kingdom the $3 billion the latter had spent on purchases in the United States before Lend-Lease came into full operation – purchases that had built up the munitions industries of the United States to her great advantage in what later became a common war. This retrospective contribution would be supplemented by a credit of $5 billion exercisable at any time during the first ten years after the war and carrying interest at 1 per cent with a sinking fund beginning after ten years at 1 per

6 Keynes, vol. XXIV, p. 278.
7 ibid., p. 280.

cent of the outstanding amount and increasing to 2 per cent after a further ten years. Canada would be invited to make available $500 million on the same terms. Under these conditions the United Kingdom could undertake to accept *de facto* convertibility of sterling within a year after the end of the war.

Coupled with these proposals were others for dealing with the sterling balances. Each member of the sterling area would be asked to contribute a proportion of its total sterling balances to the cost of the common victory; a proportion would be left liquid and freely convertible; the remainder would be funded. Non-members of the sterling area would be dealt with separately, partly by paying off outstanding debt from collateral already held.

Of the sterling balances held by sterling area countries, which were expected to reach £3000 million or more by the end of the war, Keynes suggested that about half might be funded and a quarter or so cancelled, the remaining £750 million being freely convertible for purposes of meeting an external deficit. India and Egypt were much the largest holders, with totals likely to reach £1500 million and £500 million respectively. They were also, in Keynes's proposals, the countries called upon to accept the largest cancellations – £500 million and £170 million out of a total of £880 million. How they were to be persuaded to accept such a settlement as justice, Keynes did not explain but he recognized that it would be an uphill task. The negotiations which he envisaged were never put in hand and we may for the present ignore this aspect of his proposals.

What if, as eventually happened, the Americans ruled out any retrospective contribution, however presented, to the cost of the war? Keynes did not regard an $8 billion loan rather than $5 billion on the terms suggested as quite unsupportable. But it was more akin to 'Temptation' than to 'Justice'. A contribution of $3 billion was peanuts to the Americans, as Vinson later remarked; 'the cost of the war to the United States for a fortnight' as Keynes put it. If the Americans declined to make such a contribution, an approach to sterling area members for their contribution would be prejudiced and it could no longer be represented as part of 'a general, agreed, redistribution of the financial burden of the war. . . . The Americans would have lost the sense of magnanimity for a financial benefit which is useless to them and even perhaps injurious'.[8]

8 Keynes, XXIV, p. 293. Keynes thought that the United States, in making a contribution of $3 billion, would be disposing of a foreign surplus 'far below what they are likely in any case to develop, a surplus of which in any case they will have to find means of riddance' (p. 292). This comes very close to depicting that dollar shortage the prospect of which Keynes emphatically denied.

They might also be damaging the chances of securing the free international economy on which they had set their hearts.

Keynes's memorandum ended by suggesting the beginning of September as the earliest practicable date for the opening of discussions in Washington. Between the time when he embarked on its composition and the dispatch of a mission under his leadership in September, many changes had occurred: Roosevelt had died and a new administration taken over; the wars with Germany and Japan had been brought to an end; Lend-Lease had been cut off precipitately; the Labour Party had come to power and Dalton had succeeded Sir John Anderson as Chancellor. One consequence of all this was that on both sides of the Atlantic policies had to be formed rapidly by men of whom many were largely unfamiliar with the state of play and with the development of thought, commitments and understandings over the preceding months and years.

From April onwards there was much discussion of Keynes's proposals. In correspondence with Lord Brand, the Treasury representative in Washington, Keynes made clear that by 'convertibility' he meant that there would be

> no pressure from us on the rest of the sterling area to refrain from any purchase in the United States which they considered themselves rich enough to make, and equally no pressure to buy preferentially in the sterling area as compared with North America, except in gradual liquidation of their funded sterling debt.[9]

In the light of after events this is an unusual definition of convertibility: first, because it relates exclusively to the use of sterling in the hands of members of the sterling area, not to the use of sterling by non-members, on which attention came to be concentrated; second, because members of the sterling area had originally felt quite free to draw on balances in London to meet any deficit in their international accounts, whether in sterling or dollars, and although all of them operated a common system of exchange control, they were still able to obtain dollars freely from the pool to meet deficits on current account payable in dollars. Keynes was defining non-discrimination rather than convertibility.

What the Americans were chiefly concerned about was the pressure to discriminate against their exports that went with currency inconvertibility. They wanted to see an end to the dollar pool, not because there was

9 ibid., pp. 312, 336.

anything objectionable about the use of sterling as a reserve currency but because they regarded the sterling area arrangements as involving discrimination against other suppliers, with the United Kingdom, as the holder of the area's reserves, orchestrating the discrimination by which dollars were economized and accumulated.

Lord Brand thought it unlikely that the United States could be persuaded to make restitution of $3 billion as a free grant, especially if her action could be taken to imply that she should have entered the war earlier than she did. It might be easier to induce her to take over $3 billion from the sterling balances since American exporters were fearful of their effect on their export prospects in competition with British exporters. This, however, as Keynes pointed out, would not provide the reinforcement of the liquid reserves of the sterling area that $3 billion in cash would provide; and it might lead to the break-up of the sterling area by encouraging members in the dangerous habit of keeping separate dollar reserves.

Another suggestion made by Brand, but one which others also favoured,[10] was that it might be better to fix up 'some temporary interim arrangement to carry us for a year or more after lend lease, during which time we should have more leisure to make our full position understood by the world at large'.[11] Keynes thought not. He doubted whether the psychological atmosphere would improve: what was needed was to strike while the iron was hot in the interests of an imaginative and far-reaching settlement. Moreover, policy had to take shape at once in ways very much affected by the support on which it was possible to count. In the absence of a known amount of assistance, Britain's import programme, especially of food, would have to be kept to a minimum and discriminate against American supplies. This could cause friction as well as pressure and make a satisfactory solution more difficult. Keynes completely agreed with Brand that, as an insurance against the sudden ending of Lend-Lease, it was important to draw up at once an alternative programme of food supplies based on obtaining as much as possible from outside the United States and pointed out that early in the war hardly any foodstuffs were being procured from there. At the end of May, however, he was still hopeful that Lend-Lease could be continued for at least six months after VJ Day and talked of an early approach by Churchill to Truman 'to seek an assurance from the President that he would not issue his decision about the

10  See Clarke (1982), pp. 55–6.
11  Keynes, XXIV, p. 318.

termination of lend lease suddenly or without giving us plenty of opportunity for discussion'.[12]

Until August the discussions were almost entirely at the official level. Keynes's paper had been circulated to ministers in May but had not been brought before the Cabinet. With an election due at the beginning of July there was little opportunity of involving ministers over the summer especially when there was general agreement that an approach to the Americans was impracticable before September. There was a clear need to give the Truman administration time to settle down: apart from doubts whether the atmosphere was right, the administration was preoccupied with the San Francisco Conference on the United Nations, the sixth Lend-Lease Appropriation, and the passage of the Bretton Woods Agreements through Congress. No one could tell how much longer the war with Japan would continue.

While Keynes dominated Treasury thinking, other views were also expressed. There were those who fully expected Lend-Lease to end abruptly after VJ Day, which might come in the course of the summer. Frank Lee, like Brand, doubted whether Congress would ever accept Keynes's proposals as 'Justice'. Others took the view that only the loan part of the proposals stood any chance of discussion. There was general uneasiness that if Keynes's proposals failed to win acceptance no fall-back position had been prepared other than the ruthless austerity of Starvation Corner. Otto Clarke in the Overseas Finance Division circulated in June a memorandum on 'Financial Policy in Stage III' which envisaged an enlargement of the sterling area through the inclusion of the French, Dutch and Belgian Empires, with a dollar pool and an Import and Supplies Board, working on the analogy of the wartime Combined Boards in Washington. The Board would necessarily discriminate against dollar imports – indeed, would have to restrict imports to the minimum consistent with current dollar earnings. But the plan would not be conceived in hostility to the United States and would be coupled with acceptance of the Bretton Woods Agreements, the early establishment of an International Trade Organization, and endorsement of the full operation of American objectives of free, multilateral trade at the end of a transition period of about five years.

These ideas had the backing of Sir Wilfrid Eady, Joint Second Secretary, but did not impress Keynes who commented that what the memorandum showed,

12 ibid., p. 341.

to express the substance of what in his Plan II Sir W. Eady says in another way, is that, if a tidal wave were to overwhelm North and South America, our subsequent financial problems would not be too bad and nothing worse than starvation would supervene.[13]

Bringing more countries into the sterling area that were themselves in deficit would do nothing to help Britain to cover *her* deficit. Most of the newcomers would have a dollar deficit like the United Kingdom and would take from, not add to, the dollar pool. As for the existing members of the sterling area why should they join in such discrimination against the United States in order to contribute to the dollar pool and lend to the European participants 'money they have not got?'[14]

These objections are unassailable. But they were coupled with a very different comment. Keynes thought that there was no 'serious risk of an overall shortage of gold and dollars in the first three [post-war] years'.[15] The United States would no doubt run a large surplus but it would simultaneously be feeding in dollars on the grand scale and there were many countries with ample reserves on which they could draw. This proved entirely accurate in the first year or so after the war. It was only in 1947 that the dollar shortage began to bite and by that time American opinion had changed.

In his posthumous *Anglo-American Collaboration in War and Peace* Clarke advanced rather different propositions, arguing that Keynes misjudged the post-war situation, was too optimistic and in too much of a hurry, obsessed by his Grand Design for a worldwide multilateral financial system, and the wrong man to conduct negotiations with the Americans. These views are discussed below (pp. 113–14). They do not meet Keynes's objection to Plan II that it did not help Britain to cover the unavoidably large deficit that he foresaw.

Towards the end of July a number of meetings were held at the Treasury to review the situation. At the first of these, on 20 July, Keynes had second thoughts on the prospective loan negotiations. He feared that his proposal for a grant from the United States of $3 billion and a credit of $5

13  ibid., p. 366.
14  As Keynes put it in addressing the House of Lords on 18 December 1945: 'The alternative is to build up a separate economic bloc which excludes Canada and consists of countries to which we already owe more than we can pay, on the basis of their agreeing to lend us money they have not got and buy only from us and from one another goods we are unable to supply.'
15  Keynes, XXIV, p. 367.

billion would be transformed by the Americans into one for a loan of $8 billion. He now suggested that it would be best to seek a grant of $4 billion, with no loan, and eke this out with small amounts of financial assistance from Canada and perhaps also Sweden. There would then be no clearing-up of sterling obligations for a year and sterling convertibility would be introduced at the end of the year. Such sterling balances as were not released and made convertible would carry no interest but would be paid off more rapidly since the saving in interest would be applied to this purpose.[16]

A few days later he returned to the subject of convertibility. He thought it quite clear that if the Americans provided the help requested Britain would have to abandon the Bretton Woods provision for a transitional period. Lord Brand, who attended the meeting, threw doubt on this and thought that the subject 'needed a lot of further exploration'.[17] Cobbold, then Deputy Governor of the Bank of England, expressed himself as against 'convertibility in the Bretton Woods sense' and pointed out that it would expose the United Kingdom to heavier demands for foreign exchange than an agreement to make sterling convertible in the hands of holders so that it could be spent anywhere. This implied a system of transferable accounts such as was later created and that, as Cobbold put it, 'moneys would only be convertible into the currencies of countries which have themselves accepted convertibility'. So far as can be judged from the minutes, these meetings were somewhat inconclusive and served mainly to brief officials in advance of a visit to London of Will Clayton, US Under Secretary of State for Economic Affairs.

After the election, in preparation for discussions in Washington, Keynes prepared two further papers, one setting out the proposals and supporting argument as they might be presented to the Americans, the other sketching for British ministers the financial prospects for sterling and the balance of payments over the post-war years. The first was discussed in the Treasury at the official level towards the end of July and circulated, after revision, along with the second paper to a limited group

16 '1945 USA United Kingdom Negotiations in Washington. Discussions leading to Washington Negotiations' in PRO T 236/450. The minutes of the meeting are in OF 110/39/29.

17 In an ink comment on Eady's memorandum of 25 June which attributed to Keynes the suggestion that if the United Kingdom received a $3 billion grant from the United States it should offer in return to make sterling area balances convertible in one year, Keynes wrote: 'my compromise is to make the sterling area balances convertible, retaining a string on the others' (PRO T 236/450).

of ministers who discussed them with Keynes on 23 August, four days before Keynes sailed for Canada en route to Washington.

In the first paper, 'The Present Overseas Financial Position of U.K.',[18] Keynes abandoned the suggestion of a combined grant-in-aid and credit amounting to $8 billion and instead argued for a grant-in-aid of $5 billion in three annual instalments 'to help to solve the international problem of war-time indebtedness', explaining that a smaller sum would be insufficient to allow sterling to be made available on the necessary scale or permit the termination of the existing sterling area arrangements by the end of 1946; while at the same time a larger grant 'might make us sufficiently comfortable to relax from full pressure' to regain equilibrium as soon as possible.[19]

The second paper, 'Our Overseas Financial Prospects',[20] put the external deficit over the first three post-war years at £950 million, £550 million and £200 million respectively or £1700 million in all – a total subsequently reduced in the material actually submitted to the Americans to £1250 million.[21] By taking credit for a drawing of £250 million on the gold reserves and further net borrowing from the sterling area of £150 million, Keynes was able to finish with a financial requirement of £1250 million or $5 billion which happened to coincide with the grant for which he proposed to ask.[22]

Keynes has subsequently been accused of misleading ministers both as to the chances of receiving a grant-in-aid and as to the conditions that the Americans were likely to attach to any assistance they provided. Dalton, for example, describes Keynes in his talks with ministers as

almost starry-eyed. He was very confident that in the coming negotiations he could obtain American aid that would be ample in amount, and on most satisfactory conditions. He told us that he thought he could get £1500 million ($6 billion) as a free gift or 'grant-in-aid'. There would be no question of a loan to be repaid, or a rate of interest on the loan. Nor did he, at this stage, say much to us about 'strings'.

---

18  Keynes, XXIV, pp. 377 *et seq.*
19  ibid., p. 395.
20  ibid., pp. 398 *et seq.*
21  *Statistical Material*, 1945.
22  Keynes, XXIV, p. 405. In fact, Keynes took credit for £450 million not £400 million.

. . . This undue optimism, as it soon proved to be, naturally pre-disposed us against concessions, which Keynes proposed later. . . .[23]

This is not, however, recorded in Dalton's diary but written many years later. The minutes and memoranda tell a different story. Keynes warned ministers that

the terms offered might vary from an out-and-out grant-in-aid, to a commercial credit. He thought that he should not be authorised to agree to anything except an out-and-out grant. Help on any less favour-able terms should not be accepted except after very long thought on the part of Ministers in London. . . . This point, namely the nature and financial terms of any help to be afforded to us, would constitute the greatest stumbling block.[24]

It was Cripps and Sir Robert Sinclair who wanted to go for a grant-in-aid 'and to stand on this line'. That, said Keynes, had been his first instinct, but he had been pushed off it in the course of discussion. He pointed out that Will Clayton 'was clearly not thinking on these lines'. Keynes expected a series of proposals and counter-proposals and as he wrote to Eady a week later from on board ship he was 'increasingly doubt-ful about the prospects of a straight grant-in-aid'. As for the amount of the credit, he made no mention of $6 billion. 'The Americans', he told ministers, 'were thinking in terms of $3 billion, rising possibly to $5 billion'.

It is true that, to judge from the minutes, he made only a passing reference to convertibility and another to non-discrimination. In his memorandum he explained that 'the Americans will almost certainly insist upon our acceptance of a monetary and commercial foreign policy along the general lines on which they have set their hearts'.[25] But he did not spell out what such a policy implied – it should not have been necessary – apart from a rather casual reference to 'the general principle of non-discrimination'. Since he did not expect a general dollar shortage, he may have thought that the crucial issue was not the power to discriminate against dollar imports but the power to restrict imports in total and he was able to assure

23 Dalton (1962), p. 73. See also Robbins (1971), pp. 206–7 and Harrod (1951), pp. 596–7.
24 Keynes, XXIV, p. 421. See also p. 409: 'it will be a tough proposition, perhaps an impossible one.'
25 ibid., p. 409.

the Cabinet that this power need not be compromised.[26] There was certainly little elaboration of the issues that came to the front in the later stages of the negotiation when convertibility was the sticking-point.

One weakness in Keynes's diagnosis was that he did not envisage the continuation of a dollar drain after the balance of payments was back in equilibrium. But, as we shall see, the gold and dollar deficit over the years from 1948 to 1952, when the international accounts were in equilibrium, came to almost as much as in the two years 1946 and 1947 when there was still a large overall deficit. In consequence, the amount for which Keynes asked at the outset of the negotiations can be seen in retrospect to have been much too low for its declared purpose even if it was more than the Americans contemplated at that stage or would ever have agreed to.

A second mistake was Keynes's assumption that he could plunge at once into substantive negotiations on aid when the Americans were insisting that negotiations on commercial policy came first. Keynes had seen no need to bring the trade experts with him and there was a delay until they arrived. Fortunately, the negotiations by Sir Percivale Liesching, then Second Secretary at the Board of Trade, were conducted with great skill in parallel with the financial negotiations and successfully concluded in good time.

But the major difficulty was that the Americans were dead against a grant or interest-free loan when Keynes's approach called for nothing less. They were not prepared to engage in any exercise in retrospective burden-sharing or reconsider what was due to Britain for the wartime dislocation of her economy. They saw no prospect that Congress would entertain the possibility of an outright grant to the United Kingdom, whatever the amount. The Lend-Lease settlement that they were offering was generous in the extreme and the terms of the loan itself were highly favourable by commercial standards. Convertibility and non-discrimination were in their view in the long-term interests of the United Kingdom quite as much as of the United States; and the case to Congress for further assistance would have to rest on the advantages to the United States of the early adoption of these principles.

All this might be so. But for Keynes the crux of the matter was whether the United Kingdom would be treated with such striking generosity that she could compel her creditors to do their best to match it and by cancelling some part of their debts make the rest more credible; and whether the

26 'In principle a non-discriminatory commitment is probably to our own interest, provided other countries enter into a similar engagement.' (ibid., p. 416.)

same generous act would put Britain in possession of liquid funds, or assure her of sufficient credit, to undertake the risks of early convertibility. On both these issues he had to accept defeat: the loan made no impression on the main creditors and proved inadequate in relation to the risks. There was no prospect that by breaking off negotiations better terms could have been secured a year later; and since ministers regarded the loan as indispensable, they had no option but to agree to it on the best terms that Keynes could negotiate.

The negotiations opened with an exposition by Keynes, extending over five afternoons in mid-September, of the United Kingdom's financial situation and prospects, followed by an outline of possible lines of policy. From then until the Financial Agreement was signed on 6 December the proceedings were long and troubled.

Keynes asked initially for $5 billion plus whatever was required in order to clean up Lend-Lease. The Americans made it clear by 26 September that a grant-in-aid was impossible and appeared to be thinking of a loan with interest. They also accepted the British proposals for the scaling-down of sterling balances and freeing a proportion of the written-down total, but concluded that it would be impracticable to link cancellation with their own generosity in the way Keynes contemplated.[27] There was then some consideration by the British team of what could be afforded annually if a *repayable* non-interest-bearing loan were offered and London was asked to approve possible formulas involving a debt service charge not exceeding $100 million a year.

On 6 October ministers, chafing at their dependence on America and increasingly resentful as the prospects of a grant receded, provided fresh guidance. They were not prepared to accept a large loan at 2 per cent: the service charge would be more than they could undertake to meet and in any event such terms were inequitable. If this were the only option they would prefer to turn to the Export-Import Bank and borrow as little as possible without strings. They would, however, accept a smaller grant of $2 billion supplemented by a credit of $3–4 billion on which they could draw as required at 1 per cent. Failing this, they set a limit of $100 million on any debt service commitment that borrowing involved, with a waiver of interest and amortization in any year when there was deflation in the United States or her international accounts were out of balance.

The Americans dismissed both a grant and an interest-free loan as not

27 See, however, the account by Keynes of some abortive proposals by Harry White (Keynes, XXIV, pp. 532–5).

practical politics even if the amount involved was 'only peanuts' to the US Treasury. Clayton suggested a loan of $5 billion repayable at $100 million a year beginning in five years. There would be an additional $50 million a year to cover interest, making the total service charge $150 million for fifty years, and there would be a waiver based on an agreed test of Britain's ability to pay. These terms, however, were unacceptable to the British government, the Chancellor reiterating his preference for a grant plus credit or, at worst, an interest-free loan.

By 18 October, five weeks after the negotiations had begun, Keynes urged the need to turn from poetry to prose and consider alternative formulas for an interest-bearing loan. How was he to answer Clayton if he pointed out that the difference between $150 million a year and $100 million dollars a year in five years' time was less than 1 per cent of the overseas income likely to be needed at that stage to balance overseas expenditure? No one could claim such precision of foresight at such a distance in time. If Britain's hesitation rested on the danger of a break-down in multilateral trade and payments, the Americans would readily accept a clause to cover such a contingency.

By this time, Keynes clearly felt that, barring a change of heart by the Americans, Clayton's proposal was as good as any likely to be offered. The risk of insisting that $100 million a year was the most Britain could afford was that the amount of aid would be adjusted downwards to match this figure. Keynes also found it necessary to remind ministers that, whatever the terms, they still needed an absolute minimum of $3–4 billion to cover an almost inescapable cumulative deficit in the balance of trade and were unlikely to be able to find from all other sources, including the sterling area, more than $1 billion towards this total. There was no prospect of even a small loan from the US government without the kind of commitments that the Americans were seeking to the Bretton Woods Agreements, non-discrimination in commercial policy and liberalization of sterling area arrangements, and the end-result might well be as heavy a debt charge as the British government was now boggling at. To reach no agreement at all with the United States on a comprehensive settlement and break off the negotiations would have the most far-reaching repercussions on economic life in Britain and her place in the world.

Ministers, however, paid little regard to this advice. Before they met on 26 October they had already been informed that the Americans were now offering only $3.5 billion at 2 per cent interest plus the balance of Lend-Lease on standard terms ($2\frac{3}{8}$ per cent, repayable over the next 30 years) and that the idea of a waiver clause had been abandoned after Keynes, on instructions from London, had rejected it. They had also heard from Keynes that he had urged on the Americans the importance of an adequate total for the loan and expressed reluctance to cut it below $5 billion. Keynes had also explored with them informally the possibility of reviving Clayton's proposal and the waiver clause for interest.

Ministers now put forward two plans. One of these, Plan B, involved borrowing $2.5 billion on commercial terms without any strings but defined commercial terms as 2 per cent interest and repayment over fifty years, beginning in five years' time. The Mission had to explain that commercial terms in practice would be very different and would cost $228 million per annum starting at once. It was also very unlikely that the Export-Import Bank could make available as much as $2.5 billion: the most that could be expected at once, over and above the Lend-Lease settlement, was $500 million, with perhaps another $500 million later.

The other plan, Plan A, was for a loan of $2.5 billion at 1 per cent interest for fifty years with an option on a further $2 billion, interest-free. The Mission estimated that the service charge involved was only $23 million per annum greater than under Clayton's proposal but put the Plan to the Americans who rejected it on 11 November.

After further proposals and counter-proposals in which ministers seemed anxious to limit the total amount while Keynes argued for more than the Americans were offering, the position was reached at the end of November in which the British hoped for a loan of $4 billion and the Americans were offering $3.5 billion. In the end it was agreed to split the difference and settle on $3.75 billion plus $650 million in final settlement of Lend-Lease obligations. The rate of interest was to be 2 per cent, beginning in five years, and repayment, also beginning in five years, was to stretch over the next fifty, so that the annual instalments of interest and capital amounted to $140 million. Actuarially, these were equivalent to 1.6 per cent over the life of the loan.

It was not only the financial terms of the agreement that caused difficulty. In the last month before the agreement was concluded, other issues came to the front: first, the waiver clause, then the sterling area arrangements and finally convertibility for non-dollar, non-sterling countries. There is no need to detail the intricacies of the negotiations on a waiver: agreement was reached that the United Kingdom would be entitled to ask and receive a waiver of interest if its average income from visible and invisible current transactions over a five-year period fell below the pre-war average adjusted for price changes.

The issue of convertibility was more complex. The negotiations had been conducted without specific reference to payments agreements with European and other countries as if all that was involved was the freedom of sterling area countries – and only sterling area countries – to convert current sterling earnings into dollars. The position of European, South American and other countries had been left almost entirely out of account and it was not until early November that the Americans woke up to the omission. They then insisted on the convertibility of *all* currently earned sterling – at first from the beginning of 1947 and later from one year after the Loan Agreement came into force. To the very end, ministers pressed strongly but without success for an extension of this period which would supersede the indefinite transition period provided for in the (still unratified) Bretton Woods Agreements.

There is no evidence that the Americans really understood how payments agreements worked or had visualized the full consequences of this provision. It was not part of a reciprocal arrangement in which the partners to the agreements shared the obligation to make their currencies convertible. Since the effect was to make it *more* difficult for the United Kingdom to get back into balance and *more* difficult to obtain credit from its partners it was clearly contrary to United Kingdom interests and not obviously in the interests of a general return to convertibility unless it made it easier for other countries to follow Britain's example. As events were to show, it discredited instead of strengthening the move towards convertibility among industrial countries.

The largest misunderstandings, however, related to the sterling area. Convertibility, as Keynes had offered it, was convertibility for the members of the sterling area. It would allow them to draw on the dollar pool against payment from their balances in London in order to meet deficits on current account with countries requiring settlement in dollars. They would also be free to make purchases of imports from any country without discrimination. This was what they had been free to do before the war and what they were sure to insist on doing once immediate post-war difficulties had been overcome. So was it really much of a concession?

From the American point of view it appeared that it was. The Americans wanted to see an end to the dollar pool and regarded the sterling area as an organized attempt to discriminate against American exporters. They were extremely vague about how the system worked but appeared to think that sterling area countries were required to deposit their dollar earnings in London and to obtain permission from the British authorities for any dollar outlay. What was objectionable was that the dollars in the pool should be rationed by the United Kingdom and that it should be easier to draw sterling than dollars for current purposes. If imports had to be reduced, it should be on a non-discriminatory basis. Equally, countries making deposits in London should be free to draw on them for payments in *any* country, inside or outside the sterling area. That might not apply to wartime accumulations surplus to normal working requirements. But countries earning foreign exchange currently should be free to decide where to spend the proceeds. So while they did not want to put an end to the sterling area, the Americans wanted access to sterling area markets on equal terms.

The emphasis on these markets was no doubt partly occasioned by American resentment against imperial preference. It had been hoped in business and official circles in America that Article VII of the Mutual Aid Agreement might spell the end of imperial preference and there had been frequent wartime exchanges on this point. In October 1945 a renewed attempt had been made in the commercial policy negotiations in Washington to secure the abolition of imperial preference, this time by coupling it with the proposed loan, but this attempt, which caused great indignation in the British government had been successfully resisted.

The British point of view stressed that there was nothing intrinsically discriminatory about the sterling area. There had been free access to balances held in London before the war and, within the limits imposed by the shortage of foreign exchange, there was still freedom to make all payments approved by the local exchange control outside the area.[28] These limits would be extended and the discrimination practised in wartime relaxed as exports recovered or the central reserves of the system were fortified from outside. It was this fortification that Britain was now seeking and the relaxation of discrimination would follow. This did not mean that exchange control or import control would cease: it would simply be less discriminatory. As for the dollar pool, it owed its existence not so much to the direct surrender by members of the area of dollars earned from their exports as to the payments made by *importers* from the sterling area who had to buy sterling for the purpose in London in return for dollars or other convertible currency which were then acquired by the British monetary authorities. Thus some member countries might never handle dollars at all. To disperse part or all of the centrally held reserves of

28  This was not entirely true. As Keynes pointed out, it did not apply to Egypt and the Middle East. 'Some fig leaves', he commented, 'which may pass muster with old ladies in London wither in a harsher climate.' (Telegram 7746 to Eady, 7 November 1945, Keynes, XXIV, p. 584.)

foreign exchange among the members would not be to the advantage of the United States. Countries running a deficit with the United States would be forced to limit their purchases still more strictly while those that were in surplus might elect to turn some of it into gold or hoard the dollars they earned.[29] It was not possible for the area to spend more dollars in dollar countries than it acquired, with or without discrimination. Until more dollars were earned, therefore, the market for American exports could not expand.

It became clear towards the end of November that there had been a major misunderstanding on convertibility within the British camp. As we have seen, Keynes had envisaged convertibility for the current earnings of sterling area countries right from the beginning. As Brand had agreed, it was a gamble, justified if the loan was big enough. It had been envisaged in all Keynes's memoranda and cables and approved, wittingly or unwittingly, by ministers at their meeting with him on 23 August. Dalton, however, raised the point as if it were undecided when the negotiations had been in progress for nearly three months. The Mission was instructed to retract its offer but urged on 30 November that the matter be reconsidered. Bridges was sent over next day at three hours' notice to lead the delegation but had little influence on the outcome of the negotiations. The American draft was considered at four more meetings, and signed, with minor amendments, on the morning of 6 December.

The Cabinet Minutes make clear how wide was the gulf between the thinking of ministers and the technicalities of the Washington discussions. The most extreme position was that of Shinwell who thought in November that 'U.S. producers would be in a difficult position if it were made impossible for us to take their produce. . . . The custom of the debtor countries [is] essential to U.S. prosperity' (this at a time when the US was suffering from excess demand and when Britain's imports from the US represented about 0.5 per cent of American GNP).[30] 'We should appeal', he went on 'to the people of this country to risk the continuance of conditions of austerity'[31] – as if, even with the loan, such conditions could be avoided. Alexander harked back to the spirit of Ottawa and the 'refusal

29  Keynes, XXIV, p. 382. For the opposite (but unconvincing) line of argument, see Gardner (1956), p. 215.
30  CM(45)50, confidential annex, 6 November 1945, in PRO CAB 128/2.
31  ibid. Shinwell repeated these views at a subsequent meeting of the Cabinet on 29 November (PRO CAB 128/2) and went out of his way at the final meeting on the Loan Agreement on 5 December to dismiss the length of the transition period as not of crucial importance.

to accept American dictation' in 1931. Bevan denounced the principles to which the projected International Trade Organization was to give effect as nineteenth-century and 'unlikely to find acceptance by States like the USSR'; and at a later meeting of the Cabinet thought that the contraction in the transition period was 'clearly to counter the advantage which we had gained by the provision in the Draft Agreement under which we were not required to take up more of the total loan offered than we might require at any time'.[32]

Bevin, Cripps and Dalton, in urging acceptance of Bretton Woods and the Loan Agreement, seemed more concerned by the political implications of breaking off negotiations and so putting Anglo-American co-operation at risk than with the positive advantages to the United Kingdom of the Agreements themselves. A loan without conditions was not available and the loan with conditions was indispensable if living standards were to be maintained; the terms of the loan compared very favourably with those which France had had to accept; and those who looked to the sterling area for help might well find that without the loan it was unable to retain its coherence while of the Commonwealth countries Canada would regard a rejection of the loan as quite unjustifiable.

The most interesting feature of the Cabinet discussions is the unreality of ministerial sticking-points. This is true not just of Shinwell who thought that 'we are not suppliants for financial assistance' when the opposite was self-evident. Dalton listed as conditions of acceptance that the United Kingdom should be free to restrict imports and to devalue when these things were never in question. He regarded it as a great concession by the Americans that the scarce currency clause would continue to apply. He recommended acceptance of Bretton Woods subject to a declaration by the British government that it was not required to deflate in circumstances in which there was unemployment although such a unilateral declaration had no force in international law. At the only Cabinet meeting at which there was a full discussion of the issues, on 6 November 1945, Dalton and Cripps both gave assurances that were not in keeping with the terms of the Loan Agreement as signed one month later. For example, Dalton pointed out that under Article XIV of the Bretton Woods Agreement the United Kingdom was free to use its judgement on the length of the transition period and made no mention of American insistence on, or the British offer of, earlier convertibility. When the

32 CM(45)50, confidential annex, 6 November 1945 and CM(45)59, confidential annex, 5 December 1945, in PRO CAB 128/2.

matter came up again at the meeting on 5 December Cripps dismissed the adverse effects of the shorter period as 'likely to be small' and there was no review of earlier assurances. Dalton in his diary entry two days later reflected that the shortening of the transitional period was 'a rather trivial point' when weighed against a loan of $4.4 billion, although it was a point on which he had contemplated breaking off negotiations. Perhaps this comment should be read in the light of a later entry on 19 December when parliament had approved the Loan Agreement:

> My cynical and secret reflection on the American Loan is that . . . it is quite certain that the conditions will have to be 'revised' long before A.D. 2001 and that even in the next year or two it may well be that this will require a considerable variation which might even be 'unilateral'.[33]

Here at least Dalton mixed cynicism with prescience.

The Agreement was not well received in Britain. It was submitted for approval to the House of Commons along with the Bretton Woods Agreements and the commercial policy proposals arising out of the discussions in Washington. Many Conservatives voted against it and the Conservative Front Bench, along with a majority of the Party, abstained. The Labour Party was divided although relatively few voted against the Loan and the far left were strongly in favour of it.[34] Many members of the Party were bilateralists at heart and felt that the conditions attached to the loan would weaken the government's power to plan foreign trade and bargain with advantage. The government offered only a weak defence and the only statement that carried any conviction was that of Keynes in the Lords where the Tories might well have scuppered the proposals. Even so, roughly half the peers who heard him abstained, though the other half was almost entirely in support.

Yet as Keynes was able to demonstrate, the financial terms at least were extremely generous by commercial standards even if they did not match the hopes for a grant or interest-free loan with which the Mission had set off. For the first five years no interest was to be paid whereas on an Export–Import Bank loan, payments equal to 48 per cent of the loan would have to be made in that time. The Bank would have been unlikely to lend more than $1 billion to any borrowing country and the loan would have been tied to purchases in America. The maximum annual payment was £35 million and would start off at £13 million. The complex waiver

---

33  Dalton's diary, Dalton Papers, entry for 19 December 1945.
34  Morgan (1984), p. 295.

provisions, if ever operated, meant that no interest at all would be paid so long as exports fell short of about 160 per cent of the pre-war volume. Even in 1946 commodity exports alone were not far short of £1000 million; by 1951, when payments began, they were over £2700 million; and by 1976, halfway through the life of the loan, total foreign exchange earnings were £40,000 million. In relation to these magnitudes the service of the loan speedily became a matter of little importance except in one or two acute balance-of-payments crises.

Approval by the British government did not bring any money. Keynes went to his grave still uncertain in April whether the loan would ever be voted by Congress. It was not until July, when the government had almost completed its first year in office, that it could count on receiving the promised funds. Before that time it had had to ask itself what would happen if it did not get the loan.

In February there was an exchange of minutes between Keynes and Otto Clarke in which Keynes agreed that, given the necessary cuts in military and political expenditure overseas, the position would not be desperate. But as he pointed out, this expenditure over the next three years was now expected to exceed the whole of the American loan so that 'it comes out in the wash that the American loan is primarily required to meet the political and military expenditure overseas'.[35] If that were cut sufficiently Britain could scrape through but 'no one, of course, has faced the virtual impossibilities of the reductions in military and political expenditure which will be required in the absence of an American loan' or, for that matter, even with one.[36] After much juggling with figures, Clarke suggested that it might be possible to balance accounts if government expenditure overseas were cut in half to £500 million over the three years but was doubtful whether in an inconvertible world such expenditure had the impact on the British balance of payments that Keynes was implying. This might well be true since the expenditure was mainly in sterling area countries and might merely add to their sterling balances or to their imports from the United Kingdom. But by the same token, if it

---

35  Clarke (1982), p. 152.
36  ibid., p. 145. The large commitments that ministers were assuming moved Keynes to submit an agitated paper (circulated to the Cabinet as CP(46)58) warning ministers that they were 'going down the drain at a great pace' and that the public would be disturbed to learn that 'not a single bean of sustenance for themselves or of capital equipment for British manufacturers was likely to be left over from the U.S. credit' (Keynes, XXVII, p. 466).

*Table 5.1*  Forecasts of balance of payments of the United Kingdom 1946–8[a] (£m.)

|  | 1946 | 1947 | 1948 | Total for 1946–8 |
|---|---|---|---|---|
| Imports, f.o.b. (excluding oil) | | | | |
| October 1945 | 1,150 | 1,250 | 1,350 | 3,750 |
| February 1946 | 1,100 | 1,225 | 1,350 | 3,675 |
| Actual[b] | 1,063 | 1,541 | 1,790 | 4,394 |
| Overseas government expenditure | | | | |
| October 1945 | 300 | 175 | 125 | 600 |
| February 1946 | 400 | 350 | 200 | 950 |
| Actual[c] | 327 | 152 | 83 | 562 |
| Exports | | | | |
| October 1945 | 650 | 975 | 1,175 | 2,800 |
| February 1946 | 550 | 1,000 | 1,150 | 2,700 |
| Actual | 960 | 1,180 | 1,639 | 3,779 |
| Net invisibles | | | | |
| October 1945 | 50 | 100 | 150 | 300 |
| February 1946 | 150 | 175 | 200 | 525 |
| Actual | 200 | 132 | 260 | 592 |
| Deficit | | | | |
| October 1945 | 750 | 350 | 150 | 1,250 |
| February 1946 | 800 | 400 | 200 | 1,400 |
| Actual | 230 | 381 | +26 | 585 |
| Deficit in gold and dollars | 225 | 1,024 | 406 | 1,655 |

*Sources: Economic Trends Annual Supplement 1981* for 'actual'; Keynes, vol. XXIV, pp. 403–5, 428–30, 555; Clarke (1982), p. 67; CP(46)53.

a  The figures in this table are intended as an impressionistic summary, not an exact transcription.
b  Including oil.
c  Net expenditure abroad, including transfers.

was dollars that had to be saved the cuts would have to be correspondingly more severe.

The outlook in February 1946 is summarized in table 5.1 which shows the Treasury's forecasts of the balance of payments in 1946–8 alongside the estimates submitted in Washington for those years and the actual outcome. Keynes's figures of October 1945 were based on a doubling of pre-war export and import prices and Clarke's figures for February 1946 were supposed to be on a comparable basis. This implied that Keynes was putting the volume of imports in 1946 at 77 per cent, and of exports in

1948 at about 120–125 per cent, of pre-war levels.[37] Both figures were too cautious: imports in 1946 were a full 13 per cent lower and exports in 1948 5–10 per cent higher than these forecasts. Against this favourable divergence must be set the effect on the balance of payments of the rise in import prices, which accelerated after 1945. By 1948 import prices were nearly 50 per cent higher than at the end of the war. Even if export prices had risen equally this would have added to the deficit since the value of exports fell short of that of imports by a substantial margin. But the terms of trade in the three years 1945–8 moved 11 per cent against the United Kingdom, adding £180 million a year to the deficit. Two other changes were favourable: income from invisibles was rather higher than even in the revised forecast of February 1946; and net government expenditure overseas, after taking credit for disposal of war surpluses and other items, worked out well below the worst fears of the Treasury (and still more of Keynes) in early 1946. As a result the current account deficit was far below any estimates under discussion during the winter of 1945–6. But this was so, primarily because overseas government expenditure was severely cut, as Keynes had insisted it must be, and because imports were held to a level of greater austerity than was contemplated in 1945.

The Loan Agreement finally won approval in Congress, largely as an 'investment in the political and economic stability of a gravely threatened Western world' – threatened, that is, by Soviet expansionism.[38] The misunderstandings that accompanied its negotiation and the gulf between the attitudes of the two legislatures that debated it boded ill for the future of that multilateral world economy it was intended to promote. But it put an end for the time being to the British government's anxieties over the balance of payments. In the second half of 1946 the changeover from war to peace was proceeding smoothly, exports were rising fast towards the pre-war level, and the reserves were actually increasing. If there were clouds on the horizon they still seemed a long way off.

Let us now look back at the loan in the light of after events. We need spend little time on the conduct of the negotiations. They started on the

37  'Pre-war' here means 1936–8. Clarke's figure of £1175 million for the Mission's estimate of exports in 1948 yields an increase over pre-war of 21 per cent. But Keynes in August was assuming that exports would reach 150 per cent of pre-war by volume in 1949 and put exports in 1948 at £1300 million or 133 per cent of pre-war (op. cit., p. 404).
38  Gardner (1956), p. 253.

wrong foot because Keynes misjudged the mood of the American administration which was neither willing to give an imaginative lead nor capable
of pursuing it successfully with Congress. It was no doubt his recollection
of the aftermath of post-war indebtedness in the 1920s that made him
persevere. But he staked too much on the opening bid and had not
prepared the ground with ministers for less palatable courses. In the words
of Thomas Hardy:

> If way to the better there be, it demands a good look at the worst.

Keynes himself had taken the measure of the worst but ministers had not.
For this Keynes can hardly be blamed since he had dwelt on other possibilities in papers which ministers do not appear to have studied with care.
Dalton in particular does not emerge with credit when he was so
obviously at sea on the cardinal issue of convertibility. The failure to
pursue Clayton's offer because $150 million per annum was too much and
then accept terms involving an annual payment of $140 million for three-
quarters of the capital is another example of ministerial confusion. Apart
from anything else it prolonged the negotiations and produced that fatal
staleness of which Keynes complained in November.[39] As for the
possibility that under different leadership the Mission might have obtained
better terms, there is no real reason to think so, and the last-minute
attempt to field Bridges was completely without effect. The fact is that the
Mission contained an abler group of experts on international finance than
was left in London to advise the Chancellor.

The most important single issue in retrospect may have been convertibility which will be further discussed in chapter 6; but the amount of the
loan, which was also part of that issue, ran it close. Yet there was a curious
half-heartedness in the British approach to the amount. Keynes himself
wondered from time to time 'if we were to be trusted' with a really large
loan; and others in the Treasury showed equal concern that ministers
might fritter it away. Ministers, once there was no question of a grant,
thought in terms of the minimum that would see them through and
imagined that $2 billion or so would be enough. Some officials shared this
attitude and felt no sense of urgency: better, they argued, to take a little at
once on commercial terms without strings and wait to see how things
developed. We have seen how Plan B, embodying this approach, infuri-
ated the Mission with its lack of realism. No doubt there was no immediate need for dollars, partly because the Americans and others in 1946 were

39  Keynes, XXIV, p. 594.

unable to keep pace with the orders they received and imports into Britain were artificially low. But if one imagines the loan negotiations set back by a year, what would the position have been had they dragged on until July 1947 (when the American credit was already nearing exhaustion)?

The financial terms seemed to many to be lacking in the generosity due to an ally that had taken such risks with its economy. But was $140 million a year (with a waiver) so intolerable a burden to a country that would have to export $6000 million a year or more by the time such payments began? Here the British attitude was coloured by awareness of existing sterling debts and the burden that repayment of these might eventually involve; and by uneasiness over a *dollar* obligation when the American market was notoriously difficult to penetrate and British exports to North America had amounted to no more than about £50 million a year before the war and were only £70 million (or $280 million) in 1946. Even so, once the dollar problem began to ease in the 1950s the extra £50 million a year at the new rate of exchange was not a major source of Britain's balance-of-payments difficulties.

To return to the amount of the loan. The sum originally asked for had been exactly equal to the prospective cumulative deficit on current account before the balance of payments was restored to equilibrium, viz. £1250 million or $5000 million. Although the American loan was no more than three-quarters of this, the Canadian credit made up the missing quarter. There was therefore an equivalence between the loan and the prospective deficit. It had also been envisaged by Keynes that the deficit would last five years before it finally disappeared while Clarke in the Treasury was convinced that three would suffice.[40]

What happened in fact was that the current account was back in balance by 1948 but the dollar drain still continued until 1952 with the solitary exception of the year 1950. Over the seven years 1946–52 the United Kingdom's cumulative deficit on current account is now estimated at £485 million, reaching a maximum of just over £600 million at the end of 1947, or less than half of what had been assumed.[41] Yet over those years the gold and dollar deficit (excluding defence aid) amounted to $9207 million with a peak in mid-1952 of $9543 million. Thus under the policies

---

40 Clarke (1982), pp. 145, 147. For details of Keynes's estimates see Keynes, XXIV, pp. 555–6 and for Clarke's figures see Clarke (1982), p. 153.

41 The figures published at the time were rather higher (£1125 million for 1946–7). See p. 80.

*Table 5.2* Sources of dollar finance 1945–52

|  | US $m. |
|---|---|
| US/Canadian line of credit (net) | 4,909[a] |
| Marshall Aid | 2,693 |
| Gold and dollar reserves | 630 |
| IMF loan | 300 |
| South African gold loan | 325 |
| Defence aid | 349 |
| Total | 9,207 |

*Source: United Kingdom Balance of Payments 1946 to 1953*, Cmd 8976, 1953.

a The Canadian loan of 1250 million Canadian dollars was equivalent to 1159 million US dollars.

actually pursued and the pressures actually experienced, the United Kingdom was unable to recover balance in her international accounts without making use of $9 billion of externally supplied finance – more than the highest figure ever suggested by Keynes. The financial requirements were grossly underestimated at the same time as the deficits on current account were substantially overestimated.

Two questions arise: where did the dollars go if not to finance a current account deficit? And where did the additional dollars come from? The second question is easier to answer than the first. Between 1945 and 1952 the finance required was provided mainly from the American and Canadian credits, from Marshall Aid and to a small extent from the reserves and other sources (see table 5.2).

Since British imports were held throughout below the pre-war level, starting at about 67 per cent of 1936–8 in 1946 and increasing to 90 per cent in 1952, it is natural to conclude that far more external support was required than either side appreciated in the Washington negotiations. Even with Marshall Aid and reinforcement from IMF and South Africa, the gold and dollar reserves ended the seven years lower than at the start and remained quite inadequate to meet the stresses to which sterling was bound to be subject.

This conclusion seems rather less certain when we turn to the question of where the dollars went. We do not have the full data on actual payments, country by country, but we do have an analysis by currency group as well as sectoral balance-of-payments accounts that give a consistent

*Table 5.3*  Analysis of the dollar drain 1945–52

|  | $m. |
|---|---|
| **Gold and dollars paid to:** |  |
| Dollar area, to meet current account deficit | −7,243 |
| Dollar area, to meet capital transfers | −591 |
| Other Western Hemisphere countries | −223 |
| OEEC countries | −1,215 |
| Other non-sterling countries | −290 |
| Non-territorial organizations (IMF, etc.) | −291 |
|  | −9,853 |
| **Gold and dollars received from:** |  |
| UK colonies | +1,990 |
| Other sterling area countries | −1,341 |
|  | −9,204 |

*Source: United Kingdom Balance of Payments 1946 to 1953*, Cmd 8976, 1953.

picture. These accounts are not fully up-to-date and do not tally with the latest balance-of-payments estimates but the margin of difference over the seven years 1945–52 is not likely to be significant.

Table 5.3 shows that most of the gold and dollars received as loans or grants went to cover the United Kingdom's current account deficit with the dollar area. This took no less than 80 per cent of the total. What was missing, except from the colonies, was the flow of dollars into the reserves that one might have expected through multilateral settlements. The United Kingdom turned out to be settling other countries' dollar deficits when it had been confidently expected to be in receipt of dollars itself from them.

Yet it was not as if the United Kingdom was in heavy deficit. The overall deficit on current account from 1945 to 1952 averaged no more than £100 million a year and was far below the deficit with dollar countries alone. As table 5.4 shows, there was a large surplus with the sterling area and only a small deficit with all non-dollar, non-sterling countries.

The trouble was that while the United Kingdom ran a deficit, year after year, with the dollar area, as it had in pre-war years, there was no adequate compensating inflow of dollars from its surplus with other countries. That surplus was almost exclusively with the sterling area and it was offset

*Table 5.4* Sectoral balance-of-payments surpluses and deficits 1945–52[a]

|  | £m. |
|---|---|
| Net gold and dollar deficit | 2,401 |
| Balance on current account with the dollar area | −2,181 |
| Balance on current account with the sterling area | +1,642 |
| Balance on current account with all other countries | −153 |
| Balance on current account of the UK | −692 |

*Sources: United Kingdom Balance of Payments 1946 to 1953*, Cmd 8976, 1953, table 21 and Cmd 9291, 1954, table 2.

a Dollar receipts under defence aid are excluded.

*Table 5.5* Transactions with the sterling area 1945–52

|  | £m. |
|---|---|
| Net investment in sterling area | 1,158 |
| Less addition to sterling balances | 220 |
| Less grants from sterling area governments | 46 |
| Net capital transfer | 892 |
| Net UK purchases of gold (including South African gold loan) | 619 |
| Net transfers to other areas on behalf of rest of sterling area | 127 |
| Other transfers | 5 |
| Current account surplus | 1,642 |

*Source: United Kingdom Balance of Payments 1946 to 1953 (No. 2)*, Cmd 9119 (1954).

largely by capital transfers from the United Kingdom. As the figures in table 5.4 indicate, there was a margin of £1700 million between the deficit on current account of £692 million and the £2401 million that the United Kingdom had to provide in foreign exchange. That £1700 million represented the net total of what was lent, repaid or invested abroad by the

United Kingdom over the seven years 1945–52. About £900 million of the net total went to the sterling area – nearly as much as the American loan (see table 5.5).

The sterling area did, however, make some contribution to Britain's dollar problem. For while it was heavily in deficit with the United Kingdom it was in surplus after 1949 with the dollar area. The British colonies indeed were in surplus throughout and paid into the central reserves nearly £600 million in dollars together with just under £50 million of currently produced gold. The other sterling area countries, on the other hand – especially the Dominions – were in heavy deficit and drew nearly £800 million in dollars against which they sold gold to the value of £500 million. The balance between 1945 and 1952 was a net contribution of £350 million in dollars, made up of a withdrawal of £210 million in 1946–9 and a positive balance of £560 million in 1950–2. But it was an expensive contribution, obtained at the cost of selling goods and services to the sterling area £1640 million in excess of what Britain imported.

The capital transfer did not take the form to any great extent of repayment of sterling balances. At the end of 1952 these balances had risen, not fallen. There had been no cancellation of sterling balances such as had been proposed in the Financial Agreement: the much discussed negotiations to secure cancellation, if started at all, never got very far because there was not the slightest chance of acceptance by any of the major creditors (India, Egypt, Iraq, Eire and Palestine). A large part of the balances was blocked, with annual releases that seemed dangerously high to one side and much too low to the other. The continuing members of the sterling area (for some, like Egypt, were thrust out) added £220 million to their balances so that what was repaid was more than offset by new accretions. Non-members and ex-members, however, withdrew a net total of £150 million. The movements in the aggregates were small in relation to the enormous total of £3500 million or so, apart from the holdings of the IMF and other international bodies. While the total remained relatively unchanged in money terms, inflation reduced the burden year by year. But this heavy inheritance from the war continued for more than two decades to weigh on the balance of payments and threaten fresh instability whenever confidence was disturbed.

The export of capital to the sterling area in 1945–52 took place at a time when Britain had the utmost difficulty in paying her way internationally and was receiving over $7.5 billion in dollar credits and Marshall Aid. It was not held back by exchange control because exchange control did not apply to movements of capital between Britain and other sterling area countries. Freedom of access to the London capital market was one of the inducements to remain in the sterling area and it was not until 1972 that the British government extended exchange control to sterling area countries.

It might seem, therefore, that exchange control applied only where it was largely unnecessary and not where it was really needed. Would a reduced flow of capital to the sterling area have been reflected in a diminution in the dollar drain?[42] The answer is less certain than the arithmetic might suggest. A smaller outflow of capital would have checked British exports to sterling area countries but not necessarily done much to promote a diversion of exports to the dollar area. In the long run there might be more to be gained by building up the sterling area with British capital as a source of supplies in substitution for dollar imports and for seeking to strengthen the area as an earner of dollars and contributor to the central reserves in London.

It was these issues rather than convertibility for sterling area members that in retrospect were the fundamental ones. They will be further discussed in chapter 6.

---

42  Keynes had foreseen that if British residents were free to invest within the sterling
    area this would add to the British deficit and the need for external finance (Keynes,
    XXIV, p. 19). But no one seems to have visualized so large an outflow as occurred.

# Chapter six

# THE CONVERTIBILITY CRISIS OF 1947

## Theme

It is generally accepted that the attempt to introduce sterling convertibility in July 1947 was premature and misguided. So early a date had been
resisted to the end by the British government which had hoped, even
when on the point of signing the Loan Agreement in December 1945, for
a transition period at least six months longer. It was nevertheless caught
by surprise when convertibility brought on the first and most dramatic of
post-war runs on the pound – a run that left no option but suspension five
weeks later as dollars drained away at an increasing rate. The total outflow
of gold and dollars accelerated more than fourfold in 1947, increasing from
$900 million in 1946 to $4100 million in 1947; in the third quarter it came
near to doubling again in comparison with the rest of the year; and in the
last full week of convertibility before its suspension on 20 August it
reached a peak of $237 million, equivalent to $1000 million per month.[1]
(See figure 6.2, p. 161.)

The failure of the experiment was a turning-point in post-war recovery.
It marked the end of the respite afforded by the American loan and roused
the government to a fuller awareness of the dollar problem. It also put off
for many years a renewed attempt to introduce currency convertibility: it
was not until the end of 1958 that it came into being *de jure* although
convertibility *de facto* had existed since the spring of 1955.

Why did the experiment fail and what were the consequences of the

---

1 Dow (1964), p. 22.

failure? We begin by tracing the sequence of events from the Loan Agreement onwards before engaging in a post mortem and reviewing the whole episode.

## Narrative

From the start there were doubts about convertibility of sterling. Keynes had regarded it as in Britain's own interests. But, as we have seen, ministers reacted strongly when they woke up at the last minute to the realization that the Loan Agreement bound them to introduce convertibility within a year. That condition was accepted with great reluctance. At the official level there was a powerful group in the Treasury convinced that the post-war world would be one of dollar shortage in which convertibility was the wrong medicine.[2] Sir Hugh Ellis Rees, looking back in 1962, recalled that he 'never heard any suggestion that we had even a sporting chance of making a success of the Agreement in its fullness; the only question was how long we could make the credit last'.[3]

By the middle of 1946 it had become clear that the world was clamouring for goods that only the Western Hemisphere could supply and was using up its reserves in order to acquire them. Of Britain's imports in 1946 45 per cent came from the Western Hemisphere as compared with just over 30 per cent in 1938 (see table 4.1, p. 66). This was not for lack of effort to find alternative sources of supply but it took time to develop new ones. Other countries had the same problem of resuming imports on the pre-war scale and being obliged to look for them from the Western Hemisphere, especially the United States. The result was a current account surplus in the US balance of payments for 1946 that reached the unheard-of total of nearly $8 billion, against which the US government provided in grants and loans $2.3 billion (see table 4.2, p. 70). From the beginning of 1947 the surplus leapt to an annual rate of $11.5 billion in the first quarter and stayed there for the rest of the year. The world dollar surplus (or shortage) dominated trade and finance throughout the early post-war years. All other surpluses were negligible in comparison.[4] Nearly every country had a dollar deficit. The problem of settling accounts with the US and establishing a new equilibrium in which that problem disappeared conditioned the achievement of convertibility, not only by the

2  Clarke (1982), p. 58; Keynes (1979), vol. XXIV, p. 536.
3  Ellis Rees (1962) (unpublished memorandum), part I, para. 8.
4  Tew (1952), p. 159.

United Kingdom but by virtually all other countries outside North America.

It was asking a great deal under those conditions to make sterling convertible: that is, as acceptable as the dollar. Not only were dollars scarce: sterling was abundant. There was far too much of it around the world – far more than had been assumed when the Loan Agreement was being negotiated. Very few other countries felt able to make their currencies convertible. The United Kingdom, to all appearances, was holding itself out as a bridge between the dollar and other currencies when it lacked the necessary strength.

*Monetary agreements*

Early convertibility had not been envisaged in the monetary agreements entered into with Western European countries in the later stages of the war, beginning with Belgium in October 1944. These agreements had a number of different purposes. They were intended to re-establish sterling as an international currency and London as a financial centre and at the same time bring the European countries more closely together and identify the United Kingdom with the strengthening of Europe. They were also intended to furnish a framework for the gradual development of multi-lateral trading relationships within the non-dollar world and encourage the growth of trade in both directions between Britain and Europe. Their more immediate purpose was to allow this growth to take place without undue use of limited reserves of gold and dollars by providing credit margins within which fluctuations in the balance of payments could be maintained.[5] They helped to get goods moving again between countries that were short of convertible currencies and 'to establish a uniform and smoothly working payments mechanism with a series of reasonable and consistent exchange rates'.[6]

The agreements were intergovernmental but used central banks as agents and consultation took place at both levels. Each central bank agreed to sell its currency against the currency of the other at the official (fixed) rate of exchange and to enforce the official rate in all transactions. There was provision for a limited amount of credit on either side, according as the balance of payments swung one way or the other. Beyond the limits of the swing, settlement had to be made in gold or convertible currency

5  Ellis Rees (1962), part I, paras 10–27.
6  Bank for International Settlements, 18th *Annual Report*, 1948, p. 143.

except under the agreements with the Scandinavian countries where the means of settlement was left for subsequent negotiation. Sterling paid to a resident of, say, Belgium could be freely transferred to another Belgian resident or to a resident of the sterling area; and these facilities could be extended beyond the Belgian monetary area and the sterling area, if the British government agreed, through what was known as 'administrative transferability'. With countries whose currencies were not of international standing all settlements were made in sterling under rather different arrangements described as 'Payments Agreements'.[7]

Since the agreed credit limits were modest and there was little provision for capital movements, the agreements tended to run into difficulties as the swings developed into semi-permanent credits and far exceeded the original intentions. This gave rise to some consolidation of the debts but, the settlements being bilateral, the debtors might have surpluses in some directions that could not, in the absence of convertibility, be set off against deficits in others. Thus while the agreements helped to sustain trade, the need to balance it on a bilateral basis restricted it below what convertibility would have allowed.

When monetary agreements were negotiated, the expectation in Whitehall was that the United Kingdom would be in surplus with most of its former allies in Europe and the credit limits were therefore drawn fairly tightly. With the Scandinavian countries, however, a deficit seemed likely and unlimited holdings of currencies on both sides were proposed and accepted. As things turned out, the only country with which there was a sizeable surplus was Denmark, where a deficit had been expected, and the United Kingdom accumulated a large holding of Danish Kroner.[8] Other European countries either added to the sterling they had acquired in wartime (e.g. from shipping earnings or exports from colonial territories) or built up an increasing balance. In 1946 payments in gold or dollars to European countries remained very small and were exceeded by receipts from France.[9]

7  Ellis Rees (1962), part I, paras 15–16.
8  *ibid.*, part I, paras 18–20. At the end of 1946 the United Kingdom had a debtor position of about $180 million under its agreements with Belgium, France, Sweden and Switzerland and a surplus of $135 million with Denmark. (BIS 17th *Annual Report*, 1947, p. 128.)
9  France had borrowed £200 million from the United Kingdom by the end of 1945 (Ellis Rees (1962), part I, para. 25). Between 1945 and 1947 the United Kingdom received about £125 million in gold and dollars from France which was approximately equal to her current surplus (ibid., part II, para. 46).

European sterling balances raised awkward problems even before convertibility became an issue. In spite of the insistence of the Belgians and, even more, the Dutch on an exchange guarantee in the light of their experience in 1931, none was offered; and where, in the case of Sweden, a guarantee had been extracted in wartime, it was now abolished.[10] The Chancellor took the line that he would do nothing that reflected on Britain's faith in maintaining the value of sterling or that opened the door to similar claims from other countries. The most he would agree to was a clause calling for consultations before any change in the official rate of exchange. Interest on the balances was limited to the Treasury bill rate of 0.5 per cent even when the lending country (e.g. Switzerland) protested that it would cost 3 per cent to raise the money in its own market. With some of the more important countries – Belgium, Sweden and Switzerland, for example – the fixed credit margins were supplemented by a further, and larger, sum to be held in sterling either derived from balances accumulated during the war or to be drawn upon as an indefinite credit from which to finance imports into the United Kingdom. No provision was made in the agreements for the liquidation of sterling balances; and when, as in August 1947, the blocking of sterling balances was under consideration, there was a grave danger that European holdings would be treated on the same footing as other sterling balances irrespective of any assurances given during the negotiation of monetary agreements. The agreements, moreover, did not seek to work off the balances or prevent their further accumulation by complementary trade negotiations. Although it was the general practice on the continent to link financial and trade negotiations so as to indicate how payments were to be balanced and conduct bilateral trade negotiations on that basis, this was not done in the British monetary agreements. No commitments were entered into for the exchange of goods although the possibilities for such exchanges were discussed.[11]

All this made the negotiation of monetary agreements a matter of some difficulty. The United Kingdom was trading on the goodwill of her allies and browbeating the former neutrals so as to obtain credits that she had not expected to require and build up the use of sterling on the back of a

10  The guarantee had applied to sterling held by the Riksbank. Swedish exporters who sought to invoice in Swedish crowns or to include an exchange guarantee clause in export contracts were unsuccessful in their negotiations with British government departments (ibid., part I, para. 36).

11  ibid., part I, para. 21.

deficit when only a surplus would restore it on any enduring basis. The reluctant grant of credit to the United Kingdom by her European neighbours contrasted with the extraordinary outflow of British capital to the sterling area. Her efforts to minimize the use of convertible currency contrasted with her ready acceptance of large gold transfers from France. She declined out of hand the offer of a loan on commercial terms from Switzerland but insisted on a credit for an indefinite period on terms that struck the Swiss as far from commercial. The system of international payments that the United Kingdom was trying to promote assumed the continuation of an ascendancy and financial strength to which she could no longer pretend. Yet in the circumstances she had little alternative.

As the European Payments Union was to demonstrate, what was required was a system of partial convertibility based on fractional gold payments. Such a system put all European currencies on the same footing. But a system based on sterling was not possible so long as Britain's reserves were so inadequate and her liabilities so enormous. Other European countries had added to their reserves in wartime or reduced their liabilities. They were less deeply committed overseas, less determined to run their economies under maximum pressure, and more sheltered from financial storms. The United Kingdom was no longer the obvious pivot of the European monetary system.

Agreements with all the main European countries except France had been signed by the beginning of March 1946. It took some time for Whitehall to consider how they were affected by the Loan Agreement and nothing could be done until it had been ratified. While a start would obviously have to be made earlier, final arrangements did not need to reach completion before 15 July 1947. It was, however, abundantly clear that a system of bilateral credit margins with limits on the use of sterling outside the sterling area was not easily reconciled with the commitment under the Agreement to a multilateral system and the unrestricted transferability of currently earned sterling. The Treasury doubted whether the monetary agreements could continue at all while the Bank insisted that they were 'an essential sub-structure to the Bretton Woods system even when that system was functioning to the full'.[12] It was common ground that credit limits should be introduced into the Scandinavian agreements and that sterling transfers could no longer be restricted. Such transfers might, however, be confined to *net* balances in excess of the credit limit.

12 ibid., part I, para. 45.

The Bank took the initiative in November 1946 in setting on foot negotiations for supplementary monetary agreements.[13] These, while leaving the existing agreements intact, would make any necessary amendments to give effect to the provisions of the Agreement. What the Bank envisaged was a network of agreements to make use of 'transferable accounts', the area within which sterling could be transferred freely being extended as one country after another became party to the arrangement. The facilities for transfer would be confined to central banks and would relate only to net holdings of sterling, i.e. holdings net of any of their own currency held by the Bank of England. The Bank would have to agree to the transfer of sterling to third countries; but the other parties to the Agreement would have to agree to accept sterling from any source. Why any country should hesitate to accept sterling when it was assured from the start that its sterling could be transferred freely to North America (i.e. into dollars), as well as to the sterling area, Argentina and Brazil, was far from clear. But the Bank appears at that stage to have expected that countries might resist acceptance of sterling without limit.

The supplementary agreements were presumably aimed at encouraging other countries to hold transferable sterling (i.e. sterling that could be freely transferred within the area covered by transferable accounts) and to allow settlement to be made in transferable sterling rather than gold or dollars. In other words, their purpose was to maintain the demand for sterling and reduce the urge to take advantage of unrestricted convertibility into dollars.

It was of some importance under these agreements whether the opportunity was taken to draw on existing sterling balances for conversion into dollars. Under the agreements reached before 15 July 1947 this does not appear to have happened.[14] There was also some danger that offsetting claims by the British government (e.g. for military equipment and supplies) might not be taken into account or that sterling in private hands might be mobilized by the central bank which alone enjoyed the right to make transfers into dollars.[15] There was also no way of ensuring that withdrawals by non-residents were made for current purposes only. It was left to the monetary authorities in each country within the system of transferable accounts to satisfy themselves on this point since it was thought

13  For a list of the 14 countries with which these agreements were concluded, see Clarke (1982), p. 185.
14  Clarke (1982), pp. 182, 185.
15  Ellis Rees (1962), part I, paras 72, 75–7 and 80 for the case of Belgium.

impracticable to examine each individual transaction in London. There was a risk, therefore, that transfers into dollars might be swollen by capital movements that Britain could not afford, yet was powerless to check.[16]

The effect of the monetary agreements was to make convertibility operative over a gradually expanding area and when the time came for the obligation to become general, there were only fourteen countries still to be covered. Under the 'exceptional cases' clause of the Loan Agreement, the United States granted a postponement until 15 September 1947 of Britain's convertibility obligations in respect of those countries.[17]

Even before the first supplementary monetary agreement – that with Argentina – had been signed on 3 October 1946 it was proving difficult to prevent dollar payments to countries outside the dollar area. Argentina had made it clear in September 1946 that she would not export to the United Kingdom unless paid in gold, dollars or convertible currency.[18] In November 1946, while discussions with Belgium were still in progress, she was encouraging her debtors to settle in sterling and within a week of the conclusion of an agreement on 27 February 1947 she had converted £4 million into dollars.[19] In the first five months of the year she accepted from other European governments in settlement of debts nearly £13 million in transferable sterling which was promptly sold for dollars in New York. These transactions were regarded with some disfavour in Whitehall. Yet what the Belgians were doing was what they had been asked to do in November: namely, accept sterling from any source. This was not, however, the sum total of conversions by Belgium: at the end of May she was said to be converting sterling at a rate equivalent to $150–200 million per annum and by the end of the year she had drawn $208 million.[20]

There is no indication that other countries with which agreements were reached before July converted sterling on an appreciable scale. The Netherlands had large sterling debts to set against her holdings of sterling and Portugal was not expected to make use of her rights of convertibility. The only other agreements in the second quarter were with Italy, which was in deficit and Brazil. Both Portugal and Brazil did reduce their sterling

16 Gardner (1956), p. 313, points out that the Americans had not been consulted on these arrangements nor had they endorsed them.
17 For the list, which included France, Denmark, the USSR and five East European countries, see Tew (1952), p. 132n.
18 Ellis Rees (1962), part II, Annex, p. 32.
19 They also did what they could to mop up sterling in private hands, which was not what the agreement was intended to encourage (Ellis Rees, part I, para. 80).
20 ibid., p. 31n.

balances a little and Brazil no doubt converted her current surplus as she could probably have insisted on doing under *any* monetary agreement.

By February there was increasing concern at the acceleration in dollar payments. The Chancellor of the Exchequer seems to have meditated a possible approach to the Americans on the commitment to convertibility.[21] But he took no action then or subsequently before the suspension of convertibility in August. There were strong reasons against asking the Americans for a change in the terms of the Loan Agreement. Those with influence in the administration and Congress were not expected to show much sympathy and there was likely to be criticism of British policy, for example, over the lack of progress on sterling balances. It would not have helped to expose to debate in Congress the state of the British balance of payments: to do so would have been to run the risk that the undrawn credit might be frozen. Added to this was the doubt whether convertibility was having much effect on the dollar drain and whether other factors did not rank higher in producing it.[22] It was not until the visit in June of Will Clayton, the American Under Secretary of State, that the deterioration in the economic situation was explained in detail to a senior representative of the American government; and by that time it was too late to think of revising the Agreement since, as Clayton explained, Congress was about to go into recess.

The Bank of England had expressed some disquiet in February when they commented that 'full transferability is going to cost a good deal more but no one can say how much more'.[23] They made a number of suggestions in April, when there was renewed talk of freezing sterling balances, proposing that the Americans should be persuaded to take over some of the balances and liquidate them by payments in gold and that, while the obligation to treat current earnings of sterling as convertible should be adhered to, releases from sterling balances might somehow escape this obligation.[24] Nothing came of these suggestions or of the possibility that balances might be frozen.

As July approached the Bank remained confident that, since most countries had already been granted administrative transferability before the formal obligation to make the pound convertible took effect on 15 July, no major upsets would follow. They communicated their confidence to Eady at the Treasury and he in turn to the Chancellor. Speaking in the

21 ibid., para. 91.
22 ibid., part II, para. 3.
23 ibid., part I, para. 89.
24 ibid., part II, para. 10.

House of Commons on 8 July, a week before formal convertibility, Dalton was confident that 'in large measure 15 July has already been discounted and the additional burden of assuming these new obligations under the Anglo-American Loan Agreement will be noticeably less than many people suppose'.[25] Others showed equal optimism that 'the fateful day [has] brought with it no consequential disaster, nor is any in sight'.[26] *The Economist* spoke of 'the uncertain and probably small additional cost of convertibility' and the *Manchester Guardian* of 'some extra drain [which] is unlikely to be very large'.[27]

But this overlooked the effect on confidence of the publicity attaching to convertibility and the expectation that it might have a short life. As Ellis Rees points out, 'since [15 July] had been a significant date in relation to the Washington Agreement, the Press took the opportunity of commenting in detail on the operation as a whole and of speculating on the exhaustion of the credit and what that entailed'. A run on the pound had already started in July. When no fresh measures were announced in a State of the Nation debate in the House of Commons on 6 and 7 August, when the Prime Minister and the Chancellor were at pains to emphasize the seriousness of the threat to the reserves, it was hardly to be expected that the run would diminish. Ten days later the government decided to suspend convertibility.

### The dollar drain

The dollar problem had been looming up all through the first half of 1947. It had not arisen acutely in 1946. This was not because of inconvertibility but because dollar expenditure was held down by inability to obtain supplies while exports recovered unexpectedly rapidly to their pre-war level by the middle of the year. The dollar drain, on the figures then available, was actually lower than the current account deficit (although later estimates have almost wiped out the difference between the two) and the current account deficit itself was less than a third of what had been expected. But the situation was not one that could last. Imports had been held down to 68 per cent of the 1938 level and it had been necessary to draw on stocks of food and raw materials. In 1947 the deficit might well

---

25  *H. C. Deb.* 15th ser., vol. 439, col. 2150, 8 July 1947. It is interesting that Dalton's diary makes no reference anywhere to *convertibility* (not even in August 1947) although there are several references to the dollar drain.
26  *The Banker*, July 1947, p. 59, quoted Gardner (1956), p. 312.
27  Gardner (1956), pp. 314–15.

be larger once imports could be more freely obtained. Very little could be purchased from South-East Asia except for rubber and on the continent of Europe recovery had hardly begun. The raw material situation was worse than in 1945. Food supplies from non-dollar sources had hardly eased at all. Once primary production had had time to regain pre-war levels and traditional suppliers were back in the market it would be less necessary to turn to the United States but in the meantime there was little alternative.

Added to all this was the rise in American prices and the fall in the terms of trade. Later in 1947 Dalton reckoned that higher prices had knocked $1 billion off the value of the loan. The terms of trade fell by about 7 per cent between 1946 and 1947 and were at least 10 per cent lower than before the war. Then there were the dollars that the United Kingdom had to find for subscriptions to the new international institutions, to feed the Germans and to help with relief and rehabilitation. The United Kingdom's contribution of £750 million for the latter purpose alone was equal to $15 billion if raised to the dimensions of the American economy.[28]

By March 1947 there was evidence of an acceleration in the dollar drain. Even in 1946 when things seemed to be going well it had doubled, from an average of $65 million a month in the first nine months to $135 million a month in the fourth quarter. It continued at about that rate in January 1947. Unfortunately the monthly figures for the first quarter available at the time fell well short of the rate to which later figures point. They do show a rapid increase throughout the first quarter of 1947 to over $300 million in March. But since we now know that the *average* for January to March was over $300 million per month (and not just $200 million), the actual rate in March was probably even higher. It was certainly enough to disturb the Treasury. In the middle of March the Chancellor warned the Cabinet that 'we were racing through our United States dollar credit at a reckless, and ever-accelerating, speed'; and a few days later spoke of 'a looming shadow of catastrophe. . . . I will not have it said', he went on, 'that I have left my colleagues unwarned until the eleventh hour'. The loan, if spending continued unchanged, would run out by June 1948. But he had few proposals by way of remedy except to sustain the export drive and hold down imports, even if this meant rejection of 'many attractive proposals such as an early increase in the sugar ration'.[29]

28  Brief for negotiations with the US after suspension of convertibility (undated) in PRO T 236/782 ('European Reconstruction (Marshall Plan): Dollar Crisis May–June 1947').
29  'Exhaustion of the Dollar Credit', memo by the Chancellor of the Exchequer, 21 March 1947, reprinted in Clarke (1982), pp. 156–7.

The acceleration in the first quarter may have been affected by the February coal crisis which cost foreign exchange in reduced exports and may have produced some speculative efforts to get out of sterling. The second quarter, however, was just as bad, indeed slightly worse. In March the Treasury was expecting that the second quarter rate would average $40 million per week when it was already running at double that figure.[30] At the end of June the dollar drain in the previous six months had swept away $1890 million or more than half the US loan of $3750 million. The third quarter loss of $1537 million removed nearly all that was left.

As the drain continued in the second quarter, the Chancellor invited his colleagues to take some 'hard . . . but necessary decisions'. At the beginning of May he circulated a report by the Balance of Payments Working Party ('a drastic and well-written document') which showed a prospective deficit on current account of £550 million in 1947–8 and an even larger dollar deficit of £650 million.[31] Since this would have absorbed all that was left of the American and Canadian credits by the middle of 1948, and left nothing but the reserves to meet the continuing drain thereafter, action was urgently needed. Dalton sought a reduction in the hard-currency import programme of £200 million, of which £150 million was on food, so as to leave $800 million to be carried forward at the end of the year and help to sustain the level of imports in 1948–9. By the middle of the month he was noting in his diary that there was 'indecision about the import programme on which my original Treasury paper seemed to my Inner Colleagues to be much too drastic'.[32] Debate over the proposals continued into June, both at official and ministerial level. The Minister of Food, John Strachey, fought hard against the cut in food imports, bringing in Sir Wilson Jameson, his Chief Medical Officer, to testify to the dangers. Other ministers shared his fears that health, morale and productivity would all suffer if rations had to be cut further. Yet as the Treasury paper made clear, the programme as it stood was intended to improve food rations quite substantially. Whatever the doctors might say, it was not obvious to the layman why there should be anything unthinkable in a reduction of one-seventh in an import programme for food due to increase from 63 per cent of 1938 in 1946 to 86 per cent in 1947–8.[33]

30  'The Dollar Crisis', 30 May 1947, in PRO T 236/782.
31  Clarke (1982), p. 81.
32  Entry for 15 May 1947.
33  Clarke (1982), p. 167.

In the course of the ministerial debate, the import cuts on food were reduced first to £100 million, then to £80 million and finally to £50 million. Thus the total saving in dollars fell by half from $800 million at the outset to $400 million at the end. It was agreed, however, that the reduced programme should be authorized for the next six months only and reviewed in September.[34]

In explaining the situation to his colleagues the Chancellor had pointed out that the US credit was not as large as had originally been asked for and thought necessary, and that it had been reduced in real terms by a rise of 40 per cent in US wholesale prices since December 1945 when the loan was negotiated. The country remained more dependent than had been foreseen on American supplies because of slow recovery in the non-dollar world and dollars could not be earned through multilateral trade. Finally, scarce dollars had to be used to feed the Germans: $60 million had gone on this alone in the first three months of 1947 and after the fusion of the British and American zones Britain had even had to pay for the American share of food supplies as well as her own.[35]

Treasury officials were more outspoken. 'This crisis', they argued,

> has been developing inexorably since the early years of the war and has been concealed successively by lend-lease, borrowing for sterling, and the United States and Canadian credits. We have been living beyond our means, not only in consumption levels but also in overseas financial commitments.[36]

In analysing the dollar drain, the Treasury was handicapped by an inadequate statistical apparatus. Until the crisis it had no statistical unit of its own. There was no regular comparison between programme and actual outgoings. No provision was made for consultation with the rest of the sterling area. It was left to the Bank to supply the figures, usually well after the event. At the end of May the Treasury had identified a number of special factors underlying the drain.[37] The first quarter figures for South Africa were indicative of a flight of capital to that country which appeared to be continuing. Over the year, $200–400 million might be lost in this way through diminished receipts of gold and demands on the reserves for

34 'Import Programme 1947/48', memo by the Chancellor of the Exchequer, 28 May 1947, reprinted in Clarke (1982), pp. 157–9.
35 ibid.
36 'Import Programme 1947/48', memo by the Treasury, 28 May 1947, reprinted in Clarke (1982), pp. 159–67.
37 'The Dollar Crisis', 30 May 1947, in PRO T 236/782.

dollars. But since there was no control over capital movements to South Africa, the movement could be stopped only by putting South Africa out of the sterling area. Then there was India, heading for independence, with very serious food problems and an administration that was breaking down. Here, too, there was a possibility of capital flight (e.g. from India to South Africa) and it might be necessary to remove her from the sterling area in order to avoid a consequent dollar drain. The same applied to Egypt and Iraq; and they, like India, would be more likely in those circumstances to borrow dollars from the United States and ease the general shortage. Then Belgium, which had been expected to be short of sterling and even pay in some dollars, had been acquiring a lot of sterling and converting it into dollars at a rate equivalent to $150–200 million a year. Some of it might have come from Norway's accumulated sterling balances; but whatever the source, if Belgium remained in surplus and went on drawing gold and dollars, existing trade arrangements with Belgium would need to be reconsidered. Then there were Norway and Iceland, both running down sterling balances; Germany, about to raise her drawings for the half-year to $125 million; the oil companies who were making heavy drawings; and finally Canada, now in acute difficulties in settling accounts with the United States, had to be given from the beginning of 1947 a 50 per cent payment in US dollars (alongside an equal use of the Canadian credit) for imports from Canada.

In addition to all this, there was doubt as to the promptness with which dollar earnings by UK and sterling-area exporters were brought home. There was also no real check on the remittance of sterling proceeds by British exporters to countries in the sterling area. The possibility of leads in dollar payments was mentioned, but only in passing.

Reviewing the situation, the Treasury offered two important conclusions. One was that if there were any question of removing countries like India and South Africa from the sterling area in advance of convertibility on 15 July it would be preferable to bring forward the date from which the new Exchange Control Act came into operation and represent the changed arrangements as part of a new and enduring plan. This was one of the few occasions before the 1970s on which an extension of capital controls to the rest of the sterling area was contemplated.[38] But in fact nothing was done. The new regime did not start in mid-July nor did it include capital controls within the sterling area. Egypt did leave the

38 The spring of 1952 was another. See p. 244.

sterling area in 1947 and South Africa ceased to be a participant in the dollar pool, while remaining a member of the sterling area.

The second conclusion was more important. The Treasury argued that it was desirable to encourage the holding of sterling by the rest of the world by making it transferable or convertible. We should find ourselves obliged to settle in transferable sterling if we were in deficit and even if we were in surplus we should still find it hard to acquire the things we most wanted except for convertible currency. Transferability of sterling under safeguards was of less consequence than the power to discriminate once alternative sources of supply became available. Restrictions on the use of our buying power were more to be feared than inability to control (current) sterling once it got into foreign hands. It was a sound conclusion but not one given much prominence in later post-mortems.[39]

Even at the end of May the Treasury was underestimating the drain. This would have exhausted the American credit, without any further acceleration, shortly after the end of the year, not at the end of June 1948 as Dalton told the Cabinet. A fortnight later he predicted exhaustion by November. By then a little blue sky had appeared with Marshall's speech at Harvard which proved to be the starting-point of Marshall Aid. But it was to be some months before anyone could be sure of assistance from that source.

Meanwhile Dalton, having failed to win the battle on imports, appears to have become reconciled to the worst and had no fresh proposals to offer. Although thoroughly alarmed by the dollar drain, he does not seem to have regarded convertibility as an added danger of much significance. His officials advised him that the dollar shortage was worldwide and not confined to the United Kingdom.[40] Britain was simply the point of junction between the dollar and non-dollar worlds and exposed to all the stresses set up by the imbalance between the two. It was a diagnosis that

39 The argument used by the Treasury was that transferability took the sting out of convertibility. It created an incentive to use and hold sterling rather than dollars; and the more this happened the stronger Britain's economic position. 'If at some future date sterling becomes a fluctuating currency vis-à-vis the dollar and the rest of the world has holdings of and an active interest in sterling, the rest of the world has an inducement to follow sterling; if sterling is more or less out of use for an active international currency, and exists only in the form of frozen pockets of bad debts, the same inducement does not exist. As a buyer in world markets the consequences for us might be stupendous.' ('The Dollar Crisis', 30 May 1947, in PRO T 236/782.)

40 'The World Dollar Crisis', memo by R. W. B. Clarke, 16 June 1947, reprinted in Clarke (1982), pp. 168–74.

ministers accepted readily: in mid-June they concluded that 'we were staving off a collapse in the world dollar economy by the use of our rapidly dwindling dollar resources'.[41]

It was soon clear, especially after a visit to London by Will Clayton in mid-June, that no further bilateral aid was likely from the United States. A month later, in mid-July, there was still no certainty about Marshall Aid and the loan was running out fast. The alternatives were clear. Ministers might gamble on Marshall Aid; but the country would be in desperate straits if it did not begin to flow until the reserves were gone and if it proved to be too little as well as too late. The prospect of aid would itself inhibit the drastic reversal of policy that would be required if none were forthcoming. There could be no abandonment of the loan obligations (non-discrimination and convertibility) and no postponement of the fresh obligations involved in the ITO while negotiations for Marshall Aid were still in progress; and without a free hand in bilateral bargaining it would be impossible to organize alternative sources of supply or to influence the terms on which supplies could continue to be obtained from countries like Canada and Argentina. With no or inadequate aid there would have to be radical changes in internal policy with 'direction of labour and total national mobilisation as far-reaching as that of 1940'.[42]

As July wore on, Dalton circulated a fresh paper. By this time it was clear that there could be no Marshall Aid before early 1948 since there was to be no autumn session of Congress. The Chancellor was anxious that the Americans should be informed of the position and that comprehensive measures to meet the balance-of-payments crisis were planned. Parliament ought also to be informed of what was proposed. But although he raised the question of obligations under the Loan Agreement, no approach had been made to the Americans for the postponement or suspension of convertibility.

What Dalton proposed was that the prospective hard-currency deficit in 1947–8, which he now put at £600 million (compared with £650 million minus £100 million, or £550 million after the June cuts) should be reduced by fresh cuts. He wanted a further £200 million off imports, £50 million off government expenditure overseas, and an additional £150 million in exports. Once again he received inadequate support. The Lord President

---

41  'World Dollar Shortage, European Rehabilitation and United Kingdom Import Programme 1947–48', GEN 179/3rd meeting, 13 June 1947, in PRO CAB 130/19.
42  'Alternative Courses of Action', memo by R. W. B. Clarke, 23 July 1947, reprinted in Clarke (1982), pp. 175–80.

and Foreign Secretary were lukewarm, pointing to the need to stop paying out dollars on behalf of the Germans before making further import cuts. Morrison, advised by the Economic Section, wanted more to be done through domestic policy to make demand less inflationary. There was talk of tighter restrictions on the drawing down of sterling balances, for example by India and Egypt.

It was a remarkable display of the art of fiddling while Rome burns. Great faith was placed in an approach to the Americans, but only 'after cool reflection', not in a crisis atmosphere.[43] The brief, prepared on 11 August, asked that the Americans should be warned 'in good time' that the credit would be exhausted by October and that HMG 'would no longer be able to carry out the obligations imposed on them by the Financial Agreement'.[44] The Mission, headed by Sir Wilfrid Eady, was to seek relaxation of these obligations in bilateral agreements and elasticity in the interpretation of non-discrimination requirements. It was also to ask for greater liberality in dollar drawings from the IMF, in the forlorn hope of making the dollar eventually a scarce currency. The Americans were also to be warned that Britain would incur no further dollar expenditure on behalf of Germany after October.[45] By the time Eady reached Washington, the Cabinet had agreed on Sunday 17 August to suspend convertibility and ministers, who had interrupted their holidays for the meeting, had already resumed them. Three days later, on 20 August, the suspension was announced publicly.

While the Treasury received most of the blame for the débâcle, the entire government emerged with little credit. Morrison, who was in charge of economic policy, contributed virtually nothing to the elucidation or handling of the problem. Other ministers – Strachey, Bevan, Alexander, Shinwell – were if anything actively obstructive. Neither Bevin nor Cripps gave Dalton much help. Attlee provided no leadership. The Cabinet, instead of thrashing out a policy consistent with the dangers, was content with drift. Most of its energies in the last critical weeks were wasted in wrangling over the nationalization of steel when steel had become the main bottleneck, next to coal, in the export drive. One minister after another felt obliged to 'consider his position' or threaten resignation: Dalton in January and again in July; Cripps on more

43  P. Cottrell (1982) 'The Convertibility Crisis' (unpublished).
44  ibid.
45  ibid.

than one occasion; Bevan; all three together on 31 July.[46] By the end of August the air was full of rumours of ministerial intrigue involving all of the leading ministers.[47]

Nor did the Bank of England play a very helpful part. On 17 August, the day on which it was decided to suspend convertibility (and on which Cripps approached Bevin to take over from Attlee), Dalton noted in his diary that Lord Catto, the Governor of the Bank, 'saw me today and thought we were inclined to move too fast. We are getting no very useful guidance from this nice little man in this critical hour.'[48]

The Bank was consistently over-optimistic and had 'hazarded a guess that the "convertibility drain" would run itself down before the end of August'.[49] One of the few specific proposals which they put forward was that of Cobbold, to ease the road to convertibility by dealing with sterling balances (which had not in fact been the major problem although commonly so regarded). He wanted one-third to be frozen for five years with a gradual discharge thereafter; one-third was to be taken over by the United States and cancelled against provision by the United States of their equivalent in gold at the official price either as a free contribution to the United Kingdom or as a loan; the remaining third would then be cancelled as representing the gap between the official and the local price of gold in India and the Middle East.[50] The proposal had no chance of acceptance and does not appear to have got any further.

The line taken elsewhere in the Bank was that until the dollar shortage was checked, the strain of convertibility would be higher than had been forecast. The large dollar payments to Canada, Argentina and Belgium were said to be a direct consequence of convertibility.[51]

Until the dispatch of the Eady Mission, which arrived in Washington on 18 August, the British government had done very little to keep the

46  Donoughue and Jones (1973), p. 409. Dalton's threat in January over the failure of the Cabinet to agree to a cut in the armed forces was the first in the life of the post-war Labour Government. (Diary, Dalton Papers, entry for 27 January 1947.)
47  Donoughue and Jones (1973), chs 30–1.
48  Dalton, diary, entry for 17 August 1947.
49  Ellis Rees (1962), part II, para. 58.
50  'Sterling Balances', note by C. F. Cobbold, 28 May 1947, in PRO T 236/782.
51  This was not true of Canada or Argentina: American dollars continued to be paid to both countries after the suspension of convertibility.

Americans abreast of developments.[52] They had shown extraordinary insensitivity to the need to carry American opinion with them and delayed an approach until the very last minute without putting in hand a credible programme of self-help. No doubt they could see little to be gained by asking for postponement of convertibility, especially if they thought it a relatively minor element in the dollar drain. The provisions of the Loan Agreement were tightly drawn and the escape clauses did not provide for the situation in which Britain found herself. There seemed no possibility of postponement without legislative action and a long debate in Congress, just when Marshall Aid was opening up altogether new prospects. Suspension seemed equally irreconcilable with the terms of the Loan Agreement unless the British government could give an assurance that convertibility would be resumed in a comparatively short time as soon as appropriate measures had been taken. No such assurance was offered: the British government was unwilling to bind itself to resume convertibility within the foreseeable future. John Snyder, the US Secretary of the Treasury in place of Vinson, could see no alternative to a public acceptance of the fact of default on the obligations assumed in the Loan Agreement.

This was an unpromising beginning to Eady's negotiations. The Americans had frozen the remaining $400 million of the US credit and were now proposing to brand the United Kingdom publicly as a defaulter. Such action would do nothing to arrest the dollar drain or prepare American opinion for helpful action. However in two days of negotiation, concluded on 20 August before any public announcement of suspension, agreement was reached on an exchange of notes. The American government was notified that suspension was

> of an emergency and temporary nature which His Majesty's Government consider to be within the intentions and purposes of the Financial Agreement and which they hope will enable them to take appropriate action to insure that the limited dollar resources of the United Kingdom are available for the purposes contemplated by the United Kingdom and are not diverted to other ends.

The 'full and free convertibility of sterling' was still a 'long-run objective'. Snyder, for his part, took sympathetic note of the drains on Britain's

---

52  At the beginning of June the interdepartmental group concerned with the Loan Agreement still expected Britain's current account deficit in 1947 to be about the same as in 1946 (Gardner (1956), p. 321, n.). It took some time for the British government to wake up to the need for the kind of economic expertise in the Washington Embassy that had been so important in wartime.

dollar resources 'at a rate greatly in excess of the normal flow of current transactions with consequent peril to the re-creation of the multilateral payments system which is a major objective of the Anglo-American Financial Agreement'.[53]

This exchange allowed the two governments to maintain that the suspension of convertibility was within the terms of the Agreement since it was 'of an emergency and temporary nature' but at the same time left open the possibility of further negotiations for permanent suspension.[54] It did not dispose of the inconsistency between the Loan Agreement and unilateral suspension of convertibility. Nevertheless when Britain was in desperate need of the frozen $400 million in December 1947, the United States had to grasp the horns of the dilemma and allow the withdrawal of the last of the credit although convertibility showed no sign of being resumed. Congress, busy with Marshall Aid and inflamed with anti-Soviet alarms took remarkably little notice and raised no objections.[55]

Gardner's verdict may stand:

> The convertibility provision had been tightly drafted to ensure that an important step toward multilateralism would be achieved. In fact, the provision advanced multilateralism not at all: it proved no stronger than the genuine determination of the two Governments to take all the measures necessary to assure success. Indeed, the very specificity and rigidity of the provision – the fixed time limit and the inadequate opportunity for escape – actually set back the cause they were designed to serve. For they encouraged an abortive try at convertibility which brought considerable discredit to the multilateral goal.[56]

The suspension of convertibility did not arrest the dollar drain. Far from it. Even in the last quarter of 1947 $700 million were paid out and a mere $300 million of the American loan remained. Some years later Sir Hugh Ellis Rees gave it as his view that 'the convertibility crisis was in many ways more acute after the suspension of the formal obligation than before it'.[57]

---

53  Gardner (1956), p. 233.
54  ibid.
55  Dalton in July confided to his diary that the Americans 'never felt as badly before the war about the Germans as they feel about the Russians now'.
56  Gardner (1956), p. 325.
57  Ellis Rees (1962), part II, para. 66.

The possibility of borrowing on any appreciable scale in New York was ruled out by Eady on his return at the end of August. 'If we want [over $100 million]', he reported to Bridges, 'it can only be through the U.S. Government'.[58] His judgement carried the more conviction because it was he and Clarke who had argued two years earlier in favour of commercial loans of $1 billion or so.

In mid-October a paper was circulated to the Cabinet, for the first time over the joint names of Dalton and Cripps.[59] They expected the dollar drain to continue at the rate of $2 billion a year in 1948. This would bring down the reserves to £325 million by the middle of the year and to £90 million at the end of the year. Some mitigation would result if the United States agreed to 'unfreeze' the last $400 million of the loan (as it did in December) and if another drawing was made in 1948 on the IMF (none in the end was made). No one could foretell what appropriation would be made by Congress for Marshall Aid nor what share would eventually fall to the United Kingdom. Credit had already been taken for a gold loan from South Africa of £80 million and for what remained of the Canadian credit. Arrangements had also been made with South Africa that the United Kingdom would not have to find dollars as in 1947 to cover a South African deficit.

The two ministers proposed that steps should be taken to bring down the drain in 1948 by £175 million or $700 million so as to leave at least minimum reserves at the end of 1948 and reduce the prospective gold and dollar deficit in 1949 to manageable proportions. The improvement of £175 million was to come partly from savings in government expenditure overseas (£10 million), partly from additional exports to the Western Hemisphere (£45 million, mainly in the second half of the year) and partly from cuts in imports (£120 million).

Of these, the cut in government expenditure overseas was probably ritualistic since these things are not easily judged to the last £10 million. The revision to the export programme, which involved a doubling of exports to American markets within a year, smacked a little of wishful thinking: the government had few means of influencing its achievement. As usually happened, it was the import cuts that took the centre of the

---

58 'Raising the Wind', minute from Sir W. Eady to Sir E. Bridges, 29 August 1947, in 'Suspension of Sterling Convertibility', PRO T 236/1667.
59 'Dollar Programme in 1948', note by the Chancellor of the Exchequer and the Minister of Economic Affairs (with annex by officials), CP(47)283, 16 October 1947, in PRO CAB 129/21.

stage. Food cuts were now put at £75 million out of the total of £120 million so that, with the inclusion of the £50 million cut already agreed, the total would fall even lower than Dalton has proposed in May. Figures were put round, showing how it would be possible to save, not just £75 million, but £100 million in hard currency. On the other hand, it was calculated that a cut of £75 million would reduce the average calorie intake to between 2650 and 2725 in the first half of 1948 compared with 3000 in the latter years of the war. The intake of protein would suffer even more. Sir Wilson Jameson was wheeled in again. The Ministry of Food, having already promised a cut in food imports by £12 million a month under the 'Stop buying food' instructions of September now pointed out that a large part of their buying programme was on long-term contracts so that the cuts could not be made or only under heavy penalties. Canada had set herself in the war to supply the British market with bacon and cheese and it would not be easy to suspend purchases. Besides, Canadian supplies were cheaper than those from other sources and we were not allowed to discriminate against her.

The argument raged desperately. Attlee scribbled on his copy of the paper that we should need to mobilize gold and sell our art treasures. Others suggested stopping the showing of all US films but were told that under non-discrimination this meant a ban on *all* foreign films and would shut down 80 per cent of British cinemas. Eventually, when the food cuts were reduced from £75 million to £66 million, the proposals were accepted. Rations were to be adjusted accordingly and any sugar and meat surplus to requirements that was imported under long-term contracts was to go into store. The Canadian contracts, amounting to £38 million were to be renegotiated.[60]

The cuts in dollar imports were reinforced by the Budget introduced in November by Dalton – his last act as Chancellor. With this and the Cripps Budget next April, the pressures on sterling relaxed. The current account deficit with the dollar area was cut in half in 1948 and the dollar drain sank quarter by quarter to $300 million in the third quarter of 1948. The reserves fell gradually but ended 1948 only $200 million down on the year.

Yet the first half of 1948, like the first half of 1946, was a period of acute uncertainty until in July Congress at last voted Marshall Aid as it had voted the loan two years previously. The efforts to make dollar economies had proved less successful than was hoped, exports to dollar markets had

60  CM(47)82, 23 October 1947 in PRO CAB 128/13 and PRO PREM 8/733.

risen less strongly, and the switch to non-dollar sources had moved bilateral balances into deficit, with a consequent danger that dollars would have to be paid after all and at higher prices.[61]

When the dollar position was reviewed in February the gold and dollar deficit was expected to exceed £400 million in 1948, leaving reserves of only £270 million at the end of the year if no Marshall Aid was received. This was less than the expected dollar drain in 1949 so that in under two years the reserves, on existing policies, would have gone completely. It might yet be necessary to conduct 'an operation as grave and as difficult as that needed on the outbreak of war' and recast entirely the country's defence and foreign policy.[62] Even later, in June, when it seemed safe to count on Marshall Aid, the Chancellor circulated to the Cabinet a memorandum prepared three months previously in which the dire consequences of having to survive without Marshall Aid were spelt out in considerable detail.[63] Imports from the dollar area, already cut to £395 million in the programme for 1948–9 from the 1947 level of £570 million, might have to be slashed to about £200 million, with cuts in rations that would reduce average calorie intake to 2670 per day, halt the agricultural expansion programme for lack of feeding stuffs and spread industrial dislocation and unemployment for lack of raw materials.[64]

Meanwhile all thought of resuming convertibility evaporated. The United Kingdom entered on a new phase of external economic policy by taking the lead, with American encouragement, in building up OEEC. Instead of moving precipitately towards non-discrimination, Britain headed in quite the opposite direction as a member of a trading bloc of just the kind that the United States had hitherto anathematized. For the next few years economic recovery rested on the less ambitious and more limited forms of multilateralism represented by the sterling area on the one hand and the European Recovery Programme on the other.

61 '1948 Dollar Position', memorandum by the Chancellor of the Exchequer, 5 February 1948, CP(48)35 in PRO CAB 129/24; 'Import Programmes July 1948–June 1949', annex C, 9 July 1948, CP(48)177 in PRO CAB 129/28.
62 '1948 Dollar Position', para. 14.
63 'Economic Consequences of Receiving no ERP Aid', memorandum by the Chancellor of the Exchequer, 23 June 1948, CP(48)61 in PRO CAB 129/28. The paper was by David Butt of the Economic Section.
64 The estimate of 2670 calories per day compares with one by the Minister of Food that the further cuts proposed by Cripps in February 1948 were already calculated to reduce the average intake to 2590 calories per day ('1948 Dollar Position', memorandum by the Minister of Food, CP(48)49, 11 February 1948, in PRO CAB 129/24).

### Post-mortem

Before we proceed to a post-mortem we need to be quite clear what difference convertibility makes. Might not the same situation have arisen in 1947 in the absence of convertibility?

First of all, it is important to appreciate what it did *not* change. It did not affect the power of the United Kingdom and other members of the sterling area to exercise quantitative or direct control over their imports. They were quite free to place restrictions on imports, provided they did not discriminate between suppliers. They could practise exchange control and ration their earnings of foreign exchange. They could also engage in state trading and enter into long-term bulk purchase arrangements with any country. Under Article 9 of the Loan Agreement, however, they were required to refrain from using import restrictions in order to discriminate against purchases from the United States, except in special circumstances set out in the Agreement. This obligation was, in a sense, a separate obligation from that requiring currency convertibility by 15 July 1947 but the two things, non-discrimination and convertibility, did tend to go together. There is obviously no advantage in saving dollars by paying higher prices in sterling if the sterling paid out is cashed at once for dollars by the seller.

Secondly, if convertibility did make a difference, the difference could show itself in the British balance of payments in one of two ways. Either current transactions would be affected by the non-discrimination provision through larger purchases requiring payment in dollars or through lower sales bringing in dollar receipts: or the capital account would be affected because convertibility allowed suppliers who were previously content to accumulate sterling to ask for dollars instead or induced some holders of sterling to make transfers out of sterling into dollars.

Thirdly, convertibility might have resulted in a loss of gold and dollars because of its impact on the rest of the sterling area. It made no difference to their freedom to draw from the dollar pool against sterling balances in London. But they might be moved by the prospect of convertibility to import more freely from countries that were in a position to require dollars in settlement and this would add to the dollar drain. Any sterling they held became as good as dollars; and since they held a good deal, the danger of a *capital* transfer into dollars was a very real threat to the reserves: all the more because scrutiny of such transfers rested, not with the British but with the local exchange control.

*The current account*

Most of the dollar drain in 1947 can be accounted for by a current account ✕
deficit with the dollar area. Almost all the sterling area countries, Malaya
excepted, were in deficit.[65] The net deficit of the United Kingdom alone
with the dollar area amounted to £510 million to which must be added the
rest of the sterling area's deficit of £222 million,[66] making a total equal to
nearly three-quarters of the gold and dollar drain of £1024 million. There
was no question of this deficit being met in any currency other than
dollars. The material question is whether it was enlarged by convertibility: whether, as Cobbold put it in a letter to Bridges in September, 'the
emphasis on convertibility and non-discrimination in the Loan Agreement
. . . encouraged sterling area controls to relax both as to the amount they
bought and as to where they bought it from'.[67]

In the case of the United Kingdom, whose current account deficit
accounted for half the loss of gold and dollars, any relaxation in the import
programme was much more likely to be induced by the loan itself than by
the conditions attached to it. The Treasury was alive to the dollar problem
by the middle of 1946, i.e. by the time Congress had approved the loan,
and could have hardly imagined that convertibility would make the task of
coping with a dollar shortage *easier*. The more obvious danger was that it
would feel obliged to sanction purchases from the dollar area which, had it
been free to discriminate, it would have preferred to make from non-dollar
sources and so save dollars. There is not much evidence that this was
happening to any great extent in 1946 when the difficulty was to find
supplies from *any* source to meet the import programme and there was a
substantial shortfall. It was a difficulty that continued, but to a lesser
degree, in 1947 when harvests were poor and dependence on American
supplies remained acute. Up to the middle of the year it would not have
been easy to shift the pattern of imports away from dollar sources: the
dollar economies discussed in May and June meant buying less from the
dollar area, not switching to higher cost supplies payable in other
currencies.

65   Clarke (1982), p. 186. For the overall balance of payments of the main sterling area
     countries see table 6.5 (p. 158).
66   This includes capital transactions with the dollar area. These were probably small and
     the possibility that they were affected by convertibility, actual or prospective, is not
     pursued here.
67   Letter from C. F. Cobbold, Deputy Governor of the Bank of England to Sir E.
     Bridges, 11 September 1947, quoted in Clarke (1982), p. 182.

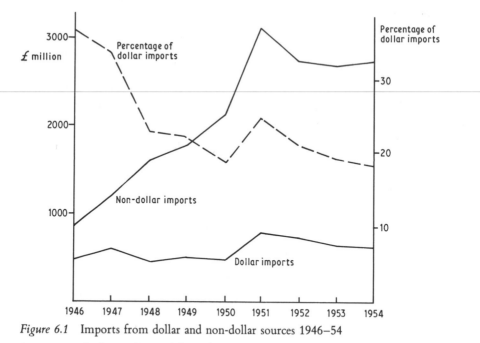

*Figure 6.1*  Imports from dollar and non-dollar sources 1946–54

*Sources: Annual Abstract of Statistics for 1953,* table 211, and *1958,* table 267.

Whether or not convertibility and non-discrimination affected British trade in the first half of 1947 they certainly would have affected it in 1948 and later years had they continued in force. As will be seen from figure 6.1 the proportion of imports from countries in the American Account area fell by half (from 36.3 per cent to 18.4 per cent) between 1946 and 1950. The big drop was in 1948 when dollar imports were cut severely after the convertibility crisis while other imports continued to grow rapidly. Most of the drop had nothing to do with convertibility and reflected no more than the need to make drastic dollar economies together with a steady improvement in the availability of supplies from elsewhere. But so big and sudden a change in the pattern of trade could hardly have been effected without overt discrimination such as was precluded by the Loan Agreement. Thus it is possible to argue that the main source of trouble in 1947, so far as the current account was concerned, was an excessively large import programme, with dollar imports no more swollen than the rest, rather than a forced abstention from discrimination; but that, had there been no crisis in the summer, the obligation not to discriminate would have been increasingly embarrassing in efforts to stem the dollar drain without a general deflation. For Europe as well as for Britain, discrimination was a necessary element in the balance-of-payments adjustments required by the dollar shortage.

The current balance may have been affected by the prospect of convertibility in another way. There was increasing doubt how long it would last after it came into effect and this may have disposed importers, so far as it lay in their power, to hasten imports from the dollar area, so bringing forward part of the dollar drain to an earlier point in time. Sir Hugh Ellis Rees, looking back at the situation in July and August, argued that:

> The widespread publicity on drawings on the credit and the knowledge that the final date for convertibility had passed must have tempted even the most redoubtable holders of sterling to turn it into goods or other convertible currencies: importers were hastening to acquire dollar goods, including, of course, importers in the United Kingdom and the rest of the sterling area.[68]

The scale of such anticipatory purchases, however, cannot have been large. No less than 98 per cent of dollar imports were either on government account or under strict government control[69] so that there was not much scope for imports beyond what the government permitted and usually no gain from unnecessary delay.

There was also the possibility that convertibility might affect the pattern of trade with countries outside the dollar and sterling areas. It gave those countries an incentive to reduce their purchases from the sterling area and to increase their sales to the sterling area so as to earn more sterling for conversion into dollars. It virtually made the United Kingdom (and indeed the whole sterling area) part of the dollar area and turned a dollar shortage into a sterling shortage from the point of view of third countries. The incentive to discriminate against Britain was therefore almost as powerful as the incentive to discriminate against the United States. Such an incentive would not have had time to make its full influence felt by August 1947 but it must have exercised *some* influence on commercial policy and aggravated (however slightly) the sterling area's deficit during the year.

This *a priori* reasoning can be supported by at least one example – that of Sweden. The Supplementary Monetary Agreement, concluded on 14 July had obliged the Swedish government 'to change their import policy and to

68  Ellis Rees (1962), part II, para. 56.
69  Dow (1964), p. 174.

*Table 6.1*　UK trade with non-dollar, non-sterling countries 1946–51[a] (£m.)

|  | 1946 | 1947 | 1948 | 1949 | 1950 | 1951 |
|---|---|---|---|---|---|---|
| *Imports:* OEEC | 146 | 239 | 339 | 456 | 573 | 923 |
| Western Hemisphere (non-dollar) | 96 | 154 | 170 | 105 | 160 | 182 |
| Other non-sterling countries | 66 | 106 | 218 | 211 | 262 | 381 |
| Total imports | 308 | 499 | 727 | 772 | 995 | 1,486 |
| *Exports:* OEEC | 262 | 260 | 393 | 421 | 599 | 705 |
| Western Hemisphere (non-dollar) | 38 | 60 | 89 | 108 | 114 | 115 |
| Other non-sterling countries | 93 | 135 | 169 | 195 | 205 | 260 |
| Total exports | 393 | 455 | 651 | 724 | 918 | 1,080 |
| Balance of trade | +85 | −44 | −76 | −48 | −77 | −406 |

Source: *United Kingdom Balance of Payments 1946 to 1953*, Cmd 8976.

a The figures are on a payments basis.

treat the Sterling Area as a hard currency area'.[70] No doubt other countries were in course of changing their import policy too. But, as the Swedish example illustrates, the interval between the conclusion of the agreements and the suspension of convertibility was generally a very short one, the exceptions being Argentina, Belgium, the Netherlands and Portugal.

If we look for corroboration to the statistics of trade with non-dollar countries we find no lurch in the balance of trade in 1947 such as one might expect. As will be seen from table 6.1, imports into the United Kingdom show no obvious sign of abnormal influences but increase fairly steadily between 1946 and 1948 from each of the three main groups of countries outside the dollar and sterling areas. The one conspicuous aberration is in the behaviour of exports to OEEC countries where there was a marked setback (by volume at least) in 1947. It is conceivable that part of this was contrived so as to enhance the power of the importing country to ask for payment in dollars. The more obvious explanation is that it was associated with supply difficulties after the fuel crisis rather than with a deliberate limitation of demand. But there is not much sign of the fuel crisis in the continuing rise in exports to *other* markets, especially the 40 per cent increase in 1947 in exports to the sterling area. As we shall see, sterling area markets were bolstered by large capital imports while several

70　Ellis Rees (1962), part III, para. 71.

of the main European countries were running short of foreign exchange. The OEEC countries, faced with growing foreign exchange difficulties, may have imposed additional restrictions in 1947 on British exports. Although the United Kingdom remained in balance with the OEEC group of countries on current account, the rest of the sterling area was in deficit and the UK itself was in deficit with some countries like Belgium, that could insist on settlement in dollars.

Third countries outside the dollar and sterling areas received in all £198 million in dollar transfers from the sterling area in 1947. These ranked as the third largest item in the dollar drain behind the United Kingdom current account deficit with the dollar area of £510 million and the deficit of the rest of the sterling area of £222 million. The balance of the dollar drain of £1024 million was made up of two special items – a subscription of £51 million to the IMF/IBRD and a repayment of £36 million to the US government – neither of which was affected in any way by convertibility.[71] Of the total of £198 million, OEEC countries received £125 million, countries in Latin America £58 million and other non-sterling countries £14 million.

The fluctuations in these dollar transfers were comparable in magnitude with the fluctuations in the two other principal items in the dollar drain: the United Kingdom's deficit on current account with the dollar area and the rest of the sterling area's deficit with the dollar area. If we leave out the minor and exceptional items – the United Kingdom's subscription to the IMF, the South African gold loan, capital transactions between the United Kingdom and the dollar area, and ERP grants – we get the picture shown in table 6.2.

The swing in dollar transfers to third countries between 1946 and 1947 was the largest single element affecting the dollar drain but the improvement between 1947 and 1948 was the smallest. This might be interpreted as meaning that, while there was a downward trend in the deficit with the dollar area and an opposite trend in dealings with third countries, trade with both groups of countries was affected in much the same way in 1947. There are grounds for suspecting, however, that capital movements played a larger part in the fluctuations in transfers to third countries than in the case of transfers to the dollar area. It is possible to reconcile the sterling area's deficit on current account with the dollar area and the loss of dollars to the dollar area without postulating any substantial movement

---

71  There was also a small net transfer of £7 million to the dollar area on capital account, including a reduction in sterling balances held by countries in the dollar area.

*Table 6.2*  Fluctuations in gold and dollar payments 1946–7 and 1947–8

| | Gold and dollar payments in (£m.) | | | Swing between (£m.) | |
|---|---|---|---|---|---|
| | *1946* | *1947* | *1948* | *1946 and 1947* | *1947 and 1948* |
| UK deficit on current account with dollar area | −301 | −510 | −252 | −209 | +258 |
| Rest of sterling area (RSA) deficit with dollar area | +9 | −222 | −10 | −231 | +212 |
| Gold and dollar transfers to non-dollar, non-sterling countries | +53 | −198 | −72 | −251 | +126 |
| | −239 | −930 | −334 | −691 | +596 |

*Source: United Kingdom Balance of Payments 1946 to 1953,* Cmd 8976.

of capital; but when it comes to the balance of payments with third countries this is not so easy. Payments on trade account by the United Kingdom to these countries moved between 1946 and 1947 from +£85 million to −£44 million (see table 6.1), i.e. by £129 million and this falls a long way short of accounting for a swing of £251 million in gold and dollar transfers, especially when one would expect the payments agreements with many of these countries to have absorbed a substantial part of the swing. It is true that this leaves out invisibles, which would add £21 million to the £129 million. It also leaves out the deficit of the rest of the sterling area if indeed there was such a deficit. The official estimates of inter-area transfers show a transfer of £59 million from the rest of the sterling area but this is neither a figure of any reliability nor a measure of the current account with third countries. There is no way of establishing what part of the £198 million received by these countries represented a capital transfer, still less how much of it was the result of convertibility.[72]

72  The accountancy of inter-area transfers is necessarily imperfect. Transfers of sterling between non-sterling countries were not separately estimated in 1946–8. The figures used consisted of 'the adjustments necessary to complete the UK regional balance of payments with each of the non-sterling, non-dollar areas; the entry under the Rest of the Sterling Area [i.e. £59 million in 1947] is a residual, the entries under all areas necessarily adding to nil' (*United Kingdom Balance of Payments 1946 to 1953,* Cmd 8976, p. 77). There is no complete set of regional balances of payments with the non-sterling, non-dollar areas so that much of what is said above about these

We can, however, take the analysis a little further. The £125 million collected by the OEEC countries was paid when they were probably in slight deficit on current account, as a group, with the United Kingdom. They were lent £86 million net of repayment by the British government and were estimated to be in credit on sterling account with the rest of the sterling area and other countries for £97 million. These receipts enabled them to add £56 million to their sterling balances and convert the excess of £125 million into gold and dollars (ignoring some small items which get in the way of an exact balance). Thus some of the sterling that OEEC countries converted can be traced to government lending and some to transfers from the rest of the sterling area and other non-sterling countries. The latter in turn had sterling to offer largely because of a net transfer of capital to them from the UK. The big increase in OEEC holdings of sterling in 1947 does not suggest indecent haste to transfer into dollars. Belgium, it is true, drew $208 million in 1947 and was thought to be unhelpful. But at 31 August 1947 Belgium's sterling balance had fallen by only £3 million since the beginning of the year;[73] and as she had a large dollar deficit she could hardly be blamed for converting her current earnings while she had the chance.

What may be true is that in the absence of convertibility OEEC countries would have been less willing to run such a large out-of-balance position in sterling or that sterling area countries might have had to take steps to check their imports from countries unwilling to accept payment in sterling without limit. But as we have seen, most of the dollar drain in 1947 can be accounted for by reference to factors not closely connected with the move to convertibility. The £58 million drawn in dollars by the Western Hemisphere countries was somewhat less than their current account surplus of £65 million with the United Kingdom. It was much more than was drawn in 1946 or 1948 but does not seem to have had much to do with convertibility, especially as these countries added to their sterling holdings both in 1946 and 1947.

---

balances is necessarily rather speculative. Moreover capital movements between the UK and other areas are very difficult to identify. In 1947 the balancing item of some £150m is attributed to capital movements, including variations in commercial credit, but could be accounted for to some extent by errors in the current account (Cmd 8976, p. 63). That is, nearly half the net estimated capital exports to the rest of the sterling area are simply unaccounted for but would seem from other evidence to be a reasonable guess.

73  Clarke (1982), p. 185.

This leaves the £14 million taken by other non-dollar countries. Unlike the first two groups they ran down their holdings of sterling quite heavily (by £59 million) but used most of it, together with an inflow of British capital (£20 million) to make settlements with other non-dollar countries, mainly in OEEC. What they took in dollars was small in comparison with the sterling passed on to other countries and used by them to strengthen their claims for dollar payment. Much the same situation was repeated the following year in respect of this group of countries except that they had then a rather healthier current account with the United Kingdom and a good deal more sterling to pass on than in 1947.

Some element of the £198 million taken in dollars by these three groups of countries must have reflected the influence of convertibility. With two of them the United Kingdom was marginally in surplus on current account, and might seem to have been as likely to receive as to pay dollars in settlement. What upset the reckoning were changes in holdings of sterling and capital movements. Belgium, for example, which collected nearly half the dollars paid to OEEC countries, cashed a good deal of sterling held by Belgian residents or transferred by governments and others in settlement of debts when much of it would have remained as an outstanding liability in the absence of convertibility. Even more important was the outflow of capital from the United Kingdom. How this outflow affected the working of the convertibility obligation we shall discuss presently.

### Changing estimates of capital movements

Before considering capital movements it is necessary to emphasize how uncertain some of the figures are and how much they have changed since 1947. It is difficult to appreciate how limited and imprecise was the information available to the authorities. The figures at their disposal were often incomplete and what figures there were usually related to a period several months in the past. Even the dollar drain, on which one might suppose the figures to be accurate and up-to-date, was seriously understated. At the end of May, for example, the loss in the first quarter of 1947 was put at $684 million in Treasury minutes when the true figure was $917 million.[74] The run of figures for the first three months (in million dollars) 137, 224 and 323 make it easy to understand why the Treasury did not begin to

74 'The Dollar Crisis', 30 May 1947, in PRO T 236/782.

react until well into March. In the autumn, minutes explaining how the American loan was spent may seem convincing in their arithmetic but had to be amended in successive editions as the Bank of England and the CSO obtained a fuller picture. The current account deficit for 1947, once thought to amount to £675 million, is now put at £381 million so that anyone starting from the *Economic Survey*'s projection of £350 million in February 1947 might wonder why it should have been so readily dismissed afterwards as disastrously wrong. Unfortunately, although some figures have been updated, others have not, so that even now we do not have the details necessary for a consistent picture of the different elements in the balance of payments. It is necessary to piece things together from figures of different vintages and reliability.

The main reason why the deficit has been cut nearly in half by later statisticians is an improvement in information about invisibles. The first guess at net invisible earnings in February 1948 was −£226 million. By October 1953 this had come down to −£28 million and there has been no great change since then, the latest estimate being −£20 million. While there was a small upward revision over those five years in the estimate for shipping earnings and a rather larger one for interest, profits and dividends, the biggest single change was in the figure for miscellaneous earnings which was pushed up progressively from −£20 million to +£233 million. The visible deficit has also been reduced very considerably from a first estimate of £449 million to one of £415 million in 1953 and now £361 million in 1984.

These revisions in balance-of-payments estimates have important consequences for an analysis of events in 1947. A deficit of £675 million went a long way by itself to explaining why it was necessary to draw so heavily on the American and Canadian credits. But a deficit of £381 million, seen alongside a gold and dollar deficit of £1024 million, leaves a good deal more to be explained. The difference between the two figures must correspond to an outflow of capital from the United Kingdom since the excess of payments was not matched by any current services, visible or invisible. The outflow instead of amounting to £349 million, as estimated at the beginning of 1948, can now be seen as reaching £643 million (see table 6.3). Given the straits to which the British economy was reduced in 1947, when it was necessary to ration even bread and potatoes, an outflow of capital equal to about 8 per cent of net national income and nearly equal to total net domestic capital formation (including stock-building) is a very extraordinary event. It was certainly not the purpose for which the American and Canadian loans were procured.

*Table 6.3* Current account, gold and dollar deficit and net capital exports 1946–52
(£m.)

| | Current account deficit | | Gold and dollar deficit<sup>c</sup> | Net capital exports | |
|---|---|---|---|---|---|
| | Initially reported<sup>a</sup> | Latest estimates<sup>b</sup> | | On first estimates | On latest estimates |
| 1946 | −450 | −230 | −225 | −225 | −5 |
| 1947 | −675 | −381 | −1,024 | 349 | 643 |
| 1948 | −120 | +26 | −406 | 286 | 432 |
| 1949 | −70 | −1 | −348 | 278 | 347 |
| 1950 | +229 | +307 | +308 | −79 | −1 |
| 1951 | −521 | −369 | −407 | −114 | 38 |
| 1952 | −58 | +163 | −174 | 116 | 337 |

a In *Economic Survey* for the following year.
b In *Economic Trends Annual Supplement 1981*.
c *United Kingdom Balance of Payments 1946 to 1953*, Cmd 8976.

It is not possible to show exactly how the £643 million was made up. Table 6.4 provides some guidance as to the major constituents and takes us up to the point at which the capital outflow was estimated at £581 million. We should not, however, exaggerate the precision of such estimates. Quite apart from the large changes made over five or six years, there is always a residual or balancing item and its absence from table 6.4 merely implies an element of guesswork somewhere in the figures to make them balance. The two items that grow steadily with each amendment are 'other RSA capital transactions' and 'other capital transactions with non-sterling area'. We are not likely to be far wrong if we assume that a further and equal addition should be made to each of these to bring up the total to £643 million. On that basis we can put the outflow of capital to the rest of the sterling area (including the rundown in sterling balances) at £(131+338) million or £469 million and the outflow to other countries at £(36 − 9 + 126) million or £153 million.[75] In addition, £51 million had to be paid in subscriptions to the IMF and IBRD and £30 million was received as a free gift from Australia and New Zealand.

These figures direct our attention to capital flows, especially those to the sterling area, as a source of pressure on the United Kingdom's

75 The total of £469 million for the sterling area compares with the total of £455 million (allowing for the donation of £30 million from Australasia) in table 6.5, p. 158. The latter figures excludes some countries but includes capital inflows from outside the sterling area.

*Table 6.4*   Successive official estimates of UK balance of payments for 1947 (£m.)

|  | Feb. 1948 | March 1949 | April 1951 | Oct. 1953 | 1981 |
|---|---|---|---|---|---|
| UK deficit with dollar area | −626 | −604 | −571 | −510 | ? |
| UK subscription to IMF/IBRD | −51 | −51 | −51 | −51 | −51 |
| RSA deficit with dollar area | −273 | −286 | −273 | −306 | ? |
| New gold from RSA | +84 | +84 | +84 | +84 | +84 |
| Net payments of gold and dollars to other countries | −157 | −167 | −173 | −198 | ? |
| Other transactions | .. | .. | −40 | −43 | ? |
| Gold and dollar deficit | −1,023 | −1,024 | −1,024 | −1,024 | −1,024 |
| Gift from Australia and NZ | +30 | +30 | +30 | +30 | +30 |
| Repayment of US/Canadian loans | −36 | −36 | −36 | −36 | −36 |
| Subscription to IMF/IBRD | −51 | −51 | −51 | −51 | −51 |
| Rundown of RSA sterling balances | −165 | −145 | −129 | −131 | (−131) |
| Rundown of other balances | +23 | +3 | +9 | +9 | (+9) |
| Other RSA capital transactions | −181 | −209 | −270 | −307 | (−338) |
| Other capital transactions with non-sterling area | +32 | +14 | −32 | −95 | (−126) |
| Capital transactions | −348 | −394 | −479 | −581 | −643 |
| Current account of UK | −675 | −630 | −545 | −443 | −381 |

*Sources: United Kingdom Balance of Payments* for: 1946 and 1947 (Cmd 7324); 1946 to 1948, no. 2 (Cmd 7648); 1946 to 1950, no. 2 (Cmd 8201); 1946 to 1953 (Cmd 8976); and *Economic Trends Annual Supplement 1981.*

reserves. What was the relationship between the outflow of £643 million in capital and the dollar drain of £1024 million and how did convertibility affect that relationship?

## Capital movements

There were various ways in which capital flows might be set in train by convertibility or might give rise unexpectedly to dollar obligations. Countries might draw on their existing holdings of sterling for conversion into dollars either because the dollar seemed more likely to hold its value or because they needed dollars to finance current purchases. They might also find themselves in possession of additional sterling as a result of a capital outflow from the UK and again swap the currency so obtained for dollars.

The first kind of capital movement, the conversion of existing balances, was limited by arrangements to block a large part of the wartime sterling balances and to release to the countries concerned a ration of 'free' sterling negotiated from year to year. In 1947 total releases of blocked sterling amounted to £156.5 million.[76] This is a great deal more than the 'annual releases of £43 million tentatively accepted as a reasonable rate of release at the time of the Washington loan agreement'[77] but falls well short of the total of £267 million in 1948 when there was no similar crisis.

The second kind of capital movement, the flow of funds for investment abroad, was freely permitted only to other sterling area countries. Transfers into other currencies, wherever made within the sterling area, came under exchange control and required official sanction. The countries that banked in sterling usually looked on London as an important source of capital and the freedom of movement allowed within the area was accepted as part of the price of keeping the area in being. There may also have been some tendency to assume that, so long as the movement of funds was confined within the limits of the sterling area, transfers from the United Kingdom to other member countries would not put pressure on the exchanges and run down the central reserves. If so, such an assumption was unwarranted. Any substantial outflow of capital, even within the sterling area, could hardly fail – especially under the conditions of shortage ruling in 1947 – to affect the exchanges.[78]

There was also a third kind of capital outflow: what later became known as 'leads and lags' in commercial credit. It was this kind of movement that seems to have been the main cause of the sudden acceleration of the dollar drain in August to its peak of $35 million a day. The trade account was weak over the year as a whole but could not have given rise by itself to the remarkable surge in the drain over the third quarter. It is to the capital account that we must look for an explanation of the acceleration and the capital account also helps to explain the size of the dollar deficit over the year as a whole.

76 Tew (1952), p. 139.
77 ibid., quoting *The Economist*, 13 May 1950, p. 1076.
78 Financial transfers were liable to be reflected sooner or later in a real transfer of resources through adjustments in the domestic economy that added to imports or held back exports. There could be no guarantee that those adjustments were confined to transactions with other members of the sterling area. If the adjustments took the form of additional imports of dollar goods, there was no way of stopping the resulting drain except by appealing to the country concerned to cut its dollar imports or, in the last resort, by excluding it from the sterling area and so from access to the dollar pool.

It was the capital account which was blamed at the time. But the capital flow on which attention was concentrated was the withdrawal of sterling balances which it was thought should have been more effectively blocked or were not blocked at all. Unfortunately for this explanation, the decline in sterling balances in 1947 was too small to account for much of the drain. Countries outside the sterling area increased their holdings of sterling and so did the colonial territories. The other sterling area countries ran down their balances by £137 million compared with £84 million in 1946 (and £663 million in the year from mid-1951 to mid-1952).[79] This does not go very far to explain a dollar deficit of £1024 million. Of the countries that drew on their balances India and Egypt made by far the largest drawings. In the thirteen months from mid-1946 to 31 August 1947 their balances fell by £136 million and £39 million respectively. It is true that over that period India took only £40 million in dollars from the central reserves and Egypt and Sudan only £10 million.[80] But this does not provide a full measure of the effect on the dollar drain of the rundown in their sterling holdings since the transfer of sterling made it available to third countries that were free to convert it into dollars. Making all allowances for effects of that kind, the fall in sterling balances remains of secondary importance.

This conclusion applies even more strongly to sterling balances held by countries with which monetary agreements had been reached before convertibility. Fourteen such agreements were entered into between 3 October 1946 and 15 July 1947.[81] There was very little change in the total sterling balances of those countries, measured from the end of the quarter preceding the date at which the agreement became effective and the end of August 1947. There was also little change for any of them if 30 June 1946 is substituted as a starting date, the exceptions being Norway, with a fall of £40 million and Greece, with one of £14 million.[82]

One source of capital flows was government lending. During the year the UK government lent £88 million to OEEC countries and £27 million to sterling area countries. It also repaid £36 million in dollars and received £14 million in repayment of loans in sterling, nearly all from countries

---

79  The total of £137 million relates to the sterling area as constituted in 1953 and so does not include Egypt which ceased to be a member in 1947.

80  C. F. Cobbold to Sir Wilfrid Eady, 16 October 1947 (Clarke (1982), p. 184).

81  ibid., p. 183. The countries covered included Argentina, Brazil and Uruguay in Latin America and nine European countries (Belgium, the Netherlands, Spain, Portugal, Norway, Sweden, Finland, Czechoslovakia and Italy).

82  ibid.

*Table 6.5*  Balance of payments on current account of sterling area countries 1946–51[a]
(£m.)

|  | 1946 | 1947 | 1948 | 1949 | 1950 | 1951 | Total |
|---|---|---|---|---|---|---|---|
| Australia | +27 | −21 | +51 | −9 | −38 | −162 | −152 |
| New Zealand | +29 | −9 | −4 | −5 | +17 | +20 | +48 |
| India | −25 | −80 | −75 | −136 | +46 | −63 | −333 |
| Ceylon and Pakistan | +6 | −14 | +8 | −39 | — | +66 | +27 |
| South Africa | −63 | −180 | −175 | −114 | — | −109 | −641 |
| Southern Rhodesia | — | −11 | −13 | −24 | −21 | −43 | −112 |
| Ireland | +9 | −30 | −20 | −10 | −30 | −62 | −143 |
| Other independent countries | −28 | −37 | −20 | — | — | +10 | −75 |
| Colonies | −56 | −43 | −6 | −32 | +150 | +180 | +193 |
| Total | −101 | −425 | −254 | −369 | +124 | −163 | −1,188 |

*Source: The Sterling Area* (BIS, 1953), p. 42. See also *The Sterling Area* (FCA, 1951), tables 78 and 90.

a The current balance includes gold production rather than the net movement of non-monetary gold. The total excludes Hong Kong, Libya, Jordan and the Trucial Sheikdoms. Burma, Iceland and Iraq are included under 'other independent countries'. Private donations, but not official donations, ERP aid, drawings on the IMF, etc., are included.

outside the sterling area. These sums are comparable in size with the run-down in sterling balances and represented a bigger net transfer through government lending operations than in 1946 or 1948. They certainly contributed to the dollar drain.

Next, there were private capital transfers. These took two forms. There was an outflow of long-term capital, especially to South Africa and Australia; and at the same time, there was a movement of commercial credit in which for the first time it was necessary to wrestle with leads and lags. It was the outflow of capital that made it possible for the sterling area to run so large a deficit without drawing down its reserves in sterling by more than £100 million or so.

A general picture of capital flows to the individual members of the sterling area is given in table 6.5 and a consolidated balance for the group in table 6.6. It need hardly be said that these figures are subject to a considerable margin of error and they do not tally exactly with one another. The first table, showing a total of £425 million in 1947 for the balance of payments on current account (and hence also for the net inflow of capital) understates the gross capital inflow which was £30 million higher because of the free gift of that amount to the United Kingdom by Australia and New Zealand.

While every country was in current account deficit, much the biggest single deficit was that of South Africa. Most of this represents an inflow of capital from Britain, with a further amount of refugee capital from India, itself in heavy deficit. It has been estimated that all but £5 million of the net inflow into South Africa of £180 million came from the sterling area.[83] This inflow was partly the result of the new investment opportunities created by the discovery of gold in the Orange Free State and the boom in construction, engineering and manufacturing that was then in progress in South Africa (assisted, of course, by the inflow of capital itself). But it was widely believed that some of it reflected fears of a depreciation of the pound sterling or of a prohibition on the transfer of funds to South Africa. Such transfers were likely to have accelerated in the atmosphere of uncertainty in the summer of 1947 but they were already in evidence by March when the Treasury began to bombard the Bank of England with requests for further information.[84]

*Table 6.6*  Balance of payments of rest of sterling area (RSA) 1947

|  | £m. |  | £m. |
|---|---|---|---|
| Deficit of RSA with dollar area | 222 | Net capital exports from UK to | |
| Deficit of RSA with UK | 127 | RSA | 338 |
| Transfers to other areas from | | Reduction in sterling liabilities | 131 |
| RSA | 59 | | |
| Gift from Australia and New | | | |
| Zealand | 30 | | |
| Residual | 31 | | |
| Total deficit of RSA | 469 | Capital transfer to RSA | 469 |

In table 6.6 the capital inflow is shown as somewhat higher. It is made up partly of drawings on sterling balances of £131 million and partly of a net movement of capital amounting to £338 million. It will be observed

83  *The Sterling Area* (ECA, 1951), p. 263.
84  R. W. B. Clarke complained to Sir Wilfrid Eady in September 1947 that the Bank had 'stone-walled for several months' and that with proper information £200 million might have been saved – a claim received with some scepticism by others in the Treasury.

that the use of sterling balances constituted only a limited part of the capital inflow. At the time it was widely thought that this was the means by which the sterling area was coming into possession of large amounts of sterling. But the rundown in sterling balances, however substantial in comparison with other post-war years, was dwarfed by the outflow of capital in other forms.

The transfer of £469 million financed the deficit of sterling area countries with the UK. It also financed their deficit with the dollar area. The sterling area recipients of the capital were able to turn £222 million into dollars to meet this deficit and add correspondingly to the dollar drain. They were also able to use £59 million to make transfers in settlement of their deficit with countries outside the dollar and sterling areas. The transferable sterling with which the deficits were met was available to be cashed by the recipient countries, mainly in Europe and Latin America, for gold and dollars from the central pool.

Lastly there were leads and lags. These movements of funds which exchange control was powerless to prevent were in 1947 a new phenomenon and little understood. Any business extending credit to a foreign supplier or in receipt of credit from its supplier abroad had no need to make use of an authorized dealer in foreign currency in order to move out of sterling and into foreign currency. It needed simply to make prompter payment in sterling and delay payment in foreign currency.

It is doubtful whether leads and lags played much of a part in the early months of 1947. But there was widespread uncertainty as to the United Kingdom's power to sustain convertibility in an inconvertible world. Such doubts grew once there were indications of a large-scale dollar drain and were greatly strengthened when Dalton, in a speech in the House of Commons on 7 August 1947 emphasized the rate at which the country had run through the dollar credits in the first half of the year. To anyone holding such doubts, the risk of an early devaluation was apparent. It is not surprising, therefore, that there was something of a flight from the pound in the third quarter of the year.

In September Harold Wilson, looking back on the crisis, reported to the Chancellor that:

> There was some expectation overseas not only that sterling would be blocked but that it would depreciate sharply. Thus foreigners would tend to postpone payment of debts incurred on current imports from the United Kingdom and sterling area generally, in the hope that they would be able to obtain the necessary sterling more cheaply in the near

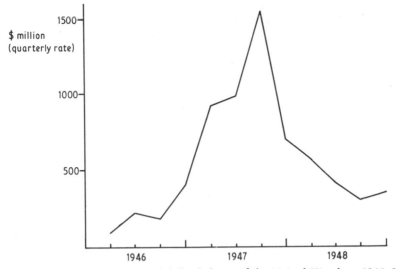

*Figure 6.2*    Quarterly gold and dollar balance of the United Kingdom 1946–8

*Source: United Kingdom Balance of Payments 1946 to 1953* (Cmd 8976), table 22.

future. Added to this was undoubtedly some speculative movement against sterling.[85]

What had not previously been appreciated was that a flight of capital could take place in spite of exchange control. It was to occur again in 1949 on a similar scale but without the complicating factor of convertibility. When one compares the two years, the natural reflection is that if a similar crisis could arise without convertibility, perhaps convertibility did not, after all, play such a big part in 1947.

The progressive acceleration is illustrated in figure 6.2. From an average of $166 million per quarter in the first nine months of 1946 the dollar drain climbed to $406 million in the fourth quarter and $917 million in the first quarter of 1947 before there was any suggestion of capital flight, except perhaps to South Africa in March. The figure for the second quarter, when the alarm bells were ringing, was not much higher – $973 million. There was then a leap to $1537 million in the third quarter when, for about half the time, there was full convertibility; and a fall to $704 million in the final quarter when convertibility was suspended but some of the imports put on order by sterling area countries with the prospect of

85 'Report on Balance of Payments Statistics' by Harold Wilson, 22 September 1947, in '1947–8 Organization a) Report by Mr H. Wilson b) Formation of OF (Statistics) Division', PRO T 236/1560.

convertibility ahead of them were still arriving. The peak rate of loss was in the last full week to 20 August when it amounted to $237 million – more than in any of the first three *quarters* in 1946.

The natural conclusion to draw from these figures, in the absence of a rundown in sterling balances exceeding $500 million, is that while the *prospect* of convertibility, and the *partial* convertibility embodied in the monetary agreements, may have added to the drain in the first half of 1947, most of the drain at that time reflected the state of the current account of the United Kingdom and the rest of the sterling area with the dollar area. After 5 July some countries may have presented sterling for conversion that they would otherwise have continued to hold or that they would not otherwise have accepted. But the big increase over the third quarter must, in the main, reflect leads and lags in commercial payments and speculative positions by those in a position to manipulate their sterling holdings or liabilities. If one puts the net effect of convertibility at perhaps $100 million in each of the first two quarters and, at most, $600 million in the third we get a total of $800 million or £200 million out of a total dollar drain five times as large. It is very unlikely that the effect was greater than this and it may well have been a good deal less.

A total of £200 million is equal to the whole amount drawn from the dollar pool by non-dollar, non-sterling countries. Unless the current account either of the United Kingdom or the rest of the sterling area was affected, this would obviously be too high. A large part of the £200 million can be accounted for by transfers to OEEC countries from the rest of the sterling area using funds remitted from the United Kingdom. The inflow of capital, whatever the reasons for it, allowed the recipient member of the sterling area to add to its imports and settle the excess in dollars from the London pool. But there is no reason to suppose that much of the movement of capital in 1947 was associated with convertibility in any way. On the contrary, it was only the leads and lags and speculative transfers, almost entirely in the third quarter, that were prompted by it. On this showing, one might put the total effect at $500–600 million for capital movements plus whatever separate influence on the current account one can detect; and that, though potentially large, seems unlikely to have amounted to much in the first half of 1947. It is hard to avoid the conclusion that £200 million in all is likely to be on the high side for the total addition to the dollar drain resulting from convertibility.

*Conclusions*

The conclusions to which this analysis points can be briefly summarized:

(i) convertibility did not by itself add substantially to the current dollar deficit in the first half of 1947;

(ii) it might, however, have exercised an increasingly powerful effect thereafter and would certainly have proved a serious hindrance to European recovery;

(iii) the main cause of difficulty in 1947 lay in the deterioration of the current account, both of the United Kingdom and of the sterling area, and the concentration of this deterioration on the dollar area;

(iv) hardly less important was the large outflow of capital to the sterling area;

(v) a relatively small part of the outflow came from existing sterling balances;

(vi) the acceleration after 15 July was largely due to leads and lags brought about by speculative forces.

In the light of these conclusions could the government have acted differently and avoided a crisis?

There is first a question of diagnosis. Was the government adequately informed and able to establish what lay behind the dollar drain? We have seen that there was no statistical unit attached to the Treasury and that, even if there had been, estimates of the balance of payments were of limited reliability. While this was an undoubted handicap, the Treasury was able, by May at least, to form a fairly accurate judgement of the factors at work and had drawn the correct conclusion that a substantial cut in dollar imports was indispensable. It had set out in October 1946 with the expectation of limiting the drain on the reserves in 1947 to £500 million (twice the current account deficit) and was aware by March that this estimate had become much too low. The divergence could be blamed largely on unforeseen developments – the 10–15 per cent rise in import prices over the winter, the fuel crisis, poor harvest prospects, the high dollar cost of feeding the Germans – but even in October there was an obvious risk of *some* of these developments and of the arrival in 1947 of imports not immediately available in 1946. The errors in the estimation of the current account, however, were small compared with the error in the forecast of the dollar drain. The current account forecast was less than £200 million out while the loss of reserves was more than £500 million above the October forecast. It was the scale of capital exports that was the biggest surprise.

The main criticism to be made of the government was that, starting out with a dangerously optimistic import programme, it delayed far too long making cuts appropriate to the situation. The main cuts were not made until *after* the suspension of convertibility and it was these cuts, not the suspension, that checked the dollar drain. There is a striking contrast with the situation in the spring of 1952 when what the Treasury had seen as a hopeless struggle to maintain the parity was eventually successful after a succession of cuts in imports. Had strong action been taken in March or even May 1947 the run in July and August, had it occurred at all, would have been far less overwhelming.

A second criticism is that the government made little attempt to alert the British public to the dangers ahead and took no action to ensure that the Americans were properly informed. In contrast to later exchange crises, it refrained from the kind of consultations with the Common-wealth that might have cut short the spending spree in the first half of 1947. Joint action with the rest of the Commonwealth, however, would have required the British Cabinet to show the way when it seemed incapable of decisive action. It might also have obliged the Common-wealth either to accept some control over capital movements or them-selves to have collaborated in limiting such movements.

Other criticisms have been made.[86] Releases from blocked sterling balances, it is claimed, were too generous. There was no need for the Bank of England to bring convertibility into operation quite so early by conclud-ing agreements with countries like Belgium and the Netherlands in the winter of 1946–7. But whatever force there is in these criticisms it must be very doubtful how long a crisis could have been averted and whether it was not just as well that convertibility had been suspended by the time the flow of Marshall Aid began.

---

86 For example, by Ellis Rees (1962), part IV.

# Chapter seven

# DEVALUATION, 1949[1]

The possibility that sterling might have to be devalued after the war was under discussion in Whitehall from at least as far back as the end of 1941. It was also present to the thinking of foreign exchange markets throughout the post-war period.

The Treasury view, as expressed by Sir Wilfrid Eady to Lionel Robbins, then Director of the Economic Section of the War Cabinet Office, was that devaluation would be of little help in dealing with the problem of the sterling balances and would provoke unhelpful reactions among American bankers. The Economic Section initially took a somewhat similar line, seeing no great value in devaluation when overseas income was denominated in sterling and imports were limited by controls rather than by price.[2] In December 1943, however, James Meade was willing to contemplate exchange rate variations during the transition period extending for perhaps four years after the war.[3]

In June 1945 R. W. B. ('Otto') Clarke, who had recently joined the Overseas Finance Division of the Treasury from the Ministry of Production, circulated a memorandum entitled 'Towards a Balance of Payments'.[4] This was based on earlier work by the Economic Section and

1 The main source used in the preparation of this chapter was the collection of Treasury papers contained in PRO T 269 and labelled 'Devaluation 1949 and Consequent Measures'.
2 'UK Post-war Balance of Payments 1940–2' and '1942–4', PRO T 230/4 and 230/5. I am indebted to Professor L. S. Pressnell for these references.
3 ibid.
4 Clarke (1982), pp. 96–122.

argued that if international trade recovered to pre-war levels by 1949–50 the United Kingdom should be able to balance her international accounts by that time provided there was an early and modest devaluation of sterling. Keynes, who did not see 'any serious risk of an overall shortage of gold and dollars in the first three [post-war] years', took issue with Clarke over the need for a devaluation. In his view, a comparison of inflation rates in Britain and America indicated some overvaluation of the dollar, and he concluded that British exporters would retain a residual cost advantage at the end of the war.[5]

A purchasing power parity test of competitiveness such as Keynes proposed does not, however, dispose of the issue. It pays no regard to capital flows on the one hand or to the scale of adjustment required in the balance of trade on the other. The United Kingdom had emerged from the war with enormous external debts such as no other belligerent had contracted, had sold a large proportion of her foreign assets, and was bound to come under pressure in due course to supply capital to Commonwealth and other countries; this affected the choice likely to be made by holders of assets between pounds and dollars. At the same time, the current account could be balanced or brought into surplus only if large changes occurred in the volume and pattern of British trade, and these changes in trade flows might well call for substantial changes in exchange rates, in favour of the dollar and against the pound.

On the other hand, however great the trade imbalance at the end of the war, and however necessary an eventual devaluation of sterling to its removal, there was a strong case for deferring an adjustment for some years. To have devalued immediately would have done little or nothing to accelerate the process of reconversion from war to peace. Price was not the significant limiting factor in the recovery of exports from the low level to which they had sunk. At the same time, imports were largely under the direct control of the government. The balance of trade would have responded very slowly and probably very little to a devaluation, while the terms of trade might have changed sharply for the worse. Higher import prices would also have given an additional fillip to inflation unless the government had intervened with higher subsidies; this would have been particularly awkward at a time when there was already an enormous budget deficit.

In the early post-war years not much was heard of devaluation. The immediate problem was how to cover an inevitable deficit by borrowing

5 Keynes (1979), vol. XXIV, p. 367; Clarke (1982), pp. 108–9, 122–5.

from the countries in surplus. In the ten months between the opening of negotiations for long-term loans from the United States and Canada and the final vote in Congress in the middle of 1946 no one seems to have proposed devaluation in the event of failure. Thereafter a second problem came to the front: the problem of hard and soft currencies when a surplus in the latter proved of no help in meeting a deficit in the former because of currency inconvertibility. When the current account was brought back into balance at the end of 1948 and the deficit disappeared, the second problem became all the more apparent because the gold and dollar deficit with hard-currency countries continued while the export drive to other countries yielded a surplus of inconvertible currencies, leaving the excess of exports 'unrequited'. It was this imbalance, not the disappearing deficit, that suggested to some officials that devaluation might be necessary in order to make hard currencies softer and soft currencies harder.

In February 1948 Clarke returned to the subject. 'It is clear', he wrote, 'that foreigners are expecting the devaluation of the pound sooner or later and probably sooner. . . . Where do we want to go?'[6] Exchange rates did not give expression to the world dollar shortage and price incentives were consequently working in the wrong direction. Raw materials and foodstuffs procured in Europe were 50 to 100 per cent dearer than if obtained for dollars from the United States. Prices of manufactures were also higher in Britain's traditional export markets than in dollar markets so that it was difficult to get exporters to switch from one set of markets to the other. As a result, the earnings of Britain and her colonies in the Western Hemisphere covered only half of her purchases of imports from there. Not that prices and wages were relatively high in the United Kingdom. If the price relationships of 1937 still held, the pound would be worth, not $4, but $5.93 on a comparison of retail prices and $5.59 on a comparison of wages. In countries like France, Italy and Belgium, however, prices and wages had moved up in relation to the dollar and stood at levels twice as high as in the United Kingdom at current rates of exchange. 'I would expect', Clarke concluded, 'another instalment of dollar crisis (even with ERP) some time in 1949'.

A month later George Bolton, an Executive Director of the Bank of England, argued against devaluation in a long memorandum but recognized that international opinion since the end of the war had regarded the

---

6  R. W. B. Clarke, 'The Future of Sterling', 27 February 1948, in 'Sterling-dollar exchange rate: future policy 1948', PRO T 236/2398.

dollar rate of $4.03 with some scepticism.[7] A staff memorandum prepared by the IMF came to a similar conclusion, after a balanced and sophisticated analysis but it, too, emphasized that 'widespread private comment' treated devaluation as desirable.[8] In June R. G. Hawtrey, now in retirement, wrote to *The Times* advocating *appreciation* against the dollar.[9] Meanwhile the debate within the Treasury continued in a rather desultory way with a note by Eady recalling that the Bank of England (and Hubert Henderson too) used to argue that if it came to a devaluation the pound should be allowed to fluctuate for a time before a new rate was fixed.[10] In early September, however, after discussion with Robert Hall, George Bolton and Stephen Holmes (Second Secretary at the Board of Trade), Rowe-Dutton (a Treasury Third Secretary) reported agreement that the pound should not be allowed to float.[11] By that time the debate had died down, Clarke minuting on 5 June that he saw no compulsory devaluation ahead but remained convinced of the desirability of a voluntary devaluation 'as the only means of mobilising ordinary commercial incentives for the task of righting our balance of payments'.[12] There is no evidence that ministers took the slightest interest in the argument or were shown any of the papers.

In December 1948 when the current account had reached rough balance and seemed likely to be in surplus in 1949 it was urged on the Board of Trade that the time had come to make use of devaluation as the only effective way of redirecting sterling area exports towards dollar markets and helping to reduce the dollar deficit rather than generate larger balances of inconvertible currencies. It would be wise to act before the issue came to be publicly debated, and there might be at most six months for ministers to make up their minds.[13] The proposal when made in December 1948 had no effect then or when revived in March 1949. The senior officials in the Board of Trade were dead against the idea. The President, Harold Wilson, showed no enthusiasm and made no move to discuss it.

---

7  'Devaluation of Sterling', 30 March 1948, in PRO T 236/2398.
8  IMF staff memo no. 204, 16 March 1948.
9  *The Times*, 7 June 1948. Later letters on the subject appeared on 15, 16 and 29 June and a leading article on 23 June 1948.
10  PRO T 236/2398.
11  'Sterling exchange rate: the question of a floating rate', in PRO T 236/2311.
12  PRO T 236/2398.
13  As Economic Adviser to the Board of Trade, I minuted the Permanent Secretary (Sir J. H. Woods) to this effect on 24 December 1948 and the President on 21 March 1949 setting out eight reasons in favour of devaluation. Later, at the end of March,

Had devaluation taken place in April, it could have been represented as a considered move, inevitable in the long run and necessary in the general interests of the world economy.[14] It certainly would have been a good deal smaller and less disruptive. Unforunately, it occurred under pressure after vociferous public debate. By August it was reported that the almost universal belief in the City was that sterling would be devalued or allowed to float.[15]

Outside opinion favouring devaluation did so largely in the belief that a rate sustained by import and exchange controls must be artificially high. Some critics took for granted that if the rate were allowed to fall the balance-of-payments problem would vanish and a whole catalogue of government controls could be got rid of simultaneously.[16] How far the rate might have to fall and what the consequences of such a fall might be were matters left unexplored. It was certainly not self-evident that devaluation was the best strategy for effecting the major structural change required in order to raise exports 75 per cent in volume above their pre-war level while holding imports to or below their pre-war volume. On the contrary, direct action to limit imports, encourage exports, and restrict the export of capital, coupled with measures taken in conjunction with the countries of the sterling area, and later those of Western Europe, to minimize outlay in hard currencies and develop alternative supplies, looked a more hopeful way of producing the very large swing that was necessary in the balance of payments.

Financial opinion, especially in North America, was more influenced by the gap between the official and black market rates for sterling, which was taken as evidence of the need for a devaluation. At a later stage some ministers were inclined to treat the discount on the official rate as an indication of the size of the devaluation required. By 1949 sterling traded at a discount – 'cheap sterling' – had become an important preoccupation

Austin Robinson, who had recently returned to Cambridge University, told me that in his view the time had come for Britain and other Western European countries to consider what changes would be appropriate in their exchange rates and that this and other problems might suitably be discussed at a World Economic Conference. He also warned me that Dennis Robertson would be making a similar suggestion in an address in Brussels the following week and was likely to come out openly in favour of devaluation.

14  Dow (1964), p. 41.
15  *The Banker*, August 1949, p. 71.
16  Jewkes (1948), p. 233.

of the government, especially because of the commodity shunting operations that flourished because of its availability.[17] But in fact, 'cheap sterling' was probably more a reflection of exchange control and the blocking of capital transfers than a measure of the appropriate rate of exchange. Black market rates continued to show a discount on the official exchange rate even after a 30 per cent devaluation.[18]

Early in 1949 there were signs of an incipient depression in the United States which did not bode well for the United Kingdom's balance of payments. The US index of industrial production began to fall and by the middle of 1949 was 10 per cent below the level in the previous October. Stock-building declined from the autumn of 1948 onwards and this reacted on US imports which fell in value between the third quarter of 1948 and the low point a year later by $1.5 billion or over 14 per cent. Against this background, the market for sterling area materials weakened and the British balance of payments on current account moved back into deficit.

This situation brought renewed talk of devaluation. Before the end of March the Economist Intelligence Unit was already predicting that the

17  'Cheap sterling' was sterling traded in irregular markets outside the jurisdiction of the Exchange Control at rates involving a discount in relation to the official rate of exchange. 'Commodity shunting' took the form of transactions in goods bought with cheap sterling and sold for dollars; or it might involve conversion into dollars from a sterling account through the unauthorized diversion of goods for disposal in a dollar market that had been acquired for use in a sterling market. Transhipment figures assembled in the Treasury pointed to a diversion of some of the main primary products of the sterling area amounting in all to $5 million in the sample month of April 1949. This represented 7 per cent of imports of these products into the United States from sterling area sources. Wool and hides from South Africa and rubber from Malaya were the largest items affected, the main centre of the trade being the Netherlands. See 'Cheap Sterling' in '1948–49 Commodity Markets and Sterling–Dollar Cross Rates', PRO T 231/445. Quotations for later years are given in PRO T 236/3242 (see chapter 9).

18  Hawtrey (1954), p.45. The rate for what Pick (1955) calls 'hand payments' in London (illegal cash payments delivered by hand to the payee's residence) fell from $3.09 to £1 at the end of March 1949 to $2.83 at the end of August and to $2.55 at the end of September. The rate then fell to a low point of $2.38 at the end of the year before rising again over the first half of 1950 to $2.57. Thus, the discount, which had never been less than 23.5 per cent before devaluation, fell to a maximum of 15 per cent in the months immediately following devaluation and to 8 per cent in the middle of 1950. Quotations for transferable sterling, security sterling and sterling bank notes from 1949 to 1952 are shown (graphically) in *The Sterling Area*, Bank for International Settlements (1953), p. 85.

pound might be devalued during the next few months.[19] The *Financial Times* had also raised the issue and Graham Hutton had suggested that devaluation was probably necessary in a broadcast on the *Economic Survey*. There was also pressure from the Canadians who feared that Britain was cutting herself off in a high cost area protected by import restrictions and driving Canada into increased dependence on the United States.[20]

In these circumstances, Robert Hall (Director of the Economic Section of the Cabinet Office) urged that an inquiry should be undertaken as soon as possible, pointing out that since deflation, the classical remedy for a deficit, had been given up, the onus was on those who opposed devaluation to prove their case. Bridges was persuaded to set on foot the proposed inquiry and Hall, once his mind was made up, set about converting some of his colleagues, including Edwin Plowden (Chief Planning Officer) and Roger Makins (Head of the Economic Division in the Foreign Office). He also put the case to the Chancellor who, however, was unconvinced. This was the beginning of a long campaign in the course of which the Treasury was gradually converted, although for some months it remained doubtful and divided. The Board of Trade, both at ministerial and official level, stuck to the other side while the Bank of England also remained strongly against devaluation.

Speculative pressure increased from April onwards. American officials were convinced of the need for changes in European exchange rates to avoid a collapse in European production when Marshall Aid ceased in 1952. John Snyder, Secretary of the US Treasury, had raised the issue of exchange adjustments when he appeared before a Congressional Committee in February and again in a speech in Minneapolis in April. A resolution calling for an inquiry into European exchange rates had been forced through the IMF on 6 April under American pressure.[21] The US Congress, in cutting down the appropriation for Marshall Aid in the spring, took the line that less aid would be needed if exchange rates were adjusted.[22] While presidential statements and official assurances accepted that internal policy, including exchange rate policy, was entirely a matter for the British government to decide, the US administration spoke with

19  *Foreign Report*, 24 March 1949.
20  Robert Hall, minute to Sir E. Plowden on 'Sterling-Dollar Rate', 28 March 1949, in PRO T 236/2398.
21  For the growth of American pressure see Milward (1984), chapter IX, 'Devaluation and the search for a new American policy'. For British reactions see '1949 USA Sterling-Dollar Exchange Rate: future policy', PRO T 236/2399.
22  Hawtrey (1954), p. 33.

many voices.[23] The pressure to devalue, as Robert Hall later summed up the position, 'inspired at first by the U.S. Treasury and ECA, had built up by the end of May into something like an international attack on sterling, which, once launched, was carried along by the facts themselves'. Fuel was added to the fire in May by the conclusion in a report of the Economic Commission for Europe that 'European currencies in general are over-valued in relation to the dollar'.[24] It is hardly surprising that a speculative run on the pound should have developed, and this at a time when the reserves, at their lowest level since the war, were inadequate to withstand sustained pressure.

At the beginning of May, the Chancellor of the Exchequer, Sir Stafford Cripps felt it necessary to scotch the rumours in a speech in Rome which seemed to leave no scope for any subsequent change of front. Neverthe-less, a few days after Sir Stafford's speech, George Bolton was cabling the Treasury from Washington on 12 May to warn them of 'the spate of rumour regarding exchange readjustment, sterling depreciation, etc.' in the United States. He also wrote to the Governor of the Bank of England that Snyder, Hoffman and Harriman were all in favour of devaluation and that fifty of their officials were spreading their views around Wash-ington.[25]

Later in May the British ambassador in Washington, Sir Oliver Franks, reported to Cripps and Bevin that a number of influential American economists favoured a devaluation of sterling and that it would be desir-able to engage in consultations with the US government before things got out of hand.[26] Official consultations started with a visit to Washington at the beginning of June by Robert Hall and one of the Second Secretaries, Henry Wilson Smith. This was followed by ministerial consultations in

23  In September, for example, the US Executive Director of the IMF, who had enough votes in his pocket to be sure of a majority, insisted – almost certainly in agreement with the US Treasury – on the inclusion in the Fund report of a strong passage practically calling on the UK to devalue, and tried to override the efforts of his British colleague to secure an adjournment so that he could consult his government. This was agreed to only after a recess of an hour, presumably to allow the US Executive Director to consult *his* government, which happened to be in Washing-ton, on the proposed adjournment. In campaigning for exchange rate adjustments, the US Executive Director argued that the IMF was the appropriate forum rather than talks between the American and other governments. (See annex A in PRO T 236/2311).
24  Dow (1964), p. 41.
25  Bolton to Cobbold, 9 May 1949 in PRO T 236/2399.
26  Hennessy and Brown (1980a).

London early in July attended by John Snyder, Averell Harriman and
Ambassador Lewis Douglas.

The talks in Washington had a powerful effect on Wilson Smith who,
as the official in charge of the Overseas Finance Division of the Treasury,
was in a key position and carried great weight with the Permanent
Secretary, Sir Edward Bridges. Up to that point Hall and Plowden had
been almost the only officials in favour of devaluation, but by the beginning of July Wilson Smith had come round and from then on a fairly solid
front developed inside the Treasury, so that by the time Gaitskell came on
the scene, official advice was no longer divided.[27]

Hall and Wilson Smith reported on their return that, according to
William McChesney Martin, Assistant Secretary of the US Treasury,
'practically all officials of the US Government were firmly convinced that
devaluation of sterling was inevitable.'[28] They went on to tell the Economic
Policy Committee on 17 June that, when they put the case against
devaluation, the Americans 'admitted that if we did [devalue] they would
follow suit and "quicker than last time" (1933). Recording this in his
diary, Hugh Dalton, now back in the Cabinet, noted that 'Americans have
now swung back to mood of 1945. Convertibility and non-discrimination
are now their principal aim – not helping Europe or resisting communism.'
The Secretary of the US Treasury, John Snyder, 'advised by some new
economists, is quite sold on devaluation'.[29]

By this time there were indications that the recession in the United
States was having a serious effect on sterling. Dalton quoted Wilson
Smith as reporting at the same meeting that 'all Americans expect [the
recession] to go deeper and to last at least a year'. The Committee's
attention had been drawn by Cripps to

a lot of items in [the] dollar balance sheet all going wrong at once . . .
our exports to the US very low in April and recession will keep them
low; colonial dollar surplus has vanished, US no longer buying Malayan
rubber and tin: Commonwealth countries spending too much, especially

27  By this time Hall was treated by the Treasury as if he were a member of the Depart-
    ment, although the Economic Section, of which he was Director, remained until
    1953 in the Cabinet Office.
28  Annex to 'Report on a Visit to the United States in June 1949' by H. Wilson Smith
    and R. L. Hall, EPC(49)63, 6 June 1949, in PRO CAB 134/222.
29  Dalton's diary (Dalton Papers), entry for 17 June. The fear of an American devalu-
    ation persisted. In a paper to the Cabinet on 10 November Cripps maintained that
    'there were interests in the United States who might make a determined effort to
    compel the Administration to devalue the dollar.'

Australia and South Africa; forestalling, postponement of orders, etc. on devaluation talk.[30]

The drain on the reserves was gathering speed. Between the first quarter and the second it rose from £82 million to £157 million and the reserves fell to just over £400 million. According to Dalton, Cripps warned the Economic Policy Committee that 'within twelve months all our reserves will be gone. This time there is nothing behind them and there might well be a "complete collapse of sterling"'. Attlee, not easily perturbed, turned to Dalton as they left the meeting with the words '1931 over again'. To which, recalling the convertibility crisis of two years previously, Dalton replied: 'It reminds me awfully of 1947.'[31]

But there was no sign at that stage that any member of the Cabinet was taking immediate devaluation seriously. Cripps was inclined to regard devaluation as wrong in principle and the expression of a policy of laissez-faire. As late as 7 July he was reiterating in the House of Commons that 'the Government have not the slightest intention of devaluing the pound.' Harold Wilson had gone out of his way, in a long report on his visit to Canada, to dismiss the idea.[32] Some ministers, including Wilson, were giving more thought to the possibility of an autumn election than to the merits of devaluation. For them the question was: could an election be held before devaluation or would devaluation delay an election until the spring?[33]

Cripps was anxious to be seen to be taking action to stop the dollar

30  ibid.
31  ibid.
32  Over the previous year the Canadians had been indicating that, having built up trade with the United Kingdom, they would like to see a devaluation of the pound as a way of maintaining that trade. Wilson, however, claimed that 'the [Canadian] Government advisers . . . accept the view that devaluation would merely add to the difficulties in which the already adverse terms of trade have involved us'; and that 'practically all the leading Canadian financial advisers (unlike some of their opposite numbers in the United States) reject devaluation as a means of overcoming Anglo-Canadian economic difficulties.' Nevertheless he referred later in his report to 'the unfortunate and fairly general – though erroneous – expectation of devaluation'. While emphasizing that 'our prices of consumer goods are far too high' to compete with American goods in the Canadian market, he refrained from any suggestion that only devaluation could close the gap, and while in Canada 'repeated the Chancellor's recent clear statement on devaluation' (paras 20 and 40 of EPC(49)65, 23 June 1949, in PRO CAB 134/222).
33  Nye Bevan was arguing in favour of an early election in May, and in recording this in his diary Dalton added, 'Douglas Jay argued this way with me last week. If we have to devalue sterling the cost of living will jump up and that will lose us the election.'

drain before the quarterly statement of the reserve position due on 5 July was published. On 22 June he put round a paper to the Economic Policy Committee, which met every Friday morning, indicating that the dollar reserves would run out by January or at latest by March if current trends continued.[34] His proposals for dealing with the situation included the summoning of a Commonwealth Conference in July, a cut of 25 per cent in dollar expenditure over the twelve months to July 1950 (to be announced on 5 July), and the suspension of fresh dollar payments, apart from exceptional cases, until 30 September. This was not a strategy likely to appeal to all his colleagues and had the disadvantage that it meant reviving and tightening controls that might be dispensed with in the event of devaluation. Nevertheless the proposals were accepted. The Commonwealth Conference, ending on 17 July, just before Cripps's departure to a sanatorium in Switzerland, agreed to make the cuts proposed. There was a sharp fall in sterling area imports from the United States in the third quarter, and over the 12 months July 1949–July 1950 the fall was in fact 25 per cent as planned.

Before the Economic Policy Committee met on 1 July Cripps circulated a long memorandum reviewing the issues raised by the decline in the reserves, and outlining three possible lines of policy: the current policy of improving competitive power through higher productivity; severe deflation; and devaluation.[35]

He rejected the second of these both because it was contrary to party policy and because it would jeopardize unnecessarily the results of the forthcoming election. But he accepted that a mild dose of deflation might reinforce existing policy by bringing about 'voluntarily helpful adjustments, calculated to assist price movements and to encourage enterprise'.[36] If the various supplementary estimates, including one of £57 million for the National Health Service, were added to public expenditure, he would have to find an equivalent saving by reducing food and other subsidies, although this would add to the cost of living and give rise to demands for

(Dalton's diary, entry for 24 May). Much later, writing from Zurich to the Prime Minister on 8 August after seeing Cripps, Harold Wilson reported that the Chancellor felt it 'more necessary than ever to have an early election', and took the view that, if one were held, devaluation should not take place until later. The letter, which is manuscript, is in PRO PREM 8/1178 part I, 'Financial Policy in 1949–50'.

34 'The Dollar Situation', memorandum by the Chancellor of the Exchequer, 22 June 1949, EPC(49)66 in PRO CAB 134/222.
35 'The Dollar Situation', memorandum by the Chancellor of the Exchequer, 28 June 1949, EPC(48)72, in PRO CAB 134/222.
36 ibid., para. 29.

higher wages. A tightening of monetary policy had also been suggested by the Treasury and the Bank of England but money had already become dearer because of a fall in the price of gilt-edged securities and the only point in raising short rates would be to propitiate capitalist opinion that this was the right medicine. Some degree of compromise might be necessary in a capitalist world but it was self-defeating if carried too far. The mere mention of a rise in Bank Rate set off a strong attack by Dalton who noted in his diary 'I say "Montagu Norman walks again". I thought we had buried all this stuff about Bank Rate.'[37] He could see no sense in higher interest rates because capital expenditure 'is not now determined by what people want but by what the government permits'.[38]

Cripps also dismissed devaluation except as 'part of some great new and imaginative scheme to solve the world's dollar problems' (which, of course, was precisely what devaluation was). He circulated a memorandum by the Bank of England setting out the arguments against devaluation, with which he concurred; and a second memorandum summarizing the opposing views within the Treasury.[39] All his advisers, he emphasized, were agreed that 'devaluation alone is not the answer'. They also accepted that it would be necessary to proceed in agreement with the United States and Canada.

This left only the first line of policy which was plainly inadequate. How should it be modified? Cripps began by listing dollar economies on the part both of the United Kingdom and the Commonwealth, a strengthening and reaffirmation of policy on money wages and productivity, strict limitation of government expenditure, and help from the United States and Canada in holding the dollar position. He went on to add to these some method of preferential treatment for dollar earners such as selective remission of taxation, premiums on dollars earned, or outright subsidies. Finally he wanted freer trade with Europe to balance the further restriction of trade with the dollar area.

In the course of the discussion on 1 July (which Cripps attended after a meeting of OEEC Ministers in Paris which ended at 2 a.m. that morning) only Morrison spoke in favour of devaluation which seemed to him the least of the evils to choose from.[40] Cripps thought it impossible to say to

---

37 Dalton's diary, entry for 1 July 1949. Douglas Jay is quoted to the same effect, denouncing 'awful old stuff like rise in Bank Rate'.
38 ibid.
39 These are appended to EPC(49)72.
40 Donoughue and Jones (1973), p. 438. Attlee is said to have offered some support but this seems highly unlikely.

what level the pound should be devalued or whether the rate could be held. He believed that by planning and control it was possible to achieve all that could be got by devaluation. Nye Bevan was also strongly against devaluation which in his view was a step in the direction of deflation. Perhaps, he suggested, the Canadian Government might be induced to hold sterling. The Foreign Secretary, Bevin, laid stress on the political factors involved and wanted 'a wholly new approach' to bring the sterling and dollar areas into equilibrium with one another.

Meanwhile, officials remained divided. Sir Edward Bridges, summing up official opinion on 18 June, told ministers that 'most of us, with differing degrees of emphasis, are opposed to devaluation *now*' but he did not exclude the possibility of a forced devaluation in the autumn or of devaluing some time later in more propitious circumstances. He was anxious that devaluation should be regarded not as a panacea but in the context of other measures designed to reduce the overload on the economy. It would be fatal if one devaluation were followed by a second, and it should therefore not be attempted when conditions were too inflationary, as those opposed to devaluation maintained they were. Under such conditions prices and wages would rise and the initial competitive gains would speedily disappear. The disadvantages were certain, the advantages uncertain. Devaluation would contribute little, if at all, to the development of export earnings in the United States, especially when the outlook in the American market remained obscure. This uncertainty posed a further difficulty in deciding how far the rate should go in the event of devaluation, and the Bank of England insisted that there should be no question of a floating rate, even for a limited period.

Those who opposed devaluation were chiefly concerned to see immediate cuts in public expenditure. Without such cuts, devaluation would not work; with them, it would prove unnecessary. Bridges pointed specifically to the food subsidies, suggesting that they should be cut by £100 million. Supporting measures in the credit field would also be necessary and should include a rise in Bank rate, higher interest rates generally and restriction of bank credit. Those who favoured devaluation (named by Bridges as Edwin Plowden, Leslie Rowan and Robert Hall) recognized the need for some accompanying measures but thought in terms of milder cuts in government expenditure and efforts to contain the rise in costs by a form of incomes policy.

Robert Hall himself put the case rather differently. He pointed out that although the process of reconversion after the war was largely complete and was likely to be followed by the recovery of some of our most important competitors, there was no end to the dollar deficit in sight, not even in the so-called 'Four Year Plan' for the years 1948–52 recently submitted to the OEEC. The country had run through borrowings and gifts from abroad at a rapid rate all through the post-war years and was still living on Marshall Aid without fully appreciating the precariousness of the situation. Moreover, there was plenty of evidence that exporters were handicapped by high costs. The Canadians were constantly complaining that American goods were cheaper, and in the markets outside North America there were similar complaints. How, if not by devaluation, was it proposed to close the gap, both in export prices and in the dollar balance of payments?

The Governor of the Bank of England, C. F. Cobbold, was strongly against devaluation 'at the present time and in present conditions'. It was not, he told Bridges on 23 June, 'an alternative solution' and would not remedy 'for any length of time . . . the main causes of the present malaise'. These he saw as the depression in the United States, excessive government expenditure and the burden of sterling liabilities. When he saw the Chancellor on 5 July he insisted that the main thing necessary in order to restore confidence in the pound was action to reduce public expenditure. The Chancellor, on the other hand, made it clear that no deflationary policy, such as cuts in expenditure would involve, stood any chance of acceptance by the government or, in his view, any other government. Undeterred, the Governor wrote to Bridges a week later that 'the two things that would really change the atmosphere in North America . . . would be a real attack on government expenditure and a deferment of further nationalisation plans.'

In the Governor's view the fundamental issue was whether, after devaluation, we could be 'reasonably certain of seeing equilibrium in our balance of payments and avoiding pressure against sterling at the new rate over, say, the next two years'. He wanted a new agreement with the United States and Canada to 'take some of the rest of the world's demand for dollars off our back' by assuming some of the burden of sterling liabilities. On the one hand, our cost structure was too high and inflexible, and on the other, overseas holdings of sterling were excessive: too much sterling was 'chasing too few dollars'. He accepted the need for complementary action in the monetary field if the pound was devalued but expressed doubts about direct action to restrict credit. By the end of July, when a decision had been all but taken, he was reported by Sir Wilfrid Eady to be very much alarmed by the absence of any proposals for a cut in government expenditure and determined to resist a tightening of monetary policy without complementary budgetary action. If there were no reduction in government expenditure, he would refuse outright to restrict credit or raise interest rates.

A few days later, on 3 August, he wrote to the Prime Minister to express his fears of a second devaluation if no action were taken to reduce inflationary pressure and deal with overseas sterling balances. These fears would lead him to recommend a larger devaluation than would be appropriate if it were undertaken as 'part of a general plan' (i.e., with the necessary accompanying measures). American pressure for devaluation was founded on the hope that it would be a step to convertibility and the relaxation of controls generally. But this was an illusion, since convertibility called for a strong pound whereas the pound would be 'convalescent' after devaluation and this would make it necessary to tighten restrictions on the use of sterling by third countries. Devaluation so soon after the Commonwealth Conference, which had just been held, was 'a hasty retreat to an unprepared line of defence'. It would cause other industrial countries to move in line with sterling so that there would be no improvement in the balance of payments with third countries. In dollar markets there was 'no reason to foresee any immediate increase in the dollar income of the sterling area'. Imports were already controlled and were unlikely to contract. The immediate effect of devaluation on net dollar earnings, in his view, was likely to be unfavourable.

This view of the effect on net dollar earnings was shared by others, including Douglas Jay, Economic Secretary of the Treasury. In a brief to the Chancellor before the meeting of the Economic Policy Committee on 8 July he argued that 'the issue [of devaluation] rests entirely on whether or not we should earn more dollars as a result and I do not feel that this has yet been established.' In June he had dismissed the 'thoroughly hypothetical economic gains' of devaluation and criticized the case submitted against it as 'altogether understated'. But by mid-July he had swung round.[41] After a meeting on 21 July at the Treasury on the possible use of

---

41  In his autobiography (*Change and Fortune*) Jay says that he was much influenced by the evidence produced by Edgar Whitehead, Finance Minister of Southern Rhodesia, at the meeting in London of Commonwealth Finance Ministers at the end of June 1949 to the effect that British exports were almost all too dear in relation to competing supplies. He made up his mind after his 'usual Sunday walk around Hampstead Heath' on Sunday, 17 July, and found the next day that Gaitskell had reached the same conclusion, also on 17 July, for the same reasons. When he told Cripps that he favoured devaluation, Cripps commented, 'What, unilaterally?' (Jay (1980), pp. 186–7).

tax rebates on dollar exports, he exclaimed: 'I wish to God we had done it a year ago.'

The chances of an early expansion in dollar earnings as a result of devaluation were much debated, particularly by those who were opposed to devaluation. Even after a recommendation to devalue had gone to the Prime Minister from the ministers in charge of economic policy, Treasury officials reported that it was unlikely that devaluation would affect the loss of reserves for nine months, 'unless the devaluation was so savage, e.g. down to $2.50 as to affect the internal standard of living in the country'. Yet when a letter (drafted by Douglas Jay) was sent to Stafford Cripps at the beginning of August by the Prime Minister, it opened with a reference to 'the ever-accumulating evidence that the universal expectation of devaluation is holding back purchases of British exports day by day and discouraging the holding of sterling all over the world'. Thus, while some were concentrating on time-lags, low price elasticities and non-price elements in marketing, others focused on expectations, capital movements and short-run effects.

Opinion changed quickly in the last week of June and the early days of July. Robert Hall claimed to have converted Douglas Jay on condition that there would be no cut in food subsidies. He thought that opinion among officials was now fairly solidly in favour, with one or two conspicuous exceptions, while, of the ministers, Morrison and probably also Bevin could be counted as supporters. Harold Wilson, reacting against overstatements of the case for cuts and deflation by officials, was coming round, and his Parliamentary Secretary, John Edwards, was strongly in favour of devaluation, regarding it as the traditional alternative to wage cuts.

Nothing of this was apparent from the meeting of the Economic Policy Committee on 1 July or from Stafford Cripps's public rejection of devaluation five days later in the House of Commons. When the Secretary of the US Treasury, John Snyder, arrived on 7 July, the Chancellor's line was that devaluation would be feasible only within the limits of a 'general settlement', the nature of which was left extremely vague. Although Cripps conducted the talks over the next two days with his usual skill, he had not slept for some days and had already made arrangements to go off to a Swiss sanatorium in less than a fortnight's time. The one concrete result of the Snyder visit was agreement that official talks should take place in Washington at the end of August on possible lines of action, with ministerial discussions following immediately.[42]

42 At a meeting at the Treasury Cripps persuaded Snyder to refrain from uttering public hints about devaluation and to offer his advice in private (Jay (1980), p. 186).

In the course of July Hugh Gaitskell (Minister of Fuel and Power), now in a key position in Cripps's absence, joined the ranks of those favouring devaluation, and he and Douglas Jay set about proselytizing their colleagues. Gaitskell's conversion is said to have been largely the work of Paul Rosenstein-Rodan in the course of a long walk on Hampstead Heath on 17 July; but others also (including Lord Kaldor, who put the case to him on 18 July) have claimed the credit.[43]

However he became convinced of the case for devaluation, it made a great deal of difference that he found Robert Hall in favour, with other Treasury officials of the same mind. Gaitskell might have taken longer to convince if officials had held a different view, and Attlee might have hestitated to override Cripps in his absence.[44]

Two days after Cripps's departure, on 21 July, Gaitskell, Jay and Wilson, the ministers who had been left in charge of economic policy, met and decided to recommend devaluation. Of the three there is no doubt that Gaitskell's was the decisive voice. It was he and Jay who brought Attlee round.[45] Harold Wilson, when the three saw the Prime Minister later in the week argued against devaluation and at a subsequent meeting still 'took refuge in ambiguity'.[46] At the beginning of the year he had seemed the likely successor to Cripps as Chancellor, but as Douglas Jay subsequently wrote of events in July 1949, 'it was this chapter which left no doubt in the minds of those few who knew the facts that, if Cripps's health failed, Hugh Gaitskell was the only possible Chancellor.'[47]

A few days later, on 26 July, a note on the economic situation was submitted to the Prime Minister, who had taken over Cripps's duties, over

43  Williams (1979), p. 199. On 20 July Gaitskell set out in his diary five reasons for devaluing the pound. Williams (1983), p. 130:
(1) exchange control had not prevented a substantial dollar drain and would not by itself bring the money back;
(2) it was clear that the US government would offer no help in the short term and would offer long-term aid only on stiff conditions;
(3) the controls over dollar expenditure by Commonwealth countries were looser than had been supposed and were weakened when sterling prices were relatively high;
(4) since devaluation would make exports to dollar markets much more profitable, the prospects of an expansion in dollar earnings were favourable;
(5) there was a danger of a currency collapse if the reserves continued to fall.
44  Letter from Lord Roberthall, 22 October 1981.
45  Harris (1982), p. 436.
46  Jay (1980), p. 197.
47  Jay in Rodgers (1964), p. 95.

the names of the three top officials in the Treasury, the head of the Economic Planning Staff and the director of the Economic Section of the Cabinet Office.[48] This stressed the danger that all power of manoeuvre might be lost if the reserves ran out. The measures taken had been insufficient, negotiations with the Americans were about to begin, and it was important that they should be told what further steps the government proposed to take. The inescapable fact was that British costs were out of line and that, while British costs were rising, American costs were falling. At the Commonwealth Conference it had been 'reiterated time and time again by representatives of the principal Commonwealth countries that one of their major difficulties in discriminating against dollar purchases was that so often dollar products were far cheaper than sterling'. In those circumstances a substantial readjustment of the sterling–dollar rate was necessary. The officials then went on to argue that, in order to be effective, devaluation would have to be accompanied by cuts in public expenditure and by some tempering of the cheap money policies that had been pursued since the war.

This minute seems to have had some weight with the Prime Minister, although he still had difficulty in seeing any connection between the balance of payments and the Budget and noted, on an attempt by Robert Hall to explain matters, 'I don't think much of this paper.'

When the Cabinet met on 29 July the Prime Minister was given authority to take whatever action he thought necessary. A few days later he wrote to Cripps in Switzerland (in a letter drafted by Douglas Jay and delivered by Harold Wilson) telling him that 'All of us are now agreed, including the responsible officials, that [devaluation] is a necessary step (though not of course the only step) if we are to stop the present dollar drain before our reserves fall to a [dangerous] level.'[49]

The letter went on to give three reasons for this decision: that the expectation of devaluation was discouraging the holding of sterling and deterring purchases of British goods; that the United States and Canada were unlikely to take any short-term action of material assistance; and that substantial help from the Americans after the projected talks in Washington in September could not be expected sufficiently early to prevent a fall in the reserves to 'a dangerously low level'.

Next, the letter referred to official advice calling for a reduction in

48  PRO PREM 8/1178, part I, 'Financial Situation in 1949–50'.
49  For the full text see Jay (1980), p. 188.

inflationary pressure if there was to be 'any lasting benefit from devaluation'. The Prime Minister proposed to issue 'a strongly worded directive' on government expenditure and indicated that 'supporting action in the monetary field' would be taken. If then went on to discuss the timing of a final decision and of its public announcement.

The Prime Minister stressed the importance of taking a decision before the Washington talks so as to avoid any appearance of 'trading an offer of devaluation for concessions' on the part of the Americans. The line to be taken was that the decision reflected the Cabinet's judgement that devaluation was the right thing to do, and that the US government was of the same opinion. This meant rejecting the position suggested at the end of June by the Chancellor, and taken up enthusiastically by the President of the Board of Trade in July, that a bargain might be struck with the Americans under which they would be required to offer further help as the price of devaluation.

What form the 'further help' from the Americans was to have taken is not altogether clear, but among the ideas under discussion were American support for sterling, either directly out of Marshall Aid or through stockpiling of Commonwealth materials, an increase in the price of gold and a possible take-over by the United States of part of the sterling balances. It might be supposed that a substantial dollar loan would have figured among the proposals. But this does not seem to have been suggested at any time, no doubt because of disenchantment with previous experience of loan negotiations. The draft communiqué on 9 July said flatly that the British did not want a loan from the United States and this was cut out only at the suggestion of William McChesney Martin, who was in the US delegation.

Cripps's reaction to the Prime Minister's letter, as conveyed by Harold Wilson, dwelt more on the timetable than on the issue of devaluation. Indeed, the Chancellor, who was feeling 'mouldy' from lack of sleep, had first expressed doubts as to the value of such a move but had then swung round and appeared to support it strongly. He had discussed disinflationary measures and raised the question of an autumn Budget. But it was the timetable on which he expressed himself most strongly. The timetable depended on whether there was an early election, since that would require a postponement both of devaluation and of the Washington talks. If there were no early election the matter should wait until his departure with the Foreign Secretary for Washington, when a decision might be taken either before he left or by the Cabinet while he was in Washington (he was undecided). In any event it was his understanding that there would be no question of taking a decision against his advice, and he would like to settle the matter at Chequers with the Prime Minister, the Foreign Secretary and the President of the Board of Trade. To make an announcement before the Washington talks would have the worst possible effect on the Americans and would also be contrary to the views of the Foreign Secretary, who still thought of devaluation as a bargaining counter, although Cripps did not. It would also, so Cripps was reported as saying, be 'a piece of sharp practice' and likely to undermine confidence if devaluation were announced in advance of the talks. An announcement after the Washington talks could be made in a broadcast on 18 September once he returned from the United States.[50]

At first, devaluation had been thought of for some undefined date in September. Gaitskell in July was so perturbed by the loss of reserves that he wanted immediate action; but once it had become clear that the earliest date was 24 August he agreed that it would make little difference if action were deferred until the conclusions of talks in Washington with the Americans and Canadians. Others were less confident that the reserves would be adequate by that date to permit a controlled movement to a new exchange rate, especially in view of the exposed position of the sterling area at the junction of the dollar and non-dollar world.

Partly for this reason, it had been suggested that it would be best to devalue before the Washington talks. Other arguments in favour of this course were that it might help to get useful results from the talks and to avoid any accusation of acting under pressure from the US government. But Stafford Cripps stuck to his choice of a date (18 September) when he would be back in the United Kingdom from the IMF annual meeting in Washington and could make the announcement to the British public in person. The delay extended the rundown in reserves, which was unusually heavy in the first half of September. It was also by no means obvious that the Chancellor was the right man to explain the inevitability of devaluation, or to underline its advantages, when he had come out so strongly and repeatedly against it.

A meeting of ministers was held at Chequers immediately after Cripps returned on 19 August. Attlee made it clear, 'more by silence than by sound', that the decision was as good as made.[51] Cripps was still reluctant

50 PRO PREM 8/1178, part I. Wilson's letter to the Prime Minister is docketed with the original of the letter to Cripps.
51 Harris (1982), p. 436.

to agree to devaluation but ultimately gave way, subject to three conditions, all of them involving the attitude likely to be taken by the United States. He insisted that it was necessary to secure the backing of the United States in approaching the IMF, since it would not be possible to give due notice to the IMF of the government's intentions. The United States would also require reassurance that the new rate would be held. Finally, the rate selected should not be so low as to invite retaliation by the United States. Cripps went on to explain his choice of 18 September as the date for devaluation. How, he asked, could he defend such a step on the eve of his talks in Washington when nothing had changed? By waiting until after the talks he could at least link the decision with the views expressed there. This was only one of many discussions in the summer of 1949 in which the role of the United States (and, to a slightly smaller extent, Canada) absorbed the attention of ministers to the almost complete exclusion of the rest of the world.

The decisions reached at Chequers were confirmed by the Cabinet ten days later on 29 August before Cripps and Bevin left by sea for Washington. The secret was well kept: there was very little evidence of leaks during the critical two months from the time the case was put to the Prime Minister on 21 July.[52]

The official brief for the talks in Washington describes their purpose as to work towards 'equilibrium in the balance of payments between the dollar and the sterling and non-dollar areas on a permanent basis, at a high level of trade and without the recurrence of crises'.[53] The measures for which American help was to be sought included: more favourable administration of the European Recovery Programme (i.e. more aid); a resumption of stockpiling (e.g. of tin); loans from the Export–Import Bank; drawings from the IMF; and reciprocal tariff reductions. Among the longer-term policies that the Mission should have in mind, if the progress of the talks afforded an opportunity, was an increase in the dollar price of gold. (The Treasury regarded the continuation of the pre-war price of gold as one of the most important contributing factors to the sterling area's dollar deficit.)

52  There is, however, some evidence of a leak after the Americans were told on 10 September of the intention to devalue and the range within which a new rate would be fixed. On 14 September a cable from Washington (Dedip 8749) reported that the Bank of Brazil had told the British Embassy on 12 September that 'they heard that we were going to devalue to $2.80 on 18 September'. (For Dedip 8749 see PRO PREM 8/973, 'Devaluation'.)
53  CP(49)175, 23 August 1949, in PRO CAB 129/36.

The Washington talks seem to have been fairly successful in spite of a cold reception from Mr Snyder, 'full of hostility and suspicion toward the British'.[54] Among the concessions made by the Americans were the promise of lower US tariffs, simpler customs procedures, and more American investment abroad. The US Treasury also agreed to allow the use of Marshall Aid for the purchase of Canadian wheat with US dollars. The Canadians were asked to act as a go-between and materially assisted the negotiations. But what must have smoothed the way more than anything was the disclosure 'to those of ministerial rank' of the intention to devalue the pound – a disclosure not made to any other country except Australia, New Zealand and South Africa until the weekend of devaluation.[55]

Meanwhile, important issues remained to be decided: the scale and make-up of accompanying measures; what changes in government expenditure were involved or necessary; the size of the depreciation; whether the sterling area should move together; whether and how the new rate should be controlled. Some of these matters were settled very late. Cuts in government expenditure, for example, were not announced until 24 October. A few days before devaluation, on 14 September, the President of the Board of Trade still did not know the rate, which had been decided by Bevin and Cripps on 12 September at the British Embassy in Washington.

The choice of a new rate of exchange was not the subject of long debate.[56] According to Robert Hall, Cripps wanted to ask the Americans and Canadians what rate they would suggest and was only talked out of the idea at the last moment. Before he and the Foreign Secretary met to discuss the matter in Washington, their advisers (Bolton, Hall, Plowden and Wilson Smith) had held a preliminary meeting at which they accepted Robert Hall's view that the choice lay between a rate of $2.80 and one of $3.00, and that it would be safer to be on the low side so that any pressure

---

54 Kennan (1967), p. 458; Acheson (1970), p. 322.
55 Plumptre (1977), p. 105. For the timetable of communication of the decision to devalue see PRO T 229/212, 'Miscellaneous papers on devaluation'.
56 The choice had previously been explored in a number of Economic Section memoranda. On 1 June Robert Hall considered the implications of a devaluation by one-third for the United Kingdom's competitive position; later in June Marcus Fleming discussed the impact of a 25 per cent devaluation; on 2 August it was concluded that the minimum should be 20 per cent and the preferred rate was as low as $2.75; by 28 August a rate of $2.80 (i.e. a devaluation of 30 per cent) was favoured. Colin Clark had suggested a rate of $2.50 to $3.00 in the June issue of the *Economic Journal*, as the Economic Section noted in its memorandum of 2 August. See Clark (1949).

on the rate would be upwards rather than downwards.[57] When the four advisers put these propositions to the ministers, Cripps turned to Bevin and asked what he thought. Bevin pursed his cheeks, hesitated and then said $2.80 and $2.80 it was.

When the Chancellor came to expound the decision to the House of Commons on 27 September he laid stress on two factors. First, there was the need to put British exporters to North American markets in 'a fairly competitive position'; this seemed to call for a rate at least as low as $3, especially as some cheap sterling transactions were taking place below this rate. There was, second, a need for finality: the rate had to be low enough to remove any danger of a second devaluation. He referred also to the possibility, which had been canvassed in the City,[58] of letting the pound float, but rejected it emphatically: if 'floating' meant that 'all our exchange and import controls should be taken off and the pound allowed to find its own level, we could not possibly think of such a course'.[59]

The possibility of letting the rate float was raised in an appendix to the memorandum circulated by the Chancellor to the Economic Policy Committee on 1 July. It was raised again at the beginning of August by the Economic Section of the Cabinet Office in a memorandum on 'The Choice of the New Exchange Rate'. After pointing out that in the end it was 'a matter of practical judgement' what rate should be fixed, the memorandum suggested that the IMF might be willing to accept a regime of variable exchange rates 'for an experimental period' before a fixed rate was settled. Gaitskell on 18 August had a similar idea: he wanted an announcement that the pound would be allowed to float within a band of rates, e.g. $2.60 to $2.80, with a view to creating an expectation that the pound would appreciate.[60] The Bank of England, however, was opposed to this idea on the grounds that the reserves were too low to embark on such an experiment.[61] The memorandum went on to suggest that it was 'presumably desirable to select an exchange rate which would enable the

57  Their advice is set out in annex C, 'Note on Exchange Rate', in 'Sterling exchange rate: the question of a floating rate', PRO T 236/2311.

58  *The Banker*, August 1949, p. 71 and September 1949, p. 159 (quoted by Dow (1964), p. 41).

59  *H. C. Deb.*, 5th ser., vol. 468, col. 12, 27 September 1949.

60  Williams (1983), p. 148.

61  In February 1950 Robert Hall commented: 'I was in favour of a floating rate last year but had to defer to the categorical view of the Bank of England that it was totally impracticable' (note to E. Playfair, 2 February 1950, in PRO T 236/2311). According to Playfair, the Bank of England was forbidden to discuss the subject (ibid). But see pp. 237, 244, below.

pound to be made convertible within the foreseeable future'. It would also be undesirable to have to devalue twice. These considerations pointed to a devaluation of not less than 20 per cent, i.e. to $3.20 or less; possibly to $3.00; and probably to a still lower rate.

Cobbold, as we have seen (p. 179), was also in favour of a large devaluation, essentially because he had no confidence that the necessary accompanying measures would be taken. He was very much afraid that one devaluation would be followed by another, and with this in mind was calling by 26 August for a rate 'midway between $2.50 and $3.00'.

Ministers do not appear originally to have contemplated so large a devaluation. At the meeting at Chequers on 19 August, Cripps was against any rate lower than $3.00. Bevin at that time favoured $3.20. Had the decision to devalue been taken earlier, before the loss of reserves reached such alarming proportions, and had it been made unanimously and deliberately with all the necessary accompanying measures, it is most unlikely that a rate below $3.00 would have been fixed, and quite possible that a rate of $3.20 would have been considered adequate.

In that event, some of the discord that resulted, especially in other parts of the sterling area, might have been avoided. There is very little mention in any of the official papers preceding the devaluation of the likely impact on other countries, even on countries holding their reserves in sterling. There are occasional references to what was seen as a dilution of the proposed devaluation if other countries — usually non-members of the sterling area — took the opportunity to devalue their currencies too. But no soundings were taken of their intentions; there was virtually no consideration of the problems presented by a 30 per cent sterling devaluation for a country like India or Australia, especially if it was given exactly two days' notice of British intentions. Although this was probably as much as such decisions allow — the IMF had less than 24 hours — and although there was plenty of speculation throughout the Commonwealth about an impending devaluation, Commonwealth countries were naturally taken aback by so large and sudden a devaluation within two months of the July Conference at which they had agreed to a 25 per cent cut in their dollar imports. Pakistan reacted by maintaining her existing parity; India expressed her displeasure at the absence of consultation; and Australia put it on record that she neither sought nor approved the devaluation.

As might be expected, the main struggle was over accompanying measures. The Prime Minister clung to the view that the external difficulties of the United Kingdom were quite unrelated to domestic policies: to suppose otherwise was 'nineteenth-century economics'. Other ministers regarded devaluation as an alternative to deflationary measures that were consequently redundant. Dalton, in particular, to judge from his diary, saw absolutely no need for any accompanying changes in the Budget. No country in the world, he maintained, had carried financial austerity and rectitude so far as the United Kingdom and to suggest cuts in public expenditure was to demonstrate how politically unreliable the government's advisers really were.

According to Dalton, after the meeting of the Economic Policy Committee on 8 July, the officials were asked to leave the room. Cripps then told the Committee that he did not trust his own officials and advisers in the Treasury (and presumably also in the Bank). They were all really, by reason of their training and their belief in a 'free economy', much more in agreement with the Americans than with British ministers. Dalton advised him to make use of Douglas Jay and Cripps agreed. Other entries in Dalton's diary make it clear that ministers were deeply suspicious of their advisers and that the grounds for this usually lay in an almost paranoic reaction to any hint that public expenditure should be cut. 'No doubt the officials, or some of them,' wrote Dalton 'are writing minutes and papers for the record to show the Tories if they *should* win the next election.'[62] At the end of July the Prime Minister complained to Dalton that he was 'being served up from the Treasury and the Bank arguments which he thinks are fallacious on evil effects of our public expenditure'. Dalton assured him that the arguments *were* fallacious.

This reluctance of the government to accept the need for accompanying fiscal measures strengthened the suspicion of officials hostile to devaluation that it was being advocated as 'an easy way out' when the real need was to trim back government expenditure and release resources. Repeatedly, officials drew the attention of ministers to the need for accompanying measures. Bridges told the Chancellor on 6 July:

We are all concerned that the proposals now before the Economic Policy Committee will not get us out of our difficulties. These proposals are in effect a continuation of the policy of exhortation to the people of this country to increase their productivity and to exercise restraint in their demand for increased wages and profits, coupled with a proposal to devalue the pound while maintaining full employment.

The minimum needed was 'a definite instruction to the Bank of England

62  Dalton's diary, entry for 19 July.

to bring about some restriction of credit and a limit of Government expenditure to the estimates put forward at the time of the Budget'. Current forecasts suggested that, without any change in policy, the estimates would creep up by £140 million over the original total for 1949–50. As for credit restriction, 'the present policy of very cheap money has meant that the monetary system has put no obstacle whatever in the way of inflationary forces generally.'

The Chancellor politely took note of this point of view in red ink, without further comment, but it no doubt contributed to the distrust of his advisers which he expressed two days later. He had already told the Governor of the Bank of England the previous day in categorical terms that the government regarded a policy of deflation, including cuts in government expenditure, as out of the question. After his departure to Switzerland, Bridges tried again in a private minute to the Prime Minister, insisting on the importance of a cut in public expenditure. This was spelled out three days later in the paper referred to earlier (pp. 181–2) which was submitted on 26 July over the names of five top officials. This argued that, since it was not possible to act by increasing the weight of taxation, public expenditure should at least be kept within the estimates and preferably be cut by 5 per cent as proposed by the Lord President, Herbert Morrison. There should also be a 'moderation in money rates of interest to make the present Bank rate [then 2 per cent] effective'.

Later still, when the ministerial brief for the Washington discussions was being prepared, Treasury officials insisted on including a paragraph on the need for stronger measures if only to carry conviction with the Americans. The paragraph got as far as the Economic Policy Committee but no further. In the end, no commitment to cut public expenditure was made in advance of devaluation and nothing was done to tighten monetary policy until 24 October when the expenditure cuts were at last announced. Even then it was limited to a letter from the Chancellor to the Governor calling on the banks and accepting houses to 'use every endeavour to ensure that inflationary policies are held in check'.

On the other hand, it was recognized that some form of incomes policy was highly desirable, and Bevin and Cripps eventually persuaded the Trades Union Congress to continue the standstill in wages introduced in 1948 so long as prices did not rise by more than 5 per cent. This made it necessary to work out measures conforming to this acceptance and to refrain from action that would have more than a limited impact on the cost of living.

The only deflationary measure on which Cripps and Bevin agreed before devaluation was an increase in the price of bread coupled with a reduction in the extraction ratio. Although Stafford Cripps favoured wholemeal bread and a high extraction ratio, Bevin, who was inclined to belch, thought that the working man would accept a higher price of bread more readily if offered a whiter loaf and the trade unions were thought also to regard the colour of bread as a first-class political issue. After some argument between the two, Cripps conceded the point with the un-realistic proviso that no increase in dollar expenditure should be involved.[63] Their proposal that the price of the loaf should be raised by $1\frac{1}{2}d.$ and the extraction ratio reduced to 82.5 per cent was, however, rejected by the Cabinet. The loaf went up by $1d.$ No other measures were agreed upon until after devaluation.

Other measures were, however, discussed. These included the impo-sition of a tax on capital gains (since devaluation would bring stock profits); an increase in profits tax to balance the wage freeze (the rate on distributed profits was raised from 25 to 30 per cent immediately after devaluation); the possibility of a rebate of tax on profits derived from exports (dismissed as contrary to GATT); a price stop over the first month following devaluation (this was an earlier proposal of the Chancellor). When the Chancellor at last put round a paper in mid-October he proposed a cut of £280 million, half falling on government expenditure and half on capital investment. These were cuts in programme, not from the current level of expenditure, and are correspondingly difficult to trace afterwards. The Chancellor based his total of £280 million on a calculation by Robert Hall that final demand was running at least £200 million above what had been assumed in the 1949 Budget, and that a further cut of £100 million was required to free resources for the improvements in the visible balance that devaluation would permit. The £300 million was whittled down to £280 million, and the final cuts by another £20 million. It would be broadly true to say that the cuts did little more than aim at restoring the pressure of demand to what had been contemplated in the spring before any question of devaluation arose. The proposed cut in public expendi-ture, by some curious logic, took credit for an increase in profits tax and a small prescription charge of a shilling under the National Health Service. It left the social services and food subsidies virtually intact, except for animal feeding stuffs and fish, and made only a very modest reduction in

63  The dispute is described in Hennessy and Brown (1980b); but it took place at least a week before the meeting at the British Embassy at which the new rate for the dollar was settled.

defence. The cut in investment was largely on paper except for housing, where it was bound to be somewhat problematic and was in fact restored early in 1950. The cuts were announced on 24 October and to the casual reader seemed to be made up largely of miscellaneous trimmings such as the Treasury might normally make in examining departmental estimates.

The expenditure cuts could be the subject of an instructive case-study in their own right and have been dealt with above in very summary fashion. At the meeting of the Cabinet on 28 July, at which the Lord President's memorandum calling for a 5 per cent cut was discussed, the Economic Policy Committee was asked to 'scrutinise Government expenditure with a view to securing such economies as were consistent with the continued application of major Government policies'. Some ministers, however, insisted that the main cause of the dollar drain was not the government's internal financial policy but the fall in sales of sterling area commodities for dollars. On 4 August the Prime Minister put round a paper asking for proposals to meet the aim of a 5 per cent cut in expenditure by the civil departments (about £100 million).[64] The government was satisfied that measures of retrenchment must be introduced 'if only to offset the increases which must automatically follow from the expansionist policies already approved'.

Little more was heard of the 5 per cent cut until after devaluation. Then, at the request of the Chancellor, Robert Hall prepared a paper on the internal financial situation which was circulated to the Economic Policy Committee on 5 October.[65] This attempted to work out the size of the cut in government expenditure and investment that should accompany devaluation. Hall started from the fact that the government had spent £221 million more in the first six months of the fiscal year than in the corresponding period in 1948 and that the Budget surplus, to judge from supplementary estimates, was likely to be about £160 million less than had been hoped. There were also indications of a fall in personal savings: small savers were drawing down their deposits at a rate of about £40 million per annum. All this pointed to the need for cuts of the order of £200 million merely in order to limit the pressure of demand to what had been judged appropriate in the 1949 Budget. The changes in the foreign balance over the past six months pointed to a similar figure. As a supplementary memorandum pointed out, since the six winter months of 1948–9 when

64 'Government Expenditure', memorandum by the Prime Minister, 4 August 1949, CP(49)170, in PRO CAB 129/36, part 1.
65 EPC(49)102. Both this paper and the supplementary memorandum (EPC(49)110) referred to below are in PRO CAB 134/222.

the current account was roughly in balance, the visible balance had worsened by over £20 million per month or £240 million per annum. Although exports were lower, unemployment was falling quite sharply: in the first eight months of 1949 it had come down by 115,000 compared with 30,000 in the same eight months in 1948. The home market was booming, with industrial production up by 6 or 7 per cent in spite of the fall in exports, and more imports were being absorbed. Investment, which had been consistently underestimated, was at least up to expectations. Quite apart from devaluation, a stiff dose of disinflation was called for.

But devaluation made still larger cuts necessary. To the estimate of £200 million for disinflation, Robert Hall suggested adding a further £100 million to free resources for improving the balance of payments and changing the pattern of production. It was important to act quickly or the chance of profiting from the new exchange rate would slip away. Failure to remove the inflationary tendencies at once would be irremediable, whereas if the cuts made proved to be excessive there would be no difficulty in relaxing them later, for example in or before the next Budget.

Robert Hall was obviously a little doubtful whether he had pitched his total high enough. On 10 October he warned the Chancellor that, if he did not start with the idea that he would have to go for the whole of the £300 million, he would never get anywhere with his colleagues. Politically difficult items might, however, be knocked off the list at a later stage in the bargaining process. Three days later, in a minute to Plowden, he was querying his own total. Government expenditure was running at a level that made him suspicious that some supplementary estimates were being delayed; investment might again have been underestimated; the additional expenditure in which departments might be involved by devaluation was not fully known, and departments also had a way of circumventing restrictive policies and failing to keep within agreed limits; in addition, there could be no guarantee that wages and salaries would hold steady.

At a meeting of the Economic Policy Committee on 5 October, Robert Hall's assessment was attacked on a number of grounds. Dalton dismissed it as 'another flank attack by officials' and 'not really a proper "estimate" at all'.[66] There were those who disliked quantification in principle, although the need to quantify the cuts in expenditure was inescapable. There were others who looked to higher import prices to do the job of disinflation without assistance from cuts in government expenditure: they found it hard to accept that there would be no net disinflation once the

66 Dalton's diary, entry for 10 October.

higher cost of imports was being met from a larger volume of exports. The economies forced on consumers would be offset by a fresh demand on resources. There was also some disposition to argue that exports might be redirected to dollar markets at the expense of sterling markets without any increase in volume, and hence without any need to cut other claims on resources. This would have been a valid argument had it been possible to disregard the low level of reserves, the commitments to sterling area countries already entered into, and the relatively modest allowance made by Robert Hall for the diversion of resources from domestic to external use. But £100 million hardly seemed excessive as an initial bid. Others argued that increased production – possibly via longer working hours – would do the trick. Finally, ministers fell back on the proposition that devaluation brought higher profits to trading departments such as the Ministry of Food and urged that these profits be brought into the budgetary reckoning. It was accepted in the end that the starting figure of £300 million might be abated by £15 million on this account.

It was assumed throughout that the budgetary change could be equated with the change in the level of final demand. The Chancellor, in asking for economies of £280 million, referred to a reduction in consumption but was clearly thinking of claims on resources since half of his total was to take the form of a cut in investment.

When Cripps defended the cuts in front of his 'openly dispirited supporters' in the House of Commons on 26 October,[67] Anthony Eden maintained that the proposals had been 'just scratched together in the last fortnight, and they represent the maximum that can be agreed without Cabinet resignation'.[68] This was fair comment. The cuts in expenditure were fought over until the very last minute. Nye Bevan contemplated resignation if they fell on the social services, Bevin and Alexander if they fell on defence and Cripps, still suffering from insomnia and nearing the end of his tether, if his proposals were not accepted.[69] Fortunately, Attlee and Gaitskell gave Cripps full support. Nye Bevan was induced to accept a small prescription charge in principle while successfully resisting a charge to hospital patients and a charge for dentures and spectacles, all three of these being designed to raise £10 million.

When the proposals were brought before Cabinet on 21 October they still fell short by £24 million of the £280 million for which Cripps had

67  Donoughue and Jones (1973), p. 447.
68  H. C. Deb., 5th ser., vol. 468, col. 1360, 26 October 1949.
69  Dalton's diary, entry for 12 October 1949; Donoughue and Jones (1973), p. 438.

asked. His suggestion that this amount should be found by reducing the subsidy on milk by ½*d*. a pint (while those in need continued to be supplied free) was strongly resisted and it was agreed instead to withdraw the subsidy on fish. The Minister of Health insisted that the cut in new house-building should fall exclusively on construction for private owners but since this was negligible in Scotland separate arrangements had to be made to allow of some cut there.[70]

Many of the cuts were not to come into effect at once and there were some that might never take effect. For example, the withdrawal of the feeding stuffs subsidy (put first at £30 million and later at £36 million) was to take effect only after the next Annual Review in February 1950, but how much of the cost would then fall on the farmers would depend on the outcome of the Review. The subsidy on fish was to be discontinued after decontrol at 'a convenient date' in the spring of 1950. Defence was credited with a cut of £30 million per annum, but this meant only that an intended supplementary, estimated by the Treasury at £30 million (a 'conjectural figure', accepted by the Ministry of Defence 'because they cannot think of a better') would now be limited to £17.5 million.

At the end of the day, the score board for expenditure cuts read £122.5 million instead of the target of £140 million and £79 million of the total represented feeding stuffs, defence and additional profits tax. 'Adminis-trative economies' were put at £28 million, and the £10 million for the prescription charge of a shilling was the other main item. The latter, although publicly announced on 24 October, never came into effect and was killed by the Chancellor in April.

As for investment, the cuts in the programme are not visible in the figures for 1950, which increased by £100 million, exactly as had been expected originally. It is possible that some of the cuts (e.g. in power and transport) really did take effect, partly in 1949 and partly in 1950.[71] But it would be hard in retrospect to stigmatize them, like Douglas Jay in 1964, as 'excessively deflationary'.[72]

On the contrary, they lacked drama and appear to have fallen short of common expectations. They certainly made little impression on the City. By the end of October Dalton was commenting on 'the widespread mood in Whitehall and the City' that 'our reserves may not revive nor even hold up and that we shall have another and worse crisis in a few months'

70 For the discussion in Cabinet on 21 October see CM(49)61 in PRO CAB 128/16.
71 Dow (1964), p. 46n. The cuts in housing were revoked within six months and investment in new dwellings fell by no more in 1950 than in 1948 or 1949.
72 Jay in Rodgers (1964), p. 95.

time'.[73] The Bank and the Treasury began to agitate again for higher interest rates, provoking from Dalton the classic expression of post-war monetary doctrine: 'You can't allow higher interest rates while resisting higher wages rates.'[74] No fresh measures were taken. Nevertheless, by the end of the year the gold reserves had recovered strongly and the gold and dollar deficit had virtually ceased.

## Lessons of the 1949 episode

Before turning to examine how devaluation worked, there are some points in this narrative worth emphasizing.

1 Those who favoured devaluation did so for quite different reasons, and often for bad ones. Some wanted devaluation to improve the competitive position of British industry, although the current account had already reached balance in 1948. Some hoped that devaluation would improve the competitive position of British exports in dollar markets, or simply in the United States. Some saw no other way of resisting the speculative pressure against the pound. At the meeting of the Cabinet on 29 August at which the crucial decision to devalue was confirmed, Cripps himself accepted that: 'An atmosphere had . . . been created . . . in which the pound could not reach stability without devaluation.'

2 These arguments were usually advanced as if devaluation were a sufficient device for the purpose favoured, without regard to other necessary accompanying measures, or to less drastic and more effective ways of achieving the same purpose. In the end, the compelling factor in the situation was the lack of adequate reserves; but the corollary was not drawn that ways must be found of reinforcing reserves either at once or at least in time to withstand future pressure of the same kind. The rundown in reserves was attributed rather too readily to a falling-off in sterling area sales in the North American market, while the speculative movement of funds in anticipation of a devaluation of sterling was never analysed and the causes of it were little discussed.

3 The debate in Whitehall was dominated by short-run considerations when it was arguable that the decisive factors were long-term. It should have been obvious that at some point in the post-war years it would be necessary to reconsider the sterling–dollar rate of exchange. That point

73  Dalton's diary, entry for 30 October 1949. For the demoralization of the market in early November see p. 441.
74  Dalton's diary, entry for 14 December 1949.

was most likely to be reached when the first surge in British (and non-dollar) exports was beginning to lose momentum, or when exports had reached a level at which the prime requirement was not to expand the total but to effect a redistribution between dollar and non-dollar markets. In 1949 for the first time there was a margin in hand for this purpose. The surplus on trade with non-dollar markets, which accrued in the form of a balance of soft, inconvertible currencies, was balanced in 1948 by a deficit in trade with dollar countries that had to be discharged in dollars. The United Kingdom was thus in danger of running out of dollars as a result of settling its deficit in hard currencies and at the same time of running up equal or larger inconvertible balances in soft currencies through the sale of 'unrequited' exports. It was necessary to make the soft currencies harder and the hard currencies softer; there could be no more effective way of doing this than by making hard currencies dearer in terms of soft currencies. This in turn could best be brought about by devaluing sterling against the dollar and inducing other countries to devalue their currencies simultaneously.

4 From this point of view, the British balance of payments was largely irrelevant to the case for devaluation since what was in question was the value of the dollar rather than the value of the pound. The issue was not how to restore British trade to balance, since it already was in balance, but how to respond to the dollar shortage. At some stage this response would have to include currency realignments. It would, however, have been premature to embark on these when exports were rising strongly and there was nothing in hand to permit a *redirection* of exports to dollar markets.

5 Except in the papers prepared for the meeting of the Economic Policy Committee of 1 July and in the memoranda by the Economic Section, there does not seem to have been a careful weighing of the pros and cons in a submission by officials, much less at a meeting of ministers. In the last resort, it was the loss of reserves that settled the matter. Although the Economic Section had given thought to the choice of rate, it was largely a matter of accident that $2.80 rather than $3.00 to the pound was the rate selected. The significance of getting other countries to move simultaneously was rarely stressed. The measures to accompany devaluation were considered separately and almost as an afterthought (although two months later the Chancellor had so far forgotten the sequence of events that he insisted that the economy cuts were decided 'side by side' with devaluation).

6 Devaluation took place in spite of repeated declarations by the

Chancellor that he would not countenance it. This in itself hardly contributed to careful pre-planning. As in 1931, and in contrast to 1967, the Chancellor did not resign, although Cripps might have been thought more ready to do so than Callaghan.

7 Devaluation was delayed well beyond the point of maximum advantage: ministers were unwilling to contemplate action that would have had the advantage of surprise. As Cripps pointed out in his Mansion House speech on 4 October, 'Our action had been discussed, debated, and indeed almost expected, throughout the world. . . . Though the actual date and the degree of change in the sterling exchange rate may have taken people by surprise – no one can suggest that it was a matter suddenly sprung upon an unsuspecting world.' While this is substantially correct, it hardly lay with Cripps to say so, since those who *were* taken by surprise were those who took him at his word. The uncertainty that seemed to him to justify devaluation need never been created had he taken action earlier.

8 Devaluation was seen by Cripps as an act of foreign policy quite as much as of economic policy. He was constantly insisting that 'the relationship between the dollar and the sterling worlds is not one to which the United Kingdom alone can find a remedy. It is a problem', he told the House of Commons in July, 'in which our friends and partners in the USA and the Commonwealth are especially involved.' In this he was undoubtedly right: the problem was part of the post-war dollar problem and intimately concerned the United States and her trading partners in the Commonwealth and elsewhere. But to say this was not, as Cripps at times implied, to voice an objection to devaluation. For if that were so, it was necessary to come forward with some other equally powerful instrument for restructuring the world economy. And the most that was ever suggested by those who preferred a 'general settlement' to outright devaluation was trivial in comparison.

9 An important byproduct of devaluation was an improvement in USA–UK economic relations, which had become far less close than in the days of planning for the post-war world. Following the consultations by Hall and Wilson Smith in Washington, an economic minister was attached after devaluation to the British Embassy, with a member of the Economic Section on his staff. The minister was nominated alternately by the Bank of England and the Treasury; he reported to both and acted as vice deputy governor on the Boards of the IMF and IBRD. This not only allowed economic affairs to be handled more professionally by the Embassy, but also made for closer consultation and more satisfactory relations with the United States.

10 Finally, it is instructive to see who finally decided. Not Cripps, though he acquiesced. Not Bevin, though he had shown in 1931 that he had no inhibitions about devaluation. Not Morrison, though he favoured it. Not the Prime Minister, who had perhaps the oddest view of all as to what was involved. It was left to three young and relatively junior ministers – Gaitskell, Wilson and Jay – all of them economists, accidentally in a position to decide, and accidentally led by a minister (Gaitskell) of principle and determination who was not even a member of the Cabinet.

## The economic background

Let us now turn to the economic background to devaluation. In 1949 the British government continued to make extensive use of many of the controls introduced in wartime, adapted and sometimes strengthened for the purposes of peacetime economic management. Imports, for example, had to conform to a programme specifying the quantity and source of the imports to be purchased by the government or to be admitted for sale if purchased privately. For exports there was also a programme, consisting more of targets at which industry was encouraged to aim than of quantities whose sale in foreign markets was assured. The government's powers over the balance of payments were further supported by exchange control over payments in foreign currencies. All the members of the sterling area operated a system of exchange control which aimed at an enforced economy in the use of foreign exchange while leaving payments by one member of the area to another free of control.

There were of course protagonists of the free market who wanted to see the controls done away with: usually without much consideration of what would follow de-control. There were also sceptics, who thought that the controls leaked badly and traced the leaks to excess liquidity and over-full order books. There is no doubt that at the end of the war the money supply was greatly inflated in relation to normal requirements, and that the banks were seriously under-lent and awash with liquid funds while business was also highly liquid. It might be thought that this would quickly seep through into price inflation and into the consequences of excess liquidity with which the world has become familiar. In fact, however, the rise in prices, given what was happening elsewhere in the world and to import prices in particular, was comparatively modest. Bank deposits grew at roughly the same rate as prices over the period, i.e. at an average rate of 5 per cent, so that there was no contraction in real money balances. But in 1949 and again in 1950 the increase in bank deposits was only 1 per cent or less, and even in 1951 it was no more than 2.5 per cent. Throughout these years the rate on Treasury bills remained steady at around 0.5 per cent.

The government's neglect of monetary policy may have been misguided; the weight of excess liquidity, as Hawtrey argued, may have held down exports a little and reduced the effectiveness of some of the controls. But there is nothing in the statistical record to suggest that the controls did not bite or that excess liquidity was fatal to their use for the purposes intended by the government. What the controls could not do was to redress the imbalance between the dollar and the non-dollar world. Nothing but devaluation could do that.

'Underlying the whole situation', as the ECA study, *The Sterling Area*, explained later,

> was the fact that at the existing exchange rate [£1 = $4.03], the free market demand for goods and services from the Dollar Area was greatly in excess of what could be paid for. Only by the use of controls was it possible to limit the actual size of the current deficits – there was no natural tendency to equilibrium. Progress in the rearrangement of trade patterns and the narrowing of the dollar gap had been substantial, but the difficulties in making the necessary controls work effectively when market forces were pulling so strongly against them were great. Objections against the use of controls, too, were beginning to be strongly heard in some non-sterling countries.[75]

In this passage, the controls referred to relate to import and exchange controls operated within the sterling area, but the thesis holds true also of domestic controls designed to limit expenditure on dollar imports, and used by a much wider group of countries.

The pressures that led to devaluation are not very evident from the trade accounts for the United Kingdom or from the estimates of the current balance of payments (table 7.1). The annual figures are in no way suggestive of a crisis in 1949. Exports continued to rise, the deficit on visible trade continued to fall, and the current account remained close to balance.

Even if we concentrate exclusively on trade with the dollar area (table 7.2), there is little that makes 1949 look unusual. Clearly, there was a setback in exports, and the trend in both the visible deficit and the current account deficit was reversed. But the size of the changes was hardly enough of itself to smack of crisis.

75 Economic Co-operation Administration, *The Sterling Area* (1951), p. 75.

*Table 7.1*  British trade and payments 1946–52 (£m.)

|  |  | 1946 | 1947 | 1948 | 1949 | 1950 | 1951 | 1952 |
|---|---|---|---|---|---|---|---|---|
| Exports and | (a) | 960 | 1,180 | 1,639 | 1,863 | 2,261 | 2,735 | 2,769 |
| re-exports | (b) | 900 | 1,125 | 1,550 | 1,790 | 2,221 | 2,708 | 2,836 |
| Imports | (a) | 1,063 | 1,541 | 1,790 | 2,000 | 2,312 | 3,424 | 3,048 |
|  | (b) | 1,100 | 1,574 | 1,768 | 1,970 | 2,374 | 3,497 | 2,927 |
| Balance on visible | (a) | −103 | −361 | −151 | −137 | −51 | −689 | −279 |
| trade | (b) | −200 | −449 | −218 | −180 | −153 | −789 | −91 |
| Balance on invisibles | (a) | −127 | −20 | 177 | 136 | 358 | 320 | 442 |
|  | (b) | −250 | −226 | 98 | 110 | 382 | 268 | 261 |
| Balance on current | (a) | −230 | −381 | 26 | −1 | 307 | −369 | 163 |
| account | (b) | −450 | −675 | −120 | −70 | −229 | −521 | 170 |

(a) As estimated in 1980.
(b) As estimated at the time.

*Sources:* For (a), *Economic Trends Annual Supplement 1981*; for (b), *Economic Survey for 1947* (and later years to 1953).

*Table 7.2*  British trade with the dollar area 1946–52 (£m.)

|  | 1946 | 1947 | 1948 | 1949 | 1950 | 1951 | 1952 |
|---|---|---|---|---|---|---|---|
| Exports and re-exports | 100 | 130 | 196 | 195 | 324 | 393 | 410 |
| Imports | 390 | 567 | 406 | 442 | 439 | 742 | 606 |
| Surplus or deficit on visible trade | −290 | −437 | −210 | −247 | −115 | −349 | −196 |
| Surplus or deficit on invisibles | −11 | −73 | −42 | −49 | 27 | −87 | 23 |
| Total surplus or deficit | −301 | −510 | −252 | −296 | −88 | −436 | −173 |

*Sources:* For 1947–52, *Annual Abstract of Statistics for 1958*, table 275; for 1946, *United Kingdom Balance of Payments 1946 to 1953*, Cmd 8976.

The most the figures for the dollar deficit in table 7.3 suggest is a slight wobble in 1949 in the favourable trend between 1947 and 1950. Even the dollar deficit of the outer sterling area (table 7.3), of which so much was made at the time, was if anything less in 1949 than in 1948. There was a check to the gradual replacement of a deficit by a surplus, but it was not catastrophic. None of the main components to be financed in gold and

*Table 7.3* UK gold and dollar accounts 1946–54 (£m.)

| | 1946 | 1947 | 1948 | 1949 | 1950 | 1951 | 1954 |
|---|---|---|---|---|---|---|---|
| UK balance on current account with dollar area | −301 | −510 | −252 | −296 | −88 | −435 | −72 |
| Balance of rest of sterling area with dollar area | −73 | −306 | −65 | −54 | 170 | 102 | 27 |
| Gold sales to UK by sterling area | 82 | 84 | 55 | 68 | 100 | 78 | 138 |
| Net credit or debt from transactions with non-dollar countries and organizations | 46 | −260 | −95 | −89 | −12 | −67 | −23 |
| Capital transactions | 21 | −32 | −49 | 23 | 137 | −84 | 57 |
| Gold and dollar balance | −225 | −1,024 | −406 | −348 | 308 | −407 | 127 |
| Financed by: | | | | | | | |
| US/Canadian loans and ERP | 279 | 812 | 256 | 345 | 268 | 63 | — |
| Drawings on reserves | −54 | 152 | 55 | 3 | −575 | 344 | −87 |
| South African gold loan/IMF dollars | — | 60 | 95 | — | — | — | −40 |
| Gold and dollar balance | −225 | −1,024 | −406 | −348 | 308 | −407 | 127 |

Sources: *Annual Abstract of Statistics for 1958; United Kingdom Balance of Payments 1946 to 1953*, Cmd 8976.

dollars shown in table 7.3 changed very much between 1948 and 1949, nor did the total itself. The biggest single change is due to a special transaction unconnected with events in 1949: the gold loan of £80 million by South Africa in 1948. Moreover, what stands out in both years as the biggest single factor in the deficit to be financed is the United Kingdom's own deficit on current account. And if one looks ahead to 1954 to see what sustainable pattern might emerge in the 1950s, it was in this item that the biggest change fell to be made.

But the annual figures do not tell the whole story: there were large fluctuations within the year. The gold and dollar reserves, for example, fell from £471 million at the end of March to £406 million at the end of June, to £372 million on 20 August and to £330 million by 18 September – a fall of 30 per cent within six months. The movement in the dollar deficit from quarter to quarter (figure 7.1) tells a similar story.

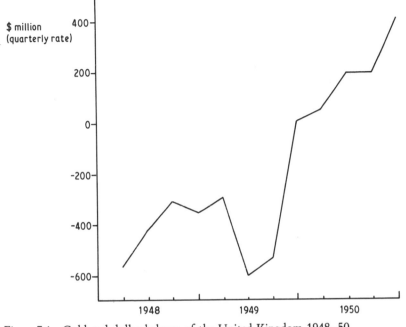

*Figure 7.1*   Gold and dollar balance of the United Kingdom 1948–50

*Source: United Kingdom Balance of Payments 1946 to 1953* (Cmd 8976).

How are these figures to be reconciled with the comparative stability of the annual totals? Most of the discussion at the time laid emphasis on the depressed state of the US market between the spring and autumn of 1949.[76] The recession, although short-lived, had serious repercussions on imports of materials from the sterling area, especially rubber, wool, jute and tin, reducing both the volume and the price paid for them. Taking these four commodities together, the fall in sterling area exports to the

76 Between October 1948 and June 1949 the US index of industrial production (season-ally adjusted) fell by 10 per cent. Stock-building began to decline in the autumn of 1948 and imports fell off from the third quarter onwards. The fall in the value of imports between the third quarter of 1948 and the low point a year later was $1.5 billion or over 14 per cent.

*Table 7.4*  Sterling area trade with the United States 1948–50 ($m. per quarter)

|  | Sterling area exports to USA | Sterling area imports from USA | Balance of trade | UK imports from USA | Rest of sterling area exports to USA | Excess of RSA exports over UK imports |
|---|---|---|---|---|---|---|
| 1948 average | 346 | 501 | −155 | 161 | 274 | 113 |
| 1949 (I) | 345 | 504 | −159 | 170 | 297 | 127 |
| (II) | 281 | 561 | −280 | 222 | 217 | −5 |
| (III) | 231 | 413 | −182 | 155 | 162 | 52 |
| (IV) | 297 | 385 | −88 | | 252 | |
| 1950 (I) | 326 | 348 | −22 | 122 | 280 | 158 |
| (II) | 361 | 318 | 43 | | | |
| (III), (IV) | 457 | 321 | 136 | 140 | 352 | 212 |

*Source:* Based on Economic Co-operation Administration, *The Sterling Area* (1951), table 36 and p. 77.

United States in 1949 was about 25 per cent, or $150 million.[77] This, though substantial, seems hardly sufficient to account for the crisis. From the annual figures we may turn to the fluctuations from quarter to quarter in the sterling area's trade with the United States (table 7.4). Estimates are given in the ECA study of the sterling area published in 1951, and although they are only approximations they indicate the magnitude of the swings during the year.[78] It will be seen that the trade deficit of the sterling area nearly doubled in the second quarter and improved thereafter quarter by quarter until, by the middle of 1950, the deficit was running $200 million per quarter below the 1948 average. The experience of the second quarter of 1949 stands out as exceptional.

It is not possible to assign the deterioration in the second quarter with any precision to its various sources, but it is clear that it cannot all be attributed to the trade deficit with the United States. The rise in the dollar deficit in the second quarter was $300 million compared with the first quarter, and $200 million compared with the quarterly average for 1948. Even if we take the latter basis of comparison, the rise in the trade deficit of the sterling area with the United States (table 7.4) by $125 million per

77  *Economic Survey of Europe in 1949* (Economic Commission for Europe, 1950), p. 96.
78  Economic Co-operation Administration, *The Sterling Area* (1951), p. 76.

quarter does not account for much more than half the change in the total dollar deficit of $200 million.

To some extent, the higher deficit in the second quarter was foreseen. In a brief for the Chancellor before the meeting of the Economic Policy Committee on 17 June, Sam Goldman (in OF Stats) pointed out that the Treasury had been expecting the deficit to increase since early April because of heavier expenditure on food and materials (for stockpiling), the usual seasonal reduction in the dollar surplus of the colonies, bigger losses to Belgium and Switzerland, and an unfavourable turn in the working of the South African Loan Agreement. April had been in line with the target, but in May there was an overshoot of $80 million, divided in roughly equal terms between the United Kingdom, the colonial territories and the rest of the sterling area. It is rather remarkable that so small an addition to the drain on the reserves should so quickly have produced an exchange crisis, and is one more illustration of the inadequacy of the reserves in the post-war years.

In addition to the special factors mentioned in the brief, we can distinguish four different elements in the deterioration during the second quarter.

1 A large part of the increase in the dollar deficit in the second quarter – about $60 million – was due to a 38 per cent increase above the 1948 level in British import expenditures in the United States. Some of this corresponded to the stockpiling of food and raw materials already referred to. Since there was never any intention of maintaining this level of expenditure over the year, some falling back was to be expected and did occur. In addition, the alarm generated by the growing deficit led the British government to cut its import programme, and this reinforced the fall.

2 The check to activity in the United States reacted on imports, particularly of raw materials, and on commodity prices, so that sales of materials such as rubber, tin and wool to the United States were depressed on both scores. Imports into the United States from the outer sterling area fell by $80 million in the second quarter and by a further $55 million in the third. When business conditions improved later in the year, inventories of materials were built up again and the movement was strengthened by a rise in the dollar price of most of the commodities supplied. Full recovery to the 1948 level did not, however, take place until the first half of 1950.

3 The expectation of devaluation led to deferments of purchases payable in sterling and of actual disbursements in sterling. It also encouraged a corresponding acceleration of imports from the dollar area and the

immediate discharge of dollar obligations. This speculative element must have influenced the purchases of materials referred to above, delaying them before devaluation and accelerating them thereafter. British exports to the United States may also have suffered prior to devaluation, if only through delays in payment. American companies in London were known to be taking no chances in transferring their profits to dollar accounts as fast as possible. The fall in gold sales to the United Kingdom in the middle quarters of 1949, by 27 per cent and 20 per cent respectively below the 1948 level, reflects the same influences. Since gold sales were much the same in 1948 as in 1949, it is natural to suspect that the distortion in the pattern of sales over the year was associated with the expectation of devaluation that developed from the spring onwards.

4 Finally, one has to take account of all the government measures designed to reduce the drain on the reserves and of devaluation itself. The American and Canadian governments, for example, had undertaken in September to review their stockpiling programme for tin and rubber so as to enlarge the field for imports. The Commonwealth governments had agreed to cut their dollar outgoings by 25 per cent from the 1948 levels. The British government had also made various cuts in order to improve its dollar deficit. Some of these measures began to take effect well before the end of the year. They are not likely to have been much reinforced at that stage by the impact of devaluation on trade flows, but the reversal of the speculative factors referred to under point 3 must by then have been at work.

It is not easy to demonstrate the relative importance of these four factors. But the evidence suggests that the speculative element was probably at least as important as the check to domestic activity in the United States.[79] It is significant, for example, that, although the trade deficit of the sterling area with the United States fell by $100 million in the third quarter, the loss of reserves up to 18 September was higher than in the second quarter, and in the last 30 days before devaluation amounted to £42 million (compared with £65 million in the whole of the second quarter). Although a decision to devalue had been taken before the outflow reached such proportions, the loss of reserves played a decisive part, and to that extent devaluation was a capitulation to market opinion and another of many demonstrations of the weakness of government in the face of an exchange crisis.

79  In retrospect, the Treasury came to a similar conclusion. See 'The Dollar Crisis 1949' memorandum by the Chancellor of the Exchequer, 11 January 1950, EPC(50)13, in PRO CAB 134/225.

It was the perception, not always very clear, that devaluation was a necessary ingredient in the restoration of international equilibrium that fuelled speculative pressure; and it was the speculative pressure that in the end compelled devaluation. But if it had not been for the additional uncertainty generated by the mild depression of 1949, it is doubtful whether the pressure would have been sufficient to force devaluation in 1949, and it might have been possible to refrain from action before the outbreak of the Korean War in June 1950. Thereafter, to judge from the frequency with which revaluation was urged, the issue might not have arisen for some considerable time.

## The impact of devaluation

The war in Korea began nine months after devaluation and swept through the world economy like a tornado. World prices, international trade and payments, national budgets – all were pulled into new orbits. By the time the storm died down the devaluation of sterling was a distant, almost forgotten, event and its effects hard to trace with certainty in the new pattern of trade flows.

The effects of devaluation must be judged against the expectations entertained in advance. To those who looked to devaluation primarily as a means of stopping the dollar drain, it justified itself in the increase in the gold and dollar reserves by 70 per cent in the first nine months and the still larger increase in the nine months that followed. Those who stressed the need to improve Britain's competitive position could claim that most of the advantage conferred by a 30 per cent devaluation outlasted the Korean War. Between 1949 and, say, 1954 the American GDP price deflator rose by 13.3 per cent while in Britain it rose by 16.4 per cent; nearly the whole of the cost advantage remained for some time. Even those who looked to devaluation to pave the way for a surplus on the current account of the balance of payments could take satisfaction from the outcome: a surplus in all but one of the five years 1950–4 and a cumulative surplus of well over £500 million.

But what of the hope that devaluation would lay the basis for a new relationship between the sterling and the dollar worlds? Some evidence of the change after 1949 appears in table 7.3, which shows a fall in the UK deficit on current account with the dollar area in 1950 by £200 million and a slightly larger improvement in the dollar balance of the rest of the sterling area. The first of these changes was reversed in the Korean War but reappeared when the war was over. The improvement in the dollar

*Figure 7.2*  British trade with dollar and sterling areas 1948–54

Sources: *Annual Abstract of Statistics for 1953*, tables 211, 212, and *1958*, tables 267, 268.

balance of the rest of the sterling area was not sustained, but after 1950 there remained a small and consistent surplus where in the years prior to 1950 there had been a consistent deficit.

Another way of bringing out the change that took place is to compare trade with the dollar area and trade with the sterling area (figure 7.2). The most notable feature of this comparison is the sharp change in 1950: the proportion of British exports sold in dollar markets rose abruptly, and the proportion of imports from dollar markets fell equally abruptly. The reaction in 1951 presumably reflects the disturbance to trade and prices brought about by the Korean War. But if one takes an average of the three following years (1952–4) and compares it with the average for 1948–9, there is a striking shift in both ratios in exactly the way one would expect: up from 19.5 per cent in 1948–9 to 28.2 per cent in 1952–4 for exports, and down from 60.0 to 44.6 per cent for imports.

It is true that were other factors in the shift quite unconnected with devaluation. Sterling area sources of supply were recovering from wartime dislocation and post-war difficulties, so that there was an upward trend in the area's trade, not only external but also internal. In 1946 and 1947 supplies from the sterling area to the British market had been exceeded by supplies from the dollar area but by 1950 were twice as large. On the other hand, one might have expected the British authorities to take a more relaxed attitude to imports costing dollars as their reserves improved, and this may help to explain the sharp rise in the proportion of dollar imports in 1951 and the later recovery in 1954–7. However, discrimination did not extend to dollar exports, and the continuing climb in the proportion of British exports reaching dollar markets is evidence of the durability of the competitive advantage brought by devaluation.[80]

British trade, however, is only half the story: the change in parities went far beyond sterling and the sterling area. In Western Europe, for example, only Sweden and Switzerland abstained from devaluing in September, Sweden having already devalued by 30 per cent the previous year. Denmark, France, Ireland, the Netherlands and Norway all devalued by 30 per cent and Germany by 20 per cent. Belgium, Italy and Portugal made more modest devaluations while Austria, Greece and Iceland made larger ones. The rest of the world also took the opportunity to make devaluations against the dollar: even the Canadian dollar was devalued by 9 per cent. The trade-weighted devaluation of sterling may be estimated at approximately 9 per cent, too – rather larger on the import side and smaller on the export side. Thus accompanying devaluations in the first year played a larger role than in either 1931, when the ratio of effective to nominal devaluations was approximately 0.5 or 1967, when that ratio exceeded 0.95.

The net result might have been expected to be a marked check to the growth of US exports and a spurt in US imports. The record, as shown in table 7.5, bears out that this occurred in 1950 although the simultaneous recovery in economic activity also contributed powerfully to the change.

Even if we allow for a downward trend in US exports as Europe recovered and an upward trend in US imports with the renewed growth in GNP, the size of the adjustments on both sides of the account in 1950 is striking. But the very speed with which they followed devaluation makes it doubtful how far they were caused by it. In the first half of 1949 exports were running (on a seasonally adjusted basis) at $17.9 billion per annum

80 Allowance should, however, be made for the increase in American GNP by 13 per cent between 1949 and 1951, after a growth of only 1 per cent in the previous two years.

*Table 7.5*   US trade and national income 1948–54

|  | Exports from USA (including services) ($b.) | Imports into USA (including services) ($b.) | Current balance of USA ($b.) | US GNP at constant prices (1948 = 100) |
|---|---|---|---|---|
| 1948 | 16.88 | 10.37 | 6.51 | 100.0 |
| 1949 | 15.86 | 9.64 | 6.22 | 98.9 |
| 1950 | 13.91 | 12.01 | 1.90 | 105.7 |
| 1951 | 18.93 | 15.09 | 3.84 | 112.4 |
| 1954 | 18.00 | 16.01 | 1.99 | 113.6 |

*Source: National Income and Product Accounts of the USA, 1929–74.*

and had already fallen to $15.5 billion in the third quarter (i.e. before devaluation). In each of the next three quarters they remained below $13.5 billion and rose above $14.0 billion only in the final quarter of 1950. Imports of goods and services fluctuated between $9 and $10 billion per annum in the five quarters between the beginning of 1949 and April 1950, but had risen from $9.5 billion in the last quarter of 1949 to $10.6 billion in the second quarter of 1950 and $13.4 billion in the third. It would seem from these quarterly movements that most of the turn-around in 1950 that can be disentangled from the effects of the Korean War came on the import side. Some of the rise in imports can be attributed to the recovery in economic activity in the United States in the winter of 1949–50. But it is not unreasonable to treat devaluation as contributing to the rise, particularly when one finds it continuing after hostilities had ceased. Making all allowances, the reduction in the current surplus of the United States after 1949 was materially assisted by the series of devaluations in 1949.

Thus whether we start from the composition of British trade or from the American current account, there is evidence of a change in the balance between the dollar and the non-dollar world that persisted into the 1950s and was an indispensable element in post-war reconstruction. From the British point of view the adjustment was by no means painless. Although in trade-weighted terms, the devaluation was under 10 per cent, import prices rose between June 1949 and June 1950 by 17 per cent while export prices rose by only 5 per cent. The shift in the terms of trade represented a real cost even if it was small by comparison with the much larger shift that followed the outbreak of the Korean War.

Finally, what of the danger that costs and prices would rise so as to extinguish the competitive gains of devaluation and raise the spectre, so much feared in 1931, of a *dégringolade* of the exchanges? In spite of the rise in import prices and the relaxed stance of monetary policy, the cost of living was remarkably steady. In the year to September 1949 retail prices had risen by 3.2 per cent; in the year that followed the rise was only 2.0 per cent. Food prices, which had risen by 8.8 per cent in the year before devaluation, rose only by a further 4.5 per cent in the following year. The government kept well within its bargain with the trade unions, who had agreed to hold wages steady if the cost of living rose by under 5 per cent. The trade unions, for their part, were almost equally successful during the first post-devaluation year. Basic hourly rates for men rose by 1 per cent and although hourly earnings, measured in the biennial October survey, increased rather faster, there was no acceleration compared with the previous year, the rise being limited to 3.5 per cent.

If there was no substantial inflation of prices, this was not because of a tighter fiscal stance. Neither public expenditure nor revenue changed much in 1950, and the pressure of demand, as reflected in the level of unemployment, was also stationary. The improvement in the trade balance was at best a modest one, and the improvement over the year, as happened again in 1967, was heavily concentrated on invisibles. This may not have been quite what the advocates of devaluation would have predicted, but in other respects they had good reason to be satisfied with the way things worked out. In particular, they could point to the absence of a faster rate of inflation and the shift in exports from sterling to dollar markets. The politicians for their part could take comfort that they had largely avoided the cuts in public expenditure that their advisers kept insisting were indispensable.

# Chapter eight

# REARMAMENT, 1950-1

After the rapid rundown in defence expenditure in the first two years after the war, the size of the armed forces continued to contract until the middle of 1950 when the numbers serving in the Army, Navy and Air Force all reached a minimum. In spite of the cold war, the coup d'état in Czecho-Slovakia, the Berlin blockade, the change of régime in China, the atom bomb in the USSR and other disturbing developments, the reduction in the armed forces over the three years 1947–50 came to nearly half. Defence expenditure, which had reached a peak of over £5000 million in 1944, dropped to about £750 million in 1948–50. When the *Economic Survey for 1950* appeared in March 1950, defence was given a single paragraph indicating that in the coming year a further reduction was planned in the size of the armed forces although some increase was expected in the numbers in industry engaged on defence work because of the exhaustion of wartime stocks of equipment.

The outbreak of the Korean War produced an abrupt change in these plans, reflected in the prominence given to rearmament in the *Economic Survey for 1951*. 'The execution of a greatly enlarged and accelerated rearmament programme', said the *Survey*, 'has now become the first objective of the government's economic policy'.[1] It was proposed to double defence expenditure within the space of two years when it already absorbed 7 per cent of GNP.[2] The demands on production included in the

---

1 *Economic Survey for 1951*, Cmd 8195, April 1951, para. 7.
2 The actual increase in this proportion did not carry it above $10\frac{1}{2}$ per cent in 1952.

total, largely on the metal and engineering industries, would expand four and a half times by 1953–4.[3]

The change began at the official level. In a visit to Washington at the beginning of June, Plowden and Hall had been struck by American comments on the deteriorating international situation, the lack of confidence in Western Europe's will to defend itself, the evidence of hostility to the West in South-East Asia, the tendency to trim and jump on the bandwagon of the winning side. They concluded that there was need for greater concentration on defence and that, in comparison, the economic and commercial issues were now secondary. Three weeks later came the invasion of South Korea. At a meeting of senior Treasury officials on 27 June, Hall found himself alone in expecting a vigorous American reaction. He took the view – which proved correct within a matter of hours – that the United States would not acquiesce in the overthrow of its whole foreign policy. US intervention was likely to prove a turning-point in post-war history.

Next day the Defence Committee authorized the C.-in-C. Far East to put his fleet at the disposal of General MacArthur and to urge collaboration on all Commonwealth countries. At this stage no longer-term action appears to have been contemplated either by ministers or by the Chiefs of Staff. Plowden and Hall agreed, however, that the time had come for an increase in defence expenditure. This would be possible without overloading the engineering industries on which the main burden would fall. On 11 July at a meeting with Edward Bridges, Norman Brook and senior Treasury officials, Hall emphasized the dangers in a situation in which the United States had taken up a firm position from which it could not retreat so that, unless the USSR backed down, there was every chance of a major collision.[4] He pointed also to the urgent need to build up stocks and add to strategic reserves rather than allow them to run down. These views had some effect and it was agreed to review the position on stock-building.[5] An approach by Hall to Rowlands at the Ministry of Supply had already set on foot an inquiry into what the engineering industries could do without trenching on exports.

3 'Economic Implications of the Defence Proposals': memorandum by the Chancellor of the Exchequer, 19 January 1951 (CP(51)20 in PRO CAB 129/44).
4 Hall doubted whether the anxieties felt by himself and Plowden were shared by his official colleagues.
5 The follow-up to Hall's warning on stocks was leisurely and inadequate. See minute of 25 March 1951 by R. L. Hall to R. W. B. Clarke on 'The Fall in Stocks' in PRO T 230/177 ('The Dollar Drain'). Hall was pointing out early in August 1950 that the United States would look with less disfavour on an increase in stocks of goods than one in foreign exchange reserves in deciding whether to continue Marshall Aid.

While the possibilities of expanding the defence programme were being pursued at the official level, the United States approached the United Kingdom and other NATO governments on 26 July for information both as to what additional expenditure they proposed to undertake on their own and what larger programmes would be physically possible with American help. There had been an earlier approach in March 1949 when the five leading NATO powers were invited to submit lists of their deficiencies in military equipment and requests for aid under the Mutual Defence Assistance Programme. On that occasion the requests submitted by the United Kingdom for the year to 30 June 1950 had totalled £232 million and in February 1950 there had been a further bid for £302 million in respect of military aid in 1951–2. But British requests had been scaled down severely and only 70 B29 aircraft (worth about £50 million) had so far been received.[6]

The British government was as disturbed as the American by the latest evidence of Soviet expansionism. There was no disagreement among the ministers and senior officials concerned on the need to join with the Americans in an immediate effort of rearmament and, as by far the strongest country in Western Europe, to give a clear military lead to America's allies in NATO.[7] Rearmament on any scale, however, carried obvious dangers to the balance of payments and the government felt able to approve a programme making full use of Britain's potential only if assured of American help. Although the enquiries received officially from the Americans involved no commitment, Attlee had received informal assurances from the US Ambassador, Lewis Douglas, to the effect that the United States would 'pick up the cheque'.[8] The Cabinet felt justified in assuming that at least the balance-of-payments effects of rearmament would be underwritten. The assumption proved to be unwarranted.

Before the Cabinet met to consider its reply on 1 August additions had already been authorized to the programme for the next few years totalling £200 million, of which half consisted of an increase in the pay and numbers of the armed forces and half of orders for urgently needed items of military equipment (see table 8.1). A further £137 million was to be spent over four years on civil defence. They were now advised that it would be

6  Minute of 17 October 1952 in Foreign Office file no. UR 1027/2, in PRO FO 371/82983.
7  About 90 per cent of NATO defence production came from the United States, the United Kingdom and France.
8  Note of meeting between the Prime Minister and the American Ambassador on 24 July 1950, in PRO T 237/82.

*Table 8.1*  Defence expenditure 1950–3 (£m.)

|  | 1950/1 | 1951/2 | 1952/3 | 1953/4 | Total 1951–3 |
|---|---|---|---|---|---|
| *Programme at end of 1949* | 780 | 780 | 780 | 780 | 2,340 |
| Additions by 31 July 1950 | | | | | |
|   Pay and numbers | 30 | 70 | (70) | (70) | (100) |
|   Defence production | 10 | 30 | 30 | 30 | (100) |
|   Civil defence | — | 20 | 30 | (40) | (50) |
| *Programme at 31 July 1950* | 820 | 900 | (840) | (850) | 2,590 |
| Additional programmes agreed on | | | | | |
|   1 August | 4 | 175 | 293 | 342 | 810 |
| *Programme at 3 August 1950* | 824 | 1,075 | 1,133 | 1,192 | 3,400 |
| Maximum with own resources | | 950 | 950 | 950 | 2,850 |
| *Programme at 12 September 1950* | | (1,100) | (1,200) | (1,300) | 3,600 |
| Chiefs of Staff on 30 October | | 1,187 | 1,289 | 1,402 | 3,879 |
| *Programme at 19 January 1951* | | | | | |
| Fighting services | 830 | 1,250 | 1,532 | 1,694 | 4,475 |
| Civil defence | 5 | 30 | 65 | 85 | 180 |
| Total (excluding stockpiling) | 835 | 1,280 | 1,597 | 1,779 | 4,655 |
|   Of which | | | | | |
|   Production (incl. civil defence) | 204 | 464 | 709 | 881 | 2,054 |
|   Works and building | 82 | 129 | 144 | 119 | 392 |
| Strategic stockpiling | 30 | 160 | 180 | 106 | 446 |
| Grand total | 865 | 1,440 | 1,776 | 1,885 | 5,101[a] |
| Actual *at current prices*[b] | 777 | 1,110 | 1,404 | 1,365 | 3,879 |

*Sources:* EPC(50)52 in PRO CAB 134/225; EPC(50)76 in PRO CAB 134/226; CP(50)181 in PRO CAB 129/41; CM(50)52 in PRO CAB 128/18; CP(50)248 in PRO CAB 129/42; CP(51)20 in PRO CAB 129/44; *Annual Abstract of Statistics for 1958*, table 299.

a  This total excludes £65 million for machine tools over and above £50 million already included.
b  Excluding strategic stockpiling.

physically possible to add a further £800 million to the programme over the three financial years beginning in April 1951. This yielded a total for those three years of £3400 million. Instead of asking the United States for the whole of the £800 million which could, with financial support, be added to the approved programme it was agreed to accept the Chancellor's proposal to ask for half the increase from the pre-Korea programme of £2300 million to the maximum physically possible of £3400 million, i.e. £550 million (see table 8.1). On this basis the United Kingdom would be representing £950 million a year as the limit of what it could do on its own. The £550 million would cover the cost of additional imports and provide compensation for any sacrifice of exports, so protecting the balance of payments.[9] The new programme, prepared and approved within about a week, was announced on 3 August without any formal assurance from the Americans that they would be able to provide the aid requested.[10]

The press announcement described the programme as the largest that was practicable within the period envisaged without restoring direction of labour, requisitioning of factories or arranging for the building of additional industrial capacity.[11] To embark on the programme would slow down the recovery of an economy already fully stretched; and a larger programme would be inconsistent with the view of the US government that the continuation of recovery, although perhaps at a slower rate, was indispensable to the immediate aim of greater military strength. How far the British government would go in carrying out the programme would depend on the amount of American aid forthcoming.[12]

The calculations on which the increased programme was based were the work of the Economic Section and Central Statistical Office rather than of the Ministry of Defence, as was later to become clear when the programme continued to expand. Looking at what actually happened (and allowing for the sharp rise in prices), the figures of defence expenditure were close to what in the end proved possible and the claim for £550 million, had it been met, would have covered the current account deficit of £60 million over the three years 1951–3 and left a surplus of £160 million a year, which, in the circumstances, would have been very satisfactory.

Discussions with the United States were, however, in a state of extreme confusion. In Washington, the ECA claimed the power to dispose of Mutual Aid Defence Funds and were carrying on conversations in Paris as well. The NATO deputies operated independently in London. All sorts of

9  CM(50)50 of 25 July and CM(50)52 of 1 August (PRO CAB 128/18) and CP(50)181 of 31 July 1950 (PRO CAB 129/41). The Treasury had originally put the British share at £900 million, rather arbitrarily, until Cripps explained to Gaitskell that he had meant £950 million (Williams (ed.) (1983), p. 194).

10  As Gaitskell explained on 14 September to the House of Commons (H. C. Deb., 5th ser., vol. 478, cols 1126–1132). He did not, of course, mention any figure for the amount of aid requested.

11  Keesing's Contemporary Archives, 4 August 1950.

12  ibid.

other discussions were taking place on the side. It was not clear where the seat of authority was, what assurances the United States had offered and how far the American government was committed when the last word lay with Congress.

At the beginning of September a crisis was precipitated by a bombshell from the State Department. It appeared that US aid to NATO of $4 billion would be used almost exclusively for the supply of finished items from the United States. Only $475 million would be available for direct aid, mainly in the form of materials and components.[13] Even this sum was conditional on defence expenditure by European countries far in excess of what had hitherto been pledged. Instead of receiving the balance-of-payments support on which she was counting, British would receive at most one-sixth of the small total available.

The changed American position on burden-sharing presented ministers with a twofold dilemma. If they said that they could get little or no help from the United States it would be bad for relations between the two countries; but if they were not free to say this, how was it possible to explain the gap in arrangements for the finance of rearmament? If the impact of rearmament on the economy was said to be small, this would throw away the case to be made to the US; but if it were represented as severe it would alarm the government's supporters, already disturbed by the rising cost of living.

Robert Hall's recommendation was to go ahead with the programme but insist to the United States that it was indispensable to receive more help than was now proposed. His suggestion that it might be possible to get by with £350 million rather than £550 million did not satisfy Plowden who saw no justification for the lower figure and was uneasy at the way in which the external balance was being sacrificed. The Cabinet on 8 September took the same line, rounding on their official advisers as wildly optimistic and neglectful of the balance of payments.

Nevertheless, as the situation in Korea became more desperate, with only one beachhead remaining to the UN forces at the end of August when the first British troops arrived, the Cabinet decided at the same meeting on a further increase in the defence programme to £3600 million and extended conscription from eighteen months to two years. This, said Attlee, was 'the maximum we can do by expanding and using to the full

13  In the end Congress voted $6 billion for North Atlantic Defence in 1951/2 of which $5 billion was for military equipment and $1 billion for economic aid.

our industrial capacity without resorting to the drastic expedients of a war economy'.

Before the end of September it had been made clear by the Americans that there was no chance of their paying £550 million or any fixed sum. Instead they proposed to try to find what sums they could pay on account in various *ad hoc* ways and supplement these on the basis of a formula for fair shares applicable to all NATO countries (including the United States).[14] It was not easy to reconcile such a procedure with the Cabinet's stipulation for a fixed sum payable in advance, estimated at £550 million. Gaitskell, however, who was being groomed for the Chancellorship, squared the Prime Minister and the Foreign Secretary and set off for Washington on 6 October to settle the method of assessing contributions to NATO. He accepted – although it came as news to the Prime Minister two months later – that the bid for £550 million should lapse and that it would be necessary to rely on the United States to make something available on account and provide additional aid under the agreed formula. He also suggested that higher payments might be made to the United Kingdom for the support of American armed forces in Britain and that orders for military equipment might be placed there. A year later, in November 1951, it was noted that nothing had come of these suggestions.[15]

In the Washington discussions the UK representatives pointed out that the original American initiative had been on a bilateral footing. The United Kingdom had been asked for an estimate of the 'financial aid that would be required to offset the adverse effect on our economy of the diversion of productive resources to defence purposes'. Now the approach was multilateral and in terms of sharing the burden. The United States agreed that the initial impact of an expanded defence programme would inevitably fail to correspond with an equitable sharing of the total burden. Adjustments would be necessary, taking the form of transfers across the exchanges. But the countries in receipt of the sums transferred were not in their view the recipients of *aid* – the transfers would be merely 'the

14  This was referred to as the Nitze formula. The memorandum setting it out is in CP(50)247 in PRO CAB 129/42.

15  Minute to Prime Minister (Churchill) by Chancellor of the Exchequer (Butler), 6 November 1951, in PRO PREM 11/141. The Americans did, however, meet the dollar cost ($84 million) of items included in the first £200 million of additional orders placed by the UK government (mainly for machine tools) and offered to place some orders for equipment in the UK. This offer, amounting to $28 million, was declined.

practical expression of the carrying out of a joint effort'.[16] Lengthy discussions ensued as to the machinery for settling what transfers should be made. The machinery proved to be cumbersome, slow and unproductive.

As October wore on, the defence programme continued to expand. At the end of the month the Ministry of Defence put in a programme totalling £3879 million, well above the agreed limit of £3600 million, arguing that with an allowance for slippage expenditure would work out within the limit.[17] The Chiefs of Staff, however, were pressing for more and were soon calling for the completion of the £3600 million programme in two years instead of three (by December 1952 instead of March 1954). Thereafter they wanted to meet the requirements of the NATO Medium-Term Defence Plan which assigned as the British share a total of £6000 million.[18] Shinwell, while in Washington in October, was understood to have given his approval to this part of the Plan, without Cabinet authority, 'as an ultimate objective though not as an immediately practical project'.[19]

Meanwhile the military situation had changed again. By the end of September the North Korean army had been driven back beyond the 38th parallel with heavy losses. General MacArthur, in command of the UN forces, then advanced into North Korea and this brought in the Chinese who, on 24 November, attacked across the Yalu River, and routed the UN troops. British fears of a major extension of hostilities were aggravated by a statement in which President Truman appeared to be threatening the use of the atomic bomb against China. Attlee decided to intervene personally with Truman and flew to Washington on 3 December. His objectives were primarily military and political but in view of the acute shortages of materials limiting British production, he took the opportunity also to press for international control of raw materials on the model of the Combined Boards of World War II.

The Americans called for still higher – much higher – expenditure on

16 US *aide mémoire* of 3 October 1950, UK memorandum of 19 October 1950 ('Sharing the Defence Burden under the North Atlantic Treaty') and minute of meeting at the State Department between Gaitskell and Spofford on 12 October 1950, in PRO FO 371/86933. For Gaitskell's own account see his diary, Williams (ed.) (1983), pp. 204–11, 296–9.

17 Annex IV to CP(50)248, 30 October 1950, in PRO CAB 129/42.

18 'Defence Programmes 1951–54', memorandum by Chiefs of Staff, CP(51)16, 12 January 1951, in PRO CAB 129/44.

19 Gaitskell's diary, Williams (ed.) (1983), p. 298n; Jay (1980), p. 204. According to Lord Roberthall, Shinwell also asked for £1000 million in arms from the United States although in July he had seen no possibility of using so much.

defence. The Prime Minister concluded that this could no longer be avoided and gave his support, on his return, to an acceleration of the defence programme. He told the Cabinet on 18 December that the US Secretary of State, addressing the NATO Council of Ministers in Brussels that day, would be asking his European allies to double their pre-Korean rate of defence expenditure. The US government was already committed to spending nearly $42 billion in the fiscal year 1950–1 and was now aiming to complete its ambitious Medium-Term Defence Plan in two years instead of three.[20] NATO's plans for an integrated military force stationed in Europe with Eisenhower as Supreme Commander were announced immediately after the Brussels meeting and a Defence Production Board was set up to co-ordinate production in the member countries.

Bevin was authorized by the Cabinet on 18 December to announce (to the NATO Council) the government's agreement to some acceleration of the defence programme but without giving any new total in place of £3600 million. The Prime Minister suggested that it would be best on this occasion to begin by considering what was needed, what was physically possible and what the cost would be before agreeing to an enlarged programme.[21] No general financial assistance was to be expected from the United States. Public opinion, said the Prime Minister, had greeted the termination of Marshall Aid with relief and would not welcome a new form of dependence on US aid.[22] But as Gaitskell explained in the subsequent debate in February, although the programme was not contingent on American aid as the previous programme had been, the NATO burden-sharing exercise had still to be carried out, so that it was too soon to say what aid in the form of equipment or dollars might yet be received.[23]

An increase in the defence programme from £3600 million to £4700 million for the three years 1951–4 was agreed on 25 January 1951.[24] Again the decision was taken largely on the basis of a paper submitted to the

20  CM(50)87, 18 December 1950, in PRO CAB 128/19.
21  ibid.
22  ibid.
23  *H. C. Deb.*, 5th ser., vol. 484, col. 661, 14 February 1951. See also Gaitskell's diary, Williams (ed.) (1983), pp. 296–9. In his paper to the Cabinet on 19 January 1951 Gaitskell said that the chances that any general financial compensation would be received under mutual aid arrangements remained highly uncertain.
24  CM(51)7 and 8, 25 January 1951, in PRO CAB 128/19.

Cabinet by the Chancellor[25] who found himself obliged to make the running in the absence of the Minister of Defence and the Foreign Secretary.[26] He explained that the new programme was £500 million higher than the original (end-1949) programme in the first year (1951–2), £800 million higher in the second (1952–3) and £1000 million higher in the third (1953–4). Whereas the September 1950 programme would have required a diversion of, at first, 200,000 workers and, later, 375,000 workers to defence the scale of diversion would now be about 650,000. This would mean a considerable upheaval. The economy was already under strain because world rearmament had caused a sharp adverse turn in the terms of trade and serious shortages of key materials, including coal and steel.[27] Rearmament would now threaten exports and investment through the demands it made on the metal and textile industries. While some weakening in the balance of payments was inevitable, the most that could be afforded was to let the current account surplus be eaten up. Apart from this, the necessary resources would have to be found largely by reducing consumption since any substantial cut in investment would impair future productivity. How the transfer was to be brought about was left rather vague except that some of the capacity making durable consumer goods would be turned over to munitions and some orders for equipment would be placed with foreign suppliers. The supply of manu-factured consumer goods would be down by 5 per cent at the end of the programme's second year.[28]

In announcing the programme to the House of Commons, Attlee stressed that its completion in full and on time depended on an adequate supply of materials and components as well as the prompt delivery of machine tools from the United States: it might not be possible to spend the full amount within the three-year period.[29] The 'clear aim' of the government was to meet the cost of rearmament from current production,

25 'Economic Implications of the Defence Proposals', memorandum by the Chancellor of the Exchequer, 19 January 1951, CP(51)20, in PRO CAB 129/44.
26 Gaitskell's diary, p. 229. Treasury officials were not very happy to see the Chancellor of all people taking the lead in a campaign for higher expenditure.
27 Gaitskell told the House of Commons on 14 February that less favourable terms of trade had cost £250 million in the past year and were likely to cost £300 million more in 1951. In spite of the raw material shortages, he was still talking of a 4 per cent increase in industrial production in 1951 (*H. C. Deb.*, 5th ser., vol. 484, cols 644–6, 14 February 1951).
28 CM(51)7, 25 January 1951, in PRO CAB 128/19.
29 *H. C. Deb.*, 5th ser., vol. 483, cols 582 and 584, 29 January 1951.

not by running into debt abroad or by reducing investment and prejudicing future productivity.

It was natural to ask how a programme which had been represented six months previously as the maximum physically possible could be replaced by a programme 40 per cent larger. Attlee's answer was that the earlier programme was 'the most we could manage without taking special measures. We are now taking the special measures'.[30] It is not at all clear what 'special measures' Attlee had in mind and hard to point to any that were calculated to clear the way for an increase in armaments production from about £1480 million in September to £2200 million in the new three-year programme.[31] Moreover the planned increase was much steeper than this if measured in terms of the fourfold rise between 1950–1 and 1953–4.[32] In the September programme there had been a fairly sharp rise in the first year, 1951–2, but thereafter total defence spending was scheduled to increase by only £100 million a year in the next two years so that the peak rate was not far above the average for the three years. Now production would have to double and more than double in the first year and double again in the next two.

The increase in production had to be concentrated on a narrow sector of the economy. The crucial figures are those for the metal and engineering industries which accounted for over 40 per cent of total British exports and about half of fixed capital investment. The Cabinet, however, was supplied only with the figures for the first two years of the programme and not with the peak rate to which the planned expansion was (or should have been) geared. Later figures, given subsequently in the *Economic Survey for 1951*, were on a different basis and yield a picture somewhat as shown in table 8.2.

To double the output for defence from the metal and engineering industries in one year and double it again in the next two was bound to have severe repercussions on exports and fixed investment. It was estimated that at least one-third of the motor-car industry would be engaged in defence work. The output of military aircraft would come to exceed the

---

30  ibid., col. 590.

31  In September Gaitskell put the increase in the programme for armaments production at £850 million in 1951–4 (*H. C. Deb.*, 5th ser., vol. 478, col. 1129, 13 September 1950); the total for 1948–51 was about £630 million (including research and development) and for 1951–4 about £2200 million (*H. C. deb.*, 5th ser., vol. 484, col. 417, 14 February 1951).

32  Attlee, *H. C. Deb.*, 5th ser., vol. 483, col. 583, 29 January 1951.

*Table 8.2* Planned expenditure on defence production 1950–4[a] (£m. at prices in March 1951)

|  | 1950–1 | 1951–2 | 1952–3 | 1953–4 | Total (1951–3) |
|---|---|---|---|---|---|
| Metal and engineering industries | 170 | 360 | (590)[b] | (700)[b] | 1,650 |
| Works and buildings | 82 | 145 | (160)[b] | (170)[b] | 475 |
| Clothing and textiles | 10 | 55 | 77 | (90)[b] | 675 |
| Other | 83 | 140 | (153)[b] | (160)[b] | |
|  | 345 | 700 | 980 | 1,120 | 2,800 |
| Metal and engineering industries (actual)[c] | 170 | 275 | 470 | (510) | 1,255 |

*Sources: Economic Survey for 1951*, Cmd 8195; CP(51)20, in PRO CAB 129/44; *H.C. Deb.*, 5th ser., vol. 484, col. 644, 15 February 1951; *Economic Survey for 1953*, Cmd 8800, p. 49.

a These figures include research and development, expenditure on civil defence, and, under 'Works and buildings', expenditure on government factories, research establishments and storage for strategic stocks (£15 million in 1950–1, £30 million in 1951–2) but not expenditure on stock-building as such. The total of £2325 million for production, excluding building and works, is £270 million higher than the figure for production in CP(51)20 and £125 million higher than the figure given by Gaitskell on 14 February 1951. It does, however, tally broadly with figures given by him later in his speech (col. 644) where he puts metal and engineering output at £1700 million, building at £500 million, textiles at £250 million and the aggregate for production, research and works at £2850 million.

b Figures in brackets are rough guesses.

c At current prices; civil defence is excluded; the figure for 1953–4 is a forecast.

output of all aircraft in 1950. The building work to be done would require a work force more than half as large as that employed on the housing programme.[33]

It was almost inevitable that the programme should stretch out over a longer period than three years as the usual delays over the design of new equipment and delivery of jigs and tools made themselves felt. These difficulties were paraded later, along with shortages of materials, components and skilled labour, in extenuation of the various shortfalls that occurred; but they were foreseeable.

Apart from the dislocation likely to be produced in a group of key industries, there was an obvious danger of setting back the whole process of recovery. A tremendous additional effort was contemplated in a

33 CP(51)20, 19 January 1951, in PRO CAB 129/44.

country which had been in doubt two or three years previously whether it would ever be able to make ends meet and stop the dollar drain. Devaluation had been almost forced on the government by the dwindling of the reserves just over twelve months before. Since then there had been a rapid but fragile recovery. Was it now possible to step up government expenditure steeply, in competition with exports and investment, in a fully employed economy already under strain, without plunging back into an insupportable deficit?

It was a question that troubled ministers. They had been warned by November that Marshall Aid was coming to an end. But they had also been encouraged at the outset by promises of American financial assistance if they agreed to a substantial enlargement of the defence programme. In July 1950 they understood the Americans to have made a definite offer to meet the whole of the additional cost of any expansion beyond what the British government would have sanctioned unaided. They asked for half and saw the promised aid vanish into thin air, to materialize again as the Nitze formula. This in turn seemed to be fading away. When the accelerated programme announced in January was taken on, ministers thought that they had at least an insurance policy in the NATO burden-sharing exercise. But by the first week in April the United States government was putting an interpretation on the formula that implied no aid for Britain during the next fiscal year. American officials in Washington explained that excessive defence burdens showed up in external deficits and loss of reserves. The United Kingdom, however, was adding to her reserves; and the fact that this reflected a sterling-area, not a British, surplus would carry no weight with Congress. The rest of the sterling area, Congress would maintain, ought to make a contribution to the defence of the West, even if it was not represented in NATO. In any event it would not vote money to a country whose rearmament effort left it with rising reserves. This arbitrary principle, of which the British government was previously unaware, did not debar the United Kingdom from assistance under other conditions and in the end Defence Aid was received amounting to £4 million in 1951, £121 million in 1952, £102 million in 1953 and diminishing amounts thereafter. But these sums were agreed long after. They were negligible when most urgently required, in the balance-of-payments crisis of 1951–2. In the spring of 1951 the government was entitled to feel that it had been led further and further up the garden path.

This feeling was intensified by the rapid deterioration in the economic situation, particularly in the balance of payments. The previous year had seen a healthy surplus, originally put at £229 million in the *Economic*

*Survey for 1951* and since revised upwards to £307 million.[34] The government was reconciled to seeing this disappear in 1951 as a contribution to the finance of rearmament and regarded a small deficit of £100 million as a legitimate offset to a similar expenditure on strategic stocks, reserves of commodities taking the place of reserves of foreign exchange. The Board of Trade at the end of 1950 thought the deficit might be as high as £250 million.[35] But it proved to be still larger at £369 million so that the swing in the balance of payments was not far short of £700 million. This was largely because of a disastrous rise in import prices which had increased by 25 per cent during 1950 (partly under the influence of the 1949 devaluation), and now rose twice as fast in the first six months of 1951, ending up 60 per cent higher in June 1951 than eighteen months previously. The acceleration in the rise in import prices was not fully appreciated until well into March when it was brought home by figures showing a big increase in December and January. But it did no more than reflect the boom in commodity prices that followed the outbreak of the Korean War and the intense rearmament activity that began in 1950.

That the economy would be under strain in 1951, even in the absence of heavy defence expenditure, was evident well before the end of 1950. The American economy had rebounded from the depression of 1948–9 and was in a state of boom. World industrial production in 1950 had risen by no less than 13 per cent over the previous year. Defence expenditure was now planned on an enormous scale: in the United States an annual rate of expenditure of $50–60 billion – twice the pre-Korea rate – was already under discussion in the autumn of 1950. The rush to buy raw materials of all kinds had not only driven up their price – in some cases fourfold – but had created physical shortages that threatened to hold up production and were endangering the growth of exports. There were shortages of non-ferrous metals (especially zinc), sulphur, cotton, linters, and other materials and some danger of a new coal crisis in the course of the winter. These shortages also put in question the 4 per cent growth in productivity on which the government was counting. The TUC, as far back as 30 June 1950, had called off the wage freeze and as the cost of living moved up more steeply with import prices, the threat of a wage–price spiral intensified. For Gaitskell preparing his Budget for presentation on 10 April 1951 this was a sombre background.

34  Dow (1964) gives a figure of £370 million for the earliest assessment of the current balance (p. 57n). This includes grants of £139 million (*Economic Survey for 1951*, Cmd 8195, table 11).
35  Minute by David Butt in PRO T 229/270.

The Chancellor's advisers took the view, throughout the winter, that the raw material shortages and the rising cost of living gave most cause for concern. The balance of payments, in view of the competitive level of costs after devaluation and the favourable outcome of 1950, seemed to them in no great immediate danger even if it turned negative for a time. Excess demand might also pose no great threat. As Robert Hall pointed out to the Budget Committee at the beginning of February, in what they were at first inclined to dismiss as 'budget gymnastics', an extra £700 million in defence expenditure would be largely offset by the swing in the balance of payments. A curb on investment would also contribute. An additional £100 million in taxation – later increased to £150 million – might prove sufficient to limit the pressure on resources. Gaitskell accepted this advice although he still felt some qualms about the balance of payments.

The Budget, however, precipitated problems of a different character. With the departure of Cripps in October 1950 the Cabinet had begun to lose some of its most prominent members.[36] In April 1951, just after the Budget, Bevin died after a long period of failing health. The Budget proposals for a charge on false teeth and spectacles became the occasion for the resignation of Nye Bevan, followed two days later by that of Harold Wilson and, next day, of John Freeman, a junior minister. These resignations, and the loss of Cripps and Bevin, greatly weakened the government and contributed to its downfall six months later.

While the ostensible reason for Bevan's resignation was the proposal to levy a charge for false teeth and spectacles so as to raise £13 million (£23 million in a full year), Bevan had throughout the previous nine months opposed a large increase in the rearmament programme and in his letter of resignation made more play with this ground for disagreement. He first expressed his misgivings at the meeting of the Cabinet on 25 July 1950, insisting that the burden of additional military expenditure should not fall on the social services or investment. On a number of occasions he developed the argument that it was part of the Russian strategy to oblige the western democracies to rearm on a scale that would impair their economies and embitter their peoples. By delaying in this way the efforts of the West to promote the development of the Third World, the USSR also hoped to woo these countries more successfully. He was sceptical of the appreciations submitted by the Cabinet's military advisers of the strength

---

36 Cripps was said to have been persuaded by Attlee in mid-July not to resign but to take three months' leave of absence. He went off to a clinic in Switzerland leaving responsibility to Gaitskell and at the end of three months resigned.

and equipment of the Russian forces. In any event it was a mistake to give the impression that we would equal the US effort of rearmament. At one of the last Cabinet meetings he attended, he argued that shortages of raw materials and machine tools would make it impossible in practice to spend effectively on defence all the money allocated for the purpose in the Budget. The United Kingdom was trying to do too much too quickly under American pressure.[37] This argument as to feasibility was made the grounds of Harold Wilson's resignation and it was no doubt from him that Bevan derived it.

The essence of Bevan's position was that the social services should not suffer and he might have been expected to make his sticking point a refusal to agree to a ceiling on the National Health Service. Once this had become the basis of government policy the only question was how to reduce the estimate for the following year to the agreed ceiling and on this the Cabinet Committee concerned was in agreement that the best way of making the necessary economy was by levying charges on false teeth and spectacles. As was pointed out in Cabinet, Bevan had already accepted the *principle* of prescription charges in 1949, so there was a possibility of a compromise by repeating the 1949 procedure of passing the legislation and holding it in suspense until it was clear whether the rearmament pro- gramme was being fulfilled. Bevan said at the meeting of the Cabinet on 19 April that 'his difficulties might be met if a statement could be made to the effect that the charges authorized by the Bill were of a temporary nature and that no further charges were contemplated'. The Chancellor refused. He regarded expenditure on the National Health Service as on the same footing as food subsidies, to be looked at each year in the light of the general financial situation, and had made it clear that any savings he could make would go on family allowances and old-age pensions rather than on the withdrawal of the health charges.[38] So what appeared to be a disagree- ment over a trifling £13 million in a Budget total of £4000 million – 'the economics of Bedlam' as Bevan put it – was more fundamentally over the inviolability of a free National Health Service although complicated by personal antipathies and resentments, distrust of American policy and reluctance to face the consequences of rearmament.

37  See, for example, conclusions of Cabinet meetings on 25 July 1950, 15 January, 9 April 1951, PRO CAB 128/18 and 128/19.
38  A year previously (on 21 March 1950) Gaitskell had noted in his diary a wish to see a definite limit to NHS expenditure sufficiently below the estimates to ensure that 'we should be quietly committed up to the hilt to finding the rest of the money . . . by making charges of some kind.' (Williams (ed.) (1983), p. 174.)

By the end of 1951, 'it was already clear', according to the *Economic Survey for 1952*, 'that the original programme could not be completed within . . . three years'.[39] This was put down partly to difficulties over design and production planning, partly to shortages of labour, materials, components and machine tools. But in addition to these predictable limitations on the logistics of expansion, rising import prices and the loss of Iranian oil were creating serious balance-of-payments difficulties which 'made it necessary to ease the burden of defence on the metal-using industries so that engineering exports can be expanded more rapidly'.[40] The overloading of the building industry and the shortage of steel had also forced cuts in the constructional part of the defence programme. The shortfall in 1951–2, excluding civil defence, was put at £120 million, over three-quarters of it in metal products, and the revised programme for 1952–3 was about £200 million below the amount originally projected.[41]

While it is difficult to make precise comparisons because of changing prices and coverage, it would seem that rearmament reached its peak in 1952 at a level unlikely to have been more than about £1250 million at end-1950 prices and so more than £500 million or 30 per cent below the peak planned in January 1951. This would imply that the expansion from the pre-Korea level was about two-thirds. The expansion in production for defence was a good deal more. For metal and engineering goods the most coherent picture is given by a table in the *Economic Survey for 1953* (table 8.3).

What table 8.3 shows is that defence never absorbed more than 12 per cent of the output of this group of industries; that far from quadrupling, defence requirements did little more than double; that production of metal goods increased rather little – by at most 8 per cent in two years (compared with over 14 per cent in the previous two years and 12 per cent in the following two years); and that defence absorbed nearly the whole of the increase in supplies in those two years while the amount taken by the principal other uses hardly changed.

Even allowing for the exports that were forfeited, rearmament in Britain probably did less harm to the economy, in the short run at least, than the rise in import prices that resulted from rearmament elsewhere. Import prices had risen all through 1950 and rose still more steeply in 1951. This had a twofold effect, first on the terms of trade and the balance of payments and secondly on the rate of inflation.

39  *Economic Survey for 1952*, Cmd 8509, para. 36.
40  ibid.
41  ibid., para. 37.

*Table 8.3*  Distribution of supplies of metal goods 1950-2 (£m. at 1951 factory prices)

|  | 1950 | 1951 | 1952 |
|---|---|---|---|
| Supplies | | | |
| Production | 3,125 | 3,350 | 3,335 |
| Imports | 65 | 80 | 110 |
| | 3,190 | 3,430 | 3,445 |
| Used for | | | |
| Defence | 185 | 275 | 410 |
| Exports | 1,000 | 1,050 | 1,010 |
| Investment | 965 | 985 | 940 |
| Other industrial goods, repair work, etc. | 735 | 790 | 745 |
| Passenger cars for home market | 65 | 65 | 95 |
| Consumer goods for home market | 240 | 265 | 245 |

*Source: Economic Survey for 1953*, Cmd 8800, table 24; for the run of years from 1948 to 1956 at 1948 prices see *National Income and Expenditure 1957*, table 16.

A 9 per cent shift in the terms of trade against the United Kingdom in 1951, coming on top of an 8 per cent shift in 1950 after devaluation, produced an unexpectedly large deficit in the balance of payments. While defence expenditure absorbed about 1½ per cent more of available resources in 1951 than in either of the two previous years, the shift in the terms of trade between 1949 and 1951 represented a loss of over 3 per cent in real income. Even if one discounts a substantial part of the shift as the outcome of devaluation, the loss in income in 1951 alone from this source and from the drag on production of raw material shortages was at least as great as the additional burden of arms production and other defence expenditure. It is true that rearmament had not reached its peak in 1951, that it grew by a further 2 per cent in 1952 and did not fall back afterwards to the pre-Korean level. But by 1952 import prices were well past their peak, the terms of trade had improved and were back to where they were in 1950 and these changes were softening the impact of rearmament instead of imposing an additional burden.

The reversion of the terms of trade to their earlier level and the see-saw of the balance of payments back into surplus in 1952 did not remove the threat of inflation through rising import prices. It was this more than anything that had precipitated the sharp rise in wages and earnings after

1949 — a rise faster even than in the war and not far short of 20 per cent in two years. The threat did pass as import prices receded but in other circumstances it might have taken on still more serious proportions.

Rearmament, as Attlee had predicted, involved the partial restoration of a war economy. Controls were renewed or extended in many different directions: over raw materials, investment, consumption (including hire-purchase controls), prices, and employment. The most stringent of these were the outcome of raw material shortages. Sulphur, zinc and copper were rationed in relation to their consumption in a base period and restrictions were placed on the use of aluminium, nickel and softwood. The allocation of new motor cars to the home market was cut. Some firms making durable metal consumer goods were required to switch over to defence orders (e.g. for radio and radar equipment) or to release labour for defence work elsewhere. Fresh import restrictions designed to save £600 million were introduced after the October election. Price controls were reimposed in July. A bill to limit dividends to the average of the previous two years was announced but not proceeded with and abandoned after the election. A system of labour preferences at the Labour Exchanges was introduced to guide workers to key jobs.

The controls were evidence of the difficulties of making the necessary adjustments even if they were of limited assistance in bringing them about. In macro-economic terms it might seem not too difficult to provide for the absorption for defence purposes of resources equal to $3\frac{1}{2}$ per cent of GDP, the maximum additional strain attributable to defence expenditure. After all, this was little more than the normal annual increment in GDP in post-war years. But the upset produced by rearmament was much greater than such a comparison might suggest. The changeover to defence production coincided with a marked slowing down of growth in 1952 when GDP fell by $\frac{1}{2}$ per cent instead of increasing by the normal 3 per cent. Over the two years 1950–2 GDP grew by only 2 per cent, not 6 per cent. During those two years fixed investment (although it was swollen by an element for defence) marked time; consumers' expenditure fell slightly in both years — the only years between 1944 and 1974 in which such a fall occurred; exports, which the government hoped to see go on expanding,[42] were 7 per cent lower in volume in 1952 than in 1950. Of all the components of output, other than government purchases, only stock-building showed a pronounced increase and the additional purchases for stock were made in the year (1951) when import prices were at their peak.

42 *Economic Survey for 1951*, Cmd 8195, para. 101; *Economic Survey for 1952*, Cmd 8509, para. 19.

The check to consumption in 1951–2 was clearly associated with the rise in import prices and the lag in money incomes behind the soaring cost of living. Real incomes were depressed by the adverse turn in the terms of trade but the resources released did not find the employment in exports that would have put the balance of payments straight. In 1951 stock-building took up the slack and industrial production continued to grow, but in 1952, with commodity prices beginning to fall, consumption checked and a tightening of credit, the rise in stocks came to an end and this curtailment of demand was more than sufficient to offset the expansion in the defence programme. The depression in activity and in consumption in 1952 cannot be laid at the door of the British rearmament programme which was plainly an expansionary influence; it was due in large part to world rearmament and the commodity boom (and shortages) which this provoked.[43]

What British rearmament did do was to halt the rise in investment and reduce exports at a critical stage in their build-up to the target proposed six years before. It left Britain with a heavier defence burden than her continental competitors and a more precarious balance of payments than the efforts of earlier years had promised.

Some writers have reached a more categorical conclusion and have argued that rearmament checked fatally the momentum of the British export drive and industrial investment, attributing Britain's relative decline as an industrial nation over the post-war years to this diversion from what should have been the central aims of policy.[44] It may be so; but it is not a thesis that can be easily substantiated.

It is true that the volume of exports of manufactures ceased to increase in 1951, then fell by nearly 9 per cent in 1952 and did not recover to the 1950–1 level until 1955. But the main setback was to textile exports, not to engineering products. Exports of those remained fairly flat between 1950 and 1954 while most other groups ended the four years lower than at the beginning. Within the engineering group, exports of machinery

---

43  The check to industrial production in 1952 was not confined to the United Kingdom. It affected all the leading industrial countries including Germany and Japan where expansion was not arrested but slowed down perceptibly. World industrial production grew by 2 per cent while in the United Kingdom there was a fall of about 4 per cent.

44  Dow (1964), p. 64n; Lord Croham in *The Times* (interview with P. Hennessy), 9 January 1978, and in Cairncross (1981), p. 142; Sir E. Boyle in J. K. Bowers (1979), pp. 3–4.

continued to increase in 1951 and 1952 and fell, though not heavily, in 1953 and 1954 before resuming steady growth over the next three years. Road vehicles and aircraft, on the other hand, fell continuously from 1950 to 1953, by which time they were about 14 per cent below the 1950 level. In this case most of the reduction in exports can be traced to increased sales on the home market rather than to the diversion of capacity to meet defence requirements. There is not much in the record of export growth to bear out the idea that those industries which were most involved in the rearmament programme made least headway subsequently in export markets.

A large part of British industry was not much involved in rearmament. The engineering industries, which took the brunt of it, were not affected uniformly and even some of those branches that were major exporters in 1950 such as shipbuilding could hardly attribute their subsequent difficulties to a temporary diversion to arms production. The big increase in the output of armaments was heavily concentrated on a limited range of engineering industries: aircraft, electronics, shipbuilding and ordnance factories. Of these four, only electronics looks in the least a plausible example of an industry that might suffer a loss of momentum and competitive power as a result of rearmament. If other British industries were complaining of inability to find or resume foreign markets after 1952 this is much more likely to have reflected the disappearance of the post-war seller's market and the rise of competition from Germany and other continental countries. Between 1950 and 1952, while British exports of manufactures were falling in volume, German exports more than doubled. Four years later they had doubled again while British exports had crept up by 20 per cent and were only some 10 per cent higher than they had been in 1950. By that time Japan's exports were rising faster than Germany's and had increased nearly threefold since 1950. It is hardly surprising that the re-entry of these two countries into world markets should have reduced Britain's share of trade in manufactures which, as late as 1955, ten years after the war, was almost as large as that of Germany and Japan combined.

## Conclusion

Why was it, one may ask, that the Labour government adopted so ambitious a rearmament programme and inflated it beyond the country's capabilities and economic strength? The fundamental answer lies in British fears of being left alone by the United States to face the USSR across a defenceless Europe. At all costs there must be no repetition of the weakness of the 1930s, if the USSR continued to push forward into any vacuum of power left by the retreating West. American help was indispensable to effective opposition. But the price of such help was that Britain should provide a lead that other, weaker powers on the continent would follow. It was not possible to limit the British response to a realistic programme such as was at first contemplated or to avoid a disproportionate burden on the United Kingdom. Not for the first time, falling in with American wishes exposed the British economy to stresses that precipitated a crisis — a crisis greatly intensified by coincident pressures on the world economy and, as a consequence, on Britain's terms of trade and balance of payments.

# Chapter nine

## ROBOT, 1952

The 1949 debate on whether to devalue the pound was succeeded within eighteen months by proposals to revalue it upwards and these in turn, a year later, by a furious controversy within the government over a plan to make the pound convertible and let it float downwards. In these debates, which were the outcome of events unforeseen at the time of devaluation, there were some curious somersaults in opinion, the Economic Section defending a fixed rate while the Bank of England and the official Treasury took the other side and favoured a floating pound.

Initially the pound recovered strongly, largely under the influence of an upswing of activity in the United States. This helped to replenish the reserves which were higher in dollar terms by the middle of 1950 than they had been for three years. Even before the end of 1949 the dollar deficit had disappeared and in the following year it was replaced by a growing surplus that continued until the spring of 1951. The current account also swung round and was in healthy surplus throughout the year.

These changes produced a revival in American pressure for a bolder approach to convertibility and for active participation in the campaign for European integration. In May came the Schuman Plan, in which Britain did not find it possible to take part, and in June the outbreak of war in Korea. These events and their sequels are discussed more fully in chapters 8 and 10. Here we confine ourselves to the balance of payments consequences of the boom produced first by the recovery in America and then by rearmament there and elsewhere.

Early in July it had been recognized that there was a need for immediate action to build up stocks of imported materials but the moment passed and

it was not until October that the Treasury began to press supply departments to increase their purchases for stockpiling. By then it was too late.
Apart from the sharp rise in commodity prices and the difficulties of
procurement, the continuing growth in exchange reserves, to which the
stockpiling of imports was an obvious alternative, aroused Congressional
disapproval of further aid to the United Kingdom. As far back as June, the
Treasury thought it 'perfectly clear . . . that Congress were going to take
some kind of a cut off our share of aid because of our rising reserves'.[1] By
the beginning of November the Chancellor (Hugh Gaitskell) and Foreign
Secretary (Ernest Bevin) were reconciled to the suspension of aid in 1951
although they hoped that additional dollars would be made available
before the end of 1950. In a paper to the Economic Policy Committee they
pointed out that the Snoy-Marjolin formula for the allocation of aid had
been specifically devised to leave countries with an incentive to improve
their balance of payments and that to change the formula so as to cut off
aid from the United Kingdom alone was unfairly to penalize success. In
agreeing to extend an initial credit of $150 million to the European Pay-
ments Union in July 1950, the Chancellor had counted on receiving in
1950–1 the full $400–450 million which would have been allotted under
the existing formula, not just the $175 million so far received.[2] A month
later, on 11 December, the Cabinet was informed that Marshall Aid
would be suspended from 1 January 1951.[3]

Meanwhile the strength of sterling was influencing opinion elsewhere.
Early in October Gaitskell referred in Cabinet to rumours that the pound
would be revalued upwards. The reserves at the end of the year, he said,
would be 'startlingly high'.[4] The rumours spread. At a meeting of the
Economic Planning Board on 2 January 1951 Lincoln Evans, a leading
trade unionist, suggested revaluation as a way of escape from the fall in the
standard of living that rearmament was likely to involve.[5] This set off a
discussion within the government that continued for the next six months.
A paper was prepared for the Planning Board by Sir H. Brittain, one of the

---

1 E. Playfair to Professor R. F. Kahn, 16 June 1950 in 'Consultations with outside
economists on the future of IEPS', PRO T 237/30.
2 'Suspension of ERP' (EPC(50)115 in PRO CAB 134/227); memorandum by
Foreign Secretary and Chancellor, 7 November 1950, in PRO CAB 134/227.
3 CM(50)84, 11 December 1950, in PRO CAB 128/18.
4 CM(50)70, 2 October 1950, in PRO CAB 128/18. The reserves increased in the final
quarter of 1950 by $546 million, the biggest increase in any quarter since the war.
5 '1951 Revaluation: general papers', in PRO T 236/2944.

Treasury Third Secretaries, making a strong case against revaluation. Frequent changes in the rate would encourage speculative pressure and capital movements. In any event a swing in the balance of payments was already in progress that was expected to produce a dollar deficit in the second half of the year. A revaluation would impede the growth of exports to the dollar area just when it was becoming important not to aggravate the effects of rearmament on the balance of payments. If the pound were in fact so strong that revaluation could be justified it would still be preferable to relax the restrictions on dollar expenditure and this was certainly how the Americans would view the matter.[6]

A similar conclusion was reached in a long paper by Nita Watts of the Economic Section. To revalue would raise doubts in the United States and elsewhere about the United Kingdom's commitment to stable exchange rates and freer trade. Short-term difficulties in the balance of payments were supposed to be dealt with by varying quantitative restrictions on imports while changes in the exchange rate were reserved for the correction of fundamental disequilibrium. The pound had been in fundamental disequilibrium in 1949 and events since then hardly demonstrated that it could be corrected at a higher rate. A revaluation by 25 per cent might knock 2 per cent off the cost of living and improve the balance of payments by £140 million by shifting the terms of trade in Britain's favour. But this was not enough to justify revaluation. Perhaps the right lesson to be drawn was that in future the rate should be allowed to float for a while before any commitment was made to a new parity.[7]

Robert Hall was in full agreement that there should be no revaluation but was troubled by the prospect of importing inflation at a fixed rate. The American economy was in the early stages of a violent inflationary expansion with a rearmament boom superimposed on a high level of investment supported by an expansion of credit. Must the British economy be dragged along by the American inflation and what limit should be set to the piling-up of gold?[8] Otto Clarke, to whom these questions were addressed, produced confident answers that contrasted strikingly with his views a year later. He expected the value of money to fall for the next five years but with pauses along the rising curve as the Federal Reserve Board under Governor Martin took action to restrict credit, Congress being unwilling to vote the necessary taxes. The United

---

6  ibid. Draft by Sir H. Brittain, 10 January 1951. In the end, no paper was submitted
   to the Planning Board, the request for one being deliberately 'forgotten'.
7  ibid. Draft paper by Nita Watts, 12 March 1951.
8  ibid. Robert Hall, minute to R. W. B. Clarke, 15 March 1951.

States was more likely to be in deficit than surplus: indeed, only Canada, Latin America, the outer sterling area and the Middle East would be in surplus. The United Kingdom would be in deficit and would need all its gold. It should not ease its restrictions on imports of inessential like canned salmon because of a purely temporary surplus. As for revaluation, it would *worsen*, not improve, the balance of payments, increase the burden of sterling balances, and expose the entire sterling area to stiffer competition from other manufacturing countries. He then launched into an attack on floating rates. 'I am opposed to a floating rate. It is bad for traders; it is bad for planners; it is a complete destruction of the IMF. But I think the real objection is that it is incompatible with exchange control'.[9] A floating rate, he went on, would not solve the problem of price stability: it was not capable of isolating the United Kingdom from the effects of inflation in the United States.

An equally strong attack on floating rates came simultaneously from the Bank of England. George Bolton argued that, with an international currency like sterling, stability in exchange rates was necessary in order to give confidence to the holder.[10] 'There appears', he said, 'to be a permanent temptation to consider revaluation through the experimental machinery provided by a fluctuating rate of exchange.' This was the result of failure to appreciate the lessons of the years 1931–9 when the Exchange Equalization Account was never in a position either to hold any particular range of rates or to decide what the right rate of exchange should be. If the United Kingdom were tempted to experiment with floating rates, the gold reserves would prove totally inadequate and it would be quite impossible to damp down fluctuations even to the limited extent achieved in 1931–9 by intervention in the market. A fixed gold price was essential to the management of the sterling area, to the system of monetary agreements and to the European Payments Union. There was no system of administration whereby fluctuating rates could be transmitted to all the sterling area controls 'so as to enable all traders and producers in the Area to have comparable and similar facilities to all the others'.[11]

9  ibid. R. W. B. Clarke, minutes to Robert Hall and Sir H. Brittain, 21 March 1951 (R.W.B.C. 4276, 4280, 4281).
10 Nevertheless he claimed, many years later, to have begun canvassing for a floating rate along the lines of the Robot plan as early as 1950 (Seldon (1981), p. 171).
11 PRO T 236/2944, memorandum by G. Bolton, 'Floating Sterling', 22 March 1951. Edwin Plowden minuted subsequently that Bolton's arguments had converted him from an inclination in favour of variable rates of exchange to support for a fixed rate (27 April 1951).

A month later, when the Chancellor asked for a paper on the subject, he was supplied with those by Nita Watts, George Bolton, and Otto Clarke. He invited comment from the Economic Secretary and Financial Secretary and Douglas Jay alone responded. He was strongly against floating but thought that the rate chosen in 1949 had been too low. However, to revalue in 1951 might revive the dollar drain and that was more than he could bear.[12] There was a discussion with the Chancellor on 1 June and it was decided to take no action.

In the meantime Professor Kaldor had been agitating for a floating rate and Roy Harrod had publicly supported revaluation. The Economic Commission for Europe, no doubt under Kaldor's influence, had proposed concerted action by European governments to raise the gold value of their currencies and pursue a policy of flexible exchange rates. Overby, Deputy Managing Director of the IMF, had commented to the Treasury that John Snyder would 'take a poor view' of any revaluation if no simultaneous relaxation were made in restrictions on dollar imports. Such a move would be taken as proof that no further economic aid was needed.[13] The issue lingered on through May and June but by the end of June there had been an unmistakable change in trend in the balance of payments and the reserves were no higher than two months previously. Treasury ministers were unanimous that this disposed finally of the case for revaluation.[14]

From the first quarter of 1951 onwards the balance of payments, as expected, showed a progressive deterioration caused largely by rising import prices and stockpiling of imported materials. The loss of the Abadan refinery had also reduced income from oil sales and made it necessary to purchase oil for dollars. Exports of metal products were limited by a shortage of steel and a diversion of capacity to the rearmament programme so that it was not possible to take advantage of exceptionally favourable market opportunities. Exports of textiles were beginning to suffer from a recession in world demand. These unfavourable trends in the United Kingdom's balance of payments coincided with a sudden swing into deficit in the balance of payments of the rest of the sterling area, which continued to spend heavily on imports out of the high incomes earned in

12 ibid. Minute of 8 May 1951.
13 ibid. Minute by Sir H. Brittain, 10 May 1951.
14 ibid. Minute by Douglas Jay, 20 June 1951. John Edwards, while agreeing, commented enigmatically, that he did not necessarily share the conclusion that the figures strengthened the case against revaluation.

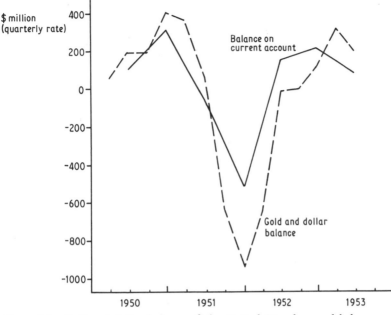

*Figure 9.1*  Gold and dollar balance of the United Kingdom and balance on current account 1950–3[a]

a The current account takes credit for defence aid.

*Sources: United Kingdom Balance of Payments 1946 to 1953* (Cmd 8976) for 1950–2, and *1946 to 1954* (Cmd 9291) for 1953.

the post-Korean commodity boom just when the collapse in commodity prices was producing a corresponding contraction in export earnings.

The balance in gold and dollars, which had shown a surplus of $371 million in the first quarter, fell to $61 million in the second and had been transformed by the third into a deficit of $635 million which grew in the fourth to $937 million – over £100 million per month (see Figure 9.1). Even with the other members of the European Payments Union the United Kingdom deficit was reaching alarming proportions – £387 million or $1084 million in the last six months of the year. By February 1952 80 per cent of this deficit was payable in gold or dollars and in another month the proportion would rise to 100 per cent. A further large loss of reserves – perhaps as much as $800 million – was inevitable in the first quarter of the year, so that when the quarterly statement of the gold and dollar reserves was released at the end of March it was expected to show a balance of no more than about $1500 million and might well set off an exchange crisis.

Meanwhile the Labour government had been defeated at the general election in October. The new Conservative government on taking office accepted the need for prompt action. Its first moves, announced a fortnight later on 7 November, did little more than implement Labour's plans except for the addition of a rise in Bank Rate from 2 to $2\frac{1}{2}$ per cent. Import restrictions were introduced, including restrictions on 'liberalized' imports from OEEC countries, and further cuts were made after a meeting of Commonwealth Finance Ministers in London in mid-January. There was also some talk of 'freeing the pound'. At the meeting of Cabinet on 10 January to prepare for the Conference of Finance Ministers it was suggested that 'the ultimate aim should be to achieve total convertibility based, not on fixed rates of exchange, but on flexible and variable exchanges. Such a system would render unnecessary any trade discrimination through the methods employed at present'.[15]

The conclusion reached by the Cabinet was more cautious. The aim of United Kingdom ministers at the Conference should be: 'to avoid any commitments on non-discrimination and to treat non-discrimination as secondary to currency convertibility which, though it might not be practicable for a long time, should be the prior aim'.[16]

The stress on convertibility at the Conference, combined with the distaste expressed for discrimination, must have seemed rather odd in the circumstances. It led to the acceptance of a policy inviting each member country to live 'within its means' even if this meant cutting imports from other sterling countries as well as from outside the sterling area.[17] Agreement was reached to take concerted action to bring the sterling area into balance with the non-sterling world in the second half of 1952 instead of running a deficit, as in the second half of 1951, of about £750 million.[18] The United Kingdom, which accounted for nearly £600 million of this total, aimed to eliminate its deficit while the rest of the sterling area undertook to transform a deficit of about £150 million into a small surplus of £100 million with the non-sterling world. The main instrument in this transformation would be import restrictions, including in the case of Australia – then in heavy deficit – cuts in imports from the UK and other sterling countries which would do little to improve the deficit of the sterling area.

15  CM(52)2, 10 January 1952, in PRO CAB 128/24.
16  ibid.
17  Dow (1964), p. 72.
18  *Economic Survey for 1952*, Cmd 8509, para. 14.

The United Kingdom's plans for checking the dollar drain included, in addition to import cuts, a tightening of credit, hire-purchase restrictions, a reduction in investment and a severe Budget. Senior officials took the view that the economy was heavily overloaded and that only a ruthless reduction in government expenditure – in particular, in food subsidies – would get rid of the external imbalance.[19] Some felt, however, that more drastic action was required. The Chancellor, disquieted by the continuing loss of reserves sought advice from officials on the emergency measures that could be taken in his forthcoming Budget, announced for 4 March.

It was a difficult time at which to reach decisions on major issues of high policy: the Cabinet was preoccupied with the death of King George VI on 6 February. Two days after his death, on 8 February, a paper prepared by officials was submitted to the Chancellor.[20] This started from the Chancellor's forecast in a memorandum which he circulated in January that the reserves would fall in the first quarter of 1952 by at least a further $700 million and would be down by June to the low level of $1400 million at which the pound was devalued in September 1949.[21] A downward revision of some $225 million was now necessary in this forecast because of American decisions on aid. Of $300 million which the Treasury had been counting on by the end of June it was unlikely that more than $125 million would be received within that period.[22] A further $50 million due under the Katz–Gaitskell agreement of June 1950 was also likely to be delayed until the second half of the year and might in the end come only at the expense of other economic aid.[23] On top of all this the reserves had fallen in January alone by $300 million, throwing doubt on the forecast of $700 million for the quarter. It would be unwise to count on a balance of more than $1400 million in the reserves at the end of April even if confidence factors were neutral, and this was a large assumption. It was not

19  Minute of meeting of Second Secretaries at the Treasury, 27 November 1951 in '1951–2 Sterling Convertibility: Operation Robot' in PRO T 236/3240.
20  'Emergency Action', 8 February 1952, in Sir Robert Hall papers 1952, PRO T 236/3245. This paper, presumably by T. L. Rowan (The Treasury Second Secretary in charge of external finance), was seen and agreed by Robert Hall. It makes no mention of the plan for a floating pound that surfaced a week or so later.
21  'Balance of Payments', memorandum by the Chancellor of the Exchequer, 19 January 1952, CP(52)10 in PRO CAB 129/49.
22  This was near the mark. Only $144 million in defence aid was received in the first half of the year.
23  This too proved an accurate forecast. Only $10 million was received before July as part of the 1951–2 allocation, and $42 million after July as part of the 1952–3 allocation.

only likely but 'certain' that the reserves would fall far below $2000 million so that at some time in the next few months a point would be reached at which no effective opposition could be offered to a crisis of confidence in sterling.

Looking further ahead, the paper underlined the uncertainties in the plan agreed upon at the Commonwealth Conference to stabilize the reserves in the second half of 1952. Other sterling area countries might fail, or might not be able, to live up to their undertakings: Australia and New Zealand, for example, might have to contend with still lower prices for wool. Prices might also go against the United Kingdom; sales of exports to the non-sterling world might be insufficient; leads and lags might develop in the expectation of a devaluation of sterling; the US aid promised might never be forthcoming.

The frustrations felt on the latter score are expressed with a rare vehemence:

> Our whole experience since . . . July 1950 has been most unfortunate. Indeed, the results of the United States' actions – stoppage of Marshall Aid, tin and rubber policy, virtual abandonment of burden-sharing, Battle Act, failure to find means to finance U.K. defence production, refusal to settle their Katz–Gaitskell liabilities, and the repeated changes of front on the $300 million – would be more readily understandable if their purpose was to weaken the U.K. economy, rather than to strengthen it.[24]

The prudent course, it was argued, was to make plans on the assumption that they must be carried out unaided. Nevertheless, as the next paragraph points out 'our plans for stopping the dollar drain in the second half of 1952 rely heavily upon United States help, which is not yet in sight, nor likely to be for many months'. The US administration should be told that 'we really must have the $300 million by the end of June and . . . an assurance of a definite sum (in usable form) for 1952–53'. In the absence of such assurances America should be warned that the defence programme would have to undergo radical revision.

To this self-contradictory remedy were added a long list of others. In internal policy the balance of payments would have to enjoy unquestioned precedence over all other objectives if confidence in sterling was to be restored. This meant removing competitive loads on resources through a firm Budget: a further reduction in the defence programme, already cut

24 'Emergency Action', para. 46.

for 1952–3;[25] measures to reduce fuel consumption and increase the flow of coal exports; curtailment of the housing programme with its heavy calls on dollars in payment for imported timber and metals; and cuts in food rations in order to leave more in store for emergencies. In external policy a wide range of possibilities was canvassed and six lines of action recommended. Of these three were for consideration rather than immediate action: a further cut in liberalized imports from OEEC countries; cancellation of import contracts and licences in emergency; and borrowing from the IMF and Ex–Im Bank after the Budget. The second of these was very much a last resort and no great enthusiasm was shown for the third; even the first was advanced hesitantly since the import programme had been thoroughly combed in the latest round of cuts. The remaining three recommendations were also pretty unconvincing: further exhortation of other sterling area countries; action to reduce consumption of imported materials and put more into stock where purchasing commitments could not be quickly altered; and credit restriction to make it more difficult for foreigners to borrow in Britain and oblige them to make prompter payment for exports.

More interesting than the recommendations submitted were the proposals rejected. A second devaluation, coming thirty months after the first (which was judged to have brought only transient gains) would lead foreigners to believe that 'sterling was going the same way as the French franc' and destroy its chances of remaining an effective international currency.[26] Action to restrict transfers of sterling between foreigners or to block sterling balances held outside the sterling area would also be damaging to the international role of sterling. As for the sterling area, one radical proposal, for dollar rationing, was impracticable, whether it took the form of a limitation of net drawings from the pool or direct restrictions on dollar imports, and could not be imposed on an unwilling sterling area. A second radical proposal, for freezing sterling balances and forcing sterling area members to get into balance without drawing on them, was also rejected as involving the dissolution of the sterling area, a political fracas, and an end to the international role of sterling.

It was a curious document exuding distrust of the sterling area and yet seeking to keep it in being; insistent that the defence programme must be cut and that US aid should not enter into British planning, yet turning to

25  The Defence Estimates for 1952–3 (excluding civil defence) were reduced by about £200 million below the amount originally projected (*Economic Survey for 1952*, Cmd 8509, p. 19).

26  ibid., para. 24.

America for help; and painting a picture of an almost inevitable exchange crisis while accepting the need to continue working on the assumption that the drain on the reserves could reasonably be expected to stop in the second half of the year.[27] It is hardly surprising that simpler and more drastic proposals pushed the Treasury paper aside and monopolized the attention of ministers: or that these proposals showed a more cavalier approach to other members of the sterling area. Within a week a short note was submitted by the Governor of the Bank of England outlining a new and radical plan which was given the code name ROBOT, presumably to suggest an automatic regulator. After its existence began to leak, the code word was thought to be connected with the names of its most active advocates, Leslie ROwan (Treasury Second Secretary), George Bolton and OTto Clarke.

The ideas behind the plan came from Bolton and Clarke who, as we have seen, held very different views a year previously. In a paper dated 25 January 1952 Clarke argued in favour of immediate convertibility combined with the blocking of sterling balances and a floating rate of exchange. The Conference of Commonwealth Finance Ministers had shown that South Africa and Ceylon would not be content to remain indefinitely in an inconvertible sterling area and colonies like Malaya and the Gold Coast would follow them out of it as soon as they were free. Clarke proposed to make sterling convertible for all non-residents, abandon discrimination between non-sterling sources of imports throughout the sterling area and introduce exchange control on capital movements to other sterling area countries. He accepted the risk that a lot of gold would be lost and that the rate of exchange might fall to a very low level and be highly unstable. But desperate situations called for desperate remedies.[28]

On 12 February Clarke circulated a further minute elaborating the plan, already christened 'Robot', and making it clear that the Bank of England would be giving it full support.[29] Two days later, on 14 February, Rowan circulated a short paper which the Governor had handed to the Chancellor, with an annex on 'Inconvertible Sterling' by Bolton, whose own exposition of the plan arrived on 16 February.

27  ibid., para. 12.
28  Minute by R. W. B. Clarke on 'Convertibility', 25 January 1952 in PRO T 236/3240. I have found no later reference to Clarke's proposal for exchange control on capital movements to the sterling area.
29  Clarke's minute drew a note of disagreement from a colleague, E. G. Copleston, who pointed out that 'convertibility cannot make a weak currency strong or restore confidence'.

The controversy that ensued was perhaps the most bitter of the post-war years in Whitehall and continued long after it had been decided by the Cabinet on 28–29 February that the scheme should not be announced in the Budget speech.[30] The plan was supported wholeheartedly by the official Treasury and the Bank of England and accepted by the Chancellor, R. A. Butler. It was strongly opposed by the Minister of State for Economic Affairs (Sir Arthur Salter), the Paymaster-General (Lord Cherwell) and the principal advisers of these ministers (Edwin Plowden and Robert Hall in the first case and Donald MacDougall in the second).[31]

The main features of the plan were: (i) a floating rate of exchange for sterling; (ii) full convertibility into gold, dollars or other currencies on a free market in foreign exchange for what was described as 'overseas' or 'external' sterling; (iii) compulsory funding of 80 per cent of the sterling balances held by members of the sterling area and the funding or blocking of nearly all balances held by non-members outside the dollar area.

The first of these elements reflected the view that it would prove impossible to maintain the existing parity for lack of reserves and that it was better to float at once before the reserves ran out rather than wait and lose control or devalue a second time. By letting the exchange rate 'take the strain' it would be possible to introduce convertibility of sterling simultaneously – a move which would be gratifying to the United States and Canada and to those members of the sterling area who chafed at the burdens imposed on them by inconvertibility. Convertibility would also put an end to dealings in 'cheap sterling' which were on such a scale that those who wanted to switch into dollars were said to have little difficulty in doing so at about $2.40 to the pound, with a consequential loss to the reserves. It was not possible, however, to take on the conversion into

---

30 Most of the official papers relating to the controversy over Robot between November 1951 and May 1952 will be found in PRO T 236 3240, 3242, 3243 and 3245. The last of these was prepared by Robert Hall but now lacks two papers originally contained, one by the Paymaster-General and one by the Chancellor. Both can be found in T 236/3240. The Cabinet Minutes lack any record of discussions of Robot although three meetings, mainly on this subject, were held on February 28 and 29. One of the only two copies of the Minutes can, however, be found in T 236/3242. I have found no record of later ministerial discussions. (Files T 236/3241 and 3244 have not yet been released and are being withheld for fifty years.)

31 MacDougall was in close touch with Robert Hall throughout the episode. An account of Cherwell's part in the controversy is given in chapter X of Birkenhead (1961). Salter gives his own account in *Slave of the Lamp* (1967), chapter 15.

dollars of outstanding sterling liabilities, most of which would have to be funded or blocked. Nor could residents of the sterling area – as distinct from their central banks – be allowed freedom to use any sterling they held or earned in order to acquire gold and dollars. Convertibility would be limited to unblocked sterling balances and new sterling earned abroad by non-residents or acquired currently by the monetary authorities of sterling area countries. Sterling coming under these headings was 'overseas sterling'.

The sterling balances to be blocked consisted partly of the holdings of countries within the sterling area and partly of the holdings of other countries, mainly in Europe or the Middle East. The latter, amounting to £866 million at 31 December 1951 would be frozen and 10 per cent (or less than £90 million) transferred to 'overseas sterling' accounts, the remainder being funded 'in, say 50-year Serial Funding Stock'.[32] Central Banks and traders of these countries would be able to convert in the London market without restriction this 'overseas sterling' and any new sterling coming into their hands from any source. The introduction of full convertibility, it was recognized, was incompatible with the partial convertibility which was an integral part of the EPU Agreement and further consideration was being given to the implications for EPU and for trade with Europe. It was also recognized that the new arrangement, by permitting countries earning a surplus in sterling to convert it freely into dollars, invited discrimination against the United Kingdom on the same footing as against the United States.

Monetary authorities and currency boards in the sterling area would also be credited with 10 per cent of their sterling assets as 'overseas sterling', the remainder being funded or used to meet pre-zero commitments or, in very special circumstances, drawn upon for economic development. Commercial banks and traders would not hold 'overseas sterling' but 'home sterling' available only for transactions within the sterling area. Thus an Australian holding sterling would be able to make a payment with it to the United Kingdom but not to any other country. If he chose to deposit the sterling with the Commonwealth Bank in exchange for Australian pounds it would automatically change from 'home' to 'overseas' sterling in the hands of the central bank. There would still be no exchange control over transfers within the sterling area but the sterling area dollar pool would disappear. Private holdings of sterling in the hands

32 'Plan for Overseas Sterling', memorandum by R. W. B. Clarke, 19 February 1952 in PRO T 236/3245.

of banks, traders or individuals within the sterling area would not be blocked but in most of the larger countries these holdings were exceeded by private liabilities in sterling.

The plan might look attractive in Whitehall but how would it strike other countries? A proposal to freeze 90 per cent of their reserves was sure to cause consternation among other members of the sterling area like Australia even if the balance of 10 per cent was freely convertible. They were not likely to be much impressed by the Bank of England's suggestion that the proposal was tantamount to a sharing out of the central gold reserves among members and that the alternative was, in all probability, a collapse in the value of their existing sterling balances. The powerful community of interest between members of the sterling area that inconvertibility created would no longer exist and the sterling area itself might well disintegrate. The United States might welcome the introduction of sterling convertibility: indeed it might enquire why such a scheme had not been proposed in 1945 and introduced along with the American Loan. But it would find it very hard to stomach a deliberate decision to let the pound float in contravention of the Bretton Woods Agreement or the setback to European integration which the scheme involved. The further proposal to reopen the London gold market and allow premium sales of gold would also be disliked in America and, still more, by the IMF. There was of course no question but that the proposals in their totality breached many of the Fund Articles. However, in view of the importance of retaining rights to make use of the Fund's resources and of avoiding drawings of sterling by other members, the sponsors of the plan hoped that the IMF could be persuaded to suspend judgement until the international exchange situation had settled down.

In the Bank of England's version of the proposals there was to be a substantial rise in short-term money rates in order to put them above New York market levels. This would put a brake on the use of credit both by residents and by non-residents and would be reassuring to foreign opinion 'about British determination to use all means to restore sterling'.[33]

The Bank took an optimistic view of the likely response to their plan in other sterling area countries. They expected Australia, South Africa and the gold-producing colonies to be attracted by the proposal for a free, international, gold market in London. It would be necessary to make special arrangements with Iraq and the oil-producing sheikhdoms in the

33 'Plan for "Overseas Sterling"', para. 8, memorandum by the Bank of England, 16 February 1952 in PRO T 236/3245.

Gulf, already disturbed at the possibility that their sterling assets might be blocked. But since their future net royalties would be convertible into gold on demand the oil producers might see advantages in the scheme. Pakistan, Burma and Ceylon were singled out as the least likely to offer willing acceptance. Some members of the sterling area might be moved by the wider fluctuations in the sterling–dollar rate to wish to peg their currency to the dollar. If so, they would have to leave the sterling area, expose themselves to the 'convulsive changes which appear to be inherent in the U.S. . . . economy' and forfeit the advantages derived from freedom of transfer inside the sterling area. What these advantages would be when sterling and dollars were freely convertible was left obscure.

The Bank wound up by urging an early decision on the plan in time to put it into effect by the beginning of April when disclosure of the large fall in the central reserves over the first quarter would add to public disquiet, however 'good' the Budget, and precipitate a still more rapid drain. There was very little time to spare for 'the immense task of technical re-adjustments (especially in domestic monetary arrangements) and Common-wealth negotiations'.

The Bank's paper was briefly discussed in the Treasury on 19 February and when officials saw the Chancellor afterwards the general view appeared to be that the plan required further study: in particular, its internal consequences were thought to be too drastic.[34] That evening, however, the Chancellor dined in the House of Commons with the Prime Minister, the Leader of the House and the Governor of the Bank of England. It was agreed that if the government intended to make such radical changes it would be wrong to introduce a Budget that gave no hint of them: if the new plan was to be adopted it should be announced on Budget day, Tuesday 4 March. Robert Hall, learning of this decision next day, was dumbfounded that such a complex issue with such far-reaching implications should be so hurriedly resolved. Since telegrams would have to go to Commonwealth countries a week in advance of any announce-ment the time left for discussion of the plan was impossibly short. He pressed this view on Sir Edward Bridges and the Chancellor who agreed on 21 February to recommend postponement of the Budget for a week.[35]

The heads of the main government departments concerned met at the Treasury on the morning of 21 February and were shown the proposals. They were asked to return in the afternoon with an indication of what

34 'Note for the Record' by Robert Hall, 4 March 1952, in PRO T 236/3245.
35 ibid. The postponement was announced on 25 February.

they would have to do if, as might well happen, ministers approved them for inclusion in the Budget speech on 4 March. Neither meeting was invited to comment on the merits of the proposals but doubts were expressed by Sir Frank Lee (Permanent Secretary of the Board of Trade), William Strath (representing the Central Economic Planning Staff) and Robert Hall.

Meanwhile Butler had put his proposal on 20 February to a small group of ministers including Churchill, Lyttelton and Cherwell, hoping to obtain immediate agreement, and had encountered opposition from Cherwell.[36] Two days later he circulated to a larger group of ministers a draft memorandum hastily prepared by Otto Clarke and briefly discussed with the Chancellor on the evening of the 21st. At this second meeting it was agreed that the impact of the plan on Britain's foreign relations made it indispensable to have the acquiescence of the Foreign Secretary who had gone to Lisbon for a meeting of NATO. Two officials, Sir Herbert Brittain of the Treasury and Mr Berthoud of the Foreign Office, were sent to explain the proposals to him, taking with them, at Bridges' suggestion, a letter from Robert Hall to Sir E. Plowden (who had also gone to Lisbon) outlining his views.[37] Plowden seems to have been influential in persuading Eden to press for postponement of a decision until his return and this allowed time for the objections to the plan to be more fully considered.[38]

At the meeting of ministers on 22 February Cherwell seems to have been alone in expressing outright opposition to the plan although Lord Swinton was also doubtful.[39] After the meeting Cherwell sent for Robert Hall who had already expressed his misgivings to the Chancellor and had come to the conclusion that the plan was not likely to be successful except at very great cost. He gave his views very briefly to Lord Cherwell and set them out more fully next day, on Saturday 23 February, in a memorandum copied to the Chancellor. Cherwell in the meantime had also drafted a note criticizing the plan and sent it to the Chancellor.[40] In a

36  Seldon (1981), p. 172, quoting diary entry for 20 February 1952 in Crookshank Papers.
37  The letter is in PRO T 236/3240.
38  Sir E. Boyle in J. K. Bowers (1979), p. 8; Seldon (1981), pp. 172–3.
39  Sir E. Bridges to Sir E. Plowden (then in Lisbon), 22 February 1952. Of the eight ministers present, all except Cherwell were in favour of the plan. A second draft of the Chancellor's memorandum on 'External Action' was circulated on 26 February but does not appear to have reached the Prime Minister until 28 February. It is contained in PRO PREM 11/140. (The first draft is in PRO T 236/3245.)
40  The note is in PRO T 236/3240.

minute to the Prime Minister he argued that the fundamental problem was to close the gap between exports and imports. This required a diversion of resources to exports or import-saving from armaments, investment or consumption. But the Robot proposals would widen the gap by letting the exchange rate slide, so making a still bigger increase in exports necessary. Some exports were held back by supply difficulties so that the adjustment to be made in other exports was correspondingly greater and would become greater still if Robot were accepted. The plan was a gamble which might well result in galloping inflation as import prices rose. It would be much better to hold the rate steady and borrow from the IMF or against the security of the dollar portfolio and the promise of $300 million in US aid.[41]

Cherwell's minute arrived simultaneously with one from Oliver Lyttelton, which strongly supported the plan. If the pound were allowed to float, the speculators who were selling sterling short would have to think again and the drain on the reserves would fall away.[42] Cherwell rejoined that this meant relying entirely on the reactions of speculators to save the situation. He suggested a series of measures, beginning with cancellation of import licences for all imports not absolutely necessary and continuing with cuts in expenditure on defence and investment; a rise in Bank Rate and a courageous budget; borrowing abroad; and pressure on the Commonwealth to take supporting action.[43] Lyttelton in turn responded two days later with a dilemma. Either the United Kingdom's accounts would balance or they would not. If they did, why should the sterling rate of exchange remain low? If they did not, why should the country be worse off under the Chancellor's proposals than under Cherwell's?[44]

Within the Treasury the division of views was sharpened by the return of Plowden from Lisbon on 24 February. He supported Robert Hall in representations to the Chancellor without, however, dissuading him from putting it to the Cabinet. Sir Arthur Salter, the Minister of State for Economic Affairs, was also briefed by them and joined with Lord Cherwell in opposing the plan.[45]

The issue came before the Cabinet at three successive meetings on 28

41  Minute to the Prime Minister, undated, in PRO PREM 11/140.
42  PM(52)6, 26 February 1952 in PRO PREM 11/140.
43  Minute to the Prime Minister, 26 February 1952 in PRO PREM 11/140.
44  PM(52)7, 27 February 1952 in PRO PREM 11/140.
45  His paper to the Chancellor is in PRO T 236/3240.

and 29 February.[46] By this time the Foreign Secretary, back from Lisbon, had come down against the scheme. The Chancellor refrained from any categorical assertion about the future loss of reserves but argued that, even if it were possible to scrape through till the second half of the year, the remaining reserves would be too inadequate to prevent the collapse of the sterling area at the first adverse turn of events. In his outline of the proposals, he suggested that, while the pound would be allowed to float, the reserves might be used to keep the rate within limits of 15 per cent on either side of the official parity i.e. within a range of $2.40–$3.20. This aim would not be made public but would be communicated privately to Commonwealth governments and banks. The United Kingdom and other members of the sterling area would retain full exchange control and there would be no change in the existing structure of the sterling area. Of sterling balances held by other member countries 'not less than 80 per cent' would be funded; and of the balances held by foreign countries (other than the USA, and Canada), 90 per cent would be funded. The balance of 20 per cent in the one case and 10 per cent in the other would be fully convertible (like all American and Canadian balances) and so would all newly acquired sterling. Finally, the London gold market would be reopened and the price of gold allowed to fluctuate freely. Residents of the sterling area, however, except gold producers, would be excluded from the market.

The Chancellor stressed the advantages of the plan while admitting some of the disadvantages. The dollar drain would cease automatically, apart from official intervention to check swings in the rate. Cheap sterling operations would be virtually eliminated. The exchange rate would take the strain of any imbalance and its fluctuations, however inconvenient, would bring into play equilibrating forces cutting down imports and boosting exports. The funding of sterling balances would remove the greatest potential danger to the reserves and strengthen confidence in sterling. The plan was also a major step on the road to convertibility and the meeting of Commonwealth finance ministers had made it clear that sterling could not survive on an inconvertible basis. He proposed to announce the plan at the same time as the Budget.

On the other hand, the Chancellor recognized that the plan would mean abrogating monetary and payments agreements with non-sterling countries, disruption of the EPU, the possible departure from the sterling area of some of its members, and 'mixed feelings' in the US government.

46  The minutes are in PRO T 236/3242.

He made light of the domestic effects in higher unemployment and more unstable prices as if these would arise only in 'the initial stages' or were an inescapable part of the adjustment process.

The Paymaster-General could find no sufficient grounds for so violent a change in policy. The only new facts were that we had failed to get $300 million in aid from the United States and that it was doubtful whether the EPU could honour its obligations and pay out gold if the UK achieved a credit balance. The Chancellor's proposals were not addressed to the central problem of restoring balance between imports and exports. A variable rate would not help to get rid of the trade deficit but, by turning the terms of trade against Britain, would initially make it worse. Exports might become more competitive but that did little good if they were limited by difficulties of supply rather than price. Similarly, making food and raw materials dearer was a slow and unattractive way of cutting down imports. It would be better to make cuts directly by further import restrictions, and by putting pressure on other sterling area countries to do the same. These measures should be coupled with a firm Budget and borrowings from the IMF and the United States.

The ensuing discussion followed familiar lines. The Paymaster-General was attacked for having it both ways: he was against a variable rate because it would not bring trade into balance and yet in favour of a fixed rate that assumed balance in the second half of the year. If such an improvement took place there would be no need to draw down the reserves in order to maintain the rate at $2.40 – it would rise automatically well above $2.40. If sterling was so weak that the risks of adopting the plan could not be faced, it would not be long before the reserves ran out and the country would have to cope with imminent economic collapse without a plan of any kind. Sterling was over-valued and the sterling balances at call were so large that there was little prospect of stability on the exchange market without floating and blocking. Ministers in favour of floating saw virtue in a moderate rise in import prices (and no doubt in unemployment too) as a way of bringing home the reality of the economic situation. They favoured making use of the price mechanism in order to encourage more gradual adjustments to changing circumstances than 'the violent upheavals which seemed inseparable from Government planning'. Ministers in favour of blocking took the line that it was unreasonable that it should fall to the United Kingdom to undergo the hardships of redressing the dollar balance of payments when her efforts might be frustrated by unrestricted drawings from the reserves by countries like Australia.

The opponents of the plan brought forward a mixture of economic and political arguments. What were Commonwealth finance ministers to think of a plan so different from the one they had agreed to a month ago? To this the Chancellor replied that he had indicated at the end of the meeting in January that the measures then discussed might not be sufficient and that much more drastic action might yet be necessary before the end of the year. He had drawn the attention of Commonwealth finance ministers to the increasing gravity of the situation early in February. But would the plan not come as a great shock to Commonwealth governments and risk a major political upheaval? On this point the Commonwealth Secretary offered reassurance. It was unlikely that Australia would leave the sterling area although Pakistan and Ceylon might well do so. Other Commonwealth countries were unlikely to object and Canada, not a member of the sterling area, would welcome the plan. The critics also underlined the setback to European unity that would result. The EPU would suffer an immediate death-blow and the United States would react against the damage done to the defensive strength of Western Europe.

The Cabinet was advised that the economists in government service who had been consulted were against the plan and their arguments were outlined: in particular it was pointed out that immediate convertibility would lead to a general restriction of world trade and induce other countries to discriminate against the United Kingdom. So violent a reversal of economic policy would also destroy any prospect of united action in face of a grave economic crisis: the argument was even advanced that it might exclude all possibility of forming a National Government to handle such a crisis if it occurred.

One compromise suggestion was that the plan might be carried out in two stages beginning with a severe Budget, drastic reductions in the defence and housing programmes and a sharp rise in Bank Rate. This would be followed at the end of March by a further Commonwealth Finance Ministers' Conference to produce an agreed plan for a floating currency and the funding of sterling balances. The Chancellor pointed to the paramount need for secrecy in devising a plan and to the primary responsibility of the United Kingdom government in coming to a decision. He himself was anxious to take immediate action as part of his Budget proposals and believed that by waiting nothing was gained and much was lost.

The Prime Minister concluded that the division of opinion within the Cabinet made it too hazardous for the Chancellor to proceed with the plan. The Chancellor then outlined the alternative course of action which he would feel bound to follow. It might, he suggested, prove just as unpalatable in its political and economic consequences as his original plan.[47] The Budget would have to include a substantial reduction in food subsidies; Bank Rate would go up to 4 per cent; a further cut would be necessary in the defence programme and perhaps also in the housing programme; investment might have to be discouraged by the cancellation of depreciation allowances; imports would have to be cut by £200 million, partly through running down stocks; open general licences to import would have to be suspended; deliberalization of imports from Europe would have to be carried further and would produce retaliation against British exports; and finally, other Commonwealth governments would have to be urged to be even more drastic in their efforts to economize gold and dollars and some way of limiting their freedom to draw on their sterling balances would have to be found.

Thus instead of a radical new plan to make sterling convertible the Cabinet accepted quite a traditional package of measures focusing on import restrictions. It was these which occupied them at their final meeting on 29 February. The minutes record a ritual reaffirmation of ministers' desire to get rid of physical controls, move to 'a more free economy in which there would be scope for the operation of the price mechanism' and approach 'the ultimate goal of convertibility of sterling'. It was suggested that the time would perhaps come later in more favourable circumstances (or if the reserves ran out) for action to make sterling convertible at a floating rate of exchange. It was not until the end of June that the plan was again discussed by ministers.

Underlying the whole controversy was the assumption that the drain on the reserves would continue and probably accelerate. Otto Clarke was urging on 24 February that 'at the level to which the reserves are certain to fall . . . it will be impossible in any event to maintain a fixed rate'.[48] Measures of the kind proposed were therefore inevitable. Even at the end of March the Treasury still thought that the reserves would be down from

47  The alternative plan was that submitted to the Chancellor by Plowden and Hall although their proposals did not altogether coincide with the Chancellor's oral presentation of them. They asked for a cut of £150 million in the engineering component and £50 million in the building component, of the defence programme; credit restriction and higher interest rates on hire-purchase contracts; a cut in housing by 25 per cent; the withdrawal of depreciation allowances; enforced economy in coal so as to release exports; and other quite specific measures (the paper is in PRO T 236/3245).

48  R. W. B. Clarke, personal letter to Robert Hall, 24 February 1952 in PRO T 236/3245.

$2.3 billion on 31 December 1951 to $1.1–1.3 billion by mid-year and between $0.6 billion and $1.25 billion by the end of the year.[49] Robert Hall was much more cautious. 'No one', he commented, 'is very good at predicting the future in economics'. The movement of reserves had not been much worse so far than was forecast by the Treasury on 21 January and there was some evidence that the changes needed in the economy were already at work. The terms of trade had improved, unemployment was rising, more capacity was available for exports, while the January import figures, 11 per cent above the new programme, pointed to the likelihood of an early drop.[50]

It was soon evident that caution was justified. When the Cabinet met on 28 February the reserves had fallen by $521 million in the previous eight weeks; in the remaining five weeks of the first quarter they fell by only $114 million and in the last week of March increased by $50 million. As the *Economic Survey for 1952* commented, there had been a marked revival of world confidence in sterling in March and some special, non-recurring factors had operated in favour of sterling.[51] Even at that point it should have been obvious to the unprejudiced eye that the downward trend in the reserves was slackening perceptibly, before the full impact of the import cuts had had time to make itself felt.[52] Over the next six months, contrary to the forecasts with which the Chancellor was plied, the reserves remained steady.[53] By the last quarter of the year they were rising strongly and at 31 December had reached $1850 million, well above the most optimistic of the Treasury's predictions.

The revival of confidence in sterling in March followed a Budget which was well received partly no doubt because it gave the lie to widespread

49 'The Future of Sterling', comments by Overseas Finance Division (presumably R. W. B. Clarke) on a paper by Robert Hall, 27 March 1952, para. 11, in PRO T 236/3245. In a paper on 'The Balance of Payments Position' circulated by the Chancellor to the Cabinet on 9 April 1952 (CP(52)111 in PRO CAB 129/51) the reserves at the end of 1952 were put at $450–1350 million – an even wider spread, but with an upper limit still far below the $1850 million actually reached.

50 Minute to the Chancellor by Robert Hall and Sir E. Plowden, 25 February 1952, in PRO T 236/3245.

51 *Economic Survey for 1952*, Cmd 8509, para. 13.

52 Leaving out special receipts and EPU settlements, the deficit in gold and dollars fell from $224 million in January to $171 million in February and $96 million in March.

53 In 'The Balance of Payments Position' the second quarter deficit was put at $375 million ± $150 million, allowing $100 million for US aid. This meant that the March outcome was not allowed to affect the forecast which turned out to be hopelessly wrong.

rumours that it would provide for a further devaluation or a floating pound.[54] The Budget proved to be milder than had been expected, the cut in income tax which it included more than offsetting a reduction in food subsidies and an increase in petrol duty in its impact on consumption.[55] An excess profits levy was also introduced but did not affect revenue until the following year. Bank Rate was raised to 4 per cent, and measures were taken to check investment through the suspension of 'initial' depreciation allowances and pressure on manufacturers of capital goods to increase the proportion of their output devoted to exports. Fresh cuts were made in imports, bringing the total since November to £600 million, measured against the current import programme. In relation to the previous year, however, the cuts, in volume terms, came to only £300 million or so and much of the reduction that ensued would have occurred in any event because of the inventory recession then in train.[56] It was this recession, more than anything else, that came to the rescue of the balance of payments. Stock-building fell off, import prices were lower and the terms of trade improved. Nothing of all this was foreseen in March.

The Cabinet decision of 29 February did not discourage the protagonists of the plan. The Prime Minister remarked a week later that he still looked forward to the day when it would be possible to 'free the pound'. Lord Cherwell, hearing the remark, was sufficiently alarmed to send him a further memorandum on 18 March urging that there should be no reconsideration of the decision until the sterling area was in surplus and the reserves rebuilt.[57] Almost on the same day, Rowan submitted to the Chancellor a memorandum on the 'External Sterling Plan' restating the case for immediate action.

This agreed that the Budget had been helpful and that there had been some recovery of confidence. Other members of the sterling area had been urged to raise their sights. But it was no good thinking that the problem would be solved by running down stocks and cutting industrial investment. There was no time to lose. The United States was running a surplus of $6 billion, American opinion was not favourable to the continuance of economic aid and the possibility of a fresh decline in American activity was

54  'The Budget may well have helped to stem the outward flow of short-term capital as much by what it did not do as by what it did.' (Butler (1971), p. 158). See also Dow (1964), p. 81n.
55  Dow (1964), p. 200.
56  Dow (1964), p. 73.
57  PRO T 236/3242.

looming up.[58] These circumstances, each of which appeared to make *against* any possibility of early convertibility, were urged in favour of the plan. Alternative measures from borrowing to devaluation or discontinuing transferability of sterling, were all dismissed. For the first time a reply was offered to the obvious objection that if the pound were made convertible, other countries would treat exports from sterling countries on the same footing as exports from dollar countries and discriminate against them. If they did so, it was argued, they themselves would be treated as in the dollar area. But if everybody was treated as in the dollar area there would indeed be that downward spiral of trade in a beggar-my-neighbour struggle for dollars to which Robert Hall pointed as the likely consequence of premature convertibility. Even more obviously there was the difficulty of distinguishing between existing import restrictions and those that were consequential on the plan. How was it proposed to identify the countless non-quota restrictions – far commoner than quotas – against sterling area supplies through the refusal of import licences and in other ways?[59]

At that stage the Treasury still hoped for action before Easter Friday (11 April). But the Chancellor contented himself with a paper on 9 April suggesting that no action should be taken on sterling balances until a comprehensive plan had been prepared. He took the opportunity, however, to warn his colleagues 'against the risk of thinking that our balance of payments difficulties and our external financial policy can be treated as though they were in a separate compartment isolated from our internal financial and economy [*sic*] policy. . . . It is probably true to say that nothing in the administration of the Socialist Governments since the war was more disastrous than failure to grasp this simple truth'.[60]

New suggestions and amendments were put forward and new difficulties were found. There was, for example, the problem posed by the commitment to continue EPU after 30 June – a commitment made by the Chancellor himself when in the chair at the meeting of the Ministerial Council of OEEC at the end of March.[61] There were questions about

58  The US surplus on merchandise account in 1951 was only $3 billion and in 1952 less than $3 billion; on current account, excluding unilateral transfers of all kinds, it was $3.8 billion and again lower in 1952; including unilateral transfers it was negligible in both years. US industrial production and GNP both continued to rise quite normally in 1952. On both scores the Treasury was exaggerating.
59  Edgar Cohen, Board of Trade, to R. W. B. Clarke in PRO T 236/3242.
60  'The Balance of Payments Position': CP(52)111 in PRO CAB 129/51.
61  Minute by T. L. Rowan, 28 April 1952, in PRO T 236/3242.

British relations with Europe if the French allowed the franc to float while the Germans held to a fixed rate for the mark. There were doubts whether it would be easy to sell sterling oil for dollars and whether Middle Eastern oil producers like Iraq might not switch to dollar invoicing and leave the sterling area.

A suggestion was put forward by Cherwell on 28 March that export proceeds should be surrendered within three weeks instead of six. The Chancellor of the Exchequer advised the Prime Minister that this would mean a sacrifice of exports and that, in any event, the use of cheap sterling was a more important source of loss to the reserves.[62] This reply was far from satisfying to Cherwell and his rejoinder elicited a fuller statement from the Chancellor three months later. He cited various enquiries into lags in payment and emphasized that 85–90 per cent of exports had all along been paid for within six months. As for cheap sterling, with which the Bank of England was obsessed, the turnover in the New York market varied between £$\frac{1}{4}$ million and £1 million per week; New York was by no means the only market and many deals were arranged without coming on any market. The total loss from this one cause might be as high as $200 million.

The flow of paper continued throughout March and April. On 25 March Robert Hall submitted a lengthy paper on 'The Future of Sterling' recapitulating the case as seen by the Economic Section. This drew a brief, critical response from Cobbold and a much lengthier one from Otto Clarke.[63] It did not convert the Chancellor. Shortly afterwards, on 4 April, he received a memorandum from the official Treasury that ran to 60 pages and expounded the case for Robot and the arguments that had been advanced against it.[64] Various memoranda were also prepared on particular aspects of the plan: for example, on cheap sterling, the likely reactions of countries outside the dollar and sterling areas, the possibility of a return to bilateralism and a 'downward spiral' in trade and employment.

Robert Hall tried to put the issue in the perspective of a continuing dollar problem. The United States had 'signally failed to make the changes in commercial policy which, by permitting an increase in her imports of

62 The exchange of minutes is in PRO PREM 11/130 'Financial Policy in 1952'.
63 'The Future of Sterling', memorandum by Robert Hall, 25 March 1952, is in PRO T 236/3242. The Governor's note of 27 March 1952 and R. W. B. Clarke's memorandum, 'U.S. Dollar Shortage and U.S. Exports', 26 March 1952, are in the same file.
64 'External Sterling Plan', report to the Chancellor of the Exchequer, 4 April 1952 in PRO T 236/3243.

manufactures, could help to redress her balance'. Nor had she made the large-scale investments in primary production in the non-dollar world that might have reduced the dependence of industrial countries on US exports of primary products. The persistent dollar shortage had now undergone 'a short-term intensification' just when American aid was shrinking. If the strain on the reserves was to be reduced and freedom of trade in the non-dollar world maintained what was required was 'greater insulation from the effects of world dollar shortage rather than the removal of what we have already'. Robot would be a move in the wrong direction, weakening or destroying the machinery and institutions built up since the war to cope with the dollar shortage. The imbalance in trade would not be easily removed by price adjustments, given the very low elasticity of demand for essential imports and the limitations preventing any rapid response in many of the leading export industries; the fall in the rate of exchange would have to be drastic and would be reinforced by speculation. In a world short of convertible currency, other countries would have a new incentive to earn dollars by restricting imports from Britain; and retaliation would merely add to the damage since British exports were less essential to buyers in other countries than imports from those countries. With the exchange rate taking the strain of the dollar shortage there would be a substantial increase in the cost of living and, in due course, pressure on wages that would push up prices still further, depress the exchange rate and destroy confidence in sterling. The blocking of sterling balances would make it more difficult to obtain credit from other countries and the abandonment of a fixed rate might prejudice any attempt to borrow from the IMF.[65] The sterling area would have little incentive to co-operate in supporting the sterling–dollar rate and would indeed have an incentive to discriminate *against* the United Kingdom since increased trade with the dollar area would depress the rate and improve the terms on which they parted with primary products in return for British manufactures.

The international repercussions would be equally unfortunate. The breakdown of the EPU would be regarded as an unfriendly act both by the other members and by the United States. Robot would also deal a blow to the IMF and its effect on the sterling area might well be serious. The blocking of sterling balances could be damaging to relations with the

---

65 The Chancellor, however, noted on his copy of the memorandum: 'this is not the confidential advice I have received.'

countries concerned. But above all, 'the unemployment, rising prices, and contraction of trade which would follow throughout the non-dollar world from such an attempt to force it into equilibrium with the dollar area without the benefit of discrimination could not help but lessen both the strength and the cohesion of the free world'.

Hall's alternative proposals included some that could be taken within the framework of the existing system such as further cuts in imports and borrowing from the IMF. His more radical proposals were directed to removing automatic gold payments from the mutual trade of non-dollar countries. The dollar pool would be abandoned and the reserves divided up between the independent members of the sterling area, leaving each to balance its own dollar trade bilaterally. The United Kingdom and Colonies would continue to operate as one unit. There would be no blocking of existing sterling balances and trade within the sterling area would remain free. The EPU would also be reformed so as to reduce or eliminate automatic gold payments and widen credit margins until it could almost be said to be absorbed into a reformed sterling area. In this way it would be possible to avoid the progressive restriction of non-dollar production and trade as non-dollar countries tried to acquire each other's dollars by deflation or by cuts in imports.

Hall recognized that insulating the non-dollar world from the dollar world ran the danger of increasingly divergent price levels between the two worlds and inadequate incentives to develop the dollar exports and dollar substitutes that would eventually bring the two worlds together again. But, as had been recognized in 1949, the bridge between the two worlds could only be built from both ends; all the strain of adjustment should not fall on the weaker party. Some adjustment in exchange rates was almost certain to be required. But such an adjustment should not be made as violently as Robot would require, at great cost and when the systems were badly out of balance.

In commenting on Hall's paper, Cobbold expressed satisfaction that there seemed to be agreement that the situation was 'too dangerous to risk going on as we are'. This was a shrewd thrust, for although the paper started out from the *hypothesis* that 'the present position of sterling is untenable', the hypothesis was not challenged and the radical measures presented as an alternative to Robot were of no relevance unless it were accepted. Cobbold pointed to the difficulties of persuading countries in and outside the sterling area 'to join a league to discriminate against America' and, still more, of maintaining 'an artificial two-price economy based on more or less unlimited credit'. From the outset there would be a complete divergence of interest between the Government and the public in every country within the area – the public wishing to sell 'easy' inside the area and the Government wishing to sell for dollars, the public wishing to buy in the cheapest market and the Goverment wishing to buy from inside the area. This situation, and the need to prevent leakages . . . via black markets, would mean ever stricter trade and exchange controls. . . . Each country in the Union would be jostling the others for dollar earnings and . . . running co-operation would be impossible even if initial membership could be achieved.

The policy would presumably mean withdrawal from the IMF, with whose aims it was in complete contradiction, and an end to the EPU in its existing form.

Otto Clarke took issue with Hall's starting-point. 'The dominating factor in the current situation', he argued, 'is the weakness of sterling, and not the strength of the dollar'. In the eighteen months before devaluation in 1949 the Americans were drawing in gold from everywhere: they gained $1\frac{1}{4}$ billion while the United Kingdom lost $\frac{3}{4}$ billion. In the next eighteen months to March 1951 the position was reversed: the Americans lost $2\frac{3}{4}$ billion and the United Kingdom gained $2\frac{1}{4}$ million. Then in the last nine months of 1951 the United States gained $0.9 billion and a further $0.6 billion in the first ten weeks of 1952, whereas the United Kingdom lost, first $1.4 billion and then $0.6 billion. Thus the reserve position of the United Kingdom tended to reflect the balance between the United States and the rest of the world. But the figures pointed to a change between the first period and the last in the reserves position in third countries. Before devaluation they were probably not, on balance, gaining or losing gold; in the eighteen months after devaluation third countries and private hoarders probably absorbed over $1 billion; in the next nine months they took perhaps another $1 billion; and even in 1952 they were probably still adding to their reserves the equivalent of newly-mined gold. It was an illusion, therefore, to suppose that the rest of the world shared the United Kingdom's predicament in coping with the dollar problem.

The root fact, Clarke argued, was the United Kingdom's lack of competitive power in an inflationary world. In a year when the volume of British exports had hardly increased, American exports had leapt from below $10 billion to nearly $15 billion.[66] This was not the outcome of

66  Clarke exaggerated a little. The increase by value in British exports in 1951 was 22 per cent while the figures he gives later in his memorandum show a rise in US exports (excluding military equipment) of 38 per cent.

policy decisions by the US government: it reflected the superior competitive power of American industry which had pushed up production by about 20 per cent in twelve months between the spring of 1950 and the spring of 1951 and had been able to supply its export markets in spite of the pressures of rearmament. British exports were conspicuously failing to make headway in the markets that had dollars to spare and were heavily concentrated in 'soft' markets where there was little competition. Half of Britain's exports went to sterling area markets where imports from America were severely restricted to no more than one-third of imports from Britain. The other half went to markets where the proportion was reversed: America sold more than three times as much as Britain in non-sterling markets. Moreover in 1951 this contrast had been sharpened. British exports to non-sterling markets had risen by only 10 per cent in value (and fallen in volume by about 6 per cent) whereas American exports to the same markets had risen in value by one-third. So long as America outsold her leading competitor in third markets with such success, Britain's lack of competitive power would continue to manifest itself as a dollar shortage. She could not hope to dodge the issue by two-world devices designed to isolate the United States from the rest of the free world, including in particular her trading partners in Canada and Latin America who supplied half her imports. There was no evidence that the stronger European countries and the rest of the sterling Commonwealth would join with Britain in such an effort. In fact if she were strong enough to build up a 'two-world' system she would be strong enough to live happily in a 'one-world' system.

In the paper submitted on 4 April to the Chancellor by the official Treasury many of the arguments already outlined reappear. The 'two-worlds' policy was rejected. 'Soft trade' policies, both in the sterling area and in the EPU, had been taken as far as other countries were prepared to take them. If the independent members of the sterling area were forced to finance their own deficits with the dollar area, the trading relations within the area would dissolve. In the EPU, opinion had moved away from the idea that members should not seek to earn gold from one another and to press it on recalcitrant members would disrupt the Union. The likely outcome of the policy was a great narrowing of the soft currency area and a corresponding widening of the hard currency area. It would perpetuate the dollar shortage in a high-cost, inflationary group of countries unable to compete effectively with the dollar countries. It would be anathema to the United States and would probably lead Canada to give up her attempt to steer a middle course between the United States and the sterling area.

The exposition of Robot made a number of new points. The official parity of $2.80 would be maintained with 'constructive intervention' to keep the rate as steady as possible, initially within the range of $2.50–$3.10. Technically, sterling was to be 'freed', not devalued. 'Cheap sterling' transactions would cease. The turnover in the New York market was now estimated at $300 million a year and emphasis was put on the loss of competitive power when materials were acquired by other manufacturing countries through dealings in 'cheap sterling'. It was admitted that with convertibility some countries would have an incentive to restrict their imports of 'less essentials' from Britain. But this would not be true of countries in the sterling and dollar areas which accounted for two-thirds of British exports. It was only the remaining third, or that part of it which consisted of 'less essentials' – perhaps 35 per cent – which was at risk. This implied that, at most, about $12\frac{1}{2}$ per cent of total exports might be exposed to discriminatory restrictions. But many countries that were heavily dependent on the British market might hesitate to take provocative action and would be vulnerable to retaliation. Examination case by case tended to narrow rather than widen the likelihood of conflict with other countries over trade in less essentials. The losses might well be less than those suffered currently through Australian import restrictions.

The paper envisaged that most European currencies would either float with sterling or be devalued to a new fixed rate against the dollar. The ability of continental countries to reach a common decision would put to the proof 'the brave words of the last four years' about European economic unity. The rest of the sterling area was expected to float at unchanged rates against sterling. It might be difficult to get them to cooperate in support of the rate since, as Robert Hall had pointed out, this was not in the interest of primary producers whose exports were priced in dollars. But their reserves were held in sterling and they would not wish to see them depreciated.

There remained the question how to consult the sterling Commonwealth once the scheme was approved in principle. On the one hand was the danger of leakage, on the other the obligation to consult. All of the member countries were likely to be anxious about and perhaps hostile to some essential feature of the scheme. One way of proceeding would be to send a senior Treasury official on a 5–6 week tour of the Dominions to invite the reactions of finance ministers to key features of a plan for early convertibility and allow the plan to be adjusted in detail before putting it forward for acceptance. Alternatively and preferably, the plan once decided upon should be communicated to the Dominions by telegram a few days before zero hour and then explained by a senior official from the Treasury.

The proposal to send out a senior Treasury official in advance of a discussion in Cabinet did not find favour with the Chancellor. Both Bridges and Arthur Salter advised against it. In a minute of 3 May Salter referred to a possible meeting of the Cabinet 'to deal with the main question' in June and accepted that something would have to be said to the Australian Prime Minister, Mr Menzies, who would be making a visit in the near future.[67] The Chancellor was in no hurry to make up his mind and noted on Salter's minute: 'the "tempo" is not at the moment "staccato".' The Governor, however, pressed him for 'a definite line of policy'. Were the safety of the currency and the maintenance of the reserves to be a first objective? The 'present easement' should not be mistaken for recovery. And was early convertibility the aim of policy or the further development of inconvertibility?[68]

Six weeks later, on 25 June, the Governor tried again, predicting an exchange crisis by the end of August unless Robot was adopted at once. The Chancellor held a meeting with his advisers, including some from other departments,[69] and it was agreed that the matter should now be put to Cabinet. Butler had by this time become a good deal less enthusiastic about the scheme. He was said to be at odds with the Governor by the middle of May and to have lost confidence in Leslie Rowan.[70]

When Robot was again considered by ministers, in the evening of 30 June, it was not at a meeting of the full Cabinet, as in February, but at a less formal gathering of the main ministers concerned. On this occasion Butler found himself the only supporter of the proposal, apart from Oliver Lyttelton. In its original form it had virtually been ruled out although an amended version was considered by the Commonwealth Economic Con-

67 Minute to the Chancellor of the Exchequer from the Minister of State, 3 May 1952, in PRO T 236/3242.
68 Minute on 'Exchange Policy' to Chancellor from Governor of the Bank of England, 6 May 1952, in PRO T 236/3242.
69 These included Roger Makins of the Foreign Office who had taken a sceptical view of Robot since the discussion in Cabinet at the end of February. According to Lord Roberthall, Makins told the Chancellor that so many people had been told about the plan by the Bank that it would no longer be a bombshell as it would have been in February.
70 Information from Lord Roberthall.

ference in the autumn under the guise of 'The Collective Approach to Convertibility'.[71]

We need not pursue Robot further than the summer of 1952 since that would take us far beyond the scope of this book. The alarms and excursions of 1952 were soon forgotten and when convertibility *de facto* came in February 1955 – only two and a half years later – it took the form of support, at a fixed rate of exchange, for transferable sterling without the blocking or funding of any sterling balances. The sterling area, the European Payments Union and the International Monetary Fund carried on as before without any of the fatal consequences predicted under Robot. The balance of payments continued to fluctuate, the reserves remained grossly insufficient and exchange crises recurred with almost predictable regularity. But the dollar shortage was never again so acute and the spectre of two worlds which had haunted Anglo-American economic policy since the war vanished completely.

What is one to make of this extraordinary episode? The most obvious comment is that the forecasts round which the debate revolved proved completely untrustworthy. The reserves did not fall to $600–1250 million by the end of the year as the Treasury predicted in March but rose to $1850 million; the drain had ceased completely by the end of March and was never resumed. The balance of payments in the second half of the year was also very different from expectations in January. Then it had seemed very unlikely that the target set at the meeting of Commonwealth finance ministers would be met: that is, that the sterling area should be in balance in the second half of 1952 with the non-sterling world.[72] At the end of

71  For an account of the later history of Robot see Birkenhead (1961) pp. 289–93 and for 'the collective approach' see Dow (1964), pp. 83 *et seq*. Instead of blocking sterling balances it was proposed to approach the United States for a contribution of $5 billion towards an exchange support fund. It was also proposed to act in conjunction with the leading continental countries. The Paymaster-General continued to attack the plan as one liable to 'lead to the worst financial crisis in history' (see 'The Collective Approach to Convertibility', memorandum by the Paymaster-General, 31 October 1952, C(52)377 in PRO CAB 129/56).

72  Nevertheless the target was later revised upwards to one calling for a surplus of 'at least £100 million' with the non-sterling world in the second half of 1952. The target included defence aid which ultimately amounted to £58 million in the first half of 1952 and £63 million in the second half. At the end of March, however, only £18 million had been received out of the £122 million appropriated by Congress for the purchase of US machine tools in the years 1949–50 and 1950–1 and only $1 million out of £300 million allocated to the United Kingdom under the Mutual Security Act for the year to mid-1952 (*Economic Survey for 1953*, Cmd 8800, para. 18).

*Table 9.1* Imports into the sterling area from the dollar area and OEEC countries 1950–2 (£m.)

|  | 1950 July–Dec. | 1951 Jan.–June | 1951 July–Dec. | 1952 Jan.–June | 1952 July–Dec. |
|---|---|---|---|---|---|
| Imports into UK from: | | | | | |
| Dollar area | 228 | 305 | 429 | 354 | 242 |
| OEEC countries | 302 | 434 | 489 | 420 | 318 |
| Imports into rest of sterling area from: | | | | | |
| Dollar area | 145 | 191 | 279 | 296 | 189 |
| OEEC countries | 174 | 262 | 339 | 275 | 198 |

*Source: United Kingdom Balance of Payments 1946 to 1953*, Cmd 8976.

March the Treasury expected the deficit (and the drain on the reserves) to be $275±$250 million.[73] Seven months later they put before the Commonwealth Economic Conference a figure of –$28 million[74] and in due course the *Economic Survey for 1953* recorded a current surplus with the non-sterling world (excluding defence aid) of $123 million for the UK alone and $182 million for the rest of the sterling area, i.e. $305 million in all. The swing in the balance of payments far exceeded the most optimistic predictions in the spring. If one takes the dollar area alone, the swing in UK payments between the second half of 1951 and the second half of 1952 (excluding defence aid but including capital transactions) was from –£435 million to –£73 million while for the rest of the sterling area it was from –£22 million to +£92 million.[75] For the whole of the sterling area this amounted to a swing of £950 million at an annual rate.

These figures do not by themselves imply that there was no cause for alarm in February or that government action after February made no difference. Speculative pressure against the pound might have continued or grown in March had action not been taken in the Budget, reinforced by a rise in Bank Rate and further cuts in imports. The government was not to know at that stage that the boom of 1951 would be followed by a year of depression in 1952 moderating the demand for imports throughout the sterling area. Yet it ought to have been alive by March, and certainly by

73 'The Future of Sterling: O.F. Comments on Mr R. L. Hall's Paper', 27 March 1952 in PRO T 236/3242.
74 CEC(O)(52)24 attached to CP(52)373, 31 October 1952 in PRO CAB 129/56.
75 These estimates are from the *United Kingdom Balance of Payments 1946 to 1953*, Cmd 8976, October 1953, tables 19 and 20. South Africa is not included.

June, to changing trends that made the second half of 1951 stand out as exceptional.

The fluctuations in imports into the sterling area from the dollar area and OEEC countries were particularly striking (table 9.1). Imports into the United Kingdom from the dollar area had almost doubled in value between the second half of 1950 and the second half of 1951 and were back a year later to about the level from which they started. Since most of these imports were on government account it must have been possible to predict the fall in 1952 with some confidence. Imports from OEEC countries followed a similar path, increasing in value by 60 per cent in the first of those years and falling back almost to their starting-point in the second. Again, this should have been predictable. Greater uncertainty attached to imports into the rest of the sterling area. Imports from the dollar area were very much depressed in 1950, the fall in that year lagging behind the fall in the value of exports a year previously when the US was in recession. Much the same lag depressed imports from OEEC countries in 1950 although these had already begun to rise in the second half of the year. Between that half-year and the second half of 1951, imports from the dollar area and from OEEC countries – exactly as in the British case – doubled. Imports from OEEC countries then sank back, like imports into the United Kingdom, to about their earlier level a year previously. Exceptionally, imports from the dollar area did not reach their peak until the first half of 1952 after which they, too, fell by half in the ensuing year. The reason for the delayed peak lies in the very strong surge in sterling area exports in the first half of 1951, when they were some 50 per cent higher than in the previous half year, and in the one-year lag behind exports that was characteristic of sterling area imports at that time. When there is such volatility in imports – exports, except in the first half of 1951, followed a remarkably steady trend – it is easy to go wrong; but the Treasury's judgement in the spring of 1952 seems to have been unduly influenced by distrust of the professions and advice tendered by Dominion governments.

Even more striking was the change in payments by the rest of the sterling area. In the first half of 1951 they had a net surplus with the non-sterling world (including sales of newly-mined gold to the United Kingdom) of about £320 million followed by a deficit in the next half-year of about £170 million – an astonishing turnround to which they were bound to react in their own interests. But in the first half of 1952 the deficit completely disappeared, giving way to a renewed surplus in the second half of the year. Even in the first six months of 1952 the outer sterling area sold more gold to the central pool than it took out to settle its accounts with other countries; and in the second six months it contributed over £90 million.

This analysis points to a second conclusion. The government appeared in 1952 to have lost faith in its power to control the balance of payments through import restrictions. The action it took was sufficient but it was uncertain of its sufficiency and was in doubt whether a fixed rate could be held. Up to 1949, and especially in 1947, import cuts and exchange control had proved a sufficient remedy for a balance-of-payments crisis. Perhaps, even in 1949, the government could have sat it out until the upswing in the United States removed the pressure. But in 1952 the moral drawn from that experience was that devaluation by itself did little good. There had to be, so Lyttelton argued, some uncertainty about the rate to keep market pressure within bounds; and there must also, the Bank maintained, be convertibility to cut out black markets and guarantee a future for sterling as an international currency. Yet in the end neither of these things was necessary. A mild depression, a little de-stocking, the almost inevitable rebound in the wake of the boom, were enough to do the trick, reinforced by drastic cuts in imports.

But what of the longer-term aspects of the proposals? Was Clarke right in urging that the fundamental problem was lack of competitiveness, not a renewal of the dollar shortage? If he *was* right, it would have been appropriate to devalue again but not necessarily to accept the need to float, either as a temporary expedient or out of inability to defend a new fixed rate. But he was not right. The 1949 devaluation was quite large enough. The United Kingdom moved back into surplus on current account in 1952 and remained in current surplus throughout the 1950s except in 1955, losing ground steadily to her competitors but not at a rate incompatible with external balance and full employment. There are no strong grounds for supposing that she would have done better with a lower rate of exchange.

Similarly, it was an error to judge the nature of the dollar problem from experience in 1951–2. American exports did respond elastically to the world boom brought about by rearmament. But so also, as Clarke himself pointed out, did the exports of Germany and Japan. If British exports grew less rapidly, this was largely because of the overloading of the economy to meet the new defence programme: there was a far smaller margin of capacity to spare in Britain than in other industrial countries. After 1951 American exports fell for two years and it took two more for them to regain the 1951 level. The aggravation of the dollar shortage in 1951 was a relatively mild and evanescent affair. The current account surplus, before taking account of unilateral transfers, increased from $1.9 billion to $3.8 billion and then fell to $2.4 billion in 1952 and $0.5 billion in 1953. *After* taking account of unilateral transfers, the surplus in 1951 was no more than $325 million and in the next three years there was a deficit. The dollar shortage as such had disappeared although still surviving in the twin forms of a hunger for additional reserves that could be satisfied with dollar balances and a need to limit purchases of dollar goods through discrimination if the hunger was to be satisfied.

While Clarke was right to emphasize the changing character of the dollar shortage, he was too easily satisfied that no great harm would be done if sterling were made convertible. So long as the American balance of payments left countries shorter of dollars than they would like and they still had doubts whether sterling would ever be as short, they were bound to give preference to the acquisition of dollars and treat convertibility as a convenient and easier way of earning dollars by running a surplus in sterling. If it was necessary for Europe to maintain restrictions on dollar imports in order to balance accounts with the dollar area it was bound to be dangerous to put sterling on a level with the dollar and invite the same treatment of imports from the United Kingdom. In the absence of discriminatory import restrictions, adjustments in the balance of payments would have to be made either through variations in price that were liable to be slow, limited and comparatively ineffective or through variations in the level of employment and activity that were effective but painful and wasteful. There was also a danger that adjustments would have to be made more quickly and violently for lack of the cushion of credit afforded by sterling balances and the credit arrangements within the European Payments Union. With sterling convertibility, as Robert Hall argued, 'the tendency would certainly be for countries to try to accumulate gold and dollars as their only cushion. In a world short of dollars this seems to me likely to lead to the mutual restriction of trade'.[76]

Whether Robert Hall's own scheme would have worked better than Robot is hard to say. Just as the proponents of Robot made too much of the dangers ahead in the absence of a radical change of policy, so he made too much of the universality of the dollar problem. Had the position been as desperate as the first group thought, their recipe might well have been the best available. Had the dollar shortage been as acute and widespread as Robert Hall implied, his proposals would have been more appropriate.

76 R. L. Hall, 'External Sterling Plan, Notes on Brief for Mr Menzies', 26 May 1952, in PRO T 236/3242.

But neither diagnosis was correct and in the end neither remedy was applied.

The debate over Robot is not without its interest in comparison with other debates over exchange-rate policy. It was more protracted than in 1949 although not as protracted as in 1964–7.[77] In all three cases, there was extensive debate at the official level and less debate at the ministerial level. The fullest debate was over Robot and it was also the most sophisticated. Those among the government's advisers who took part had nearly all participated in 1949 in the debate over devaluation with the notable exception of Donald MacDougall. Curiously enough, none of them on the second occasion recommended devaluation to a fixed rate. Robert Hall who had wanted a floating rate in 1949 fought for an unchanged, fixed rate in 1952. Otto Clarke, who was strongly against a floating rate in 1950 and again in 1951, was on the other side in 1952. The official Treasury, which in 1949 had seen little virtue in exchange rate changes of any kind, was now reconciled to daily variations. The Bank of England, strongly against a floating rate in 1949 and (in the person of George Bolton) in 1951, saw no alternative in 1952.

There were other paradoxes. Otto Clarke had been the main exponent of the dollar shortage ever since 1947 (or even 1946) and had presided over the putting in place of much of the apparatus of dollar inconvertibility. As Chairman of the London Committee he had spread the gospel at OEEC in Paris as well as in London. Yet in 1952 he was in the van of those who urged immediate convertibility. Again, it was a government wedded to the idea of abolishing controls and giving freer play to market forces that rejected Robot.

The issue, as always, was decided by ministers. In retrospect, Robot would have been disastrous, politically and economically; Butler himself came to the conclusion that it would have been a mistake.[78] Yet apart from Cherwell and Salter (and at a critical moment Eden) few voices were raised in Cabinet against it. Churchill was predisposed in favour of 'freeing the pound'; and it was only 'the cautious conservatism of the elder statesmen'[79] and the spectacle of agreement between two such different figures

---

77  Cairncross and Eichengreen (1983).
78  Salter (1967), p. 224. The Chancellor later told Bridges that Robert Hall had been right all along. In *The Art of the Possible*, however, Butler still maintained that 'in the long term . . . the decision not to free the pound was a fundamental mistake'. Butler (1971), p. 158.
79  Butler (1971), p. 160.

as Cherwell and Salter that moved him to withhold approval of the scheme.[80] Salter, within the Treasury, was unable to convince Butler. So it is right to give Cherwell credit for having, almost single-handed, stymied the plan.

80  Brittan (1971), p. 196.

# Chapter ten

# BRITAIN AND EUROPE

## Performance and attitudes

In comparison with other European countries, Britain appeared to emerge from the war in a comparatively healthy condition. Employment was higher than in 1939 and industrial capacity, in spite of the bombing, was also greater. The standard of living might be somewhat lower, but with a rapid and massive changeover from wartime to peacetime outputs, that could presumably be put right fairly quickly. Wage-earners were drawing higher real incomes even if they could not buy with them what they most wanted. By contrast, the three major continental countries, France, Italy and Germany, had suffered severely from warfare, occupation and destruction. Their economic systems were disorganized and recovery delayed by shattered communications and shortages of fuel, materials and equipment. In Germany production was almost at a standstill; in France and Italy it was far below capacity.

Yet the contrast was misleading. In nearly all the countries of Western Europe, industrial capital had expanded. In some that had not been fought over or had been quickly liberated, the apparatus of productive activity had survived almost unscathed, although there had been other damage such as large-scale inundation in the Netherlands or extensive loss of shipping as in Norway. In the neutral countries production had grown during the war years. Even in the three major continental countries, the damage to productive assets was not the most serious problem. In Germany, where output had reached a level in wartime two-thirds higher than in 1936, the loss of industrial capacity through war damage, reparations, dismantling or scrapping probably still left in place 10 per cent more than in 1936.[1] In France there had been chronic underutilization of capacity before the war and a small net addition had been made during the war. In Italy metal-working machine tools had increased by 40 per cent.[2]

The biggest obstacle to recovery was not shortage of capacity. This was demonstrated conclusively in Germany after the currency reform of June 1948 when industrial production grew by 50 per cent in six months. In the previous three years the economy had been tightly controlled by the Occupying Powers and the use of money had been severely circumscribed by rationing and allocation arrangements. In these circumstances the incentive to earn or accept money had been eaten away and money had become increasingly redundant. The more inflation was suppressed by the controls, the more monetary transactions were displaced by barter, payment in kind and compensation deals – time-consuming forms of exchange that prevented the emergence of organized markets and kept the economic system in a comparatively primitive state.[3] Even so, industrial production increased between 1946 and the currency reform in 1948 from 34 per cent of 1936 to 50 per cent – exactly the same percentage as in Japan (in relation to 1937) and by no means a slow rate of growth. With currency reform, industrial production accelerated sharply and by the end of 1950 was back to the pre-war level and increasing rapidly. It does not appear to have been seriously limited by any acute shortages of capacity. Shortages of raw materials and finance and the organizational problems of rapid expansion played a much larger part.

What was true of Germany was true also of her neighbours. The very disasters which all of them had suffered and the low level from which they started contributed to the rapidity of their recovery. The need was self-evident, ample labour was available, liquid funds had accumulated in private hands. Motives of obvious self-interest in survival encouraged an all-out effort, shortened the period necessary for recovery and inculcated habits that were both consistent with rapid growth and helpful in prolonging it. The habits of co-operation developed in wartime also made it easier in some countries for a close understanding between employers and employed to be carried forward into the peace.

1 K. Hennings in A. Boltho (1982), p. 477 quoting R. Krengel, *Anlagevermögen, Produktion, und Beschäftigung der Industrie in Gebiet der Bundesrepublik von 1924 bis 1956* (Berlin, 1958).
2 *Economic Survey of Europe since the War* (ECE, Geneva, 1953), p. 3.
3 ibid., p. 73.

In almost all European countries recovery from the war was rapid. In Western Europe as a whole, manufacturing production in 1951 was 30 per cent above the level before the war in 1937 or 1938. If we take 1938 as a measure of pre-war output – although in many countries it was a year of industrial depression with a great deal of over-capacity in many industries – the increase in manufacturing output was 50 per cent in the United Kingdom, 20 per cent in France, 35 per cent in Italy and at least 10 per cent in Germany[4] Given the low level from which the continental countries started, their performance compares quite favourably with that of the United Kingdom and measured in terms of the rate of growth was consistently well above it. By the early 1950s the rates of growth in all the main European countries were settling down to their normal relationships over the next two decades.

The picture is much the same if we use the broader measure of industrial production. In France and Italy the initial recovery carried industrial production to within 10 per cent of the pre-war level in 1947. By 1951 both countries, as well as Belgium and the Netherlands, had improved on 1938 by a margin that fell 10–15 per cent short of the United Kingdom's improvement over the same period while all of the Scandinavian countries had done better than the United Kingdom. In relation to pre-war output, the United Kingdom's position in 1951 was thus a little above average – a good deal above average if Germany is included. But if one takes the rate of expansion after 1947 the record of the next four years tells a more familiar story. Industrial production in the United Kingdom grew by over one-third – by no means an unsatisfactory rate by any standard – but France and Italy achieved 50 per cent or slightly less and so also did Finland while the Netherlands did even better and Germany more than trebled her production.

If we measure economic performance simply in terms of index numbers the United Kingdom had no more to crow about in the immediate post-war years than she had afterwards. It is perhaps not surprising that countries like France and Italy should set a hot pace in the period when they were still taking in slack and that the pace in Britain should be slower when she had none. What *was* surprising was that the pace remained faster

---

4 For *industrial* production the figures given in *Economic Survey of Europe since the War* (ECE, 1953) are 34 per cent for France, 38 per cent for Italy and 13 per cent for Western Germany compared with 55 per cent for the United Kingdom. The figures in the text are based on the United Nations *Statistical Yearbook for 1954* except that for Germany the ECE estimate seems more reliable.

in these countries and capacity expanded continuously as output grew. The experience of the early post-war years proved to be typical, not abnormal. Once a steep but feasible rate of expansion had been attained, it proved possible to sustain it. But this is not the whole story, for continental countries like Belgium that grew more slowly than Britain between 1947 and 1951 subsequently pulled away and experienced a higher rate comparable with that in neighbouring countries.

It does not seem possible to explain the differences in economic performance either before 1951 or afterwards in terms of differences in economic regime: the use of planning or market mechanisms; the sophistication of the controls; the monetary and fiscal policies adopted. There is too much in common in performance and too little in common in policy. The situation differed widely from one continental country to another and the policies they pursued varied just as widely, certainly as between countries, often as between successive governments. It is more natural to enquire what was peculiar about the United Kingdom that held her back than by what magic this or that continental country advanced so fast.

There were several important points of difference. One was that the United Kingdom from the very start had full employment and an inelastic labour force. In nearly all the European countries except Sweden and Switzerland there was a large reserve of labour that could be drawn upon continuously as expansion proceeded so that the necessary momentum could be acquired to give stability to expectations of further expansion and the necessary time was provided for the extra training, the installation of new equipment, the changes in productive methods, and so on that expansion required. Apart from unemployed workers there were the discards from areas of declining employment, notably agriculture, and all the immigrant labour that flowed in from 1945 onwards. In Germany there were the millions of refugees; in Italy there were the Sicilians and others from the south; in France the Poles and North Africans. Even in Belgium half the coal-miners had come from abroad. The United Kingdom had no unemployed to speak of, there was no manpower in those years to spare from agriculture and little use was made of immigrants in the places where they could have done most good.

It was not only that these additions to the industrial labour force gave expansion a longer run and more thrust but that an elastic labour supply made it easier to maintain labour discipline and plan the use of labour with more assurance. While the trade unions in Britain were remarkably accommodating under conditions in which they enjoyed unprecedented bargaining power, the average British management still had to spend far more precious time in struggling with labour problems than their competitors on the continent. The pace of change was slower because it was more difficult to find the necessary labour and because the work it did had to be the subject of negotiation.

There was, secondly, a difference in incentive. The need to earn money was more acute on the continent and the possibilities of large rewards were greater. The scope for an expansion in production and the importance of finding new ways of achieving it were all too obvious whereas Britain was more content to slip back into traditional ways. It was distribution of income, not production, that preoccupied the United Kingdom as tax rates of up to 19s. 6d. in the pound testified: a social revolution had priority over a revolution in productive methods.

It is true that these differences apply more strongly to France, Germany and Italy than to a country like Sweden. But they were not the only differences. There was, for example, a marked contrast in respect of external indebtedness and external responsibilities. The continental countries had no large external debts such as Britain had incurred, no enormous liquid liabilities threatening instability in the exchanges, no debt service weighing against their importing power. Germany and Italy had also none of the economic and military obligations that Britain continued to discharge all over the world: towards the Commonwealth, in occupation of the countries of defeated enemies, feeding the population of the Ruhr, re-establishing order, or preparing to withdraw once a new government had taken over. On the one hand were the sterling balances and the demands soon to be made by the Dominions on the London capital market; on the other, was the military presence Britain sought to maintain in Greece and Palestine as well as Germany: in Egypt and Iraq, Malaysia and Malta, as well as India.

Another factor was the difference in market structure. The United Kingdom's markets lay traditionally outside Europe, especially in the sterling area and in the less developed countries. In 1948 the sterling area took half of British exports and the Western Hemisphere one-sixth more. The countries of continental Western Europe in OEEC took less than one-quarter. By contrast, the European countries traded mainly with one another. Taking France, Italy, Germany and Benelux as a group, their exports to other Western European countries amounted in 1948 to 55 per cent of their total exports and the proportion was increasing with the recovery of Germany. This difference in market structure had two consequences. The first was that the United Kingdom was supplying a wider assortment of markets with widely different requirements whereas her competitors on the continent could cater for a market of greater uniformity in immediately adjacent countries. The difference in market density and propinquity made for longer runs and greater specialization on the continent and contributed to a rapid increase in real incomes. This was the second point of difference: the continental market was expanding faster than the non-European markets supplied by the United Kingdom. The gradual disappearance of Commonwealth preferences was also reducing the competitive advantage of British producers in Commonwealth markets while at the same time the calls made by Commonwealth countries on the London capital market added to the burdens on the British economy. Thus in various ways the continental countries were sustained by their association with one another in what became eventually the Common Market while the United Kingdom, after the first few years, found her dependence on extra-European markets, comparatively speaking, a handicap.

At the time, the United Kingdom was little aware that her record of growth over the first half-dozen post-war years would come to look disappointing in comparison with the experience of other industrial countries over the next two decades. It seemed in those years that the United Kingdom was ahead of the game in making the structural adjustments in her trade that the post-war situation required. She was not only earlier than nearly every other European country in getting back into balance but she was also bending every effort with some success to wipe out her dollar deficit by exporting more to dollar markets and cutting imports from dollar sources. This was the gospel she preached to her fellow-members of OEEC and it was a gospel preached in Geneva as well by the ECE.[5] The one thing on which the United Kingdom felt she could unite with the rest of OEEC was a common endeavour to get on top of the dollar problem.

If the United Kingdom had a false picture of her achievements so also had her neighbours on the continent. They had accepted her leadership in wartime and hoped that she would continue that leadership in peace. It was of course *political* leadership they most wanted: above all, the prospect of an end to war with one another and some closer relationship that would hold out that prospect. But since, as it proved, the straightforward way of achieving that relationship within a close-knit defence community was not feasible, they looked instead to closer economic relationships in

---

5 See *Economic Survey of Europe since the War* (ECE, 1953), ch. 6, 'The inadequacy of structural readjustments'.

which, again, Britain might take the lead. These were desired not only for their own sake but for what they might bring.

The hopes of integration led by Britain did not seem so misplaced in the late 1940s as they do now. It is difficult in the 1980s to appreciate the dominant position of the United Kingdom in the years immediately after the war. In 1947 Britain's exports were nearly five times those of France, and as large as those of France, Germany, Italy, Belgium, Luxembourg, Netherlands, Norway and Denmark combined. Four years later in 1951 they were still above those of France and Germany combined. Similarly, the United Kingdom's industrial production in 1951 was still as great as that of France and Germany combined and one-third of the total industrial production of all OEEC countries taken together.[6] These proportions should be contrasted with a situation in 1985 where Germany alone has an industrial production nearly three times that of the United Kingdom, and France not far short of double.

Britain was also in a powerful position as a creditor country *vis-à-vis* Europe. Whereas by 1948 the United Kingdom had balanced her current account and was in surplus with most European countries, practically every other European country except Sweden and Switzerland was in continuous deficit on current account until 1951. The deficits of France, Germany, Italy and the Netherlands were not only continuous but very large: the totals for the four years 1948–51 worked out at $3.0 billion, $2.6 billion, $0.9 billion and $0.9 billion respectively.[7] These were deficits incurred after the first two and a half years of peace and help to explain why the United Kingdom despaired of seeing an end to the succession of deficits and the need for Marshall Aid. They also help to explain why the United Kingdom saw herself cast indefinitely in the role of creditor in her dealings with the continent while at the same time running a dollar deficit which looked increasingly difficult to extinguish by means of surpluses with third countries.

But in a Europe unwilling to join forces for her own defence, it was the United States that was the dominant power not the United Kingdom. Militarily in NATO, politically in the United Nations and economically in OEEC, the lead had to be taken by the United States. The United Kingdom was heavily dependent on the United States and far weaker than her neighbours perceived. As the French were well aware, Europe came

6 *Economic Survey of Europe since the War* (ECE, 1953), appendix A, tables I and XI.
7 At the end of 1948 all four countries had expected to remain in deficit with non-members of OEEC after Marshall Aid came to an end. (OEEC, *Interim Report on the European Recovery Programme*, p. 193.)

well down the list, after the Commonwealth and after the United States, in the areas of greatest concern to the United Kingdom. The United Kingdom had neither an overriding desire for closer links with Europe at the expense of links with other continents nor a confident belief that the forging of such links would ensure the kind of integration that would stick.

In the first two years or so after the war Britain's economic relations with Europe were governed by the series of monetary agreements already discussed (pp. 123–9) and by grants and credits on a large scale. By April 1947 these had reached a total of £710 million, of which £325 million represented non-recoverable expenditure, £245 million loans and credits and £140 million economic assistance to Germany.[8] Later, in August 1949, Churchill claimed that payments to Europe since 1949 had reached a total of over £900 million.[9] The heavy dollar cost of feeding the Germans, amounting to $175 million in the first eight months of 1947 alone, was the subject of frequent outbursts from Dalton. But it was relations with France that dominated the European scene. These were far from happy in spite of well-intentioned efforts by Britain to help French recovery.[10] The French resented their dependence on Anglo-American aid and their exclusion from what the British counted their 'special relationship' with the United States.

From 1947 to 1950 various proposals were put forward for closer collaboration with France. At a Cabinet meeting in January 1947 Bevin asked for consideration of 'some special economic régime falling short of complete customs union between the United Kingdom and France'.[11] In the autumn Alphand, the leading French official in the Quai D'Orsay dealing with economic matters, suggested a Five-Year Plan for collaboration between the two countries and Bevin replied that 'we don't do things like that in our country; we don't have Plans; we work things out practically'. But he had proposed to Bidault, then Foreign Minister, a form of planned industrial specialization that would allow each country to

---

8  Bank for International Settlements, 17th *Annual Report*, June 1947, p. 123, quoting H. C. *Deb.*, 5th ser., vol. 436, Written Answers, cols 223–4, 30 April 1947. The total includes the value of surplus military stores and equipment, a contribution of £155 million to UNRRA (for 'relief and rehabilitation', not exclusively in Europe) and a loan of £100 million to France at ½ per cent interest.

9  Dalton (1962), p. 325.

10  ibid., pp. 156–7.

11  CM(47)13, 28 January 1947, in PRO CAB 128/9.

concentrate on certain lines of production: Britain on heavy steel products, France on light, with similar demarcations in textiles and other industries.[12] At the beginning of 1949 Cripps was all agog to go to Paris and prepare a plan for Europe with Plowden in OEEC as chief planning officer.[13] Nothing came of this but shortly afterwards Cripps and Bevin made arrangements with French ministers for Plowden, Hall and Hitchman to talk to Monnet at his country house. At the talks, which took place between 21 and 24 May, Monnet argued in favour of some dramatic gesture that would catch the imagination of Europe and the ECA such as a big swap of British coal for French meat. In November 1949 Monnet returned to the proposal in conversation with Robert Hall arguing that some such deal was necessary as a demonstration that the two countries believed in one another. Agricultural investment should be cut in the United Kingdom and coal investment in France, and the deal pursued even if it meant that France had to ration meat and the United Kingdom had to go short of coal.

Ideas of this kind struck the British as insubstantial. Apart from the difficulty of accomplishing a changeover to meat from grain production in France, or expanding the British coal supply to allow of bigger exports, there was nobody with the political standing and energy to carry through such projects. It would have been more to the point to open up the channels of trade and allow comparative costs to shape the resulting pattern. But European co-operation at that stage was talked of in general terms without enthusiasm for concrete action to do the specific things that were feasible. Economic integration was felt by the British to be little more than a slogan and a façade behind which each country went its own way.

The devaluation in 1949 did not improve matters. The French complained that they had not been consulted even although Cripps had warned Petsch in July that if it proved necessary to devalue, only two days' notice would be possible. When this was pointed out to Monnet he had replied that the two last days could have been used as a cloak for consultation. As it was, nobody now thought that Britain cared a damn about consultation.

Meanwhile the Marshall Plan had got under way and Britain was under increasing pressure from the Americans on three fronts: to honour her obligations under Article 9 of the Loan Agreement and make some move

12  Dalton, op. cit., p. 325.
13  Information from Lord Roberthall.

towards convertibility of sterling; to make some commitment on economic integration; and to help to remodel the scheme for intra-European payments.

## Convertibility and non-discrimination

The suspension of convertibility in 1947 did not absolve the British government from its undertaking under Article 9 of the Washington Loan Agreement to refrain from discrimination in its use of quantitative import restrictions. The commitment to convertibility as an ultimate aim of policy also remained. In practice the government was able to discriminate against dollar imports after 1947 with considerable freedom – and not just in favour of 'war-shattered' countries under clause 9(b) of the Agreement. The State Department continued to turn a blind eye on these practices as the European Recovery Programme got under way but the US Treasury viewed them with some uneasiness and had not lost sight of the 'emergency and temporary' nature of the suspension of convertibility.

By the middle of 1949 the British government was contemplating a considerable relaxation of import restrictions in favour of OEEC countries but found itself in a dilemma because of its unwillingness to extend these relaxations to similar imports from the dollar area. The possibility of withdrawing Article 9 was raised during the visit of Wilson Smith and Robert Hall to Washington in June 1949 when they were asked why it should be necessary for the British government to bring the matter up and so draw public attention to Britain's failure to implement the Agreement when the Americans had allowed discrimination to go on quietly without objection. Wilson Smith explained that the relaxations were intended to put an end to the worst features of bilateralism and would take the form of a published list of items to be allowed entry under Open General License. The 'under the counter' arrangements practised hitherto would not suffice: it would be necessary to engage in open and public discrimination. The British representatives suggested that perhaps the case could be met through the substitution for Article 9 of the provisions of the proposed International Trade Organization but the Organization was stillborn and nothing came of this idea.[14]

These exchanges were followed by the high-level tripartite talks in September 1949 that preceded the sterling devaluation later in the month. It was always intended that after these talks there should be continuing

14  Note of meeting in Washington, 8 June 1949, in PRO T 230/177.

discussion of fundamental issues in financial and economic policy but, during the winter, conversations were mainly on other, *ad hoc* difficulties such as trade in oil.[15] Meanwhile the United Kingdom had taken action to liberalize imports, and OEEC had passed two resolutions at the instance of the United Kingdom, the first on 4 July 1949 and the second on 2 November, calling on its members to free half their imports on private account from quota restrictions. Discussions had also begun in December on a new European payments arrangement and had revealed wide differences in approach between the United Kingdom and the ECA. Further progress on liberalization was also in some doubt since Gaitskell, who became Minister of Economic Affairs in February 1950, expressed strong reservations to the Economic Policy Committee on the abandonment of quota restrictions.[16]

In February Rowan reported from Washington increased interest in US circles in the trend of British policy and two months later Snyder wrote to Cripps inviting him to submit 'a full statement of the trade and payments policies which your Government expects to pursue' in the context of the Washington Loan Agreement.[17] These communications set off a lengthy debate on 'fundamentals' within the Treasury, with Gaitskell participating in the preparation of an official brief.[18] This took the line that it was impossible to contemplate full convertibility, even on current transactions, or the abandonment of discrimination against dollar supplies without much greater reserves in gold and dollars and an elimination of the United States surplus in its balance of payments. Although the reserves were increasing, they were still in April 1950 below the level when Marshall Aid began and in a matter of twenty months loan obligations to the United States and Canada would start to absorb about $200 million a year. Not only the United Kingdom but the whole of the non-dollar world needed to rebuild its monetary reserves and the United States must be ready to acquiesce in the loss of its own reserves that this implied. What was required for this purpose was a combination of policies designed to make dollars plentiful and sterling scarce; and a long list of appropriate policies – a good deal longer under the first head than under the second –

15  'Fundamental Discussions with the United States', memorandum by the Chancellor of the Exchequer, 27 April 1950, EPC(50)44, in PRO CAB 134/225.
16  See pp. 329–32.
17  Letter from John W. Snyder, Secretary of the US Treasury, 11 April 1950, annex B to EPC(50)44.
18  The papers are in PRO T 232/199; the final text is annex A to EPC(50)44.

was set out.[19] Unless a better balance was struck and reasonable equilibrium regained between the dollar and non-dollar worlds, the United Kingdom would find herself facing a continuous drain of gold and dollars as the rest of the non-dollar world sought to earn dollars from the sterling area in order to cover its direct deficit with the dollar area.[20] If the disequilibrium became worse, as it would in the likely event of a US depression in the next few years, discrimination, instead of being watered down, would have to be more severe in the interests of avoiding a general deflation.[21]

In the end, Cripps suggested to Snyder that conversations should begin with British representatives in Washington who would be briefed for the purpose. It was not until 21 June 1950 that Snyder was able to take advantage of this offer. It then became clear that the US Treasury was not seeking to review the working of the Loan Agreement but was looking for an explanation of the economic strategy by which Britain hoped to achieve the agreed objectives of convertibility and non-discrimination. The Americans felt that they had taken considerable political risks to help the United Kingdom and now needed some unmistakable sign that Britain, too, would take some chances. They argued that the specific actions that Britain had taken were sometimes a move away from the agreed objectives, instancing the emergency cut of 25 per cent in sterling area imports in 1949 which now appeared to have become settled policy. Even the EPU and trade liberalization tended to be written off as intensifying discrimination against the United States. The EPU scheme in particular was very different from the one originally proposed by the United States.[22]

The ensuing discussion followed familiar lines, with the British representatives emphasizing the disaster that would follow a second premature advance to convertibility and the Americans contending that the imbalance between the United States and the non-dollar world was a simple reflection of lack of competitive power which reliance on discrimination would aggravate. The Americans were also concerned to see so much of their aid going into reserves as the non-dollar world progressively reduced its dollar imports (without any equivalent expansion in exports to the American market).

19  Annex A to EPC(50)44.
20  Letter from Cripps to Snyder, annex C to EPC(50)44.
21  Annex A to EPC(50)44.
22  Note of meeting held at US Treasury on 21 June 1950 in PRO T 232/199. On this, as on other matters, the US Treasury took a less sympathetic view than the State Department and ECA.

The debate was one that continued long after 1950. But within a few days of the meeting in Washington, war had broken out in Korea and from then on Anglo-American discussions were preoccupied with other, more urgent matters.

### European economic integration

From the beginning, Britain had seen the central problem of Europe as 'the restoration of dollar viability'.[23] The Conference in the summer of 1947 that examined the plans of participating countries found that in 1951–2, the last year of the European Recovery Programme, their collective deficit with the Western Hemisphere was expected to amount to $3\frac{1}{4}$–$3\frac{1}{2}$ billion and their dollar earnings, even on an optimistic basis, would pay for only two-thirds of their imports from the Western Hemisphere. All European countries had the same problem and they could not hope to achieve independence of American aid without putting in hand a substantial modification of their industrial and agricultural structure. Co-operation for this purpose would automatically bring their economies much closer together and might lead on to a pooling of resources and perhaps complete economic union. But the immediate need was to organize for ultimate viability.

This was a programme that left considerable freedom of action to the United Kingdom and avoided difficulties with the Commonwealth. Indeed, since little came of the pooling of resources by member countries the freedom of action was much greater than at first seemed likely. It was a programme conceived in opposition to the various projects for a customs union favoured by the French which the Treasury dismissed as contributing nothing to the major problem of viability and more likely to divert resources to the production of less essential goods for the European market than lead to a concentration on the saving or earning of dollars. A general increase in intra-European trade should not be encouraged since it was 'more likely to hinder than to help the process of readjustment'.[24]

In the course of 1948 ministers and officials found themselves forced to look further ahead and consider whether, and in what circumstances, they would enter a Western European Union. The state of official opinion emerges clearly from the record of a discussion on 5 January 1949 between

23 R. W. B. Clarke, 'Western European Economic Policy', 27 February 1948, in Clarke (1982), p. 193.
24 ibid., para. 9.

senior officials from the main departments concerned.[25] The United Kingdom, it was agreed, must look to the United States, not to Europe, for her defence. She had a major interest in the economic recovery and economic stability of Europe and was pledged, as a condition of the ERP, to economic co-operation in OEEC. British policy should therefore be to assist European recovery, for example by letting them have supplies, or earn sterling. It also meant taking the lead in OEEC since otherwise it would break down and with it the whole ERP programme. But long-term co-operation with Europe held no attraction and would be at best a drain on Britain's resources. Co-operation 'in a structural sense (e.g. Customs Unions, integration in extreme forms) is impossible without political federation. This must be ruled out of practical consideration.'

In a longer memorandum a few months earlier Otto Clarke, who was much the most influential thinker in the Treasury although still only an Assistant Secretary, explained how he had been obliged to abandon his earlier hope of a pragmatic advance towards integration:

> an Open Conspiracy of bureaucrats and business men would link the affairs of the Western European countries closer and closer together, and we should advance by almost imperceptible stages to a point at which so many questions were in fact being settled internationally that one had the substance of Western European Government without its form. . . . I am now inclined to think that the political steps have to be taken first.[26]

It would be difficult, for all the achievements of the Common Market, to contend that in this respect Clarke was mistaken although his advocacy later in the memorandum of an Atlantic Union between the United States and the British Commonwealth, after independence of American aid had been achieved, nourished other illusions.

The lead taken by the United Kingdom in OEEC in 1949 was for liberalization of intra-European trade. In the British case this implied freer entry of less essential imports from the Commonwealth as well as from Europe and was only possible because Britain was moving into surplus with the non-dollar world. The surplus exposed her to the criticism that a substantial part of her exports was 'unrequited' i.e. brought no imports in

---

25 'Policy towards Europe' in Clarke (1982), pp. 208 et seq.
26 'Western and other Unions', memorandum by R. W. B. Clarke to Sir E. Bridges, 27 September 1948, in Clarke (1982), pp. 201 et seq.

return, and to the equally damaging criticism that a surplus with soft-currency countries had to be financed out of capital that was simultaneously being furnished by America to promote recovery, not for lending to other countries. A move towards liberalization not only answered these criticisms but might help to satisfy American opinion by demonstrating the ability of European countries to co-operate in helping trade to recover.

The campaign was opened at the end of March 1949 with a paper by Cripps and Harold Wilson informing their colleagues in the Economic Policy Committee of a review which they were conducting of goods that might be put on soft currency Open General License, subject to a dispensation from the conditions of the Loan Agreement governing non-discrimination.[27] They hoped to submit recommendations representing £200 million of imports from all sources, perhaps more. As they emphasized in a later paper, quota restrictions were not intended as protective devices and had to be justified on balance-of-payments grounds. The interests affected might submit a case for higher tariffs but the prior need was to remove the administrative burden of unnecessary controls, expose industry to more competition in order to improve efficiency and bring down prices and costs, and reduce the rigidities and distortions introduced by bilateralism. Where British producers were obliged to limit sales on the home market, however, either because of severe shortages of raw materials or the need to give priority to export targets, import quotas would have to be retained until the restrictions on British producers were relaxed.[28]

At the end of May the Chancellor was authorized to put a resolution to the Council of the OEEC calling for the progressive elimination of quantitative import restrictions in order to achieve as complete a liberalization of trade as possible by 1951. The Chancellor indicated that such a move might help to divert American pressure for a new European payments arrangement that could cost the United Kingdom dollars. The power to reintroduce restrictions under certain conditions would have to remain.

27 'Import Policy', memorandum by the Chancellor of the Exchequer and the President of the Board of Trade, 29 March 1949, EPC(49)30, in PRO CAB 134/221. In the absence of such a dispensation any relaxation would have to be confined to 'war-shattered' European countries and the colonies. A dispensation would also be necessary from Canada.
28 'Liberalisation of Trade', memorandum by the President of the Board of Trade, 18 June 1949, CP(49)137, in PRO CAB 129/35; 'Import Licensing Restrictions', memorandum by the Chancellor of the Exchequer, 28 May 1949, CP(49)124, in PRO CAB 129/35.

The resolution was adopted by OEEC on 4 July and set in motion a stage-by-stage withdrawal of import restrictions, the next being acceptance of a resolution on 2 November in favour of liberalization of 50 per cent of total imports on private account by all member countries by 15 December. This requirement was to apply to each of the three main categories of imports: food and feeding stuffs, raw materials and manufactured goods. Most member countries fulfilled or improved upon this requirement and their success encouraged the Council to adopt on 31 January 1950 a further resolution from the French and Belgians calling on members to remove quantitative restrictions on at least 60 per cent of imports on private account in each of the three categories of imports as soon as the new payments scheme then under discussion came into operation. The Council would decide as soon as possible after 30 June what progress could be made in 1950 towards substituting 75 per cent for 60 per cent. Agreement on a European Payments Union was reached on 7 July and was followed by the adoption of a Code of the Liberalization of Trade. This prescribed liberalization of 75 per cent of imports on private account from other members by 1 February 1951.

Thereafter the Code was modified from time to time and in the course of the 1950s extended to imports from other areas including North America. There were, however, retreats by individual countries when in balance-of-payments difficulties. The United Kingdom, for example, reduced the proportion of liberalized trade with Europe from 90 per cent to 61 per cent in November 1951 and to 46 per cent in March 1952. Germany had suspended liberalization entirely in February 1951 and France had done the same in February 1952.[29] But these were brief episodes that did not arrest the progressive expansion in intra-European trade or prevent the gradual extinction of import quotas. Between 1948, the base year for calculations of the liberalization proportion, and 1952, the last year of Marshall Aid, intra-European trade grew in dollar value by about 70 per cent (in volume by 80 per cent). Of this increase one-third was trade with Germany; only 5 per cent was with the United Kingdom.

## The European Payments Union

The recovery of intra-European trade had been facilitated by the network of bilateral payments agreements concluded after the war. But these had proved increasingly restrictive as recovery proceeded. The credit provisions of the agreements had brought into existence by the end of 1947

29 Rees (1963), p. 128; Triffin (1957), p. 186.

credit lines totalling at least $1.5 billion and this stimulus had helped to raise the level of intra-European trade to 60 per cent of its pre-war volume by 1947.[30] Then progress began to slacken, largely because foreign exchange reserves were running down but also because the agreements, being bilateral, were insufficiently elastic and far more credit was absorbed by the system than would have sufficed if each country's debits and credits could have been offset against one another.

A beginning was made with multilateral settlements in November 1947 but in the aftermath of the convertibility crisis Britain was not party to it. A further step was taken once the Marshall Plan was in operation in two successive Intra-European Payments Agreements in October 1948 and September 1949. These agreements introduced a system of 'drawing rights' under which countries in receipt of Marshall Aid could be required to make part of the aid 'available' to other participating countries to finance their forecast bilateral deficit with the country concerned. Drawing rights did not involve a country in passing on dollars but only in allowing its own currency to be drawn upon up to the amount forecast, this amount being made good in additional aid. The system, however, was highly unsatisfactory. Its operation was haphazard and unpredictable, largely because settlements were monthly and bilateral, not cumulative over the year and net of surpluses and deficits with other countries.[31] The assignment of drawing rights was on the basis of forecasts which were subject to large errors, the errors being aggravated by the incentives built into the scheme to redirect the flow of trade. The net effect was to distort trade patterns still further and stimulate bilateralism rather than help to strengthen competitive forces.

By the end of 1949, as the currency devaluations took effect, it was accepted that a simpler and bolder scheme was required as the natural counterpart to the liberalization of trade. Agreement would have to be reached by 30 June 1950 when the existing scheme was due to expire. Proposals were put forward by the United Kingdom and a number of other countries, by the Secretariat of the OEEC and by ECA. The ECA's proposals, devised by Robert Triffin, formed the basis of the scheme ultimately accepted. One feature was that settlements should be fully multilateral i.e. they should be on the basis of the net surplus or deficit in payments between each country and all the other participants taken together. A second feature was that the scheme was cumulative in the

30  Triffin (1957), p. 145.
31  ibid., pp. 152–3.

sense that at any time the net position would represent the outcome of all surpluses and deficits since it began. Thirdly, the scheme as adopted provided for settlement of the net balance up to an agreed limit partly in gold and partly in credit, with the ratio of gold to credit increasing gradually for debtors from zero up to 100 per cent at the agreed limit or quota and for creditors abruptly from zero to 50 per cent once the cumulative surplus reached 20 per cent of the country's quota. This arrangement was designed to put increasing pressure on debtors to correct persistent disequilibria in payments and at the same time oblige persistent creditors to offer credit to their trading partners.

Although the scheme once in operation was an outstanding success and the greatest achievement in European co-operation of the post-war period, the United Kingdom was extremely hesitant in giving it support. To some extent this reflected concern over the international position of sterling and the emergence of a system which might to some extent displace it: this appears to have been uppermost in the thinking of the Bank of England.[32] The Treasury was more concerned at the possibility that it might lose more gold and dollars than under existing arrangements. It had never taken kindly to losses of gold to European countries like Belgium and Switzerland and had no particular wish to earn gold from them.[33] It would have liked to exclude gold and dollar payments from settlements between European countries but recognized that this stood no chance of acceptance and aimed, therefore, to maintain as high a credit margin as possible. Since the United Kingdom already had payments agreements with several member countries that made no provision for gold settlements but involved settlement in sterling, she had no wish to supersede these by more onerous arrangements. The proposed clearing union, in the British view, should be a lender of last resort after existing credit lines were fully drawn upon – an additional means of payment rather like gold – and existing payments agreements should be disturbed as little as possible. The American proposals, however, envisaged all settlements taking place through the clearing union and the abandonment of

32 'It is a cardinal point in the policy of the United Kingdom', the Chancellor told the OEEC, 'that the multilateral facilities offered by sterling shall be not only maintained but increased.' 'European Payments Union', 27 January 1950, annex to 'Proceedings at the Meeting of OEEC Ministers in Paris', Report by the Chancellor of the Exchequer, 10 February 1950, EPC(50)28, in PRO CAB 134/225.
33 'Fundamentals: Gold and European Payments', memorandum by the Minister for Economic Affairs (?), 17 April 1950, in '1950 Fundamental Discussions with the United States,' PRO T 232/199.

bilateral agreements. They could see no reason to accept arrangements that would allow the United Kingdom to meet deficits with countries like Sweden in sterling and channel all its surpluses through the union to meet deficits with countries like Belgium to which it would otherwise have to pay gold.[34]

On the other hand, the United Kingdom feared that sterling held securely by trading partners like Sweden might be converted through the operation of the scheme into credits on which gold would eventually have to be paid.[35] This would have occurred if, for example, Sweden used some of her sterling to meet a deficit with Belgium and Belgium had a surplus in the union. The Belgians indeed were just as responsible for prolonging the negotiations for a new scheme as the British. They were reluctant to grant credit within the union for indefinite periods or to agree to fractional gold settlements with other members that reduced their chances of earning the gold and dollars they needed in order to meet their 'structural' deficit with the dollar area. They would have liked the scheme to require settlement of debit balances with the union in gold at the end of a year[36] – an arrangement that was tantamount to full convertibility and at the opposite extreme to the British dream of settlements that made no use of gold and dollars (but might, with advantage, be in sterling).

A second major issue was the use of discrimination. It was not only the Americans who wished to outlaw discrimination in trading relationships. Continental countries felt strongly that it was inconsistent with economic co-operation within the OEEC and more akin to economic warfare.[37] The bilateral agreements which the United Kingdom wished to retain not only allowed her to make the utmost use of her superior bargaining power but incorporated quota arrangements that were inherently discriminatory. The Americans wanted to replace all bilateral by global quotas, which in principle were non-discriminatory, but the United Kingdom did not regard this as practicable or desirable and pointed out that some bilateral restrictions, covering perhaps 10 per cent of trade, were indispensable adjuncts of the dollar export drive.[38] There was particular hesitation over

---

34  Rees (1963), p. 104.
35  Dow (1964), p. 51n.
36  'Meetings of the OEEC Ministers in Paris', memorandum by the Chancellor of the Exchequer, para. 6, 17 January 1950, EPC(50)20, in PRO CAB 134/225.
37  Williams (ed.) (1983), p. 180.
38  'A New Scheme for Intra-European Payments', memorandum by the Chancellor of the Exchequer, para. 4, 7 January 1950, EPC(50)10 in PRO CAB 134/225.

extending relaxations of quota restrictions to countries in chronic surplus with other members of OEEC. Any member of the proposed union should be free to reimpose restrictions on trade against a member whose currency had become scarce. Otherwise, Britain urged, creditors would escape all responsibility for any lack of balance and debtors would either have to deflate or to restrict imports from all the members without distinction. Quite apart from the issue of discrimination Britain was anxious to retain freedom to cope with a serious external deficit by re-imposing import restrictions – as she did, in fact, in 1951–2.

A third difference of view related to the powers of the Managing Board. The United Kingdom wanted an automatic arrangement working to an agreed set of rules while the Americans visualized a Board with extensive powers of inquiry into the affairs of member countries. In the end, the Managing Board's functions were broadly in accordance with British ideas.[39]

This particular issue was tied up with the relationship between the union and the IMF, which viewed the negotiations with some suspicion but took no part in them. There was a deep division in Washington between the ECA and other agencies including the Treasury and the Department of Commerce over a scheme that departed so obviously from the path of convertibility and multilateralism and enshrined discrimination against the dollar for an indefinite period. ECA was successful, however, in winning from Congress the necessary appropriation of $500 million to provide working capital for the union.

The various differences of view with the United Kingdom came to a head at the end of January, just before the general election in February. At that stage the Americans warned Cripps that they might have to establish a payments union without sterling area participation but thought that a scheme could be worked out to meet British objections.[40] In March fresh British proposals were submitted which asked for special treatment of sterling and offered to forgo the right to borrow from the union.[41] ECA argued, however, that the proposals would virtually have meant Britain's contracting out of the EPU or at least allowed her 'to pick and choose the claims and debts which she would settle bilaterally and those which she

39  Rees (1963), pp. 101–2.
40  EPC(50)28, paras 4 and 10, in PRO CAB 134/225.
41  'European Payments Union', memorandum by the Chancellor of the Exchequer, 3 March 1950, EPC(50)31 in PRO CAB 134/225.

would pass on to the Union'.[42] For a time the negotiations were dead-locked. At the same time efforts were made to resolve British apprehensions. Surplus countries, it was suggested, might be authorized to exchange the *credit* portion of their claims on the union for equivalent sterling balances provided these remained usable in future settlements within the union and not only for the settling of deficits with the sterling area. This helped to remove British fears that countries willing to hold sterling in their reserves would be required automatically to convert a surplus with the sterling area into a claim on the union in the monthly compensation arrangements. A second amendment dealt with the use of sterling balances accumulated prior to the EPU Agreement. Such use could not be restricted bilaterally by the United Kingdom but had to be channelled through the EPU. It was, however, limited – leaving aside balances on which a specific amortization schedule had been agreed between Britain and her creditors – to the amount necessary to cover the net deficit of the creditor country towards the union. ECA undertook to reimburse the United Kingdom for any gold payments to the union resulting from the use of sterling in this way. Although these amendments were apparently crucial to British participation, neither was of any practical importance when the scheme was in operation.[43] Similarly, although Britain was fearful of an immediate loss of gold under the scheme, there was a large initial surplus, only reversed in 1951.

The acceptance by the United Kingdom of the final scheme was due in part to the rapid increase in her reserves of foreign exchange in the first half of 1950. From a low point of $1340 million just before devaluation they had nearly doubled to $2422 million by the end of June 1950 and were still rising strongly. A second factor may have been the replacement of Cripps by Gaitskell in the later stages of the negotiation and the more elastic view of the scheme which he came to take. The paradox of Britain's position in the previous three years had been that she had had to pay dollars to some of her continental neighbours even though she was in current surplus with them as a group.[44] Such a situation was unlikely to

---

42  Triffin (1957), p. 165.

43  ibid., p. 167.

44  In the three years 1947–9 the United Kingdom made net payments from the reserves of £260 million to OEEC countries (*Annual Abstract of Statistics for 1948*, table 277). Not only was the United Kingdom in current surplus over those three years but the rest of the sterling area was in surplus on trade account and almost certainly on current account (Rees, op. cit., p. 65).

arise under the proposed clearing union: if there were a net surplus with the participants (including, however, *all* transactions in sterling), no loss of reserves would occur and even if there were a deficit the loss, up to the quota of £379 million, would not exceed one half of the net amount.[45] Moreover the credit that the United Kingdom would enjoy would be a great deal more, if the worst came to the worst, than the quite limited credit of which she could hope to take advantage under her bilateral agreements.[46] No doubt some such considerations were urged on Gaitskell between March and May and broke down his previous reservations to the proposals.

Thus the inclusion of the United Kingdom, and with it the whole of the sterling area, in the EPU was something of a fluke. It so happened that the negotiations came to a head when for once the reserve position was strong and just before the Korean War let loose its destructive influences. The scheme was adopted initially for two years only and before these two years were up the United Kingdom, as we have seen, was contemplating very different arrangements that would have ruled out further British participation and might have brought the Union to an end.

It was fortunate that satisfactory payments arrangements covering a large part of the non-dollar world came into existence before the full impact of the war in Korea was felt. The EPU helped to contain the

45  No specific provision was made for settlements beyond the quota but when in May 1952 the United Kingdom reached that limit the whole of the subsequent excess was paid in gold.

46  J. R. Sargent (in Worswick and Ady, 1952) p. 527. The United Kingdom's quota amounted to 1060 units of account or £379 million and of this, one-fifth or £76 million was a gold-free tranche (i.e. it represented unconditional credit from the Union) while only half the remaining £303 million was payable in gold. On the other hand, existing payments agreements with five members of OEEC only entitled the United Kingdom to £39.5 million in credit before gold payments became due; and the three countries (Italy, Norway and Sweden) that undertook to hold sterling without limit were unlikely to have accepted substantial amounts without protest. In the year July 1950–July 1951 when the sterling deficit with the EPU reached the extraordinary total of £540 million (of which £284 million represented the United Kingdom's current account deficit and the balance the deficit of the rest of the sterling area plus sterling transfers to OEEC countries), £340 million was covered by a swing in credit from the Union and only £200 million had to be met in gold and dollars (*United Kingdom Balance of Payments 1946 to 1953*, Cmd 8976, table 25). It is conceivable that had the United Kingdom not joined the Union, she might have acted earlier or more strenuously to cut imports and reduce the deficit; but it is *not* conceivable that she would have benefited from a net change of anything like £340 million in credit from OEEC countries.

imbalances generated by the war and subsequently by rearmament. It also underpinned the efforts of OEEC to remove trade barriers through its programme of liberalization. It provided a very tangible basis of economic co-operation between European countries. Above all its represented the kind of advance towards convertibility that proved sustainable and satisfied American hankerings after such an advance in contrast to the disastrous experiment that followed the American Loan Agreement.

## The Schuman Plan

The various arguments and negotiations – over 'fundamentals', economic integration and the European Payments Union – were all in progress simultaneously in May–June 1950. At the beginning of May the Foreign Office was wrestling with a memorandum by US officials accusing Britain of dragging her feet over integration. A paper agreed by Robert Hall was prepared in reply pointing out that different meanings could be attached to 'integration' and protesting that 'we have always recognised that we would have to take the leading part in OEEC if it were to be successful, and in our view we have in fact done this'.[47] Joint consideration of economic problems in OEEC did not necessarily lead to freer trade or to acceptance of the view that the primary requirement for a stronger Europe in the economic field was the removal of all restrictions on the movement of goods, people and capital. In a country not suffering from inflation but with a weak balance of payments, restrictions on imports might be a less harmful remedy than deflation or frequent changes in the exchange rate. In any case it was the United Kingdom that had been largely instrumental in initiating the move for greater liberalization of trade, a move that was acceptable because of the need to test and strengthen the competitive position of British industries.[48]

Less than a week after receipt of the US memorandum, on 9 May, the French government announced the Schuman Plan for coal and steel, referring only in their public statement to Franco-German production and leaving the basis of control over these industries extremely vague.[49] Bevin,

47 PRO FO 371/87012, 4 May 1950.
48 ibid.
49 As Attlee pointed out in the House of Commons on 11 May, a treaty entrusting control of Germany's basic industries to an international authority required the concurrence of the Occupying Powers. No reference was made in the French announcement to the limitations imposed on German steel production by the Occupying Powers and no indication was given as to the powers of veto that would be reserved to ministers.

who had not been consulted, was told of it by the French Ambassador on the same day. There ensued lengthy discussions within the British government, punctuated by an ultimatum from the French government on 1 June requiring unconditional acceptance of the plan or exclusion from subsequent discussion.

It looked from the start as if the French did not envisage British participation and the British, while they welcomed the move and were anxious to pursue discussion of it in association with other countries, were not prepared to commit themselves without further examination of its implications. On 2 June Bridges submitted an official report to the Cabinet pointing out that 'it has been our settled policy hitherto that we should not commit ourselves irrevocably to Europe either in the political or in the economic sphere unless we could measure the extent and effects of that commitment'. The report recognized that the most important aspect of the plan was that it represented ' a new and constructive approach to the problem of Franco-German relations' but thought it unlikely that 'by refusing to join in now on the French terms we shall be prevented from participating in European discussions in some manner later on'.[50]

A month later a Ministerial Committee including Cripps, Gaitskell and Wilson (but not Bevin, who was ill) reported that the outgoing French government had been deeply divided on the plan and that the United Kingdom might yet have to offer its own proposals. It noted that there had been virtual unanimity in the debate in parliament that the United Kingdom could not accord powers of decision over the coal and steel industries to a supranational body or participate in a federal system limited to Europe. But if a suitable chain of responsibility to ministers could be devised, a large measure of control could then be delegated. A possible structure meeting this requirement, with an Executive Council of 'industrial statesmen' reporting to a Council of Ministers, was outlined. This would have permitted a link with the OEEC through the Council of Ministers and the grant of a power of veto over investment projects to the Executive Council.[51]

Officials had gone rather further than this. A lengthy report by a Committee under Strath, a member of the planning staff, concluded:

In short it is our view that there is a case for concerted international action on economic grounds in regard to the coal and steel industries of

50  CP(50)120, 2 June 1950, in PRO CAB 129/40.
51  CP(50)149, 1 July 1950, 'Integration of the European Coal and Steel Industries. Report by a Committee of Ministers', in PRO CAB 129/40.

Europe; that the more we depart from scarcity conditions the more important the need for international action will become and that, therefore, the sooner a suitable organisation is established the better.[52]

In endorsing these views, Bridges argued that the High Authority's powers to veto new investment should be advisory not mandatory but added that this was not the unanimous view of officials.

After much discussion at a succession of meetings the Cabinet gave its approval in principle on 4 July to a scheme for the integration of the coal and steel industries of Western Europe subject to the reservation of a power of veto to a Council of Ministers and to terms of reference emphasizing the need for expansionary policies and deprecating anything of the nature of a producers' cartel. However, it was agreed after argument that the scheme should not at that stage be submitted to other governments and nothing more was heard of it.[53]

Soon after the announcement of the Schuman Plan Bevin had seen Schuman and Acheson, and Schuman had explained that he envisaged economic integration after 1952 (i.e. after the Marshall Plan) along lines that associated the United States and Canada with the OEEC. This was partly, he said, to avoid Western Germany's becoming associated with the Atlantic Pact Organization. This met with disagreement from Bevin who wanted to leave the way open for such an association under Article 2 of the Atlantic Treaty.[54] It was a curious inversion of roles for Bevin to find himself in disagreement both with Acheson and with Schuman in seeking greater freedom for Germany within the Atlantic Community. The incident was not without significance since Britain's attitude to integration with Europe was coloured by her efforts to give substance to the idea of an Atlantic Community while the United States, although nominally in support of the idea, was more anxious to thrust Britain into Europe and disengage herself from both.

Barely a month after the announcement of the Schuman Plan, and while it was still under discussion, the Korean War broke out. A new set of problems took the stage and for the rest of the life of the Labour government economic policy was increasingly dominated by rearmament.

---

52  CP(50)128 covering FG(WP)(50)38 of 16 June 1950, 'Integration of Western European Coal and Steel Industries', in PRO CAB 129/40.
53  CM(50)42, 4 July 1950, in PRO CAB 128/18.
54  CP(50)115, 22 May 1950, in PRO CAB 129/40.

# PART THREE

# Chapter eleven

## THE PLANNED ECONOMY

### What is planning?

The war had been planned and planned successfully, so it appeared. Why then, it was asked, should planning prove any less successful in peace?

It was a question that was much debated in the early post-war years. Speeches, pamphlets and books abounded in expositions of the virtues or failures of economic planning, often without any clear account of what distinguished planning from non-planning.[1] Before the war it had usually been identified with the system of economic management in the USSR and it was still associated in popular thinking with the compulsions and cruelties of the Soviet regime. On the other hand, there was widespread concern that if the economy were left unregulated and unplanned, it might undergo a repetition of the inter-war depression. Wartime experience seemed to show that full employment was attainable with no more than limited and acceptable restraints on individual freedom. At the same time, there were obvious difficulties ahead in the transition to peace that seemed unlikely to disappear if the state held itself aloof but might yield to the kind of action in which only the state could engage. So past experience

1 The publications of the 1930s on planning either concentrated on employment policy, monopoly and redistribution of income, or on the issue of decentralization, as in Oscar Lange's attempt to reduce planning to a few simple rules: for example, instructing government-owned businesses to charge a price equal to marginal cost. Even Barbara Wootton's *Plan or no Plan* (1934), in spite of its title, leaves the reader with a very hazy notion of what constitutes planning as distinct from government intervention of any kind. For one of the few pre-war discussions of the changes in government machinery that planning would require see Cole (1938).

and immediate prospects united in commending a much expanded role for government intervention. In what sense that role meant economic planning, and what the purposes and machinery of such planning should be, were questions that few stopped to pursue.

At first the debate turned largely on the retention of wartime controls which are described and discussed in chapter 12. The Conservatives wanted to get rid of them as soon as possible but agreed that they might be needed in order to keep demand in check during a short, transitional period. As Churchill put it in the Conservative election manifesto: 'We stand for the removal of controls as quickly as the need for them disappears. . . . As long as shortage of food remains, rationing must obviously be accepted: the dangers of inflation also must be guarded against.'[2]

The Liberals took much the same line. With the experience of 1919–20 in mind, they too were afraid of inflation: 'This war has forced us to accept controls which cannot be suddenly relaxed without incurring the dangers of soaring prices and inflation.'[3]

The Labour Party in their election manifesto, 'Let us Face the Future', made no reference to inflation although they agreed that money must not be allowed to lose its value. Their emphasis was on the need to retain controls, including control of 'rents and the prices of the necessities of life',[4] in order to ensure fair shares and to prevent profiteering. It was distribution, not production, that was uppermost in their minds. But they also foresaw a continuing need for controls as an instrument of economic management. Slumps would inevitably be 'too severe to be balanced by public action'[5] unless the sphere of government was extended. Controls would be necessary over investment, over the allocation of materials, for the promotion of exports, and for the bulk purchase of food from abroad. But how the various controls were to be combined was left unexplained. 'We stand for order', said the manifesto, 'as against the chaos which would follow the end of all public control . . . the chaos of economic do-as-they-please anarchy.'[6] Investment was to be planned by a National Investment Board which was to 'determine social priorities and promote better timing in private investment'. There was to be nationalization of

2  Craig (1970), p. 94.
3  ibid., p. 110.
4  ibid., p. 98.
5  Craig, op. cit., p. 99.
6  ibid., p. 98.

key industries, public supervision of monopolies and cartels, planning of food supplies and of agricultural production, and a wide array of policies in relation to housing, health, education and so on. Labour would 'plan from the ground up – giving an appropriate place to constructive enterprise and private endeavour in the national plan'.[7] But apart from this incidental use of the phrase there was no attempt to dwell on the idea of a national plan or to bring out what shape planning would eventually take.

To most ministers the need for controls seemed obvious and the use made of them constituted planning. Controls arose out of scarcity and some of them at least could be dispensed with as scarcity faded away. But scarcity is a function of price so that the question remained when and how far it would be proper to let a rise in price take over the work done by a control. An appeal to 'fair shares' was not a complete and convincing answer since some things were not controlled and the prices of those that were did not remain absolutely fixed. Moreover some controlled items were subsidized, adding to the scarcity, and the subsidies, too, were not fixed.

The justification for controls in wartime was that they allowed the government to impose its own priorities on the market directly when these priorities might mean victory or defeat. In peacetime it was more difficult to find good reasons for limiting the freedom of consumers and producers but it was arguable that if, within a measurable space of time, demand and supply were likely to come into balance at the existing price, every effort should be made to hold that price steady in the meantime. If this meant limiting demand, then the rationing process should be as equitable as possible. It was also arguable that if controls were removed prematurely, not only would demand, which was already excessive, increase but the price of 'necessities' (which were controlled) would increase sharply in relation to the price of 'luxuries' (which were not) and to the level of money wages (the most important price of all). Such a sharp upset in relative prices would undoubtedly be strongly resisted and the resistance would take the form of inflation – first wage inflation and thereafter a general and continuing rise in prices. This was the more likely if there was plenty of money available and the budget was in heavy deficit.

Justification along these lines, however, extended only to the period of recovery from wartime scarcities. It did not provide a rationale for long-term planning through the use of controls. If, for example, an ample supply of copper became available at the current price, there was no need

7 ibid., p. 99.

of a machinery of allocation. What controls was it intended to preserve in the long run? It became increasingly clear that there were only five candidates of any importance: controls over investment, whether financial or direct; controls over imports and foreign exchange; labour controls; controls over industrial location in the interests of regional planning; and general financial controls operating through the budget and monetary policy. Of these, the government was reluctant to continue the use of labour controls and never succeeded in tying them at all closely to the manpower budget which, for a time, it made the centrepiece of its economic planning under the illusion that the route to full employment lies through manpower budgeting. The others were operated in close association with one another, reinforced at times by price control and other instruments of policy, in pursuit of the government's economic objectives such as full employment, faster growth, greater economic equality, and the avoidance of wide differences in prosperity between different parts of the country. But it was only gradually that the government singled out the more enduring from the transitory among peacetime controls, began to focus on the broad, strategic instruments of economic management and came to rely increasingly on financial rather than physical controls.

James Meade had said most of what needed to be said on economic planning in a memorandum to Bridges in September 1945.[8] Planning, he argued 'should take place in terms of the broad categories of demand upon the community's resources' and these he listed as current government expenditure, public and private investment, the balance between exports and imports and personal consumption. For each of these, targets should be fixed in such a way that the aggregate was in balance with a similar target for national income based on estimates of the manpower likely to be available and the future course of productivity so far as it was possible to forecast it. These targets would be expressed in a common unit of measurement which would necessarily be money. Given all the uncertainties, any plan must be flexible and seek to preserve the right balance between total economic resources and the claims likely to be made on them under existing policies and programmes. While local imbalances in particular industries and regions would need study and the plan should strive to reduce them, it was inconsistent with the freedom of choice of consumers and producers to try to fulfil a rigid plan for each industry and

8 'Economic Planning', undated but almost certainly September 1945, in PRO CAB 124/890.

region. What Meade visualized was first an Economic Survey with fore-casts over the period of the plan (which he took to be five years), an indication to ministers of the options of policy arising out of these fore-casts and a set of ministerial decisions allowing the various targets making up the plan to be established.

Ministers did not engage in much discussion of what they meant by planning. As Sir Richard Clarke has pointed out, Stafford Cripps was the only one of them in the 1945 government who thought in terms of economic planning, rather than in terms of nationalization (Morrison) and fiscal policy (Dalton).[9] The only reference to planning in the index to Hansard from the end of the war up to November 1946 is to town and country planning.[10] Ministers' views of the planning process were nebu-lous but exalted and they dismissed anything that extended over a single year and did not carry the planning label as 'experimental'. It was never clear whether they had some fixed objectives – for particular industries or for aggregates like the volume of investment – to which everything else was to be subordinated, and which would be upheld even if circumstances changed radically, or whether they meant no more by planning than intro-ducing forethought and consistency into the framing of economic policy. They thought of planning as issuing in a plan but had not asked them-selves whether the essence of good planning was not re-planning. For all their talk of 'democratic planning' they took no pains until 1947 to explain to the public how their various decisions were intended to fit together in relation to the economic outlook as they saw it. Even then, large elements of economic policy, for example monetary policy, were not even mentioned and the role of prices was left entirely out of the picture.

Cripps wanted 'a central and co-ordinated production plan worked out by the Government';[11] and he wanted it, not on purely ideological grounds, but because he foresaw a prolongation into the peace of the stringencies of wartime. Even before the war was over he was issuing warnings that 'unless there was some general plan to achieve the necessary level of exports . . . when Lend-Lease from the United States ended . . . we should be in a very serious economic position. . . . It is going to be one of the most difficult and trying periods in the history of the country.'[12]

9  Clarke (1982), p. 79.
10  D. N. Chester in Worswick and Ady (1952), p. 341.
11  Cooke (1957), p. 330.
12  ibid.

Not only was he aware of the central importance of the balance of payments in planning the allocation of resources under post-war conditions. He was anxious not to underestimate the difficulties of industrial planning in a society as complex as Britain. 'Those of us', he told the Labour Party Conference in June 1945,

who have been concerned with the planning of war industries – in my particular department we had 15,000 firms to control and plan – realise that when we come to the broader national plan that will be required . . . we shall be faced with a very difficult technical task . . . [for which] no preparations have been made.[13]

Cripps's ideas on planning did not find full expression until the appearance of the first *Economic Survey* in the middle of the fuel crisis that began on 7 February 1947 and underlined, rather forcibly, the limitations of government planning. The *Economic Survey for 1947* contained the first and only attempt to explain what economic planning entailed ever to appear in an official British publication. It had a preliminary section headed 'Economic Planning' that we now know to have been drafted personally by Cripps, at that time President of the Board of Trade but playing an important role in the absence of Morrison, who was ill, in the co-ordination of economic policy.[14] His share in the drafting was unsuspected. In the debate on the document on 12 March Winston Churchill singled out for special commendation one of Cripps's paragraphs insisting on the need to compete with the rest of the world in price, quality and design and went on to speculate on 'who was the civil servant who wrote this for his Socialist masters. Out of the 2,000,000 we have at present, he should be the last one to be sacked.'[15] The author, sitting on the Front Bench opposite him, made no response.

In his exposition of planning Cripps took pains to distinguish between his concept of economic planning in a democratic society and totalitarian planning. The contrast that he was anxious to draw was in respect of the freedom of choice enjoyed in a democracy. But, of course, so far as

13  ibid., p. 328n.
14  Clarke (1982), p. xx.
15  *H. C. Deb.*, 5th ser., vol. 434, col. 1355, 12 March 1947.

*consumers* were concerned, their freedom of choice was circumscribed by the controls inherited from wartime in a way reminiscent of similar totalitarian controls. To that extent there was really no difference in principle between British and Soviet arrangements to bring consumption into line with what the authorities chose to make available. It was the compulsions to which producers were subject that Cripps had in mind – for example, the wartime power to direct labour. This power had been used sparingly. What had mattered more in manpower planning in wartime was the Control of Engagement Order under which employers were required to engage their workers, and workers were required to take their jobs, through the machinery of the national employment service. This order, and the requirement that certain categories of unoccupied persons should register for employment, were supported by the government's powers of direction to specific employment. The power of compulsion was a necessary sanction but there was little need to use it. In view of Cripps's emphasis on the abandonment of compulsion, it is rather ironical that the wartime manpower controls, including the power to direct labour, were resumed shortly after the appearance of the *Economic Survey for 1947* and only abandoned in 1950 (although the power of direction was not in fact used).

Planning, as expounded by Cripps, was divisible into three elements. First, there were long-term plans for a few 'basic' industries, of which six were mentioned: coal, power, steel, agriculture, transport and building. These plans were to be 'pressed forward as fast as possible and kept in proper relationship with each other and with the rest of the economy'. The 1947 *Survey* did not, however, give output targets for the six industries named but only for coal, electric power, building and ship-building (the last not included in the list of six).

Second, there were 'economic budgets' for manpower and national income and expenditure over the coming year. These were the macro-economic counterpart to the micro-economic industrial plans and would be prepared by 'an organisation with enough knowledge and reliable information to assess our national resources and to formulate the national needs'. The budgets related these needs to the available resources so as to 'enable the Government to say what is the best use for the resources in the national interest'. In the light of the budgets the government would use 'a number of methods', drawing on wartime experience but 'less drastic' than wartime measures, to 'influence the use of resources in the desired direction'.

The comparison between resources and requirements could be either in terms of manpower or of national income.[16] If in terms of manpower, the estimated future working population would be compared with the number of workers required industry by industry. If in terms of national income, the comparison would be between the estimated value of total output and the value of all the goods and services required. Ministers tended to prefer the manpower approach, to which they had become accustomed in wartime when the allocation of resources between departments had been made in terms of manpower, not finance. But in a peacetime world where money, not manpower, was the universal measuring rod and control was exercised over expenditure, not over employment, it was an approach that became increasingly out of place.

How were the requirements, however measured, to be arrived at? Cripps wanted them to be prepared, like the estimates of future output, by

> a central staff, working with representatives of the Government departments concerned under an official committee. . . . Some [requirements], such as the man-power for the Armed Forces, originate within the Government machine. Others originate outside the areas of Government control, but are sponsored by Government departments. . . . Others again, where no government control operates, are estimates of what the market will claim.[17]

Here, as with the plans for individual industries, there is no explanation of the process of estimating future output or of balancing supplies and estimated requirements, especially when these requirements were not wholly under the government's control but depended upon 'what the market will claim'.[18]

The third element in planning, as seen by Cripps, would supplement the manpower and national income 'budgets' by analysis of particular

---

16 Nothing was said as to which took precedence if there were any conflict between them. 'If we had balanced the manpower budget and showed an inflationary gap nevertheless, would we then create unemployment in order to close it?' (Clarke (1982), p. 77.) This was a false antithesis unless inflation originated in cost-push rather than excess demand. Manpower was simply a measure of potential output on the one side and final demand on the other, i.e. it was an alternative accounting unit. It did not make sense to talk of manpower requirements except in terms of demand as expressed in expenditure; and if labour was not the limiting factor in production because earlier limits were imposed by capacity or raw material supply, the resulting unemployment would show up equally in the manpower budget.

17 *Economic Survey for 1947*, Cmd 7046, para. 16.

18 Devons (1970), p. 68.

problems: the balance of payments, capital investment, shortages of raw materials or of fuel and power. In each of these sectoral analyses there would again be a comparison between supplies and requirements in order to arrive at a programme equilibrating the one with the other and consistent with the two key 'budgets'. For example:

the investment statement compares the estimate of what is required to be spent on capital equipment and maintenance with the labour and materials available for the industries which produce equipment, such as building and engineering. It is also necessary to make sure that the plans under this head are consistent with the funds which are estimated to become available for financing capital work, which is an item in the national income 'budget'.[19]

But as to how the various budgets were to be reconciled with one another so as to form a consistent plan, very little was said. The central problem of co-ordination was dealt with in a single paragraph. Planning, viewed as a way of 'deciding which out of a number of claimants must go short', was

precisely the same problem, only on a national scale, as the housewife has to solve every week. On the one side are the resources which we have to spend, on the other side are the things upon which we want to spend them. The two must be made to match. After full examination of possible means of attaining a balance, the official committee submits to Ministers a report on what measures should be taken and their decisions form the basis for subsequent action.[20]

The *Survey* then turned to the problem of implementation. It pointed to the apparatus of government controls that can be used 'to guide the economy in the direction which is indicated by the plan', including government expenditure, taxation and various direct controls. It then underlined the limitations of this apparatus which could not of itself

bring about very rapid changes or make very fine adjustments in the economic structure. To do this, they would have to be much more detailed in their application and more drastic in their scope. Indeed, the task of directing by democratic methods an economic system as large and as complex as ours is beyond the power of any governmental machine working by itself, no matter how efficient it may be. Events

19 *Economic Survey for 1947*, para. 19.
20 ibid., para. 25.

can be directed in the way that is desired in the national interest only if the Government, both sides of industry, and the people accept the objectives and then work together to achieve the end.[21]

There are two curious features of this exposition. The first is the absence of any mention of the price mechanism. There is no hint that there are always powerful forces at work to close any gap between supplies and requirements and that it may be well to pay regard to these forces. If the market's priorities are wrong, as the references to 'too many toys and . . . greyhound tracks' imply, by what criteria are they to be superseded and at what cost? It is not necessary – indeed it is not possible – to set market forces aside merely because they do not allocate resources in the most desirable way. As James Meade kept insisting in 1945–6, when he was Director of the Economic Section and effectively the government's Economic Adviser, planning and the price mechanism have to be used jointly. In no other way can the government free itself from the need to make innumerable decisions on petty details or introduce consistency into the limited number of major decisions that cannot be devolved. In wartime when the government's priorities take precedence over everything else, the price mechanism may play only a minor part. But when in peacetime the public can insist on expressing its own priorities, it is through the price mechanism that these are registered in the first instance. To talk of planning or economic co-ordination without reference to the price mechanism is to overlook the existing machinery of economic co-ordination.

This neglect of the price mechanism was no accident. It corresponded to a fundamental cleavage between two approaches to economic planning: a socialist, egalitarian, approach which saw planning as a purely organizational activity akin to the planning that goes on within a productive enterprise, an army or, for that matter, a political party; and a liberal, Keynesian, approach which saw planning as a corrective to the operation of market forces and dwelt particularly on the need for a level of effective demand adequate to maintain full employment. Although the emphasis of the two approaches was very different they were not in flat contradiction since the socialist approach did not by itself assure a high level of employment while the liberal approach was consistent with the use of controls for particular purposes. Where they tended to clash was in their view of the utility of price changes as a remedy for an imbalance between supply and demand. When scarcity developed at a given price socialist ministers

21  ibid., para. 27.

regarded rationing as the appropriate way of ensuring 'fair shares' while their economic advisers were more disposed to allow prices to respond, except under special conditions, and rely on the tax system or welfare payments to redress any inequity. Ministers rarely explained why the particular price at which demand and supply failed to balance was more 'right' than any other: why, for example, food subsidies should not be increased almost indefinitely. Their advisers pointed to the distortion of the price structure that resulted from a combination of food subsidies and high indirect taxes on 'conventional necessities' like beer and tobacco and 'luxuries' of all kinds and proposed the substitution of larger pensions or family allowances.

A second curious feature of the exposition in the *Economic Survey* is the conception of economic planning as a guide to the individual producer and consumer. The government may 'lay down the economic tasks for the nation' in a plan. But how does the individual learn from it what he ought to do? No doubt there are ways in which the government can elucidate economic problems and rally support for measures to resolve them or on occasion encourage the public to take specific action that would be helpful. But this is very different from the proposition that 'it is only by the combined effort of the whole people that the nation can move towards its objective of carrying out the first things first, and so make the best use of its economic resources'.[22]

The success of economic planning, like any other policy, may depend on favourable reactions from the general public; but it can hardly depend on freely adopted changes of conduct traceable exclusively to an intellectual grasp of the plan's objectives.

The nearest approach to a situation of that kind in the post-war period was the issue of a series of export targets by Cripps himself while still at the Board of Trade. His officials were sceptical of the utility of publishing figures which they regarded as little more than conjectural arithmetic, but Cripps saw virtue in announcing specific targets to which industries could be asked to work and was not unduly troubled by the difficulty an individual enterprise might experience in identifying its share in the industry total. In the event, the targets probably did serve to make industry more export conscious and did induce firms to put more effort into the export drive.

A similar example that may have been in Cripps's mind was the issue by the government in February 1948 of its *Statement on Personal Incomes, Costs*

22  ibid., para. 29.

*and Prices.* This was an attempt to enlist the support of employers, workers and their organizations in maintaining stability in prices and wages. As such, it had considerable success and wages in particular remained remarkably steady for over two years. We have become familiar since then with similar efforts to develop some form of incomes policy. But it has also been apparent that the price-mechanism does not operate in the labour market as it does in commodity markets since changes in *relative* wages are far more difficult to effect than changes in relative prices. The scope for voluntary restraint is correspondingly greater.

## Wartime planning

Apart from long-term plans for basic industries – plans which, as we shall see, never amounted to very much – the methods of planning described by Cripps were not very different from those in use in wartime. However, in the course of the war manpower came to be the currency in which decisions on the allocation of resources between departments were expressed; and from 1941 onwards financial decisions such as entered into the annual budget were taken in the light of an elementary system of national accounts and took stock of the probable flows of expenditure and the pressures that these flows would exert. There was also a whole range of controls at different points of the economy that had somehow to be co-ordinated with one another and with the manpower and national income budgets.

But there was an essential difference between wartime and peace. That difference lay, not in the power to direct labour in accordance with the manpower budget, as Cripps imagined, but in the dominant role of the government on the side both of control of resources and formulation of needs. The government was itself the employer of half the manpower, the importer of nearly all the food and raw materials, and the borrower of nearly all the country's savings. It could dictate to the labour market, the commodity markets and the capital market. It could do so because it was the agency through which the nation's efforts to achieve victory in war could find expression. This single, unifying objective resolved any problem of co-ordination in the use of resources because the final test of priority was what use of resources would contribute most to the winning of the war, and the final judgement of priority had to be made by the government. Not that the government was automatically right in its judgement: far from it. Nor need one suppose that 'the government' was ever more than George Unwin's 'group of bald-headed men, sitting in offices' or that it was always conscious that there was an issue of priority and devised appropriate administrative machinery. The point is that, in principle, there was a simple measure of value in arriving at administrative judgements as to the utility of alternative courses of action. This measure of value was on all fours with that of a business enterprise aiming at maximum profit; and organization for war was, by the same token, on all fours with the organization of a business enterprise for competition with its business rivals. That organization took the form of a planned economy, expressing itself in programmes of production, purchasing and sales, as well as in plans for the recruitment of labour, the raising of capital and so on.

All this, it need hardly be said, is in striking contrast to a world in which public goods like defence occupy a subordinate place in the economic scheme of things and it is the individual consumer who, by his expenditure, directs the flow of production. The measure of value in such circumstances is then established in the market in the familiar form of a price, and co-ordination comes about through the price-mechanism. Again, there is no need to idealize market forces any more than administrative judgement and there are many grounds on which it may be desirable for governments to intervene. The only point that needs emphasis is that when values reflect the judgement of millions of consumers, rather than of governments carrying proxies for limited purposes, planning necessarily takes a different shape and has to be married with market forces more effectively.

What was carried over from wartime was fundamentally the practice of drawing up programmes of various kinds. In the war it was through programmes that administrative decisions were expressed. If these related to outputs, like the aircraft programme, they represented a set of instructions to the manufacturers, to their suppliers and to their customers. More than that: they conveyed instructions over a period ahead that afforded a sufficient horizon for immediate decisions and that provided information as to quantities and times in one set of figures. Programmes were the means by which demand and supply could be reconciled over time by administrative decision. They gave concrete expression to the policy of the government and were changed whenever that policy changed.

Thus when it is said that resources were allocated through manpower planning this is not entirely accurate. The programmes were based on certain expectations as to the availability of manpower and were adjusted upwards or downwards when the government made a fresh manpower allocation. But what was really being decided was the size of, say, the aircraft programme, not how many men should be herded into aircraft manufacture. Manpower 'planning', in other words, rested on the power of the government to influence final demand (as, for example, the demand for aircraft), and hence the *demand* for labour, with only limited pressure on labour to comply, just as in later years planning for full employment was accomplished through demand management of a rather different kind.

Broadly speaking, programmes were a way of organizing *supply*; and the controls that accompanied them were designed to keep supply or production within the limits set out in the programme. They were at the opposite end of the spectrum from *demand* management which in principle aims at a given level of effective demand and is concerned only with a few key sub-divisions of demand (consumption and investment, imports and exports, public and private expenditure), not with organizing the flow of production. It is not surprising that ministers who took for granted that it was production that should be planned were glad to preserve most of the wartime controls, regarded them as symbols of a planned economy and took some persuading that it was more important (and much less cumbersome) to plan demand. There were, in any event, good reasons why the transition to reliance primarily on demand management should be protracted and incomplete. Some controls – those over imports and, to a lesser extent, investment – lay at the heart of post-war policy and could not be abandoned without the risk of severe deflation.

Responsibility for wartime economic planning was diffused among a number of departments administering particular programmes or particular controls: for example, the Ministry of Food, the Ministry of Fuel and Power, the Ministry of Labour, the Board of Trade, the Ministry of Supply, the Ministry of Aircraft Production, the Treasury and the Ministry of Production. Co-ordination of economic activity took place at different levels, some within the authority of a single department, some requiring interdepartmental resolution. The Board of Trade, the Ministry of Supply, the Ministry of Production and the Treasury had each some co-ordinating duties in relation to commercial policy, raw material supply, munitions production or financial control respectively. But the main responsibility for settling the more important issues in domestic economic policy rested with the Lord President's Committee. This increasingly powerful Committee was presided over in turn by Neville Chamberlain, Sir John Anderson and Clement Attlee, and was able to relieve the War Cabinet of business which, in wartime, was not of overriding importance. Anderson in particular built up the role of the Lord President and his

Committee into one of dominance on the home front, so that it was to him or to his Committee that problems and proposals, and matters that were in dispute between departments, were normally submitted. This did not, of course, apply to the larger problems of military–economic planning such as the size of the armed forces or the programmes for the production of weapons: these were settled by the Defence Committee, the Ministry of Production or in full Cabinet. Nor did the Lord President deal with the Budget or with overseas financial negotiations: these were the province of the Treasury.

So far as staff was concerned, planning duties were carried out by economists and administrators in many different departments. One group in the Prime Minister's Statistical Branch took a prominent part from time to time in major issues of economic policy. But the main responsibility for assembling economic intelligence and advising on economic problems lay with the economists and statisticians attached to the War Cabinet Secretariat, the economists in the Economic Section and the statisticians in the Central Statistical Office. The latter had in a few brief years revolutionized government statistics while the Economic Section, especially after it came to brief the Lord President and to act as his professional staff, assumed a key role in the formulation and co-ordination of economic policy which continued into the peace.

Before the war no provision had been made for the employment of professional economists in government. If some administrators like R. G. Hawtrey did emerge as skilled economists they were self-taught on the job. The economists who served during the war had been recruited from the universities and were likely to return there when it was over. It was, however, envisaged (in the only reference to post-war planning machinery made by the Coalition government) that some of them would remain in Whitehall. The government declared its intention, in the White Paper on *Employment Policy* (Cmd 6527) issued in 1944, 'to establish on a permanent basis a small central staff qualified to measure and analyse economic trends and submit economic appreciations of them to the Ministers concerned' (para. 81). This was presumably a reference to the Economic Section which was put on a permanent footing after the war and took planning for the maintenance of full employment as its principal duty.

The White Paper had set out, in general terms and not very convincingly, how this was to be done. In particular it had pointed to the need to stabilize the flow of total expenditure, or final demand, by operating on its various components such as consumer spending and capital investment.

This would involve a more complete analysis of the constituents of national income and expenditure than had been previously attempted and would require direct estimates of the various types of capital expenditure and the various sources of savings. Side by side with the financial analysis there would be a parallel study of the manpower position by the Ministry of Labour which was 'specially well-equipped . . . to direct attention to the employment aspects of national policy' and would indicate 'the probable supply of labour over the coming period, the prospective changes in employment in the different industries, and the effects upon employment of Government projects designed to modify the volume of investment or expenditure' (para. 85).

Thus the White Paper gave its blessing both to what developed into demand management and to what led a short life as the manpower 'budget'. The one occupied the Economic Section from then on while the other was never entrusted to the Ministry of Labour, which had no experience of economic forecasting and had no basis on which to predict 'prospective changes in employment'. The analysis called for by the White Paper was developed in a series of Economic Surveys, starting during the war, but remaining unpublished until 1947. These did, as the White Paper suggested, include a manpower 'budget' alongside a 'budget' of national income and expenditure and a forecast of the balance of payments. The Economic Surveys and the budgetary and other decisions based on them were about as close to economic planning as post-war governments ever got.

### Regional planning

One aspect of economic planning to which the White Paper gave particular prominence was the need for what was described as a 'Balanced Distribution of Industry and Labour'. This treated as an indispensable element in employment policy the need to prevent the emergence of local unemployment on the scale associated with the pre-war 'distressed areas'.

It was in these areas – Scotland, Wales, the north-east coast and west Cumberland – that the heavy industries supplying a high proportion of the country's exports were concentrated. Throughout the 1930s these industries, already depressed in the aftermath of the First World War, continued to suffer from chronic unemployment and present an obstinate problem of structural adjustment while the government attempted, without much success, to find palliatives. As the war approached, rearmament provided a partial substitute for lost export markets but even in August

1939 recovery from the depression had been very lopsided. While unemployment among insured workers averaged only 5.8 per cent in the London area at the outbreak of war, it was 11.3 per cent in Scotland and 14.8 per cent in Wales.[23]

In those days the problems of the depressed areas were viewed in terms of local circumstances without much reference to the state of economic activity elsewhere. The decline of the staple industries and the absence of newer industries or their failure to expand in those localities were treated as facts of life rather than as by-products of a world depression or an inappropriate exchange rate. The remedies proposed accorded with this view of things. They took the form of schemes of labour transference involving retraining for work available in other regions, schemes of work creation to provide temporary employment and to improve social amenities, schemes for providing finance for promising small businesses, and schemes for creating trading estates to bring in new branches of manufacturing industry. All of these had fairly modest results. Most workers who moved did so without benefit of government help; the schemes of work creation did little to change the balance between regions; the small businesses remained small; the trading estates were usually dominated by firms dependent on government orders. So long as the world depression continued, the regional contrasts did not fade away.

Experience in wartime of the wide variations from one locality to another in the ease of recruiting additional labour showed that the regional problem was bound to return if free play was allowed to the greater gravitational pull of London and the Midlands. To offset this would require more stringent policies than those favoured in the 1930s.

One might have expected that the White Paper on *Employment Policy*, in discussing localized unemployment, would dwell on differences in the pressure of demand and examine the measures necessary in order to secure a more equal pressure. Instead there is only a brief reference to the inadequacy of a policy of relying on the general maintenance of purchasing power to solve all the problems of local unemployment. A solution that relied on creating labour scarcity in the more prosperous areas, attracting a flow of migrants and producing a displacement of industry and orders towards the areas with labour to spare, was rejected as 'too long drawn out and [likely to] involve the partial depopulation of industrial regions'.[24]

23 *Ministry of Labour Gazette*, September 1939, p. 357.
24 *Employment Policy*, Cmd 6527, para. 24. But of course *any* solution to acute regional problems is long drawn out and usually involves partial depopulation.

The White Paper took diversification not pressure of demand to be the sovereign remedy. It dwelt on the need to restore 'proper industrial balance' to areas that had specialized too narrowly and were over-dependent on industries subject to sudden fluctuations or unpredictable changes in demand. These 'development areas' were to be assisted in establishing a more diversified industrial structure through the provision of training facilities to fit workers for jobs in expanding industries, the removal of obstacles to movement such as a shortage of accommodation and the location of new enterprises that would diversify the area's range of industries.[25]

The measures contemplated included:

(i) the construction of new factories in development areas on individual sites or on trading estates with a view to sale or lease to small firms;

(ii) priority in the grant of building licences to firms seeking to build or extend premises in development areas;

(iii) early release for conversion to civilian production of factories making munitions in development areas;

(iv) preference for those areas in the placing of government contracts;

(v) efforts to ensure access to adequate facilities for obtaining loan- or, where necessary, share-capital on behalf of enterprises with good commercial prospects and locating themselves in conformity with government policy;

(vi) powers to require industrialists to notify the government at an early stage of their intention to build a new factory or transfer a factory from one area to another; and powers to prohibit establishment of a new factory where further industrial development would be undesirable and to offer special inducements where it would be desirable.

The government also expressed its intention of creating in the development areas an adequate social infrastructure of communications, housing and public services and committed itself hopefully to research into the type of industry best suited to 'the long-term economy of each of these areas'.[26] There would be no fixed list of development areas since some would regain their prosperity and be removed from it while others would be added; and the measures, too, would vary since what was needed in one

25  ibid., paras 23–5.
26  ibid., para. 27. What was done in fulfilment of this commitment is a mystery.

area would not be appropriate in another. Responsibility for the policy within the government was to rest with the Board of Trade which was also to assume responsibility for 'all general questions of industrial policy'.[27]

The White Paper by no means envisaged that local unemployment should be dealt with exclusively by 'taking the work to the worker'. It accepted that some isolated communities, especially in mining areas, might have no hope of industrial revival and that it should be made easier for workers to move, even if large-scale labour transfers were not the right solution. The only concrete proposals, however, were for 'a substantial proportion of the new houses erected after the war [to be] available at a rent which is within the means of the average wage-earner' and for resettlement allowances for workers transferred under approved schemes. It cannot be said that much came of either of these proposals under the conditions of housing shortage in post-war years. Labour continued to move on its own, with or without benefit of government policy, on a scale comparable with internal migration in the inter-war years.

When the policy came to be applied in the Distribution of Industry Acts of 1945 and 1950 and the Town and Country Planning Act of 1947, what stood out, after the initial provision of surplus factory space, was the element of compulsion: not positive compulsion to go to particular areas but denial of the right to locate in areas judged to be already at full employment.[28] The post-war period started off under the influence of two dominant ideas: first, that action should be concentrated on the provision of factory space and the location of branch factories; and second, that this action should be governed by the level of unemployment in each region. The idea of growth or of a change in the long-term balance between regions did not enter because in 1945 attention was fastened on short-term issues of employment, not long-term issues of growth.

There can be no doubt that the government had a powerful influence on the location of industry in the post-war years. The influence was greatest on branch factories and warehouses, particularly those that were built by multinational enterprises. But new branch factories rarely add more than, at most, 2 or 3 per cent to employment in any year and some of the

27  ibid., para. 30.
28  The Town and Country Planning Act, 1947, required all new factories of over 10,000 square feet to obtain an Industrial Development Certificate from the Board of Trade. In consequence of this, existing factories usually elected to make extensions within the limit of 10,000 square feet.

employment they provide may displace other employment in the neigh-
bourhoods. Thus it takes time for a policy confined to new branch
factories to change the regional pattern of employment and unemployment and the results have to be judged with a time horizon stretching far
beyond the six years of Labour rule. To many the results were disappointing, especially if the test of success was a narrowing of regional unemployment differentials. The regional pattern of unemployment rates remained
remarkably stable from 1945 until the 1970s when it changed under the
joint influence of world depression and North Sea oil. But at least the
development areas suffered no greater unemployment than had been
experienced before the war in the most prosperous regions in the country.

Regional planning continued long after 1951: new approaches were
adopted and new devices introduced. But within the period of Labour
government before 1951 the shape taken by the policy did not differ substantially from that sketched in the White Paper. Those years saw the
application of ideas worked out in wartime, largely by Douglas Jay,[29]
much as employment policy reflected the ideas worked out by Keynes. In
both cases it is a matter for argument how far regional development and
full employment were the fruit of government policy and how far they
were determined by forces which owed little to the intervention of
government.[30]

## Post-war machinery

The new Cabinet had hardly been appointed when Cripps made a take-
over bid for the Economic Section which he saw as meeting in conjunction
with the CSO the need for an 'organisation to work out a national plan in
order to decide how much of our resources should be devoted to consumption goods, the export trade, capital goods, etc.'. Morrison who, as Lord
President and *de facto* Minister of Economic Affairs, had inherited the
Economic Section resisted the bid. At the end of July he put it to Cripps
that there would be serious disadvantages in the move to the Board of
Trade, pointing out that attachment of the Section to the Lord President's
office gave it a certain independence of departmental views which it would
lose if attached to the Board. Departments would feel the loss if the
Section's impartiality in offering advice could no longer be relied upon.

29  For Douglas Jay's own account of the development of the policy, see *Change and
Fortune* (1980), ch. 6.
30  For a fuller treatment of post-war regional policy, see McCrone (1969).

But of course if Cripps wanted to avail himself of the services of the Section, any request for their advice would be treated sympathetically.[31]

Cripps persisted and in the end the matter was resolved in Morrison's favour by the Prime Minister at a meeting on 20 August in which Dalton also took part. It was presumably in the light of discussion at this meeting that Attlee decided to set up the Ministerial Committee on Economic Planning, consisting of Morrison, Cripps, Dalton and Isaacs although it was not formally constituted until some weeks later and did not acquire its title until later still. The Prime Minister did not, however, pursue an idea he had floated of appointing a junior minister with planning responsibilities.[32]

In August and September there was much discussion among officials as to how they should set about preparing an economic plan. The lead was taken by Bridges, as Secretary of the Treasury, prompted by John Maud, Permanent Secretary to Morrison, and drawing in James Meade who had taken over from Lionel Robbins as Director of the Economic Section. Maud was anxious to involve the Treasury more deeply in economic planning: their position was 'cardinal' and he hoped to induce them to accept far more responsibility for the preparation and execution of the plan and for keeping it under continuous review. He urged Bridges to chair the official Steering Committee that would be in charge of the plan. Bridges needed little persuasion. The Treasury had already set up a full employment division; and since, in Bridges' view, there was 'no real distinction between the working out of a national plan on the line suggested and the task of devising a full employment policy' a merger between the two jobs was inevitable.[33]

By the beginning of October the necessary administrative machinery had been agreed. The Steering Committee on Economic Development was made up of the Permanent Secretaries of the four departments represented on the Ministerial Committee together with the Director of the Economic Section, the Permanent Secretary of the Ministry of Supply (Franks) and another Treasury official (Gilbert). Reports from this Committee would be submitted to the Lord President's Committee by the Chancellor. The work supervised by the Committee – for it was not intended that it should undertake the work itself – would be divided

---

31 'Central Planning', PRO CAB 124/890.
32 ibid.
33 ibid.

between five sub-committees covering investment, the balance of payments, manpower, statistics, and economic development and prospects. The first two of these had Treasury chairmen while the manpower committee was chaired by Ince of the Ministry of Labour and the statistics committee by Campion of the CSO. The last, which seemed likely to be the key committee, was entrusted to James Meade.

Meade set about the preparation of an economic survey as the first stage in a National Economic Plan. He had already advised Bridges at the end of August that the survey should be based on information supplied by departments on the prospects as they saw them for the coming year and should seek to establish the probable changes in employment, output, and other macro-economic aggregates over the year. The governing idea was that of full employment and the closing of any inflationary or deflationary gap that threatened to disturb the balance of the economy. The survey would also comment on the major implications by region and industry and would present alternative lines of policy to deal with the situation. It would be submitted to ministers through the Steering Committee which would add its own suggestions and recommendations and so provide a basis for ministerial decisions.[34]

This procedure, as *The Economist* put it a year later, meant

trimming the edges of departmental policies rather than . . . determining their shape; and more effort goes into seeing that nothing is done contrary to sound policy than into thinking up policies and urging them on the departments. . . . Policies are still born in the outer departmental darkness, away from the planners' fluorescent lights, out where the winds of unplanned economic pressure blow.[35]

On 9 October 1945 a letter was sent to departments from the Treasury asking them to submit information on their expected manpower requirements and demands on resources in 1946 for the 'central planning of economic development'. This information was used to prepare the draft of an economic survey circulated at the beginning of December 1945 to a group of officials from the Treasury, Board of Trade and Ministry of Labour.[36]

34  Meade, Diary (MS), entry for 1 September 1945; PRO CAB 124/890.
35  *The Economist*, 26 October 1946, p. 657.
36  The text of the first post-war 'Economic Survey' was prepared in the Economic Section in collaboration with the CSO. Most of the drafting was done by R. C. Tress of the Economic Section supported by Jack Stafford of the CSO. The Treasury was represented on the advisory group of officials by R. W. B. Clarke and P. D. Proctor; the Board of Trade by E. A. G. Robinson and W. B. Reddaway; and the Ministry of Labour by A. Reeder. (See '1945 Economic Survey', PRO T 230/54.)

It was not until 21 January 1946 that the survey was considered by ministers. It came first before the small group who had been charged with responsibility for economic affairs: Morrison, Dalton, Cripps and Isaacs. Morrison proposed that a White Paper should be published giving an outline of the planning machinery, a description of the current economic situation and a statement of the government plan for dealing with it. Publication should coincide with the Budget and would contribute to a widening of the Budget debate. Dalton pointed out that the Treasury played a major part in economic planning and that it was not altogether desirable that its plans (e.g. for tax changes) should be given a wide circulation. Cripps was also against publication. Would it be wise, he asked, to issue a document like the 'Economic Survey' if it gave warning of an approaching slump? In any event the government could not publish its plan because as yet it had none. It would be enough to represent the government's policy as one of 'extending into the first year of peace the machinery for the allocation of resources . . . which had proved its worth during war-time'.[37]

When the 'Economic Survey for 1946' finally came before the Cabinet on 7 February Morrison, briefed by Max Nicholson, explained that it had been prepared on an experimental basis and that 'until it was projected further into the future, [it] could not form the basis for a long-term economic plan'. Since it was experimental and could not be coupled with a statement on the machinery of economic planning (not, it will be observed, a statement on the government's economic plan), he thought publication undesirable. He promised, however, to prepare 'a broad statement of the economic problems of 1946'.[38] Unfortunately the statement that was submitted a few days later to the Prime Minister was so dull and badly written ('a pretty awful document' the Prime Minister's private secretary commented) that it went no further.[39]

When Morrison came to explain matters to the House of Commons on 28 February he was remarkably uncommunicative. Nicholson had advised him earlier that 'great care should be taken to avoid any references which might suggest to the public that any cut and dried plan exists or can be expected during the next few months of transition' in case this gave rise to

37 PRO PREM 8/319, 'Economic Survey for 1946'. The minutes of the meeting appear under GEN 115/1st meeting.
38 CM(46)13, in PRO CAB 128/5.
39 PRO PREM 8/319.

'clamour for facts and figures and the disclosure of planning machinery which would cause serious embarrassment to the Government'.[40]

Morrison contented himself with a general reference to the Economic Section and the Central Statistical Office and assured the House that 'economic co-ordination has undoubtedly improved enormously during recent years'.[41] It was an assurance he might have hesitated to repeat a year later in the middle of the fuel crisis.

A second 'Economic Survey' was begun early in April 1946 covering the period April 1946–April 1947. It reached ministers early in July but again it was decided not to publish. Like the earlier survey it did, however, provide the Steering Committee with an opportunity to highlight critical economic problems and push ministers into decisions that they had been in no hurry to take.[42] Like the earlier survey also, it concentrated on macro-economic issues, especially the inflationary gap and the balance-of-payments deficit.

Meanwhile Meade was much exercised because the 'Economic Survey' was usually in calendar year terms while the Budget was in terms of the financial year. He was anxious that any plan should relate to the financial year so as to make sure that the Budget would be regarded as 'the main instrument of carrying out the Plan'.[43] This idea attracted little support and he was finally persuaded in July to stick to the calendar year and present the survey in advance of the Budget. This would be less likely to scare the Treasury and would reduce the risk that the Chancellor would be pilloried if he failed to carry out the financial side of the Plan.[44]

By the time the next 'Economic Survey' was put in hand in September the Economic Section had begun to give more thought to the pattern of saving and spending in the absence of controls. It continued to make use of the idea of an inflationary gap and presented two estimates of its size according as income-earners saved the same proportion of their income as in 1938 or the higher proportion that was implied in the estimates of requirements submitted by departments. The draft, submitted to the

---

40 'Economic Survey for 1946', in PRO T 230/55. Nicholson's brief is dated 21 January 1946 and was incorporated in the Lord President's memorandum on the 'Economic Survey', CP(46)32 in CAB 129/6. Attached to the memorandum are the comments of the official Steering Committee and the draft 'Economic Survey' prepared by the Economic Survey Working Party.
41 H. C. Deb., 5th ser., vol. 419, col. 2131, 28 February 1946.
42 The draft 'Economic Survey for 1946–47' is in MEP(46)5 and the Steering Committee's comments are in MEP(46)7, in PRO CAB 134/503.
43 Meade, MSS Diary, entry for 6 April 1946.
44 ibid., entry for 27 July 1946.

Steering Committee in December 1946, showed the usual alternative presentation of the inflationary gap in terms of a manpower budget that did not balance. It was evident then, as on previous occasions, that ministers found the alternative version more intelligible and congenial than hypothetical figures of income and expenditure that did not match. When the *Economic Survey of 1947* was eventually published in February 1947, all financial estimates of national income and expenditure had disappeared and the argument was conducted entirely in manpower terms.

Before then, however, there had been the customary reluctance to sanction publication. It was necessary for officials to remind ministers that the Lord President had promised in November that, as background to a full-dress economic debate, a White Paper would be issued early in the new year in order to 'enable the House to take stock of the national position in the light of a more comprehensive economic survey than has hitherto been made available'.[45] The government was too deeply committed to withdraw. But it was also unwilling to publish the text submitted to it and a completely new document was hastily prepared, Stafford Cripps, as already explained, providing the introduction on economic planning and 'Otto' Clarke, a Treasury official, the Survey proper.

Thereafter *Economic Surveys* appeared annually. As the years went by they lost progressively any resemblance they had ever had to a plan. The manpower budget was an early casualty.[46] It never, in the published versions, lived up to its billing in the 1947 *Survey* as a comparison of 'the estimated future working population with the number of workers required industry by industry' (para. 15). The figures in 1947 showing the distribution of the working population at the end of the year were said to be 'neither an ideal distribution nor a forecast of what will happen . . . [but] the approximate distribution which is needed to carry out the [government's] objectives' (para. 128). A year later only the labour forces proposed for coal, agriculture and textiles were to be regarded as 'targets in the full sense' (para. 186). In 1949 the only target was for coal-mining; in 1950 there were none; and in 1951 no table of any kind for manpower distribution was included. The manpower budget had disappeared without trace.

The plans for individual industries underwent a similar process. The targets were thinned out until by 1951 only figures for coal, steel and

45 *H. C. Deb.*, 5th ser., vol. 430, col. 889, 20 November 1946.
46 Devons (1970), pp. 72–3.

agricultural production were left. The text accompanying the figures evolved into a review of recent events and current problems; and what figures were given for the coming year were tentative and hedged about with qualifications.

Detailed investment plans had also disappeared from the *Economic Survey* by 1951. The figures published from 1948 to 1950 proved very accident-prone, both in detail and in total. 'Usually the sectors where investment was planned to increase increased less than the plan; and where reductions were called for, the reduction did not fully materialisc.'[47] The total was equally subject to error. Total fixed investment rose in 1948 when the plan called for some reduction; and the plan was also thrown out by confusion over the treatment of repair and maintenance.[48]

The two 'budgets' that continued to be prepared and used in government planning were the forecasts of national income and expenditure and of the balance of payments. Balance-of-payments forecasts were published only briefly. In 1947 estimates were given of imports, net invisible income, planned borrowing and exports (as a residual) for the whole of the year. In 1948 and 1949 figures appeared for the first half of the year only. But in 1950 all forecasts of imports and the foreign balance, export targets and the rest had disappeared, never to return until the late 1960s.

National income forecasts made their first public appearance in 1948 when calculations were set out of the inflationary gap along the lines of the *draft* 'Economic Survey' for 1947: that is, through a comparison between the level of personal savings needed to finance prospective capital expenditure, given other sources of finance, and the level actually prevailing in earlier years. By 1949 more regard was paid to key economic indicators and in later years inflationary pressure was measured in ways more in keeping with later usage.

Meanwhile in 1947 planning had got its second wind. The fuel and convertibility crises roused the government to the need for a firmer grip on the economy even if they simultaneously demonstrated the difference between planning in practice and in theory. It was agreed that the planning staff must be strengthened; and at the same time ministerial arrangements underwent a succession of changes.

Early in March, Bridges submitted proposals for the appointment of a full-time Chief Planning Officer in the Cabinet Office, with departmental planning officers under his direction in six of the main economic depart-

47  ibid., p. 76.
48  Investment planning is discussed in detail in chapter 17.

ments.[49] Each of these planning officers would have a staff of his own and there would also be a small, picked staff in the Cabinet Office under the Chief Planning Officer which would report to ministers through the official Steering Committee of permanent secretaries. These proposals were accepted and announced a few days later by Cripps in the House of Commons in the course of a debate on the economic situation.[50] Cripps explained that the new arrangement was on the model of the joint war production staff which had also been drawn from different departments under common direction. But the interdepartmental staff, which was to work in close association with the rest of the Cabinet Secretariat, especially the Economic Section and the CSO, never came into existence. Only the small staff under the Chief Planning Officer was ever appointed. It began life in the Cabinet Office, was attached to Cripps as Minister of Economic Affairs and moved with him in November to the Treasury.

A second change, announced simultaneously, was the decision to create an Economic Planning Board for purposes of consultation with industry. This would include representatives of both sides of industry as well as members of the planning staff and would meet from time to time 'to follow development of the plan'.[51]

It took some time before these arrangements were implemented. Sir Edwin Plowden was named as Chief Planning Officer in March and what became known as the Central Economic Planning Staff took up their duties in May and June. The Economic Planning Board was not appointed until July.

The primary task of the CEPS, Attlee told the House of Commons, was 'to develop the long-term plan for the use of the country's man-power and resources'. The Chief Planning Officer would work directly under the Lord President, with access to all ministers concerned with production. Decisions on planning policy would continue to be made by the Cabinet and responsibility for them would rest wholly on ministers. In one of his rare efforts to explain what planning signified, Attlee went on:

> The function of planning is to enable decisions to be reached as to the best allocation of available man-power, materials, services and manu-

49  'Proposals for Strengthening the Staff for Economic Planning', memorandum by Sir Edward Bridges, 7 March 1947, in PRO PREM 8/646.
50  *H. C. Deb.*, 5th ser., vol. 434, cols 69–71, 10 March 1947.
51  ibid. The Planning Board proved to be something of a fifth wheel, duplicating the observations of the Steering Committee without doing much to engage employers or employed in support of the government's plans. In contrast to NEDC no ministers attended.

facturing capacity. Planning is itself no substitute for the increased effort and efficiency which are essential to our national prosperity.[52]

Throughout the fuel crisis and preparations for the new planning arrangements the Lord President had been ill. He was out of action from mid-January until May and in his absence Dalton had taken over while Cripps took an increasingly active part. Ministerial disquiet grew when the convertibility crisis took them by surprise in the summer and after various manoeuvres Cripps emerged on 29 September as Minister of Economic Affairs. Six weeks later, on 13 November, he had become Chancellor and in full control of economic policy.

From then on there is a coherence to the government's planning that was previously lacking. Economic and financial policy were united under a strong minister with a clear line of policy. No doubt things were easier for Cripps in many ways. The Cabinet was more alive to the need for firm action: the balance of payments was nearing equilibrium and any deficit in dollars was looked after by Marshall Aid; Dalton had given the Budget a push into surplus. But Cripps was also more willing to listen to advice, more perceptive in his reactions to it and more successful in communicating to the public what he aimed to do. Plowden enjoyed his confidence and had great influence on him; and Plowden in turn was well advised, particularly by Robert Hall, the new Director of the Economic Section.

## Long-term planning

The new team concentrated first on the investment programme, then turned their attention to long-run issues and set about the preparation of a 'Long-term Programme' for the OEEC. There was nothing particularly novel about trying to look several years ahead in economic policy. There had been attempts in wartime to foresee the future of international trade once the war was over and estimate the likely course of the British balance of payments. The Board of Trade in 1945–6 had carried out a massive study of British long-term export prospects. The briefing for the Washington loan negotiations had also involved studies of the prospective economic situation several years ahead.

The first post-war long-term survey, which may have formed part of the briefing, was circulated by the Economic Section and the CSO on 29 September 1945.[53] It made forecasts of net national income in 1946, 1947

52  *H. C. Deb.*, 5th ser., vol. 435, col. 1413, 27 March 1947.
53  The memorandum is in PRO T 230/54 and is numbered EC(S)(45)32.

and 1948 which proved remarkably accurate. For example, it put the increase in national income between 1939 and 1948 at 11 per cent which, as it happens, agrees exactly with Feinstein's estimate for the increase between those years.[54] In reaching this total it allowed for a fall in the size of the armed forces to 1 million by the end of 1946 (in this it was too optimistic); a rise in unemployment to not more than 4 per cent in 1947 and 1948; and an improvement in labour productivity by 1948 of 10 per cent above the 1939 level (here again it was remarkably near the mark since the number in civil employment was about $1\frac{1}{2}$ per cent higher and the national income up by about 11 per cent). The same document puts the increase in wage rates from mid-1945 to mid-1948 at about $7\frac{1}{2}$ per cent compared with a rise now put at $17\frac{1}{2}$ per cent. The rate of inflation was less accurately foreseen than other changes in the post-war years.

While there are frequent references to work on a long-term plan after 1945, none was submitted to ministers until 'The Long-Term Economic Survey', subsequently published in a somewhat bowdlerized form as *The Long-Term Programme of the United Kingdom*[55] in 1948. When the *Economic Survey for 1947* was under consideration by ministers in February 1947 officials informed them that work had been proceeding on a sketch plan for 1951 but that there had been no time to submit it to ministers and in any event 'in present circumstances of shortage' a long-term plan would be of limited value.[56] In the published version of the *Economic Survey for 1947* Cripps explained that the budgets and programmes discussed in it extended over the year ahead but that the same technique of planning could be applied to longer periods of, say, five years. The most urgent job was to provide a framework for 'the vast number of decisions which had to be taken in the short-term allocation of resources'. It was

> too early yet to formulate the national needs . . . with enough precision to permit the announcement of a [five-year] plan in sufficient detail to be a useful practical guide to industry and the public. There are still too many major uncertainties, especially in the international field.[57]

From the middle of 1947 a renewed effort was made to put together a long-term plan. But what gave fresh impetus to this effort was the request

54  Feinstein (1972), table 5: net national product at factor cost.
55  *European Co-operation: memorandum submitted to the OEEC relating to Economic Affairs in the period 1949 to 1953.* Cmd 7572, 1948. 'The Long-Term Economic Survey' is in PRO T 230/144.
56  PRO PREM 8/646.
57  *Economic Survey for 1947*, Cmd 7046, para. 14.

from OEEC in August to prepare a statement showing how it was proposed to achieve external balance without Marshall Aid at a satisfactory level of economic activity by 1952. Countries were also asked to produce a forecast of their balance of payments in 1952–3 on the assumption that they would not be able to earn dollars from one another.

*The Long-Term Programme* was the first and only long-term economic plan to be issued by any British government before the National Plan of 1965. It was more modest in its approach to planning than the *Economic Survey for 1947*. Starting from 'the administrative fact that no economic planning body can be aware (or indeed ever could be aware) of more than the very general trend of future economic developments'[58] it went on to point out that 'for a nation with an open economy like the United Kingdom, the assumptions and forecasts underlying long-term plans are largely assumptions and forecasts about events overseas and these plans cannot be effectively prepared in isolation in its own capital' and went on to conclude that: 'for the United Kingdom, therefore, a long-term plan can be no more and no less than a statement of economic strategy'.[59]

*The Long-Term Programme* was submitted in September 1948 at a time when the United Kingdom had already achieved external balance and the main planning decisions necessary to maintain it, apart from the decision to devalue, had all been made. Thus in approving the document ministers were not being asked to take fresh decisions such as the *Economic Survey* normally required. They were being presented with a picture of how things might work out over the next few years to meet the OEEC prescription if nothing untoward happened and other countries played the part allotted to them. They were, however, also being asked to visualize the continuation until 1953 or later of restrictions on imports to their 1948–9 volume and a limitation of net capital exports (including the release of blocked sterling balances) to £100 million a year.

With the completion of *The Long-Term Programme* interest in long-term planning seems to have died. Economic planning was increasingly seen in terms of measures to maintain full employment, check inflation and preserve external balance. Demand management, rather than intervention to control the use of resources directly or improve their efficiency, was the order of the day. Controls that were not helpful to demand management were removed as the shortages that had given rise to them were overcome. The key instruments in the management of the economy

58  *The Long-Term Programme*, para. 3.
59  ibid.

– and 'management' rather than 'planning' became the 'in' description –
were the budget, credit control, the exchange rate and, for the next few
years, import control and investment programming.

## The end of the story

Some ministers, however, were by no means convinced that these instruments were sufficient. When in 1949 the Chancellor took the initiative in
persuading OEEC to adopt a programme of liberalization of trade there
were those who felt some qualms at the loss of control over the balance of
payments that this appeared to involve. The Chancellor had told the
Economic Policy Committee in December 1949 that 'in the management
of our general balance of payments indirect measures of control must play
an increasing part, primarily by anti-inflationary internal policies and a
strict external financial policy'.[60]

Gaitskell, then Minister of Fuel and Power, dissented and later, in
consultation with Douglas Jay, circulated a memorandum giving one of
the few expositions of economic planning by a minister in the Attlee
government.[61]

Gaitskell pointed out that in maintaining incomes and demand at a level
that virtually guaranteed full employment the government was unable to
meet the demand for a number of essential goods at the controlled price
and had therefore to resort to rationing over a wide field. He admitted that
food subsidies had widened the gap between demand and supply but
argued that it was right to ration in the interests of fair distribution rather
than leave things to the power of the purse. Much the same applied to
other controls: over building resources and raw materials and over finished
goods diverted from the home market. The purpose of direct controls was
to restrain both consumption and investment below the level which they
would otherwise reach with current money incomes and this was done
either in order to secure fair distribution or to improve the balance of
payments. The use of controls in this way was 'the distinguishing feature
of British socialist planning' and the abandonment of controls by non-
socialist European governments had brought 'a certain amount of unemployment and/or a much less equitable distribution of income'.

60 Memo by the Chancellor of the Exchequer, 13 December 1949, EPC(49)157, in
   PRO CAB 134/223.
61 'Economic Planning and Liberalisation', memorandum by the Minister of Fuel and
   Power, 7 January 1950, EPC(50)9, in PRO CAB 134/225.

Gaitskell did not explain why rationing should take place at one price rather than another. Nor did he discuss the danger that a system which gives weight only to considerations of equity, if pushed far enough, may result in some diminution in what is available for distribution, fair or unfair. The danger in his mind was one of having to rely exclusively on fiscal and monetary policy if the controls were removed. Unless deflation was pushed to a point at which unemployment increased to a million or so, prices would rise, the balance of payments would weaken and a crisis would probably follow. Exchange control and import control, he concluded, were not temporary devices but would be necessary *permanently* as vital instruments of policy.[62]

The great danger, however, was not that the Labour government would abandon controls but that it would be pressed by the ECA and the 'unplanned' economies of OEEC to relax specific controls. Liberalization of European trade was the prime example of such pressure. Given that it was Cripps who took the lead in pressing for liberalization this was rather odd doctrine.

Gaitskell developed his argument on liberalization at some length. Much of it rested on a sharp distinction between 'essentials' and 'inessentials' which other European countries regarded as spurious and which could never be sustained in bilateral negotiations.[63] No mention was made at any point of unrequited exports. Yet by 1950 Britain was moving rapidly into surplus. The desirability of balancing trade at a higher level was met with the objection that Britain and her trading partner might merely be deflected from an effort to sell more in the dollar area. Finally, it would obviously be unfair to admit imports on OGL (Open General License) in competition with British firms that could not sell freely on the home market or were restricted in their access to raw materials. But this

---

62 ibid., para. 8.
63 Essential goods were 'those of which we need more according to our plan', mainly food and raw materials. But it takes two to engage in trade and the categories of the buyer are unlikely to coincide with the categories of the seller. On how things worked in practice see Ellis Rees (1962), part V, paras 31–7. For example: 'I remember having a difficult discussion with Dr Salazar . . . about a quota for pineapples. I explained that this fruit was regarded as the height of luxury at home, and a sudden influx would not accord well with the enforced austerity under which many simple foodstuffs (e.g. one egg a week) were denied to the people; he merely shrugged his shoulders and said that pineapples were the only product of the Azores, and ours was a traditional market; if we wanted an agreement, we must extend a quota to Portugal.'

was not a point in dispute and had already been urged by Harold Wilson when Cripps's original proposals were advanced.[64]

Having rejected the argument that liberalization would be of advantage to the United Kingdom Gaitskell then turned to the impact on the dollar shortage and could see no reason to suppose that there would be any advantage there either. What was needed was a switch of productive resources away from industries producing inessentials for European consumption into industries producing essentials either for domestic consumption or for export to North America. But there was little reason to expect such an outcome from liberalization. The idea that a widening of the market in Europe would bring down costs and make industry more competitive was a theoretical argument that might have some validity in the very long run but hardly applied to the immediate situation. The British car industry would sell *fewer* cars in North America if it sold more in Europe. The textile industries were already working to capacity and the demand for steel sheets was far in excess of the supply. Were conditions so different in Europe?

Costs might also be lowered as a result of more intense competition from European suppliers. But this too was debatable. Britain's best dollar earners were whisky and motor-cars where foreign competition in the domestic market was virtually non-existent; and this was precisely why the industries concerned were such successful dollar earners – they were enabled to concentrate on export markets by the absence of competition in their home market.

It will be observed that the argument paid no regard to third markets. Yet in 1950 the United States was still the principal supplier, not just of Europe but of markets all over the world in which European exporters, after the devaluations of 1949, enjoyed a much more competitive position.

The interest of Gaitskell's paper for present purposes lies not in whether he was in the right – for he very soon withdrew his objections to liberalization – but in the sophistication and trend of the argument. The essence of his position was that a planned economy was necessary for full employment, external balance and an equitable distribution of income. Physical controls were indispensable to achieve these aims but were likely to be undermined if the policy of liberalization was carried any further. Although he had bowed to market forces over devaluation he was still reluctant to make use of the price mechanism for other purposes and

64 'Liberalization of Trade', memorandum by the President of the Board of Trade, 10 June 1949, CP(49)7, in PRO CAB 129/35.

hankered after the planning of foreign trade in parallel with the planning of the domestic economy. He quite rightly took the view that the more external trade was free of control, the more difficult it would be to plan domestic economic activity. Whatever one may think of the validity of his argument under conditions of expanding trade in the 1950s and 1960s, it had considerable force as a rationale of government economic policy in the transition from war to peace.[65]

In his Budget speech in April 1950 Cripps insisted that the press was mistaken in claiming that planning had been abandoned. The truth was, rather, that planning in a democratic society was *different*. It was not possible to use the 'violent compulsions . . . appropriate to totalitarian planning': a great part of the direction of the economy must be accomplished by agreement, persuasion and consultation. Nor was it sensible to decide from the centre all the details of planning and distribution. But how the details were to be decided and what role the price mechanism should be allowed to play remained obscure. What he saw more clearly than he had seen in 1947 was the need to control inflation by removing excess purchasing power through the budget. The Budget, he now conceded, 'can be described as the most powerful instrument for influencing economic policy which is available to the government';[66] and with that admission he may be said, ironically enough, to have pronounced a requiem on economic planning as he had once conceived it.

---

65  When he came to deliver his Budget speech in April 1951 Gaitskell was still insisting on the need for physical controls but conceded that they were less effective when working against the tide. A strict monetary and fiscal policy was therefore necessary but if carried too far would result in 'losses, unemployment and austerity at home without any substantial benefit to our external position'. (H. C. Deb., 5th ser., vol. 486, col. 828, 10 April 1951.)

66  H. C. Deb., 5th ser., vol. 474, col. 39, 18 April 1950.

# Chapter twelve

# DIRECT CONTROLS

Nearly all the controls over the economy introduced in the course of the war were continued at the end of the war. By 1951 most of them had gone or were on the way out and by 1960 practically nothing remained of them except exchange control. It is natural to ask why, if they could be dispensed with later, it was necessary to retain them during the transition. Few other countries relied on them so heavily. Were they any the worse for it?

Thus there is first a question of purpose and justification. Underlying that is a second question: were the controls effective in serving that purpose? What was the impact of the controls either individually or in total on the economy?

The first of these questions has already been briefly discussed in chapter 11. Before returning to it it is necessary to be more specific about the controls under discussion since some of them served one purpose and some another, some were very tight or relatively extensive while others were much looser or more limited.

A catalogue of all the controls in use would be very extensive. For raw material controls alone the Board of Trade published a guide running to ninety pages. David Butt, in what he described as a 'brief list', outlined eighteen different types of control with many variants and questioned whether control at so many different points in so many different ways was not counter-productive. Perhaps, he suggested, it would be wiser to concentrate on fiscal controls and steel allocation.[1]

1 D. Butt, 'Controls', May 1947, in PRO T 230/25.

We can confine our discussion to six broad headings: consumption, prices, investment, raw materials, labour and foreign trade. Since we are discussing physical controls only, we can leave out of account the use of monetary and fiscal policy, including controls over capital issues, hire-purchase controls, exchange control, and so on.

### Consumer rationing

First of all there were various forms of consumer rationing, including 'single line' rationing of specific items, points rationing of canned and processed foodstuffs, clothing and furniture, and limitations on tourists' expenditure abroad. These covered less than one-third of consumer spending at their most extensive in 1948, and from 1949 never more than one-eighth. The main items were food, clothing, furniture and coal. Of consumer spending on food over half was not subject to rationing even in 1948.[2] Nevertheless, spending on rationed foodstuffs was almost as large as on all other rationed goods. Clothing, which was next in importance, was almost all subject to rationing throughout the first three post-war years and the same was true of new furniture, the sale of which was largely confined to newly married couples and bombed-out families. Coal continued to be rationed until 1958, food until the summer of 1954, when fats, butter, cheese, bacon and meat were all de-rationed, and clothing and furniture until June 1948 and March 1949 respectively.

The mere extent of rationing tells us little about its effects. When clothing was taken off the ration, for example, there was no great surge in demand. Similarly, when bread was rationed for two years between July 1946 and July 1948, or when potatoes were rationed in November 1947, the main effect was probably to reduce the amount fed to animals. On the other hand, when sweets were de-rationed in April 1949 they very soon disappeared 'under the counter' and rationing had to be resumed later in the year.[3] Rationing may be presumed to have *some* limiting effect on the demand for rationed goods, especially the demand of richer consumers. But once it affects only 10–12 per cent of consumer spending, as it did from 1949 onwards, this effect can hardly be very large.

Rationing was only one form of control over consumption. Over a wide range of products, a licence to produce or distribute was required and

2 Dow (1964), p. 173. Fish, fresh fruit and most vegetables were not rationed and consumers were free to make use of restaurants and canteens to supplement their rations.
3 Worswick and Ady (1952), p. 286.

the volume of production was limited by raw material supplies or allocations. There were also many sumptuary restrictions on production, often to facilitate price control or free supplies for export. Examples are the various utility schemes; the uniform extraction rate for wheat flour; and the ban on sales of decorated pottery in the home market.

## Price control

Coupled with consumer rationing there was extensive price control. At the end of the war this covered about one-half of total consumer spending. Making allowance for items that could not be controlled, like the imputed annual value of owner-occupied dwellings, items already subject to government influence like gas, electricity and post office charges, and items where taxes formed half or more of the purchase price, the proportion covered by price control where control made sense was a good deal higher, perhaps 60 per cent.[4] No appreciable relaxation took place until 1949–50 when some of the least effective parts of price control – non-rationed foodstuffs, ironmongery and some items of clothing – were abolished. The rise in prices after the outbreak of the Korean War and the rearmament that followed led to the reimposition of control on a miscellaneous list of consumer goods in July 1951 and efforts to strengthen existing controls. But this move was always intended as a temporary (and probably not very effective) expedient. Although a few items (rents, bus and railway fares and coal) continued to be controlled, and price control over some foodstuffs lingered on for a little longer, the system of price control was effectively abandoned in 1952–3 with the repeal of the Enabling Acts of 1939 and 1941.[5]

As with consumer rationing, the extensiveness of price controls is a poor guide to their effects. There was an obvious difficulty in enforcing price control without an inspectorate and without precise definition of the goods whose prices were being limited. As Gaitskell pointed out in 1951

There are inherent limitations . . . in price control. . . . Without standardisation and close control of specifications, it is difficult to ensure the maintenance of quality, and a form of price control evasion may develop. . . . Where the costs of different firms diverge there is bound to be a problem of settling what maximum prices are appropriate.[6]

4 Dow (1964), p. 164.
5 ibid., p. 166.
6 *H. C. Deb.*, 5th ser., vol. 491, cols 2340–2, 26 July 1951 (quoted by Dow (1964), p. 166).

Price control may be either 'tight' or 'loose'; and on one classification about one-third of total consumer spending was 'tightly' controlled.[7] Rationed foodstuffs, for example, had to be tightly controlled since most of them were subsidized and they could be controlled because the government was the sole supplier. Clothing and furniture were controlled under the 'utility' arrangements which limited and defined the goods included in the scheme and at the same time fixed their price.[8] In general, tight control and rationing went hand-in-hand although rationing was abandoned more quickly than price control.

Tight or loose, price control was obviously incapable of containing all the pressures towards higher prices for an entire decade. All it could do was to slow down the rise as import prices, wages and other costs increased. Prices do in fact appear to have risen in line with costs throughout and there is no evidence of widespread inflation of profits. Evasion, as with rationing, seems to have been remarkably limited. We return to this point below.

## Control of investment

A third type of control, over investment, is discussed in chapter 17. The government could exercise control either through its influence over public investment, or by building licensing, or by controlling allocations of steel and timber, or by inducing manufacturers to increase their exports of machinery.[9] We can leave aside the first of these as a normal element in demand management not relevant to the influence on the economy of direct controls. The last two types of control were used to some extent in conjunction with one another, steel allocations providing a bait or sanction in fixing export targets for metal-using industries. Similarly the allocation of timber could be used to divert building activity in directions favoured by the government, such as house-building. It could also be reinforced by production controls such as the limitation imposed on the amount of timber allowed per house. While the government was undoubtedly able to exercise restraint over the scale or pattern of domestic investment through raw material controls – as, for example, by forcing car manufacturers to starve the home market until the 1950s – it relied also on its informal influence over various sections of the engineering industries to procure the desired results.

7  Dow (1964), p. 164.
8  Utility products benefited from exemption from purchase tax.
9  Dow (1964), p. 149.

In principle, building licensing appeared to be a powerful control and extended to most building work until 1955. Until July 1948 even minor jobs costing over £10 in any six-monthly period had to be licensed. But in practice the volume of work licensed or authorized in the first three years after the war far exceeded the volume of work carried out. Not only was there an over-issue of licences on an enormous scale but there was also an acute shortage of raw materials, notably bricks.[10] It was only from the end of 1948 that building licensing can be said to have had any effect on the volume of building although it may have allowed more house-building to be put in hand at the expense of other building work.

What building controls did affect very strikingly was the proportion of factory-building in the development areas. Between 1 January 1945 and 31 November 1951, of factory construction granted building licences, 37 per cent by value was in the development areas and of factory construction completed, over half by value was in the development areas (which normally employed only about 5 per cent of the total working population). After the crises of 1947, however, the development areas did not enjoy such high priority and these proportions were dropping rapidly in the last years of Labour government. The numbers employed in the new factories were small in comparison with the size of the working population: whatever their long-term contribution to employment in the development areas, it was the high pressure of demand throughout the country that transformed the current employment prospects of the areas, not the small addition made possible through building controls and (from 1947) Industrial Development Certificates.

### Raw material allocation

A fourth form of control was over the allocation of raw materials. Initially all raw materials of any importance were subject to allocation, the three most important being coal (which in turn affected others such as steel and bricks), steel and timber. Apart from coal and steel nearly all raw materials were imported; and as imports increased the need for control diminished. Aluminium, wool and rubber ceased to be allocated in 1947; tin, cotton and most hardwoods in 1949. At that stage softwood was regarded as the most persistent shortage, with the smallest increase in consumption since 1946 of any raw material and no prospect of improvement in 1949 or 1950.[11] Of the input into industrial consumption of the fifteen main raw

10  ibid., pp. 150–1.
11  *Economic Survey for 1949*, Cmd 7647, para. 30; Dow (1964), p. 159.

materials, 94 per cent by value is estimated to have been subject to allocation in 1946 and 47 per cent in 1950, the main fall occurring after 1948.[12]

The process of de-control was arrested by the Korean War and rearmament. Steel, which had been de-restricted in May 1950 (except for sheet and tinplate) was again allocated between February 1952 and May 1953. Many other controls had to be reimposed and the proportion subject to allocation rose in 1952 to 64 per cent.[13] But by 1953 the main shortages were over and apart from coal and tinplate all allocation schemes had been dropped by 1954.

The effects of the raw material controls are not easy to assess. As Dow suggests, they were a way of organizing for scarcity and promoted the acceptance of shortages. So long as the government was in a position to make the controls effective – as it was during the period when it was the sole importer – it could also prevent businessmen from bidding up the price so that they reinforced the system of price control. They also allowed the government to effect some economy in imports. It is true that since 'it was at most times the government's intention to provide all the raw materials which were essential to production, provided supplies were available',[14] such economies must have been small. But a shortage of imported materials could also deflect demand to goods and services making less demand on imports or force producers to make do with other materials; and these effects were reinforced when the government imposed production controls (e.g. on the amount of timber allowed per new house) that enforced economy in the use of materials.

## Labour controls

By 1947 labour controls were very limited. The Essential Works Order and the parallel system of labour direction had been almost entirely discontinued. Control of Engagement Orders, which put a 'ring fence' round an industry in which the call-up of workers was deferred, applied only to men in the building and civil engineering industries, coal-mining and agriculture. The Ministry of Labour could, however, exert influence on recruitment to particular industries through training schemes, persuasion at employment exchanges and organized immigration. The possibility of bringing government influence to bear on wages, which was for ever under discussion, is dealt with in chapter 14.

12  Dow (1964), p. 175.
13  ibid.
14  ibid., p. 162.

## Import controls

We may take as a last example, and one of great importance in the post-war period, import controls. During the war virtually all imports were either purchased on government account or imported by private traders under licence. In 1946 the government continued to import four-fifths both of the food and of the raw materials entering the country and two-thirds of total imports including manufactures.[15] No manufactures of any kind could be imported without a licence. Given the need to limit imports, to switch to non-dollar sources of supply and to engage in inter-governmental negotiations for trade agreements, it was perhaps inevitable that the government should wish to exercise direct control over a large part of the import programme and do much of the buying itself. There was also a strong disposition to favour bulk-buying on long-term contracts in the expectation of striking a better bargain than the private trader. Nevertheless the proportion of import business conducted by the government fell gradually but steadily and was down to 50 per cent by 1950.[16] All rationed foodstuffs continued to be bought by the government until that year when cheese, cocoa, tea and various fruits were restored to private trade.

The position as seen by the government at the end of 1949 is summarized in table 12.1. This shows how the imports included in the import programme for 1950 would have been distributed between the different categories under the policies then in force. All imports of oil, whatever their source, were purchased privately subject to quantitative controls; they are not shown separately in the table but are included in the totals. At least four-fifths of total imports of food, feeding stuffs, drink and tobacco, both from dollar and from non-dollar sources, were on government account, with most of the dollar purchases, and a smaller proportion of the much larger non-dollar purchases, on long-term contracts. Raw materials were mainly imported privately, subject to quotas, but with a rising proportion on Open General License. Machinery and manufactures were all privately imported but formed a relatively small proportion of the total. In their case, too, the use of Open General Licenses for imports from soft currency sources had already been taken quite a long way. The picture, as seen at the time, was one of a steady weakening in the power to control

15  ibid., pp. 154–5.
16  ibid., p. 155. See also table 12.1.

*Table 12.1* Analysis of 1950 import programme according to degree of control exercised (percentage)

|  | Food, drink and tobacco | | Raw materials | | Manufactures and machinery | | Total (incl. oil)[b] | |
|---|---|---|---|---|---|---|---|---|
|  | $ | non-$ | $ | non-$ | $ | non-$ | $ | non-$ |
| Government purchases | | | | | | | | |
| Long-term contracts[a] | 60 | 33 | — | 1 | — | — | 25 | 17 |
| Other | 23 | 48 | 36 | 29 | — | — | 22 | 35 |
| Private purchases | | | | | | | | |
| quantitatively controlled | 17 | 8 | 62 | 40 | — | — | 39 | 25 |
| policy controlled | — | 2 | 2 | 1 | 100 | 51 | 14 | 5 |
| OGL (from OGL countries) | — | 9 | — | 29 | — | 49 | — | 18 |
| Total | 100 | 100 | 100 | 100 | 100 | 100 | 100 | 100 |

*Source:* ED(49)22, appendix, table 1.

a For more than one year.
b All oil imports, dollar and non-dollar, were private purchases, quantitatively controlled.

the volume of imports from non-dollar sources except after an interval and through the application of general policies.[17]

Restrictions on private trade had continued with little change until 1949 when the United Kingdom and other OEEC countries embarked on a joint programme of 'liberalizing' imports from one another. This gathered speed in 1950 with the creation of the European Payments Union and the concessions then made by the United Kingdom were extended to other non-dollar countries outside the Soviet bloc (imports from sterling area countries were already admitted relatively freely). 'Liberalization' meant freeing imports from control and by 1950 half the imports made by private traders, or a quarter of total imports, were unrestricted.[18] In the payments crisis of 1951–2, however, the process of liberalization was temporarily interrupted and import cuts totalling £600 million were made in three successive bites: in November 1951, in January 1952 and again in March 1952. These took effect not only on imports still under control but

17 'Balance of Payments in 1950', appendix, 29 November 1949, ED(49)22, in PRO CAB 134/223.
18 Dow (1964), p. 156.

*Table 12.2* Extent of import control 1945–58 (percentage of imports purchased by government or subject to government restrictions)

| Year | 1946 | 1947 | 1948 | 1949 | 1950 | 1951 | 1952 | 1953 | 1957 | 1958 |
|---|---|---|---|---|---|---|---|---|---|---|
| Government imports | 64 | 58 | 57 | 54 | 46 | 38 | 37 | 24 | 2 | — |
| Restricted private imports | 32 | 33 | 34 | 37 | 27 | 16 | 28 | 24 | 7 | 10 |
| Total controlled imports | 96 | 91 | 91 | 91 | 73 | 54 | 65 | 48 | 9 | 10 |
| Uncontrolled imports | 4 | 9 | 9 | 9 | 27 | 46 | 35 | 52 | 91 | 90 |
| Total imports | 100 | 100 | 100 | 100 | 100 | 100 | 100 | 100 | 100 | 100 |
| Controlled imports by commodity class | | | | | | | | | | |
| Food | 97 | 98 | 97 | 97 | 88 | 72 | 78 | 55 | 6 | 6 |
| Raw materials | 96 | 73 | 75 | 74 | 48 | 36 | 53 | 32 | 8 | 6 |
| Fuels | 82 | 100 | 100 | 100 | 100 | 32 | 31 | 32 | 32 | 32 |
| Manufactures | 100 | 100 | 99 | 99 | 68 | 61 | 73 | 65 | 24 | 13 |
| Controlled imports by currency area | | | | | | | | | | |
| Dollar area | 94 | 98 | 98 | 98 | 98 | 95 | 95 | 68 | 47 | 37 |
| Non-dollar non-sterling | 96 | 98 | 98 | 98 | 63 | 44 | 70 | 51 | 15 | 12 |
| Sterling area | 97 | 81 | 81 | 81 | 69 | 44 | 43 | 36 | — | — |

*Source:* Hemming, Miles and Ray (1959), quoted by Dow (1964), p. 174. For definitions see Dow. Each category of imports is weighted by value of imports in 1955. Items shown as controlled in any year if controlled on 30 June.

also on imports that had been freed from control and were now 'deliberalized'.[19] Later in 1952 the government decided to take 'deliberalization' no further and by the following year the process of de-control was again in full swing. The share of imports freed from all control reached 50 per cent in 1953 and 90 per cent in 1957, with discrimination against dollar imports continuing until 1959 (see table 12.2).

The gradual handing back of imports to private trade and the process of freeing trade from restriction did not determine the severity of control over the volume of imports. The shifting outlook for the balance of payments produced frequent changes of policy as the import programme was cut or enlarged and efforts were redoubled or relaxed to make do with lower imports from dollar sources and find alternative, but often dearer, supplies elsewhere. Sometimes, as in 1949 and 1951, action to cut imports was taken in concert with other Commonwealth countries just as action

19 ibid. About a quarter of the cuts were intended to fall on deliberalized imports, mainly unrationed foodstuffs and timber.

to agree on measures of liberalization was taken in conjunction with other members of OEEC. Sometimes, as when the pound was devalued in 1949, the import programme was radically affected by government action outside the apparatus of control.

Of the effectiveness of control during the six years of Labour government there was never much doubt. In the 1947 crisis, for example, the cuts made in dollar imports produced a fall in their value of nearly 30 per cent between 1947 and 1948 and reduced the proportion of imports coming from the Western Hemisphere from 43 per cent to 30 per cent.[20] Some of the change represented an improvement in 1948 in the availability of supplies from non-dollar sources which would have produced a shift away from the dollar area even without the cuts. On the other hand, import prices were some 13 per cent higher in 1948 than in 1947 so that the fall in volume must have been appreciably larger than the fall by value of nearly 30 per cent.

The import cuts of 1951–2 provide a second example. The restrictions did not exert their full effect until well into 1952 and by that time the domestic economy was in the middle of a minor recession. This by itself would have checked the growth of imports so that the cuts were not responsible for the whole of the reduction in 1952 by £400 million. A detailed study by W. M. Corden suggests that perhaps £250 million of the reduction can be attributed to the cuts, the main items affected being food from non-sterling sources, tobacco and timber and other materials for the strategic stockpile.[21]

The effectiveness of import control was tested not only in periodic cuts like those in 1947 and 1952 but also in the persistent lowering of imports as an element in final demand. The volume of imports remained well below the pre-war level when GDP was already well above it. This was partly the result of structural changes such as the relative decline in the textile industries with their large import requirements. There was no rapid recovery in the volume of imports in relation to GDP once import control was relaxed: for example, imports in 1954 were only 25 per cent higher than in 1947 when GDP had grown by 23 per cent over the same period. But if one looks a little further ahead to 1957, imports were growing more than twice as fast as GDP over the three years 1954–7. It took time for the effects of prolonged import control to wear off and restore a more normal relationship between imports and GDP.

20  *Economic Survey for 1950*, Cmd 7915, pp. 17–18.
21  Corden (1958) quoted by Dow (1964), p. 157n.

Efforts to influence exports usually involved the use of the controls already described: for example, by making the allocation of steel or a licence to manufacture conditional on meeting an export target. It was much more difficult to find effective controls over the *direction* of exports, e.g. to dollar markets. Indeed this was one of the clearest examples of the superiority of the price mechanism as an instrument of policy over administrative control, since devaluation redirected exports far more effectively than the Dollar Exports Board.

## The purpose of controls

We can now return to the questions with which we started. What was the purpose of the controls and how far did they serve that purpose?

At times the Labour Party had laid stress on the controls as a planning device. They also attached importance to them as contributing to equity by ensuring 'fair shares'. In the election campaign the need to retain controls was related above all to the danger of a repetition of the inflationary boom and subsequent slump that followed the First World War.

The first comment to be made is that since nearly all the controls were gradually abandoned the government cannot have held to a consistent view that they were indispensable to economic planning. After 1945 economic planning took a different form and the controls had to serve different purposes. In wartime they had a positive role to play in the allocation of resources between competing government requirements as well as the negative role, which alone continued in peacetime, of denying resources in excess of some fixed amount to civilian consumers. In the post-war years government needs no longer took automatic precedence over those of the private sector and the government's share of total resources was shrinking rapidly. Where the government had previously been obliged to plan and co-ordinate its own activities for the prosecution of the war, leaving the minimum to be shared out in meeting civilian requirements, there was no such compelling need in peacetime when the whole purpose of production was to meet those very requirements. It was not only possible but inevitable that a multiplicity of consumer demands should be linked with the activities of thousands of productive units through the price mechanism, subject only to such intervention as the government thought necessary.[22] So long as those units remained in private hands and supplied most of what private consumers bought,

22 Devons (1947).

economic planning by the government was necessarily limited to efforts to achieve specific macro-economic objectives such as stability of employment and prices, except to the extent the government chose to impose its own view of social priorities.

This did not mean, however, that the controls had no place in meeting those objectives. It might be a diminishing role as circumstances returned to normal and it was found possible to discontinue or relax some of the controls. But the fact that the controls lingered on into the 1950s suggests that governments, rightly or wrongly, did regard them as useful, even after the transition, in the management of the economy.

The two principal objectives that the controls might be thought to have served were the avoidance of inflation and the restoration of external balance. Let us take these in turn.

## Inflation

The threat of inflation took four distinct but related forms. There was first of all, the threat of a distortion of the price structure that might meet with resistance in the form of a general inflation: the kind of distortion that arose with the big rise in commodity prices in 1973 and led on to the worldwide inflation of 1974–5. Secondly, there was a danger that money wages might begin to rise and then go on rising in a wage–price spiral. This can be regarded as a variant – a specially important variant – of the first threat since it was likely to be a response to an initial rise in prices of importance to wage-earners. There was, thirdly, a danger that excessive pressure of demand might push prices up. Finally, a continuing external deficit might make it necessary to devalue the currency, forcing up import prices and the cost of living, and setting off a general inflation.

Rationing was, from one point of view, a way of countering the first type of threat. It was a response to shortage when the alternative was to allow prices to rise and bring demand and supply back into balance. When elasticities were low the rise was liable to be large and might communicate itself to other prices. It is true that the fear of contagion was not the only – and often not the most important – reason for electing to make use of rationing. It was often the non-economist's instinctive reaction to shortage or reflected a judgement that letting the price rise would serve little or no useful purpose and would be unfair to poorer consumers on whom the shortage would be concentrated. But where there was no great risk of 'contagion', as in the case of luxury foodstuffs, demand was often left unrationed or price control was looser.

The main risk of 'contagion' lay in the reactions of wage-earners to a succession of sharp increases in price. In an effort to protect their standard of living they were likely to make demands for higher wages which, under conditions of acute labour shortage, would be very difficult to resist and, if granted, would raise prices still higher. If rationing allowed prices to be held, this danger would be greatly reduced. No doubt rationing also would involve a reduction in living standards that workers might, with equal justice, resist. But it is one thing to accept a limitation in which everyone shares and a quite different matter to stand back and renounce the use of undoubted bargaining power while others make unrestrained use of their spending power. Inflation, once it takes a grip, is hard to shake off and rationing may help to make it less likely.

While rationing may be an alternative to letting prices rise, it does not by itself hold prices down if costs nevertheless increase. To counter such an increase it would be necessary for the government to help out with a subsidy, shifting the burden to the taxpayer.[23] From 1941 onwards the rise in procurement prices for a group of key foodstuffs regarded as making up an 'iron ration' was covered by food subsidies on an increasing scale. The Labour government continued this policy, setting no limit to food subsidies until 1948 when the total was over £400 million, and undertaking to hold the cost of living index steady. However expensive food subsidies may have been, they do appear, taken in conjunction with rationing, to have been comparatively successful in limiting the rate of inflation. With unemployment no more than one tenth of what it had been in the early thirties the rise in wages was not much more than twice as fast as it was then.

*Mutatis mutandis*, what applies to the introduction of rationing controls applies equally to their removal. So long as supply and demand were seriously out of balance at current prices and it would have required a large increase in price to restore the balance, there was a case for maintaining control in order to reduce the risk of inflation. The case was all the stronger if there was every prospect of a gradual recovery of the supply at the going price so that the control could be relaxed progressively until it became redundant. To retain the control when supply and demand were

23 Where a reduction in purchases by the government of supplies to meet the ration would have allowed it to drive a better bargain, reducing the size of the ration was an alternative way of steadying the price. It would seem, however, that in the post-war period, food rations were limited by considerations of foreign exchange rather than of Exchequer finance.

back in balance would mean contriving a renewed scarcity by refusing to make available what was freely obtainable at the going price.

The scarcity giving rise to controls had its origin in various underlying shortages affecting not just a single commodity or group of commodities but whole sectors of the economy. For example, there was a general shortage of manpower because nearly half the manpower in wartime was in the armed forces or supplying them. This shortage could be expected to pass or at least become less acute as demobilization proceeded. Hence the derived shortages could also be expected to become less acute with the passage of time and control of the commodities affected by manpower shortages could be defended as transitional.

These considerations applied also to goods obtained from abroad. The supply of these, too, might improve through time as the countries producing them recovered or additional foreign exchange became available to pay for them. De-control could then follow as the supply became sufficient to meet the demand frustrated by rationing.

Critics of the government asked, as time went on, whether these wider shortages – of manpower or of foreign exchange – could not have been cured by other means. If there was a *general* shortage of manpower was that not much the same as an excess demand for labour and would a tighter monetary and fiscal policy not have removed the excess demand? Did it make sense to allow excess demand to develop and then introduce controls in order to hold it back? A second question raised by some of the government's critics was why the shortage of foreign exchange could not be removed by allowing the price to rise i.e. by devaluing the pound. This is perhaps the easier question to answer.

Had the pound been devalued at the end of the war it is likely that a very large devaluation would have been necessary before import control could have been abandoned. Exports were not held back by lack of competitiveness but by the logistical difficulty of expanding supplies quickly under the handicaps of immediate post-war conditions. Imports, on the other hand, were strictly controlled but far greater than exports. The large gap between imports and exports that opened up with the cessation of Lend-Lease was bound to be slow in closing and would have widened had imports entered freely. The simultaneous removal of rationing and other controls at that stage would have raised prices abruptly and put further pressure on the exchanges. If the exchange rate had been allowed to find its own level it would almost certainly have fallen steeply and caused import prices in sterling to rise correspondingly. They had already doubled in the course of the war – a much bigger increase than had taken place in consumer prices – and, in spite of all the controls, rose by a further 30 per cent in the first two post-war years and by 50 per cent at an unchanged parity in the four years to 1949. The rise would have been much greater in the absence of the controls and wages would not have been long in following, so producing a fresh fall in the pound and setting off the next inflationary cycle. We need only think of how the big rise in import prices in 1973–4 brought on a major bout of inflation and drove down the pound to an all-time low in 1976 in order to appreciate the dangers.

This leaves the issue of excess demand. Did the controls reduce the danger of inflation from this source?

During the war consumer spending was reduced in a variety of ways: through high taxation, through shortages of the goods consumers wanted, through controls that either created these shortages by limiting supplies or rationed what was still available, and through public acceptance of the need to restrain demand either by voluntary saving or by the exercise of government control. Personal saving was inflated from about 5 per cent of personal disposable income before the war to over 15 per cent at the height of the war. On the other hand, gross fixed investment fell heavily from 15 per cent of GNP to a negligible amount. Thus, in wartime, controls and shortages together would appear to have had at least as large an effect in checking demand as higher taxation, which took an additional 20 per cent or so of GNP.[24]

It was apparent from what happened after 1945 that it was shortages rather than controls that were chiefly responsible for this result, at least on the side of consumer spending. Although most of the controls remained in being the personal savings ratio plummeted as the flow of consumer goods recovered. It may be that the controls still acted to restrain demand in the post-war period since the savings ratio could have become negative as consumers drew on their accumulated wartime savings. But it is clear that the fluctuations in the savings ratio were not closely related to the removal or relaxation of controls on consumer spending.

The same is true of the fluctuations in fixed investment. It is true that the fall in wartime owed a good deal to the promptitude with which timber for house-building was cut off and the strictness with which steel was withheld from private investment. But the pace of the subsequent increase at the end of the war was set more by the greater availability of materials for these purposes as government demand fell off than by the machinery of control and allocation which was capable only of *limiting*

24 Dow (1964), pp. 169–70.

supplies to particular uses. Here, too, the more important influence was shortage, not control.

Such a conclusion is not surprising in view of what has already been said about the limited impact of controls over consumption and investment. Rationing never covered more than one-third of consumer spending and by 1948 the proportion was no more than 12 per cent. Controls over investment did not do much to limit the volume of building activity and, in the case of engineering, were largely confined to informal agreements with manufacturers.

But if demand was constrained chiefly by shortages why did these shortages not result in higher prices, i.e. in inflation? The answer, as Dow has convincingly argued, is that, in face of the shortages, private traders operated

> their own schemes for rationing their sales, and their own constraints over prices. That such private 'controls' existed in many lines is indeed a matter of common knowledge: commodities ranging from cars to cigarettes and drink were either queued for, or 'kept under the counter' and handed out to old customers, usually at standard prices. Unless this had been the case, official controls would not have had much effect, for they were too partial in their coverage to be, on their own, an effective barrier to total demand.[25]

The inflexibility of 'administered prices' under extreme conditions of excess demand is not, however, unlimited. As the margin by which prices fall short of what the market will bear increases, the temptation to break ranks and raise prices becomes stronger. Once a move begins, it may quickly become widespread and the barrier to inflation will be broken. On the other hand, the habit of keeping prices fixed and resisting the pressure of demand can be strengthened if statutory controls are introduced with similar aims. This indirect effect of the controls in reinforcing the practices of private traders may have been a more powerful contributor than their direct impact to the inflexibility of prices.

Paradoxically, however, as Dow points out, direct controls are unlikely to do much to contain inflationary pressure except under conditions when excess demand is severe i.e. when the danger of inflation is greatest.[26] Controls can be imposed only where there is scarcity; and unless the

25  Dow (1964), p. 172.
26  ibid.

scarcity is widespread the controls cannot be sufficiently general to provide much of a barrier to spending.

So far as inflation is concerned, therefore, the conclusion to be drawn is that the controls made a fourfold contribution to holding it in check:

(a) by helping to hold down key prices, particularly of foodstuffs, and to avoid the resentments that inequality of access to foodstuffs would have bred;

(b) by helping, in conjunction with the food subsidies, to temper wage claims;

(c) by improving the balance of payments and allowing devaluation to be postponed to a time when it would have less damaging consequences;

(d) by reducing to some extent the pressure of demand and reinforcing the inflexibility of prices under that pressure.

We have already dealt implicitly with the balance of payments. But in view of the critical importance of the balance of payments something more needs to be said about the contribution of controls to limiting the deficit. Fortunately a thorough study by Maurice Scott provides us with estimates, which are the best available, of the annual savings in imports resulting from controls over the four years 1946–9. In comparison with the years 1935–8, retained imports were 23 per cent less in volume while GDP was 10 per cent larger so that there was a very marked reduction of 30 per cent in the ratio of imports to GDP. Scott's estimates or 'best guesses' imply that half or more of this reduction can be ascribed to controls. The annual rate of imports of food, he suggests, would have been greater by over £200 million or about 25 per cent had all controls been removed and supplies been freely available abroad at unchanged prices.[27] For imports of materials he puts the saving in imports at £40 million, for manufactures at £70 million and although he makes no estimate for coal and oil he points out that rationed consumption was well below the level of free demand.[28] The total of over £300 million compares with average annual imports totalling £1940 million.[29]

These estimates are rather crude and it would be unwise to put too

27 Scott (1963), p. 17.
28 ibid., pp. 71–2.
29 This total includes drink and tobacco where it is assumed that imports were unaffected by controls.

much weight on them. For example, in the first year or two after the war some supplies were simply not obtainable and the controls were determining the size of the ration, not holding back imports. In other cases the removal of the controls would have raised prices, including import prices, and this in turn would have checked demand. The *volume* of imports would not have increased to the extent Scott calculates but the value of imports very well might.

One has also to take account of other controls affecting invisibles (e.g. tourist expenditure), exports (e.g. via steel allocations) and foreign investment (mainly through exchange control). Taken together, these must have had an appreciable effect on the balance of payments which has to be added to that of import control. On the other hand, the higher the estimate the more difficult it is to explain the subsequent behaviour of the balance of payments. By the mid-fifties the controls had virtually gone and the balance of payments had to absorb the effect of their removal. But it was more, not less favourable than in 1948–9 (although not, admittedly, than in 1946–7). What, then, had offset the removal of controls? Devaluation? Perhaps so. But the volume of exports was only 10 per cent higher in 1955–7 than in 1950. There is clearly a danger of overstating the total impact of the controls on the balance of payments even if it was uncontestably of major importance.

There is not the slightest doubt, also, that import controls played a key role in disposing of the dollar problem. The controls were not intended to affect all imports alike: they were devised after 1947 to bite specially hard on dollar imports and there is plenty of evidence that they did so. A similar point stands out in reviewing other controls: they were all, in some measure, selective and many of them were geared to the balance-of-payments problem. After the first two years it was the scarcity of foreign exchange, and particularly of dollars, that shaped the import programme and hence the size of the ration in the case of foodstuffs and the availability of supplies in the case of raw materials. The degree of control exercised over the economy from 1947 is largely a function, not of the threat of inflation but of the weakness of the balance of payments.

Import controls, moreover, were usually remarkably effective. In the succession of crises they may have been introduced belatedly: but there is no doubt that they worked. It is difficult, if one concentrates on the balance of payments rather than control of investment or prices, to agree with Dow that the attempts to make use of controls as instruments of economic planning in the early post-war crises were 'accompanied by a certain air of failure. . . . The apparatus of control came to appear a cumbersome and vexatious way of not doing precisely what was intended'.[30]

For some purposes the controls may have been a charade taking up the energies of officials and ministers in reaching decisions that 'were sometimes represented as part of a national economic strategy . . . [but] were for the most part merely decisions called for by the existence of a complex of controls'.[31] But for the overriding purposes of avoiding inflation and restoring external balance they were far from a charade. They were at the heart of a successful strategy with just such aims and it is very doubtful whether any strategy dispensing with them would have succeeded.

## The case against direct controls

Controls had their drawbacks as well as their advantages. In the first place they were costly to administer, inflating the manpower requirements of the public service to an extent difficult to assess. They were irksome both to consumers and producers, whose efforts to spend or earn as they thought fit were blocked by various forms of rationing or by regulations as interpreted by officials. This not only caused annoyance and frustration but was damaging to the incentives to extra effort. If prices were held fixed, shortages would persist that could be made to disappear if market forces were allowed freer play. Controls tended to perpetuate existing methods and channels of supply and exclude new and more efficient competitors. Finally there was the problem of ensuring that the controls were (and remained) effective and that market forces did not find an alternative outlet in 'black' or 'parallel' markets.

It is generally agreed that black markets were relatively unimportant in Britain during and after the war. One of the few official inquiries on the subject was that conducted by the Russell Vick committee into petrol rationing in 1948 after persistent allegations of widespread evasion. The committee put black market consumption at 3 per cent of total petrol consumption in 1947, a conclusion implying that 10 per cent of supplies to private motorists were illegitimately acquired.[32] Since the black market in petrol was the most widely publicized of all, this hardly suggests that the controls were ineffective. The fact that many of the key controls were over raw materials and foodstuffs imported from abroad by the government

30 Dow (1964), p. 168.
31 ibid.
32 Worswick, 'Direct controls', p. 287, in Worswick and Ady (1952).

may have contributed to the absence of a substantial black market such as existed elsewhere.

## Controls and emergency powers

Economic controls rested largely on emergency powers continued in force by the Supplies and Services (Transitional Powers) Act, 1945 which expired in December 1950. The Act could be renewed from year to year but at some stage, if the controls were to continue, parliament would have to be asked for permanent powers. Ministers decided to ask for such powers in March 1950. By October the proposed 'Economic Powers Bill' had been renamed the 'Economic Planning and Full Employment Bill' and was now intended to start, not from the Supplies and Services Act, but from the government's full employment policy.[33] In commenting on the change of title, Gaitskell pointed out that economic planning was neither well understood nor very popular whereas this could not be said of full employment, which required very much the same powers. But what were those powers?

Throughout the post-war period the trend had been away from physical to financial controls. By the end of 1950 the question had become what physical controls should be retained to supplement financial controls whether for purposes of economic planning or in the interests of full employment. In Gaitskell's view, the need for physical controls arose largely from the difficulty of maintaining an even pressure of demand on the economy. If the pressure on the building industry was excessive, building controls would be required. If unemployment persisted in the Development Areas when the pressure was already excessive elsewhere, special steps would have to be taken to even up the pressure. There was also a problem of keeping exports and imports in balance without varying the pressure on domestic resources. The necessary powers of control could be divided into those needed in order to boost demand, which would very largely take the form of fiscal and monetary measures to stimulate invest-ment, and those needed for purposes of control. Gaitskell listed six: power to control prices, building activity, imports and the proportion of output sold in the domestic market, and power to ration essential consumer goods

---

33 'Future of Emergency Powers', brief from Sir Norman Brook to Prime Minister, 29 March 1950, in PRO CAB 21/2247; 'Economic Planning and Full Employment Bill', memorandum by the Chancellor of the Exchequer, 9 November 1950, GEN 343/2, in PRO CAB 130/65. I owe these references to Dr Andrew Chester.

and allocate materials. On the other hand, he expressed doubts over general powers to manufacture and to purchase on government account.

None of the powers of control listed by Gaitskell was ever put on the Statute Book. The Full Employment Bill was dropped in February 1951 and the use of direct controls continued to rest on emergency powers as they fell steadily into desuetude.

# Chapter thirteen

# THE COAL CRISIS

Of all the shortages constraining government policy over the post-war period, the shortage of energy – and particularly of coal – was among the most damaging, taking second place only to the dollar shortage. The danger that the shortage would gradually develop into a crisis was well recognized from the start. In the Debate on the Address in August 1945 Attlee named housing and coal as 'the two main anxieties that beset us'.[1] It had been necessary to draw on stocks during the previous winter and unless output improved or consumers showed 'self-control' in their use of coal, the same thing would happen again – and it did. There was a physical limit to the rundown in stocks, and as Douglas Jay emphasized in his minutes to the Prime Minister in 1945–6, that limit was likely to be reached after two more winters in February or March 1947 unless measures were taken well in advance to recruit more labour.[2] What was apparent to the Prime Minister and his advisers was apparent also to other observers. Shinwell, the minister responsible, was not one of them. But he was entirely accurate when he declared in October 1946, 'Everybody knows that there is going to be a serious crisis in the coal industry – except the Minister of Fuel and Power'.[3]

The output of deep-mined coal had fallen year by year since 1939 from 231 million tons in that year to 175 million tons in 1945. In spite of this it had been possible to meet domestic requirements of coal throughout the

1 *H. C. Deb.*, 5th ser., vol. 413, col. 102, 16 August 1945.
2 Jay (1980), p. 143.
3 ibid., p. 151.

*Table 13.1*  Output, consumption and stocks of coal 1938–52[a] (m. tons)

| | Saleable output | | Total available supplies[b] | Inland consumption[c] | Exports and bunkers | Distributed stocks at end of year |
|---|---|---|---|---|---|---|
| | Deep-mined | Open-cast | | | | |
| 1938 | 227.0 | — | 224.1 | 177.8 | 46.3 | 14.6[d] |
| 1943 | 194.5 | 4.5 | 197.4 | 190.4 | 8.0 | 17.7 |
| 1944 | 184.1 | 8.7 | 191.8 | 187.3 | 6.1 | 16.0 |
| 1945 | 174.7 | 8.1 | 184.3 | 179.4 | 8.6 | 12.3 |
| 1946 | 181.2 | 8.8 | 191.1 | 186.2 | 8.9 | 8.3 |
| 1947 | 187.2 | 10.3 | 198.3 | 184.7 | 5.5 | 16.4 |
| 1948 | 197.7 | 11.8 | 207.9 | 193.4 | 16.3 | 14.6 |
| 1949 | 202.7 | 12.5 | 214.8 | 195.3 | 19.4 | 14.7 |
| 1950 | 204.1 | 12.2 | 216.9 | 202.1 | 17.1 | 12.4 |
| 1951 | 211.9 | 11.0 | 224.6 | 209.2 | 11.7 | 16.1 |
| 1952 | 214.3 | 12.2 | 223.4 | 208.1 | 15.1 | 16.3 |

*Source: Annual Abstract of Statistics for 1953.*

a  All figures refer to Great Britain.
b  Including imports (in 1947, 1948, 1951 and 1952) and change in undistributed stocks at colleries and open-cast sites.
c  Including shipments to Northern Ireland.
d  1939.

war because of the cessation of exports (36 million tons in 1939) from the fall of France onwards. Consumers had been rationed and supplies had been augmented from open-cast sites. But distributed stocks had begun to drift down after 1942 and there was a danger at the end of the war that this process might accelerate.

What gave cause for concern was not just the low level and downward trend of coal production over and against the expansion in domestic requirements as industrial output increased. There was also an urgent need to resume exports of coal both to earn much-needed foreign exchange and to assist European recovery. That recovery might yet prove the key to the dollar problem by providing alternative sources of supply for a wide range of imports. Moreover in the bilateral deals in which the United Kingdom engaged in the post-war years nothing did more to improve her bargaining position than the ability to offer substantial coal exports. 'The lack of coal exports', the Prime Minister was told in January 1946, 'is already depriving us of Swedish timber for housing and acutely needed Argentine wheat'.[4] As the *Economic Survey for 1947* insisted after the crisis had broken, 'Coal is the basis of our whole programme'; and, it went on, 'the loss of our coal exports since pre-war days is roughly equivalent in value to the whole of our wheat imports'.[5] But although the Ministry of Fuel and Power showed great zeal in laying claim to future markets for coal it was a long time before it could supply them.[6] Exports of coal were limited to 4.5 million tons in 1946 and barely exceeded 1 million tons in 1947.

The low level of output was partly due to the loss of manpower in war-time. With the call-up of miners to the armed forces the unemployment of pre-war years had vanished and the number of workers on the colliery books had fallen from 773,000 in the middle of 1939 to 694,000 at the end of 1945. An even bigger fall took place in output per man-year from 302 tons in 1939 to 259 tons in 1946. Some of this fall could be accounted for by the difficulty of sparing resources in wartime for maintenance and new development and by the increased proportion of older workers.[7] The high rate of wastage which this produced made it all the more urgent to find younger workers and add to the labour supply.

But the trend in employment was flat or obstinately downwards. Memories of pre-war conditions in the industry discouraged recruitment. The intake of juveniles in 1945 was not much more than one-third of what it had been in pre-war years.[8] The return of 8000 ex-miners from the forces in the last quarter of 1945 did no more than hold the strength steady. Employment in 1946 was 10,000 below the average level in 1945 and between July and November 1946 fell by over 8000 just when an increase was of the greatest urgency. This fall reflected an unusually high wastage rate after relaxations of wartime regulations that were thought to have detained in the industry workers who made little net contribution to output.

The Ministry of Fuel and Power took a fatalistic view of recruitment possibilities. 'Because of the unlikelihood of raising the labour force', they were reported in the draft 'Economic Survey for 1946' (prepared in October–November 1945) to have asked for 'no greater labour force in

---

4 ibid., p. 144.
5 *Economic Survey for 1947*, Cmd 7046, para. 92.
6 In September 1946 the Ministry still hankered after bilateral commercial deals in which to force the sale of British coal in competition with Polish coal (Meade, Diary (MS), entry for 21 September 1946).
7 In 1950 the average age of coal-miners was 40 and only 30 per cent of them were aged 30 or less compared with some 45 per cent in the 1920s (NCB *Report for 1950*, p. 10).
8 Jay, op. cit., p. 144.

Table 13.2  Employment, recruitment, wastage and absenteeism in coal-mining 1938–52  (000s)

| | Average number of wage-earners on colliery books | Recruitment during year | Of whom ex-miners | Wastage during year | Net increase in manpower during year | Effective employment at coal-face[b] | Absenteeism (%) | Output per man-shift at coal-face (tons) |
|---|---|---|---|---|---|---|---|---|
| 1938 | 781.7 | | | | | | 6.44 | 3.00 |
| 1945 | 708.9 | | | | | 249 | 16.31 | 2.70 |
| 1946 | 696.7[a] | 72.8 | 49.1 | 77.0 | −4.2 | 249 | 15.95 | 2.76 |
| 1947 | 711.4 | 94.2 | 46.2 | 68.0 | +26.2 | 260 | 12.43 | 2.86 |
| 1948 | 724.0 | 73.7 | 28.0 | 65.9 | +7.8 | 265 | 11.64 | 2.92 |
| 1949 | 719.5 | 52.1 | 18.3 | 68.5 | −16.4 | 264 | 12.34 | 3.02 |
| 1950 | 697.0 | 55.3 | 24.0 | 75.8 | −20.5 | 257 | 11.96 | 3.11 |
| 1951 | 698.6 | | | | | 257 | 12.15 | 3.17 |
| 1952 | 715.6 | | | | | 264 | 12.10 | 3.15 |

*Sources: Annual Abstract of Statistics for 1953; Report and Accounts of the National Coal Board for 1950.*

a  A change in recording methods reduced the number on colliery books by approximately 2500.
b  Wage earners who worked at least one shift or part of a shift during any given week.

coal-mining than at July 1945' by the middle of 1946 and an additional 10,000 men by the end of 1946.[9] This would still have left the labour force more than 50,000 below the pre-war level; but it would none the less have required a net addition in 1946 of 25,000 workers – a good deal more than the draft 'Economic Survey' took to be implied, and in striking contrast to the actual fall in 1946 of a further 4000. Nott-Bower, the Ministry's Deputy Secretary, reflected the prevailing mood when he wrote: 'We are planning a fairly ambitious recruiting campaign designed to lend some reality to what would otherwise be the expression of a pious hope.'[10] Unfortunately, something more than a 'fairly ambitious' recruitment drive was necessary.

When the next 'Economic Survey' was drafted in June 1946, a much gloomier picture was presented. The additional manpower required to maintain the domestic fuel ration and exports at their current level and to keep industry fully supplied with coal was put at 40,000 while an increasing rate of wastage and falling rate of recruitment might bring about a *reduction* in manpower of 40,000 over the year to March 1947. Only 7000 ex-miners had still to return from the forces and the number of ex-miners returning from other industries was also expected to dwindle. Yet the Ministry of Fuel and Power hoped that there would be no fall in output in 1946–7 and were equally optimistic about demand. The increase in gas and electricity requirements, for example, was put at just over 4 per cent[11] and the increase in industry's requirements at $2\frac{1}{2}$ per cent. No increase was provided for in household consumption. Even allowing for a cut in exports, there was a prospective deficit of 10 million tons which various expedients, including drawing on stocks, might reduce to 6 million tons but not sufficiently to avoid a 'very considerable' increase in industrial unemployment during the winter months.[12]

Meanwhile Jay in No. 10 Downing Street kept plugging away at Attlee who in turn prodded Shinwell, but without effect. In June 1946 Jay

9 Draft 'Economic Survey for 1946', p. 13, CP(46)32 in PRO CAB 129/6. The Board of Trade was planning simultaneously (presumably on advice from the Ministry) to expand exports of coal in 1946 on a scale that would have raised employment on exports from 25,000 to 50,000 and reduced employment to meet domestic requirements correspondingly.

10 Letter from W. G. Nott-Bower to S. R. Dennison, 3 November 1945, in PRO CAB 124/891.

11 Six months later Harold Hobson, Chairman of the Central Electricity Board, told Shinwell that the substitution of electric fires for coal had by itself increased the demand for electricity by 10 per cent (Hannah (1979), p. 314).

12 Draft 'Economic Survey for 1946–47', paras 57–9, in PRO CAB 134/503.

reported that the Labour Exchange officials were under the impression that housing and building materials had priority over coal.[13] He suggested a differential increase in food rations to the miners, higher wages, shorter hours and various health and welfare improvements. The situation, he argued, was now very serious. Distributed stocks at the end of the winter had fallen seasonally to 6–8 million tons in April 1946, not much above the operational minimum, and it looked as if the winter of 1946–7 would begin with stocks 3 million tons down on the autumn 1945 level. This pointed to an impossibly low level of 3–4 million tons in April 1947 and spelt uncontrollable industrial dislocation. Coming at almost the exact moment when the National Coal Board was due to take over the industry, the dislocation would be as devastating to the government's credit as to the economy of the country. Jay called for a recruitment drive with top priority for coal-mining at the Labour Exchanges, and in the allocation of workers brought over from Ireland. Shinwell's proposal for a five-day week and special concessions on holiday pay – 'roundabout methods of raising wages' – should be adopted but only on condition that the NUM accepted the need to use Poles in the mines as extensively as possible.[14]

This last suggestion came from James Meade who had sent 'a strong minute' to Morrison warning him of the danger in the coming winter that factory workers would be unemployed and householders left shivering for lack of fuel.[15] Morrison, 'xenophobic as he is', expressed agreement and urged the proposal on the Cabinet. But the NUM refused to accept Polish workers and a few months later Shinwell explained to his ministerial colleagues that there was widespread dislike of the Poles among British miners 'who believed that because the Poles did not wish to return to Poland they must be fascists'.[16] Whatever the truth of this, Shinwell had already refused point-blank to have Poles in the coal-mining industry; and although the Cabinet had explicitly made negotiations for a five-day week conditional on the introduction of Poles, he told the NUM that it was quite unnecessary.[17]

13  Jay, op. cit., p. 146.
14  ibid., pp. 146–8.
15  James Meade, Diary (MS), entry for 30 June 1946. See also the paper by the Lord President, CP(46)242 in PRO CAB 129/10, discussed below.
16  GEN 94/6th meeting, 18 October 1946, in PRO PREM 8/729.
17  Jay, op. cit., p. 151. James Meade noted in his diary on 27 July that Fergusson, the Permanent Secretary in the Ministry of Fuel and Power, simply wouldn't hear of the recruitment of foreign labour for fear of disturbing the NUM. Meade briefed Morrison that 'he had better accept as inevitable a serious shortage next winter' and concentrate on making sure of the best possible allocation of what coal there was.

Morrison had also proposed in his paper to the Cabinet in June on 'Output, Recruitment and Conditions of Employment in the Coalmining Industry'[18] that there should be a definite target for recruitment of 2000 per week with first priority for coal-mining at the Labour Exchanges; that male labour recruited from Eire by the Ministry of Labour should be placed in coal-mining for the next six months; and that all unemployed men in coal-mining districts should be interviewed and pressed to go to the mines. These proposals were endorsed by the Cabinet. Although wastage was abnormally high over the next four months it was in balance with recruitment in November, by which time 130 men per week were being drawn from Eire and a smaller number from Northern Ireland.[19]

It was not until January 1947, however, that agreement was reached on the employment of Polish miners between the National Coal Board, the Ministry of Labour and the National Union of Mineworkers. None were to be taken on without the agreement of the local branch of the NUM. All recruits were required to join the NUM and undergo at least three weeks' training at residential training centres. In the event of redundancies Polish workers would be the first to go. It was March before the first group of Poles began their training and during the early months some branches of the NUM continued to oppose the employment of Poles, a few until well into the autumn, so that at one time '1000 Poles who had completed their preliminary training had been waiting several weeks to be found jobs'.[20]

The Poles proved to be excellent workers and in the end relations between them and British mineworkers were good. Of 8600 who offered themselves for employment in 1947, 6000 were accepted and given jobs.[21] This represented less than 1 per cent of the number on the colliery books so that, even if recruitment had begun a year earlier, the contribution to output would have been relatively small. But even an extra 1 million tons of coal in stock by the end of January would have made a perceptible difference in the crisis that followed.

Until very late in the day the Ministry of Fuel and Power argued that

18 CP(46)242, 20 June 1946, in PRO CAB 129/10.
19 CC(46)1st meeting, 9 December 1946, in PRO CAB 134/62.
20 *Report and Accounts of the National Coal Board for 1947*, p. 47.
21 In addition 1230 European Voluntary Workers were recruited and by the end of 1947 688 were actually at work (*ibid.*, p. 103). In 1948 a further 8700 foreign workers were recruited, mainly European Voluntary Workers, after renewed opposition by some branches of the NUM. The recruitment of Italian miners, who formed nearly half the labour force in the Belgian mines by 1949, was not attempted until 1951.

'more labour was not needed in the industry', taking their cue from Shinwell who said much the same publicly.[22] Even in September 1946 he obliged his officials to decline priority at the Labour Exchanges after the Prime Minister had issued instructions calling for it to be accorded to employment in coal-mining.[23]

On 17 October 1946 – a week before his public denial that there was any cause for alarm – Shinwell at last put round a paper warning his colleagues that inland consumption was increasing faster than output and that there was a prospective deficit over the coal year April 1946–April 1947 of 2–5 million tons.[24] Demand was running 6 per cent higher than over the previous winter at 196 million tons per annum while output, including 9.5 million tons of open-cast coal and 0.4 million tons of briquets, looked like reaching only 190 million tons over the year. How the paper squared these figures with an estimated deficit for the year of only 2–5 million tons was not clear but it appeared to exclude from the deficit a drawdown of stocks by 1.5 million tons.

Not that any but the most obvious conclusions were drawn from the situation disclosed. Shinwell was content to deduce that either production must increase or consumption would decrease. Neither possibility was explored. The only concrete proposal was that supplies should be curtailed *after Christmas* to 'wasteful industrial consumers' if the measures already taken (and presumably discounted in the forecasts) proved insufficient.

At the ministerial meeting in October Shinwell maintained that there was 'no call for the immediate imposition of cuts'. He proposed to deal with the situation by making allocations for the winter to each industrial consumer at the beginning of December.[25] Since there was insufficient coal to meet the allocations, this was little more than an exercise in arithmetic and no cure for a shortage.

Cripps, profoundly disturbed, wrote to Attlee in November.[26] He insisted that 'an ordered and planned reduction in consumption' was essential. Shinwell, he said, was still arguing in favour of a voluntary scheme of rationing when both sides of industry were in full agreement that what was needed was a compulsory scheme.

22  *The Economist*, 12 October 1946, p. 594.
23  Jay, op. cit., p. 151.
24  GEN 94/11, 17 October 1946, in PRO PREM 8/729.
25  GEN 94/6th meeting, 18 October 1946, in PRO PREM 8/729.
26  Cripps to Attlee, 12 November 1946, in PRO PREM 8/729.

In mid-November Shinwell circulated a paper to the Cabinet containing proposals by his officials together with his own suggestions.[27] Officials proposed that there should be no cuts in allocations to iron and steel, coke ovens, railways, collieries and small users with no regular allocation; a cut of 5 per cent for high priority industries; and a cut of $12\frac{1}{2}$ per cent for the rest, with provision for a pool using part of what was saved in this way to provide *ad hoc* assistance where necessary. Shinwell 'was not satisfied that all the apprehensions expressed in the paper [were] justified'. He wanted no public announcement since this was quite unnecessary and would have 'a severely depressing political effect'. Rather than cut allocations when the quantities of coal available might be increasing, he would make cuts of 5 per cent and 10 (not $12\frac{1}{2}$) per cent in deliveries and notify firms of the extent of the cut. Firms would be asked to make a cut of 10 per cent in their November consumption of gas and electricity and told to keep down their consumption of coal over the four months December to March to the average weekly level in November, with iron and steel, coke ovens, etc., alone excepted. On this basis he reckoned on saving 2.45 million tons, including 850,000 tons from reduced consumption by gasworks and power stations – an optimistic estimate higher than that promised under the officials' scheme.

Although Shinwell's proposals, backed by Morrison, were accepted by the Cabinet, other ministers expressed concern, nearly all from a narrow, departmental angle. Cripps would have preferred an outright cut in allocations so that industry could know on what basis to plan and regarded a cut in deliveries as inequitable both to new and expanding enterprises and as between districts in receipt of widely different proportions of their allocations.

Shortly afterwards, a ministerial Coal Committee was appointed under Dalton as a sub-committee of the Lord President's Committee.[28] The Committee had a short life, beginning on 9 December and giving way on 12 February to a Fuel Committee over which the Prime Minister himself presided, adding Cripps to the four ministers who had served on the Coal Committee.

The Coal Committee concentrated initially on transport problems and the loss of output for lack of waggons. Shinwell then and later made much

27 CP(46)423, 15 November 1946, in PRO CAB 129/14; and CM(46)98, 19 November 1946, in PRO CAB 128/6.
28 In addition to Dalton and Shinwell, the other members were Barnes (Minister of Transport) and Isaacs (Minister of Labour).

of these problems[29] and Lord Wigg in his autobiography takes a similar line: 'our difficulties', he writes, 'were rooted in transport, not in coal production'.[30] It is true that there was a loss of 290,000 tons of deep-mined coal in December from this cause; but thanks to the priority accorded to coal transport these losses were cut to 29,000 in January and over the first three months of 1947 were limited to 214,000 tons, mainly in the first two weeks of February, in spite of the appalling weather conditions that began on 23 January. Gaitskell, at the meeting of the Committee on 6 January, asked for overriding rail priority for one month similar to the priority enjoyed before D-Day by military traffic. His proposal was rejected as likely to do more harm than good, the Committee preferring other, less extreme measures such as delaying the movement of commodities like iron ore which competed for traffic facilities with coal; suspending the movement of government stores for a month; mobilizing all the road haulage vehicles that could be used for coal transport; and making greater use of sea transport.

These measures and others approved by the Cabinet on 7 January were effective. Gaitskell at the meeting on 6 January of the Coal Committee complained that the amount of coal in transit had increased between October and December by 750,000 tons above a normal winter figure of 3 million tons.[31] On 23 January it was claimed that 600,000 of this excess had already been cleared from the pipeline[32] and on 6 February the Cabinet was assured that the movement of coal had been 'substantially maintained'

29  In defending in his autobiography his role in the fuel crisis (Shinwell (1955), pp. 180–5), he dwells mainly on transport difficulties and the measures which he proposed for overcoming these difficulties, leaving it to the reader to suppose that he was alone in the battle, the sole author of worthwhile suggestions and unable to gain the wholehearted support of his colleagues. This would be a travesty of what occurred. Other departments, including the Ministry of Transport, were only too anxious to help but found Shinwell grudging, intemperate and slow to act. The measures eventually taken represented a combined effort that was remarkably effective. Even when the weather was at its worst, the loss of output due to transport difficulties was relatively small. On the other hand, Shinwell has little to say on the key issue of manpower, apart from emphasizing the need to make the industry more attractive to recruits and to offer special concessions such as the extra ration of meat granted to miners from July 1946. Nearly the whole of his first year in office is passed over in silence.
30  Lord Wigg (1972), p. 127.
31  CC(47)1st meeting, 6 January 1947 and CC(O)(47) 1st meeting, 13 January 1947, in PRO CAB 134/62.
32  CC(O)(47)2nd meeting, 23 January 1947, in ibid.

throughout the severe weather then being experienced, although the railways were finding it hard to keep the coal moving, particularly to London and the South. Coal in transit was put at 220,000 tons above the normal winter level.[33]

When the Cabinet considered the coal situation on 7 January they were given figures showing that after meeting requirements for public utilities, essential industries (including iron and steel), railways, bunkers and domestic consumption, there was a shortfall of 300,000 tons a week in relation to industrial requirements of 760,000 tons a week.[34] The situation varied between one region and another and was particularly bad in the north-west and in the Midlands (where only 50 per cent of requirements were currently being met). In view of this inequality Cripps recommended a uniform cut in allocations of about 40 per cent on all industries except iron and steel, where he suggested a cut of $17\frac{1}{2}$–20 per cent. This would allow a reserve to be built up for allocation by the Regional Fuel Allocation Committee.

The Cabinet also reviewed the position at the power stations where coal consumption at the end of January was up by one-third on the previous year, sales of electricity to domestic consumers had grown particularly rapidly and a shortage of generating plant equal to 1.2 million kW was expected to grow to 1.8 million kW over the next two years. It was agreed to accept a recommendation from the Coal Committee that larger deliveries of coal (an extra 50,000 tons a week) should be made to the power stations at the expense of industry.[35] A proposal in favour of selective cuts in electricity supply to specified works for specified times was opposed by Cripps who preferred a directive to industry to cut its

33 Annex to minutes of CM(47)17, 6 February 1947, in PRO CAB 128/9. The Ministry of Fuel and Power agreed on 10 January that the road haulage vehicles which were to have begun moving dumped coal in December were now available in adequate numbers. Lord Wigg who makes much of the delay makes no mention of this (op. cit., p. 127).

34 CM(47)3rd meeting, and CP(47)6 (in PRO CAB 129/16). This way of putting the matter took no account of any possible further rundown in stocks or in coal in transit or any economies that might be made by consumers of the other 3 million tons. Although some factories were working intermittently or going on short time, the figures of industrial production are not easy to reconcile with a level of actual *consumption* equal to 58 per cent of current requirements.

35 CC(47)1st meeting on 6 January in PRO CAB 134/62. This followed an earlier diversion from industry of 20,000 tons per week.

November consumption of gas and electricity by 40 per cent.[36] He asked also that the Lord President should prepare a new list of industries or firms to be given special treatment, having regard both to the importance of the industry and the need to avoid creating unemployment in industries making little use of coal per worker. The Cabinet, in approving these proposals, asked that they should be announced as revised allocations, not as cuts in existing allocations. They were clearly very touchy on the political aspects of the coal shortage without appreciating how little these niceties would matter in the end.

In addition to these efforts to deal with shortages much thought was given to methods of procuring economies in the use of gas and electricity and to the conversion of apparatus (including generating equipment and locomotives) from coal to oil. The second of these could yield little or nothing immediately although the full programme, when completed in 1948, was expected to save 8 million tons of coal;[37] the first depended ultimately on the co-operation of consumers since rationing was held to be virtually impossible and penal surcharges to be ineffective.

In the meantime the coal industry had been nationalized. A National Coal Board was appointed on 15 July 1946. Vesting day, however, was not until 1 January 1947 when the Board was due to take over and operate the assets of the coal industry. The Ministry of Fuel and Power had also to divest itself of some of its responsibilities and surrender them to the Board. Over the winter, therefore, a transfer of responsibilities on the grand scale was in progress at the very time when a major crisis was looming up. The changeover was complex and protracted and by no means complete on 1 January. For example, it was not until 1 April that the Board took full charge of labour recruitment. However smooth and efficient the changeover, there were bound to be delays, confusion, and divided loyalties and responsibilities during the period of transition and the marvel is that they were so little in evidence. This was no doubt largely because the machinery of distribution through Coal Supplies Officers which had been in existence all through the war was left undisturbed.

Soon after the Board took over, it received instructions to give effect to the new allocation arrangements and these came into force on 20 January.

36 CP(47)18, 6 January 1947, in PRO CAB 129/16. Cripps was mistaken in thinking that this cut was similar to the proposed cut in coal supplies which was in relation to allocations, not November consumption.
37 CC(O)(47)9, 7 February 1947 in PRO CAB 134/62. The programme had been launched only in May 1946 and had received no help from tax measures.

Priority over other customers was given to power stations, gasworks, waterworks and ships' bunkers and their allocations were to be met in full. The railways and house-coal depots were also to be allowed full allocations. The iron and steel industry and the coke ovens were to be given three-quarters of their allocation and the rest of industry one-half. A notional pool of 100,000 tons per week was to be used to supplement the allocations of some important industrial consumers.

It proved impossible before the crisis broke to build up the proposed reserve in the right qualities and places or to meet even the reduced allocations to industry. Cripps's hopes of improving distribution between regions had been defeated by transport difficulties. The industries selected for preferential treatment had to be denied their priority when coal was conveyed to more accessible consumers. The changes in any event came far too late.

On 23 January there began the longest and most severe spell of icy weather of the century: for six weeks the average maximum day temperature remained close to freezing point, the average for the whole period being 34°F. The effect on coal production was almost negligible: weekly production of deep-mined coal in February was only 3 per cent below the average for two normal weeks in the middle of January. Nearly half this loss, which was confined to the first two weeks of February, could be accounted for by the shortage of railway waggons: the loss on that score over the fortnight was estimated at 150,000 tons. Even so, this was no more than the rate of loss through transport difficulties in December. The effect on inland consumption was also comparatively small: making the same comparison between February and mid-January the reduction works out at 6.3 per cent. But the effect on industrial production and on employment was devastating. Industrial production fell heavily and unemployment soared to over 2 million. The loss of industrial production was concentrated on exports which fell in the first half of the year and took a long time to regain momentum. It was estimated at the time that the cost in lost exports alone was £200 million or over one-sixth of the total for the year.[38]

The severe weather had disrupted the normal flow of coal traffic and the number of factories obliged to work on short-time or to close for lack of

38 This was, I believe, my own estimate, supplied to Cripps after the crisis, but I have no recollection how it was arrived at. Exports in 1947 fell £100 million short of the average for 1946 and 1948. The rate of expansion was falling off and it would be reasonable, therefore, to take £100 million as a minimum estimate of the loss, although £200 million now seems rather too high.

fuel increased. A sudden crisis developed. The Cabinet met on 6 February to discuss the situation. Commenting on the discussion in his diary, Dalton showed no great concern: 'Our coal and electricity supplies are in a pretty poor way. It will be a great relief to get through to March and into the period when more coal is being produced [sic].'[39]

His entry for the following day, Friday 7 February, tells a different story:

> Today, at this morning's Cabinet, Shinwell suddenly asks permission to tell the House of Commons this afternoon that all electricity must be cut off from industry in London, South-East England, the Midlands and the North-West, and from all domestic consumers all over the country between nine and twelve, and between two and four each day. This is a complete thunderclap, following the usual rather hopeful tales we have had from him during the past week.[40] Only two days ago he was saying that he supposed we ought to give a priority to keeping all the generating stations well supplied, even if this meant cutting off some other people.
>
> This afternoon he made a very poor performance in the House, with a lot of the usual Party polemics, blaming the coalowners, etc., and only in the last few sentences of a forty-minute speech made a very rapid and garbled announcement of the proposed cuts. No one really understood what he was saying, and neither the Press nor the public had any warning.[41]

Dalton had good reason to be shocked by the slapstick preface to one of the most extraordinary announcements ever made in the House of Commons. It is doubtful whether the House has been treated with such contempt by any post-war minister about to convey news of the gravest importance. Shinwell sought to minimize the calamity by suggesting that the stoppage would 'not last for longer than three or four days, or at the most for a week', whilst 'as regards the Lancashire area, it may be possible to avoid the cut – at any rate after the first day or so'. In fact, the electricity ban lasted for three weeks.

39 Entry for 6 February 1947.
40 Shinwell had outlined the same proposal to the Cabinet the previous day and the Cabinet had rejected it. So it was hardly a 'thunderclap'.
41 Entry for 7 February 1947. See also Dalton (1962), pp. 203–4; H. C. Deb., 5th ser., vol. 432, col. 2179, 7 February 1947; Jewkes (1948), p. 182. The fact that the announcement had to be made at a very inopportune time, on a Friday afternoon, should be held against the Cabinet, not Shinwell.

At the Cabinet meeting on 6 February Shinwell warned the Cabinet that 'a very serious situation might arise' early in the following week.[42] Production of open-cast coal had stopped completely; gales were holding up ships loaded with coal in north-east coast ports and ships that had unloaded coal in south coast ports; transport in Northumberland, Durham and Yorkshire had been seriously interrupted; loading machinery in the Cardiff and Barry docks was frozen; and miners in many parts of the country were unable to get to work. The Central Electricity Board had suggested that in London and the south-east, the north-west, and the Midlands all supplies of electricity to industrial consumers should be cut completely and supplies to domestic consumers cut from 9 a.m. to noon and 2 p.m. to 4 p.m. Shinwell, while in agreement that detailed plans to this effect should be got ready, thought that it might be possible to avoid such severe cuts if supplies of coal were concentrated on the more efficient power stations. Cripps said that even before the recent severe weather 120 factories in the north-west and 30–40 in the Midlands were on short-time. He thought that the time had come for ministers to consider whether the whole of the coal shortage should continue to fall on industry while no restrictions were imposed on domestic consumers.

The Cabinet, however, gave approval neither to the CEB's proposal nor to Cripps's. They agreed that there should be no drastic cuts in electricity consumption, whether by industry or by domestic consumers, 'for the present'. Most of their suggestions for immediate action were extremely vague: more flexibility at the regional level; concentration of supplies on 'more efficient' producers; a larger reserve pool at the expense of basic allocations; an examination of the possibility of double summertime.

The following day Shinwell told a different story.[43] The cuts in electricity supplies proposed by the CEB were now inevitable and it would not be sufficient to limit industry to two days a week or reduce household consumption. Essential services and factories operating continuous processes would, however, be supplied. The restrictions he proposed would be introduced on Sunday, 9 February and might last 3–7 days. Taken aback, the Cabinet asked that the restrictions be deferred for a day since the industrial load was light on Sundays and there would be no substantial saving, while consumers would suffer 'grave inconvenience'. Exports

---

42  CM(47)17, 6 February 1947, in PRO CAB 128/9; CP(47)50, 5 February 1947, in PRO CAB 129/16.
43  CM(47)18, 7 February 1947, in PRO CAB 128/9.

were to be suspended. The embargo on loading bunker coal into ships proceeding overseas, which Shinwell had imposed the previous evening without consultation, much to the indignation of the Minister of Transport, was withdrawn and officials were asked to discuss in what circumstances they should be provided. It was agreed also that Shinwell should announce that the restrictions would last, not for 3–7 days but for 'at least a week'; this, as we have seen, he did not do.

Further meetings of the Cabinet on the coal situation were held on 10 and 11 February. The railways were to give absolute priority to the movement of coal irrespective of any inconvenience to passengers and the Navy was to help in bringing ships up the Thames and into north-east coast ports. In the usual miscellany of suggestions it was agreed to take steps to prevent the use of electricity by greyhound-racing tracks. The Prime Minister in a broadcast on the evening of the 10th was to invite the co-operation of the public in overcoming the crisis.

Other measures taken by the government were designed to get the coal away from the pits and prevent any hold-up in production. Army lorries were used to move coal, distributors in the coastwise trade were required to pool plant and coal supplies, and waggons were relabelled to enable full trains to be dispatched over routes that could accept them.[44] These measures appear to have been effective. Although difficulties of transport conditioned the distribution of coal between different consumers and different routes the resulting loss of output after the middle of February was very small and was less during the whole period of icy weather than it had been in the month before it began.

The government also took more active steps to improve recruitment. In the middle of January it had agreed to exempt underground coal-workers from call-up to the forces for the next five years. It had also, in June 1946, announced its readiness to accept a five-day week in the mines 'of a kind which will secure the output of coal necessary to meet the country's needs'. The National Coal Board, soon after its appointment, concluded that a five-day week was desirable and embarked on negotiations with the NUM in December. These were successfully concluded in March, received government approval in April and brought the five-day week into operation on 5 May. In February the government sanctioned the construction of more houses in the coalfields and asked the local authorities to give

---

44 *Report and Accounts of the National Coal Board for 1947*, p. 3. Between 14 and 17 February 120 trains were relabelled at East Midlands Collieries alone.

priority to the housing needs of coal-miners. It also approved an expansion in training facilities and a relaxation of training requirements.

It was not altogether clear at first what the criteria were to be for withdrawing the restrictions on electricity consumption. At the first meeting of the new Fuel Committee, the Central Electricity Board wanted to increase stocks at the power stations from just over one week's consumption to two weeks' consumption before lifting the restrictions on industry.[45] The Ministry of Fuel and Power thought that one and a half weeks' consumption would be enough for power stations near the coalfields. No one seems to have queried these targets. In consultation with the CEB the National Coal Board made arrangements to increase stocks at the power stations to two weeks' consumption by 10 March at the latest. The government gave instructions that coal for this purpose was to be found at the expense of industry.

Since the power stations had been using about 700,000 tons of coal a week out of a total weekly output of 3.75 million tons, this implied setting aside, at the height of the crisis, nearly 5 per cent of current output for four weeks to put into stock by denying industry a corresponding amount. It is hard to understand how so extraordinary a decision could have been taken so lightly. It is not as if the power stations, with a few exceptions, were below some operational minimum. Even in London and the south-east, stocks of coal on 7 February were equal on the average to a little over nine days' consumption and in the Midlands to just over seven days' consumption. That these low stocks imposed severe restraints on electricity generation is not in question. The coal uncovered as stocks fell might have been lying under a heavy weight for several years and in consequence might be seriously degraded. Stocks were lower than they had ever been before or have ever been since. Mechanical handling equipment, moreover, worked less satisfactorily near the bottom of the heap. If one power station had to close, others might be incapable of taking over the load. There were no doubt good technical reasons why higher stocks eased the difficulty of keeping the power stations going and meeting what were judged to be crucial requirements. The fact remains that at a time when industry in three of the main industrial areas of the country had to shut down for lack of electric power, the consumption of electricity in three out of the four weeks following 8 February was well in excess of consumption in the corresponding weeks of 1946. In January 1947 11 per cent more coal was consumed in electricity generation than in January 1946; in

45  FC(47)1st meeting, 12 February 1947, in PRO CAB 134/272.

February 1947, *with the shutdown*, coal consumption was nearly 12 per cent above the level a year previously. Similarly at gasworks the *excess* above the corresponding month in 1946 was greater in February than in January – 6 per cent compared with 4½ per cent.[46]

The stock position at power stations and gas works is shown in table 13.3:

*Table 13.3*  Stocks of coal at power stations and gasworks 1946–7 (000 tons)

| *End of period* | *Power stations* | *Gasworks* |
|---|---|---|
| March 1946 | 1,176 | 1,053 |
| 25 January 1947 | 1,254 | 1,112 |
| 1 February 1947 | 1,130 | 1,015 |
| 8 February 1947 | 974 | 915 |
| 15 February 1947 | 1,076 | 852 |
| 22 February 1947 | 1,351 | 934 |
| 1 March 1947 | 1,483 | 971 |
| 8 March 1947 | 1,535 | 952 |

*Source:* National Coal Board Marketing Department. (Professor W. Ashworth kindly supplied me with the figures.)

At the end of January 1947 coal stocks at power stations were only a little below the lowest level reached in the winter of 1945–6 but were falling rapidly. They reached their lowest point in the week ending 8 February when they fell by 155,000 tons. They then climbed even faster than they had fallen and within the three weeks ending 1 March had risen by just over 500,000 tons. This represented 4½ per cent of total domestic consumption of coal over those three weeks – enough, one might reasonably suppose to have avoided the worst of the crisis, and certainly enough to have allowed the power stations to work to capacity.

By 1 March stocks in London had reached 2.08 weeks' consumption and at Shinwell's suggestion the restrictions on industry were removed on Monday 3 March. Electricity supplies to industry in the Midlands had already been restored a week earlier. Meanwhile no other group of consumers – railways, coke ovens, the iron and steel industry, industry generally, house-coal merchants – held on the average more than ten days'

46  Consumption of coal at gasworks increased in February above the pre-crisis level; at power stations the fall in consumption from the high January level was insignificant.

*Table 13.4*  The summer coal budget May–November 1947 (m. tons)

| | Programme | Actual | | Programme | Actual |
|---|---|---|---|---|---|
| Inland consumption | 77.9 | 84.0 | Stocks on 1 May | 5.0 | 6.4 |
| Less saving in | | | Deep-mined production | 83.0 | 90.1 |
| consumption by | | | Open-cast disposals | 6.0 | 5.8 |
| oil conversion | −2.0 | | Fall in colliery stocks | | 0.2 |
| Exports and bunkers | 3.1 | 2.6 | Imports | | 0.6 |
| Stocks on 1 November | 15.0 | 16.4 | | | |
| | 94.0 | 103.1 | | 94.0 | 103.1 |

Source: *Report and Accounts of the National Coal Board for 1947*, pp. 71–2.

consumption in the second half of February. Broadly speaking, the government selected the one sure way of forfeiting industrial production for the sake of adding to stocks at the power stations just when the winter was drawing to an end. Had the target been to maintain the pre-crisis level of stocks until the end of the cold spell, most of the loss of production would not have occurred.

On 8 March the allocation arrangements introduced on 20 January were restored except that industrial firms were to receive one-third instead of one-half of their allocations and there would be a larger pool from which supplementary allocations could be made.

A further example of inexperience in planning was the National Coal Board's proposal to build up stocks to 18 million tons by the beginning of the winter of 1947–8.[47] Cripps succeeded in getting agreement early in March on the more realistic figure of 15 million tons, which still meant putting 10 million tons into stocks over the summer, and a coal budget was drawn up on this basis (see table 13.4). It was a budget that proved much too cautious since it allowed only 76 million tons for inland consumption while it proved possible to provide 84 million tons without trenching on the ambitious stocks target.

Towards the end of March the Cabinet finally decided against a rationing scheme for gas and electricity, Cripps protesting that it was the *minimum* required, given the risk of 'a complete economic collapse'.[48] It was agreed, however, to prohibit the use of both gas and electricity for the heating of homes and, a little later, factories and other places of work as well. Railway passenger services were cut by 10 per cent. Two million

47  FC(47)10th meeting, 4 March 1947, in PRO CAB 134/273.
48  CM(47)32, 25 March 1947, in PRO CAB 128/9.

tons of coal were to be saved over the summer by the conversion of locomotives, steelworks and other plant to oil burning. Industry remained the
residuary legatee and only two-thirds of its estimated needs were provided
for. In April, however, Cripps was able to announce that the outlook had
sufficiently improved to permit an upward revision in the amount
allocated to industry. Firms would receive an amount equal to their
consumption during the previous summer but would be expected to build
up their stocks to at least three weeks' winter consumption by November
on the firm understanding that any extra accumulation (or any shortfall)
would not affect their subsequent winter allocations.

As so often happens, the government had swung from excessive complacency to excessive caution. It could not, of course, foresee how output
would be affected by the introduction of the five-day week and no one
could be sure how long the efforts of the miners to respond to the crisis
would continue – the South Wales miners, for example, worked voluntarily on seven successive Sundays. But it was increasingly apparent that
there had been a marked change in trend from the crisis onwards. Distributed stocks were never as low as 5 million tons and production was running ahead of consumption from the last week in March. In April nearly
600,000 tons of coal were put into stock whereas in April 1946 stocks had
continued to fall. By the beginning of May when production had risen
above 4 million tons a week the estimate of 83 million tons for deep-mined
production over the twenty-six weeks to the beginning of November was
already out-of-date. It was exceeded by 7 million tons or 8.5 per cent.
Fortunately the government did not hold to its budgeted allocations and
was content to let stocks increase by the 10 million tons originally planned
while consumption benefited by the whole of the unforeseen improvement in supplies. Nevertheless over the twenty-six weeks industrial
consumers received less coal than in the same period in 1946. The margin
was small – less than 1 million tons and under 5 per cent. It was a good
deal smaller than it had been in February and March when it averaged
nearly 20 per cent. But even in those months the reduction on the previous
year never came near the horrific proportions of the cuts in industry's
presumed requirements represented by allocations of one-third or one-
half.

## Anatomy of the crisis

We can now turn back to ask what did happen to the consumption of coal
over the crisis months and whether the best use was made, under prevailing conditions, of the supply available. The fears of the Ministry of Fuel

and Power were concentrated on the power stations and on the needs of certain users of electric power such as the hospitals, sewage and water works and other public utilities. Indeed, the Ministry is said to have been afraid by Sunday 9 February that if coal could not be shipped in within three days to supply the London power stations 'sewerage and water supplies would break down and the capital might have to be evacuated'.[49] Did these fears lead them, as was argued at the time in the Board of Trade, to allot too much coal to the power stations or to deprive industry unnecessarily of electricity?

Different power stations were differently circumstanced and some no doubt did run out of supplies. But total stocks at the power stations increased in February and again in March. The power stations had been using an exceptionally high amount of coal in January, consumption in the two weeks before the crisis averaging 730,000 tons per week. In the ensuing four weeks consumption fell to 565,000 tons. It is fair to conclude that over those four weeks the total saving of coal in electricity generation cannot have exceeded 660,000 tons – much the same as the amount put into stock. A similar calculation applied to total inland consumption shows a drop of 300,000 tons a week or 1,200,000 tons for the four weeks.[50] These also are relatively small figures. They show by how narrow a margin the crisis was produced. But they also suggest that it would have been wise to set about economies in consumption much earlier if a million tons of coal could make such a difference; and that it should not have been necessary to pick on economies in the use of electricity (mainly by industry) in order to effect half the total savings in coal consumption. No other economies would have been nearly as costly in lost output and lost exports. If it was feasible to make additional deliveries, the power stations should have had more, not less coal; but to oblige them to add to their stocks in the middle of a crisis was perverse and to cut off supplies of electricity to industry at the same time was to get the worst of both worlds.

When the ban on the use of electricity in the restricted areas was ended on 3 March the rise in electric power consumption was comparatively modest. Coal consumption at the power stations rose initially by 50,000–70,000 tons a week and from the middle of the month began to fall to levels below those of the previous year. The index of manufacturing

49  Williams (1979), p. 136 citing Arthur Horner (1960), pp. 179–80.
50  About one-third of the drop was in consumption by industries other than iron and steel.

production which had averaged 100 in 1946 and reached 106 in January 1947, dipped to 81 in February but was back at 100 in March and 107 in April. For a minute economy in fuel – the coal equivalent of the electric power of which the factories were deprived in February – something like a quarter of February's manufacturing output was thrown away.[51]

It may be that fuller examination would reveal a different picture. The dislocation in transport all through the crisis period was a great handicap to efforts to move the coal to the places where it was most needed and different kinds of coal were not interchangeable. There was no escape from shortages of fuel and power in the least accessible places. The ban on electricity consumption announced by Shinwell does, however, appear to have had an unnecessarily drastic effect on industrial production.

Was the crisis inevitable? Given the severity of the weather, *some* loss of output was more or less unavoidable. A similar spell of severe weather in January 1963 when there was no shortage of coal raised unemployment by about 1 per cent over the first quarter and reduced industrial production by 2–3 per cent (compared with about 10 per cent in 1947). But what of the additional unemployment and loss of output resulting from the coal shortage? Could the output of coal have been greater had measures been taken in time or could greater economies have been effected in the use of coal so as to allow larger distributed stocks to be built up?

That output was disappointingly low is not in question. Output per man in 1946 was 16 per cent below the pre-war level. Absenteeism among face workers was not far short of 20 per cent and well over double the pre-war rate. Productivity, as measured by output per man-shift worked at the coal-face, was down by about 5 per cent.

It might be argued that some of the disappointing performance was attributable to the uncertainties resulting from nationalization but of this there is little direct evidence. Ministers argued that without nationaliz-ation the men would not exert themselves for the sake of higher profits while their critics pointed to the additional burdens on the Ministry of Fuel and Power of nationalizing three major industries in quick succession and the complications and loss of incentive for colliery managements. But if one looks at the run of figures (see table 13.2, p. 357), the rise in output

51  Manufacturing production was increasing at about 12 per cent per annum (in the first half of 1948 it was 28 per cent higher than in the first half of 1946) and would appear to have been roughly on trend in the second quarter of 1947. The fall in the index suggests a loss of about 10 per cent of manufacturing output in the first quarter, nearly all of it in February.

per man-shift and the fall in absenteeism proceed fairly steadily from 1945 onwards without any obvious reflection in them of such influences. The introduction of the five-day week on 5 May 1947 made absenteeism dip more sharply and output per man-shift improve perceptibly but since working hours were extended again in November 1947 these changes are less apparent in the annual averages.[52] The one variable that does not show a fairly consistent trend over the post-war years is recruitment. The fluctuations in recruitment bear out the contention that this was the critical factor on which to operate in efforts to avoid a crisis.

It must be admitted that the National Coal Board itself was a little equivocal on this point. In its 1947 *Report* it gave estimates of the various factors behind the improvement in output in 1947.[53] These were summarized as follows:

|  | million tons |
| --- | --- |
| Increased manpower | +5.0 |
| Better attendance | +9.5 |
| Greater output per man-shift | +5.5 |
| Reduction in number of working days | −14.0 |
|  | +6.0 |

But at least two of these are part of a common factor – the introduction of the five-day week which reduced the number of working days and the amount of absenteeism simultaneously. If we attribute the improvement in productivity to the same factor we are left with increased manpower as by far the most important contributor to increased output. Elsewhere, however, the Board argues that 3.5 million tons of additional coal was produced in 1947 through the introduction of new machinery and re-organization of pits i.e. as a result of purely technical measures.[54] This leaves only the remainder of the improvement in deep-mined production – 2.8 million tons – to be attributed to better efforts and attendance and to the increase in the total labour force. Moreover the Board indicates that

52 *Report and Accounts of the National Coal Board for 1947*, pp. 13–14. In May and June output per man-shift improved over the two previous months, by about 4 per cent and absenteeism fell from 15 per cent to 9 per cent. These improvements, which were not fully sustained later, meant that output was little affected by the change.
53 ibid., p. 121.
54 *Report and Accounts of the National Coal Board for 1947*, p. 41.

the larger number of recruits could involve setting aside faces for underground training 'at the expense of immediate production or of the development of new production faces'.[55] In spite of the training of more face workers there was no substantial increase in the number of face workers.

Apart from technical changes, which necessarily took time, recruitment was virtually the only factor on which the government could operate with any hope of quick results. If recruitment was improving there was a strong likelihood of an early improvement in output too and conversely if recruitment was falling off output was likely to suffer.

The most obvious way of improving recruitment was by improving pay and working conditions in the coal-mines. This was urged by the miners themselves when the NUM sent a 'Charter of Demands' to the Minister of Fuel and Power. Among other things, the Charter asked for a five-day week without loss of pay; average wages not inferior to those of any other industry; a seven-hour day for underground workers and a 40-hour week for surface workers; an additional week's holiday with pay; and pensions at 55 for those who had to give up work in the mines. A definite timetable was sought for the introduction of each of these items.[56]

Some of these demands were liable to reduce output in the short run. For example, it was estimated that shorter hours would mean sacrificing at least 5 million tons a year and extra holidays a further $3\frac{1}{2}$ million tons, apart from adding £10 million to labour costs; but no one could really foretell the repercussions of shorter hours on the high rate of absenteeism or on output per man-shift. As for wages, the average hourly wage of miners was third in the list of all industries and underground workers were at the top of the list, although for weekly wages the ranking was very different because of the high rate of absenteeism.[57]

The Cabinet naturally hesitated to endorse proposals that offered no immediate relief to the shortage of coal and was in any event reluctant to enter into direct negotiations with workers whom it did not employ. It would also have hesitated to require the National Coal Board to raise pay outright when it took office for fear of setting off a general rise in wages and was in some embarrassment in the course of 1947 when it found concessions made in favour of the miners claimed by other workers in the

55 ibid., p. 48.
56 For a full discussion of the government's reactions see Chester (1975), pp. 796 et seq.
57 In its 1951 Report, the NCB commented that 'wages in the mining industry have risen further than in any other. In 1938 they were low in the list of wage-rates; at the end of 1951, they were at the top' (p. 73).

employment of the NCB. The government in the end had to leave negotiations on pay and conditions to the Board. The one exception was the
five-day week to which it declared in June 1946 that it offered no objection
in principle provided the miners gave their full co-operation in securing
the necessary output of coal – construed by Shinwell in addressing the
miners as acceptance in principle.

It is conceivable that the introduction of the five-day week, various
other changes made by the Board and the improved image and prospects of
the industry after nationalization lay behind the increase in recruitment in
1947. But the five-day week was not finally agreed until April 1947 or
introduced until the following month while recruitment had begun to
improve in the last quarter of 1946. The main explanation is more likely to
lie in administrative arrangements.

In the first year after the war recruitment was swollen by the return of
miners from the forces but wastage was also high because of the large
number of older men in the industry and the loss of wartime recruits such
as the 'Bevin boys'. An initial fall in employment was checked towards
the end of 1945 and reversed in the first quarter of 1946 when the number
of ex-miners returning from the forces reached a peak of 11,000. Total
recruitment exceeded wastage by over 4,000 and employment continued
to increase slowly until July. From the peak at the end of July there was a
fall of 8,000 to mid-November. Then began a steady climb which brought
total employment to a fresh peak at the end of July 1947, 20,000 higher
than a year before. It was the climb in numbers in the first half of 1947 that
was the decisive factor in removing the danger of a fresh crisis in the
winter of 1947–8.

Closer examination (see table 13.5) shows that the improvement in the
first half of 1947 was partly due to a big drop in wastage from 44,000 to
30,000 (in 1948–9 wastage remained fairly steady at about 33,000 in each
half year) but even more to an unusually high rate of recruitment. Indeed,
recruitment in the first half of 1947 was roughly equal to recruitment over
the whole year in 1949 or 1950. This was not due to a high rate of recruitment of miners released from the forces. Nearly two-thirds of the
improvement came from the recruitment of adult workers from other
industries, especially ex-miners. Some 12,500 more workers from other
industries were recruited than in the second half of 1946 and an extra
4,500 workers from Training Centres, many of them foreign workers.

It is difficult not to associate this picture with a strengthening of the
recruitment drive in the final quarter of 1946 and with more resolute
efforts by the NCB once they took full charge of recruitment on 1 April

*Table 13.5*  Recruitment to coal-mining 1946–7 (000s)

|  | 1946 | | 1947 | | Total |
|---|---|---|---|---|---|
|  | First half | Second half | First half | Second half |  |
| **Recruitment** | | | | | |
| Ex-miners from forces | 19.2 | 8.7 | 6.4 | 5.9 | 40.1 |
| Ex-miners from other industries | 9.2 | 10.7 | 17.9 | 11.0 | 48.8 |
| Other workers from other industries | 2.1 | 4.1 | 9.4 | 8.1 | 23.7 |
| Juveniles | 6.3 | 6.4 | 10.0 | 4.6 | 27.4 |
| Men from residential training centres | 1.8 | 3.1 | 7.7 | 8.1 | 20.7 |
| Other | — | 1.4 | 2.1 | 2.9 | 6.4 |
|  | 38.5 | 34.3 | 53.7 | 40.5 | 167.0 |
| *Wastage* | 33.2 | 43.8 | 30.0 | 40.0 | 145.0 |
| *Balance of recruitment over wastage* | 5.3 | −9.5 | 23.7 | 0.5 | 22.0 |

Source: Report and Accounts of the National Coal Board for 1947, table 14.

1947. If we leave out coal-miners returning from the forces, recruitment was steady at around 10,000 per quarter throughout the first three quarters of 1946. It then jumped to 15,000 in the last quarter, 25,000 in the next quarter and 22,000 in the following quarter, tailing off to 16,000 and 18,000 in the second half of the year. The coal crisis may of itself have caused more men to present themselves as recruits from February onwards. But the improvement probably reflects in the main a more vigorous recruitment drive, beginning some months before the crisis and involving the co-operation of the Labour Exchanges in giving priority to the needs of the coal industry.

If this is so, would a recruitment drive, conducted with the same urgency, have had less effect a year earlier? The rundown in the armed forces was proceeding rapidly throughout 1946 and offered far greater opportunities of pressing men to enter (or return to) the coal-mining industry than existed in 1947. If employment, instead of falling by 4,000, had risen by 26,000, as in 1947, manpower over the year before the coal crisis would have been on the average 15,000 or over 2 per cent greater; and if output had been correspondingly enlarged and consumption no higher, distributed stocks would have been nearly 4 million tons greater by the beginning of 1947 – quite enough to allow the worst of the damage to industrial output to be avoided. Even an extra 1 per cent put into stock would have eased the shortage perceptibly.

Suppose that Cripps and not Shinwell had been Minister of Fuel and Power. In February 1946 he had expressed concern that exports might be hit by a shortage of coal for industrial purposes[58] but his absence in India later in the year delayed his intervention until it was too late to do anything effective. There can be little doubt that, had it been his responsibility, he would have put far more pressure behind recruitment and that the output of coal would have been appreciably higher in 1946. If it had been as high as in 1947 there would have been no coal crisis: any loss of industrial output would have reflected weather conditions, not a shortage of coal. Without going quite as far as that, one can conclude that much of the loss was avoidable.

It is more difficult to be sure that the government could have procured greater economy in the use of coal. There were only two ways in which that could have been brought about. One was by greater insistence on the danger of an acute shortage but, as we have seen, the Minister concerned took exactly the opposite line and pooh-poohed the danger. The other was by cutting allocations so as to allow of a larger accumulation of stocks under government control. This would have meant, in practice, larger allocations to the power stations and other utilities at the expense of exports, domestic consumers and industry generally.

A year after the crisis the situation seemed transformed. Employment had risen by nearly 4 per cent; output per man-shift in 1947 was 3 per cent higher than in 1946; the level of output had grown correspondingly and was still increasing. As a result, distributed stocks at the end of the year were over 16 million tons and higher than they had been at that point in the year since 1944.

Exports, too, had been resumed. In July when the crisis had passed but it was still uncertain what the future had in store, the government committed itself in Paris as part of the Marshall Plan, to the supply of 13 million tons of coal a year for exports and bunkers of which 6 million tons would go to markets in OEEC, 6 million tons would be delivered as bunker coal at British ports and the remaining 1 million tons would be bunker coal delivered to foreign ports. More cautiously, the government explained that not much could be expected before April 1948. On this occasion boldness was rewarded. In December, restrictions on bunker coal supplies were removed and the National Coal Board was authorized to

58  CM(46)20, 11 February 1946, in PRO CAB 128/5.

resume exports up to 200,000 tons per week within the framework of trade agreements with foreign governments. In March 1948 this limit was withdrawn and by April shipments were already up to an annual rate of 13 million tons. Meanwhile the *Economic Survey for 1948* had revised the export target upwards to 'more than 15 million tons'. In fact the total for 1948 reached 16 million tons, the annual rate at the end of the year being nearly 20 million tons.

Earlier in 1948 export targets had been set for later years under the Marshall Plan of 22 million tons in 1949, 33 million tons in 1950 and 41 million tons in 1951.[59] These targets proved too ambitious. A peak of 19.4 million tons was reached in 1949 but thereafter there was a drop. So far from reaching 41 million tons by 1951, exports and bunkers were no more than 11.6 million tons, of which exports proper amounted to only 7.7 million tons.

Although output continued to expand after 1947 there was still cause for anxiety. Coal was rationed to householders and exports were less than half their pre-war volume. Manpower had begun to fall, stocks were declining slowly from one year-end to the next and the annual growth in output was progressively smaller. Distributed stocks at the end of 1950 were back to the low level of January 1946 and domestic consumption was rising strongly. For a time it looked as if there might be a replay of the 1947 crisis. Noel-Baker, the new Minister of Fuel and Power, going to the opposite extreme from Shinwell, went so far as to propose that the BBC should shut down at 11 p.m. so as to save 50 tons of coal. The rate of exports was cut quite drastically from August 1950 onwards and bunker supplies reduced from November. In 1951 widespread working of Saturday overtime was introduced throughout the year except in the summer months and arrangements were made for the importation of some 2 million tons of coal. But the alarm died down as recruitment and production improved. Stocks recovered by October 1951 to as high a level as in any previous post-war year.

From then on throughout the 1950s there was no recurrence of an acute shortage of coal. Employment fluctuated within narrow limits, output also remained fairly flat, exports never regained even the level of 1949 and oil increasingly took over as the source from which the increment in demand was met.

How did the post-war effort made by the British coal industry compare with that of its European neighbours? In all of them coal was scarce and

59 *Report and Accounts of the National Coal Board for 1947*, p. 116.

there was every incentive to expand production. Most of them, unlike Great Britain, were consuming less coal, even in 1951, than they had before the war largely because the imports on which they had then relied, from Great Britain and Germany, were no longer available in anything like the same quantity. Instead of 100 million tons of coal and coke, as in 1937, European countries were able to import only 60–65 million tons in the years between 1947 and 1950, and as their European neighbours could supply only about two-thirds of what was required, they had to turn for the remainder to the United States. Imports from America in the five years 1947–51 reached a total of nearly 90 million tons. This dependence on American coal was at its height in 1947 when 34 million tons were imported at a substantially higher cost per ton than supplies from European sources.[60] Imports from the United Kingdom into OEEC countries in the same year were under 1 million tons. But between the first quarter of 1947 and the last quarter of 1948 the situation changed radically. There was a rise in total imports into OEEC countries from the four leading exporters – the United States, the United Kingdom, Poland and Germany – from 2.5 million tons a month to 5.5 million tons a month; and there was a switch from American supplies, which were down to 2.5 million tons in total in the last three months of 1948, to European supplies which totalled nearly 11 million tons over the same three months, Britain supplying 2.6 million tons out of this total. American imports continued, however, and in the winter of 1950–1 there was a renewed surge to meet the exceptional rise in consumption after the outbreak of the Korean War.

Britain's coal exports to Europe were lowest when the need for them was greatest. It was the absence of British (and German) supplies that was the main cause of post-war dependence on American supplies and it was not surprising therefore that as output improved Britain contributed to a reduction in this dependence. But she was not the main contributor to this reduction. Nor was the recovery in employment and production in Britain as complete as in other European countries. At the end of 1947 more miners were at work in Europe than before the war; in Britain there was still a shortfall of 6 per cent. Coal output was above the pre-war level in France, Poland and Czechoslovakia, 80–90 per cent of pre-war in Belgium and the Netherlands, and 65 per cent in West Germany; in Britain it was

60  The United Kingdom imported 600,000 tons of coal from the United States in 1947 at an average cost of $11 a ton (75s., or £3.75) and made a loss on the sale of 45s./10d. (£2.30) per ton (*Report and Accounts of the National Coal Board for 1947*, pp. 75–6).

about 85 per cent. This meant that production was at the level of pre-war inland consumption (including bunkers) with little or nothing to spare for exports. Thus, leaving West Germany on one side, Britain's recovery was slower or at best no faster than that of other European producers when the fastest possible recovery was in the interests of all.

### Lessons of the fuel crisis

In retrospect the fuel crisis has a fivefold interest:

(1) It was a striking example of incompetence in industrial planning by a government dedicated to economic planning. What stood revealed were not the limitations on which the textbooks insist — the problem of decentralizing and yet achieving co-ordination, the uncertainties and lack of adequate information. On the contrary, the uncertainties were minimal, the information abundant, the organization impressive.[61] The lesson was rather that planning depends on planners, that when ministers plan they may have no sense of magnitudes and dismiss statistical analysis with an airy reference to 'imponderables',[62] and that the biggest errors in planning are likely to be errors in human relations: making the wrong appointments or persisting in them; inability to visualize the scale and mode of action necessary; failure to convince others of the need for action and arouse in them the responses required. Planning has its technical side: but it is also a political art and one in which on this occasion the Labour government fell down badly.

(2) It was an early demonstration of the vulnerability of an industrial society to a shortfall in the supply of fuel and power. Like all short-falls it can be made to yield in time to price changes; but when it

61 In one important respect this needs qualification. If an insufficiency of coal was inescapable the only thing to do was to apportion the shortfall with the minimum of damage to industrial output (as well, of course, as to other kinds of economic activity). This required information as to the level of output that individual consumers could sustain with different supplies of fuel below the optimum. Little attempt was made to collect such information and the cuts that were made in coal deliveries were correspondingly random. It must be very doubtful, however, how far it would have been possible, by collecting additional information, to move from a system that took account of differences between industries and services to one that also took account of differences between establishments in the same industry or service on the loss of output they would suffer if coal supplies were cut proportionately.

62 Jay (1980), p. 149.

arises suddenly, the elasticities on both sides are extremely low and it may be impossible to close the gap without major disruption.

(3) In a controlled economy the signals of impending shortage take the form of changes in stocks rather than in prices and the responses are mediated through officials and ministers, not through the market. If ministers and their advisers are incapable of reading the signals or are determined to misread them, the result is likely to be disastrous. Since in this case the Prime Minister was repeatedly warned by his advisers of the danger and knew that the Minister responsible was turning a blind eye on the signals but took no action to move him in good time – nor even for some months after the crisis – he must share the blame for the fiasco.

(4) The margin between sufficiency and insufficiency can be a very fine one especially when sufficiency is measured in terms of the adequacy of stocks. In the last three weeks of February 1947 coal output actually exceeded consumption by 140,000 tons but it was in these three weeks that the heaviest loss of industrial production took place.

(5) The coal crisis set back the export drive by at least six months and delayed to the same extent the achievement of external balance. In judging its importance one has therefore to weigh up the damage resulting from that delay. To the extent that it was the *dollar* deficit that mattered and that the loss of dollar exports was relatively small, the damage may have been limited. But suppose that there had been no Marshall Aid. In the absence of the coal crisis the United Kingdom would have been not far from external balance in the second half of 1947. This might not have reduced by very much the outflow of dollars on trade account. But it would have improved the United Kingdom's credit greatly and increased her bargaining power in what would have been an extremely serious situation, not only for the United Kingdom but for her European neighbours as well. On the other hand, it is just possible that it was such events as the fuel crisis that alarmed the United States and persuaded her that further help to Europe was necessary. The most reasonable conclusion is that the fuel crisis added to the risks of an external breakdown in an already dangerous situation: the risks were real even if in the end the harm done was limited.

# Chapter fourteen

## MANPOWER AND THE LABOUR MARKET

Many of the early economic decisions taken by the government were couched in terms of manpower. It may not have been prominent in the government's thinking at the outset since they had no legislatgion in mind and were content with the scheme for demobilization drawn up earlier by the Ministry of Labour. But they were soon made aware of a threefold problem. First there was a general shortage of labour that brought into sharp conflict the needs of the armed services and civil industry. This was accompanied by a maldistribution of labour, with some 'essential' industries undermanned while other industries that seemed to the government less 'essential' were able to recruit labour with more success. Finally, the shortage of labour, by adding greatly to its bargaining power, created a serious danger of wage inflation.

The first two of those problems emerged from consideration of the manpower budgets prepared by the Economic Section. In conditions of labour shortage it was impossible to balance these budgets without cuts and the armed forces were an obvious target. The budgets also posed the question how the distribution of manpower between industries could be made to conform to government plans. But it was hardly necessary to appeal to a manpower budget to show how much larger the armed forces would be at the end of 1946 than in 1939 and to point in that direction for relief from a shortage of manpower; while the difficulties of industries like coal, textiles and agriculture in attracting labour were only too apparent. Nevertheless a manpower budget gave an appearance of precision to estimates of shortage and posed the issues for ministers in the context of a comprehensive picture of labour market developments. The allocation of

manpower in wartime had regulated the scale of departmental programmes and had accustomed ministers to approach planning decisions in
terms of manpower rather than money, employment rather than the
expenditure giving rise to it. In peacetime they still hankered after the
power to control employment directly and allocate manpower between
one industry and another. Many of them were at a loss to understand how,
without such power, they could ensure full employment or get rid of
undermanning. For this reason they were at first reluctant to give up the
powers of direction which the government had assumed in wartime.

## The manpower budget and demobilization

The first problem, that of labour shortage, was not strictly one of manpower at all. It reflected excess demand and was simply an alternative way
of presenting the inflationary gap. It was in this way that it was presented
in December 1945 in the draft 'Economic Survey for 1946'. This showed a
manpower 'gap' of 940,000 in June 1946 and 1,346,000 in December
1946, and suggested ways of reducing it, including a faster rundown in
the armed forces, economy in their demands for new supplies, persuading
more women to remain at work, avoiding localized pockets of unemployment, and so on. But it did not attempt to show how the gap could or
would be closed in manpower terms. Instead, the arithmetic of its proposals was geared to a financial gap of £470 million between the likely
level of effective demand and available supplies. Financial gaps, however,
excited no great interest except in the Treasury. Ministers had yet to
recognize in the 'Economic Survey' the groundwork of the plan they
hoped for.

When the 'Survey' came before the Lord President's group on 21
January 1946, discussion of its recommendations was rather desultory.
The Chancellor, however, took the main point. The first conclusion, he
said, was that the armed forces and supply services were too big and
should be cut by half a million. Cripps, however, was more disturbed 'to
find the "Survey" assuming that we must accept over $2\frac{1}{2}$ million people
in distribution at the end of 1946' and wanted a cut in distributive margins
once this could be done 'as part of a general economic plan'.[1]

Meanwhile the size of the armed forces was also being pursued in other
ministerial committees. Norman Brook, the Secretary to the Cabinet,
drew the Prime Minister's attention at the beginning of February to the

1  GEN 115/1st meeting, 21 January 1946, in PRO PREM 8/319.

overlap between three different ministerial committees each discussing the same problem.[2]

The situation was clearly set out in the draft 'Economic Survey'. This showed 9 million workers in the armed forces and supply services in June 1945 and 12.5 million in civil employment. The 9 million were expected to fall to 2.6 million at the end of 1946 but this was still 850,000 higher than in June 1939. Civil employment would not benefit by the full drop of 6.4 million because in the changeover to peacetime conditions there would be a large efflux from the labour market. Perhaps as many as 2 million workers would opt for domestic or other duties or retire. If so, the total working population would fall back to its pre-war level or even below it (see table 14.1). Civil employment would then be below the pre-war level in spite of a heavy fall in unemployment since 1939. On the arithmetic of the 'Economic Survey' the number in civil employment would rise over the eighteen months from June 1945 to December 1946 by one-third to 16.60 million. But this would still leave it below the pre-war level and 1.35 million below the level of manpower requirements as estimated by departments.

These calculations had obviously no great claim to precision. They concentrated attention on the apparent intention of the military to retain manpower in December 1946 on a scale far above the pre-war level and underlined the undeniable excess demand for labour in 1946. Their fallibility was revealed when it emerged that employment on supplies for the armed forces at the end of 1945 was 450,000 higher than the 'Survey' showed (presumably 1.9 million instead of 1.45 million). This did not, however, dispose the Cabinet, in its consideration of the matter, to raise the target level for December 1946. The Prime Minister on 5 January recommended a cut in the armed forces to 1.2 million (from a forecast of 1.75 million) and in the supply services to 650,000 (from a forecast of 850,000). This cut was confirmed by the Cabinet a month later except that the rundown in the supply services to 650,000 was now to be completed by June 1946. It would seem that this stiff target – it represented a cut of two-thirds in six months – was all but achieved (see table 14.1). While employment on munitions in mid-1946 was reduced to not much more than half what it had been in mid-1939, the armed forces by contrast still retained over four times as many men.

The Cabinet decision meant the release of an additional 750,000

2 Minute to the Prime Minister from Sir Norman Brook, February 1946, in PRO PREM 8/319.

Table 14.1  The progress of demobilization 1945–8 (millions)

| | mid-1939 actual | June 1945 actual | June 1946 actual | end-1946 forecast[a] | end-1946 actual | end-1947 actual | end-1948 actual | end-1953 actual[b] |
|---|---|---|---|---|---|---|---|---|
| Armed forces | 0.48 | 5.09 | 2.03 | 1.20 | 1.46 | 1.12 | 0.81 | 0.85 |
| Supply services | 1.27 | 3.83 | 0.72 | 0.65 | 0.46 | 18.89 | 19.15 | 19.42 |
| Civil employment | 16.73 | 12.59 | 16.70 | 17.35 | 17.82 | | | |
| Unemployed or on release leave | 1.27 | 0.14 | 1.08 | 0.60 | 0.70 | 0.42 | 0.37 | 0.35 |
| Total working population | 19.75 | 21.65 | 20.53 | 19.80 | 20.44 | 20.43 | 20.33 | 20.62 |

Sources: Economic Survey for 1947, Cmd 7046; Economic Survey for 1949, Cmd 7647; draft 'Economic Survey for 1946'; Monthly Digest of Statistics.

a  As in draft 'Economic Survey for 1946' amended to show Cabinet decision in February 1946 reducing armed forces from forecast of 1.75 million to 1.20 million and supply services from 0.85 million to 0.65 million.

b  Manpower figures were on a different basis from 1948 onwards. The figures shown for 1953 are estimates on the pre-1948 basis i.e. they add to the 1948 total the increase in the working population on the new basis and assume that no change need be made in the figures for armed forces and unemployed.

workers, making the increase in civil employment by December 1946 nearly 40 per cent. Half the manpower gap, if one chooses to accept the arithmetic of the 'Economic Survey', was successfully closed. The rest of the gap was closed by the retention in the labour force of 640,000 more workers than had been assumed in the 'Economic Survey', of whom, however, an extra 100,000 were on release leave or unemployed. Large discrepancies in detail remained. The rundown in the armed forces was 250,000 less than the Cabinet had ruled. On the other hand, there was a shortfall in distribution of 250,000 and in building and engineering of 110,000.

When the next 'Economic Survey' was prepared in June 1946 (MEP(46)5), the calculation then made put the manpower gap at the end of 1946 at the more reassuring level of 230,000. The Steering Committee of Permanent Secretaries commented that inflationary pressure persisted and looked to a damping down of investment for relief. But it thought the most serious threat was a coal shortage during the winter which might seriously disrupt the government's plans and was doubtful, quite apart from coal, whether the government had adequate powers to implement their plans (MEP(46)7).

When the third post-war 'Economic Survey' was submitted to ministers in December 1946 the inflationary gap was again presented in dual form: first as a manpower gap and then as a financial or spending gap. Manpower requirements as estimated by departments or implied in their programmes were 630,000 in excess of expected labour supply. This represented a lesser degree of labour shortage than a year previously when it had been put at 1.35 million but a greater degree of labour shortage than in the previous 'Survey' in June when it was put at 230,000.[3]

It was not very easy to give an unequivocal meaning to the gap since departmental requirements had been 'scaled down to take account of the realities of the situation'. It was recognized that in the absence of the various controls, effective demand would be substantially greater and the gap correspondingly increased. The availability of additional manpower would also not eliminate the gap since additional employment would simultaneously add to spending power. If the gap was a truly inflationary gap it could only be removed by withdrawing demand, not by adding to supply unless the extra supply added nothing to purchasing power and the flow of expenditure.

3  For the draft 'Economic Survey for 1947' and subsequent discussion see PRO PREM 8/646.

Explanation of the gap in terms of consumption and saving proved rather confusing and not pointed enough to form the basis of a ministerial decision. Not surprisingly, the issue was posed by the Steering Committee in terms of manpower. Officials suggested that the gap of 630,000 could be closed by the following series of measures:

| | |
|---|---:|
| (a) Employment of Polish labour | 100,000 |
| (b) More rapid reduction in military requirements | 168,000 |
| (c) Postponement by six months of raising of school-leaving age | 160,000 |
| (d) Less rapid increase in employment in building (shortage of timber) | 70,000 |
| (e) Reduction in civil service, local government employment and engineering employment; call-up of women aged 20 for two years' national service | 140,000 |
| | 638,000 |

Ministers rejected (c) and accepted (a) and part of (b). They took credit also for an economy of 230,000 workers because there would be insufficient steel to allow of additional employment in the metal-using industries. Manpower for the services was to be cut by 30,000 not by the 168,000 suggested, still less by the 300,000 that had originally figured in the proposals. (Dalton was so disgusted that he contemplated resignation.)[4] These 'economies' added up to 430,000. Where the remaining 200,000 was to come from was left obscure unless it corresponded to ministers' hopes that higher productivity would offer a way out of their difficulties. It is not a bad example of the tendency of ministers to decide what they have little or no power to influence and leave undecided what is plainly within their discretion. The standstill in employment in the building and metal and engineering industries might or might not reduce inflationary pressure. But it was not a matter of decision since it was the presumed consequence of a shortage of timber and steel. As for higher productivity, however welcome that might be, it would do little to extinguish excess demand if it added to purchasing power as well as output: the suggestion illustrated the confusion that might be created by thinking too exclusively in terms of manpower. In any event, the prospective shortage of materials seemed unlikely to go with a marked improvement in productivity (although the Prime Minister quite correctly predicted that it would be higher than in 1946).

4  Diary, entry for 27 January 1947; Dalton (1962), ch. XXIII.

When the *Economic Survey* did appear it made no reference to an inflationary gap: the word 'inflation' does not appear. Where there was originally a reference to a shortage of 250,000 workers, the figure, on the Prime Minister's instructions, was deleted but the text continued to maintain that 'the prospective labour force of 18,300,000 men and women at December 1947 falls substantially short of what is needed to reach the national objectives'.[5]

In the *Economic Survey for 1947* the Economic Section's original assessment of labour supply prospects stood up fairly well to the actual progress made (see table 14.1). The armed forces were still 1 million above the pre-war level and substantially higher than the Cabinet had ruled. But this excess was more than made up by the fall in unemployment and the unexpectedly high level of the working population. Some 600,000 women more than before the war had elected to continue in employment, an increase of about 12 per cent. Employment in civil industry, including the supply services, was rather higher than had been expected and more than before the war. In the eighteen months from the middle of 1945 employment to meet civil requirements had grown by 5 million.

The reluctance of the Cabinet to insist on a larger reduction in the armed forces reflected the disturbed state of the world and the widespread responsibilities of a country still professing to be a great power. The armed forces were stationed in many countries lying within the British sphere of influence where conditions remained unsettled, from India and Malaya to Palestine and Greece. It was necessary also to discharge the duties of an occupying power in Germany and Austria and on the frontiers of Italy. The growing estrangement between East and West disposed the government to look to its defences in a world of dictators and warring creeds in which the 1930s were seen as an object-lesson in the risks of military weakness. The burdens weighed heavily on an enfeebled economy and were not much lightened by Commonwealth contributions to their own defence. But they were at first judged to be the necessary price of an independent diplomacy.[6]

The succession of crises in 1947, however, forced the Cabinet to reassess its priorities. Bevin, who had been a powerful opponent of a rapid run-down in the armed forces, agreed that it should be possible to release additional men, and Attlee also had second thoughts. A review of policy

---

5 *Economic Survey for 1947*, Cmd 7046, para. 124.
6 George Peden, 'Economic aspects of British perceptions of power on the eve of the Cold War' (unpublished MS), pp. 16–17, and references given there.

had been undertaken by the Chiefs of Staff on the basis that the risk of a major war in the next five years could be ruled out and that any risk in the five years after that would increase only gradually. The Defence Committee accepted that until the country recovered its economic and industrial strength, the most it could afford to spend on defence was £600 million per annum compared with Estimates for 1948–9 that would otherwise have reached £900 million.[7] This did not prevent the Minister of Defence from submitting manpower plans to the Cabinet that were expected to yield Estimates of £711 million in 1948–9. He proposed to cut the armed forces from 1227 million at 30 September 1947 to 713,000 in eighteen months' time. But at 31 March 1948 only 150,000 more men would have been released than had previously been planned. To this had to be added 100,000 who would be shed from the industrial manpower supplying the services and, in the year following 31 March 1948, there would be a further net release of 225,000 from the armed forces.[8]

These proposals, which were accepted by the Cabinet on 2 October 1947, made a useful contribution to Dalton's disinflationary Budget a month later. They involved withdrawal by March 1948 from Austria, Greece, Italy and Japan, a big reduction in strength in the Middle East and a decidedly lower profile in the Far East. British troops would also be out of India by the end of 1947.

The actual reduction in numbers in 1947 was 350,000 and in 1948 300,000 (see table 14.1): but from then on there was little change in the size of the armed forces. The number on release leave dwindled to negligible proportions and unemployment remained low. Although the working population fell slightly, partly because of the raising of the school-leaving age to 15 in 1947 and the withdrawal of 160,000 juveniles from the labour market, nearly a million more workers were absorbed into civil employment by the end of 1948. Thereafter the changes in manpower were comparatively minor. In the five years to the end of 1953 the working population grew by some 300,000. The armed forces dipped a little further and then recovered to a level slightly higher than in 1948. The main changes, especially from 1950 onwards, reflected the expanding claims of rearmament on industrial manpower. From about 450,000 at the end of 1949 (excluding non-industrial workers engaged in the Defence

7  DO(47)68, 15 September 1947, in PRO CAB 129/21.
8  'Defence Requirements', memorandum by the Ministry of Defence, CP(47)272, 30 September 1947, in PRO CAB 129/21.

departments, research and development, etc.) the total was expected to more than double by 1953–4.[9]

In the three and a half years from June 1945 to the end of 1948 the working population dropped by 1.33 million or 6 per cent while the numbers employed to meet civil requirements (including exports) grew by nearly 6 million or not far short of 50 per cent. In the next five years the working population expanded by 300,000 and most of this was employed in meeting civil requirements. The changes in the second period were obviously very small in comparison with those taking place in the first.

With the completion of demobilization the manpower budget faded into the background. Its chief function had been to focus attention on the size of the armed forces and once ministers had tumbled to the link between manpower shortage and inflation they were more willing to think in terms of finance rather than labour supply. In the 1948 *Economic Survey* it was argued that

labour is not at present, and is unlikely to be in 1948, the limiting factor in economic activity as a whole. Any projected distribution . . . is therefore largely a forecast of the results of other factors, and if some figures turn out differently it is not necessarily in every case a matter for regret.[10]

Shortages of imported raw materials and uncertainty over the prospect of Marshall Aid had for the time being put an end to the government's preoccupation with a general labour shortage. The danger of unemployment had become real; it was the avoidance of unemployment, not how to add to the labour supply, that had to be planned. The balance of payments occupied the centre of the stage; and when by 1950 these anxieties became less acute the balance of the economy was studied more and more from the side of demand rather than supply. The development of macro-economic management is discussed later, in chapter 15.

## Undermanned industries

When we turn to the distribution of manpower between industries, a rather similar distinction can be drawn between the period up to 1948 and

---

9 *Economic Survey for 1951*, Cmd 8195, p. 10.
10 *Economic Survey for 1948*, Cmd 7344, para. 186. How one was to judge which cases were a matter for regret was not revealed.

*Table 14.2*  Employment in the 'undermanned' and other industries 1939–53 (000s)

|  | June 1939 | June 1945 | Dec. 1946 | Dec. 1947 | Dec.ᵃ 1948 | Dec.ᵃ 1948 | Dec. 1953 |
|---|---|---|---|---|---|---|---|
| Agriculture and fishing | 950 | 1,041 | 1,081 | 1,090 | 1,126 | 1,178ᵇ | 1,087ᵇ |
| Coal-mining | 773 | 738 | 730 | 758 | 766 | 788 | 784 |
| Textiles | 798 | (500) | 615 | 652 | 690 | 971 | 1,002 |
|  | 2,521 | 2,279 | 2,426 | 2,500 | 2,582 | 2,937 | 2,873 |
| Metals and engineering | 2,278 | 3,345 | 2,822 | 2,876 | 2,908 | 3,921 | 4,314 |
| Building and contracting | 1,310 | 722 | 1,289 | 1,364 | 1,357 | 1,480 | 1,401 |
| Distributive trades | 2,887 | 1,958 | 2,309 | 2,351 | 2,406 | 2,739 | 2,704 |
| Total (including all other industries) | 18,000 | 16,416 | 18,276 | 18,888 | 19,153 | 22,011 | 22,288 |

*Sources: Economic Survey,* various years; *Annual Abstract of Statistics for 1953* and *1958.*

a  Labour statistics were reorganized in 1948 and the figures given for that year are shown first on the old and then on the new basis.
b  Mid-year, including forestry.

the ensuing period (see table 14.2). The industries causing most concern to the government (agriculture, textiles and coal-mining) were not those that had lost most labour during the war. The building industry, for example, had lost nearly half its labour force and the distributive trades not far short of a million workers. The three 'undermanned' industries were regarded with special favour because of the contribution they could make to the balance of payments either by displacing imports or by contributing exports that were particularly useful as bargaining counters in trade nego-tiations.

Agriculture, which had already taken on more labour in wartime, was the subject of a large new expansion programme which initially created an acute shortage of labour although after 1948 it was found possible to pursue expansion and yet shed labour. The textile industries on the other hand had contracted their labour force in wartime by over one-third and never regained the pre-war level of employment. They were able to get more than half-way back to the pre-war level by the end of 1948 but in the next five years made little progress in building up their labour force and eventually, like agriculture, began to shed labour. Coal-mining was an intermediate case. There had been some reduction in employment – less than 5 per cent – in the war years; and so far from increasing, the number of miners fell slightly immediately after the war. In this, coal-mining was unlike almost every other industry except engineering. In the coal crisis of

1947 there were fewer miners at work than there had been when the war ended. In the next two years the number was increased to just below the pre-war level; but again, little change occurred over the next five years and soon afterwards the numbers began to drop. In each case, the post-war increase had virtually ceased by the end of 1948, the next five years were more or less flat, and in due course a steep decline in employment set in.

The problem facing the government at the end of the war was how to get rid of 'undermanning'. Drawing up a target distribution of labour by industry and calling it a 'manpower budget' did little to procure labour for the coal industry or limit the steady build-up of employment in distribution. A variety of enticements were used. More houses were provided for particular groups such as coal-miners. Better rations might be offered in exceptional conditions. In publicly-owned industries action could be taken to improve working conditions – pithead baths, canteens and other amenities – and in privately-owned industries the application of an Essential Works Order was dependent on acceptance of minimum requirements for working conditions. A cut in hours – the five-day week, for example – might bring in more workers but did little to increase output in the short run. Men might be released earlier from the services or their call-up delayed. The possibility of using European Voluntary Service workers and other immigrant labour was frequently canvassed: there were said to be 420,000 German prisoners of war available for work in the summer of 1946 and a further 30,000–40,000 who might be brought from Norway.[11] Later, it was pointed out that there were 100,000 Poles who might be found employment in the undermanned industries;[12] and in fact 85,000 foreign workers were recruited under official schemes and placed in employment in 1948 alone, over half of them going into mining, agriculture or textiles.[13]

The most obvious ways of increasing the labour force in an industry, however, were to raise wages or apply labour controls. The government liked neither course. Raising wages risked inflation and labour controls spelt compulsion. Their advisers in the Economic Section were strongly in favour of getting relative wages right but had to accept that this was by no means a simple matter. For example, when the Agricultural Wages Board awarded agricultural workers an extra 10s. a week so as to improve recruitment, the wages of roadmen were almost immediately put up by

11  CM(45)64, 20 December 1945, in PRO CAB 128/2.
12  Draft *Economic Survey for 1947*.
13  *Economic Survey for 1949*, Cmd 7647, para. 90.

12*s*. a week.[14] As for labour controls it was hard to see how they could be retained for long.[15]

In November 1945 the Lord President's Committee reported to the Cabinet that they were 'satisfied that a long-term policy for a planned distribution of man-power could be applied only by means of a rational and effective wages policy'. The urgent question, however, was how to find labour for essential industries over the next 6–9 months. A short-term policy had to be devised to cover the period during which releases from the forces were still incomplete. While it was simply not practical politics to announce to a public ill-educated in the need for controls that all controls over labour would be retained, a decision to relax the controls should be deferred. They should not be rigorously enforced at once, not until after an interval for public education in their use in securing 'a proper distribution of man-power'.[16]

No agreement was reached and a second unsuccessful attempt to secure agreement on labour controls was made on 20 November. A publicity campaign was needed because 'the conviction that labour controls would not be enforced was spreading daily'. Even if they were not enforceable in particular cases, however, it might be unwise to modify them since a large body of workers complied and the industries in difficulties were likely to lose more than they would gain by any overt relaxations.

The Minister of Labour's proposal was that workers over 30 should be given sympathetic consideration if they wanted to return to their previous employment and should be subject to direction only for industries like

14  Meade, Diary (MS), entry for 27 July 1946.
15  Of the wartime controls the most important was the power to direct labour to any employment subject to a 'fair wages' clause. This power was rarely used but the knowledge of its existence reinforced the efforts of the Ministry of Labour to supply labour by persuasion where it was most urgently needed. Workers in particular age-groups were also required to register for employment: younger women and men over military age could then be called up for work in the munitions industries. Under the Essential Works Order employees of scheduled undertakings were forbidden to leave or be discharged or transferred without the permission of a National Service Officer. An Essential Works Order was made for coal-mining in 1941 and the labour force in other industries (shipbuilding, the docks, building, iron and steel) was tied by ring-fence variations of the Order. Firms in the engineering and building industries were also required to engage workers only through employment exchanges so as to prevent 'poaching' from other firms. (Hancock and Gowing (1949), pp. 307–9; Worswick and Ady (1952), pp. 237–8.)
16  Report of Industrial Sub-Committee of Lord President's Committee, CP(45)260, 1 November 1945 (see CM(45)48 in PRO CAB 128(2)).

building and coal-mining. Workers under 30 would remain subject to the Control of Engagement Order and would be liable to direction 'without hesitation'. One minister after another opposed the first of these proposals and feared that the industries they sponsored would lose manpower.

At the third attempt on 3 December the Cabinet finally reached agreement. The power of direction was to be limited to men under 30 except for the purpose of enforcing Essential Work Orders or ensuring that workers demobilized so as to take specified employment did so. There would be no direction of women of any age except for nurses under 30. At the same time, the Essential Work Order would be applied to a narrower range of industries in special need of an increase in their labour force. House-building was to receive exceptional treatment since men in the building industry could be required to transfer to this kind of work. Both in building and mining the call-up of men would be postponed until February. Otherwise no specific reference was made to the special difficulties of the mining industry.[17]

While most of the labour controls were quickly relaxed, the Essential Work Order continued for some years to apply to agriculture and coal-mining. In 1947, however, the succession of crises and the dangerous state of the balance of payments made it urgent to find labour for the under-manned industries. The government took powers under the Control of Engagement Order to require workers within certain age-limits to change their jobs only through and with the consent of the employment exchanges. These powers seem to have had some effect in 1948, particularly in textiles and agriculture. In coal-mining difficulties over the recruitment and absorption of foreign workers continued and the manpower in the industry increased by only 8000.[18] The government continued the powers in 1949 but progressively relaxed their use and left almost completely in abeyance the power of direction. Restrictions on leaving agriculture and coal-mining were dropped at the beginning of 1950 and in March 1950 the Control of Engagement Order was withdrawn and the use of powers of direction discontinued.[19]

From the end of the war until 1950 the total number of unfilled vacancies notified to the employment exchanges had fallen steadily although it remained higher than the number of workers unemployed. With the beginning of rearmament in 1950, however, the fall in vacancies

17  CM(45)58, 3 December 1945, in PRO CAB 128/2.
18  *Economic Survey for 1949*, Cmd 7647, para. 89.
19  *Economic Survey for 1950*, Cmd 7915, para. 114.

– at least for men – ceased.[20] By the middle of 1951 they were back to the level of 1947 and still increasing. The shortage of skilled engineers was particularly acute. At the end of 1950 there were nearly six vacancies for every unemployed man in the skilled engineering grades and eight months later, when the shortage was at its height in the autumn of 1951, there were nearly eighteen.[21]

The government continued in 1950–1 to operate a system of labour preferences in the placings made by the employment exchanges, i.e. to use persuasion in the filling of selected vacancies. It did not, however, revive labour controls. In February 1952, the new Conservative government introduced the Notification of Vacancies Order requiring employers to engage adult workers only through the employment exchanges or scheduled employment agencies, and this Order remained in force until 1956. This enabled the exchanges to bring what they regarded as the most important vacancies to the attention of workers and seek to persuade them to fill them, but without any powers of compulsion. The Conservative government also sought to revive the wartime system of Labour Supply Inspection which gave power to inspectors to review an employer's requirements for skilled labour whenever he notified vacancies and discuss with the employer whether these requirements might not be met by training, upgrading and other arrangements.

The acute labour shortages of 1951 had largely vanished by the following year. In the course of 1952 the labour market eased more perceptibly than at any time since the war and for over a year unemployment was in excess of unfilled vacancies, a situation almost unknown until the 1960s. Even vacancies for skilled engineers fell during the year by one-third and were down from eighteen to four times the number unemployed in December 1952.

It cannot be said that labour controls succeeded in the end in relieving 'undermanning' more than marginally. It is impossible to trace the influence of surviving controls in the years of rapid demobilization. In the next two years, while total civil employment increased by nearly 1 million, the three main 'undermanned' industries added 150,000 to their strength, expanding by 6.4 per cent compared with 4.8 per cent in the total. Given the precarious state of the foreign balance and the damage that a marginal

20  In 1949–50 the vacancies were distributed roughly equally between men, women and juveniles under 18. Thereafter, vacancies for men increased sharply while vacancies for women continued to fall.
21  *Economic Survey for 1952*, Cmd 8509, table 8, p. 21.

shortage of coal could do, such a result was worth a considerable effort and an indication of what an earlier effort might have done. Even marginal effects on key industries were well worthwhile at that stage. After 1949 the controls were no longer in use and when revived in 1952 were much milder and more limited in their purpose.

## Wages and inflation

A shortage of labour carries with it an obvious danger of wage inflation. In six years of war the rise in wages had been about 50 per cent, much the same as the rise in prices; and although there had been a slowing down in the latter years of the war when mobilization was complete, it had by no means ceased in spite of all the controls and subsidies by which the government sought to check the rise in the cost of living. The White Paper on *Employment Policy* in 1944 recognized that there were limits to what the government could do, without the wholehearted co-operation of employers and employed, to secure reasonable stability in wages and prices and that without such stability it could not ensure the high and stable level of employment at which it now proposed to aim. Co-operation would be needed to root out restrictive and monopolistic practices and maintain international competitiveness. Labour would have to be mobile between occupations and places. But above all there would have to be 'moderation in wage matters'. If labour took advantage of its enhanced bargaining power to force up money wages, prices would follow, the value of money would fall progressively and a retreat from full employment would become inevitable.

The need to avoid such a situation made many people look with sympathy on the idea of a wages or incomes policy. As far back as November 1939 the Stamp Survey of Economic and Financial Plans urged the adoption of a system of centralized review and authorization of wage rates.[22] Others took the more optimistic view that the unions would 'learn habits of greater responsibility and do less harm to the general working of markets if they are left free to make their own policy . . . and their own mistakes'.[23] Throughout the war a debate went on between those who, like James Meade, believed that a moderate wage policy was a *sine qua non* of employment policy and those who, like the Ministry of Labour, put their faith in free collective bargaining.[24]

22  Russell Jones (1983), unpublished MA thesis, p. 34.
23  Lord Robbins (1971), p. 231 quoted by Russell Jones, op. cit., p. 51.
24  Russell Jones, op. cit., pp. 40 *et seq*.

The debate was resumed after the war on an Official Working Party on Wages Policy which was authorized by Bridges in October 1945 and reported at the end of March 1946 to the Lord President's Committee.[25] Emmerson, the Ministry of Labour representative, made light of the wage increases which were then occurring, emphasized the success of wartime policy as reflected in harmonious relations between employers and employed, and came down firmly in favour of continuing the status quo. Others, however, were less optimistic. There were suggestions for a National Wages Commission, a tripartite body which would make periodic statements on wages in relation to the general economic situation and sit in on all major negotiations; for a schedule of priority industries that would be allowed greater freedom in fixing wages during the transition period; and for a negotiated limit to annual increases in the national wage bill on the basis of productivity growth, the terms of trade and room for profit-squeezing. These suggestions did not, however, find their way into the report, which was largely an expression of the Ministry of Labour's point of view. It did retain, however, under pressure from the Economic Section, the idea of a National Industrial Conference to promote understanding of the bearing on wage negotiations of conditions of full employment.

In due course this idea took shape in a decision to reconstitute the National Joint Advisory Council (a tripartite body which had been set up in October 1939 to deal with labour problems). Apart from this, the Lord President's Committee was content to endorse the report. Morrison, however, in summing-up, indicated as 'the general view' that the government was likely to have to take 'a more and more positive part in shaping wages policy' as time went on.

While negotiations over the reconstitution of the NJAC were in progress the TUC released a statement in April describing the arguments for a national wages policy as 'academic and unconvincing'.[26] Whitehall was becoming increasingly doubtful, however, whether it was possible to trust to the good sense of the unions, whatever the steps taken to educate them in the national predicament. The draft 'Economic Survey for 1946–47' prepared in June dwelt on the wage problem posed by full employment and drew attention to the acceleration in wage adjustments

25 The report is in PRO CAB 124/783. See also PRO T 230/111, 'National Wages Policy'; and Lord President's Industrial Sub-Committee, 'Working Party on Wages Policy, 1946: minutes and memoranda' in PRO CAB 132/88.
26 Russell Jones, op. cit., p. 83.

in the first five months of 1946. The annual rate of increase had become 11 per cent – more than twice the average for the previous four years of war.[27]

The draft was considered by the Ministerial Committee on Economic Policy in July. Ministers expressed some concern over the difficulties experienced in implementing planning decisions, including the difficulty of keeping wages and prices reasonably stable, and a report was put in hand by the official Steering Committee. When completed this was submitted to the same Ministerial Committee, reaching it in December 1946 along with the first draft of the 'Economic Survey for 1947'.[28]

The report started from the proposition that 'a successful policy of maintaining full employment will in itself produce a continuing inflationary tendency' and argued that, whatever the merits of the existing wage system, 'the urgent immediate task is to find some means of exercising effective restraint against a further general increase of wage rates or other labour costs without an appropriate increase in productivity'.[29] Some members of the Steering Committee favoured a measure of direct government participation or intervention in wage-fixing as the only effective means of preventing inflation and securing the necessary recruitment to essential industries such as coal-mining. The government could not, in any event, stand aloof from wage negotiations in the socialized industries and its involvement in other wage disputes was a matter of degree. The majority of the Committee, however, shrank from the industrial unrest that might follow such intervention and from anything that would weaken the sense of responsibility of the leaders of both sides of industry. They put their faith in the National Joint Advisory Council and hoped that the government would find a way of turning it into a forum for discussion of claims for higher wages or other improvements in conditions of service. They also suggested a single central body for arbitration awards and, as a first step, a co-ordination of existing forms of arbitration so as to allow all arbitrators to draw on a common stock of knowledge 'of the wider economic considerations'.[30]

These recommendations led to the issue in January 1947 of a White Paper *Statement on the Economic Considerations Affecting Relations between*

27 Draft 'Economic Survey for 1946–47', MEP(46)5, 11 July 1946, paras 34–8, in PRO CAB 134/503.
28 'Wages and Price Policy and Means of Carrying Out Planning Decisions'. Report by the Steering Committee, MEP(46)17, 21 December 1946, in PRO CAB 134/503.
29 ibid., paras 11 and 14.
30 ibid., paras 14–21.

*Employers and Workers*.[31] This was intended to educate the participants in collective bargaining in 'the wider economic considerations', for example the need to increase productivity and restrain increases in wages and prices for the sake of competitiveness and ability to buy necessary imports. A draft of the White Paper had been submitted to the NJAC before publication and in the course of a paragraph-by-paragraph discussion, the emphasis on wage restraint had been watered down to meet trade-union objections.[32]

In the middle of the coal crisis during February the Steering Committee submitted a second report, this time specifically on Wages Policy.[33] Ministers had commented that the earlier document did not deal clearly enough with the long-term objectives of wages policy and officials now sought to meet this criticism. They began by reiterating that in wage negotiations the matters at issue extend far beyond the interests of the parties immediately concerned and include matters that may be given little or no consideration in the settlement arrived at. In conditions of acute labour shortage employers might be more concerned to get the necessary labour than to avoid increases in wages; many of them were cushioned against higher costs by government subsidies (e.g. in agriculture and building) and the food subsidies had a similar effect on the wage-earner by encouraging the view that higher money wages were a real gain; wage rates were increasing faster than the cost of living with no corresponding increase in productivity to close the gap; and finally, justifiable demands for increased wages or better conditions in one industry tended to give rise to similar but unjustifiable demands in other industries in order to restore traditional relativities that were no longer appropriate.

The report then recapitulated the division of view outlined in the earlier document and made similar recommendations. On long-term objectives it pointed out that these were interwoven with the structure of society and the economic conditions prevailing. For example, was full employment and some degree of inflationary pressure to be assumed? Would economic planning go as far as direction of labour? Wages policy, they suggested, should be related to a manpower budget, showing the target allocation of labour. 'This would establish the magnitude of the transfers that it was desired to effect, and the readjustments in customary relationships

31  Cmd 7018.
32  Minutes of the NJAC Joint Consultative Meeting, 8 January 1947 (in PRO CAB 124/786), quoted by Russell Jones, op. cit., p. 84.
33  'Wages Policy'. Further Report by the Official Steering Committee on Economic Development, MEP(47)4, 21 February 1947, in PRO CAB 134/503.

between wage-rates that would operate in the right direction'.[34] They saw no reason to associate changes in wages in one industry directly with changes in productivity in that industry unless greater effort on the part of the workers was involved. Other long-term objectives included encouraging the acquisition of special skills and the promotion of good relations between employers and employed.

These reports, which were the forerunners of many others dealing with the same problem, began from what was seen as the urgent problem of wage inflation and ended with some rather fundamental questions about the flexibility of economic institutions. They did not examine how far wage inflation might be eliminated if the pressure of demand were reduced or what the links were between the two. The recommendations to which they led were nearly all couched in long-run terms that contrasted with the urgency attributed to the problem.

It was inevitable, however, that attention should be drawn to the interaction between wage pressure and inflationary pressure. James Meade kept insisting that no satisfactory wage policy was possible so long as the economy was thrown out of balance by excess demand.[35] Partly for this reason the Economic Section had for some time pressed for a reconsideration of food subsidies and the automatic pegging of the cost-of-living index. In their view the benefit of the subsidies in reducing the size of wage claims was more than offset by the heavy budgetary cost, the distortion of consumption and the weakening of employer resistance. They argued for a reduction or withdrawal of the subsidies and their replacement by child allowances and cuts in indirect taxation.

In the summer of 1947, debate was transferred to the Lord President's Committee with Shinwell arguing strongly for comprehensive control of wages and prices and Cripps proposing the consolidation of the existing machinery for arbitration into a central arbitral body, while Isaacs, with support from Dalton and Morrison, defended free, collective bargaining.[36] These discussions were overtaken by the convertibility crisis in the middle of which, on 6 August, the Prime Minister made an appeal to all workers not to press for increases in wages. In letters sent out by the Ministry of

34  ibid., para. 20(c).
35  See, for example, PRO CAB 124/898. Meade to Lord President, 24 December 1946 (quoted by Russell Jones, op. cit., p. 85).
36  Minutes of the 16th meeting of the Lord President's Committee, 6 June 1947, in PRO CAB 132/6; memoranda by Shinwell, Isaacs and Morrison, June–July 1947, in PRO CAB 129/9.

Labour, negotiators were urged to keep the Prime Minister's appeal fully in mind, much to the annoyance of many trade unionists.[37] Later in the year the TUC felt it necessary to insist to the Prime Minister that the trade unions were not being given proper credit for their forbearance; and in a later release they issued a warning that:

> any attempt on the part of an outside body to regulate or directly control wage movements would have disastrous effects in undermining the industrial authority of trade unions . . . if there was to be greater restraint upon wage movements it could only come from within the trade union movement itself.[38]

Yet another 'Working Party on the Stabilization of Wages' was set up in August with a Ministry of Labour chairman. After lengthy discussion in the Committee and in Cabinet, a *Statement on Personal Incomes, Costs and Prices* (by the Prime Minister) was issued in February 1948, without, on this occasion, any prior discussion in the NJAC.[39] The Working Party had ruled out the more radical proposals such as:

> to make the National Joint Advisory Council bear responsibility for, or at least express a view on, major wage claims, to deter wage increases by the imposition of a uniform tax on all workers employed, to impose a statutory wage freeze, to impose a public sector wage freeze, to set up a 'Central Appeal Tribunal' . . . and to allocate a government representative to all major wage negotiations.[40]

The White Paper refrained from making any such proposals and accepted the undesirability of direct interference by the government in wage negotiations. Instead, it called for strict adherence to the terms of collective agreements. But it went on to say that 'in present conditions . . . there is no justification for any *general* increase' in wages (or in 'incomes from profit, rent or other like sources'). There might be cases in which the national interest justified an increase: for example, in an under-manned industry which could not attract the necessary labour in any other way. There was certainly no case for perpetuating established differentials in changed circumstances. Exceptional cases apart, wages should remain

37 Russell Jones, op. cit., pp. 87–8.
38 TUC, *Interim Report on the Economic Situation* reprinted in TUC, *A Policy for Real Wages* (1948); quoted by Russell Jones, op. cit., p. 88.
39 Cmd 7321 (1948).
40 Russell Jones, op. cit., p. 89; Interim Report of the Working Party on the Stabiliz-ation of Wages, 23 September 1947, CP(47)264 in PRO CAB 129/21.

steady; and 'all those engaged in negotiations or decisions which might result in an increase in wages or other personal incomes' should act on this principle, as the government themselves would, 'in order to avoid the undesirable necessity for any interference with the existing methods of free negotiation and contract'. It was to be clearly understood that there could be no presumption that increases, if they occurred, would be taken into account in the control of prices and margins.

The TUC responded to the White Paper by calling a conference of 1500 trade-union executives in March 1948 which accepted the call for a voluntary wage freeze, with two provisos. They insisted on the need to maintain skill differentials in the interests of industrial efficiency and higher productivity; and on the need to raise wages where they were below a 'reasonable standard of subsistence'.[41] The TUC had in the meantime been made aware, in a meeting with the Prime Minister and some of his senior colleagues on 11 February, that the government was taking action to secure more effective control over prices, profits and dividends. In March a price stop was imposed by various Price Control Orders on a wide range of foods not previously subject to effective control. About the same time the need to exercise voluntary price control and to limit dividends to the rate of distribution in the previous year was accepted by the Federation of British Industries.

The agreement of the TUC to the government's policy was a considerable achievement, all the more because the White Paper had been preceded by an announcement by the government of its intention to set limits to the food subsidies and so abandon its commitment to the pegging of the cost-of-living index number. In the event a ceiling on the subsidies was not introduced until the 1949 Budget and they were allowed to go on rising in 1948.

The White Paper policy undoubtedly slowed down the rise in wages and prices. In the first two post-war years from June 1945 to June 1947 hourly wage rates had increased, first by 9 per cent, then by 8.5 per cent. In the next nine months to March 1948 the rise continued at nearly 9 per cent per annum. From then until the devaluation eighteen months later, the annual rate of increase fell to 2.8 per cent and, as we have seen, it fell again to not much more than 1 per cent in the year following devaluation.[42] Retail prices in the meantime had increased after March 1948 at an

41 Worswick and Ady (1952), p. 329.
42 See p. 211. The figures of hourly rates are taken from tables 27 and 28 in *British Labour Statistics: Historical Abstract 1886–1968* (Department of Employment, 1971).

average of 3.3 per cent per annum before devaluation, with a sharper increase at about 5 per cent per annum in food prices. Over those eighteen months, therefore, real wages were stationary or falling; and with a rise of about 2 per cent in retail prices the same was probably true in the first year after devaluation.

That money wages rose so little when real wages were stationary or falling and unemployment was down to 300,000 is striking testimony to the influence of the trade-union leaders. Hourly wage rates after March 1948 rose no faster than in the mid-1930s, between 1934 and 1938, when unemployment was around 2 million. Even if one takes the first five years after the war, before the full effects of devaluation and the rearmament boom were felt, the annual increase in hourly wages averages only 5.6 per cent i.e. about double the pre-war rate. But whereas pre-war increases were not appreciably higher than the underlying growth of productivity, the post-war increases, at least in the first half of the period, were plainly well above it.

The contrast between the two halves of the five-year period may suggest that the unions' claim to have exercised moderation before March 1948 is not well-founded. But, as we shall see, the pressure of demand was much greater in the early post-war years: unfilled vacancies were falling steeply until the end of 1948 by which time the pressure had eased. The rise in import prices was also a good deal faster in the first two post-war years, driving up the cost of living and spreading discontent among the rank and file.[43] The unions may well have felt that they were doing what they could to avoid embarrassing the government.

There was a limit, however, to the degree of moderation that the unions could show and to the time-span of any freeze or near-freeze. It took the shock of devaluation in September 1949 to prolong and tighten the policy. Cripps and Bevin, as we have seen, were successful in their approach to the TUC for a wage standstill, subject to the proviso that the cost of living was held within 5 per cent of its pre-devaluation level.[44] A recommendation to this effect from the General Council, providing also for the suspension of existing sliding-scale agreements, was approved by a narrow majority at a conference of trade-union executives in January 1950. Ministers continued to fear an increase in wages and meditated budgetary concessions in order to hold the position but were advised by

43 Between 1945 and 1947 import prices rose by roughly 30 per cent; between 1947 and 1949 the rise was 15 per cent.
44 See p. 190.

Tewson, the General Secretary of the TUC, that no concessions could guarantee the success of the standstill since trade unions would not accept the idea of a 'social wage'. Tewson expected that the agreement would hold for a few months more and was anxious that the Chancellor should not compromise his Budget in the hope of influencing wage settlements.[45]

At the end of April Cripps made another approach to the TUC to arrange that officials should work out a policy for wages but nothing seems to have come of this. The fear that wages might get out of hand continued even although the wage index remained flat throughout the first nine months of 1950. Anomalies and exceptions were multiplying and the TUC was finding it increasingly difficult to secure adherence to the standstill. At the end of June, within six months of its adoption and a few days after the outbreak of war in Korea, the General Council advised affiliated unions that 'there must be greater flexibility of wage movements in future'. From then on the policy began to crumble although it was not until November that wages began to climb steeply to a level 11 per cent higher one year later.[46]

Cripps's reaction to the TUC statement was to suggest a new working party on wage policy and to revive the idea of a central council to offer guidance. He was persuaded by Tewson, however, not to include the latter suggestion in his public statement on wages on 3 July. As for the idea of a working party, it was suggested by Robert Hall that this should be on employment policy so that the wages issue was treated in the right context. By this time Cripps was withdrawing from the direction of policy, leaving Gaitskell in charge. He, too, wanted a new study of wages policy with a view to the issue of a White Paper.

In his Budget Speech in April 1951 Gaitskell dwelt on the danger of a progressive loss of confidence in the value of money resulting, not from excess demand, which he could prevent, but from pressure for higher wages. If wages rose faster than productivity it was not usually profits that suffered: inflation bore most heavily on the lower income groups. He found nothing surprising in proposals that wages should be controlled by 'some central independent authority' or index-linked in some way with the cost of living or the growth of productivity. But such proposals involved 'far-reaching risks and difficulties – some economic, some

45  Information from Lord Roberthall.
46  For a full analysis of the decay of the first British incomes policy, see John Corina, 'The British experiment in wage restraint with special reference to 1948–50' (1961), unpublished D.Phil. thesis.

psychological' and would imply 'greater changes than either side of industry is at present willing to contemplate'.[47] His initial idea was that there should be a National Advisory Panel which would have to be consulted during all important wage negotiations but would exercise no powers of compulsion. He also took up a suggestion of Nicholas Kaldor's for dividend limitation on a new formula that would have allowed companies to distribute either the same dividend as in the previous year or some pre-determined rate of return on equity earnings, whichever was the higher.

In the end nothing came of these ideas. A paper was duly produced at the end of November. A Full Employment Bill was drafted but dropped in February 1951. Approaches to the TUC in February by the new Minister of Labour (Nye Bevan) had got nowhere and the proposed White Paper had been abandoned.[48] In March Bevan and Gaitskell agreed to drop the ceiling on wages and the cost of living. There remained the idea of dividend limitation by statute. It was announced by the government in the summer that legislation for this purpose would be introduced. Before that could be done a new government had come into office.

---

47  *H. C. Deb.*, 5th ser., vol. 486, cols 829–31, 10 April 1951.
48  Bevan had told Gaitskell that since he was on intimate terms with all the union leaders he would have no trouble. (Information from Lord Roberthall.)

# Chapter fifteen

## FISCAL POLICY, DEMAND MANAGEMENT AND INFLATION

Budgetary policy was a matter for the Treasury throughout: but by the same token it was not a matter for the Lord President. Morrison might be responsible for economic planning but finance lay in a separate domain over which he had no jurisdiction. It was not for Morrison to decide how financial instruments of policy should be used even if, as became increasingly evident, it was these instruments and not physical controls that were to prove the more enduring regulators of economic activity. At the ministerial level, the division of responsibility led to error and confusion in the framing of policy and at the official level weakened the influence of the Economic Section, to which Whitehall in wartime had been accustomed to look for guidance. The Section remained in the Cabinet Office, rather like a stranded whale, between the shallow waters of the Lord President's Department and the dry land of the Treasury.

It was hardly surprising, in these circumstances, that there was at first no explicit link between the budget and inflationary pressure or the level of employment. The White Paper on *Employment Policy* had played down the role of fiscal policy and rejected the idea of continuing surpluses and deficits of the budget. Equally the Labour government, while it had strong views on taxation and public expenditure, began by attaching little importance to varying the balance between the two. Dalton, it is true, converted a large budget deficit into a substantial budget surplus two years later. But until the convertibility crisis and the Budget of November 1947 this was in no way the result of deliberate increases in taxation or of cuts in civil expenditure: it was largely the automatic consequence of the rundown in expenditure with demobilization and the replacement of public employment by private. Dalton was never at pains to relate the size of the surplus to some measure of excess demand or to expound the tax changes he was proposing in the Budget, like his wartime predecessors, against a macro-economic background. Equally, in contrast to his immediate successors, he made no use in his Budget speeches of the *Economic Survey*. He was 'robustly sceptical' to the end of attempts to measure inflationary pressure 'with any close precision'.[1] The tests to which he appealed were 'the financial and economic situation, the movement of prices, the level of employment, the relative dangers of inflation and deflation'.[2] In his third Budget in April 1947 he accepted that the Budget had a part to play in the fight against inflation arguing that 'we must earn the right to a Budget deficit in another year by recording a Budget surplus this year'.[3]

But it was only in his last Budget in November 1947 that he explicitly related the additional taxation he was imposing to the need to 'strengthen still further and without delay our defences against inflation'.[4] Indeed, the sole purpose of the Budget when he first thought of it in August was to lessen inflationary pressure.[5] In the opening words of his Budget speech he dwelt particularly on the need to counter the inflationary effects of the recent crisis measures to reduce the large deficit in the balance of payments. Dalton made no attempt, however, to refine the analysis of Exchequer Accounts so as to yield a more accurate gauge of the economic impact of the Budget on the economy and was content to use for this purpose the surplus 'above the line' even when it included revenue from the disposal of war stores or money 'clawed back' from previous budgetary allocations.[6]

In the Dalton years there was a marked contrast between the ministerial view of inflation and that of Keynesian officials such as James Meade in the Economic Section. Meade, starting from the ideas sketched in the White Paper on *Employment Policy*, thought in terms of a continuing task of

---

1  *H. C. Deb.*, 5th ser., vol. 444, col. 395, 12 November 1947 quoted by Dow (1964), p. 28n. The extent to which inflationary pressure was held back by controls was not something easily measured.
2  Dalton (1962), p. 230.
3  *H. C. Deb.*, 5th ser., vol. 436, col. 55, 15 April 1947.
4  *H. C. Deb.*, 5th ser., vol. 444, col. 394.
5  PRO T 171/392.
6  Before the 1946 Budget, Keynes pointed out to him that expenditure was understated by £162.5 million ($650 million) because supplies obtained after the ending of Lend-Lease had been financed on credit without cash passing (PRO T 171/386, meeting on 3 April 1946).

demand management, avoiding both excessive pressure and a deficiency of demand. Ministers were more preoccupied with the immediate danger of a repetition of the short inflationary boom and subsequent slump that followed the First World War. It was this danger that had featured in their election programme as the main justification for the retention of controls. They were reassured when no runaway boom developed but continued to fear the expected slump: as the first danger faded, the other became an obsession. A fall in world prices seemed always round the corner and the least tremor in world markets seemed to herald a major slump. Thus although unemployment was almost negligible and prices moved steadily upwards it was never the danger of inflation that was uppermost in their minds. As Dalton put it in October 1946 – and Cripps might well have echoed him in the years of his Chancellorship – 'the risk of inflation now is less than the risk of deflation later'.[7] Ministers, moreover, tended to think of inflation in terms of rising prices rather than excess demand, although this changed after their first two years in office. They recognized the danger of wage inflation under conditions of labour shortage since this inevitably worked through into prices. But whether they took the danger of inflation seriously or not, few of them would have conceived of the budget, or of a budget surplus, as a powerful anti-inflationary instrument.

The Economic Section, on the other hand, was preaching against inflationary pressure from the start and implying the need to make use of budgetary measures. In the draft 'Economic Survey for 1946', circulated at the beginning of December 1945, the background to economic planning is expounded in terms of inflationary pressure.[8] Emphasis is also laid on the limits of control in peacetime when the distribution of manpower between different jobs might well diverge from government targets and be very difficult to change.[9]

The 'Survey' included a table C comparing the income likely to be generated by the resources available with the demands implicit in existing departmental programmes, and showed a gap between the two of some 6 per cent (see table 15.1). This 'inflationary gap' was purely notional in the sense that it would automatically be closed by rising prices if nothing was done to withhold excess demand. Action could be taken to reduce it – for example, by higher taxation, cuts in departmental programmes or an

7  Dalton (1962), p. 165.
8  Draft 'Economic Survey for 1946', CP(46)32, December 1945, in PRO CAB 129/6.
9  Draft 'Economic Survey for 1946', paras 23–33.

Table 15.1  National income and expenditure 1946 (£m.)

| | 1938 | 1944 | Target 1946 | | 1938 | 1944 | Requirements[a] 1946 |
|---|---|---|---|---|---|---|---|
| Wages | 1,735 | 2,930 | 3,100 | Personal expenditure on consumption at market prices | 4,157 | 5,216 | 6,100 |
| Salaries | 1,100 | 1,473 | 1,650 | Government net current expenditure on goods and services | 814 | 5,221 | 2,705 |
| Pay and allowances of HM Forces and auxiliary services | 78 | 1,171 | 820 | Government net fixed capital formation | 125 | -42 | 345 |
| Rents | 380 | 384 | 400 | Private net fixed capital formation at home | 266 | -146 | 710 |
| Profits and interest | 1,326 | 2,376 | 2,150 | Change in value of inventories and work in progress | -50 | — | 550 |
| Net national income | 4,619 | 8,334 | 8,120 | Change in value of exported goods not yet paid for | — | — | 150 |
| Gap | — | — | 470 | Deficit on balance of payments in current account | -70 | -655 | -750 |
| | | | | Subsidies less indirect taxes, etc. | -623 | -1,260 | -1,220 |
| Total | 4,619 | 8,334 | 8,590 | Net national expenditure | 4,619 | 8,334 | 8,590 |

Source: Table C of Draft Economic Survey for 1946.

a 'Requirements' represent what departments 'are willing to sponsor'.

intensified savings campaign but in planning such action it would be wise to assume that table C underestimated the gap. This was because private investment had been estimated at only a little above the pre-war level whereas business firms might wish to undertake substantially more; and consumption expenditure presumed a savings rate of 20 per cent of disposable income compared with only 8 per cent in 1938[10] and a peak rate in wartime of 17 per cent. A variety of ways of closing the gap was then discussed.

The 'Survey' was attacked by Keynes on technical and logical grounds. He agreed that government current expenditure was 'shamefully high', a view which he subsequently developed in a pungent attack on military expenditure overseas which Dalton took pleasure in circulating to his Cabinet colleagues.[11] He took issue with the 'Survey's' estimate of the wage-bill, arguing that it was £250 million too high, but was answered effectively by Jack Stafford of the Central Statistical Office who pointed out that Keynes's calculations took no account of special bonuses that increased earnings by treating as overtime what were previously standard hours, payments above agreed minimum levels, more generous rate-fixing and miscellaneous allowances that were all creating wage drift in ways later to become familiar. Keynes was also sceptical of other estimates including private fixed capital investment which in his view was liable to be consistently *over*-estimated.

It was the 'logical absurdity' of the inflationary gap between national income and expenditure when the two must by definition be equal that formed the nub of Keynes's criticism. 'Table C in its present form does [not] make sense, either logical or statistical', he argued. 'Some figures represent what is likely to happen, some what simply cannot happen'.[12] The conclusion which he drew was that in the transition period while the controls were still operative a little excess demand was desirable. There could be no exact balance across the board and it was better to leave some excess demand to be thwarted until supplies improved rather than try to cut it out completely by deflationary measures that would leave pools of unused resources and unemployment.

10 These ratios include business savings and are net of depreciation. Gross savings in 1938 have since been revised downwards from £691 million to £554 million (*National Income and Expenditure 1957*, table 6). Personal savings in 1938 are now estimated at 5.5 per cent of disposable income (gross of depreciation).

11 CP(46)58, 8 February 1946, Annex on 'Political and Military Expenditure Overseas', in PRO CAB 129/6.

12 Keynes to Meade, 15 January 1946, in '1945 Economic Survey', PRO T 230/54.

There followed a correspondence between Keynes and the authors of the draft 'Survey' in which Meade defended his exposition in terms of an inflationary gap, pointing out that he could not show a balance between available supplies and the demands upon them without knowing which departmental programmes would be jockeyed out of position, something requiring ministerial decision. He agreed, however, that once the gap was rather smaller, demand should be expressed, not in terms of 'working departmental programmes' but as estimates of what individuals, departments and other bodies 'would like to spend regardless of supply difficulties'.[13]

In April, shortly before his death, Keynes returned to the attack. By this time he was not only against publication but also against work of the Economic Survey type. The forecasts were too uncertain and he distrusted the statisticians who helped to prepare them. He was also against fine tuning: control had to be imprecise and did not permit of small adjustments. The margin of error was large and the range of possibilities wide. It was better to rely on 'intuitive hunch'. In addition the investment forecasts were always higher than the work it proved feasible to carry out so that any advice based on them had a built-in deflationary bias. It would be a mistake to cut demand to the point at which unemployment emerged. It was wise to err on the safe side by allowing some inflationary pressure.[14]

The reaction of ministers to the 'Survey', as we have seen, was to fasten on the manpower budget rather than on the financial aspects of the gap and to make large cuts in the manpower working in, or on behalf of, the armed forces. This enabled them to avoid encroaching on the Chancellor's territory and to continue to nourish expectations of an early slump.

When the next 'Economic Survey' was prepared early in 1946 the danger of inflation was again stressed. The inflationary gap, which had been put at £470 million in 1946 in the December draft before the cuts in the armed forces, was now put at £187 million in the financial year 1946–7, with some indication that it would widen in 1947, as exports continued to grow. The gap, however, was 'merely a measure of the mutual consistency of existing departmental plans and programmes' and would be far larger if demands were not held back by rationing and other controls.[15]

13  Meade to Keynes, 18 January 1946, in PRO T 230/54.
14  Meade, Diary (MS), entry for 6 April 1946.
15  Draft 'Economic Survey for 1946–47', MEP(46)5, para. 27, 11 July 1946, in PRO CAB 134/503. The draft had been completed by 6 April 1946.

In spelling out the threat of inflation the *Survey* listed four elements: the accumulation of unspent balances in liquid form, including £3800 million added during the war to 'small savings'; the curtailment in supplies of consumer goods and services in relation to current incomes; the large backlog of demand for investment goods, backed by unspent depreciation allowances and undistributed profits; and finally the rise in import prices and in wage rates.[16]

The Steering Committee in submitting the 'Survey' to ministers passed rather lightly over this analysis and preferred to couch its recommendations in manpower terms. 'Although a significant gap still remains', it commented,

> it would not be sensible to insist on a further pruning of departmental programmes merely for the sake of closing it because (a) some of the programmes are certain to be upset by unforeseen hitches, (b) the instruments of control are not sharp enough to effect the finest adjustments, and (c) there is necessarily a margin of error in the statistical estimates.[17]

The Committee did, however, emphasize the need to postpone public investment as much as possible and the need to make the undermanned industries more attractive even if this involved wage adjustments that ran the risk of generating irresistible pressure for corresponding increases in wages elsewhere in order to restore previous relativities.[18]

Meade continued to stress the problem of excess demand. In a long memorandum circulated to the Budget Committee later in July he emphasized the disadvantages of direct controls as a means of containing inflationary pressure and pointed to the alternative of using fiscal policy to promote a better balance between supply and demand. Price control was bound to become less effective as a bulwark against inflationary pressure and shop shortages would become progressively more irksome; it was damaging to incentives if extra income could not buy what consumers wanted; freezing prices also froze the economic structure by making it impossible to use the price mechanism and preventing local adjustments in prices and wages from dispelling the most acute shortages; finally, resort

16 ibid., paras 28–34.
17 Draft 'Economic Survey for 1946–47'. Note by the Chairman of the Official Steering Committee on Economic Survey (MEP(46)7, para. 2, 11 July 1946, in PRO CAB 134/503.
18 ibid., para. 14.

to administrative controls was not only costly in manpower but might end by discrediting the very idea of state planning through the petty annoyance caused by innumerable controls. On those grounds the immediate need was for an early budget surplus, coupled with an enlarged flow of consumer goods at the expense of current investment plans and of some delay in bringing exports and imports into balance. The cost-of-living subsidies should be 'rapidly tapered off' and the funds so saved should be used either to add to family allowances and other benefits or to institute an Employment Stabilization Fund by setting aside £200 million annually for this purpose.[19]

In December 1946 yet another draft 'Economic Survey', this time for 1947, was submitted. This once again emphasized 'the inflationary risks of the general excess of demand over supply'.[20] Not only was the draft a lengthy one but the Steering Committee's covering memorandum amounted almost to a fresh version. Yet a third, completely new, document was eventually published in February 1947.

The Economic Section had now moved away from departmental programmes as the basis of their estimates of demand and were using hypotheses as to the behaviour of final consumers under the conditions assumed. 'The question of policy', they concluded, 'is not whether consumption goods should be restricted but how austere the restrictions should be'.[21]

They reached this conclusion on the basis of national income forecasts showing an inflationary gap that varied in amount with the assumption made about savings behaviour. Consumer demand, still restrained by controls, would support a level of consumption 10 per cent higher than in 1938 even if savings reached the 1938 rate now put at 7.3 per cent. This would, however, generate excess demand of £650 million, equal to 7.5 per cent of national income. If savings reached 12 per cent and consumption was correspondingly less, excess demand would be reduced to £250 million but would not be entirely eliminated. On the other hand, if savings fell to zero, as was quite possible since consumers had ample liquid funds to overspend on the things they had not been able to buy in wartime, excess demand could be as high as £1250 million.

The Steering Committee, commenting on the 'Survey', made a large number of recommendations, mainly on manpower and materials. But

19  22 July 1946 in PRO T 171/389.
20  Draft 'Economic Survey for 1947: covering memorandum' (by the Steering Committee), MEP(46)16, para. 1, 21 December 1946, in PRO CAB 134/503.
21  Draft 'Economic Survey for 1947', MEP(46)15, para. 67, 21 December 1946, in PRO CAB 134/503.

they found the situation so serious (the coal crisis was still two months away) and the decisions to be taken by ministers so difficult that they did not feel able to carry out their intention of submitting the draft outline of a White Paper for eventual publication. On inflationary pressure they contented themselves with the following paragraphs:

> We have considered what measures we would advise Ministers to adopt which would produce an early and substantial reduction in this general inflationary pressure. The traditional correctives would include a sharp rise in the rate of interest and substantial increases in taxation. For various reasons this medicine must be ruled out in the present situation. After the war years of austerity such a policy would be difficult to defend and would certainly have a depressing effect on incentive. To increase the rate of interest at a time when large expenditure on investment is vitally necessary for the economic recovery of the country might hamper our subsequent competitive efficiency, apart from possible consequences on some aspects of social policy. To attempt to operate through an increase of taxation on current incomes ignores the over-hang of the enormous amount of accumulated savings.

> We must firmly avoid any measures which have the risk of increasing the pressure of demand on supply. But in present circumstances we do not see any practical solution of the problem by a global financial policy of the kind mentioned.[22]

The Steering Committee, and ministers after them, preferred the more hopeful (not to say Panglossian) remedy of relying on efforts to increase production which they described as 'by far the more urgent' of the measures required, paying no regard to the increased demand that such measures (if successful) would generate simultaneously. Action should also be taken, they added, 'to curtail specific demands by devoting our resources to the things which are of the most urgent importance in the national interest'. But the only guidance offered as to the specific demands to be curtailed related almost exclusively to the building industry plus a suggestion that there might not be enough steel to justify any increase in employment in the metal-using industries.

When the *Economic Survey for 1947* finally appeared, all mention of inflation had been removed. Various circumlocutions were used. Part I concluded that 'it is essential that costs and prices should be held steady and if possible reduced [sic]' while part III opened with the words: 'The

22 Draft 'Economic Survey for 1947: covering memorandum', paras 12–13.

central fact of 1947 is that we have not enough resources to do all that we want to do. We have barely enough to do all that we must do.'[23] But of inflation or inflationary pressure there is no mention.

If ministers saw no need to dwell on inflation in the *Economic Survey* this may have been because they imagined that it had been scotched by pegging the cost-of-living index number. Dalton had taken action to hold it steady for a year, extended later for another year, and had relied mainly on food subsidies to achieve this result. These had involved very large outgoings from the Exchequer: from about £200 million in the last year of the war, food and agriculture subsidies had grown to £350 million in 1947 and reached a peak of £450 million the following year.[24] By that time they amounted to 20 per cent of personal expenditure on food and nearly 13 per cent of current government expenditure. Taken in conjunction with indirect taxes, which were about four times as large, they changed the price structure radically and in ways that were not always defensible. Although they went some way to offsetting the increased cost of imports and labour, they did not prevent some rise in the cost of living. The old cost-of-living index, with a pre-1914 base, did remain virtually constant from 1 September 1945 thanks to the subsidies and a good deal of statistical 'massage'. But more up-to-date deflators, using 1938 as a base, unite in yielding increases between 1945 and 1947 of 9–10 per cent.[25] This is close to the increase at 5 per cent per annum predicted by the government's advisers in September 1945 for the years 1946–8, on the basis of past trends in costs and the likely movement of wages.[26] By the standards of other countries (including the United States) it was a very satisfactory outcome and there can be little doubt that the food subsidies made an important contribution to price stability. But inflation, whether open or suppressed, was not scotched.

On the contrary, in the course of 1947 the overriding problem was seen by officials and by outside commentators more and more in terms of excess demand.[27] The Treasury became increasingly alarmed at the steady rise in

23  *Economic Survey for 1947*, Cmd 7046, 1947, paras 28 and 61.
24  *National Income and Expenditure 1955*, table 37, for 1947 and 1948. The cost of milk and welfare food schemes is excluded. Subsidies to agriculture in 1948 amounted to £48 million.
25  The LCES index, Feinstein (1972) and *National Income and Expenditure of the UK, 1947* (Cmd 7371), appendix III, all point to this result.
26  'Memorandum on Net National Income in 1946, 1947 and 1948' by the Central Statistical Office and the Economic Section, EC(S)(45)32, 29 September 1945, in PRO T 230/54.
27  See chapter 16, p. 442.

food subsidies which it saw as an important source of inflationary pressure, whatever their impact on wage settlements. When Dalton's Budget
of November 1947 was under preparation, the Budget Committee took a
line very different from that of the Steering Committee the year previously. Bridges warned him that even with additional taxes that were
estimated to bring in about £220 million in a full year, and the cuts in the
investment programme and reductions in the armed forces that had just
been agreed, the Budget proposals made 'a wholly inadequate contribution to the relief of the inflationary pressure', now aggravated by the
emergency measures to improve the balance of payments. The physical
controls, lacking adequate support from the Budget, would be unable to
stand the strain and the government's economic planning was likely to
fail. It was important both to the success of the government's financial
policy (i.e. cheap money) and to confidence in Britain and abroad in the
stability of sterling to have an adequate Budget that dealt resolutely with
the subsidies; and in the view of the Budget Committee nothing less
would do than a statement limiting the total in 1948 to £300 million (or,
preferably, a lower figure) compared with the 1947 Budget estimate of
£435 million.[28]

To this Dalton rejoined that from the point of view of a Budget surplus
one cut was as good as another and food subsidies, which redistributed
purchasing power, ranked below cuts that released resources directly.
Raising the price of food was not the way to make workers do a better
job; it would hit the poorest hardest, stimulate demands for higher wages
and increased benefits and cause 'the maximum political commotion'.
Finally, all the wrong people politically had been advocating big cuts in
food subsidies and putting it about that advice in Whitehall was to the
same effect.

In his November Budget he contented himself with a statement that 'it
would be impossible to justify a further increase' in food subsidies above
the £392 million in the Estimates but announced the removal of the subsidies on clothing and footwear. The new taxation imposed was no greater
than proposed. Nevertheless the November 1947 Budget was a turning-
point in post-war fiscal policy: inflationary pressure, which had been

28 Bridges to Chancellor of the Exchequer, 'Autumn Budget', 22 October 1947 in
   PRO T 171/392. The total of £435 million included the subsidies on clothing and
   footwear as well as on agriculture and food. I owe this reference to Dr Andrew
   Chester.

increasing steadily all through 1947, fell perceptibly in 1948 (see figure 2.1, p. 23).

During the first two post-war years the material issue had been how far and how fast to reduce taxation as expenditure fell and this was not an issue that could be resolved by forecasts extending over one year or at most two. It was clearly necessary to aim at a surplus although not altogether clear how a surplus was to be measured since budget accountancy and economic accountancy were two very different things. It was also clear that tax revenue would have to exceed the pre-war figure by a substantial margin in view of the new duties laid on the state. But some reduction from the high wartime level of taxation was obviously desirable and possible when abundant manpower was being released for civil employment even if most of it was required for work on exports and investment.[29]

The main changes in the balance of the budget took place in those two years. They were concentrated on the expenditure side of the budget. As demobilization proceeded, defence expenditure fell from £4.4 billion to £0.85 billion, i.e. by £3.55 billion, between 1945–6 and 1947–8 and changed little thereafter until rearmament in 1951–2. Expenditure on other supply services trebled over those first two years, rising from £0.6 billion to £1.8 billion and absorbing roughly one-third of the purchasing power released by the fall in defence expenditure. Tax revenue increased in spite of the reductions made in rates of tax. Thus the swing in the budget balance was not far short of the falling-off in defence expenditure. The changes between 1945–6 and 1947–8 are summarized below:

|  | £000 million |
|---|---|
| Fall in defence expenditure | 3,556 |
| Less additional expenditure on other supply services | 1,210 |
| Less other additional expenditure on consolidated fund services | 71 |
| Plus additional ordinary revenue | 560 |
| Swing in budget balance | 2,835 |

The budget surplus which emerged under Dalton was maintained under Cripps. Table 15.2 (cols 1 and 2) shows the surplus 'above the line' (i.e.

29   Between 1938–9 and 1950–1 central government revenue increased from 16 per cent to 30 per cent of GNP.

*Table 15.2*  Budget surplus or deficit and public sector savings 1946–52
(£m.)

|  | Prospective surplus[a] | Realized surplus[a] | Savings of public sector[b] | Savings of private sector[b] |
|---|---|---|---|---|
| 1945–6 |  | −2,207 |  |  |
| 1946–7 | −694 | −586 | −348 | 890 |
| 1947–8 | 318[c] | 636 | 249 | 1,170 |
| 1948–9 | 789 | 831 | 662 | 1,121 |
| 1949–50 | 470 | 549 | 757 | 1,096 |
| 1950–1 | 443 | 720 | 860 | 1,550 |
| 1951–2 | 39 | 380 | 830 | 1,934 |
| 1952–3 |  | 88 | 606 | 1,578 |

*Sources:* Col. 1, Budget speeches, 1946–51.
Col. 2, *Economic Trends*, December 1961 and (for 1951–2 and 1952–3)
*Annual Abstract of Statistics for 1953*, tables 251–2.
Cols 3 and 4, *Economic Trends Annual Supplement 1981*.

a Excess of 'ordinary' revenue over 'ordinary' expenditure.
b These figures relate to calendar years from 1946 to 1952. They are gross of
  depreciation and stock appreciation.
c After autumn Budget changes.

the excess of ordinary revenue above expenditure), for which the Chancellor budgeted at the beginning of the financial year in April, and the realized surplus at the end of the year. From a deficit of £2207 million in 1945–6 the budget swung into surplus in 1947, with a peak surplus of £831 million in 1948–9. This transformation had been almost entirely accomplished in Dalton's four Budgets; Cripps's achievement was to sustain the surplus, not to originate it.

The 'surplus above the line' was never an adequate measure of the economic impact of the budget. If what is to be measured is the net contribution of the government to savings, many adjustments have to be made to what is misleadingly labelled 'ordinary' revenue and 'ordinary' expenditure. Cols 3 and 4 of table 15.2 show the outcome of these adjustments but treat the public sector as a whole i.e. national insurance and local authorities are added in. While this means that cols 3 and 4 are on a slightly different basis from cols 1 and 2, they bring out the wide divergence between the conventional view of budget balance and an economic approach. On the second view the swing in the balance was much less in the early post-war years but it continued longer, and showed less of a falling-off after 1950. On this showing, Cripps added quite substantially to the level of public savings for which Dalton had budgeted and the period of Labour government ended with the public sector contributing far more to national savings than the budget surplus 'above the line' seemed to imply.

Once budget surpluses became the order of the day, Chancellors found themselves compelled to justify them to colleagues who thought it wrong in such circumstances to withhold purchasing power from departmental spending programmes or equated a budget surplus with deflation. They were not able, like Dalton, to take refuge in the idea of a balanced budget over a series of years. Cripps was under strong pressure from members of his party to reduce the surplus and it needed all his firmness and strength of purpose to resist them. When Gaitskell succeeded Cripps, he felt obliged to circulate to the Cabinet a paper defending budget surpluses.[30] In this he emphasized the need for the government to make up a deficiency in private savings in relation to the size of the investment programme, especially when loans and gifts from abroad were fading out. Whilst a reduction in taxation might react favourably on savings, it was unlikely to be completely offset and the risk was one that could not be taken so long as the balance of payments remained weak.

### Budget changes

Dalton's first Budget in October 1945 provided for reductions in tax in a 'full' year of £385 million, mainly through increased income tax allowances and a reduction in the standard rate from 10/– to 9/–. But these were to take effect only in the next financial year beginning in April 1946 and the only immediate release of purchasing power was confined to reductions in purchase tax on space-heating and cooking appliances estimated at £10 million. In his second Budget in April 1946 the first reductions were supplemented by cuts estimated to be equivalent to £146 million in a 'full' year. Very little of this – only £17 million – was in indirect taxation. Dalton took the unpopular view that purchase tax had come to stay; but at the same time he allowed the food subsidies to go on increasing (as a kind of negative indirect tax) and undertook to keep the cost of living steady by this device until at least the end of the year. The changes he made in direct taxation took the form of abolishing the Excess Profits Tax, already reduced in October 1945 from 100 per cent to 60 per cent, and raising the earned income allowance from one-tenth to one-eighth.

30  CP(50)35, 15 March 1950, in PRO CAB 129/38.

*Table 15.3* Analysis of Budget tax changes 1945–52 (effects in a 'full' year on the revenue yield in £m.)

|  | 1945 Oct. | 1946 | 1947 | 1947 Nov. | 1948 | 1949 | 1950 | 1951 | 1952 |
|---|---|---|---|---|---|---|---|---|---|
| Taxes on: |  |  |  |  |  |  |  |  |  |
| personal incomes | −292 | −82 | −87 | — | −104 | −4 | −82 | 79 | −230 |
| company incomes | −83 | −70 | 20 | 47 | — | −62 | — | 233 | 100 |
| capital | — | 22 | 9 | — | 105 | 20 | — | — | — |
| personal expenditure | −10 | −16 | 89 | 150 | 48 | −44 | 40 | 50 | 33 |
| other expenditure | — | — | 23 | — | — | −2 | 41 | 25 | 30 |
| Total change in taxation | −385 | −146 | 54 | 197 | 49 | −92 | −1 | 387 | −67 |
| Estimated impact on consumption | +242 | +87 | −8 | −120 | +42 | +38 | +37 | −84 | +176 |

*Source:* Dow (1964), pp. 198–9.

The net effect of these two Budgets was to cut taxation by over £500 million. The impact on consumption was a good deal less and in the circumstances of 1945–7 when spending was often limited by availability it is difficult to judge what the impact was. Dow puts it at £330 million in a 'full' year or a little over 4 per cent of consumption in 1947 (see table 15.3).[31] This compares with an estimated increase in consumption between 1945 and 1947 of 14 per cent.[32]

After the Budget of 1946 fiscal changes were smaller until 1951. The one important exception was Dalton's last Budget in November 1947 following the convertibility crisis. Purchase tax and profits tax were both doubled and duties on alcoholic beverages increased. Some £200 million was taken back from the earlier concessions in 1945–6. With the increases in this and in the April Budget, when the tobacco tax was drastically increased, half the tax reductions in Dalton's first two Budgets were offset.

Under Cripps there was little change. Between 1947–8 and 1950–1 ordinary expenditure remained almost constant, within £100 million or so of a total of £3250 million. Ordinary revenue was also relatively steady within a similar margin of £3900 million. The most spectacular change was the Special Contribution introduced in 1948 (which levied up to 50

31 Dow (1964), p. 198.
32 Feinstein (1972), table 5.

per cent on investment incomes in addition to the income tax to which they were subject); but this was a once-for-all affair that was probably paid out of capital and had little effect on consumption. As Dow comments (with table 15.3 as evidence)

> Sir Stafford Cripps, despite his name for austerity, and despite the tenacity with which he strove to disinflate by fiscal means, in fact reduced taxes affecting consumption at each of his three budgets; and in three years, more or less undid Dr Dalton's last act of disinflation.[33]

Thus until 1951 the use of fiscal policy for purposes of demand management was pretty rough and ready. When there was a crisis as in 1947 and 1949 fiscal policy was tightened just as Bank Rate had previously been increased as a public acknowledgement of danger. In October 1949 in particular there was a careful assessment of the signs of increasing pressure of demand.[34] But at the official level the forecasts were still relatively unsophisticated and at the ministerial level there were few, if any, who understood the system of demand management that was evolving. Even Douglas Jay in October 1949 and Hugh Gaitskell in 1951 were at sea in discussing how changes in import prices and the balance of payments affected the pressure of demand. All one can say is that from early in 1947 there was a growing acceptance by the government of the need to enlist fiscal policy in the struggle against inflation by maintaining a substantial budget surplus.

The surplus was indeed substantial. Between 1947–8 and 1950–1, as measured conventionally for presentation to Parliament, the budget surplus averaged a little under £700 million a year (nearly 7 per cent of GNP). In April 1951, estimates of public sector savings, in the calendar years 1947–50, using economic criteria to distinguish income and capital items (and eliminating swaps), yielded an average of about £500 million a year (including a minuscule element for local authorities but over £130 million a year for national insurance funds).[35] On the latest calculations by the Central Statistical Office, public sector savings in the same four calendar years averaged £630 million. Personal savings over the same period averaged only about £65 million a year (i.e. they were negligible)

33  Dow (1964), p. 201.
34  See pp. 192–3.
35  *National Income and Expenditure of the UK, 1946 to 1950* (Cmd 8203), table 29 ('Total sums set aside through the action of public authorities'). The figures are gross of depreciation.

and company savings about £1200 million. Even on this basis the public sector was furnishing one-third of the country's savings. But if one could eliminate depreciation and stock appreciation, which are much less in public sector activities, the proportion would be substantially higher.

The biggest test of fiscal policy came in 1951 when Gaitskell had to judge what increase in taxation was called for by rearmament. The problem was a difficult one because it was necessary to take account not only of the domestic upset involved in a large increase in government expenditure, concentrated on the engineering industries, but also of the simultaneous upset in the balance of payments as import prices soared and exports ceased to expand. Most people, including Gaitskell, concluded that a big increase in taxation was required in order to bring the economy back into balance. But, left to themselves, the higher import prices that were the main cause of the external deficit would have exercised a powerful disinflationary influence. The Economic Section on these grounds argued for a limited increase in taxation and in the end Gaitskell was persuaded to accept their advice. He did, however, abolish 'initial' depreciation allowances in order to discourage domestic investment and leave more room in the engineering industries to accommodate the defence programme. The abolition of initial allowances was only one of a number of influences on company investment and is unlikely to have played a major role. But, taken together with the simultaneous increase in profits tax and income tax, it contributed to the depression in investment in 1952–4.

From 1947 onwards the Budget was seen increasingly as a governing element in the pressure of demand. The view gained currency that if the pressure were reduced the need for most of the controls retained by the government would disappear. The pressure did in fact subside from 1946 to 1950 as various measures of excess demand testify; and the controls did eventually disappear. But the changeover to economic management through fiscal and monetary policy was a very gradual one and was not completed when the Labour government lost office.

Dalton did not worry unduly about the risk that his Budget might have gone too far in the deflationary direction: Cripps did so constantly. He had hardly taken office as Minister of Economic Affairs when he asked for a paper on the inflationary situation and after each of his Budgets he was troubled by talk of impending deflation. In 1948 there were clear signs that inflation was easing: for example, there were fewer shop shortages and vacancies were falling. On the other hand, unemployment was slightly lower. Nevertheless there was alarm in some quarters that the

Budget was unduly restrictive and at the beginning of June Cripps felt obliged to withdraw some of his proposals for an increase in purchase tax. He returned to the subject several times in the debates on the Finance Bill and on 24 June held a press conference on signs of deflation. Similarly in 1949 the Budget was introduced in the middle of widespread fears of a slump and Cripps's advisers oscillated between thinking the Budget too deflationary and not deflationary enough. It was only in 1950 that no such doubts arose.

In Cripps's Budgets it was possible to edge a little way towards tightening or loosening the pressure of demand without any need to make precise calculations in face of major changes arising elsewhere. But in 1951 there was a more complex situation involving larger risks. What changes in the tax burden were appropriate to an economy grappling with large-scale rearmament, sharply higher import prices and a rapidly deteriorating balance of payments? The Budget Committee was taken aback when the Economic Section suggested no more than £70 million in extra taxation and the Chancellor himself was reluctant to accept that higher import prices would by themselves have a powerful deflationary effect. To make matters worse, the Central Statistical Office, as in previous years, kept changing its estimates of the national accounts until the very last minute. In the end, Gaitskell's Budget provided for a reduction in the budget surplus 'above the line' by £400 million and imposed new taxation calculated to bring in £387 million in a full year. Most of this (e.g. the suspension of initial allowances) fell on company incomes and was unlikely to do much to check the demand on resources in 1951–2.[36] On Dow's calculations, the impact on consumption was less than £100 million.

However this Budget and the calculations underlying it are viewed, it was fortunate that a more deflationary stance was not adopted. Even more important, it established the Budget firmly as a prime agent in the management of economic activity and confirmed the position of the Economic Section in their role as advisers on the central Budget judgement.

---

36 Gross domestic capital formation increased in 1951 by nearly 50 per cent in money terms but plummeted in 1952, largely because of fluctuations in stock-building. Gross fixed investment in manufacturing industry, which is generally thought to have suffered, rose by 25 per cent between 1950 and 1952 or about 5 per cent in real terms.

# Chapter sixteen

# MONETARY POLICY

Monetary policy during the war had been largely passive. Apart from a brief flurry at the outbreak of war, Bank Rate remained unchanged at 2 per cent throughout the nineteen years between 1932 and 1951. Short-term market rates were also held steady. The rate on Treasury Bills, which had been as low as $\frac{1}{2}$ per cent in the mid-1930s, was fixed at 1 per cent early in the war through the readiness of the Bank of England to make purchases at any higher rate. At the long end of the market, the government had set itself the target of 'a 3 per cent war' and had conducted its debt management policy on that basis.[1] The money supply grew at a rate consistent with this target, doubling over the six years of war as the banks absorbed whatever government debt was not taken up by the public. Advances to customers in the private sector, after dropping by about one-quarter in the first four years, held steady in the next two and by 1945 absorbed only one-sixth of total bank deposits. The resulting excess of bank liquidity was absorbed from the autumn of 1940 onwards in the form of Treasury Deposit Receipts – non-negotiable instruments with a life of six months and carrying a slightly higher rate of interest than Treasury Bills.

Thus the wartime situation was one of heavy government borrowing at fixed rates of interest. The different markets for government debt were catered for by the issue of a variety of instruments and the residuary requirements were met by borrowing the surplus cash of the banks in exchange for TDRs. It was an integral part of the policy that the banks

1 Sayers (1956), pp. 159–62.

had access to whatever cash they required for their own needs by disposing of Treasury Bills to the Bank of England at the fixed discount rate of 1 per cent.[2]

The cheap money policy pursued by Dalton in 1945–7 was largely a continuation of wartime arrangements. It had been Keynes's contention from the mid-1930s that the long-term rate responded to expectations of government policy and that, with war on the horizon, nothing should be done to conflict with the possibility of holding the rate firmly at an appropriate level. Wartime experience had shown that it was possible first to reduce the rate slightly and then to hold it at 3 per cent in spite of borrowing on a colossal scale (well over one-third of GNP). With the coming of peace and the prospect of a balanced budget it did not seem altogether unreasonable to contemplate some further reduction in the long-term rate. If the government was fading out as a borrower – and for that matter raising much of what it needed in the United States and Canada – lower rates might well be appropriate.

Cheap money in post-war years was by no means peculiar to the United Kingdom. In the United States, for example, the Federal Reserve Bank of New York kept its discount rate at 1 per cent from 1946 to 1948 and six years after the war, in the spring of 1951, it was still only $1\frac{3}{4}$ per cent. At the same date the discount rate of the Swiss National Bank was $\frac{1}{4}$ per cent lower and that of the Bank of Canada $\frac{1}{4}$ per cent higher. In the Netherlands, Norway, Sweden and Portugal the rate was either steady throughout at $2\frac{1}{2}$ per cent or raised latterly to 3 or (in the case of the Netherlands) 4 per cent. In France the rate stood at $2\frac{1}{2}$ per cent or less throughout the post-war years except for a brief spell in 1948–9 when it was raised to 3 per cent. Italy was one of the few countries in which the discount rate was ever in excess of 5 per cent. Only Germany of the major European countries held to relatively high rates, reaching 6 per cent in October, 1950.[3]

Cheap money was therefore *à la mode*. But even if it had not been, Britain's financial system was under tighter control, less closely integrated into the international monetary system and less at the mercy of external financial flows than now seems possible. Exchange control, control over capital issues and the informal exercise of the Bank of England's authority gave the government a freer hand in debt management and a stronger

2 ibid., p. 223.
3 Bank for International Settlements, 19th *Annual Report*, June 1949, p. 162; 21st *Annual Report*, June 1951, p. 188.

influence over market opinion. At the same time the many physical controls which the government exercised over the domestic economy made it much less certain that the influence of market forces on prices, including the rate of interest, would be allowed to prevail. If, for example, the government wished to check investment it was under no compulsion to make use of higher interest rates for the purpose.

Cheap money has come to be thought of as an automatic recipe for inflation. But this was not so in the immediate post-war years: the world-wide inflation that followed the war had been brought under control in most countries by the end of 1948 without any marked change in interest rates.[4] Wholesale prices in the United States, which had been rising rapidly in 1946 and 1947 reached a peak the following year and fell 4 per cent over the six winter months in 1948–9. Over the same period, prices fell in France and Italy (where they had been rising at about 50 per cent per annum) as well as in Belgium and Switzerland (where the rise had been gentler). In the United Kingdom the rise in wholesale prices over those six months was insignificant. Whatever brought about the change, it was not higher interest rates nor, except marginally and in a few countries, was it tighter credit. The main factors at work were the end of post-war restocking in the United States, an improved supply position elsewhere (partly as a result of better harvests) and a consequent easing in international commodity prices.

Inflation, it is true, reasserted itself later. But within the period of 'the Dalton experiment' the rise in prices in Britain was modest in comparison with most other countries: far below the American rate and not very much above the Swiss. With a fixed rate of exchange, rapidly rising import prices and no real possibility of *appreciating* the currency, it would have been very hard to avoid inflation altogether. Adding to the already heavy burden of food subsidies would have delayed the restoration of budgetary balance and would have been only partly effective in holding prices down. Raising interest rates would have been hard to justify when foreign rates were so low; and the weight of interest charges on sterling balances in London would have been directly increased. The natural line of defence against inflation was through resolute action to bring the budget into balance and if necessary into surplus; and this was the line that Dalton followed.

If it was indeed possible to hold down or reduce interest rates there were

4  BIS, 19th *Annual Report*, June 1949, pp. 51–2.

strong arguments for doing so. These are summarized by Christopher Dow in the following passage:

> From the narrowly budgetary point of view, the argument for reducing the service of the national debt remained almost as pressing as during the war. At the same time, there was general scepticism about the effects of interest rates upon investment, and thus upon the economy at large. There was general agreement that during the transition period, controls would have to remain in force, including controls on investment: this seemed to make high interest rates, even if otherwise desirable, unnecessary. The transition period was, moreover, expected to be short: and beyond it, the danger foreseen was not inflation but deflation. So far as interest rates could help at all, it would, after this phase, be low interest rates that were going to be needed.[5]

The argument for caution rested ultimately on fear of inflation. A rate of interest below 3 per cent was historically exceptional and was likely to reflect an expectation of falling prices as in the 1890s. But the immediate outlook was very different. The money supply had been inflated, the floating debt (including TDRs) was excessive and threatening, wartime issues were due to mature every year for years ahead, and to the excess liquidity held within Britain had to be added the large balances in sterling accumulated in the hands of foreigners. Controls over investment would not last indefinitely and might not prove effective. Even if full employment was not sustained, price stability was precarious so long as funds could be mobilized and brought into use on a formidable scale. If on the other hand full employment did persist, that in itself carried inflationary dangers through the bargaining power that it conferred on wage-earners. Either way, low rates of interest might prove inappropriate or might turn out to be unsustainable once market sentiment registered the magnitude of the inflationary risk.

These were not arguments advanced at the outset. Sir John Anderson, speaking as an ex-Chancellor and chief opposition speaker in October 1945 expressed his complete agreement with the action Dalton was taking. Other opposition speakers throughout Dalton's period of office took care not to attack cheap money as an objective. It was mainly a few financial journalists like Wilfred King, and some elements in the City, who took a critical line from the autumn of 1946.

5  Dow (1964), p. 223. Most of these points can be illustrated from the White Paper on *Employment Policy*, Cmd 6527, 1944.

Dalton's campaign for cheap money – it was increasingly seen in personal terms – was foreshadowed in the Debate on the Address in mid-August 1945. He proposed 'a national plan for the use of our national resources in finance not less than in materials and labour', and told the House that he was examining 'future possibilities in the field of cheap money and low interest rates'.[6] In September he announced that he was making a special study to see whether the gilt-edged rate should be brought down and in his Budget speech in October issued a further warning that 'the terms of lending may become less attractive'.

Dalton's first move was to cut the Treasury Bill rate from 30 November to $\frac{1}{2}$ per cent with corresponding reductions in other short-term rates. The new, lower rates endured throughout the years of Labour government until the increase in Bank Rate by the incoming Conservative administration in November 1951. Viewed as a measure of economy, the annual saving was about £9 million in interest on overseas sterling balances, a further £9 million or so at the expense of the clearing banks, and a maximum of £4 million from other non-official lenders – say £20 million a year in all. Viewed as an act of monetary policy, it suspended the use of Bank Rate, committed the government to a passive monetary policy except by way of debt management, and had no very marked impact on the gilt-edged market, although its initial effect was to increase the relative attractiveness of bonds.

It was on the bond market that Dalton now concentrated. He was anxious to lower the long-term rate from 3 per cent to $2\frac{1}{2}$ per cent, partly for fiscal reasons and to reduce the cost of acquiring the assets of the nationalized industries, but also because he wanted other borrowers for productive purposes, including local authorities and nationalized industries, to have the benefit of the lowest possible rates. He had little sympathy with bondholders, throwing his weight as Chancellor behind 'the active producer' who borrowed money as against 'the passive *rentier*' who lent it.

At first he confined himself to warnings that the public would be well advised to buy the two tap stocks then in issue before the tap closed on 15 December 1945 since future issues would be on less favourable terms.[7] This tactic was successful in producing a last-minute rush of subscriptions.

6  *H. C. Deb.*, 5th ser., vol. 413, cols 502 and 504, 16 August 1945.
7  He announced towards the end of November that the tap would close on 15 December on $2\frac{1}{2}$ per cent National War Bonds 1954–6 and 3 per cent Savings Bonds, 'B', 1965–75.

He then called two stocks that were redeemable from 1945, offering holders in exchange bonds carrying a lower coupon: a total of £191 million had to be repaid in cash.[8] In May 1946 he replaced 3 per cent Defence Bonds by a $2\frac{1}{2}$ per cent issue and raised the ceiling on the total holding of any individual: this brought in heavy applications for the 3 per cent Bonds before the closing date.

From May 1946 the tap for marketable stocks was reopened with an offer at par of $2\frac{1}{2}$ per cent Savings Bonds 1964–7. This was slightly below the market and brought heavy initial subscriptions from the public. At the same time a further conversion operation was undertaken into the new tap stock. This was moderately successful but £159 million had to be repaid in cash.[9]

By the end of October 'Old' Consols had risen to a peak of 99 although the public had become net sellers of gilt-edged from the autumn onwards. A new issue was made at par of undated $2\frac{1}{2}$ per cent Treasury Stock, redeemable at the Treasury's option from 1975, popularly known ever since as 'Daltons'. Of a total of £482 million in issue from 25 October 1946, £305 million was used for the conversion of Local Loans Stocks and only £177 million was subscribed in cash. Both the Local Loans Stock offered for conversion and the cash subscriptions were thought at the time to have come largely from the departments, i.e. from official subscribers handling various government funds. In addition, £125 million of the Local Loans Stock was repaid in cash on 5 January 1947.

No further issues for cash were made for the next three financial years apart from the redemption of an outstanding issue of 3 per cent Conversion Loan 1948–53 for £300 million in cash in March 1948. In the meantime there had been a series of crises, starting with the coal shortage at the beginning of 1947 and continuing with the convertibility crisis in the summer and the prolonged debate on steel nationalization. The bond market had begun to weaken in November 1946 ahead of any of these and it continued to weaken until the spring of 1948 when Consols had fallen from their peak in October 1946 by nearly 25 per cent. By that time Dalton's efforts to drive down the rate had clearly failed. Were these efforts misconceived? And were they doomed by the methods adopted?

As we have seen, there was nothing particularly new or daring about efforts on the part of the government to impose its view of the appropriate

8   The $2\frac{1}{2}$ per cent Conversion Loan 1944–9 was called for 1 April 1946 and $2\frac{1}{2}$ per cent National War Bonds 1945–7 for 1 July 1946 with the option of conversion into $1\frac{3}{4}$ per cent Exchequer Bonds 1950 up to 25 February 1946.
9   The issue called for conversion was of $2\frac{1}{2}$ per cent National War Bonds 1946–8.

level of interest rates on the market. To those who objected in principle to a policy of cheap money, Dalton could reply that he was acting with the full agreement of the Governor of the Bank of England, Lord Catto, and, for that matter, of Lord Keynes. When consulted before the 1946 Budget Keynes had suggested that there was no immediate need to reopen the taps but when that time came he would favour concentration on medium-term issues, deferring long-term issues till later. The course he would prefer was to make an issue at 2 per cent for, say, ten years with a later issue at $1\frac{1}{2}$ per cent for five or six years. If the government borrowed at long-term he would recommend an undated issue at 3 per cent with an option allowing the Treasury to redeem or convert at any time. He also thought that Bank Rate should be dropped from 2 per cent to 1 per cent although he had no wish to press this strongly on the Chancellor.[10]

If the government was successful there need be no repercussions on the money supply or on inflation. But what if the government achieved its success by levering up the price of its bonds 'artificially'? There were rumours of extensive intervention by the government broker using departmental funds, i.e. the government's own money, to support the market; and at times it was apparent that the government was successful only at the cost of increasing the money supply through diverting its borrowing from the market to the banks. Dalton's critics could not quote precise figures of departmental support since none were published; but they could trace the connection between the government's borrowing operations and the money supply.

Departmental support could mean one of two things. It could mean a switch in the holdings of government debt by the Issue Department of the Bank of England and the National Debt Commissioners from short- to long-dated securities or the retention by them of an increased amount of stock, financed out of cash balances or through the issue to the public of additional Treasury Bills. The second expedient had no effect on the quantity of outstanding government debt and was simply, like the first, a way of offering more short-term debt (or cash) to the public in substitution for an equivalent amount of longer-term debt.

Departmental support of the first kind is apparent in 1946–7 from figures published in 1961 showing the distribution at 31 March of debt held by departments and by the market between maturities of less than five years, five to fifteen years and over fifteen years.[11] Between 31 March 1946

10 PRO T 171/386.
11 'Exchequer Financing and National Debt, 1945–51', *Economic Trends*, December 1961.

Table 16.1  Exchequer financing 1945–51 (£m.)

| Year | Quarter | Total borrowing[a] | Net sales of marketable stocks | Increase in holdings of Issue Department and National Debt Commissioners[b] | Net sales to the public of marketable stocks | Non-market borrowing[c] | Increase in market Treasury Bills and TDRs |
|---|---|---|---|---|---|---|---|
| 1945 | 2 | 705 | 229 | 88 | 141 | 227 | 371 |
|  | 3 | 700 | 123 | -43 | 166 | 193 | 292 |
|  | 4 | 734 | 779 | 124 | 655 | 285 | -312 |
| 1946 | 1 | 95 | -4 | -34 | 30 | 48 | -31 |
|  | 2 | 389 | 261 | 61 | 200 | 139 | -9 |
|  | 3 | 361 | -253 | -162 | -91 | 41 | 324 |
|  | 4 | 256 | 150 | 190 | -40 | 163 | 87 |
| 1947 | 1 | 116 | -92 | 15 | -107 | -55 | -82 |
|  | 2 | -176 | -3 | 22 | -25 | 25 | -152 |
|  | 3 | 178 | — | 104 | -104 | -26 | -46 |
|  | 4 | 241 | 2 | 83 | -81 | 25 | 131 |
| 1948 | 1 | -211 | -307 | -54 | -253 | -209 | 17 |
|  | 2 | -30 | -1 | 31 | -32 | -23 | -6 |
|  | 3 | 25 | 3 | 22 | -19 | 19 | -253 |
|  | 4 | 159 | 51 | 13 | 38 | 60 | 8 |
| 1949 | 1 | -397 | 74 | -16 | 90 | -134 | -518 |
|  | 2 | 224 | 51 | 38 | 13 | 31 | 77 |
|  | 3 | 151 | 5 | 48 | -43 | 6 | 28 |
|  | 4 | 146 | 8 | 340 | -332 | 94 | 428 |

Table 16.1—continued

| Year | Quarter | Total borrowing[a] | Net sales of marketable stocks | Increase in holdings of Issue Department and National Debt Commissioners[b] | Net sales to the public of marketable stocks | Non-market borrowing[c] | Increase in market Treasury Bills and TDRs |
|---|---|---|---|---|---|---|---|
| 1950 | 1 | -499 | -52 | -91 | 39 | -179 | -477 |
|  | 2 | 123 | 154 | 155 | -1 | 74 | 128 |
|  | 3 | 167 | 77 | 15 | 62 | 47 | 95 |
|  | 4 | 175 | 282 | 211 | 71 | 80 | 236 |
| 1951 | 1 | -529 | -119 | -68 | -51 | -116 | -277 |
|  | 2 |  | 1 | -27 | 28 |  | 60 |
|  | 3 |  | 17 | -28 | 45 |  | -175 |

*Sources: Economic Trends*, December 1961; for the second half of 1951, J. H. B. Tew, 'A second look at exchequer financing under the Labour government' (unpublished MS).

a  Including receipts from extra-budgetary funds and external borrowing.
b  Departmental support, excluded from col. 1 but included in col. 2. Thus col. 1 is equal to the sum of cols 4, 5 and 6 plus receipts from extra-budgetary funds and external borrowing.
c  Small savings, tax reserve certificates, other non-marketable securities and increase in fiduciary note issue.

and 31 March 1947 maturities in official hands over fifteen years increased steeply from £616 million to £1330 million while maturities of under five years fell from £565 million to £201 million and maturities of five to fifteen years from £427 million to £374 million. Market holdings, on the other hand, rose much less for the longer maturities in 1946–7 than in either the preceding or the following year and much less proportionately than maturities of under five years. The figures also show that public bodies and the commercial banks accounted for the whole of the increase in market holdings of government bonds in 1946–7. There seems no doubt that a quite abnormal switch took place in official holdings in 1946–7 in support of Dalton's bond market operations.[12]

Departmental support in the second sense can be analysed from the same source which provides details of Exchequer financing between 1945 and 1951. It is possible to trace the scale of departmental support in each quarter as well as the distribution of the government's borrowing operations between sales to the public of marketable stocks, the issue of non-marketable securities (small savings, tax reserve certificates, etc.) and short-term borrowing on Treasury Bills or Treasury Deposit Receipts (see tables 16.1 and 16.2). An increase in departmental support, unless it reflected an enlarged flow of savings to the National Debt Commissioners, provided an alternative to sales to the public, but only at the expense of a larger issue of bills. The material change was in the balance between sales of bonds and bills and it is this, rather than the contribution of departmental support to that change, that calls for analysis.

The figures for the three and a half years from April 1945 fall into four contrasting periods. For the first six months in the middle of 1945 the government was able to borrow continuously on short-term and long at steady rates of interest. In the final quarter of 1945 and the first half of 1946 there is a change as Dalton's warnings of lower bond rates in future produced a rush to buy bonds and enabled the government to reduce its outstanding short-term debt. Then in the latter half of 1946 the opposite process occurred with renewed short-term borrowing and some re-purchase of bonds. It was in this period that bond prices reached their peak and began to weaken. There followed nearly two years of almost continuous redemption of government debt, both on short-term and long. In seven quarters from the beginning of 1947 the total marketable debt redeemed was £621 million and a further £391 million in bills and TDRs

12  The switch was very largely in the holdings of the National Debt Commissioners, the Issue Department's holdings being only about one-tenth as large.

Table 16.2  Exchequer financing and the money supply 1945–52 (£m.)

| Financial year | Exchequer borrowing | External financing | Internal borrowing[a] | Treasury Bills and TDRs | Non-market borrowing[b] | Net sales of marketable stocks to the public | Departmental support | Increase in bank deposits |
|---|---|---|---|---|---|---|---|---|
| 1945–46 | 2,234 | 64 | 2,170 | 320 | 753 | 992 | 135 | 290 |
| 1946–47 | 1,122 | 277 | 845 | 320 | 288 | –38 | 104 | 807 |
| 1947–48 | 32 | 902 | –870 | –50 | –185 | –463 | 155 | 238 |
| 1948–49 | –243 | 428 | –671 | –769 | –78 | 67 | 50 | 21 |
| 1949–50 | 20 | 91 | –71 | 56 | –48 | –323 | 335 | –32 |
| 1950–51 | –64 | –661 | 597 | 182 | 85 | 81 | 313 | 254 |
| 1951–52 | 280 | 1,063 | –783 | –1,608[c] | –36 | 834 | –110 | –150 |

Sources: Economic Trends, December 1961 and (for 1951–2) Tew, 'A second look at exchequer financing under the Labour government'.

a Cols 4–6 plus receipts from extra-budgetary funds.
b Including addition to fiduciary note issue.
c Includes issue of £1000 million of government stock to the banks in exchange for Treasury Bills.

was repaid. This was possible because the large budget deficits of the immediate post-war period were ending (although there was still a borrowing requirement of £204 million in 1947–8) and because of the use made of the American and Canadian loans in 1947 and American and other aid in 1948. When account is taken of these external funds there was not only no need for net domestic borrowing but a substantial flow of funds into the repayment or repurchase of existing government debt.

The figures in table 16.1 bear out the picture of a public disinclined to buy 'Daltons' in the final quarter of 1946. The £177 million subscribed in cash for 'Daltons', mainly in that quarter, is, as it happens, close to the £190 million made available by departmental support.[13] More significant is the sudden cessation, in the second half of 1946, of net sales of marketable stocks to the public and their replacement by a substantial figure for net redemptions. In the circumstances of 1947, when there was no need to borrow from the public, this would have presented no problem. The healthier state of the budget and the calls made on the American and Canadian lines of credit made for a steady stream of repayments of government debt, either long-term or short. But in the second half of 1946, the failure to make sales of bonds to the public pushed the government into the short end of the market; and since such borrowing involved recourse to the banking system with all the publicity attending a rapid growth in the money supply it was not easy to carry conviction that the inevitable trend in interest rates was downwards.

In the second half of 1946 the deposits of the London clearing banks increased by no less than £600 million (over 10 per cent), a rate which was bound to be alarming to financial opinion and give pause to the government. This increase was associated with an increase in the floating debt in the form of market Treasury Bills and TDRs of over £400 million, and this increase in turn is traceable to the turnround, between the first and the second halves of 1946, of £360 million in sales of marketable stocks to the public.

The sequence of events is thus quite clear. Up to about the middle of 1946, the technique of repeatedly offering the public a 'last chance' before yields fell to their eventual floor was highly successful in combining falling yields with heavy sales of government bonds. But once the floor was reached, there was nothing left for the bondholder to go for.[14] The fear of

13  The cash repayment of Local Loans Stock was not made until the following quarter when heavy tax receipts eased the financial strain.
14  Tew, unpublished MS.

*Figure 16.1* Interest rates 1946–52

*Source: Monthly Digest of Statistics,* various issues.

depreciation and the lack of any prospect of further appreciation checked the public's appetite for bonds. For over two years from the middle of 1946, net sales of marketable stocks were replaced by net purchases while the long-term rate of interest climbed almost continuously. From a low point of 2.5 per cent at the end of October 1946 the yield on Consols rose to 3.3 per cent in the summer of 1948 (see figure 16.1).

What support the market received over that period from departmental purchases was almost certainly too little to have any significant effect on the longer-term movement in yields. But Dalton's tactics did clearly have an effect on interest rates in 1945–6. These tactics, if more hectoring, were not very different from those pursued more delicately in wartime. But whereas the authorities were able to carry financial opinion with them in representing 3 per cent as a sustainable rate under wartime conditions, Dalton was not successful in effecting the necessary transformation in opinion in 1945–7. Had he persisted in 1947 he would have been obliged to put the government broker into redeeming debt through the purchase of marketable securities at a faster rate. These purchases might have been financed out of further departmental support or by borrowing more on short term. The first possibility could not have amounted to a great deal since departmental funds had just been heavily committed in the previous quarter. The second possibility would have given a further, and observable, fillip to the growth of the money supply.

No one can say what scale of operations on the part of the government broker would have been necessary to bring the gilt-edged market back to a $2\frac{1}{2}$ per cent basis in early 1947. In the first half of the year he was already buying government stock at £250 million a year without stopping the rise in yields. On the other hand, floating debt was simultaneously being redeemed at £470 million a year and the expansion in the money supply had been virtually halted. A shift between the one set of operations and the other might conceivably have stopped the fall, for the time being at least. But once the public had made up its mind that $2\frac{1}{2}$ per cent was not a sustainable rate and bond prices had been allowed to weaken, it is hard to see how Dalton could have made his view prevail.

It is just conceivable that, had the budget deficit dropped more steeply, the need to add to the floating debt would never have arisen in the second half of 1946 and the growth in the money supply would have been comparatively modest. The market, having been cajoled into a price of 99 for Consols without unloading on the government broker appreciable quantities of gilt-edged, would have seen no reason to be disturbed and might have come to accept $2\frac{1}{2}$ per cent without second thoughts. A rather tighter fiscal policy thereafter would have offset the expanding credit requirements of industry and might have stopped the slide in gilt-edged. But the probabilities are otherwise. The market was shaken by the coal crisis and still more by the exchange crisis; the question mark over the future value of sterling was increasingly prominent in City thinking; and the prospect came to be dominated by continuous full employment and steadily rising wages with their implications for the future value of money. In these circumstances the chances of holding the rate at $2\frac{1}{2}$ per cent were slight.

Indeed one can go further. The effort to push the long rate down discredited the government's judgement as to the rate appropriate to postwar circumstances. Had Dalton stuck to 3 per cent he might well have held the rate and allowed it to persist for several more years. There would have been no open challenge to market opinion, merely a prolongation of what had come to be accepted. It is not at all obvious that a level 3 per cent, had that been possible, was less advantageous to the economy than an unsuccessful attempt to get the rate down to $2\frac{1}{2}$ per cent, taking account of the rebound that followed.

By the time Cripps took over from Dalton in November 1947 the yield on Consols was over 3 per cent. Although he reaffirmed Dalton's policy, Cripps's first operations early in 1948 were on the basis of 3 per cent. This was the rate on the enormous issue of Transport Stock on 1 January 1948 and it was also the rate fixed for long loans from the Public Works Loan Board.

From the beginning of 1948 there was no declared aim of policy in relation to long-term interest rates. But the government had still to decide as the months went by how far it should apply the funds corresponding to a negative borrowing requirement to the redemption of long- or alternatively short-term debt. In the first three quarters of 1947 Dalton had followed a fairly even-handed division between the two. In the next three quarters Cripps leant more in the direction of redeeming long-term debt, notably in March 1948 when £300 million was paid out in cash for the redemption of the 3 per cent Conversion Loan 1948–53. Between the middle of 1948 and April 1949, however, the budget surplus was used mainly to extinguish short-term debt, with the result that over the financial year 1948–9 the money supply was held more or less constant. The following year shows a rather different pattern for although there was a slight increase in market Treasury Bills and TDRs, in contrast to 1947–8 and 1948–9, the money supply fell a little.

Broadly speaking, it looks as if the use made of the greater power of manoeuvre which the authorities enjoyed from the beginning of 1947 (when the domestic borrowing requirement turned negative) was to limit and later stop the growth of the money supply rather than to throw the full weight of the government's financial strength into the gilt-edged market. The government remained a buyer for nine successive quarters from the middle of 1946 but never on any large scale except perhaps when it was flush of funds and could redeem an outstanding issue as in the first quarter of 1948.

It would also appear that the gilt-edged market enjoyed departmental support on a scale comparable with the final quarter of 1946 on three later occasions: in the second half of 1947 after the convertibility crisis; in the last quarter of 1949 after the devaluation of the pound; and in 1950 at the outbreak of the Korean War and in the final quarter of the year when there was a risk of war with China. We do not have the figures for shorter periods than three months but on that basis the most anxious period would seem to have been the quarter following devaluation when departmental support, net repurchases of marketable stocks from the public and net additions to the floating debt were all higher than in any other post-war quarter. In November 1949 the government broker 'entered a market both demoralized and technically "oversold" and caused a rise of three full points in the "longs" by little more than his mere presence'.[15]

15 C. M. Kennedy (1952), p. 202.

In 1950 and 1951 the large surpluses that the government had employed for domestic debt redemption came to an end and were replaced by a growing borrowing requirement in sterling. In those two years a trickle of sales of government stocks continued, supplemented in 1950 by substantial departmental purchases, and the floating debt also increased. The money supply showed only a small increase over the two years but the rate of interest continued to rise and by 1952 had climbed to well over 4 per cent. By the time the Labour government lost office the rate on irredeemables had risen over 50 per cent from its low point in 1946. This, however, was the nominal rate. If the change were measured in terms of the real rate, after a year in which prices had risen by 10 per cent, one might be more doubtful whether the rate had risen at all.

The movement of interest rates tells us only part of the story of monetary policy. We have also to consider how monetary policy fitted into the rest of economic policy and what kind of pressures the government sought to apply by monetary means.

Both in official documents and in outside comment by economists and financial journalists, the view was increasingly expressed, from about the beginning of 1947 onwards, that the economy was suffering from suppressed inflation. Controls limited demand and kept prices from rising; but the pressures within the economy found expression in a rundown in stocks,[16] in a lack of incentive to work and innovate,[17] in a continuing deficit in the balance of payments[18] or finally in an over-ambitious level of investment.[19] All through 1947 the chorus swelled and after the convertibility crisis it was widely accepted that other methods of limiting demand must be found. The use of the budget for this purpose was discussed in the last chapter. But was it out of the question to use monetary policy as well?

We have already seen that the emergence of a budget surplus in 1948 did of itself help to make money rather tighter. In the five years from April 1947 the money supply (as measured by deposits with the London clearing banks) increased by only 5 per cent. But there were those, including Robert Hall, who would have liked a more vigorous policy of credit restriction. They could point to the rapid expansion in bank advances while the government sought to limit its own recourse to the banks and was steadily paying off TDRs. Once the government accepted, by the end

16  J. R. Hicks (1947), pp. 1–14.
17  J. Jewkes and E. Devons (1947), pp. 1–11.
18  Lionel Robbins (1947), pp. 1–28.
19  Roy Harrod (1947).

of 1947, the need to be on its guard against inflation why should the banks be left free to increase their advances in three years by 36 per cent?

It was not a question to which the Bank of England returned a very satisfactory answer. They took a view, rather like that of the 'Banking School' after 1844, which assumed that the banks should respond, within the limits of their resources, to the needs of their customers. This came to much the same, in Dennis Robertson's words, as limiting central banking operations on the quantity and value of money to 'registering and implementing the decisions of the trade unions about the rate of money wages'.[20] Nor had ministers much of an answer, as became clear when the measures to accompany devaluation were under discussion. Some who passed as economists regarded any suggestion of credit restriction as old-fashioned and misguided. Proposals to raise Bank Rate or at least to make the existing rate effective came to nothing and all that survived from other suggestions in favour of tighter money was a letter from the Chancellor to the Governor asking for 'every endeavour to ensure that inflationary policies are held in check'.[21] Shortly afterwards, in mid-November, Cobbold sent on to the Chancellor a memorandum from Lord Linlithgow representing the London clearing banks, objecting to the idea of government-imposed restrictions on credit or of a ceiling on bank advances. Cripps, unimpressed, told Cobbold that he 'could not accept the view that the volume of money was at the discretion of the Clearing Banks'.[22]

Apart from this almost imperceptible bow to monetary policy in September 1949 the government confined itself largely to using its (cash) budget surplus in order to check the growth in the money supply. As Dow points out, 'for a year or two . . . there is scarcely a sentence in any official statement which mentions credit or interest rates. . . . In the budget speeches of 1948, 1949 and 1950 there is no mention of monetary policy'.[23]

Interest in monetary policy revived with rearmament. In November the Bank of England proposed an increase in Bank Rate as a counter-inflationary measure. They tried again, equally unsuccessfully, at the end of June 1951, Gaitskell preferring to rely on selective credit restriction. In his Budget speech in April 1951 Gaitskell accepted the need for an increase in bank advances in order to meet the higher cost of stocks but called on

20  *Money* (ed. of 1948), p. 222, quoted by Thomas Wilson in Worswick and Ady (1952), p. 247.
21  See p. 190.
22  Information from Lord Roberthall.
23  Dow (1964), p. 227.

the banks to exercise moderation and in July repeated his call for restraint 'with emphasis'.[24] Although he took other action to check investment he also appears to have seen advantage in a further rise in long-term interest rates. Departmental support of the gilt-edged market, which had been pronounced in 1950 when long-term rates were relatively steady, seems to have been withdrawn. Apart from this, there is no evidence of any change of policy in relation to market intervention.

As Table 16.2 brings out, the monetary situation in 1951 was dominated by the swing in the balance of payments. Where in 1950–1 the favourable balance of payments had more than absorbed the budget surplus, leaving a positive domestic borrowing requirement for the first time since 1946–7, in 1951–2 an unfavourable balance of payments had brought large sterling receipts to the Exchange Equalization Account and the Exchequer, far exceeding the borrowing requirement that rearmament had caused to reappear. This inflow of funds into the Exchequer made it possible to reduce the floating debt and put pressure on bank liquidity. By the spring of 1952 the money supply had fallen by £150 million and the Conservative administration was pursuing an active monetary policy.

This was initiated in November 1951 with an increase in Bank Rate from 2 to $2\frac{1}{2}$ per cent. The Bank of England suspended the practice of supplying cash to the discount market at $\frac{1}{2}$ per cent, by the purchase of Treasury Bills more or less on demand, and substituted a charge of 2 per cent for advances to the market for a minimum of seven days against Treasury Bills, reserving the power to buy Treasury Bills at its discretion. A swap was also arranged with the clearing banks that left them with £1000 million of Funding Stock maturing at dates up to 1954 in return for a corresponding surrender of Treasury Bills. The Capital Issues Committee was given fresh instructions as to the purposes for which new issues could be made and the clearing banks were given similar marching orders as to advances in a letter from the Chancellor.[25]

The effect of these measures was to reduce the liquid assets of the banks near to what was then regarded as the conventional minimum of 30 per cent, to raise interest rates right across the board, and to create that 'diffused difficulty of borrowing' which is normally associated with tight money. The effect was the greater, as the *Economic Survey* noted, because

24  *H. C. Deb.*, 5th ser., vol. 486, col. 842, 10 April 1951; and vol. 491, col. 2343, 26 July 1951.
25  *Economic Survey for 1952*, Cmd 8509, pp. 41–4. This was the first time a section on monetary policy was included in the *Economic Survey*.

of 'the uncertainty about the lengths to which the new policy would be carried'.

Bank Rate was further increased to 4 per cent in the March 1952 Budget. This was done partly for the domestic reasons that had prompted the reactivation of monetary policy in November – the need to damp down investment expenditure and restrain the growth of the money supply – and partly because of the need 'to fortify the currency and improve the balance of payments'.

Thus within a few months of the change of government monetary policy had been transformed. Bank Rate had been revived and a new emphasis put on control of the money supply. The change, however, was largely confined to the short end of the market and to the hopes invested in the use of monetary instruments. There was more readiness to accept higher interest rates and more reliance on monetary policy to regulate investment and the balance of payments. But in other respects there was continuity. If the Conservative government was increasingly anxious to engage in funding, the Labour government had gone to some lengths to get rid of TDRs and reduce the floating debt. It had come to accept rising long-term rates. It had also laid stress on credit control and applied moral pressure to the banks, much as its successor did, and had devised many forms of financial control that were taken over by the new administration. But it was more conscious than they of the limitations and costs of dependence on monetary policy in the management of the economy.

# Chapter seventeen

# CAPITAL INVESTMENT

One element in planning on which the incoming government was agreed was control of capital investment. It was the only element involving an explicit reference to economic planning in the Speech from the Throne.[1] 'Machinery will be set up', it was announced, 'to provide for the effective planning of investment'.

Dalton regarded control of investment as a job for the Treasury, and was well satisfied with the way it was done. 'Here at least', he wrote in 1949, 'we have effective planning'.[2] In November 1945 he asked the Cabinet to approve a Control of Investment Bill which was intended to form 'part of wider proposals for economic planning' and to confer on the government 'far-reaching powers' over investment.[3] The Bill was introduced two months later, when the powers it conferred proved to be along the lines of the existing Capital Issues Control and to relate to access to finance, not to the construction of physical assets. The purpose of the Bill was 'to make permanent provision for control of demands on the capital market' by means of restrictions on new capital issues. But the new-issue market had been controlled for years without statutory powers, new issues on behalf of foreign borrowers were already subject to exchange control and in any event industrial and commercial investment was largely financed out of profits, a method of finance that was unaffected by the

---

1 Reference was also made to 'town and country planning' but this has little to do with general economic management.
2 Diary, Dalton Papers, entry for 1 July 1949.
3 CM(45)55, 22 November 1945, in PRO CAB 128/2.

Bill. If there was 'effective planning' of investment under the Labour government it was not because of the Control of Investment Bill.

The Bill was intended also to enable the government to assist in the reconstruction or redevelopment of private industries and for this purpose the government took power to guarantee loans up to £25 million a year. It sought to promote co-operation between public and private undertakings responsible for capital development and the agencies providing finance through the creation of an Investment Advisory Council. If the planning of investment was to be harmonized with the government's other policies, however, Dalton thought that it must be guided by the government itself. The Council was therefore purely advisory and was to meet quarterly unless more frequent meetings seemed desirable. Letters of invitation were sent out in January, in advance of the issue of the Bill, and the Council held its first meeting six months later in July. It was a large body, including, in addition to the Chancellor, the Foreign Secretary and the Governor of the Bank of England, no less than ten prominent figures from the City or business and seven leading civil servants. They were asked in their terms of reference 'to assist the government in so organising, and, when necessary, stimulating investment as to promote full employment'.[4]

How Dalton persuaded himself that such a body could serve such a purpose is a mystery. He clearly hoped that it might help to promote understanding in the City of governmental policies and provide a link between public and private sectors in the direction of investment. But its scope was restricted to finance and any advice it could offer was correspondingly limited. Its discussions never related to the current level of real investment, whether domestic fixed capital formation or stock-building, or to the impact on that level of the government's financial controls. The agenda for its first meeting ('1. Control of Borrowing Order; 2. Bonus Issues') was a fair indication of its remoteness from the planning of investment. It is hardly surprising that it faded out after the first twelve months.

Yet the traditional way of controlling investment was through financial measures: the cost and availability of finance were cited in all the textbooks as the most obvious constituents, along with public works, of any policy for regulating investment. The use of monetary policy, however, had been set on one side. Bank Rate remained at 2 per cent until after the Labour government left office. As for long rates, Dalton from the start

4 Letter of invitation, 15 January 1946 in '1945–6 National Investment Council: minutes and agenda' (PRO T 233/161).

was planning to bring them down, not use them to check or stimulate investment. In the debate on the Address in August 1945 he announced his intention to 'have a national plan for the use of our national resources in finance not less than in materials and labour' and promised to examine 'future possibilities in the field of cheap money and low interest rates' so as to get 'even further assistance . . . by cheapening still further the cost of . . . capital operations'.[5] The rationale of Dalton's policy is discussed in chapter 16. For present purposes, the fact that it put no financial impediment in the way of investment except through restrictions on new capital issues implies a correspondingly heavier dependence on other forms of control.

One obstacle to effective control, of which the government took quite insufficient account, was ignorance. It simply did not know in 1946–7 what the total level of investment was but it knew enough to be distinctly uneasy.[6] It was increasingly obvious in the course of 1946 that fixed investment was roaring away faster than any other element in GDP.

The first assessment of investment prospects appears in the (unpublished) draft 'Economic Survey for 1946' at the beginning of December 1945. Departmental programmes at that stage assumed that the building and civil engineering industries would be back to pre-war strength in terms of manpower by the middle of 1946 and yielded a total for gross fixed investment over the year 5–10 per cent above the 1938 volume. The picture presented for domestic capital investment in 1946 was as shown in table 17.1.

The figures for 1938 show just how much at sea the government was in its estimates. From this point of view it hardly matters whether the 'actuals' are correct or not since they too are based on (later) official figures. It is the discrepancies between the two sets of estimates that bring out how uncertain any calculations in 1945–6 of investment, past, present or future, were bound to be. This is particularly true of estimates of

---

5 *H. C. Deb.*, 5th ser., vol. 413, cols 502, 504, 2 August 1945.

6 In the *National Income* White Papers no estimates of the value of changes in stocks and work in progress were included before 1950; and even then no figures were given for 1946 or 1947. The successive White Papers thereafter show wide variations from year to year in the estimates for any given year. For example, the increase in stocks in 1948 was put at £75 million, £200 million, £280 million, £195 million, £153 million and £175 million in the years between 1950 and 1955. The estimate for 1950 varied between +£204 million and −£168 million in successive years and for 1951 between +£387 million and +£610 million in successive years. When even the past was so incalculable the future could hardly be reckoned with much confidence.

*Table 17.1* Domestic capital investment in the United Kingdom 1938 and 1945–7 (at current prices in £m.)

|  | 1938 | 1945 | 1946 | 1947 |
|---|---|---|---|---|
| Economic Survey 'Estimates'[a] | | | | |
| Gross domestic fixed capital formation | 831 | 309 | 1,595[a] | 1,705[a] |
| less repairs to building and works | ? | ? | –500 | –535 |
| Value of increase in stocks | –50 | — | 550 | 150 |
| Total | (781) | (309) | 1,645 | 1,320 |
| 'Actual'[b] | | | | |
| Gross domestic fixed capital formation | 592 | 350 | 925 | 1,199 |
| Value of increase in stocks | 83 | –200 | –126 | 269 |
| Total | 675 | 150 | 799 | 1,468 |
| Gross domestic fixed capital formation at 1938 prices | 592 | 190 | 480 | 560 |

*Sources:* Draft 'Economic Survey for 1946' and '1947'; Feinstein (1972), tables 2 and 5.

a These figures, which in 1946 and 1947 represent departmental requirements, include repairs and maintenance. In order to achieve comparability with the 'actuals' a reduction of about £500 million in 1946 and £535 million in 1947 has to be made. These deductions represent the difference between the figures for those years given in the White Paper for 1946 to 1950 and in the Blue Book for 1946 to 1952: that is, they are *ex post* while the 'estimates' are *ex ante*.

b 'Actual' figures are from Feinstein (1972), table 2. For 1946 and 1947 they are either identical or virtually identical with those in *Economic Trends Annual Supplement 1981*. The estimates for stock-building are highly unreliable: for example, Feinstein shows stocks in 1946 falling in table 2 and increasing in table 5. For 1938 and 1946 a slightly different picture is given in *National Income and Expenditure 1955* (which gives the same figures as *Economic Trends* for later years): gross domestic fixed capital formation is shown there as increasing from £656 million in 1938 to £905 million in 1946 while stock-building falls from zero in 1938 to –£54 million in 1946.

changes in stocks and work in progress.[7] The draft 'Economic Survey', perhaps with the stock-building boom of 1919–20 in mind, looked forward to a large build-up of stocks in 1946 as 'an inevitable concomitant of filling up the pipe-line of the peace-time economy'.[8] But in fact it now appears that stocks either rose very little or actually fell, including stocks

7 See the discussion in Devons (1970), pp. 76–9.
8 Draft 'Economic Survey for 1946', para. 17, in PRO T 230/55.

of imported goods. This was one reason why the balance of payments turned out to be very much less in deficit in 1946 than had been expected at the end of 1945 when the 'Economic Survey' was in preparation.

There was no such uncertainty about the trend in fixed capital formation. It was recognized at an early stage that it was steeply upwards and that, since there seemed to be no shortage of finance, and higher interest rates were ruled out, other means of checking it must be employed. The draft 'Economic Survey' argued that until the pressure on resources subsided 'the case for postponing long-term projects is strong' and that a cut in the investment programme for 1946 of 10 per cent, 'if carefully applied', would not be very damaging. This was a considerable understatement. Since the prospect was one of pressure on resources beyond what could conceivably be met, the only genuine choice was between letting things take their course, so allowing a shortfall on programme to take place at random, and making deliberate cuts to the dimensions of a realistic programme.

When the 'Survey' was considered by the Cabinet in February it was agreed that since it was out of the question to cut consumption so as to reduce inflationary pressure, 'the most promising course' would be to control investment and that there should therefore be a postponement of investment in areas of labour shortage.[9] How these decisions were to be implemented was not discussed. Public investment was under the direct control of the government and control over private investment could be exerted through building licensing, machinery licensing and raw material allocations. But how effective these would be under peacetime conditions had yet to be put to the test.

In July the Steering Committee, in submitting the draft 'Economic Survey for 1946–47' to ministers, commented that some damping down of investment was still required and recommended that the licensing of small building jobs down to £10 should be continued for at least six months.[10]

Fixed capital investment in 1946 did not achieve the 5–10 per cent 'target' increase above the 1938 level to which the departmental programmes in the 'Economic Survey' were thought to add up. Instead there was a shortfall on the 1938 level of nearly 20 per cent and it was not until 1948 that that level was regained. Even so, the rate of increase, by over

9  CM(46)13, 7 February 1946 (PRO CAB 128/5).
10  MEP(46)7 in PRO CAB 134/503.

150 per cent in a single year, was startling. The additional claim on resources, in a year when GDP stood still or fell, was comparable with the claims of exports and consumption.

One of the biggest increases in 1946 was in housing on which the government alone, according to the 'Economic Survey', proposed to spend £270 million. In the end, 56,000 'permanent' and 84,000 'temporary' houses were completed.[11] A much larger number were started and the housing programme got increasingly out of balance with large numbers of half-finished houses held up by shortages of building materials.

The authors of the draft 'Economic Survey' had been in no doubt that the investment targets for 1946 would prove too ambitious unless other measures were taken to reduce the pressure of demand. One reason for the shortfall was that the labour force in the building and engineering industries failed to reach the target of 1,400,000 at the end of 1946 and got no further than 1,250,000. The other reason was that output per man-year remained well below the pre-war rate. When the *Economic Survey for 1947* was prepared, ministers concluded that the shortages of timber, structural steel and clay products, which contributed to the low output per head, removed any justification for a further large addition to the industry's manpower and substituted a target of 1,300,000, i.e. the pre-war level, to be reached during 1947. Since three workers in five were engaged in work on housing and there was likely to be insufficient timber to meet the housing programme, it would have been natural in these circumstances to cut the programme. The government preferred, however, to confine itself to 'close control . . . over new construction projects in order to prevent more from being started than can be completed' and meeting any hitch in the housing programme by slowing down the expansion of the labour force, 'taking up any slack which may develop by relaxing restrictions on work which uses little scarce material, including maintenance and repair'.[12] The target set for housing was 240,000 new permanent homes and 60,000 temporary houses and housing was to form 20 per cent of total gross fixed investment.[13] No figure was given for the projected value of total fixed investment in 1947 but it was indicated that, including maintenance work and excluding new housing and housing repairs, it should

---

11  It is typical of the figures on capital investment in the post-war years that the 84th *Annual Abstract of Statistics*, dated 15 December 1947, gives these totals as 8,500 and 31,600 respectively. They were still incomplete in the 90th *Abstract*, six years later.
12  *Economic Survey for 1947*, Cmd 7046, paras 113–14.
13  ibid., paras 117–18.

be at least 15 per cent above a normal pre-war year. It was not a target that was achieved in 1947 but it *was* achieved the following year.[14]

The bad weather in the early part of 1947 set back the rate of building, particularly the housing programme, and the shortage of building materials held back construction still further. The target for house-building was therefore modified to the maximum degree of completion of the permanent houses under construction at the beginning of April. But at the end of 1947 only 141,000 had been completed (compared with 240,000 in the programme) while 100,000 houses were roofed and awaiting completion.[15] The programme had got so far out of balance that 250,000 'permanent' houses were under construction – nearly twice as many as completions in 1947 – and starts had to be further restricted in an effort to speed up completions.

Housing was only part of the story of an over-ambitious investment programme. In spite of the shortage of materials, fixed capital formation in 1947 was higher than in 1946 by about one-sixth in real terms. Employment in building and civil engineering was up by 75,000 at the end of 1947, not by the 50,000 'planned'. Investment was at a level that made excessive demands on manpower and these demands were seen increasingly as a source of inflationary pressure. The succession of crises in the spring and summer forced the Cabinet to reconsider the investment programme and cut it drastically. On 1 August 1947 the Cabinet agreed to set up a new Investment Programmes Committee of officials as a sub-committee of the Steering Committee and in the meantime asked the newly appointed planning staff to review the programme urgently in consultation with the departments concerned. There was agreement that the scale of investment should be reduced, particularly where it made no contribution to an improvement in the balance of payments, and that there should be a more concentrated effort on fewer projects.

The report when submitted to the Chancellor on 10 October 1947 met with a warm response. Dalton welcomed it as 'a real start to central planning'.[16] It envisaged a reduction of 18 per cent in the forecast for fixed

---

14 Feinstein (1972), table 40, shows an increase in gross domestic fixed capital formation, excluding dwellings, at 1938 prices, from £406 million in 1936–8 to £420 million in 1947 and £473 million in 1948, i.e. by 16.5 per cent between the pre-war years and 1948. In 1947 housing represented a quarter of total fixed investment and in 1948 a little over a fifth.

15 *Economic Survey for 1948*, Cmd 7344, para. 182.

16 '1947 Investment Programmes Committee: White Paper on investment programme 1948', PRO T 229/66.

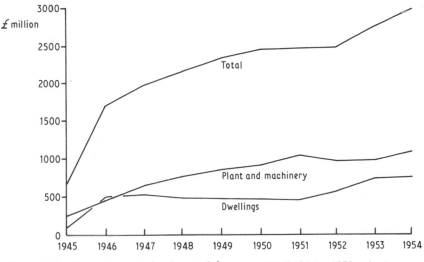

*Figure 17.1*   Gross domestic fixed capital formation 1945–54 (at 1958 prices)

*Source:* Feinstein (1972), table 40.

investment in 1948, with construction cut by 17 per cent and plant, machinery and vehicles by 22½ per cent. Steel supplies, it was pointed out, were barely adequate to meet the steel-using forms of investment in the cut programme. Housing was similarly limited by timber supplies. Starts were to be restricted to 60,000 in 1948. Total fixed investment, which was thought to be at an annual rate of £1550 million in mid-1947, was to fall to £1400 million in 1948 and an annual rate of £1300 million at the end of 1948.[17] These recommendations were approved and were made public, slightly amended, in a White Paper on *Capital Investment in 1948* (Cmd 7268).

Three reasons were given for the cuts but each of them came down to priority for exports and the balance of payments. The rapid exhaustion of the dollar credits made it necessary to put more pressure on exports even if this meant some deferment of re-equipment of domestic industries. Investment and exports were in competition for scarce materials such as steel and here again priority had to be given to exports. What was true of scarce materials was true also of manpower and of resources generally. The balance of payments came first and a cut in investment was necessary in order to clear the way for an indispensable improvement in it.

17  These figures are on a different basis from those now given in official estimates. They include repairs to building and works and omit some miscellaneous fixed investment. (Devons (1970), pp. 76–9.)

The fall in fixed capital investment planned for 1948 never took place. Investment increased continuously throughout the post-war period and by 1951 was 45 per cent higher in volume than in 1946.[18] The increase in 1948 was rather less than in 1947 – $7\frac{1}{2}$ per cent compared with 17 per cent – but any check in 1948 to the post-war expansion was little more than the slowing down inevitable at that stage. The divergence between plan and performance was explained in the *Economic Survey for 1949* in a brief reference to 'the receipt of ERP aid and the increase in steel output [which] made it possible for a less restrictive policy to be followed', but gave no particulars of any change of policy.[19] A simpler and more realistic explanation is that the control exercised over investment was not very effective.

The new Investment Programmes Committee did not come into existence until the changes in the 1948 programme had already been agreed. Its terms of reference required it to draw up general investment priorities, to approve departmental investment programmes and to scrutinize major projects costing over £500,000. These terms of reference were regarded with suspicion by Nye Bevan. They suggested to him that 'the Committee is intended to act as an official May Committee' and he wrote to the Prime Minister on 19 August to protest that ministerial responsibilities were being surrendered to officials.[20] Attlee assured him that all that was intended was that ministers should have 'the material on which policy decisions must be based'. But it was natural that Bevan should feel some uneasiness since it was the headlong expansion in house-building that was the most obvious target for attack in any review of the investment programme.

Although the new Committee interrogated the departmental sponsors of the main programmes and presented a report to ministers, it did not seek to re-vamp individual programmes or do much more than try to establish where cuts might be made if required and indicate how the total might be brought within plausible limits. It concentrated largely on public investment, including investment in the nationalized industries, and was often very inadequately informed as to the changes taking place in the private sector. There were times, for example, when it did not know whether industrial investment was rising or falling. Moreover, although the programmes submitted to it might stretch over several years, and the

18  Feinstein (1972), table 5.
19  *Economic Survey for 1949*, Cmd 7647, para. 5.
20  Bevan to Attlee, 19 August 1948 in PRO PREM 8/423.

larger projects once begun could not easily be abandoned, the horizon of control was a single year and the recommendations related to that year.

In the two years following 1948 fixed investment continued to increase; since housing and transport were held down, the expansion in other elements was correspondingly faster (see table 17.2). Manufacturing and commercial investment, investment in the various forms of fuel and power and miscellaneous public services all increased substantially. After 1950, however, the rearmament programme cut across any further expansion and for the next two years, as we saw in chapter 9, fixed investment marked time. In 1951, the Labour government's last year in office, manu-facturing investment (including construction) had climbed to 31 per cent of the total, a ratio never regained in later years.

## The machinery of control

The machinery of control changed little after 1948. It has already been sketched in chapter 12 and it is not necessary to review its operation in detail.

In wartime control had been all-embracing. The building industry was controlled by a system of licensing and most types of plant and machinery also required a licence. Even with a licence there was still the difficulty of finding the necessary materials. Some of these – steel, timber, non-ferrous metals and rubber, for example – were subject to allocation while others – bricks and cement, for example – were equally scarce. After the war, when the licensing of domestic machinery had been virtually abandoned, as happened very early, a licence continued to be required for imported equipment. The availability of domestic equipment could be reduced by putting pressure on manufacturers to meet stiffer export targets. The government could also, in principle, take action to control public investment which was not far short of half the total.

Building licensing continued until November 1954. For over three years after the war, until November 1948, all private building work *of any kind* costing above £10 in a six-month period required a licence and work above the same limit for a local authority or other public body had to be authorized by the appropriate government department. The limit for industrial, commercial and agricultural building was raised to £1000 in November 1948, lowered to £500 in February 1953 and after further vari-ations in 1952 and 1953 was removed in 1954. The limit for housing had been raised, exceptionally, to £100 in July 1948 and remained there until

Table 17.2  Gross fixed capital formation in the United Kingdom 1946–53 (£m. at 1958 prices)

| | 1946[a] | 1947[a] | 1948 | 1949 | 1950 | 1951 | 1952 | 1953 |
|---|---|---|---|---|---|---|---|---|
| Dwellings | (930) ⎫ | (523) | 486 | 476 | 465 | 456 | 546 | 711 |
| Other new building and works | ⎬ | (446) | 480 | 588 | 661 | 640 | 650 | 688 |
| Plant and machinery | (452) | (626) | 765 | 845 | 942 | 1,026 | 975 | 986 |
| Vehicles, ships, etc. | (331) | (404) | 404 | 424 | 391 | 347 | 308 | 363 |
| Total | (1,713) | (2,000) | 2,135 | 2,333 | 2,459 | 2,469 | 2,479 | 2,748 |
| Manufacturing and construction | | | 554 | 626 | 714 | 768 | 732 | 713 |
| Gas, water, electricity | | | 206 | 252 | 282 | 284 | 284 | 309 |
| Transport and communication | | | 344 | 355 | 334 | 292 | 273 | 329 |
| Distribution, road haulage, etc. | | | 187 | 231 | 251 | 250 | 248 | 267 |
| Social and public services | | | 123 | 151 | 182 | 201 | 191 | 202 |
| Agriculture, mining, etc. | | | 181 | 189 | 179 | 164 | 167 | 181 |
| Total (including dwellings)[b] | | | 2,135 | 2,333 | 2,459 | 2,469 | 2,479 | 2,748 |

*Source:* Feinstein (1972), tables 40 and 42.

a  Estimates scaled up on basis of volumes in 1946–8 at 1938 prices.
b  Transfer costs of land and buildings are not included.

July 1952 when it was increased to £200. It, too, underwent some further changes before its removal in 1954.[21]

Although there was provision for broad control from the centre, the operative control was through the regional offices of the Ministry of Works which specified a starting date when licensing private work. This was not at first co-ordinated with the sanctioning of work for public authorities but the resulting confusion caused that, too, to be brought under the starting-date procedure from April 1947.

In view of the low exemption limit, the controls must have covered virtually all new work and a very high proportion of repairs and maintenance. The unlicensed sector, however, is thought to have accounted for at least a quarter of the value of building and construction work. It included repair and maintenance work in the public sector, which was exempt, and work authorized by local authorities for war damage repairs and conversions and adaptations.

The main trouble was that until 1948 or even later far too much work was licensed or authorized in relation to what could be carried out. As Dow puts it, 'the system of control was not operated to ration demand, so much as to favour types of investment which the government considered especially urgent, in particular, housing'.[22] In other words it was the old story of trying to make a priority system do the work of an allocation system. To make matters worse, when labour gravitated towards repair work, Bevan, instead of making way by cutting the housing programme, gave the local authorities their head by authorizing them to put more work in hand and compete freely for scarce building labour.[23] Other difficulties were the lack of co-ordination at the regional level between the various authorities authorizing starts and the unexpectedly low level of output because of raw material shortages.

The changes in 1947 have thus to be seen as essentially deflationary, bringing the value of licences in issue more closely into line with the prospective value of output. This was most apparent in the housing programme where the cut in starts made it possible to complete more houses and leave fewer under construction. But the whole of the building programme was brought into better balance and under firmer control without the drop in output that was forecast.

21 For the details see Dow (1964), p. 150 on whom this account draws heavily.
22 ibid., p. 150.
23 ibid., pp. 150–51.

The rest of the investment programme consisted of engineering output and was under less direct control. The engineering industry had to meet four different sets of requirements – metal goods for domestic consumers, capital goods for domestic investment, government orders for investment or defence, and exports. The allocation of output between these different markets involved frequent discussion between the government and the larger firms and if it was necessary to enforce any limitation of domestic investment the government could do so through its control over steel allocations. This limitation could then be supplemented by informal rationing of customers by the manufacturers.

All these forms of control were supplemented by the influence of the government on public investment. This could be made effective in various ways. For the nationalized industries, then as now, ministerial approval of the investment programme was required; and for local authorities departmental loan sanction was needed for any borrowing for investment. The Investment Programmes Committee, starting in 1948, conducted a thorough annual examination of the constituent parts of the total and its report was made the basis of an approved programme.

Some clue to what was held back by the controls over investment may be obtained from observation of any marked changes in the composition of the total in comparison with the pre-war pattern or with the position later in the 1950s after removal of the controls. Total fixed investment in 1948 was only a little above the level in 1938 but for different kinds of investment the changes between 1938 and 1948 were very different. The changes after 1948 show equal diversity.

The figures for dwellings conceal the great effort that was put into house-building and repair immediately after the war. There can be little doubt as to the priority it enjoyed in government intentions, whatever the actual performance. Even when the housing programme was cut in 1947 the government boasted of the 460,000 homes provided in two and a half years since the war – a record it contrasted with the 5500 new houses completed in the first two years after the 1914–18 war.[24] From a record level in 1938 housing had fallen to negligible proportions early in the war and the build-up after the war took place in competition with other urgent demands and in face of an acute shortage of timber. The controls were designed to make the best of this situation by limiting the timber that

---

24 *Capital Investment in 1948*, para. 2. The figure of 460,000, which included permanent and temporary houses, conversions, adaptations and war-damaged houses made habitable, was probably an understatement.

*Table 17.3* Changes in the pattern of gross domestic fixed capital formation 1938–58 (£m.)

|  | 1938–48 % change | 1948–58 % change |
|---|---|---|
| Dwellings | −24 | +21 |
| Ships, vehicles, aircraft, etc. | +31 | +31 |
| Plant and machinery | +24 | +74 |
| Other new building and works | −10 | +118 |
| Total | +1 | +64 |

*Source:* Feinstein (1972), table 40.

could be used to 1.6 standards per house compared with 2.5 standards before the war and by licensing building work done outside the housing programme.

If the magnitude of the fall to 1948 is misleading so also is the increase to 1958. It so happens that housing construction dipped sharply in 1958 and in that year was over 20 per cent below the peak in 1954. The true picture for housing is of a concentrated drive, including the construction of 160,000 temporary houses and the repair of 125,000 war-damaged houses, in the first few years after the war, a slowing-down from 1948 to 1951 and thereafter a renewed drive, reaching its peak in 1954. The early drive was concentrated on local authority housing, with private construction never exceeding 42,000 houses until 1953 and that under difficulties. Then from 1953 onwards, the number of new local authority houses fell off while privately-built houses increased rapidly.

When we turn to 'ships, vehicles, aircraft, etc.' – a miscellaneous total that also includes railway rolling-stock and trams – the picture is very different. The expansion of the engineering industries in wartime left behind ample capacity and an experienced labour force when the switch to peacetime production began. Thus it was not difficult to achieve a higher level of output than before the war and to continue to meet an expanding demand over the post-war period, the main limiting factor in the initial stages being steel. Control of investment for this group consisted mainly in pressing for higher exports and limiting home demand. For motor cars, home demand was checked by a rate of purchase tax that rose by 1951 to $66\frac{2}{3}$ per cent while at the same time an export target of 75 per cent of total output was backed up by control over the allocation of steel, e.g. auto-body sheet. From the beginning of 1946 when production of motor cars was only 40,000 a year, exports took roughly half the output. By 1948 70 per cent of the output, now 330,000 cars per annum, was being exported and by 1950 and 1951 the proportion was 78 per cent of an output of about 500,000. It was not until 1955 that the proportion fell below 50 per cent. Much the same pressure was applied to commercial vehicles and the proportion of output going abroad reached 63 per cent in 1950–1. It is highly unlikely that commercial interest alone would have produced such results. There is also little evidence that the concentration on export markets did harm to the subsequent competitive position of the motor industry – it would seem more likely to have been strengthened.

Investment in plant and machinery was subject to many of the same influences as ships, vehicles, aircraft, etc. For example, it benefited from the wartime expansion in the metal and engineering industries and was quicker off the mark than investment involving new construction. There was also the same tussle between home and export markets, with a large boost in exports in the early post-war years and efforts on the part of the government to cut down supplies to the home market. In the review of capital investment towards the end of 1947 a large-scale switch of specialized plant and machinery from home to export markets was planned: by the end of 1948 exports were to be up from £45 million to £72 million per annum while production for the home market was to be down from £65 million to £49 million. At the same time the issue of licences for industrial building was severely curtailed, the monthly average falling from £11.3 million in the second quarter of 1947 to about £3.2 million in the first quarter of 1948.[25] A year later, however, it was apparent that investment in manufacturing industry had held up quite well in 1948 and that the total for plant and machinery (not just *specialized* plant) had edged up slightly instead of falling steeply.[26]

By 1948, as table 17.3 shows, investment in plant and machinery of all kinds was appreciably higher than before the war. Here, too, as the export drive lost its momentum domestic investment expanded. By 1951 it was already 34 per cent higher than in 1948. There was then a pause for three years before a further climb that continued almost without interruption

25 *Capital Investment in 1948*, p. 57.
26 Investment in plant by manufacturing industry other than iron and steel rose from £255 million to £285 million while the price of equipment increased by about 11 per cent (*Capital Investment in 1948*, p. 57 and Feinstein (1972), table 63). Feinstein (table 40) shows an increase of over 20 per cent in 1948 in *total* investment in plant and machinery.

until by 1979 investment in plant and machinery was more than four times what it had been in 1948 and five times as much as before the war.

There is not much doubt that the controls were used to limit domestic investment in plant and machinery both through the licensing of industrial building to house the plant and through pressure to meet higher export targets. Public investment programmes were also re-vamped so as to make room for exports by delaying domestic orders. The Post Office, for example, limited its requirements for telephone exchange equipment in order to allow the industry making the equipment to accelerate its exports even although this meant lengthening the long queue of applicants for telephone connections.

The main impact of the controls would seem, however, to have been on 'other new building and works'. The total was held to a level below that of 1938 until 1949 but shot up after 1953 when the controls were relaxed. In the ten years after 1948 the volume of new building other than dwellings doubled and the rate of expansion in the decade after 1958 was just as rapid. No doubt it took longer for building plans to be prepared. But the spurt in construction when building licensing ceased points to the restrictive effect of the licensing control.

Control of investment, it need hardly be said, was not the same thing as planning of investment. So far as stock-building was concerned there was no control and no planning: yet this was the most volatile and de-stabilizing element of any. As for fixed capital formation, for the first half of the period control was ineffective; for the second half it was designed to keep the total within limits, not to meet a self-consistent economic plan. So far as the approved programme represented a collection of uncoordinated plans, it went no further ahead than a year and disregarded the commitments implicitly assumed for future years. Where, as with power stations, the work extended into the future it was not really possible to limit approval to the first year's outlay. No attempt was made, however, to investigate whether trouble was building up in later years. The selection of items for inclusion, exclusion or postponement was largely arbitrary and unrelated to measurable economic criteria such as expected rates of return. There was no question of 'picking winners'. Much the same could be said of the programme total. It was not arrived at after examination of rates of saving and what could be afforded at those rates. Rather it was the rate of investment that was accepted as fixed on the assumption that savings would be adjusted by budgeting for an appropriate surplus or that the foreign balance would take up any change in pressure. In times of crisis it might be decided to cut investment rather than depress consumption still further: or in more expansionary times the restraints on investment might be relaxed. But in a world of biennial crises there was no accepted principle by which the level of investment should be adjusted upwards or downwards from year to year.

.

# Chapter eighteen

# NATIONALIZATION

Of all the achievements of the Labour government, there were few more closely identified with Labour Party doctrine than the series of measures for the nationalization of major industries. Public ownership, after all, was at the centre of the socialist vision of the future in 1945. Most of the measures taken were foreshadowed in the Labour Party's manifesto and were not seriously contested, except in detail, by the Conservative Opposition. It was only iron and steel and road haulage, on which there had been comparatively little public discussion, that gave rise to acute political controversy.[1]

No other part of the legislative programme took up so much parliamentary time. The four principal bills, covering coal, gas, electricity and transport, occupied 530 hours in the House of Commons and 675 hours in the Lords.[2] The number of amendments on the order paper in both Houses exceeded 5000. When other new legislation is added in, the number of pages needed for the various bills in the three Sessions following that of 1945–6 was twice the annual parliamentary output of the 1930s and a correspondingly heavy load was imposed on ministers and departments, already jaded by six years of war.[3]

The legislation attracted widespread attention abroad and coloured the reactions of financial markets in the various foreign exchange crises from 1947 onwards. Foreign commentators were only too ready to attribute

1 Chester (1975), p. 1002. It will be evident that this chapter is heavily indebted to Sir Norman Chester's authoritative study.
2 ibid., pp. 1004–6.
3 ibid., p. 26.

Britain's post-war difficulties to the socialization of a large tract of its economy.

Yet if one asks what nationalization contributed to economic recovery or to the resolution of the many urgent economic problems of the post-war years it is not easy to find a convincing answer. As a means of taking a grip of the economy it was essentially pre-Keynesian: it did little, if anything, to make the economy more stable and ensure full employment and it was not closely linked at any stage with the idea of economic planning. It did not purport to make any impact on the distribution of income since fair compensation was promised to the existing owners; and it was neither the most obvious way of trying to improve industrial efficiency nor seen in that light by the rank and file who were its strongest supporters. It was, however, a major upheaval, the full effects of which were difficult to foresee. Not that there had been much prior examination of the problems that nationalization was bound to create. As Mr Shinwell told the Co-operative Congress two years later, 'There was far too little detailed preparation in the formulation of schemes of nationalisation, and in consequence we found ourselves with legislation that had to be completed without the necessary blue prints.'[4]

The situation was not unlike that after the triumph of Communism in Russia. The government was quite clear on the issue of ownership but not at all clear about control. A succession of industries and services considered to be in some sense 'primary' or 'essential' were to be taken over and run by the state but beyond this, little had been settled: what differentiated these activities from others, how far various forms of control offered an acceptable alternative to nationalization, the basis on which compensation was to be paid, how the nationalized industries were to be managed, what ground rules were to be observed in relation to prices, wages and investment, what links between the nationalized activities or with the private sector were to be established or permitted, where the boundary was to be drawn eventually between public and private sectors – these and many other issues had still to be thrashed out.

Proposals for nationalization went back at least a century, the earliest candidates being the railways, land and coal-mines in that order. In 1918 the Labour Party, in Clause IV of a new constitution, called for 'the common ownership of the means of production, distribution and exchange'; and in the same year singled out coal, electric power, transport

4 ibid., p. 1008.

and communications as prime candidates for nationalization. In the inter-war years the list remained and was added to (or sometimes shortened): the Bank of England, the banking system, life insurance, water supply, the cotton industry and iron and steel were included at various stages. But in those days nationalization, even in the case of coal, was little more than a pious aspiration, never a carefully prepared plan of action.

When the Labour Party came into office in 1945 it was committed to taking the Bank of England into public ownership and nationalizing the railways, road transport and civil aviation; coal, gas and electricity; and iron and steel. It gave priority to the Bank of England, coal and civil aviation, including them in the King's Speech in August 1945. A government statement on the rest was made three months later. This put electricity supply and gas next in line. The railways, canals and long-distance road haulage were all to be nationalized and the best way of co-ordinating road passenger transport was to be the subject of further consideration. The most suitable form of public ownership for docks and harbours was under examination but shipping was not to be nationalized. As for the steel industry a decision was deferred until the government had received the development report which the industry was preparing. This report was submitted in December 1945 and in April the government announced that iron and steel would be added to the list of industries to be nationalized.

When the Cabinet returned to the matter a year later in April 1947 the choice for the 1947–8 legislative programme lay between steel and gas and if gas were given priority this might mean that it would be difficult to introduce the Iron and Steel Bill within the lifetime of the existing Parliament, especially if it were necessary to overrule a rejection of the Bill by the House of Lords through the use of the Parliament Act. The Cabinet therefore agreed that the Gas Bill should be deferred and the Steel Bill introduced in the 1947–8 Session. By August, however, the country was in a major balance-of-payments crisis, there was an acute shortage of steel and the government was appealing to the nation for an all-out effort of recovery. To some it seemed hardly the time to embark on controversial and divisive legislation which the managements of steel companies would find distracting and discouraging. A great battle ensued, the outcome of which was a decision to amend the Parliament Act at once so as to reduce the Lords' delaying powers, to proceed with the Gas Bill in 1947–8 and to defer the Steel Bill to 1948–9. The Steel Bill eventually received Royal Assent in November 1949, three months before the election of February 1950, while the vesting day was set for February 1951, after that election

*Table 18.1*  Nationalization measures

| Bill | Second reading | Vesting date | Numbers employed in 1951 (000s) | Compensation paid (£m.) |
|------|------|------|------|------|
| Bank of England | 29.10.45 | 1.3.46 | 6.7 | 58 |
| Coal Industry | 29. 1.46 | 1.1.47 | 765.0 | 392 |
| Civil Aviation | 6. 5.46 | 1.8.46 | 23.3 | —[a] |
| Cable and Wireless | 21. 5.46 | 1.1.47 | 9.5 | 32[b] |
| Transport | 16.12.46 | 1.1.48 | 888.0 | 1,150 |
| Electricity | 3. 2.47 | 1.4.48 | 178.9 | 542 |
| Gas | 10. 2.48 | 1.4.49 | 143.5 | 220 |
| Iron and Steel | 15.11.48 | 15.2.51 | 292.0 | 245 |
| | | | 2,306.9 | 2,639 |

*Source:* Chester (1975), pp. 38–9.

a  BOAC was already publicly owned and other companies were acquired by private negotiations. No provision for compensation was included in the Civil Aviation Bill.

b  Excluding £3 million for stock already held by the Treasury.

but, as it happened, not long before the election of October 1951 at which the Conservatives were returned to power.[5]

The legislation passed between 1946 and 1949 enlarged employment in the public sector by some 2 million workers. The nationalized under-takings had 2.3 million workers on their payroll in 1951 but some of these worked for bodies such as the London Passenger Transport Board, British Overseas Airways Corporation, or municipal gas and electricity under-takings which were already publicly owned.[6] These figures compare with a total in civil employment in 1951 of 22.75 million so that nearly one worker in ten was directly affected. Since the activities nationalized were more than usually capital-intensive the shift from private to public invest-ment was even larger. The nationalization programme, together with the government's involvement in the provision of housing, expanded public investment from a relatively small proportion of the total to a level com-parable with private investment, if somewhat less.

The emphasis put on nationalization by the Labour government reflected in the first instance political aims and pressures. Technical and

5  ibid., pp. 36–8.
6  ibid., p. 39.

economic considerations took second place. There were those who simply wanted to bring a larger proportion of economic activity under the direct control of the state; and there were influential groups of government supporters whose commitment to nationalization stretched back over many years. These groups included the trade unions in some (but not all) of the industries which it was proposed to nationalize. The miners and the railway workers, for example, would settle for nothing less because they assumed that nationalization would bring better pay and conditions while the iron and steel workers, in a more prosperous industry that enjoyed good industrial relations, had little interest in it. These contrasting attitudes had little to do with the merits of nationalization as such and exemplified the disposition to seek some magic cure in industries where demand contracted steadily leaving surplus capacity and rising unemployment. Nevertheless the unions representing the miners and the railway workers were in a strong position to press their views on the Labour Party. When the policy statement on nationalization was approved at the Party's Blackpool Conference in May 1945, the National Union of Mineworkers, the three railway unions and the Transport and General Workers Union, with 1,137,000 members between them, were in a position to cast nearly half the votes of the trade unions affiliated to the Party.[7]

Political support for nationalization rested heavily on antipathy to the existing economic system. This antipathy was primarily to reliance on the motive of private profit; but since the industries after nationalization were to be run on commercial lines it was not altogether clear what change there would be in the role of profit. There was antipathy also to leaving the future of important industries to be settled by market forces; this was linked with the hankering after a planned economy. But just as, in their approach to planning, Labour ministers tended to leave out the price mechanism, so in their approach to nationalization they tended to think purely of administrative control over productive units and leave out mechanisms such as competition for securing a prompt response to consumer requirements. Since what was uppermost in their minds was the idea of social control they welcomed the monopolistic powers that nationalization conferred on the industries concerned without questioning whether such powers were in the best interests of efficient production.

Not that there was ever any question of refraining from some form of public control over the industries that were ultimately nationalized. Three of these industries had been reported on before 1945 by committees of

7 Chester, op. cit., p. 14.

inquiry each of which had made recommendations for major changes in structure. In 1936 the McGowan Committee on Electricity Distribution had presented two alternative schemes of reorganization. The preferred schemes envisaged the absorption of smaller electricity undertakings by the larger and more efficient units while the alternative scheme proposed the setting-up of regional boards under public control to take over all the existing undertakings.[8] It was only the pressure of parliamentary business that prevented the pre-war government from giving effect to the first of these proposals. In any event by the end of the war 60 per cent of the electricity supply industry (taking employment as a yardstick) was already publicly owned and the local authorities had a statutory right to acquire most of the privately-owned companies, subject to payment of compensation, once their franchise expired.[9] The second of the committees, on the gas industry, was the Heyworth Committee which reported in 1945, shortly after the election. This recommended the kind of scheme for regional boards owning all the undertakings in their area which the McGowan Committee had rejected for electricity distribution. Here, too, much of the industry was publicly owned, local authorities accounting for 37 per cent of gas sales. In the case of the coal industry on which the Reid Committee reported in March 1945 the government had exercised full operational control during most of the war and in 1943 the Minister of Fuel and Power (a Liberal) had even proposed to resolve the problem of dual control by becoming the owner of the mines, and hence the employer of all who were engaged in the industry, for the duration of the wartime system of control. The Reid Committee, without expressing a view on public ownership, stressed the need for larger units of management in the interests of efficiency and recommended the establishment of an authority to ensure mergers into units of appropriate size.

Thus in each of these industries the state was already heavily involved, either directly or through local authority undertakings, and at the same time expert opinion was almost unanimously in favour of larger operational units. But none of the committees of inquiry over the previous decade had recommended units that were national in scale or had visualized nationalization on the pattern ultimately adopted, with a single authority owning the entire assets of the industry. Reorganization had been seen in terms of compulsory mergers with area or regional boards as the most obvious alternative to the enlargement of existing undertakings.

8 ibid., pp. 17–18.
9 ibid., pp. 16–17.

In the case of the Bank of England, Cable and Wireless and civil aviation the situation was rather different. The issue was not one of securing mergers but of taking over individual companies and transforming them into public corporations. Most central banks are publicly owned but some enjoy more autonomy than others: nationalization did not by itself determine the relationship between the Bank of England and the Treasury. The nationalization of Cable and Wireless, Ltd did no more than give effect to a wartime agreement between Commonwealth governments to establish a public utility corporation in each country, owned by the government of that country, and linked with the United Kingdom corporation in the operation of a telecommunications service. The two air transport corporations, BOAC and BEA, that were created under the Civil Aviation Bill, had been envisaged in the Coalition government's White Paper of March 1945; and since it was a Conservative government that nationalized the two pre-war airline companies to form BOAC in 1939 it is unlikely that, had the Conservatives been in power in 1946, they would have done anything very different.[10]

Nationalization of the railways was also not very controversial. After the First World War the 119 railway companies had been amalgamated by the Railways Act, 1921, into four main-line companies and unification of these companies in one way or another had been viewed sympathetically by the Royal Commission on Transport in its Final Report issued ten years later. Throughout the Second World War and after, the main-line railways were operated under government direction and in the latter part of the war the government was also controlling most of the canal companies and the main road-haulage firms. Road passenger transport was largely in the hands of local authorities and other public bodies, including the London Passenger Transport Board; and all bus and coach services had to be licensed by Area Traffic Commissioners who had power to specify frequency of services, fares, etc. Road-haulage undertakings, which were private except where local authorities operated their own vehicles, were subject to a rather less rigorous system of licensing by Area Licensing Authorities. Thus in the case of the railways there was a general expectation of nationalization and in the case of road transport services there

---

10 ibid., p. 19. The White Paper, however, had proposed two new airways corporations additional to BOAC, one for internal and one for South American routes, with a financial stake in both for railway, shipping and travel agency interests (ibid., pp. 104–5).

was already some state control through a licensing system and some public operation of passenger services through local authority undertakings.[11]

This leaves iron and steel, where controversy was acute. After 1931 the industry had enjoyed extensive protection, the continuation of which was made conditional on reorganization. This was co-ordinated by the British Iron and Steel Federation, formed in 1934 by the various trade associations and given wide powers by them. During the war the staff of the Federation was absorbed into the Iron and Steel Control which ran the industry under directions from the Ministry of Supply. At the end of the war the Federation prepared a five-year programme of development at the request of the Coalition government, on the assumption that if the programme was acceptable to the government and was not dependent on government finance the industry would be allowed to proceed under such public supervision as was necessary.[12] When the government announced its intention to nationalize the industry the Federation expressed its readiness to submit to whatever improvements in the pre-war machinery of supervision were thought necessary. In August 1946 the Cabinet approved a proposal to control the industry by acquiring a controlling interest in the equity of the various companies. The minister concerned (John Wilmot) told the Federation that it might be enough to base government policy not on nationalization but on financial participation in the steel companies or on a combination of this with the interim Control Board that had been set up in replacement of wartime arrangements. A partnership along these lines was considered by an official Working Party and rejected in favour of compulsory acquisition of the entire capital of the companies.[13] In later negotiations with the government, the Federation outlined a scheme which would have given statutory powers (including powers of direction) to the Control Board and the right to insist on financial participation in iron and steel companies if necessary or even to acquire them compulsorily. From start to finish the issue was never whether there should be public control of the industry but was essentially whether any realistic and effective scheme of control could be devised that fell short of outright nationalization. The conclusion to which the government was driven was that it was very difficult to reconcile thoroughgoing public control with private ownership or to find a half-way house that made provision for private participation or left some part of the industry in private hands.

11  ibid., pp. 12–14.
12  Chester, op. cit., p. 159.
13  ibid., pp. 163–5.

Apart from the idea of public control and the technical and economic advantages expected from larger units, another factor that weighed heavily in the argument for nationalization was the large capital investment that seemed likely to be required for the reconstruction of the industries concerned. It was taken for granted that those industries would have great difficulty in raising funds on the scale necessary in order to make good the very large arrears of maintenance and obsolescence that had accumulated, first in the years of depression before the war and then in the course of the war itself. Ministers expressed themselves at times as inheritors of 'a poor bag of assets' – although this was more a defence against criticism when output was disappointing than a considered assessment.

In coal-mining and rail transport where the long-term prospects did not seem particularly bright there were good grounds for doubting whether private owners would have made the large investment that the government judged to be necessary. Equally there were grounds for doubting whether the government needed to provide quite so much new capital since both industries had begun to contract again before the full effect of post-war investment had had time to make itself felt. Other industries in private hands like petroleum and chemicals raised and invested very large sums without state participation but their long-term prospects were very different.

Irrespective of the availability of the necessary funds, Dalton at least would have claimed that the state could provide them more cheaply. When the first nationalization measures were prepared, the government was borrowing on long term at $2\frac{1}{2}$ per cent per annum and even in 1951 the rate on government bonds was just over $3\frac{1}{2}$ per cent. No private borrower could raise capital on such terms. The government's credit being much better than that of business corporations it could take over assets from the private sector on terms that were highly favourable to itself but not unfair to the vendors or to those who lent the money required if payment was made in cash rather than in stock.

From another point of view the large capital requirements of the nationalized industries were seen as affording an opportunity to the government of reducing the inherent instability of the economic system. Capital investment was notoriously unstable but the more of it that fell within the public sector, the easier it would be, so it was argued, to offset fluctuations in the private sector by making provision for opposite fluctuations in public investment. Subsequent experience cast doubt on this attractive hypothesis. Efforts to change the investment programmes of the nationalized industries so as to reduce the amplitude of fluctuations in economic activity very often merely intensified them. By the time the programmes were modified and put into effect the economy had generally moved from a phase of contraction to one of expansion.

Another advantage seen in nationalization was co-ordination: co-ordination, for example, of transport facilities between road and rail and of fuel and power through public control over coal, gas and electricity. The belief in co-ordination was identical with the belief in planning and was equally oblivious of the role of the price mechanism. Labour ministers like Herbert Morrison were horrified when it was put to them by the Economic Section that road and rail would be automatically co-ordinated if each followed an appropriate pricing policy: the consumer could then choose what suited him best on the basis of a price in keeping with the social cost of the resources utilized. There was no such juxtaposition of the ideas of co-ordination and opportunity cost in the ministerial mind: co-ordination was more a device for slowing down the contraction of traditional services like the railways and requiring consumers to make fuller use of underutilized resources irrespective of cost. In the case of fuel and power it was hard to make out what co-ordination implied in practice especially under conditions in which there was a chronic shortage of coal, gas and electricity and the chief contribution to overcoming the shortage came from the development, outside the public sector and indeed outside the United Kingdom, of petroleum supplies.

## Nationalization issues

### Scope

We turn next to the problems that were encountered in the nationalizing process. First there was the difficulty of defining an industry. In any collection of undertakings there are inevitably differences in the range of activities in which they engage. If nationalization involved taking over the entire assets of the undertakings these would inevitably be found to overstep the limits of the industry as popularly conceived. The coal industry, for example, was made up of about 800 companies ranging from those that owned a single pit to those that were engaged in a variety of industries such as iron and steel, shipping, brickmaking, etc. It was necessary to decide where to draw the line by delimiting either the list of firms to be acquired or the types of assets necessary to the proper functioning of the coal industry. This difficulty was most acute in the case of iron and steel where there was no generally accepted definition of the industry and the practical choice was between taking over the largest producers, six of which accounted for half the output and thirteen for three-quarters of it, or aiming at a comprehensive take-over of all firms engaged in steel production.[14] Even this was not an entirely unambiguous prescription since steelmaking processes shaded into engineering and the making of special steels was a different operation from that of common grade steel.

Except in the case of coal the government opted for the acquisition of whole undertakings, whatever the range of their ancillary activities. The colliery companies remained in existence as private concerns but surrendered on vesting day managerial responsibility for the assets designated in the Act and those opted for by the National Coal Board. This procedure was facilitated by the special circumstance that there had existed since 1921 a definition of the industry for the purposes of what were known as the TS (Terms of Settlement) returns, used in the apportionment of the net proceeds of the industry between owners and miners.[15] These returns formed the basis on which compensation was fixed for TS assets, which were acquired as the core of the nationalized industry. But among the ancillary assets were some, such as coke-ovens, that were adjuncts of the colliery undertaking and not easily separated from it and others, such as miners' cottages, that it would be useful to retain. There were lengthy discussions with the Mining Association (representing the coal-owners) as to which ancillary assets should be taken over either automatically or at the option of the National Coal Board or by agreement. By the time the Bill was drafted the catalogue of such assets had grown steadily longer and more complex. In the end the Bill made no use of the distinction between TS and other assets, listing in a First Schedule the various assets to be transferred compulsorily or at the option of the Board or of the owners.[16]

On vesting day the National Coal Board acquired, along with the coalmines, coking plants, briquetting and manufactured fuel plants, brickworks, housing estates and farms. It was the producer of two-fifths of the

14 Chester, op. cit., p. 1010.
15 ibid., p. 93.
16 For a full discussion see Chester, op. cit., pp. 91–104. 'Some idea of the amount of detail involved in applying the vesting to the circumstances of each colliery company and relating the lists of assets to the compensation provisions may be gained from the fact that the Regulations which prescribed the information that had to be provided were 110 pages long.' (ibid., p. 100.) The valuation of ancillary assets was correspondingly elaborate: 'the average inventory was 100 foolscap sheets and the longest was 250,000 and . . . these all had to be checked by the technical staff who were engaged in running the mines.' (ibid., p. 252.)

output of metallurgical coke, 8 per cent of all town gas, a substantial proportion of various chemical products such as benzole and sulphate of ammonia, and a manufacturer of proprietary articles such as liquid water-proofers and rust-resisting paint.[17]

The problems created by the need to specify the precise assets to be nationalized strengthened the case for acquiring entire undertakings. In some cases, such as the taking-over of the Bank of England, there was really no alternative. Similarly, it was the obvious course in the nationaliz-ation of the railways, where only the four main-line companies were involved. The electricity and gas companies were relatively easy to identify and there was little overlap with other activities. These companies, like the railway companies, lost their identity on nationalization and a new managerial structure had to be created under the boards to which the whole of their assets was transferred. In the case of gas and electricity the transfer was on vesting day, while the railway and canal companies continued formally for one more year. In the case of the coal industry the continued existence of the company structure after vesting day, in private hands but without managerial responsibility for the assets transferred to the Coal Board, was of some help to the Board in the early stages of assum-ing its responsibilities. In the case of iron and steel the companies taken over remained in existence, the Corporation becoming the sole share-holder and owner with no need to prepare a new managerial structure.[18]

So far as the government had any choice – iron and steel being the prime example – it aimed at a clean sweep. As Sir Norman Chester comments:

> Deep down [this] conformed with the long-standing belief in the Labour Movement that nationalisation was an all or nothing process. Whilst one steel producer remained in private ownership it could not be claimed that 'the industry' had been transferred to public ownership. Basic to that conception was the belief that decisions in respect of any industry could only be taken from some central point. Nationalisation was based on a denial that a number of competing producers could, even with some central guidance, make decisions individually, which would result in greater efficiency of the industry as a whole than if such decisions were made by a single central body.[19]

17  ibid., p. 103. The ancillary assets acquired by the Board were valued for compen-sation at £91 million compared with £165 million for coal industry assets.
18  Chester, op. cit., p. 1011.
19  ibid., p. 1010.

Yet since there never is nor can be such a thing as absolute monopoly, competition could not be entirely suppressed but continued from outside the industry without being allowed to mould industrial structure as in a world of free competition. The structure adopted, moreover, had to take shape almost instantaneously rather than by successive acquisitions, as happens in private industry. The method used, of taking over entire companies, was bound also to carry the nationalized undertakings into activities not obviously germane to the purpose of nationalization and perpetuate in those activities the competition so assiduously avoided in the main industry.

To sum up, nationalization was embarked upon with the aim of creating 'a series of neatly defined, publicly owned industries'[20] engaged in a single activity and ended up with the reorganization, under a single national management, of the heterogeneous activities of an agglomeration of undertakings, widely different in size and scope. It was necessary to reconcile what the Labour Movement wanted in all innocence and what Parliament would approve in its wisdom with what company law had brought into existence. Whereas company law spawns commercial organizations with broad objects that are relatively easy to change, Parliament tends to insist on strict, immutable definitions of functions and powers and the Labour Movement tends to call for the nationalization of this or that 'industry' without regard to difficulties of definition.[21] 'The idea that a nationalised iron and steel industry should be able also to become bankers, brewers, builders, etc., was quite foreign to the thinking of most of those who advocated nationalisation.'[22] The end-result was not due to some fresh insight into the logic of industrial organization but to the need for simplicity in legislation, the convenience of a take-over bid for stocks and shares and the advantage of using stock exchange values as a basis for compensation.

### Organization

Nationalization nearly always involved the supersession of a large number of undertakings either by a single giant, nationwide corporation like the National Coal Board or by a small group of linked undertakings like the area boards in gas and electricity. The extreme case was road haulage

20 ibid., p. 1012.
21 ibid., p. 1013.
22 ibid., p. 1013.

where there were 3766 independent management units before nationalization reduced them to 1; in gas and electricity there were 1000 and 560
respectively; and in coal, 800. Some of these units, however, were sub-
sidiaries of large holding companies, especially in gas and electricity. The
largest coal company employed about 40,000 workers and the largest gas
company more than 20,000. To devise an organizational structure for an
undertaking seven times as large in the case of gas, and twenty times as
large in the case of coal, and to bring within that structure the enormous
number of smaller units in each industry was no mean task. Even the
GPO, the largest comparable undertaking run by the government,
employed only some 250,000 workers.[23]

In view of the difficulty of managing any large organization efficiently
and the still greater difficulty of doing so under government auspices, it is
natural to ask whether so large a change in scale was really necessary. The
answer is essentially that while private enterprise is normally a powerful
decentralizing agent, public ownership makes equally powerfully for
centralization. Having taken over an industry, governments are reluctant
to offer genuine autonomy to the constituent parts, to allow them to
compete with one another, charge different prices, pay different rates of
wages and follow inconsistent practices of any kind. If capital has to be
raised, it is easier for the Treasury to make a single issue of stock for the
whole industry and to treat it as a single financial unit that will set any
losses on some activities against the profits on others instead of coming to
the Exchequer to have the losses made good. If wages have to be fixed, the
trade unions are just as insistent on national negotiating machinery that
allows a central authority to fix wages at a uniform, national level instead
of leaving them to vary from one locality to another. Ministers also
showed a disposition towards uniform prices, irrespective of local circumstances, in an industry like electricity. The term 'nationalization' itself
seemed to imply a single national authority. For that reason Morrison
insisted that Shinwell's proposals for area boards in electricity generation
and supply was not nationalization at all but regionalization and on these
grounds opposed, and came close to defeating, the scheme for fifteen
management units rather than one.[24]

Gaitskell, who was very much alive to the drawbacks of large-scale
organization combined with public accountability, pointed out that
people talked a lot about decentralization but rarely appreciated how

23 ibid., p. 1026.
24 ibid., p. 1027.

difficult it was to make this compatible with the underlying objectives of nationalization and with control by ministers and Parliament over the boards. But nationalization need not have spelt an end to competition, or required uniformity of prices and wages, so long as Parliament was willing to allow diversity and, if necessary, inconsistency of practice between one unit and another. In the largest companies in the private sector it is not unknown for different constituent undertakings to compete freely with one another as do, for example, the subsidiary companies within the General Motors Corporation. In Britain the nationalized industries have never been encouraged to follow such practices. More than most countries, Britain has long made a fetish of consistency, largely on grounds of fairness; and it is this that has made not only for the high degree of centralization of control but also for the greater difficulty of finding a basis for co-operation between public and private enterprise.

Decentralization would have involved much more than a different managerial hierarchy. When it was proposed in 1948 that the main management unit in the coal-mining industry should be the district rather than the division because the division was too large, Gaitskell asked how independent the proposed district units would be: would they own their own assets like the electricity and gas boards and would they be expected to pay their way? If so, prices in some areas would have to rise substantially or pits would have to close.[25] This, so far from being an objection to decentralization, might seem to demonstrate the need for it; but it served in 1948 and for long afterwards to perpetuate the existing structure with its cross-subsidization and over-centralized control.

One further reason for preserving units on a national scale was the desire to leave to the industry the co-ordinating and supervisory functions that might otherwise have rested with a minister and his department. This meant a high degree of industrial self-government not easily reconciled with public control. The boards were entrusted with the functions of operation and management without departmental supervision and without even review (e.g. of their pricing policy) by a non-departmental body such as the pre-war Electricity Commissioners. No doubt the supervisory function was best exercised at the national level but it was not obvious that it could be satisfactorily combined with executive control by the same agency. A division between the two functions that left co-ordination and

25 ibid., p. 1032.

supervision to the department concerned would have made it easier to devise smaller-scale units of management.[26]

## Efficiency and public accountability

It would have been possible after nationalization to appoint a management – perhaps even reappoint the same management – and leave it to run the industry. Something like that happened in other countries.[27] But there were questions to be answered in Parliament about what had become a large sector of the economy and the ministers responsible as well as members of Parliament wished to satisfy themselves that the industries were being run efficiently and responsibly. The very fact that nationaliz-ation had been very much a party matter made the success or failure of any of the boards of immediate political interest. Apart from that, it was simply not possible to be indifferent to the affairs of major industries on which the future of the country was closely dependent.

There were two main proposals for establishing public accountability. One was that of Hugh Molson in 1948 for a Select Committee which would periodically prepare a report for the House on the basis of oral and written evidence, focus and elucidate the main issues and prepare the way for a full and free debate every two or three years on each of the national-ized industries. Such a report, and the debate following it, should avoid detailed interference and concentrate on matters of strategy and efficiency in obtaining the best results from the nation's investment. There should be no attempt to make party capital out of the review since the govern-ment of the day would feel obliged to range itself with whatever board was under attack from the opposition without much regard to the merits of the criticism.[28]

An alternative proposal was that of Morrison for an efficiency audit. In July 1947 he had suggested taking stock of relations between the socialized industries and the government and a progress report had been prepared by the Ministerial Committee on the Socialization of Industry over the winter of 1947–8.[29] Much of the time of the Committee was spent in discussing how to make sure that the boards would use the most up-to-

26  ibid., p. 1028; Clegg and Chester (1953), pp. 141–7.
27  For example, iron-ore mining in Sweden was run by the same management after nationalization without much government interference or talk of public accounta-bility.
28  Chester (1975), pp. 956–7.
29  SI(M)(48)19 in PRO CAB 134/689.

date methods for checking on their own efficiency and how, if Parliament wished to satisfy itself as to their efficiency, this wish could be met.[30] What Morrison proposed was a body of experts within an efficiency unit common to the various industries, financed and appointed by the boards, and including one or two industrial consultants, who would advise the boards on organizational issues, keeping these issues under continuous review, and issuing annual reports on the model of the relationship between the Comptroller and Auditor-General and Parliament.

This proposal encountered criticism from other ministers and from the chairmen of the nationalized industries. It was argued that the unit would undermine the position of the minister and the sense of responsibility of the board themselves. The chairmen were sceptical of the ability of outsiders to grasp the real problems of such enormous undertakings and pay full regard to the personal factors involved. They foresaw the publicity attending the operations of the proposed unit, and the pressure to make its reports available to ministers and perhaps also to Parliament and the general public, with damaging effects on the responsibility of the boards. When the Lord President, claiming that he had been misunderstood, tried again, the chairmen remained firmly opposed to the idea of an efficiency unit.

Morrison reminded them that Parliament had so far refrained from pressing for opportunities of discussing the affairs of the nationalized industries but would not be likely to persist in this attitude without satisfying itself that there were adequate methods of ensuring the efficiency of those industries. If Molson's proposal were adopted, the boards would be exposed to close parliamentary supervision and the minister would be bound to take just as close an interest in the details of management. Other ministers, however, doubted whether a common efficiency unit reporting to the boards would be regarded by Parliament as an adequate substitute for a body reporting directly to it. Securing efficiency and satisfying Parliament were two rather different things.

When the matter was once again discussed in February 1949 with the board chairmen, all of them saw serious practical objections to the proposal. Lord Hurcomb, chairman of the British Transport Commission, pointed out that there was very little in common between the different nationalized industries so that it might be better for each of them to call in consultants who were experts in their specific problems. So far as

30 The Committee thought it a debatable point whether the minister was answerable in law for the general efficiency of a board. (Chester, op. cit., p. 960n.).

Parliament was concerned, debates might be organized on the board's annual report, which should seek to satisfy Parliament's legitimate desire for full information on the conduct of the industry.[31] Lord Citrine, chairman of the British Electricity Authority, thought that the proposal reflected on the board's competence and would distract it from more urgent problems. Morrison stuck to his guns. All big concerns had common problems of organization: it was this that had given rise to industrial consultancy. There was nothing incompatible between a small efficiency unit and the use of outside consultants. The chairmen agreed to give the matter further thought but did not meet ministers again to present their views until the end of June 1950.

In the meantime ministers themselves continued to differ on Morrison's proposal. In November 1949 Cripps drew a distinction between administrative efficiency and technical and operational efficiency. In his view it was the former only that interested Parliament and the public and should be reported upon by a common unit; technical issues were better dealt with by calling in outside experts *ad hoc*. Gaitskell doubted whether the appointment of a common unit would satisfy Parliament. The problems common to the boards related to high-level questions of management, were limited in number, and were best left to the boards to settle themselves.[32] There was a stronger case for a parliamentary inquiry every five or ten years on the model of the BBC.

At this stage discussion within the government opened up on rather different issues, centring on the public relations of the boards and the ways in which parliamentary questions and discussion might be used to meet criticism of the boards or to provide explanations and justifications of their activities. An official Committee reporting on this subject emphasized that ministers 'should present themselves as spokesmen for consumers at least as much as for the Boards' and that they should take the opportunity to remind Parliament 'that the Government, representing the community, regard them [i.e. the boards] as servants of the community rather than as chosen instruments of the executive power'.[33]

31  Lord Hurcomb's suggestion was adopted in November 1949 when the annual report of the Coal Board for 1948 was debated. In 1950 the government made time available for one-day debates on the annual reports of the National Coal Board, the British Transport Commission and the Electricity Authorities.
32  Chester, op. cit., p. 967.
33  SI(M)(50)3rd meeting in PRO CAB 134/691, quoted by Chester, op. cit., p. 968.

When the election took place in February 1950 the proposal for an efficiency unit was still in play but the whole issue of accountability had never come before the Cabinet. It was only in March 1950 that a proposal to raise railway freight charges on the basis of a recommendation from the Transport Tribunal caused the matter to be raised in Cabinet. Ministers then expressed concern that they had had no earlier opportunity of expressing their views, however informally, on proposals that might have political repercussions. If the government was held accountable by Parliament and the electorate for the standard of efficiency of the transport system, was the board right to regard a reference of the proposal to the Transport Tribunal (which might then make embarrassing recommendations) as 'a matter of day-to-day administration' and consequently falling within their jurisdiction?

The irritation of ministers gave the Lord President a chance to relaunch his proposal which he now brought before the Cabinet at the end of March in a 'Memorandum by the Lord President'.[34] In this Morrison pointed to 'a good deal of disillusionment even among supporters' of nationalization – as had been apparent at the recent election – and set out nine different ways in which ministers might help to improve efficiency. He put it to the Cabinet that in default of satisfactory proposals from the board chairmen for checking efficiency within their organizations, the government would make whatever arrangement it thought best. He proposed also that the principle of periodic inquiries by outside committees should be accepted and that Parliament should have greater opportunities for the discussion of the nationalized industries. Opinion in the Cabinet, however, was very much divided with some ministers regarding external checks as premature and others wanting to go all the way to full departmental control. The Prime Minister summed up negatively on all the main suggestions.

After a second Cabinet discussion in April in which Morrison made more headway he suggested five possibilities for discussion with board chairmen, three of them for a common efficiency unit responsible to the boards, to ministers or to some semi-independent body, and two envisaging a Select Committee with a staff of House of Commons Clerks or with the addition of a kind of Auditor-General with appropriate industrial qualifications. Although Morrison wished to avoid the last two of these suggestions, it was agreed to put all five to the chairmen.

34 CP(50)60, 31 March 1950, in PRO CAB 129/39.

There followed an exchange of letters between Gaitskell (now Minister of Economic Affairs) and Morrison in which Gaitskell reiterated the objections to 'some superior body continually investigating the boards' and making it look to Parliament, the public and the boards themselves as if the government did not really trust them.[35] Since a unit appointed by the boards would not be regarded as impartial, the minister would be driven to appoint a body of so-called impartial outsiders; and there would then arise the dilemma of publishing what might include damaging criticisms or refusing to publish and being accused of hiding something. If ministers appointed to the boards the best people they could find how could they subsequently find better people to give lessons in raising efficiency? Periodic inquiries, more debates and better public relations would be a more acceptable way of establishing accountability.

Much of this, as Morrison pointed out, was rather far-fetched. Consultancy and management are two very different things and even the most efficient firms find it useful to employ consultants. Any group of men in charge of a large-scale monopoly need the stimulus of outside criticism and are in danger of neglecting the interests of consumers, failing to keep in touch with public opinion and new developments and holding back from unpleasant decisions. It might be difficult to combine the roles of watchdog to reassure Parliament and friendly critic providing advice to the boards. But some way had to be found of serving both purposes.[36]

When ministers met the chairmen of the boards at two further meetings in June and July they found them still strongly against a common advisory service, particularly at so early a stage in their experience of nationalization. The chairmen doubted whether they would be left free to decide what use to make of such a service which would be under pressure from Parliament and increasingly responsible to the government as well as the boards. They were also sceptical about finding management consultants of the necessary calibre and in the number required for an effective service. They accepted the need for periodic inquiries into questions of broad policy and structure at intervals of not less than seven years, but saw serious objections to the proposal for a Select Committee, less on the grounds of inconvenience to the boards than of the damage to ministerial responsibility. Some of the chairmen said that if the choice lay between a Select Committee and a common advisory service they would prefer the former.

35  Chester, op. cit., p. 976.
36  Chester, op. cit., pp. 976–7.

The Lord President in due course reported to the Cabinet that while there had been substantial agreement with the chairmen on everything else, there had been no agreement on a common advisory service. The proposal should therefore not be pursued for the time being. In the forthcoming debate in the House of Commons (on 25 October) he would announce, if the Cabinet approved, the intention to hold periodic inquiries. The Cabinet did approve and that, so far as the Labour government was concerned, was the end of the matter. In October 1951, as soon as they took office, the Conservative government decided to appoint a Select Committee 'to consider the present methods by which the House of Commons is informed on the affairs of the nationalised industries . . .' and two years later the Select Committee on Nationalized Industries that had originally been proposed by Mr Hugh Molson came into existence.

There were a number of reasons why this expedient was adopted rather than the Lord President's proposal for a common advisory service. One was the acceptance that a vast extension of the public sector had come to stay (iron and steel and road haulage apart) and that there was scope for bipartite investigation of the affairs of the socialized industries, in an atmosphere relatively free from party controversy. Members were ready to accord the boards substantial managerial freedom without entering into matters of day-to-day administration. But they needed some opportunity of hearing not only from ministers but from the boards themselves an explanation of their affairs. Given the extensive contacts between departments and the boards, they also needed to inform themselves on the relations between the two, especially as departmental influence was not limited to what was prescribed by statute.

On the other hand, no efficiency unit would have found it possible to encompass the full range of issues for which ministers were accountable, or all the forms of efficiency expected of the boards. A large expert body constantly investigating the affairs of the nationalized industries was not easily reconciled with the managerial independence of these industries on which Morrison himself insisted. If it was appointed by the boards, reported privately to them and was responsible to them alone it could not have satisfied the Parliamentary quest for accountability.

From the point of view of the boards themselves, a Select Committee had considerable advantages. It offered them a forum in which to explain their policies and answer criticisms. They were expected to conform to the wishes of ministers and their departments without being free to require publicity for such intervention or make public their criticisms of it. A Select Committee could allow them to bring such intervention into the open. They could state their case direct to Members of Parliament. As Lord Hurcomb said in March 1953,

> a large number of Members of Parliament would have an opportunity of satisfying themselves and conveying, not by way of attack and public speech, but by way of suggestion to the organisation, the points where they thought something might be going wrong, or, at any rate, would be worth looking into.[37]

## Relations with ministers

The more the industry was left to run itself, the less the responsibility of the minister for its affairs. In what sense then was it answerable to public control? In what way was the minister to bring to bear on the management those considerations of public policy that private enterprise was thought to neglect?

On the one hand, it was necessary in the interests of efficient management to leave as much latitude as possible to those who had been appointed to do the job. The minister could not be for ever intervening. But, equally, if nationalization had wider aims than the creation of larger, more stable, and more efficient units, the boards would need guidance in interpreting and pursuing those aims. The two things were reconciled in the nationalization legislation by a formula made up of two elements. The first required the boards to conduct their affairs on sound commercial principles with a view to securing that 'their revenues [were] not less than sufficient to meet their outgoings properly chargeable to revenue account, taking one year with another'. The second empowered the minister to issue 'directions of a general character as to the exercise and performance . . . of their functions in relation to matters [affecting] the national interest'. Thus the industries had to pay their way and would be kept in tune with the government's social and economic policy by the issue of ministerial directions.[38]

Neither of these elements was very explicit. As we shall see, pricing and investment policy was not satisfactorily encapsulated in the first part of the formula, especially when there was no indication as to how many years had to be taken one with another. As for general directions, it was soon realized that these were a very unsatisfactory device for conveying ministerial wishes to the board of a nationalized industry and not a single

37 Chester, op. cit., pp. 1048–9.
38 ibid., p. 1035.

general direction was ever issued by the Labour government. Although on rare occasions after 1951 directions were employed, it is now many years since any British government has made use of them. The Ministerial Committee dealing with nationalization accepted in March 1948 that

> General directions should only be used in exceptional circumstances. Their usual purpose may in fact be to give a board formal cover for some activity which it is undertaking in the national interest. It would never be possible to control a recalcitrant board by issuing a stream of general directions.[39]

There were a number of difficulties about relying on general directions. First of all, they smacked of confrontation and a breakdown in the harmonious relations that ought normally to obtain between the board of a nationalized industry and the minister responsible. If the minister was asking the board to conform to a stated government policy or had clear, defensible reasons for what he proposed, it would usually be possible to persuade the board to comply although on occasion it might wish first to establish that the minister felt sufficiently strongly to be prepared, if necessary, to issue a direction. A second drawback lay in the publicity attending the issue of a direction, particularly if it appeared to override the considered views of an expert body appointed by the minister to run the industry. From the minister's point of view it was much more satisfactory to exercise his influence in private and at the same time be able to disclaim responsibility in Parliament for the board's decision.[40] A third consideration was that the power to issue directions tended to be represented by the government's legal advisers as disconcertingly narrow. For example, the statutory responsibility of the boards to conduct their affairs so as to be able to pay their way took precedence over a general direction (e.g. as to price) that conflicted (or might appear to conflict) with that responsibility. The Attorney-General went so far in 1949 as to advise the government that

> The policy of the nationalisation Acts does not seem to have been expressed in such a way as to enable the nationalised industries to be used as instruments for promoting economic results outside their own economic field.[41]

39 Quoted by Chester, op cit., p. 1036.
40 ibid., p. 1037.
41 ibid., p. 1038.

Such advice raises the key question how far nationalization assisted the government's efforts to plan the economy or (to use less ambiguous language) to deal effectively with the many complex economic problems with which it was faced. Before we turn to this question we may review how ministers, in response to enquiries by the Lord President in April 1949, regarded their relations with the industries for which they were responsible.[42]

The Minister of Transport took the view that the Transport Act entrusted to the Transport Commission, and not to the minister or the government, the right and duty to decide how it should discharge its statutory responsibility to provide 'efficient, adequate, inland transport and port facilities within Great Britain'. The purpose of the Act was primarily to bring the transport services into a single, coherent organiz-ation and how it set about that task was a matter for the Commission subject to very general ministerial powers best exercised through consul-tation rather than compulsion. Other ministers were more concerned that the boards might seek to preserve too great a degree of independence of the government and resist its efforts to use the nationalized industries as instruments of economic planning.

The Minister of Supply, who had still to see his Bill to nationalize the iron and steel industry through its final stages, distinguished between those matters where the boards should be encouraged to exercise their own commercial judgement in deciding how to meet consumer needs and those where the government should make clear its determination to assert its influence, if necessary by direction. In the latter group he included control of capital investment and development, policy in relation to prices (but not wages and conditions), and the siting of new or the abandonment of old works. These were issues on which a board alive to its wider responsibilities should not decide exclusively on the basis of profit or loss and he hoped therefore that agreement would normally be reached with-out resort to direction. But in the event of disagreement there should be no hesitation in issuing a direction and, if a substantial loss was thereby imposed on the industry, the government should have power to offer a subsidy under proper safeguards.

The Minister of Civil Aviation differed in thinking that considerations

42 For a useful summary and commentary see Chester, op. cit., pp. 966–99. The questionnaire issued by the Lord President also asked more specific questions about efficiency and public accountability; pricing policy; control of investment; training, education and research; and social questions.

of public policy were for ministers to pronounce upon while boards should confine themselves to considerations of commercial and financial advantage like any good employers in the private sector. The board should enjoy the minister's full confidence in its commercial ability and in coming to a decision should normally be left to marry the two sets of considerations after consultation with the minister. In the last resort the minister's will should prevail. The kinds of issue on which it had been most necessary to intervene were the 'fly-British' policy governing the purchase of aircraft and the continued operation of uneconomic routes, mainly internal.

The Minister of Fuel and Power thought that, rightly or wrongly, Parliament treated him as responsible for the success or failure of the boards appointed by his department. How that responsibility was to be exercised had, however, been left vague in the nationalization Acts. Each nationalized industry built up a staff of engineers, accountants and other experts who ought to be the most competent, and were bound to become the most knowledgeable, in dealing with the affairs of the industry. There could be no question – indeed no possibility – of duplicating such a staff or of employing in the department others of lesser standing to pass judgement on the decisions of the boards that required such expert advice. Nor could the minister summon the staff of a board and seek to arbitrate between conflicting views without usurping the role of the Board Chairman. It would in any event be wrong to weaken the board's sense of responsibility by continually trying to teach them how to do their own job better. Interference in matters on which the boards should be competent to make up their own minds would produce either frustration or excessive dependence and would end by making it increasingly difficult to attract to the management of the industries men of the necessary calibre. Decentralization 'should begin at the top'.

While some of these considerations had been strangely neglected in the literature on nationalization, the difficulty of exercising control over any organization from without is a matter of everyday experience and the aggravation of the difficulty by obstacles to the flow of expert knowledge from the controlled to the controllers was frequently remarked on in wartime. The question remains, however, how control can be exercised without *some* understanding of the more technical and commercial aspects on the part of the minister and *some* understanding of the broader economic and social aspects on the part of the board. Some element of duplication is virtually unavoidable. How, for example, could the Treasury exercise control over monetary policy if it had no access within the department to expert knowledge of financial operations and if the

Bank of England had no staff familiar with the kinds of consideration likely to be urged by a determined Chancellor?

In the light of after events it is interesting to find as illustrations of what must be left to a board because of its superior knowledge decisions as to which mines should be developed (or, presumably, closed), the form of generating stations (although this was before the days of nuclear power), and the system of gas distribution (again before there was any talk of North Sea gas or of a grid to gather supplies from different sources).

Gaitskell's submission dealt also with the situations in which he thought that ministers would be justified in intervening. He gave three examples. The National Coal Board had sought to enter into an agreement with coal merchants to establish a fixed wholesale margin on the basis that the Board would cut off supplies from wholesalers selling below the agreed profit margin. Gaitskell told the Board that he could not countenance such a restrictive practice but had not needed to issue a directive to enforce his view. Similarly he had persuaded the Coal Board, against its wishes, to increase exports of anthracite to Canada at a price lower than that in European markets so as to make a contribution to dollar earnings. He had also insisted on the introduction in the autumn of 1948 on a differential tariff for electricity between winter and summer, the aim of this being to discourage consumption in the peak months. Apart from these instances of personal intervention by the Minister in support of some general consideration of policy, there was continual contact at the official level on less important matters either in response to an approach by one of the boards or in order to offer advice on matters affecting the national interest.[43] The Minister also felt free to discuss privately with the Chairman of the Coal Board, almost every week, a wide range of problems falling wholly within the Board's responsibility and he had informal but less frequent contacts with the chairmen of the Electricity Authority and the Gas Council.

It is hardly surprising that there should have been confusion and uncertainty in those years over the relations between ministers and the nationalized industries. It is not as if the confusion and uncertainty have disappeared forty years later. There were no precedents to which the government could turn for the management of such a large slice of

43  SI(M)(49)33 in PRO CAB 134/690 quoted by Chester, op. cit., p. 1043. Gaitskell went on: 'there has, of course, to be consultation and there is sometimes considerable discussion, but generally speaking we manage without undue difficulty on the smaller issues to persuade the Boards to do what we think desirable.'

industry in a mixed economy. The public corporations of pre-war years were too small, too far removed in political climate, too different in structure, to provide useful guidance. The government was faced with new and formidable economic problems in a rapidly changing situation so that it was not easy to decide on the appropriate role of the nationalized industries; but whatever that role, the government could hardly exert *less* control over the nationalized industries than over private industry, however anxious it might be to leave them to 'get on with the job'. When economic recovery hung on an adequate supply of coal the government simply could not disclaim responsibility for the affairs of the industry, least of all after nationalization. Equally, it was hardly realistic to pretend to impotence in dealing with transport because the Act laid certain duties on the Transport Commission. Even before nationalization the government was deeply involved in nearly all the activities covered by the legislation; and if nationalization had an economic purpose it was clearly to make these activities in some way *more* responsive to public policy. In the circumstances of the post-war situation the government felt obliged to continue many of the wartime controls over private industry and in addition to bring pressure on it to modify its pursuit of commercial advantage. It could do no less within the public sector. But just as it had to learn the best way of controlling private industry without destroying enterprise so it had to find the best way of exercising control over the nationalized industries without compromising the independence of the management within agreed limits.

*Price and investment policy*

If nationalization had any wider economic purposes than greater efficiency and better industrial relations these might be expected to express themselves in control over price and investment policy.

So far as prices were concerned, there was agreement more or less from the start that the boards should pay their way without open or concealed subsidies. The Treasury in particular was concerned lest guarantees of the industries' capital led to claims on the Exchequer. It also sought to discourage the idea of coupling general directives with subsidies to compensate for any consequential costs or loss of revenue. There was, however, no question of requiring the industries to cover their costs year by year and various forms of words were used to indicate that the requirement related to a term of years ('taking one year with another', 'on an average of good and bad years', etc.).

A major issue in price policy was raised by the Economic Section in a report presented to ministers in May 1946.[44] Were prices to be governed by marginal or average cost? There was a strong case in principle for making prices equal to the cost of additional units of output (i.e. equal to marginal cost) even if, with a falling or rising cost curve, prices would then yield losses or profits, not just occasionally but systematically. Rather optimistically, the Economic Section went on to argue that in the long run there was no reason to expect a substantial loss: the socialized industries could be treated as a group and the surpluses of some set off against the deficits in others.

Although the Economic Section received no support, even at the official level, and ministers found the idea either unintelligible or impracticable, the point was by no means purely academic. Leaving aside the familiar economic arguments, there were at least two implications of great practical importance. One was that price policy should not be tied to meeting overheads irrespective of the level of demand. The cost of servicing debt incurred in paying compensation for the industry's assets was not particularly relevant to the price appropriate to current circumstances and these circumstances might change greatly as the years went by. Other officials argued that if one of the industries could not cover capital charges, the right thing to do was to write down the capital under statutory authority. But they went on to argue in favour of meeting such a contingency by accumulating reserves; and since they also looked to such reserves for a substantial part of the capital needed for development, they were clearly willing to depart from their 'general rule' of pricing on the basis of average costs.

What officials visualized was that initially the use of government credit would enable most nationalized industries to earn their debt service with a reasonable margin. It was in fact essential that they should be capitalized on a basis that left them with a comfortable surplus in prospect. This should be used to build up free reserves so as to make it possible to meet debt obligations in bad times. On the other hand, the gains to the boards from raising capital more cheaply on the government's credit should not be recouped by the Treasury through some contribution to the Exchequer (for example, the payment of an overriding commission as proposed by the Herbert Committee on the Gas Industry)[45] but should accrue to the

44  Official Committee on the Socialization of Industries, second report, SI(M)(46)18 in PRO CAB 134/687.
45  Cmd 6699.

consumer on the grounds that the services provided were 'basic' and should be priced as low as possible. This was a rather dubious proposition that did not go well with the simultaneous emphasis on accumulating at the expense of the consumer the capital required for further development. As the Economic Section pointed out, the size of the investment programme of a nationalized industry should not turn on 'the fortuitous circumstances whether the particular industry has or has not a surplus revenue available for the finance of investment'. Nor could there be any guarantee that the state of demand might not so alter, over the long run and not just 'in bad times', that it would be quite wrong to seek to recover capital charges incurred when prospects were more encouraging.

A second, more immediate, implication of average cost pricing was cross-subsidization. There was no obligation on individual pits or individual area boards to cover their costs provided the surpluses made by other parts of the industry were sufficient to cover local deficits. Within each of the nationalized industries there were substantial loss-making sectors as well as sectors consistently in surplus. By what criterion were these losses justified? And why adopt a rule that allowed just enough losses to eat up the surpluses? When the Ridley Committee on Fuel and Power[46] reported in September 1952 Professor Arthur Lewis and three other members argued in favour of price increases that would narrow the gap between marginal and average cost but would oblige consumers to pay an extra £200 million. The Chairman and other members of the Committee feared that this would make mine-managers less cost-conscious and encourage demands for higher wages. Professor Lewis therefore recommended an excise duty of £1 per ton to raise the same amount for the benefit of the Exchequer. No action was taken, partly no doubt from fear of accelerating inflation or aggravating the balance-of-payments deficit, and the problem of loss-making pits remained.

In practice the government was not content to leave it to the boards to devise a price policy consistent with their statutory obligation to pay their way. Throughout the period after nationalization ministers (and from time to time the Cabinet) were closely involved in pricing decisions, particularly those proposed by the railways or coal-mining. Needless to say, all such decisions had to do with proposed increases.

As a rule ministerial interventions were governed by short-term considerations and had the effect of slowing down adjustments made necessary by rising costs. Sometimes, however, more general issues were

46  Cmd 8647.

involved as in the attempts to reduce the peak demand for electricity by introducing a spread between winter and summer running charges. When this proved ineffective after a single year's trial in 1948–9 it was not renewed.

It would be possible to give many illustrations of the problems that arose over prices in the relations between government and the boards. Particularly awkward were those where the government was negotiating at one level, as in trade agreements with other countries, while the Coal Board was negotiating at another – for example, over the price of coal exports. It might happen that government assurances were given in good faith only to prove completely unfounded a week or so later when the Coal Board took action.[47] In general, however, the problems of price control from the centre are much the same whether they arise in the public sector or in private industry, especially when the latter is organized in large units. We may therefore turn from prices to investment.

The government's interest in investment was heavily concentrated on the need to provide against the danger of a recession. The White Paper on *Employment Policy* had regarded investment as a prime source of economic instability and had envisaged some stimulation of public investment when activity slackened and some dampening of public investment in a boom. Ministers had to approve the general lines of programmes of capital development (as well as capital issues) and were kept informed by the nationalized industries of their plans in some detail. Without duplicating technical staff, they did not feel able to offer criticisms in detail or suggest alternative plans to the industries. All they ever contemplated was to make sure that the programmes were consistent with the general policy of the government and with the plans of other nationalized industries for which they were responsible. Beyond that they might be able to influence the timing of investment under guidance from the Investment Programmes Committee, speeding up the programme or slowing it down to offset opposite trends in the private sector.

Ministers' powers to influence the phasing of investment were, however, in doubt. First there was the practical question whether these powers could be made effective once the controls over building, raw materials and imports of machinery ceased to exist. Some of the negative powers over public (as well, of course, as private) investment would disappear with the controls. More positive powers to encourage investment would be likely to require the use of guarantees or grants-in-aid: if the Treasury was

47 Chester, op. cit., pp. 723–5.

willing to offer such assistance, private investment might be equally encouraged, so that discouragement and encouragement alike were little affected by nationalization.

Secondly, there was the legal issue whether ministers could require the boards to vary their investment programmes for reasons unconnected with eventual profit. The Attorney-General advised that there was some doubt whether the nationalization Acts gave ministers powers to direct that in the event of a slump the boards should maintain or expand capital investment. The Transport Act, for example, required the Commission to operate in a way which promoted the efficiency and economy of the industry itself, not of the country as a whole – rather a different matter. The Commission could embarrass the minister by asking for a direction if he wished it to increase its investment programme in a slump and could even decline to act on the direction, appealing to its statutory duty so to organize its affairs as to pay its way. A situation of that kind, however, would be inconsistent with the kind of relation that must subsist between minister and board and there would be no alternative but to get rid of the board.

Ministers were not much disturbed by what they were told of the legal position. They thought, rightly, that the situation would not arise in which the boards would refuse to act. In any event they did not think that there was any great urgency when the nationalized industries were anxious to *increase* their programmes. Only Cripps feared that additional powers might be required suddenly; and when he put round a paper on 'Economic Policy in a Recession' in June 1949 indicating the measures he thought necessary to deal with investment in a slump it was only a month before the provisional decision to devalue and four months before the decision to make cuts, not increases, in public investment.

As will be clear from chapter 17 investment did not conform to plan and it would be hard to argue that, except to some extent in 1947, public investment acted as a stabilizer in the way the White Paper had suggested. What is equally striking is that ministers gave remarkably little thought to investment *in detail*. They accepted the need to keep the aggregate within bounds and to delay most forms of public investment as far as possible. But the pattern was selected arbitrarily and in response to political pressure without much attempt to calculate which kinds of investment would yield the highest return. There was no talk of 'picking winners'.

## Conclusion

The Labour government's nationalization legislation has to be judged in long-run terms. It was not intended as a way of resolving the immediate and urgent problems of the economy and, with the possible exception of coal, was almost completely irrelevant to them. It was a response to strongly-held political and moral convictions and from that point of view was largely inevitable: the only real question was how far nationalization should be extended within the lifetime of the government. It was also the expression of an economic philosophy favouring large, nationwide units of control; and here there was a question whether that was the appropriate form of organization, in the public as in the private sector. Whatever the pressures and thinking behind it, the full merits (and weaknesses) of nationalization were not likely to be immediately visible and the fruits would become available only gradually.

There were some who saw nationalization in lurid terms as the first step towards Communism. In fact it was introduced by a set of rather conservative politicians whose main anxiety was to secure efficient management and give it a fairly free hand provided it followed commercial precedents. In the next forty years hardly anything else was nationalized. The whole business was practically completed in a single administration. Many other proposals for nationalization were made and still are: insurance, banking and the aircraft industry were seriously considered and all of them dropped. When a Conservative government succeeded in 1951 the only denationalization was of iron and steel and road haulage.

The economic rationale of nationalization was twofold: to improve the efficiency of selected 'basic' industries; and to give the government a better grip on the economy for planning purposes. These two objectives did not fit very comfortably together. The pressures that the government is enabled to exert from the centre in the interests of the balance of payments, or price stability, or a higher level of employment are liable to be at the expense of efficiency; and greater efficiency in turn, in the short run at least, may lead to more unemployment without offering much help in the struggle against inflation and an external deficit. There are no doubt some situations like that in the 1960s in which surplus manpower in the coal-mines is drained off to other employment, so yielding lower mining costs and at the same time relieving an acute labour shortage. But such a happy coincidence is not to be relied upon.

There is, therefore, a dilemma which greatly troubled the Labour government, between leaving the boards to 'get on with the job' and persuading, or directing them, to pay regard to the wider economic objectives of the government. The planning of a nationalized industry is not made easier if it has to fit into some national economic plan which is subject to an entirely different set of uncertainties. Even if there is no formal plan, the government's economic strategy is apt to undergo bewildering changes and what the government asks of the nationalized industries in holding down prices, or boosting exports, or cutting back investment may be far removed from what would seem to the boards the prudent course in the interests of efficiency and solvency.

In the years after 1945 the tighter grip that nationalization conferred was not altogether apparent. The wartime controls remained; and as they were removed fiscal and other measures were employed to regulate demand and keep the economy in balance. It was not clear, therefore, that nationalization by itself contributed much to the planning of the economy, particularly to full employment. It may have given some extra leverage on industrial policy but even that depended in the last resort on willingness to offer compensation for losses incurred or profit forgone; and private industry might have been induced equally readily to respond to the same bait. Unless the nationalized industries are large profit-earners (rarely a likely prospect), the state cannot escape, by a mere change in industrial structure, paying out of taxpayers' money for those non-commercial acts of policy that are necessary in the interests of its macro-economic objectives.

In one way nationalization may even have weakened the government's grip on the economy. The industries nationalized after the war, with the exception of iron and steel, catered almost exclusively for the home market. Even the coal industry had become quite a small exporter and it was only occasionally and in emergency that coal was imported. As a result, the units created by the legislation differed critically from large, private, multinational businesses like ICI, Unilever, RTZ and Shell which were engaged simultaneously in operations in many different countries and had to adapt themselves quickly to competitive situations in these countries. The force of the objection to steel nationalization lay in the need for just such adaptability and a recognition that it was not bred in the other, more autarchical, industries. The importation of coal, for example, became in forty years a 'no-go' area; and the efforts of the other nationalized industries to help the balance of payments were conspicuously unsuccessful.

Whatever the consequences of nationalization the Labour government could claim to have done the job after the most thorough discussion, in contrast to the almost total absence of discussion earlier. Little that has happened since does not find some anticipation in the mass of papers recording that discussion. On the whole, remarkably little has changed.

# PART FOUR

# Chapter nineteen

# CONCLUSIONS

The years 1945–51 set the stage for Britain's post-war economic development. In comparison with those years what happened in the next two decades was little more than an extrapolation of trends already at work. By the time the Conservative government took office at the end of 1951 the mould was already set.

It is natural, therefore, to ask whether different policies in those years might have yielded a different and better future. Such a question implies dissatisfaction with what ensued, although no one in 1945 envisaged an outcome over the next thirty years so superior to what had gone before. Taken in isolation, the British economy recorded a much improved performance between 1945 and 1975: it was only the faster growth of other industrial countries that cast a shadow on Britain's post-war development. These countries showed what was possible, indeed likely, if industry took its chances; and the shortfall in Britain hurt national pride and seemed to defy explanation. But the trend in productivity in Britain, which is what matters to the standard of living, changed little over the period and diverged from the start from the steeper trend in other countries. Could the trend have been steepened by action on the part of the Attlee government? Could they have set the economy off on a path that not only registered a big improvement on the pre-war record but compared favourably with experience in competing industrial countries?

He would be a bold man who would answer that question in the affirmative. Few governments have proclaimed more insistently the need for higher productivity. Perhaps government exhortations have no effect on industrial efficiency; but the government also took some practical steps to increase interest in productivity, including the dispatch of teams to study American methods of production. Few governments also have held back consumption more assiduously so as to let the pace be set by exports and investment, as recommended by a later generation of experts on growth. They were successful in achieving a fast growth in exports, eliminating in turn the external deficit and then the dollar deficit and sustaining a high level of industrial investment in spite of the virtual cessation of personal savings. But they did not succeed in raising the rate of growth to the level that their European neighbours proved capable of maintaining. It must be very doubtful whether any set of government policies could have done more.

The Labour government is also entitled to some credit for keeping the rate of inflation so low. It may not have achieved complete stability but in comparison with nearly every other country, including the United States, the cost of living was remarkably steady until the Korean War played havoc with international prices. Food subsidies were incapable of holding prices down indefinitely but they do appear to have contributed a good deal to stabilization over the first two or three years. The controls also helped to prevent sharp fluctuations in prices such as might have set off a wage–price spiral that was difficult to bring to an end. In addition ministers were sometimes able to use their personal influence with the leaders of the trade unions because their policies were perceived as fair to the average worker.

The maintenance of a high level of employment was only to a limited extent the government's doing. It was made easy because world markets remained in a state of boom and this reflected the buoyancy of the American economy more than anything else. Not only did it suffer only a minor interruption to a continuing state of domestic boom; America also took pains, notably through Marshall Aid, to allow the boom elsewhere to continue and prevent a dip in the level of activity in Western Europe because of balance-of-payments difficulties.

What can be claimed for the Labour government is that the one thing that it had to plan, and did plan – the balance of payments – was effectively planned. Ministers may have dragged their feet – over import cuts, over devaluation and over liberalization – but in the end they took the action necessary. The transformation in the external position between 1945 and 1951 was highly dramatic and more rapid than the government's advisers in 1947, when the four-year plan for the OEEC was under preparation, would have thought possible. But then, the recovery of Western Europe was also unexpectedly rapid and confounded the pessimists. What the experience of those years showed was that, when the balance of payments is looked after, and monetary and fiscal policy permits, industrial economies can recover very fast.

Not that the Labour government showed any great skill in planning, aside from the balance of payments. The rundown in defence could have been faster in 1946 as Keynes was urging in February. Dalton had good reason to complain of Attlee's obduracy in maintaining under arms more men than an impoverished Britain could afford. Investment in the sterling area from 1946 onwards was on much too large a scale and left almost completely uncontrolled. Monetary policy was more expansive than it should have been. Devaluation was six months too late. The rearmament programme reached excessive proportions. And so on.

If one looks at the apparatus of planning, that too was inadequate. Nearly two years went by before a planning staff was appointed. Even then, the original proposal – to use staff scattered throughout Whitehall – did not make much sense. It was only by luck that planning and finance came together under Cripps, and as luck would have it there was no need for Cripps to do more than hold to existing policies. At the Board of Trade he had been an innovator but at the Treasury he was not, and perhaps, devaluation apart, that was just as well. What he did was to give firmness and conviction to a policy of austerity that without him might have been difficult to sustain.

From one point of view the history of those years is the history of the emergence of demand management. The panoply of controls with which the government began was rapidly disappearing as they gave up office. Instead, the government was coming to rely, even in regulating the balance of payments and the level of investment, on fiscal policy rather than direct controls. It had not begun to make use of monetary policy; but it was not long before that joined fiscal policy in the 'packages' of the 1950s and 1960s.

In managing the economy the government never had to face a deficiency of demand. On the contrary the situation was always one of excess demand until the moment it handed over to the Tories at the end of 1951. Such an excess was entirely defensible during the first year or two when the controls remained in operation and a balance was being restored between demand and supply in sectors where it had been disturbed by wartime requirements and impediments. But once demobilization was virtually complete and industry back on a peacetime footing, the danger that excess demand would produce inflation became more acute and the chances of warding it off through controls looked less convincing. If the controls were fundamentally a way of handling scarcity in relation to a given price structure and the various forms of scarcity were yielding to that price structure, the controls were *ipso facto* becoming redundant. Moreover as the local scarcities were relieved, attention was bound to focus on the more general cause of scarcity in the pressure of excess demand; and the cure for that was not control but a diminution in purchasing power, whether thought of as income or cash.

It was not surprising therefore that from 1947 onwards the government began to veer away from the kind of planning with which it began, expressed in production targets and programmes, to a different kind of planning through budgetary and other measures designed to influence the level of demand. But although it was willing to let demand pressure operate freely in commodity and product markets it had major reservations about the labour market and the balance of payments. It hoped to find some way of influencing the labour market so as to prevent an uncontrolled rise in money wages; and it was deeply suspicious of any move to limit its powers to control imports from outside the sterling area.

In its efforts to agree on a feasible wages policy the government had little success. Paper after paper was produced by officials; approaches were made one after another to the TUC; but the most that was ever achieved – and it was an important achievement – was the wage freeze agreed in 1948 with the TUC. No way was found of reconciling the unions – or smaller groups within the unions on the shop floor or at the place of work – to the abandonment of their freedom to bargain with employers over remuneration (as over working conditions) in the interests of wider social obligations. The Cabinet might view such freedom as a recipe for inflation and harp on the difficulty of managing the economy so long as powerful groups in a fragmented labour market could go their own way. It was freedom to strike for rates of pay governed by what was fair, given what other workers were earning, and governed also by what employers could be compelled to offer, not by what would best serve the long-run interests of the community or of workers as a group or even of the strikers themselves. But the government was sensitive to the accusation of tampering with that freedom and preferred to rely on moral suasion. Ministers were given to thinking that they had only to ask and their old friends who were running the unions would respond. As they discovered, union leaders were not all-powerful and not always responsive. Gaitskell by 1951 was convinced that some new initiative was required. But he never had the opportunity to take it and there is little reason to suppose that his initiative would have met with a fate different from more recent initiatives.

The balance of payments was the focus of the one really determined effort of planning in which the Labour government engaged. The dollar drain dominated their thoughts of full employment and drove them as nothing else did to vigorous action. They enjoyed relief from it in the even years – in 1946, after the Loan Negotiations; in 1948 after the launching of Marshall Aid; and in 1950, after devaluation and the recovery in the United States. They also saw it cease completely for a time, only to return more alarmingly than ever as they were leaving office. But the dollars lasted out. The succession of exchange crises never resulted in the disastrous drop in employment that the government feared. Each in turn was surmounted by cuts in imports, supplemented by other measures and reinforced latterly by parallel cuts by other Commonwealth countries, the devaluation of 1949 being the one exception.

The exception is one that evokes an obvious parallel with the Labour government of 1964–70, which also held power for six years. Each inherited a balance-of-payments deficit, each borrowed heavily in its struggle with the deficit, and each reluctantly gave way to market pressure and devalued, the one after four years, the other after three. But the parallel is misleading. After 1945 sterling had an international significance far greater than twenty years later: of all international payments, visible and invisible, probably more than half were then made in sterling.[1] The devaluation of the pound in 1949 meant not only a bigger upheaval in the international economy: it was virtually a revaluation of the dollar which the Americans were unwilling to contemplate on their own account. In 1967 the devaluation of sterling was a more local and limited affair. A second difference was that in 1949 the current account was in balance while in 1967 it was not. Devaluation in that year was primarily a means of restoring Britain's competitive power while in 1949 devaluation was more akin to the removal of a wartime control that had become redundant. There had been time for the volume of exports to reach an adequate volume and what was needed was a redirection to dollar markets that only a price incentive, if powerful enough, could ensure. Devaluation provided that incentive. It was a recognition of the need to call the price mechanism into play even in a system of economic planning.

The period was one in which the consumer and the taxpayer were asked to carry unexpectedly heavy burdens. We can enquire with Roy Harrod

---

1 'European Payments Scheme', annex to 'European Payments Union', memorandum by the Chancellor of the Exchequer, 3 March 1950, EPC(50)31, in PRO CAB 134/225.

'were these hardships necessary?' Some of them undoubtedly were. Civilian consumption in 1945, low though it was, was higher than the country could have afforded if it had had to balance its external accounts unaided. Moreover it compared a great deal more favourably with pre-war consumption than did consumption on the continent. This allowed Britain to put aside for the sake of external balance a much higher proportion of annual increments in output than her European neighbours; and she did so with more urgency than they because most of them had larger reserves and could prolong their deficits. Exports and investment, as we have seen, took two-thirds of the extra output yielded by demobilization and rising productivity.

What is less clear is whether, in the distribution of these burdens, the social revolution of the post-war years was pushed too far. It was not just that consumption was inelastic in the face of a big expansion in output. Consumption was re-distributed by controls and high taxation of earned incomes in favour of the lower-paid and the poor. In Europe the redistribution was carried much less far (except in Scandinavia) and the hardships of which Roy Harrod complained fell on other, less broad, shoulders. French and German workers consequently addressed themselves to the task of earning an adequate living with a greater inducement to exert themselves. Since redistribution worked less powerfully in their favour they had every reason to see what higher production would do for them, not just as a nation, but personally.

In a defeated nation or a country recovering from foreign occupation, with production at a low level and a surplus of labour, the logic of giving priority to higher production was readily accepted. It was less apparent in a country preening itself on military success and accustomed by six years of war to 'fair shares'. British manual workers felt entitled to better treatment after the war than they had enjoyed before it, without regard to the level of production. Unique among workers in the European belligerent countries, their real earnings had risen in wartime even if their standard of living had not and they could see no reason to accept a less favourable outcome in peacetime when they were assured of full employment. The mysteries of Lend-Lease, foreign borrowing and the dollar drain were not for the likes of them to fathom. They looked to the government to ensure distributive justice whatever happened to production and no government could ignore the prevailing mood. Regardless of the case for or against redistribution of income, rationing and other controls were inevitable politically under post-war conditions in Britain.

One can also put the question the other way round: did Britain in those years move a long way towards what the government's supporters would have regarded as socialism? One could point to the nationalization measures if public ownership was the test: or to the National Health Service if an expansion in free social services was peculiarly socialist. But when the incoming Conservative government, voicing different slogans, found little to undo and much to copy, one might have cause for doubt. The role of government had been greatly extended; but then it had been growing throughout the century as the rising proportion of GNP passing through the budget testifies. The main extensions, in the development of the social services and the absorption of some of the basic industries into the public sector, were not challenged on grounds of principle and have stood ever since. But what of the effort to achieve greater economic equality through heavier taxation of the well-to-do and large food subsidies benefiting the poor? These were both inherited from the wartime Coalition government and not a socialist innovation. What the Labour government did was to maintain direct taxation at wartime levels to help finance its concessions to the less well-off. Rates of income tax that began at 50p in the £ in 1945 still began at 47½p in 1951. The food subsidies were continued and after reaching a peak of about £450 million in 1948 had not fallen very far before the change of government. Economic equality was carried almost as far as in wartime, to judge from these measures, and a good deal further than after 1951 when food subsidies and income tax were progressively reduced.

While taxation, rationing and other controls restrained the consumption of the well-to-do, from foodstuffs to motor cars and foreign travel, peace necessarily meant a resumption of the production of luxuries that were unobtainable in wartime. The return to peacetime conditions, therefore, meant some renewal of inequalities that the war had suspended. It was not until after 1951, however, that these inequalities were allowed freer play in the big surge in consumption that started in 1953.

Relations with other countries were coloured throughout by the continuing difficulties with the balance of payments. Two themes run through these relationships in the post-war period: convertibility and integration. The United States, from the moment the war was over, clamoured for convertibility at the earliest possible moment. But in a world in which the United States from its vast resources could supply the needs of every other country in a way that Britain, still struggling with shortages, could not, dollars were bound to be more attractive than pounds and there was a vast excess supply of pounds. If the United States herself had been prepared to swap sterling freely for dollars, convertibility might have been achieved: that would have been a sure test of US faith in convertibility. But there was never any chance of such a move. In moments of crisis, as in August 1947 or September 1949, the United States suspended its pressure for convertibility. But as soon as the gold and dollar reserves began to rise, as in 1950, the pressure was on again. American policy did not take kindly during the war or after, to rising reserves in Britain that accompanied, and might therefore be attributable to, American aid. But without much higher reserves, the chances of maintaining convertibility were poor. Not that higher reserves by themselves would have done the trick. So long as Britain's own trade accounts showed a dollar deficit, her chances of convertibility turned on success in earning dollars elsewhere to cover that deficit and it was a long time before much progress was made in that direction.

The inconvertibility of sterling arose partly from the weakness of the pound and partly from the strength of the dollar. The strength of the dollar in turn arose from the willingness of a devastated world to use its limited stock of gold and dollars in the procurement of goods from the one source where they were to be found in abundance. This was the essence of the dollar shortage. If the reserves fell too low for dollar goods to be bought, that was no reason why, if similar goods could be obtained from other countries at higher prices, they should be spurned as uncompetitive, particularly if those countries were willing to accept payment in the currency of the importing country. The dollar shortage did not sit well with non-discrimination. On the other hand, it was important to preserve as much competition and as much convertibility as possible. Hence the efforts in which Britain engaged so strenuously to achieve partial convertibility – complete, indeed, within the sterling area, more limited within the EPU – and to open the door more and more widely to imports for which some fraction only of their value had to be paid in dollars. The door was wide open to the sterling Commonwealth and from 1949 was opened progressively to European products through the OEEC's liberalization schemes. But it was never possible to ban the dollar completely from intra-OEEC transactions; and Europe was not able to supply the full range of goods obtainable for dollars from America.

The second main theme in economic relationships was integration. The United States made no secret of their desire to see the United Kingdom integrated into Europe. On the other hand, they showed little sympathy with the effort to maintain Commonwealth relationships, engaging throughout the war and after in denunciations of Imperial Preference and seeking to put an end to the dollar pool. In Britain, on the other hand, the

Commonwealth was regarded as an example of international collaboration which had proved its value in war and could continue to be helpful in peace. Europe was a much more doubtful affair. There was everything to be said for Britain taking the lead in the Marshall Plan and converting it into a drive to put an end to the dollar shortage: that was something practical and in everyone's interest. But the talk of European integration was likely to prove empty or dangerous. The same, it is true, might have been said of integration with the United States which appealed to many in post-war Britain. But the most influential idea was that of an Atlantic Community spanning both sides of the Atlantic and embracing in a necessarily very loose relationship the United States on one side and Western Europe on the other. The enlargement of OEEC to include the United States and Canada in what was known thereafter as OECD was a natural outcome of this sentiment. But by the time that change occurred, the Treaty of Rome had led continental Europe along a different path towards closer union.

How successful was the government? Measuring success in terms of the aims it set out in its 1945 election programme, it was obviously highly successful: full employment was maintained, to almost universal surprise; there was no repetition of the great inflationary boom of 1919–20 and the slump that followed; the entire programme of nationalization was carried out; the National Health Service was successfully launched; the welfare state was put on a solid foundation.

As usually happens, these achievements were as much dependent on external events as on Cabinet decisions. The maintenance of full employment, for example, owed as much to the American as to the British government. Not that the role of the British government was unimportant as was evident from the very different approach of some continental governments, such as the Belgian and Swiss, to employment policy. Those were years when the government was learning from experience how to maintain a steady pressure of demand, how to use fiscal policy in particular for that purpose, and what residual controls might be needed in order to even out the pressure between industries and localities. Regional policy in particular was pursued vigorously and helped to improve the industrial prospects of areas that had suffered severely before the war. At the end of the period the government had arrived at a much clearer idea of the instruments of policy required for full employment and how to use them.

The success of the government's employment policy, however, lay not so much in devising or following prescriptions for full employment as in taking the measure of the threat to it posed by a weak balance of payments and a dollar drain. Full employment policy was first and foremost balance-of-payments policy so long as excess demand persisted. It was also, at times, energy and raw material policy when the threat of a coal or steel shortage was acute or when, as in 1951, other materials like sulphur or copper were becoming serious bottlenecks.

What if there had been no America and in consequence no dollar short-age? Would the government's task have been easier? It is the very ques-tion with which Keynes confronted the Treasury officials who were against a large loan from the United States. Their plan, he argued in July 1945, amounted to saying that 'if a tidal wave were to overwhelm North and South America, our subsequent financial problems would not be too bad and nothing worse than starvation would supervene'. Ministers might insist that the dollar problem was America's problem too; but there was no getting away from the fact that it originated in the happy circum-stance of an overabundance in America of what Europe sorely needed. If at the end of the war Britain had had to find other ways of feeding herself and other sources of raw materials and equipment, her recovery would undoubtedly have been far slower and more painful: all the more so because other countries would have been stricken simultaneously and in their greater need would have followed more desperate policies, protec-tionist, bilateral and contractionary. America was a volatile neighbour with large but not always very realistic ideas. But a world without America would have left Britain with a far more difficult problem, more akin to that which turned the inter-war years into such a disaster.

The real problem for Britain was that the role she was asked to play was one beyond her strength. This was true both in relation to convertibility and to economic integration. The pound staggered on as an international currency but it took twelve and a half years to make it fully convertible. As for integration, Britain never felt she could take the lead except in urging a united onslaught on the dollar problem or launching the EPU or campaigning for liberalization of imports. She had no great confidence that she could sustain even the initiatives on which she embarked. Officials, long before Robot, sometimes meditated an end to OEEC and by 1952 were backtracking on liberalization and proposing to kill off the EPU while Chancellors indulged now and again in derisory remarks on the EPU and the IMF ('we are not in the pocket of this valueless organis-ation').[2] There was no glad, confident view such as a super-power might

2 Annotation on 'Robot – Interim Measures' in PRO T 236/3242.

adopt: more a feeling of insufficient room for manoeuvre which convertibility and economic integration would restrict still more.

All in all, the early post-war years presented the government with a much more difficult task of economic management than the two decades that followed; and its mastery of that task entitled the government to all the more credit. It pointed the economy in the right direction, rode out the various crises that the years of transition almost inevitably gave rise to, and by 1951 had brought the economy near to eventual balance. No doubt there were false starts, concentration on secondary issues, a slowness to react, an unwillingness to act with sufficient firmness, and at the end a serious error over the scale of rearmament that was feasible. There was, too, little success in changing long-standing attitudes in industry that slowed down innovation and expansion. But whether one tries to look forward from 1945 or backwards from forty years later, those years appear in retrospect, and rightly so, as years when the government knew where it wanted to go and led the country with an understanding of what was at stake.

# SELECT BIBLIOGRAPHY

## Public records

| | | |
|---|---|---|
| Cabinet | CAB 21 | (Prime Minister's Briefs). |
| | CAB 124 | (Lord President of the Council files). |
| | CAB 128 | (Cabinet Conclusions). |
| | CAB 129 | (Cabinet Papers). |
| | CAB 130 | (Cabinet Committees: minutes and memoranda). |
| | CAB 132 | (Lord President's Committee and Sub-committees: minutes and memoranda). |
| | CAB 134 | (Cabinet Committees: minutes and memoranda). |
| Foreign Office | FO 371 | |
| Prime Minister's Office | PREM 8 | (1945–51). |
| | PREM 11 | (1952–). |
| Treasury | T 171 | (Budget and Finance Bill papers). |
| | T 222 | (Organization and Methods). |
| | T 228 | (Trade and Industry Division). |
| | T 229 | (Central Economic Planning Staff). |
| | T 230 | (Economic Section papers). |
| | T 232 | (European Economic Co-operation Committee files). |
| | T 233 | (Home Finance Division). |
| | T 234 | (Home and Overseas Planning Division). |

T 236 (Overseas Finance Division).
T 238 (Overseas Negotiations Committee).
T 247 (Keynes Papers).
T 267 (Treasury Historical Memoranda).
T 269 (Papers on 'Devaluation 1949 and
      Consequent Measures').


## Official reports and papers

*United Kingdom (London, HMSO)*

| | |
|---|---|
| Central Statistical Office | *Annual Abstract of Statistics.* |
| | *Economic Trends.* |
| | *Economic Trends Annual Supplement.* |
| | *Monthly Digest of Statistics.* |
| | *National Income and Expenditure* (annual, from 1952). |
| | *Statistical Digest of the War* (HMSO and Longmans, Green, 1951). |
| Department of Employment | *British Labour Statistics: Historical Abstract 1886–1968* (1971). |
| Foreign Office | *European Co-operation: Memoranda to the OEEC and ECA covering revised United Kingdom Programme, 1st July 1948 to 30th June 1949* (1948, Cmd 7545). |
| | *European Co-operation: Memoranda submitted to the OEEC relating to Economic Affairs in the period 1949 to 1953* (including *The Long-Term Programme*) (1948, Cmd 7572). |
| | *Proposals for Consideration by an International Conference on Trade and Employment*, Miscellaneous no. 15 (1945, Cmd 6709). |
| HMSO | *Food Consumption Levels in the United States, Canada and the United Kingdom* (1944). |
| | *The Impact of the War on Civilian Consumption in the United Kingdom, the United States and Canada* (1945). |
| House of Commons | *Parliamentary Debates* (Hansard, 5th series). |
| House of Lords | *Parliamentary Debates* (Hansard, 5th series). |
| Ministry of Agriculture | *Post-War Contribution of British Agriculture to the Saving of Foreign Exchange* (1947, Cmd 7072). |

| | |
|---|---|
| | *The World Food Shortage* (1946, Cmd 6785). |
| Ministry of Reconstruction | *Employment Policy* (1944, Cmd 6527). |
| National Coal Board | *Annual Report and Statement of Accounts for the years ended 31 December 1946, 31 December 1947.* |
| | *Report and Accounts* (annual, from 1948). |
| Prime Minister | *Statement on the Economic Considerations affecting Relations between Employers and Employed* (1947, Cmd 7018). |
| | *Statement on Personal Incomes, Costs and Prices* (1948, Cmd 7321). |
| Treasury | *An Analysis of the Sources of War Finance and an Estimate of the National Income and Expenditure in 1938 and 1940* (1941, Cmd 6261). |
| | *Capital Investment in 1948* (1947, Cmd 7268). |
| | *Capital Issues Control: Memorandum of Guidance to the Capital Issues Committee* (1945, Cmd 6645). |
| | *Control of Dividends* (1951, Cmd 8318). |
| | *Economic Survey* (annual, 1947–62). |
| | *Financial Agreement between the Governments of the United States and the United Kingdom dated 6th December 1945, together with a joint statement regarding Settlement for Lend-Lease, Reciprocal Aid, Surplus War Property and Claims* (1945, Cmd 6708). |
| | *National Income and Expenditure of the United Kingdom* (annual, 1946–51). |
| | *Preliminary Estimates of National Income and Expenditure* (annual, from 1952). |
| | *Statistical Material presented during the Washington Negotiations* (1945, Cmd 6707). |
| | *United Kingdom Balance of Payments* (annual or biennial from 1948). |

*International and US*

| | |
|---|---|
| Bank for International Settlements | *Annual Reports* (Basle). |
| | *The Sterling Area* (Basle, 1953). |
| Committee of European Economic Co-operation | Vol. I, *General Report* (1947, London, HMSO). |

European Co-operation Administration — *The Sterling Area: an American Analysis* (London, 1951).

Organization for European Economic Co-operation — *Economic Progress and Problems of Western Europe*, third report of the OEEC (Paris, 1951).

*European Recovery Programme*, second report of the OEEC (Paris, 1950).

*Interim Report on the European Recovery Programme*, 3 vols (Paris, 1948).

*Report to the Economic Co-operation Administration on the First Annual Programme* (Paris, 1949).

*Statistical Bulletin of Foreign Trade* (bi-monthly, Paris).

*Statistics of National Product and Expenditure 1938, 1947 to 1952* (Paris, 1954).

—— *No 2 1938, 1947 to 1955* (Paris, 1957).

United Nations — *Economic Survey of Europe* (ECE, Geneva, annual, from 1949).

*Economic Survey of Europe since the War* (ECE, Geneva, 1953).

*Statistical Yearbook* (New York, annual).

## Newspapers and periodicals

*The Banker*
*Board of Trade Journal*
*The Economist*
*Keesing's Contemporary Archives*
*Lloyds Bank Review*
*Manchester Guardian*
*Ministry of Labour Gazette*
*The Times*

## Unpublished works

Corina, John, 'The British experiment in wage restraint with special reference to 1948–50' (Bodleian Library, Oxford University, submitted for D. Phil., 1961).

Cottrell, Philip, 'The Convertibility Crisis' (1982).

Jones, Russell, 'The wages problem in employment policy 1936–48' (Bristol University, submitted for MA, 1984).

Peden, G. C., 'Economic aspects of British perceptions of power on the eve of the Cold War' (MS, 1984).

Pressnell, L. S., 'Convertibility and the Anglo-American loan negotiations' (1983).

Rees, Sir Hugh Ellis, 'The Convertibility Crisis' (Treasury Historical Memorandum no. 3, 1962, in PRO T 267/3).

Robinson, E. A. G., 'The Long-term Demand for British Exports of Manufactures' (Board of Trade Memorandum, July 1946).

Tew, J. H. B., 'A first look at exchequer financing under the Labour government' (1960).

—— 'A second look at exchequer financing under the Labour government' (1961).

—— 'U.K. national debt policy since 1945' (1961).

## Other MSS

Cherwell Papers (Nuffield College Library, Oxford).

Crookshank Papers (Bodleian Library, Oxford).

Dalton Papers (British Library of Political and Economic Science).

Meade Diary (British Library of Political and Economic Science).

## Published works

Acheson, Dean (1970) *Present at the Creation* (London, Macmillan).

Allen, Sir Roy (R. G. D. Allen) (1946) 'Mutual Aid between the U.S. and the British Empire, 1941–45', *Journal of the Royal Statistical Society*, vol. CIX, part III, reprinted in Sayers, *Financial Policy 1939–45*.

Balogh, Lord (1949) *Dollar Crisis* (Oxford, Blackwell).

Beveridge, Lord (Sir William) (1948) *Full Employment in a Free Society* (London, Allen & Unwin).

Birkenhead, Lord (1961) *The Prof in Two Worlds: the Official Life of Professor F. A. Lindemann, Viscount Cherwell* (London, Collins).

Boltho, Andrea (1982) *The European Economy: Growth and Crisis* (Oxford, University Press).

Bowers, J. K. (ed.) (1979) *Inflation, Development and Integration* (Leeds, University Press).

Boyle, Lord (Sir Edward Boyle) (1979) 'The economist in government', in Bowers, *Inflation, Development and Integration*.

Brittan, S. (revised edn, 1971) *Steering the Economy* (Harmondsworth, Penguin Books).

Bullock, Lord (1983) *Ernest Bevin: Foreign Secretary 1945–51* (London, Heinemann).

Butler, David and Halsey, A. H. (eds) (1978) *Policy and Politics* (London, Macmillan).

Butler, Lord (R. A. Butler) (1971) *The Art of the Possible* (London, Hamish Hamilton).

Cairncross, Sir Alec (with B. Eichengreen) (1983) *Sterling in Decline* (Oxford, Blackwell).

Cairncross, Frances (ed.) (1981) *Changing Perceptions of Economic Policy* (London, Methuen).

Carter, Sir Charles (1951) 'The Real Product of the United Kingdom 1946–1950', *London and Cambridge Economic Service*, vol. 29, bulletin no. 3, August.

Chester, Sir Norman (D. N. Chester) (1975) *The Nationalisation of British Industry 1945–51* (London, HMSO).

Clark, Colin (1949) 'The value of the pound', *Economic Journal*.

Clarke, Sir Richard (R. W. B. Clarke) (1982) *Anglo-American Collaboration in War and Peace 1942–49* (Oxford, University Press).

Clegg, Hugh and Chester, T. E. (1953) *The Future of Nationalisation* (Oxford, University Press).

Cole, G. D. H. (1938) *The Machinery of Socialist Planning* (London, Hogarth Press).

—— (1939) *Plan for Democratic Britain* (London, Labour Book Service).

Cooke, Colin (1957) *The Life of Richard Stafford Cripps* (London, Hodder & Stoughton).

Corden, W. M. (1958) 'The control of imports: a case study in the United Kingdom import restrictions of 1951–2', *Manchester School*, vol. 26 no. 3.

Craig, F. W. S. (1970) *British Election Manifestos 1918–1966* (Chichester, Political Reference Publications).

Dalton, Lord (Hugh Dalton) (1962) *High Tide and After* (London, Frederick Muller).

Devons, Ely (1947) 'Economic planning in war and peace', *Transactions of the Manchester Statistical Society*, reprinted in *Essays in Economics* (London, Allen & Unwin).

—— (1970) *Papers on Planning and Economic Management* (Manchester, University Press).

Donoughue, B. and Jones, G. W. (1973) *Herbert Morrison: Portrait of a Politician* (London, Weidenfeld & Nicolson).

Dow, J. C. R. (1964) *The Management of the British Economy 1945–60* (Cambridge, University Press for NIESR).

Durbin, E. F. M. (1949) *Problems of Economic Planning* (London, Routledge).

Feinstein, C. H. (1972) *National Income, Expenditure and Output of the United Kingdom 1855–1965* (Cambridge, University Press).

Flanders, M. June (1963) 'The effects of devaluation on exports: a case study, United Kingdom 1949–1954', *Bulletin of the Oxford Institute of Economics and Statistics*.

Franks, Lord (1947) *Central Planning and Control in War and Peace* (London, LSE and Longmans).

Gardner, Richard N. (1956) *Sterling-Dollar Diplomacy* (Oxford, University Press).

Hancock, W. K. and Gowing, M. M. (1949) *British War Economy*, History of the Second World War, UK Civil Series (London, HMSO).

Hannah, Leslie (1979) *Electricity before Nationalisation* (London, Macmillan).

Harris, Kenneth (1982) *Attlee* (London, Weidenfeld & Nicolson).

Harrod, Sir Roy (1947) *Are These Hardships Necessary?* (London, Rupert Hart-Davis).

—— (1951) *The Life of John Maynard Keynes* (London, Macmillan).

—— (1963) *The British Economy* (Maidenhead, McGraw Hill).

Hawtrey, Sir Ralph (1954) *Towards the Rescue of Sterling* (London, Longmans).

Hemming, M. F. W., Miles, C. M. and Ray, G. F. (1959) 'A statistical summary of the extent of import control in the United Kingdom since the war', *Review of Economic Studies*.

Henderson, Sir Hubert (1947) 'Cheap money and the Budget', *Economic Journal*, September.

—— (1947) *Use and Abuses of Economic Planning* (Cambridge, University Press).

Hennessy, P. and Brown, M. (1980) (a) 'Deciphering the 'rose' code, (b) 'Cripps and the search for a whiter loaf', (c) '19 month progress to devaluation' (*The Times*, 3, 4 and 8 January).

Hennessy, P. and Arends, A. (1983) *Mr Attlee's Engine Room: Cabinet Committee Structure and the Labour Governments, 1945–51* (Glasgow, Strathclyde University).

Hicks, Sir John (1947) 'The empty economy', *Lloyds Bank Review*, June, new series no. 5.

—— (1950) *The Problem of Budgetary Reform* (Oxford, University Press).

Horner, Arthur (1960) *Incorrigible Rebel* (London, McGibbon & Key).

Jay, D. P. T. (1980) *Change and Fortune* (London, Hutchinson).

Jewkes, John (1948) *Ordeal by Planning* (London, Macmillan).

Jewkes, John and Devons, Ely (1947) 'The Economic Survey for 1947', *Lloyds Bank Review*, April.

Kahn, Lord (R. F. Kahn) (1974) 'On re-reading Keynes', British Academy Keynes Lecture, *Proceedings of the British Academy*.

—— (1950) 'The European Payments Union', *Economica*.

Kenen, Peter (1960) *British Monetary Policy and the Balance of Payments, 1951–1959* (Cambridge, Mass., Harvard University Press).

Kennan, George (1967) *Memoirs 1925–1950* (London, Hutchinson).

Kennedy, C. M. (1952) 'Monetary policy', in Worswick and Ady, *The British Economy 1945–1950*.

Keynes, Lord (1979) *The Collected Writings of John Maynard Keynes* (ed. D. Moggridge), vols XXIV–XXVII (Cambridge, University Press for Royal Economic Society).

Leruez, Jacques (1972) *Planification et Politique en Grande Bretagne 1945–1971* (Paris, Armand Colin).

Little, I. M. D. (1952) 'Fiscal policy', in Worswick and Ady, *The British Economy 1945–1950*.

McCrone, Gavin (1969) *Regional Policy in Britain* (London, Allen & Unwin).

MacDougall, Sir Donald (1957) *The World Dollar Problem* (London, Macmillan).

—— (1978) 'The machinery of economic government: some personal reflections', in Butler and Halsey, *Policy and Politics*.

Macmillan, Sir Harold (1973) *At the End of the Day* (London, Macmillan).

Maizels, A. (1963/1969) *Industrial Growth and World Trade* (Cambridge, University Press for NIESR).

Matthews, R. C. O., Feinstein, C. H. and Odling Smee (1982) *British Economic Growth 1865–1973* (Oxford, University Press).

Meade, James (1948) 'Financial policy and the balance of payments', *Economica*.

—— (1948) *Planning and the Price Mechanism* (London, Allen & Unwin).

Milward, Alan S. (1984) *The Reconstruction of Western Europe 1945–51* (London, Methuen).

Mitchell, Joan (1963) *Crisis in Britain, 1951* (London, Secker & Warburg).

Morgan, D. J. (1980) *The Official History of Colonial Development* (London, Macmillan).

Morgan, K. O. (1984) *Labour in Power 1945–1951* (Oxford, University Press).

Paish, F. W. (1950) *The Post-war Financial Problem* (London, Macmillan).

Pick, Franz (1955) *Black Market Yearbook 1955* (Pick's World Currency Report).

Plumptre, A. W. F. (1977) *Three Decades of Decision* (Toronto, McClelland & Stewart).

Reddaway, W. B. (1950) 'Movements of the real product of the United Kingdom 1946–1949; *Journal of the Royal Statistical Society*, vol. CXIII, part IV.

Rees, Graham L. (1963) *Britain and the Post-war European Payments System* (Cardiff, University of Wales Press).

Robbins, Lord (Lionel Robbins) (1947) *The Economic Problem in Peace and War* (London, Macmillan).

—— (1947) 'Inquest on the crisis', *Lloyds Bank Review*, October, new series no. 6.

—— (1971) *Autobiography of an Economist* (London, Macmillan).

Robertson, Sir Dennis (1948) *Money* (Cambridge, University Press).

Rodgers, W. T. (ed.) (1964) *Hugh Gaitskell 1906–1963* (London, Thames & Hudson).

Salter, Lord (Sir Arthur Salter) (1967) *Slave of the Lamp* (London, Weidenfeld & Nicolson).

Sargent, J. R. (1952) 'Britain and the sterling area', in Worswick and Ady, *The British Economy 1945–1950.*

—— (1952) 'Britain and Europe', in Worswick and Ady, *The British Economy 1945–1950.*

Sayers, R. S. (1956) *Financial Policy 1939–45*, History of the Second World War, UK Civil Series (London, HMSO and Longmans).

Scott, M. F. (1963) *A Study of United Kingdom Imports* (Cambridge, University Press for NIESR).

Seldon, A. (1981) *Churchill's Indian Summer: the Conservative Government 1951–55* (London, Hodder & Stoughton).

Shinwell, Lord (1955) *Conflict without Malice* (London, Odhams Press).

Shonfield, Sir Andrew (1959) *British Economic Policy since the War* (Harmondsworth, Penguin Books).

Tew, J. H. B. (1952) *International Monetary Co-operation* (London, Hutchinson).

Triffin, Robert (1957) *Europe and the Money Muddle* (New Haven, Conn., Yale University Press).

TUC (1944), *Interim Report on Post-War Reconstruction.*

TUC (1948), *A Policy for Real Wages.*

Wigg, Lord (1972) *George Wigg* (London, Michael Joseph).

Williams, Philip M. (1979) *Hugh Gaitskell* (London, Jonathan Cape).

—— (1983) (ed.) *The Dairy of Hugh Gaitskell 1945–1956* (London, Jonathan Cape).

Wilson, T. (1952) 'Manpower', in Worswick and Ady, *The British Economy 1945–50.*

Wootton Lady (Barbara Wootton) (1934) *Plan or no Plan* (London, Gollancz).

Worswick, G. D. N. and Ady, P. (1952) *The British Economy 1945–1950* (Oxford, University Press).

Wright, K. M. (1954) 'Dollar pooling in the sterling area 1939–1952', *American Economic Review*, vol. XLIV, September, pp. 559–77.

Zupnick, E. (1957) *Britain's Post-war Dollar Problem* (New York, Columbia University Press).

# INDEX

Abadan oil refinery, 238
Acheson, Dean, 296
agriculture, 67, 71, 82, 280, 394
aid, reciprocal, 4 n., 5, 8, 12; *see also*
  Marshall Aid
Alexander, A. V., 49, 108, 137, 194
Allen, R. G. D., 5
Alphand, Hervé, 279
Anderson, Sir John, 52, 56, 95, 312–13,
  420
Anglo-American Financial Agreement,
  Ch. 5 *passim*, 121–3, 126–30, 136–40,
  144–6, 156, 281–3, 286, 294
arbitration, 401, 403
Argentina, 127–8, 136–8, 148, 355
Atlantic Treaty, 296
Atlantic Union, 285
atomic bomb, 3, 212, 219
Attlee, C. R., xii, 3, 5–6, 312, 454, 481;
  rôle as Prime Minister, Ch. 3; in coal
  crisis, 354–6, 358, 361–2, 369, 384; in
  convertibility crisis, 130, 137; on devaluation, 174, 179–85, 188–9, 194; on
  manpower allocation, 386–7, 390–1,
  403–5, 501; on planning, 325–6; on
  rearmament, 214, 217–22, 230
Australia, 154–5, 158–9, 186, 188, 240,
  242, 246–7, 252–3, 263

balance of payments: constraint, 16, 20,
  43–6, 500–3; crises, 21, 28, Chs 6, 7
  and 9; estimates, 21–2, 79, 84, 88,
115–18, 152–5, 239; gold and dollar
  deficit, 79, 117, 150–3, 161–2, 200–3,
  239; long-term forecasts, 9, 63,
  78–80, 91, 326–8; short-term
  forecasts, 77–87, 112–13, 324; of
  sterling area countries, 158–60; wartime deficits, 4, 8–9; Working Party,
  74, 132; *see also* capital flows,
  exchange control
bank advances, *see* credit restriction
bank deposits, *see* money supply
Bank of England, 153, 159, 198, 444;
  concludes monetary agreements,
  126–30, 164; on convertibility, 129,
  138; against devaluation, 171, 176; on
  EPU, 289; on floating, 168, 187, 234,
  270; nationalized, 464–5, 474, 488;
  suggests cuts and tighter money, 176,
  189, 196, 443; supports Robot, 245–8
Bank Rate, 176–7, 190, 240, 253–4,
  266, 424, 431, 433, 443–5
Barnes, Alfred, 369
Battle Act, 242
Belgium, 45, 72, 97, 123, 125, 128, 134,
  138, 148, 152, 164, 205, 209, 274–8,
  289, 382, 507
Berthoud, E. A., 249
Bevan, Aneurin ('Nye'), 48–9, 53, 109,
  137; in devaluation crisis, 177, 194–5;
  on investment cuts, 454, 457; resigns,
  226–7; threatens resignation, 138; on
  wages policy, 408

Beveridge, Lord, 18, 36
Bevin, Ernest, 20, 47, 109, 137, 218, 235, 447; death, 48, 226; on devaluation, 172, 177, 180, 183–8, 190–1, 199; on France, 279, 294–6; on manpower allocation, 391, 406; relations with colleagues, 49; threatens resignation, 194
Bidault, Georges, 279–80
bilateralism, 72, 92, 110, 124–5, 136–7, 258, 281, 286
black markets, 261, 351–2; *see also* cheap sterling
Bolton, George: on devaluation in 1949, 167, 172, 186; on floating rate, 168, 237–8, 270; supports Robot, 244
Boyle, Lord, 61 n.
Brand, Lord, 95–7, 99, 108
Bretherton, Russell, 54
Bretton Woods Agreements, 5, 77, 88–9, 92, 97, 99, 109–10, 126, 247
Bridges, Sir Edward, 51–2, 213, 295–6, 400, 419; on devaluation, 117, 173, 177–8, 189–90; goes to US, 108, 114; on planning, 319–20, 323–4; on Robot, 248–9, 264
Brittain, Sir H., 235–6, 249
Broadley, Sir H., 81 n.
Brook, Sir Norman, 213, 386
budget, Ch. 15 *passim*; in 1945–52, 422–5; in 1951, 225–8; in 1952, 253–6, 445; Committee, 226, 415, 419, 426; as planning instrument, 322, 332; surpluses, 326, 409–11, 419–22; *see also* fiscal policy
building controls, 336–7, 352–3, 450, 455–61, 492
bulk purchasing arrangements, 300
Butler, R. A., 86, 241, 508; raises Bank Rate, 444–5; supports Robot, 245, 248–58, 262, 264, 270
Butt, David, 86 n., 333

Cable and Wireless, 17, 466, 469
Cairncross, Alec, 168 n., 366 n.
Callaghan, James, 48

Canada, 72, 80, 91, 109, 115–16, 132–8, 171, 176, 178, 184–6, 209, 237, 251, 253, 262
capital: controls, absence of in sterling area, 134, 244, 501; expenditure, *see* investment; flows, 7, 73, 80, 118–20, 133, 149, 152 *et seq.*, 180, 236, 501, *see also* balance of payments; issues, 428, 446; stock, 13, 18, 37–8
Capital Issues Committee, 444, 446
cartels, 92, 301
Catto, Lord, 138, 433, 447
centralization, 476–8, 487
Central Economic Planning Staff, 325–6
Central Electricity Board, 368, 370
Central Statistical Office, 53–5, 153, 216, 313, 325–6, 426
Chamberlain, Neville, 312
cheap money, 428–41
Cherwell, Lord, 245, 249–54, 256–8, 270–1
Chester, Sir Norman, xii, 474
Chiefs of Staff, 219, 392
Churchill, Winston, 96; on Robot, 248–50, 253, 256–8, 279, 300, 304
Citrine, Lord, 480
Civil Aviation Bill, 469
Clarke, R. W. B. ('Otto'), 55, 63 n., 285, 303, 323; on exchange rate, 165–8, 236–8, 269; on Robot, 244, 249, 254, 258, 261–2, 268–70; on US loan, 97–8, 111–15, 122, 141
Clayton, Will, 99, 101, 104–5, 114, 129, 136
coal: crisis of 1947, Ch. 13 *passim*, 20–1, 26–7, 82–3, 148, 432, 440; employment, 356–61, 376–9, 394–5, 494; exports, 243, 280; imports, 495; nationalization, 17, 365, 375
Coalition government, 14–15, 17, 57
Cobbold, C. F. C.: on convertibility, 99, 138; on devaluation, 172, 178–9, 190, 443; on Robot, 244, 248, 258–61, 264
colonies, 45, 117, 157, 205
commodity: boom, 225, 231, 239, 344; shunting, 170

Commonwealth: conferences, 75, 175, 179, 182, 240–4, 264–6; relations with, 75–6, 92, 164, 176, 183, 188, 198, 248, 251–4, 262–3, 279, 285, 391
competitive power, 36, 68, 207, 261–3, 268, 283, 503
'consideration' for Lend-Lease, 89
consumption, 11–12, 18, 23–33, 37, 230–1, 416, 426, 504–5
Control of Engagement Order, 305, 338, 397
Control of Investment Act, 446–7
controls: financial, 302–3, see also demand management; physical, Ch. 12 passim, 14, 22–3, 49–50, 175, 179, 199–200, 230, 254, 270, 286, 300–2, 329–30, 411, 416, 442, 495, 501–2, see also rationing
convertibility, Chs 5, 6 and 9 passim, 20, 62, 67, 82, 173–4, 179, 281–3, 290, 403, 432, 440–2, 505–6
Corden, W. M., 342
credit restriction, 177, 190, 231, 241, 243, 442–4
Cripps, R. Stafford, 17, 74, 411, 480, 493, 501; on coal crisis, 361–8, 372–3, 380; on devaluation, 172 et seq., 280; fiscal policy, 75, 329, 332, 422–6; on import cuts, 81, 137, 141–3; monetary policy, 440–1, 443; on planning, 303–10, 318–26, 330–2; on relations with Europe, 176, 280–1, 286, 291–2, 295, 329–30; rôle in Cabinet, 47 et seq.; on US loan, 101, 109–10; wages policy, 403, 406–7
cross-subsidization, 477, 491
crowding out of exports, 27
customs union, 279, 285

Dalton, Hugh, 95, 125, 279, 321, 326, 411, 471; on coal crisis, 362, 367; on convertibility, 129–43, 160; on devaluation, 173–4, 176, 189, 193, 195; fiscal policy, 303, 326, 409–10, 413, 418–24; on import cuts, 81–3, 136–8, 141–2; on investment planning, 446–8, 452; on manpower

allocation, 390, 392, 403, 501; monetary policy, 196, 428–41; rôle in Cabinet, 47 et seq.; on US loan, 100–1, 108–10, 114
death duties, 18
Defence Aid, 86, 115, 224
defence expenditure, Ch. 8 passim, 91, 194–5, 231, 242–3, 253–4, 391–3, 420, 501
deflation, 43, 69, 175, 177, 180, 189–90, 195, 283, 312, 411, 425–6
demand: excess, 14–16, 41, 211, 347–9, 386, 403, 410–11, 416–19, 425, 500, see also inflationary gap; management, 19, 312, 314, 328–9, 423–4; see also fiscal policy, monetary policy
demobilization, 5, 21, 23, 30, 33, 385 et seq., 409, 501
departmental support of bond prices, 433–40, 444
depreciation allowances, 254, 415, 425–6
depression, fears of international, 14, 108, 300, 411, 493, 500
devaluation of 1949, Ch. 7 passim, 20–1, 27, 56, 85, 243, 280–1, 331, 441, 443, 493, 500–1, 503
Development Councils, 17
Devons, Ely, 57
direction: of exports, 83, 91, 194, 197; of labour, 386, 396–7, 402
directions, to nationalized industries, 484–9
discrimination, Ch. 5 passim, 43–4, 62, 83, 135, 147, 240, 257–60, 281–3, 290–1; see also convertibility, liberalization
Distribution of Industry Acts, 317
dividend limitation, 230, 405, 408'
dollar: pool, 67, 95, 97–8, 106–7, 162, 243, 246; portfolio, 250; problem, 20–1, 43–6, 65–73, 130–8, 196–7, 508; rationing, 106, 243
Dollar Drain Committee, 74
Dollar Exports Board, 74, 343
Douglas Lewis, 173, 214
Dow, J. C. R., xi, xiii, 338, 348, 426, 430, 443, 457

drawing rights, 287
Durbin, E. F. M., 48

Eady, Wilfrid, 129, 168; on devaluation, 165, 178; Mission to Washington, 137–9, 141; Plan II, 97–8, 122
earnings, *see* wages
ECA (European Co-operation Administration), 78, 172, 288, 291–2, 330
Economic Commission for Europe, 238
Economic Planning Board, 53, 235, 325
Economic Section of Cabinet Office, 51–7, 78, 137, 165, 171, 182, 187, 197–8, 216, 236, 258, 313–14, 325–6, 385, 391, 395, 400, 403, 409, 411, 416, 425–6, 490
Economic Surveys, 51, 57, 80–6, 255, 266, 303–5, 314, 320–5, 356, 381, 386–92, 401, 410–8, 448–51
economists in government, 54–6, 253
Eden, Anthony, on Robot, 249, 251, 270
Edwards, L. John, 180
Egypt, 7, 119, 134, 157
Eisenhower, General Dwight, 220
electricity: cuts, 362–72; nationalization, 17, 465–8; rationing, 372
Ellis Rees, Hugh, 122, 130, 140, 147, 164 n.
*Employment Policy*, 14–15, 19, 57, 313–18, 399, 409–10, 490
Employment Stabilization Fund, 416
EPU (European Payments Union), 20, 46, 54, 77, 126, 235, 237, 246, 251–3, 257–69, 283, 286–94, 340, 508
ERP (European Recovery Programme), 143, 149, 185, 281
'essential' and 'inessential': imports, 5, 237, 330–1, 464; industries, 385
Essential Works Order, 338, 395–7
Europe, relations with, Ch. 10 *passim*, 76–7
European Voluntary Service Workers, 395
Evans, Lincoln, 235
exchange control, 75, 95, 107, 119, 134, 169–70, 199, 237, 244, 330, 333, 428, 446
Exchange Equalization Account, 237, 444
Export-Import Bank, 103, 185
exports, by value or volume, 5–6, 14, 22, 24–8, 35–6, 43–5, 83–5, 112–13, 231–2, 261–2; drive, 36, 74, 131, 290, 343, 500; targets, 9, 63–4, 74, 296, 309, 337; unrequited, 167, 197, 285–6, 330; *see also* direction, price
external economic policy and domestic, xii, 51, 61, 188–9, 257

family allowances, 309, 403
films, 75, 142
fiscal policy, Ch. 15 *passim*, 19, 75
food and feeding stuffs, 5–6, 30–2, 63, 81, 96, 131–3, 142–3; *see also* subsidies
forecasts: of national income, 326–7, 411–14, 416; of world trade, 63, 80, 326; *see also* balance of payments, Economic Surveys
France, 45, 90, 97, 109, 124, 126, 209, 258, 272–80, 287, 294–6, 382
Franks, Sir Oliver, 172, 319
Freeman, John, 48
Full Employment Bill, 352–3, 408
'fundamentals', debate on, 282–3

Gaitskell, Hugh, 48, 53–4, 56, 235; Budget of 1951, 225–7, 424–6; on coal crisis, 363–4; on devaluation in 1949, 173, 181, 184, 187, 194, 199, 331; on economic planning and control, 329–32, 335, 352–3; on monetary policy, 443–4; on nationalized industries, 476–7, 480, 482, 487–8; on rearmament, 215, 218–21; on relations with Europe, 282, 292–5; on wages policy, 407–8, 502
Gardner, Richard, 140
gas, nationalization, 17, 465–8
GATT (General Agreement on Tariffs and Trade), 191
general election: of 1945, 3; of 1950, 174–5, 183, 189

Germany, Federal Republic of, 10–11, 62, 93, 131–4, 137, 209, 258, 272–9, 382–3; as trade competitor, 8, 35, 67, 231
Gilbert, Bernard, 319
gold: market, 138, 247, 251; price, 183, 185; sales, 206
Goldman, Samuel, 205
government: broker, 433, 439–41; expenditure, *see* defence expenditure, public expenditure

Hall, Robert, 54–6, 280, 294, 326, 407; on devaluation, 171, 177–8, 186, 191–4; on floating rate, 168, 187 n., 270; opposes Robot, 245, 248–50, 254 n., 255–60, 263, 269; on rearmament, 213, 217; in Washington talks, 172–3, 198, 281
hard and soft currencies, 22, 65–8, 167, 197
Harriman, W. Averell, 172–3
Harrod, Roy, 238, 503–4
Hawtrey, Ralph, 168, 313
Henderson, Hubert, 168
Herbert Committee on gas industry, 490
Heyworth Committee on gas industry, 468
hire purchase controls, 19, 241
Hitchman, Alan, 280
Hoffman, Paul G., 172
Holmes, Stephen, 168
hours of work, 18, 194
housebuilding, 34, 192, 195, 243, 253–4, 347, 397, 451–4, 457–9
Hurcomb, Lord, 479, 480 n., 484
Hutton, Graham, 171

imbalances, international, 10–11, 66, 72, 89, 135, 200
immigration, 275, 395
imperial preference, 92, 107, 277
imports, by value or volume, 5, 10, 24–8, 43–5, 81, 83–5, 112–13, 122; control, 302, 339–42, 349–50; cuts, 141–3, 163–4, 240–1, 255, 266–7, 500, 503; licensing, 257; restrictions, 43–4, 68, 74, 230, 236, 238, 240, 254, 257, 268, 281–2, 328–32; *see also* liberalization, machinery licensing, price
Ince, Godfrey, 320
incomes policy, 190, 310, 396; *see also* wages
inconvertibility, 71–3, 244
India, sterling balances of, 7, 134, 157, 188
Industrial Development Certificates, 317 n., 337
inflation, 14–16, 21, 25, 39–42, 63, 166, 211, 225, 301, 344–51, 417–18, 429; imported, 236–7; *see also* excess demand, price, wage
inflationary gap, 320–3, 386–91, 410–14
integration, economic, 77, 234, 279–81, 294, 506–7
interest rates, Ch. 16 *passim*, 15, 177, 196, 417; long-term, 176; in other countries, 38, 125, 428; short-term, 125, 176, 190, 200, 247; on US loan, 92–3, 102–5; *see also* Bank Rate
International Bank for Reconstruction and Development, 5, 62, 88, 149, 154–5, 198
International Monetary Fund (IMF), 5, 54, 62, 77, 88, 116, 119, 137, 149, 154–5, 168, 171, 184–5, 187–8, 198, 237, 247, 252, 259–61, 265, 291, 508
International Trade Organization, 88–9, 92–3, 97, 109, 136, 281
intra-European payments, 281–2, 285
intra-European trade, 276–7, 287–8
investment, Ch. 17 *passim*; control of, 15, 19, 176, 302, 326, 336–7, 347–8, 350, 430, 450, 455–62; cuts in, 191–2, 195, 221, 231, 415, 450–3; foreign, 7–8, 13, 38, 67, 80, 446; industrial, 231, 454, 456, 460–1, 501; rate of, 24–8, 34–5, 37–8, 230, 448 *et seq.*; *see also* capital flows, capital stock
Investment Programmes Committee, 54, 452, 454–5
invisible earnings, 7, 27, 75, 153, 211
Iraq, 119, 134, 247

Isaacs, George, 51, 319, 321
Italy, 209, 272–8

Jameson, Dr Wilson, 132, 192
Japan, as competitor, 8, 35–6, 67, 231, 273
Jay, Douglas, 21, 48, 176 n., 238, 318, 329, 424; on coal crisis, 354, 358–9; on devaluation in 1949, 179–82, 189, 195, 199
Johnston, Alexander, 52
'Justice', 93–4, 97

Kaldor, Nicholas, 188, 238, 408
Katz–Gaitskell agreement, 241–2
Keynes, Lord, 6, 10, 16, 54–5, 501, 508; on Economic Surveys, 413–14; on interest rates, 428, 433; negotiates US loan, Ch. 5 passim; on post-war balance of payments, 78–80, 88 n., 166
King George VI, death of, 241
King, Wilfred, 430

labour: preferences, 230; supply, 275
labour controls, 230, 302, 305, 338, 395–9
Labour Exchanges, 230, 359, 361, 379, 397
Labour Party, 47, 463–5, 467
leads and lags, 134, 156, 160, 163, 258
Lee, Frank, 97, 249
Lend-Lease, 4–6, 88–90, 93, 96–7, 102–3, 303, 504
Lewis, Arthur, 491
liberalization of imports, 243, 254, 282–7, 294, 329–31, 340–2, 500, 508
Liesching, Percivale, 102
Linlithgow, Lord, 443
liquidity, excess, 14, 199–200, 430
London clearing banks, 442–4
London Passenger Transport Board, 466, 469
Lyttelton, Oliver, 249–50, 264

MacArthur, General, 213, 219
MacDougall, Donald, 245, 270

McGowan Committee on electricity distribution, 468
machinery licensing, 74, 455, 492
Makins, Roger, 171, 264 n.
Malaya, 7, 145, 173
manpower: allocation, 14, 26, 52; budget, 302, 311–12, 323, 385 et seq., 402–3, 414; shortages, 14, 275, 346, 411; see also labour controls, undermanned industries
marginal cost pricing, 490–1
market structure, 276–7
Marquand, Hilary, 53
Marshall, General, 135
Marshall Aid, 22, 39, 44, 71, 73, 78, 83–6, 116, 119, 135–6, 140–3, 164, 171, 178, 186, 219, 224, 235, 242, 278, 282, 287–8, 384, 500, 503
Marshall Plan, 20–1, 54, 65, 72, 280, 380–1, 393
Martin, William McChesney, 173, 183, 236–7
Maud, John, 319
May Committee, 454
Meade, James, 52, 55–7, 89, 165, 359; on excess demand, 411–16; on planning, 302–3, 308, 319–22; on wage policy, 399, 403
meat consumption, 31–2; from France, 280
Menzies, Robert, 264
military expenditure overseas, 7, 10, 62, 64, 78–9, 90–1, 276; see also defence expenditure
Molson, Hugh, 478–9, 483
monetary agreements, 45–6, 123–9, 147–8, 157, 164, 237, 251, 279
monetary policy, Ch. 16 passim, 19, 176, 182, 190, 199–200, 303, 417, 419, 425, 501
money supply, 199–200, 427, 433–40, 442, 445
Monnet, Jean, 280
Morrison, Herbert, 47, 49; on coal crisis, 359–60, 362, 365; as economic coordinator, 50–5, 318–26, 409; favours devaluation, 176, 180, 190,

Morrison, Herbert—*continued*
199; on fiscal measures, 137, 190;
ill, 48, 53, 304, 326; on manpower
allocation, 386, 400, 403; on
nationalized industries, 472, 476,
478–83, 486
motor cars, 32–3, 222, 230, 331
multinational companies, 495
Mutual Aid Agreement, 1942, 89, 107
Mutual Defence Assistance Programme
(MDAP), 214

National Coal Board, 359–60, 365, 369,
377–8, 380, 473–4, 492
National Debt Commissioners, 433, 436
national government foreseen, 253
National Health Service, 17–18, 61, 175,
191, 227, 505
national income, 18, 19 n., 24–7, 153,
230, 326–7
National Investment Board, 300
National Joint Advisory Council, 400–2,
404
National Union of Mineworkers (NUM),
359–60, 369, 377, 467
nationalized industries, Ch. 18 *passim*,
17, 20, 74, 300–1, 303, 375, 505;
accountability and efficiency, 478–84;
finance of, 471; investment policy,
466, 471–2, 492–3; organization,
475–8; price policy, 417, 472, 481,
489–92; relations with Ministers,
484–9; scope, 472–5; Select
Committee on, 478, 481–4
NATO (North Atlantic Treaty
Organization), 214, 218–20, 224, 278
Netherlands, 97, 125, 148, 164, 209,
272, 274, 382
New Zealand, 154–5, 159, 186, 243
Nicholson, Max, 52, 321–2
Nitze formula, 218 n., 224
Noel Baker, P. J., 381
Norman, Montagu, 176
Norway, 134, 157, 209, 272
Nott-Bower, W., 358

OEEC (Organization for European
Economic Cooperation), 62, 72, 77–8,
148–52, 157, 176, 240, 243, 257, 267,
277–8, 282, 288, 290–6, 329–30, 380,
500
OGL (Open General Licence), 254, 281,
286, 330, 339–40
oil, 80, 83, 228, 238, 248, 258,
282
Overby, A., 238
overseas sterling, *see* Robot

Pakistan, 182, 248, 253
Parliament Act of 1911, 465
payments agreements, 54, 91, 124, 251,
287–8; *see also* monetary agreements
pensions, 17, 309
planning, Ch. 11 *passim*, 19, 252, 275,
279–80, 343–4, 501; industrial, 305,
323–4; investment, 307, 324, 326,
461–2; long-term, 303, 326–32;
machinery of, 50–5, 318–26; regional,
302, 314–18, 357, 507; totalitarian,
304; wartime, 310–14
Plowden, Edwin, 53, 55–6, 213, 217,
280; favours devaluation, 171, 173,
177, 186, 193; influence on Cripps,
325–6; opposes Robot, 245, 249–50
Portugal, 45, 128, 148, 209
Post Office, 476
premium on dollar earnings suggested,
176, 180
price(s): commodity, 27, 63, 225, 231;
consumer, 21–2, 30, 38, 40–2, 199;
control, 230, 301, 335–6, 405–6,
415–16; export, 41–2, 63–4, 112;
import, 15, 21, 40–2, 63–4, 81, 112,
225, 228–9, 238, 406; indices, 12 n.,
14, 25, 30, 39, 403, 418; mechanism,
252, 254, 303, 308, 310, 331, 343,
467, 472, 503; relationships, 40–2,
167, 310, 502; *see also* discrimination,
inflation, nationalized industries
production, growth of, 18, 21–3, 28,
274
productivity: increase in, 18–19, 41, 68,
175, 225, 499–500; teams, 17
profits, 191, 194, 206, 415, 446, 467,
495

public expenditure, 24–8, 33–4, 413; cuts in, 141–2, 176–7, 189–96, 211, 241, 409; goods, 311; *see also* defence expenditure, military expenditure overseas

purchase tax, 422–3, 426
purchasing power parity, 166

railways, nationalization of, 17, 464–7, 469, 474
rate of exchange, 67–8, 165; floating, 168–9, 187–8, 236–8, 240, 244 *et seq.*, 270; *see also* devaluation
rate of interest, *see* interest rates
rationing, 12, 15, 23, 28–32, 91, 142–3, 243, 301, 334–5, 344–8, 505; of bread and potatoes, 31, 81, 334; of coal, 358, 361, 381; of petrol, 33, 81
raw materials: allocation of, 23, 74, 327–8, 492; shortage of, 63, 225–7, 273, 296, 451
rearmament, Ch. 8 *passim*, 21, 28, 33, 41, 44, 86, 234, 392, 397–8, 425, 444, 501
redistribution of income, 504–5
Reed Committee on coalmining, 468
refugees, 275
revaluation of sterling, 234–8
Ridley Committee on Fuel and Power, 491
road transport, 17, 463–9, 494
Robbins, Lionel, 52, 55, 165, 319
Robertson, Dennis, 168 n., 443
Robinson, Austin, 54–5, 63 n., 168 n.
Robot, Ch. 9 *passim*, 508
Roll, Eric, 54
Roosevelt, Franklin D., 3, 98
Rosenstein Rodan, Paul, 181
Rowan, Leslie, 177, 244, 256, 264, 282
Rowe-Dutton, Ernest, 168, 244
Rowlands, Archibald, 213
Russell Vick Committee, 351

Salter, Arthur, 245, 250, 264, 270–1
saving, 12–13, 34–5, 347, 415–17
scarce currency clause, 77, 109, 137
Schuman Plan, 234, 294–6

Scott, Maurice, 349
Shawcross, Hartley, 47, 485, 493
Shinwell, Emmanuel, 48–9, 108–9, 137, 221, 403, 464, 474; approves Defence Plan, 219; in coal crisis, Ch. 13 *passim*
shipping: earnings, 7–8; losses, 7; not to be nationalized, 465
Sinclair, Robert, 101
Smith, Adam, 11
Snoy-Marjolin formula, 235
Snyder, John, 139, 282–3; on devaluation, 171–3, 180, 186, 238
social security contributions, 18, 42
South Africa, 133–5, 158–9, 161, 186, 244, 247; gold loan, 45, 116, 141, 149, 202
South-East Asia, 67, 131
Stafford, Jack, 413
Stage II, 3, 89
Stage III, 90, 97
Stamp Survey, 55, 399
'Starvation Corner', 92, 97
statistics, revisions in, xii–xiii, 25, 56–7, 92, 152–3, 418, 445–7
Steel Control Board, 470
steel industry, nationalization, 17, 432, 465–7, 470, 474, 494–5
Steering Committee on Economic Development, 37, 325, 389, 401–3, 415–17
sterling: area, 45, 66–7, 75–6, 91–8, 100, 106–8, 111, 117–20, 134–5, 148, 188, 243, 289–92; balances, 7–8, 73, 80, 90–9, 111, 115, 119, 125, 134, 137–8, 156–7, 162–3, 183, 243 *et seq.*, 431; blocking, 119, 125, 129, 156–7, 243, 265, 328; cheap, 72, 169–70, 187, 243, 245, 251, 258; controls, 237; funding, 94–5, 245, 251, 253; overseas, 246 *et seq.*; trade, 203–6, 266–7; transferable, 99, 127–9, 135, 160, 257, 265
stockbuilding, 21, 24–8, 34–5, 37, 170, 185, 205–6, 213, 230–1, 234–5; strategic, 213, 215, 225
Stone, Richard, 57
Strachey, John, resists cuts, 81, 132, 137

Strath, William, 249, 295
structural adjustment, 64, 73, 169, 277
subsidies, 14, 17–18, 33, 71, 175–7, 180,
191, 195, 227, 241, 256, 301, 309,
345, 403, 405, 416, 418–19, 500
Sweden, 45, 125, 148, 209, 275–6
Swinton, Lord, 249
Switzerland, 45, 125, 126, 205, 209, 275,
289, 507

tap issues of government securities,
431–3
tariffs, 68, 185–6, 286
tax rebates, 176, 180, 191
taxation, Ch. 15 *passim*, 12, 14, 18, 42,
176, 191, 256, 276, 309, 347, 491; *see
also* budget, purchase tax
'Temptation', 92, 94
terms of trade, shifts in, 9, 42–3, 63–4,
71, 113, 131, 166, 228–30, 233, 236,
255; and real wages, 42
Tewson, Vincent, 407
tobacco, 12, 29–30, 75
trade, world, 35–6, 39, 63, 73
trade unions, 211, 275–6, 399, 405–7,
467, 476, 500, 502
Trades Union Congress (TUC), 15–16,
190, 225, 400, 404–8, 502
transition period, 3, 89, 91–2, 99
transport, nationalization, *see* railways,
road transport
Transport Act, 486, 493
Treasury bills, 200, 427–8, 431–6, 444;
deposit receipts (TDRs), 427, 430,
436
Triffin, Robert, 288
Truman, Harry, suspends Lend-Lease, 4,
96–7, 217
two worlds threat, 72, 135, 177, 260,
262

undermanned industries, 385, 393–9
unemployment, 12, 14, 21–3, 36–9, 109,
143, 193, 252, 255, 391–3, 397;
localized, 315–18, 386

United Nations, 278
United States: in dominant position, 37,
39, 65, 278; loan of 1946, Ch. 5
*passim*, 20, 64, 78–9, 132–3, 247, 438,
503; State Department, 217, 281;
Treasury, 171–2, 281; troop
disbursements, 5–6, 91; *see also* ECA,
ERP
UNRRA, 4, 62
USSR, 3, 5, 93, 109, 226–7, 231–2

vacancies, 22–3, 297–8
VE Day (9 May 1945), 4, 6
VJ Day (15 August 1945), 78, 97
Vinson, F. M., 94, 139

wage(s), 11–12, 15–16, 41–2, 229–30;
cuts, 180; drift, 413; effect of
devaluation on, 211; freeze, 190, 225,
404–6; inflation, 301, 344–5, 385,
399–408, 411; policy, 502; real,
11–12, 18, 41, 406; relative, 310;
social, 407
waiver clause in 1945 Loan Agreement,
103–5, 110–11, 115
war damage, 13, 18, 37; finance of,
12–14
Washington talks in 1945, Ch. 5 *passim*,
79; in 1949, 180, 183–7; in 1950, 213,
219, 281–4
Watts, Nita, 236, 238
Welfare State, 17–18
Western European Union, 284–5
White, Harry D., 103 n.
Wigg, George, 363
Wilmot, John, 470
Wilson, Harold, 48–9, 53, 286, 295; on
convertibility crisis, 160–1; on
devaluation, 168, 174, 180–4, 199;
resigns, 51, 226–7
Wilson Smith, Henry, 172–3, 186, 198,
281
Working Parties (Board of Trade), 17, 74

Yalu river, 219